William W.
Bleifuss

The works of
THOMAS BEER

THE FAIR REWARDS [*1922*]

STEPHEN CRANE [*1923*]

SANDOVAL [*1924*]

THE MAUVE DECADE [*1926*]

THE ROAD TO HEAVEN [*1928*]

HANNA [*1929*]

MRS. EGG AND OTHER BARBARIANS
[*1933*]

These are BORZOI BOOKS, *published by*
ALFRED A. KNOPF

HANNA

CRANE

AND

THE MAUVE DECADE

HANNA

CRANE

AND

THE MAUVE DECADE

BY

THOMAS BEER

With an Introduction by

LEONARD BACON

1941 *Alfred A. Knopf* NEW YORK

THOMAS BEER

SOME time in the year 1908 the writer of these remarks, who for the moment had achieved the ghastly
eminence of an editor of the *Yale Literary Magazine*,
found himself in earnest conversation, verging on dispute,
with a self-contained young man, who in the slang of the
period was a " heeler," that is to say an aspirant for the
same pale purple. A number of heelers confronted the editorial board in the dingy fumed-oak wainscoted room in
the basement of White Hall, for it was the important hour
of the monthly conference when editors discussed with
ambitious aspirants of letters the virtues or defects of com-
positions which had been rejected outright or returned for
necessary repairs. There was always something resembling
a contest about these occasions. Editor and contributor
alike stood fiercely to the points. One is reminded of a
Golden Gloves competition, for, however wild, punches
were seldom pulled. Men who have since become writers of distinction gnawed their lips with rage when men
who have since become stockbrokers took them for long,
painful rides. But discipline was on the whole superb.
And I, for one, always found the encounters exciting,
although, as the pugilist remarked, it was more blessed
to give than to receive. Be that as it may, it was under

such circumstances that I first tested the quality of Thomas
Beer, who, it required no special intelligence to perceive,
was more poised and observant than his competitors —
or his judges. As one of the latter, I confess that I had
a passing sense of uneasiness as I was studied by dark
brown eyes, which might not be unkind but were clearly
well designed to take the measure of men and things. That,
after all, was what Thomas Beer came into the world for.
And it is not unpleasant to me to have such a recollection
of him, young, at his ease, attentive with some rather special attentiveness, and not unnecessarily impressed.

But I think, it is fair to say, that the lot of us were immediately impressed by him, something which could not
be helped. In the first place, there was the precocious and
unusual equilibrium of his nature which protected him at
once from callowness and priggishness. In the second, writing came as naturally to him as polo to Tommy Hitchcock.
And the boyish stories and poems he wrote for the *Lit* had
something leonine about their little claws. Even when he
was at his most derivative (and O. Henry had a lot to
answer for at the time) there was an admirable ripeness in
his notions and his style that could be, and was, envied by
the less mature. And one knew instinctively that he was
already moving in the unrealized American world, which
most of us had been so well trained to ignore that we were
ill prepared to recognize it at all. In those days when it
was still practically uncivilized not to be an expatriate,
actual or spiritual, Tom Beer, who had already forgotten
more about Europe than most of us were ever to learn, was
noticing such barbaric developments as the increasing
beauty of New York, where great architects were beginning
to find notable opportunities for remarkable native imagi-
nations. And it is a matter of interest to me that it was in an

undergraduate magazine office that I first read anything like an adequate mention of the glory of sunset-light in the cross-town canyons of the newly towered city. God forgive us, I believe we rejected that poem.

To give anything like a real picture of any human creature is hard. And Beer is in some respects a peculiarly hard specimen to handle. Physically he was neither large nor small. But he looked powerful and deep-chested. And for me at least his head and shoulders had the monumental quality of a classic bust. He carried his chin in the air so that he made one think a little of Petronius Arbiter considering an arena where top-flight gladiators had been advertised but so far had not appeared. Not that he was cynical, but he was not going to be fobbed off with second-rate performers. And the proud air was really protective (as Johnson used the word), concealing as it did a wild interior universe of generosities and fiery enthusiasms. When he was sure of your interest he would unveil them with authentic shyness, or perhaps they would dance naked with abandon before you. But even as a boy his judgment about real things seemed singularly suggestive and exact. And I know we recognized in him that quality which William James considers the essence of intelligence, the capacity to perceive genuine connection between apparent irrelevances.

It is not proposed in this brief paper to give any detailed account of Tom Beer's life, his actual doing and suffering. It followed pretty much the pattern of his time and circumstances, college, the War, and so on, and would only be interesting if it were related with full realistic detail, for which I have neither the time nor ability. But this much may be said: that he came of a family that was distinguished but neither dull nor famous. His paternal grandfather was an able, effective, and honorable judge, three adjectives not always applicable to the bench. When Beer was born, in 1889, his father was a stirring and capable young lawyer who was active against the Silver Heresy, and wrote penetrating reports on the state of opinion in the pregnant Middle West for Moguls by the Waters of Manhattan. It is clear that the father had a lot to do with the son's ideas. He had been close to the burning center of politics, had seen important matters decided by persons capable of decision, and, though fully aware of crudities in the American complex before him, did not believe, like some of his contemporaries, that the bad taste of his fellow-citizens was the significant fact about them. It was not unnatural that his son should never accept the heresy that the Republic consisted of three million square miles of unstoried mountain and vacuous plain, drained by rivers which made no appeal to the imagination. On the contrary, the boy saw a part of the world cut out on too large a scale to be parochial, an organic part of the world, whether material or intellectual. This had interested him from the beginning, and from the beginning it made him interesting in contrast with boys whose idea of culture consisted in an admiration for what they supposed ran hot in Paris or Rome.

Not that this limited his curiosity. From our first contact with him I am sure most of us, to travesty the epigram on Macaulay, wished we knew as much about anything as Tom Beer knew about everything. Nor is any innuendo intended. It is a simple fact not only that he had more information than our brightest and best but that it was correlated and organized and immediately available. If we talked, say, of socialism, then as now a subject of intense interest to undergraduates (though some of the Youth Movement inform me that the whole idea is the result of the superfetation of their own intelligence), at best we had mere shadowy notions of Saint-Simon, of Fourier, of Marx, and of Lassalle. But Beer would prove to have read, to have inly digested, and to have a coherent scheme of things, with its roots in the medieval guilds, whose savage champions he had investigated with dispassionate interest and was prepared to compare, perhaps favorably, with Henry George, William Morris, and Edward Bellamy. In short, he had a mind so well organized that it was also modest. With respect to this last aspect, I have always believed that our friendship dated from our first interview, when, by happy accident, I proved to be in the right on a minor point of fact which had escaped his encyclopedic curiosity. In all our thirty years of friendly intercourse I do not remember that it ever happened again. But I am sure it broke the ice for me. Unlike too many of us, Beer was the kind of man who would value being set right even about a trifle.

I am sure he enjoyed college, perhaps more than he was to enjoy any subsequent period. Certainly his abilities won for him what honor lay in the gift of his contemporaries. And quite as certainly he did not overestimate those simple laurels. At any rate he did not leave college with any sense of that resentment which has been felt by distinguished men who have naïvely suffered because their abilities had been ignored.

But I have no information as to whether he was happy in the study or practice of the law and suspect that, like a million other young Americans, he welcomed the deracination of the War. At any rate, as the phrase goes, the law was not for him nor he for the law. And after the Armistice, which interval he had apparently spent in the absolute and engulfing absorption of all French literature, he returned to the United States to become a writer.

In some respects I think it was an unfortunate time to become one, in spite of the efflorescence of which men still talk with appropriately bated breath. Whatever timidities and inhibitions withered during the battle, something had happened, not in my opinion for the better. As someone has put it, the Art of Fiction had become Fiction, Inc. The young writers who came back from France full of released energy and connected disillusion, found themselves more than ever before the wage slaves of an industry more organized than ever before. They were to publishers and magazine-editors what shop-foremen are to production managers. The editor had come into his own and was important — and self-important. And the writer found himself writing not what he had set his heart on writing, but what an executive thought would be profitable for him to write. It is not denied that editors may be full of suggestive ideas, or that a healthy collaboration may exist. But more and more men with fixed and sometimes large salaries were to be seen at the Algonquin, of whom it was said that they had " incubated " Main Street, that they had " made " Cabell and Dreiser, or unmade the equally unfortunate. More and more it was felt or silkily suggested that practical students of a practical business were entitled to order the clothing for an idea as if the laborer who made it were a sort of tailor and must cut his cloth according to an editorial pattern. And it has even been noticed that poetry, which cannot be commanded in this manner, suffered on the whole a progressive atrophy and finally became a mere academic ribbon in the buttonhole of an occasional spring suit. The writer was to be an artist, of course, but what was actually in demand was the swift journeyman who could promptly produce an improved model in a line that had taken on well. And, as has been said, men have to live in spite of the eminent Frenchman who could not see the necessity.

Like others, his inferiors, Tom Beer was exposed to the increasing compulsion, and particularly because he was obsessed by a native generosity that amounted to a pathological condition. It is true he pretended that this was not the case. And I remember a set speech he once made me on the subject of ill-advised altruism. Others might have this weakness, but not the hard-boiled Tom Beer " contemplating with composure the absurdities of mankind." I think a hundred witnesses would bear me out in the statement that when he made that oration, or at any other time in his life, it was impossible for him to understand that it was not necessarily his duty to support persons who had no claim on him, in the style and affluence which they preferred and to which they fancied they were accustomed. Agitated by such considerations, he wrote over a hundred stories (the equivalent of a dozen volumes) for a weekly whose foundation by Benjamin Franklin has recently, and perhaps brutally, been called in question. He was properly grateful. But confronted by the spectacle of such a colossal boiling of other people's pots, with appropriate wonder, I do not acknowledge any particular obligation to the editorial mind.

All those stories were easy to read, a dozen were brilliant, and the most hack-ridden of the lot bore witness to Beer's astounding power of evoking what he wished to evoke. Wet meadows, shining weathervanes, the gleam of a colt's new curried coat, there was always something to take you into a hollow glen upstate or under the shadowy trees of a flat Ohio timber claim. And the personalities that emerged, tough horse-breeders, and women who loved to eat, had much to be said for them which he often said with grace and skill. But for all the humor, drive, and veracity in his stories, my own feeling is that he was not really at home in the short story any more than Whitman would have been at home in a sonnet.

And though I be slain for heresy, I don't think he was wholly at ease in the ampler Zion of his novels. They are immensely imaginative. And *Sandoval* at least is furiously ingenious and brings up a lost epoch superbly. *The Fair Rewards* is an elaborate and sagacious resurrection of the perished theater before Hollywood. But frankly these books are genre pictures in which he exercised an art which he knew would find its scope in a quite different direction. He needed even more room, because the images he was happiest with always had to be real ones, with three and, to be accurate, four dimensions. For Beer was one of the rarest of men, the appropriately imaginative historian.

Historians are frequently inappropriately imaginative. They write fiction which they expose for sale as history. They sophisticate fact with fancy. They defend preconceptions as if they were laws of nature, or introduce equivocations that bear a family resemblance to forgery. They paint a man's character from the epigrams of his enemies, or, still worse, of his friends. And the hidden premise in their argument is difficult to find, because it is effectually concealed in the hypocritic darkness of the unconscious.

If Tom Beer had any prejudices they were rather unusual ones, for he was congenitally opposed to suppressing what was true or suggesting what was false. In fact, in the three remarkable biographical and historical works reprinted in this volume, he became the scientific enemy of the legendary without losing sight of the reality from which legend is born. And it is accordingly with something like a shock that we learn that McKinley had a will of his own and that Richard Harding Davis was a vivid and courageous personality, not at all " like the illustrations to his own novels." And such constant revaluation helps to make a coherent and ingenious picture of a time that will excite the mirth and the pity of a century which we may hope will not be so epileptically explosive.

For, whether by accident or design, *Stephen Crane, The Mauve Decade,* and *Hanna* are supplementary angles in the arc which stretched from the cloudy horizon of 1890 to the red skyline of 1914. And there is hardly a facet of the life or thought of the period that is not touched or illuminated in the three. The area of time swept over is of course greater and less than my hasty statement could indicate, for Hanna was born in 1837 and Crane died before the new century had properly begun. But in a real sense, the nucleus and burning core of the books is the quarter-century which included the panic of 1893, the strange conflict over silver, and the building of the Panama Canal, not to mention those crescendo overtures to greater battle in Greece, Cuba, the Transvaal, and Manchuria. Federations of labor were getting new ideas in the Haymarket of Chicago, while Henry James trifled with an old one in Mayfair in London. Henry Adams notices that Hanna is in strange agreement with Goethe on a point of some historical importance. Novelists are afraid to write about America. Poets apparently have unconquerable prejudices against the subject. And it would seem that like their predecessors in the equally cloudy time before 1789, the fortunate and the instructed, with a few notable exceptions, were anxious to ignore immedicable dangers. Some time about 1907 a wise man observed to me that the wars were getting bigger. It only took seven years to give point to the remark. And Beer's three strange works have the same sort of deadly implicit meaning for us at this moment.

Strange books they are. To a hasty reader they might seem like collections of brilliant, semi-detached epigrams, whose author only occasionally condescends to straightforward narrative and explanation. At times they are almost maddeningly elliptical and parabolic. And Beer, to use the catchword, makes heavy demands on the activity of the reader's intelligence. But that same reader will suddenly grow aware that the books, so to say, reach all over themselves and that there is hardly a sentence that has not its complex and articulate connection with something of importance that went before or is to succeed. In fact, there is such a structure as the musically competent endeavor to persuade us is to be found in a Bach fugue or a Mozart sonata. It is perhaps worth while to submit not too fanciful an example. The first sentence of *The Mauve Decade* has become a cliché: " They laid Jesse James in his grave and Dante Gabriel Rossetti died immediately." People stared and gasped at a juxtaposition so satisfactory and illuminating, and perhaps ignored the less antithetic concluding passage of the book which exhibits Theodore Roosevelt heading a procession on Fifth Avenue. If that isn't a resolution there is nothing in harmony.

Apart from a mind specially qualified to distinguish what was genuine from what was pinchbeck, Beer had several other advantages. He was born near the political center of things, and was in a position to get at the sort of information that is apt to be excluded from memoirs. But beyond that he was inordinately laborious. No hack whoring after the idol of a doctorate ever explored his subject more meticulously. One quails at the mere magnitude of the reading he had done, and shudders at the realization that, when he says a story of Stephen Crane's has been imitated three hundred times, he has counted them. Yet he never lost gusto for all the expense of spirit. One of the pleasing features of all three books is the graceful compliment which he pays the forgotten or the ignored. Yet at the same time he is as detached from the time which he chose to exhibit as Voltaire's ingenuous Huron. No one could have viewed the phenomena with fewer preconceptions, although no one was more familiar with what had been preconceived or more sympathetic with the motives and passion which governed the expanding universe of the Republic. The arts might be feeble, frivolous, and divorced from life. But a boy of twenty-four made great battles march across his page with a new and unexpected emphasis. Politics might be gross and corrupt. But a man supposed to be the last word in illicit manipulation set the water running " in the little ditches of the Western desert and in the big one " that Goethe dreamed of at Panama. There was no absurdity of taste or ignorance that Beer did not have his fun with. But neither was there any nobility of mind or action that he ignored. Beer, in fact, had neither lot nor part with the debunkers with whom the thoughtless may have associated him. He saw no particular virtue whether in the " blackwashing " of men who had achieved something or in the build-up of men who had not. Each of these activities was a part of yellow journalism and divorced from reality and history as he saw it and makes us see it. Tom Beer's style may have an almost dangerous glitter, but nothing could seduce him from his interest in permanent and fundamental actuality.

And so it is that Stephen Crane steps out of the time, a

charming and entertaining boy unimpressed by " Dostoy-whatshisname," much preoccupied with the way things are, and not at all with what editorial masters of the wastebasket think they ought to be. A lord of language with a sound knowledge of inside baseball has much to be said for him. And to read Beer's brief and pointed tribute is to know the man yourself. I doubt if a more convincing portrait was ever done with fewer strokes, or more masterly ones. A dozen and the man is there, his form and pressure, as he lived. And Beer has the art to make the reader party to discovery as the Elizabethans made the spectator party to the play. When with admirable skill Beer shows you the very conception of a tale, how the wild fancy was struck by some fact gross or beautiful, you are forced into excit-ing inferences about that germination, are so to say in at the birth. As Carl Van Doren with his usual acuteness has said, Beer was the best thing that ever happened to Stephen Crane. And certainly few men have been able to exhibit another man's mind *in motion* as well as Beer was able to exhibit Crane's.

The odd thing is that he fared quite as well when he dealt with another sort of realist. With Hanna, as with Crane, a legend had to be destroyed before the vigorous and fascinat-ing creature that gave rise to it could be properly observed. Crane had been the object of private and secretive envy. But Hanna had been the oblivious or contemptuous target of all the ordure at the disposal of Mr. Hearst. Neverthe-less, just as the humorous young artist was suddenly a vital personage to a forgetful world, so was the humorous old man of affairs. You can hear him growl to Cushman Davis, as he glances at Veblen's *Theory of the Leisure Class:* " What's their theory? More damn fancy-dress balls? " The Bradley-Martin orgy of ineptitude no doubt had irritated him. Beer was not unlike his improbable hero. There was no form of cheapness that he did not abhor, whether it was the kind that ran down an American political figure, or the kind that ran up a French painter without other visible means of support. But nobility is a bed-rock thing. And there was plenty of it in the man Beer delighted to honor, who, a whole generation had been taught to believe, was Mammon himself, when he was not Belial.

At the risk of the usual charges of mawkishness and sentimentality, it is proper to remark that in a world of image-breakers Tom Beer's incredibly ingenious irony is invariably exercised in the affirmation of what is humanly substantial or in the castigation of what is not. The odd moment when the litter of Petronius halts by Barnard's statue of the two natures is perhaps not the happiest instant of Beer's invention, yet one would hesitate to unspeak that volume. It makes one familiar with a man impatient of complicated motives for doing only what is comfortable and convenient. Beer admired persons who sought to be masterly in what they undertook. And he was incurably contemptuous of those who seem to think that to take a great figure apart for fun and money is somehow as novel as it is entertaining. " Kipling," he once remarked to me, " is fair game nowadays. I don't like Kipling. But before they write him down, they ought to confess what they have stolen from him." Even *The Mauve Decade*, which some seem to think is a devastating raid across a desert, throws the emphasis on people with the root of the matter in them. Figures like Cope, William James, and Sumner set off the ephemeralities in a manner not altogether satisfactory to people who derive a meager pleasure from the consideration of the follies of their predecessors. No doubt there was plenty to deplore. And that merciless study in female

INTRODUCTION

pathology called " The Titaness " said it right out. Yet what remains to you from that extraordinary essay? The great figure of Louisa Alcott, cribbed, cabined, confined, and heroic. It will be a long cold day before she is as justly or sympathetically treated as she was by an admirer whose axe had been magnificently sharpened for nearly everything she symbolized. It did not lie in his power to mitigate absurdity, but neither was he capable of tarnishing any brightness that was charming or splendid.

As one contemplates in such leisure as is left to us the canvas where, with the detail of Breughel, the spectacle is revived, one for a moment recaptures the fancy that there is something not unpleasing about mankind, when the animal allows himself to be human. The animal permits himself this liberty occasionally — even in cock-eyed quarter centuries before such catastrophe as has overtaken us. And Beer was created by God to catch him at it.

It is bad luck that he will not discriminate further between our virtues and ineptitudes. He did not believe they were indistinguishable. And he had the fire in him that flamed up generously at the spectacle of authentic dignity and courage. As we are now going to need unlimited amounts of these uncommon qualities, it is not improper at this moment to bring out once more the three astonishing and engaging books in which a mind of the first order, curious, enthusiastic, and never sentimental, studied the time of which we are the horror-stricken heirs. If that time left us this heritage of paying the piper, it has also perhaps left us a certain wherewithal to pay him. Beer, to judge alike from his praise and his condemnation, evidently thought so. Nobility is a bed-rock thing.

LEONARD BACON

CONTENTS

THE MAUVE DECADE

STEPHEN CRANE

CONTENTS

HANNA

THE MAUVE DECADE

AMERICAN LIFE

AT THE END OF THE NINETEENTH CENTURY

". . . Mr. Whistler said: 'Mauve? Mauve is just pink trying to be purple . . .'"

FOR

ERNEST BOYD

PREFACE
ADDRESSED TO READERS
BORN AFTER 1900 A.D.

ALCOTT, AMOS BRONSON (*1799–1888*). *Born at Walcott, Conn. Pedlar, schoolmaster, lecturer, practicing philosopher. Established a communist colony for farming in Harvard township, 1843. Subsequently dean of the Concord school of philosophy. Principal works: Orphic Sayings, Tablets, Ralph Waldo Emerson: His Character and Genius.*

ALCOTT, LOUISA MAY (*1832–1888*). *Born in Germantown, Pa. Educated at random. Began literary hackwork in 1855. Health impaired by illness contracted while nursing soldiers at Georgetown in 1862–3. Principal works: Hospital and Campfire Sketches, Moods, Little Women, Little Men, An Old-fashioned Girl, Eight Cousins, Rose in Bloom, Jo's Boys, Jack and Jill and Under the Lilacs.*

ALDEN, HENRY MILLS (*1836–1919*). *Born at Mount Tabor, Vt. Educated for the ministry. Attracted attention through studies in Hellenic culture. Editorially connected with Harper's Magazine and Harper's Weekly for forty years. His volumes of metaphysic, God in His World and A Study of Death, are similar in theory to ideas of Henri Bergson.*

ALDRICH, THOMAS BAILEY (*1836–1907*). *Born at Portsmouth, N. H. His light verse and compressed, graceful*

3

tales made him popular in the '70's. He inherited The Atlantic Monthly's editorship from William Dean Howells in 1881 and held it until 1890. His importance was largely that of remarkable personal charm, although he sometimes produced pleasing effects in verse. Principal works: The Story of a Bad Boy, Marjorie Daw, Mercedes and Later Lyrics, Judith of Bethulia.

ALLEN, CHARLES GRANT BLAIRFINDIE *(1848–1899). Born at Kingston, Canada. Began to write as an undergraduate at Merton College, Oxford. Taught school in Jamaica and returned to London. He lectured extensively and wrote numbers of brilliant critical essays, uncollected, showing a considerable bent for psychology. Principal works: Physiological Aesthetics, The Color Sense, Philistia, The Woman Who Did, Hilda Wade, The Evolution of the Idea of God and a translation of The Attis of Catullus.*

BIERCE, AMBROSE *(1842–?). Born in Meigs County, Ohio. He served with gallantry in the Civil War, and was severely wounded. Even his earliest humorous sketches were grim. He was a journalist and editor in California until 1895, when he came to the East. His work was not unappreciated but, in spite of its genuine distinction, it was unpopular owing to a monotonous insistence on death and fantastic calamity. Bierce vanished in Mexico in 1916 and his end is unknown. Principal works: In the Midst of Life, Black Beetles in Amber, The Devil's Dictionary, The Monk and the Hangman's Daughter.*

BURTON, SIR RICHARD *(1821–1890). He was largely educated in Europe and acquired an amazing dextrousness in Oriental languages during his early life in India and Africa. His reputation was established by a pilgrimage in disguise to Medina and Mecca in 1852. He translated The Arabian Nights, without expurgation, as well as Il Pentamerone and the poems of Camoens. His other translations, books of travel and essays in geography make up twenty volumes.*

CARRYL, GUY WETMORE (*1872–1903*). *Born in New York. His cynical, light verse stamped him as a humorist and in Zut he used the artificial forms of Robert Louis Stevenson, but his last work, The Lieutenant Governor, showed a drift into realism and satire.*

COPE, EDWARD DRINKER (*1840–1897*). *Born at Philadelphia of a distinguished Quaker family. His aptitude for natural science appeared when he was a child and at sixteen he was already writing notes, in Quaker dialect, on fossils. He spent his life in zoology and paleontology and in exploring the west for specimens. His scientific writings and discussions are too candidly free of popular values to be read by people without an education in the subject, but his influence was tremendous both in Europe and America. He cooperated with Josiah Willard Gibbs, the American authority on thermodynamics and statistical mechanics, in forwarding the Society for the Advancement of Science. His name appears upward of five thousand times in the proceedings of European and English scientific bodies.*

DAVIS, REBECCA HARDING (*1831–1910*). *Born at Washington, Pa. She achieved an almost scandalous fame in 1861 by the publication of Life in the Iron Mills and Margaret Howth, both social studies of unusual frankness. Her temperament was realistic and her feminism took the highly practical bent of demanding respectable wages and vocational freedom for women. Her later fiction is of no great interest but her essays on celebrities and localities were amusing and vigorous to the last.*

DU CHAILLU, PAUL BELLONI (*1835–1903*). *Born in New Orleans but removed to France as a child. His first accounts of explorations in equatorial Africa were received with open derision as fabulous and for years he was involved in arguments and assertions until subsequent explorers righted him with the public. He became interested in Scandinavia and produced an excellent text on its primitive civilizations. In his later life he resided considerably in New York. He is best represented by The Gorilla Country, Explorations and Adventures in Equatorial Africa and The Viking Age.*

FORD, PAUL LEICESTER *(1865–1902). Born in Brooklyn. He was privately educated and widely travelled before he became interested in historiography. He edited the writings of Thomas Jefferson, explored Americana of the eighteenth century, wrote sketches of Washington and Franklin which show the tide of American historical writing on the turn from sentimental bombast to research and sanity. His fiction is generally banal, although The Honorable Peter Stirling is amusing as a description of a heavy politician. Mr. Ford busied himself in calling attention to the wretched preservation of documents and records in the United States and established a magazine of bibliography shortly before he was brutally murdered by his brother in 1902.*

GEORGE, HENRY *(1839–1897). Born at Philadelphia. After a roving boyhood he appeared as a radical journalist in San Francisco. The publication, in 1879, of Progress and Poverty made him famous. His advocacy of the single tax — i.e., the reduction of real estate to common property by the imposition of a tax equal to the total rental value of the land, aroused horror and admiration. He was even denounced by the Duke of Argyll. In 1886 he was a contestant for the mayoralty of New York City in a political turmoil accelerated by the priest, Edward McGlynn, who denounced Catholic interference with American affairs. Mr. George was defeated by the combined forces of conservatives and Catholics. He*

PREFACE

died in 1897 while candidate a second time for the mayoralty of New York.

GODKIN, EDWIN LAWRENCE (*1831–1902*). *Born at Moyne, Ireland. He came to the United States in 1856. In 1881 his review, The Nation, became a weekly issue of The New York Evening Post, Godkin assuming the editorship of both the newspaper and the magazine. His editorials indubitably influenced public thought in the United States and aided in the renovation of the Democratic Party in 1884. For a competent characterization see Some Newspapers and Newspapermen, by Oswald Villard, as Mr. Godkin's official biography is an atrocity.*

HUNTINGTON, COLLIS POTTER (*1821–1900*). *Born at Harwinton, Conn. At the age of sixteen he became a clock pedlar and did very well. In 1849 he transferred his abilities to California. In 1860 he, with Charles Crocker, Leland Stanford and Mark Hopkins, conceived the transcontinental railway and in 1869 the Central Pacific was finished, at the expense of a number of people and states. This line was absorbed in the Southern Pacific Railroad, of which Mr. Huntington was the controlling power. His character was constantly attacked, and when the Southern Pacific attempted to excuse itself from the debts of the Central Pacific, the financier became an object of malignant insinuations. But he built a church in his native town to the memory of his mother, donated extensively to Hampton Institute in Virginia, gave $50,000 to Tuskegee Institute in Alabama and expressed his benevolence in countless ways, so that his aid was sought by representatives of the most respected organizations for the promotion of human well-being and of reform.*

NORRIS, FRANK (*1870–1902*). *Born at Chicago. He studied in Paris and at Harvard. His first important novel, Vandover and the Brute, could not be published until after his death. He edited The Wave at San Francisco, re-*

PREFACE

ported the Cuban campaign and then lived in New York for a short period. There is no biography of this artist. His principal works are: McTeague, Blix, The Octopus and The Pit.

CHAPTER I

THE TITANESS

THEY laid Jesse James in his grave and Dante Gabriel Rossetti died immediately. Then Charles Darwin was deplored and then, on April 27, 1882, Louisa May Alcott hurried to write in her journal: " Mr. Emerson died at 9 p.m. suddenly. Our best and greatest American gone. The nearest and dearest friend Father has ever had and the man who helped me most by his life, his books and his society. Illustrious and beloved friend, good-bye! " So she made a lyre of yellow jonquils for Ralph Waldo Emerson's preposterous funeral and somehow steered Bronson Alcott through the dreary business until he stood beside the coffin in the damp cemetery and mechanically drawled out the lines of a dire poem. Under the shock the tall old idler was a mere automaton with a bloodless face that startled watchers as he stepped back from the grave into which his one importance sank. Emerson was going from him! He was losing his apologist, his topic. His fingers fell on the shoulder of a little boy who had pressed forward to see and the grip became so cruel that Louisa saw and her hoarse voice rose in the hush, commanding: " Pa! Let go! You're hurting Georgie's arm! " But her father could hear nothing. She stooped and wrenched the child's arm free.

All summer long, Bronson Alcott paced through Concord's placid loveliness, being Bronson Alcott still, still ready to let flow the wondrous volume of his stored inanity

9

on any victim. But ghosts may have stalked with him beneath the royal elms, for when his school of limp philosophers gathered in July, he said to Frances Hedges: " I am the last. They are all gone but me." And they were gone — Hawthorne, Thoreau, the obsessed Sumner and the bloody Theodore Parker; and now Emerson had left him. True, Holmes survived, and so did Lowell. But they had never been too friendly, and neither was young Howells a great admirer, nor that dapper, handsome poet, much too suave — his name was Aldrich — who once so upset a session of the Radical Club by reciting some satirical verses about an improper woman in a harem.

" Then, at a wave of her sunny hand,
The dancing girls of Samarcand
Float in like mists of Fairyland!
And to the low voluptuous swoons
Of music rise and fall the moons
Of their full brown bosoms. . . .
And there in this Eastern paradise
Filled with the fumes of sandalwood,
And Khoten musk and aloes and myrrh,
Sits Rose in Bloom on a silk divan,
Sipping the wines of Astrakhan,
And her Arab lover sits with her. . . ."

No, Bronson Alcott was wasted on this new society of fribbles and light poets in which men applauded the ribaldries of Mark Twain, whose flippancy Louisa had reproved in her " Eight Cousins," in which the Radical Club was forgotten. His occupation and his audience ceased beside Emerson's flowery casket. Emerson had approved him in all his stages — Platonist schoolmaster, vegetarian, communist, transcendentalist, abolitionist. Bronson Alcott had repaid the devotion with devotion. A new phrase of his Emerson roused in the shallow pond of his intelligence the noisy splash of a log rolled down some slope into a tepid flood. As he lounged from hotel to hotel in summers, he spoke of Emerson as warmly as he spoke of Duty or Domestic Loyalty or Purity or Unselfishness. For Alcott was not an ungrateful man, although an idealist by profession and practice. Idealism is best supported on an income and, after the death of his proud wife's father, Alcott had no banker.

He somehow married the daughter of Samuel May, a rather leonine lady, kin to the Sewalls and Frothinghams. She refused food when her husband's idiotic communist farm at Harvard failed, perhaps from sheer exhaustion, as she had toiled in the fields with her impubic children while Alcott, clad in white linen, talked to callers and explained his high purposes to Margaret Fuller under shady trees. Emerson rescued the family. Emerson brooded affectionately over the growing girls while Mrs. Alcott had an employment office in Boston, on behalf of Alcott's inexhaustible idealism. The older daughters wore frocks bestowed by cousins and an aunt. Louisa went out as a maid once, and once contemplated marriage with a wealthy unloved suitor and once considered suicide. She taught school; she wrote trash for newspapers; she ran errands. Alcott addressed her as " duty's faithful child " in one of his insufferable poems and rhetorically clasped her to his bosom in recognition of her merits, which, he wrote to a friend, gave him every satisfaction. It seems fair. Her first, forgotten novel " Moods " had just made a stir, even causing Henry James, Junior — " a very literary youth," says Louisa's journal — to commit an act of enthusiasm in print. But " Moods " did not sell and Emerson's benevolence continued. It appears that he found for Alcott a paying post in the hospital service at Washington when war broke out, but he was obliged to tell the offering powers that Mr. Alcott had " other projects," which consisted, as far as there is

11

record, in a hearty admiration of the Bostonian excitement over a situation highly profitable to Boston, together with some occasional speeches for the holy cause.

Louisa went to nursing in the hospitals and Alcott quite closely approached the rim of slaughter when he had to bring her home in icy trains, delirious with typhoid and pneumonia, all the way from Washington to Concord. What Louisa thought of his notions about tending a sick daughter we shall never know, as she destroyed much of her journal in the autumn of 1887 when she was so wrecked that she took refuge with Dr. Rhoda Lawrence and sat making penwipers of flannel in the shape of carnations, waiting for death at the age of fifty-four. But the experience gave her material for " Hospital and Campfire Sketches." She became popular, and money oozed on the arid contours of Alcott's massive debts. Then her publisher wanted a book for girls. She didn't much like girls. Girls, it is possible, had always been rather shy of the Alcott sisters with their bad gowns and their curious papa. But she could write of herself and her family, so she wrote that first part of " Little Women " — and there it is, simple and as effortless as though she had spilled bright rags of silk from her lap on sunlit grass beneath a blowing lilac-tree.

Louisa May Alcott was famous. Her bones ached; her voice had become hoarse and coarse; doctors gave her opiates and treatments that would scare a modern physician badly; she had no use for popularity and no taste for the world that now blandished before her. Pleasure? A trip to Europe with her youngest sister, May. She must nurse her mother and pay Pa's debts and make sure of the family's future. Alcott went beaming and rosy in the very best broadcloth and linen to lecture on Duty, Idealism and Emerson before larger audiences which now looked eagerly at the grandfather of " Little Women." Duty's child was hard at work, writing " moral pap for the young," in her own phrase, and paralysing a thumb by making three copies of a serial at once. Once she walked across the lawns of Vassar among the thronging girls who tore bits of lace from her dull gown, shook hands with Maria Mitchell, the astronomer, who privately held that Miss Alcott's books were namby-pamby nonsense, but thought the tall spinster a fine woman. And once at Syracuse she faced a congress of her sex and heard its applause as women wrung her fingers. She worked, and Alcott prattled to and fro. Her mother slowly died after looking up at Alcott with the odd remark, " You are laying a very soft pillow for me to go to sleep on." And in the summer of 1882 she worked still, arranging monstrous lunches and teas for the students of the Alcottian school of philosophy, scolding her adored, handsome nephews, permitting Miss Frances Hedges to help her with preserves and ginger cakes, and pausing between jobs to mend a coat or stitch a baseball for any lad who swung over the fence and came prowling around to the kitchen in search of Miss Lou. Men had no interest for Louisa, but a court of adolescents hummed about her to be lectured for sneaking off to Boston to see that awful French troupe in *La Grande Duchesse* and *La Belle Hélène*, and to be fed ginger cakes. Little Miss Hedges had come to be irradiated by the wisdom of Bronson Alcott, but she fell into subjection before Alcott's daughters and wrote to her father in crude Illinois: " I just cannot see anything remarkable or interesting in Mr. Alcott at all, but it is a *privilege* to know Miss Alcott and Mrs. Pratt [the " Meg " of " Little Women "]. They had the awfullest time when they were girls. Sometimes they did not have enough to eat and I have met some ladies here who think that Mr. Alcott has always treated his family shamefully. . . ." Alcott would probably have been much astonished to know that anybody had such thoughts of him. There is an indurating quality in the practice of idealism. It is true that Louisa's journal contains notes of restlessness under the spell of duty. In April of 1877 she wrote: " I'm selfish. I want to go away and rest in Europe. Never shall," and in August of 1882 she sent word after Miss Hedges that she was going to take her favourite nephew, Johnny Pratt, out to California and have " a good, long, selfish rest." Never did. In September her father collapsed and thereafter lay a prisoner in a pretty room lined with books, chattering more and more feebly, but chattering still.

All this while the fat volumes of Louisa May Alcott had gone swarming in ugly covers across America from the press of Roberts Brothers, spreading the voice not of Bronson Alcott but of Abba May, his wife, a Puritan lady born in 1799. Her biographer admits that Louisa was unfitted by nature to comprehend Bronson Alcott. In the journal he is " my handsome old philosopher " but it isn't evident that his child cared for transcendentalism. In " Little Women," " Little Men " and " Jo's Boys," Pa is the merest shadow, and the heroic males of the long series are either handsome lads or brisk, successful bearded doctors, men who would hardly lug a delirious lady four hundred miles in railway coaches and who always have cash in pocket. Such philosophy as the books hold is just what Abba May had taught her children, and when the young folk of the tales have flared into a moment of wilful hedonism, it is a firm, kind lady, middle-aged, who steps forward and puts them right. Louisa was writing " moral pap." She couldn't conceive an unmoral book for children, and her own morality hadn't shifted since it was pressed into her by Ma, who had Louisa analyse her small self in a diary for inspection. Pa's lessons, such as " Apollo eats no meat and has no beard . . ." seem to have faded from her completely. God's ministrant is always female, sometimes abetted in virtue by one of the bearded doctors, and always a success. The children wriggle for a breath and then are towed meekly in the cool tide of rectitude. One learns a deal of Abba May Alcott

14

in the progress. She was charmed with " Eight Cousins," in which her representative rebukes current books for boys, the nonsense of Horatio Alger and Oliver Optic, with a fleet slap for " Innocents Abroad," and comments: " It gives them such wrong ideas of life and business; shows them so much evil and vulgarity that they need not know about. . . . It does seem to me that someone should write stories that should be lively, natural and helpful — tales in which the English should be good, the morals pure and the characters such as we can love in spite of the faults that all may have. . . ." She must have been delighted with " Rose in Bloom," in which Rose Campbell gives talks on conduct to other girls in the dressing-rooms of balls, throws over her lover when he comes in a state of champagne to wish her a happy New Year, and waltzes only with her male cousins. She did not live to read " Jo's Boys," which decides that men who have been, no matter how forgivably, in prison may not woo pure young girls. Righteous diversion? A jolly picnic on the river or a set of patriotic tableaux; a romp on the sands at Nonquit; red apples and a plate of gingerbread after sledding in winters; tennis and rootbeer under the elms in summer.

It is a voice of that fading generation which crowned William Dean Howells and shuddered with pleasure as it dabbled its hands in strong Russian waters, for Miss Alcott found " Anna Karenina " most exciting and liked " Kings in Exile " with its pictures of a dissolute Europe. She would even recommend Le Père Goriot as suitable reading for a girl of eighteen, but as for " Huckleberry Finn," why, " if Mr. Clemens cannot think of something better to tell our pure-minded lads and lasses, he had best stop writing for them." . . . But she went on writing moral pap for the young and it sold prodigiously. The critics paid no particular attention. Miss Alcott wrote admirably for our little folk. It seems to have struck nobody that Miss Alcott's first audience, the girls who had wept over " Little Women " in the latter '60's, were now rearing their daughters in an expanded world on the same diet. In 1882 Joseph Choate turned on a witness in one of his cross-examinations with the cry, " Good God, madame! Did you think that your husband was one of Miss Alcott's boys? " but the lawyer was a profane fellow, given to whist and long dinners. There was no discussion of Miss Alcott's morality, and certainly nobody talked of her art: she wrote for the young.

As spring of 1888 drew near, certain improvident small Bostonians in the region of Louisburg Square's marshalled prettiness were aware of a benevolent goddess whose dark carriage came daily to a rented house. If you ran quickly to open the door, you were sure of a hoarse joke and some pennies and, if you were a small male, a kiss and the loan of a laced handerchief should your nose need wiping. The goddess, known by the rather Syriac title of " Msalkot," was in the form of a tall lady whose handsome body shivered constantly under furred wraps and whose brown hair showed no grey. Sometimes she came out of the house with a plate of some quivering dessert or a bunch of black foreign grapes untouched by the dotard upstairs in his hired shrine. Sometimes she came out weeping quietly on the arm of a grave nephew if Pa had not known her that day. Once she picked up little Patrick Keogh and held him against her weary barrenness all the way to Dunreath Place and gave him a bath in Rhoda Lawrence's tub. She had nothing left for herself. Her sister's sons were grown. Her will was made, asking that she be buried across the feet of her family, as she had always cared for them in life and would rest better so. On March 3rd some acute infant may have noted that the lady wore no furs. Chill wind pursued the carriage as she drove away. In the morning came the daze and agony of a new pain. She asked: " Is it not men-

16

ingitis? " But at noon she could not know that Bronson
Alcott had stopped talking, and before a second sunset
duty's child went hurrying after him.

The journals observed that she had been an admirable
writer for the young. Mayo Hazeltine stated casually that
" Miss Alcott has found imitators among writers who
aspired to something more than the entertainment of
nurseries." The gentle, forgotten Constance Woolson exclaimed on paper: " How she has been imitated! " and resumed the imitation of Henry James, a habit in which she
so far progressed that " A Transplanted Boy " might have
been written and destroyed by James himself. It was plain,
to be sure, that a cooing legion was now busy in devising
tales on the Alcottian formula, and one follower, Margaret
Sidney, was simply a vulgar duplicate of Miss Alcott. But
the reviewers generally had little to say of an influence,
loosed and active for a quarter of a century, embedded in
grown women from the nursery, familiar as a corset.
Louisa May Alcott passed without judgment or summary.
The critics faced thrilling importations just then and space
must be kept for the discussion of " Robert Elsmere," an
announcement by a Mrs. Humphry Ward that she had re-
ceded from strict belief in the divine origin of Jesus Christ,
a fact somehow more exhilarating than the similar reces-
sion of her kinsman Matthew Arnold. And then there was
" As in a Looking-Glass " with delicious illustrations by
George Du Maurier, in whose pages one learned of a raffish
woman who married a virtuous landholder and then poisoned herself when her past rose to be a nuisance. Its
morality had to be discussed in long columns, just as the
morality of its stepchild, " The Second Mrs. Tanqueray,"
would be discussed sixty months later. These foreign wares
had natural precedence of the case of an American spinster,
born of a dismoded philosopher, and full justice had been

done when six notices mentioned that Louisa May Alcott was a type of the nation's pure and enlightened womanhood.

Even before the Civil War, orators had flung to the female margin of their audiences some variation of a phrase that always concluded with the trisyllabic word, " womanhood." Theodore Parker used " our pure and enlightened womanhood " four times in two years. Daniel Sickles produced " our world conquering and enlightened womanhood " a few days before he shot his wife's paramour in the streets of Washington. Roscoe Conkling sprinkled his speeches with references to " a pure, enlightened and progressive womanhood " and had more than six hundred babies named for him, to say nothing of one proved " Roscina Conkling " in Ohio. Chester Arthur begot " our cultured and enlightened womanhood " shortly after he startled a dinner in his honour at Saratoga by remarking that he might be President of the United States but his private life was nobody's damned business. Ulysses Grant was also President, but he said nothing much about women and was defended by his doctors and family in his last days from committees of ladies and ancillary clergymen demanding that he sign warnings against the use of alcohol and tobacco. Robert Ingersoll spoke touchingly of the nobility of womanhood quite often, and his version of the tribute is identical with that used by Susan Brownell Anthony and Lucy Stone. There was some convention of the editorial desk and platform in favour of a noble womanhood currently to be viewed in America, and the phrase echoed broadly in 1889 when a yearning for suffrage crystallized under the leadership of Elizabeth Cady Stanton. Miss Grace Ralston caught the words from air about her and made use of " the nobility of womanhood " to a courtly, charming gentleman in a Bostonian drawing-room. " Just what," he asked the girl, " is the nobility of womanhood? "

THE TITANESS

Miss Ralston was annoyed. She had in her possession a dried rose once the property of Elizabeth Stanton and some letters from Lucy Stone. The nobility of womanhood was . . . why, it was the nobility of womanhood! The pleasant gentleman seemed amazingly dull. What precisely was the nobility of womanhood? Miss Ralston had to lecture him stringently. The nobility of womanhood meant the nobility of womanhood! Anybody knew that! " Yes," said William James, " but just what is it, my dear? "

The year 1889 is stippled with unrecorded criticism of American womanhood, besides the printed observation of Rudyard Kipling who found it wasted time to call on the grand pirates of San Francisco in their homes as wives and daughters adopted the dark young man from India. The house belonged to the womenfolk and it was vain to hint that he had come to see its owner. In March Mlle. Suzanne Beret was appalled by the strangeness of Cleveland as she taught French in a wealthy family and wrote to a cousin in New York: " The ladies talk of nothing but adultery to each other, although they never tell amusing stories of love-affairs. . . . I do not accustom myself to the rudeness with which young girls treat men older than themselves. M. Eltinoit [1] made Miss X a compliment on her costume at a dinner last week by saying she resembled Sarah Bernhardt. She responded: ' Shut up! How dare you compare me to such a woman! ' . . . They treat their sons and husbands as rudely before people as though they were bad servants. . . . They are much more loyal to each other than French-women would be. . . ." She could make nothing of such a situation. Home-sickness overcame her and she went back to Nantes and to matrimony. In June a Mrs. Edward Wharton of Boston gave offence to a matron from Chicago by remarking on the rudeness of American ladies to their sons, but was something forgiven on account of a lovely

[1] Elton Hoyt.

white parasol. In October the curious Grant Allen gave some advice to an English friend starting for New York and concluded: " Be careful about involving yourself in arguments with ladies. American women take offence easily. With them argument is not intellectual but always emotional and if you attack any little belief or vanity you will find that they can be very rude indeed." Allen knew countless Americans and was himself a Canadian. He later chose to refer rather coldly to " American girls indulged by ' poppa ' and spoiled beyond endurance by ' mamma ' who make life intolerable and ordinary conversation inaudible for a considerable distance around them," although, among his many avocations, he was a feminist and raised a storm with a feminist novel, " The Woman Who Did," in 1895. His whole literary course was unsteady and a perplexity to critics. He applauded good popular art as good popular art and found the low comedian, Dan Leno, more amusing than Sir Henry Irving. He wrote readable bits of botany, translated from Catullus, composed guide-books, and invented, in a story, a prelude to the psychological entertainments of Sigmund Freud. One comes to-day on his name in volumes of reminiscence or in dusty copies of the *Strand* with some surprise. . . . But, for all these dubious undertones, 1889 was a year of triumph for American womanhood. Without parade or notice, outside Chicago, a settlement for the poor was opened by Jane Addams and Ellen Starr in September with the name, " Hull House," and at Lake Forest, on Christmas Day, Helen Kimball, a child of ten, was asked to define the word " author " and with the speed of true intelligence answered: " An author is a dreadful person who likes to write books." The last decade of the nineteenth century could now begin.

It began with a handsome exhortation from Phillips Brooks, who urged it to be a good decade. Susan Anthony wished it well, but symptoms of frivolity appeared too soon.

THE TITANESS

In the West some young Indians imagined that they saw a Son of the Great Spirit walking the waters and their aboriginal fancy led them to represent this messenger as having nail-pierced hands and feet. The absurdity didn't prevent tribes from believing that a promise of a happier land teeming with buffalo had been made. So lone agents and commanders of outlying forts were alarmed by the Ghost Dance. Naked altogether or striped with paint and floating wolfskins, lads spun and trotted in monotonous rhythms. Some whisper ran down deserts into Mexico and there they danced with green feathers laced to ankles above feet that padded in the noise of drums. Old Sitting Bull now had callers at his shack. His attitude toward the paleface had always been tinged by a dour conservatism, and after Major Kossuth Elder translated to him Longfellow's awful poem on the death of Custer at the Little Big Horn he was heard to state a preference for Negroes. It is said that he was spider in a vast conspiracy, red and black, to drive the white man altogether from America but unhappily he was killed before his plans had time to mature. . . . In the East, too, dancing held the eye. Dandies packed Koster and Bial's profane hall nightly to applaud the stamp and flutter of Carmencita as the tall Spaniard whirled and swayed in smoky light. Ladies came veiled to inspect the prodigy and she outdid in gossip the fame of Richard Harding Davis or of Richard Mansfield, who returned to female favour in the " Beau Brummell " of a young playwright, Clyde Fitch. Carmencita's red and yellow gowns covered her legs entirely and her shoulders were hidden in sleeves. It is plain that she wore corsets and nothing lewd is recorded of her performances, in public, while in private she seems to have been an estimable, stupid creature, like most artists, but in October the peace of the *Sun's* office was invaded by five matrons from Chicago, headed by a Mrs. Walker, who demanded that Charles Dana suppress Carmencita forthwith.

The editor was habitually deferential to women and notably patient in conversation with fools, but his cynical humour roused behind the kindly mask. He asked if the committee had seen the Spaniard dance. No, but she was an immoral person and the *Sun* must wither this ribald bloom straightway. Chicago then contained a dive of ferocious note among men, mentioned discreetly in journals when it vanished and since recalled in the documents of psychiatrists. Did the ladies not think they they should suppress " the Slide " before they began to rearrange New York? They had never heard of such a place. " Well," said Dana, " you go back to Chicago and have them shut the Slide, and then I'll have Carmencita run out of town for you." The committee bustled forth. . . . Carmencita danced and danced. In 1893 male tourists went secretly and timidly to behold the odd assemblies at the Slide when the World's Fair packed Chicago. But on April 7, 1891, Dana wrote to an old friend in Illinois: " I do not see why you cannot keep your lady reformers at home. They come in here so thick and fast that I am thinking of attaching a portcullis to my office just to keep them out. If I do not let them waste my time proposing some foolish amendment to the laws they insult me by mail, and if I do see them they insult me anyhow. If you hear of any more nuisances starting for the *Sun*, tell them to try Godkin at the *Post*."

II

AMERICA had already seen the two best criticisms of its civilization produced by European authority, and neither Matthew Arnold nor James Bryce had taken much heed to the problem, simple in England, of housekeeping in the United States. It was bad enough for women of the Eastern ports to find suitable servants. Civil War and Indian troubles had kept immigration scanty in the Middle West through the '70's and '80's. The Swedes and Germans arrived, to be sure, but either as tribes or as bachelors. Life in Chicago was made more difficult by " the servant question," and life among the moneyed in Omaha and Council Bluffs was nothing less than a twisted cozenage of Karens and Ludmillas, certain to betray a mistress for the gain of another weekly dollar and always likely to announce a sudden marriage with some dumb suitor just as invitations had been sent for an important dinner. In 1882 an heiress of Omaha saw for the first time in her twenty years a house in Chicago attended by four servants, and the primary renown of Mrs. Potter Palmer outside her windy realm along the Lake was that she kept six servants. The condition supplied and made practical young wives of the midland. They must be practical or perish, socially. Dinner had to be cooked and the clock from the Philadelphia Centennial had to be dusted. Rudyard Kipling briefly bade his friends in India be thankful for their cheap and biddable hirelings after he had dashed from side to side of the continent, seeing half of the situation. As early as 1880 there began to be talk of " the lure of the great cities " and bright in the golden phantasmagory of a house in New York or Chicago stood the shape of the Hired Girl. So when Grace had scolded or cajoled Olga in the kitchen toward some pallid comprehension of boiling jelly and had bestowed Robby in his red express cart under the maples of the front yard with a hope that Sue wasn't playing with those possibly lousy Swedish children around the corner, she fell wearily into the hammock with Mrs. Constance Cary Harrison's new novel and permitted the perfume of that metropolitan world to thrill her gently. A nurse-maid for the children was usually as fantastic a dream as the English governess of mundane fiction. She could read of shopping-trips along Twenty-third Street, but if she sketched one for herself, why, who would take care of Sue and Robby? Thus Fred,

23

idling up the street at half past four, or driving in from an inspection of the farm outside town left to his namesake by Uncle Fred, might be met by a wistful suggestion about the "niceness" of living in New York or Chicago. Perhaps some second blooming of the Teutonic immigration took over the desk at the bank; one of old man Hoffmeister's nine boys leased the white farm-house built after the model of white houses in the Connecticut hills. Fred and Grace were off to fill a wooden shell on Chicago's fringe or to conciliate timidly earlier settlers in Roselle, New Jersey. Or, if Fred was obdurate, Grace resigned herself to the battle and then it must have been consoling to remember how simply the March sisters lived in " Little Women " and to hear how Miss Frances Willard deprecated the frivolities of the cities. William James could presently explain that " we are thus driven by the necessities of our condition to proclaim that condition admirable and to seek precedents for so proclaiming it," and ladies of New York or Boston, in the stinking constriction of railroad coaches, were likely to be told off-hand that society in Sioux City was just as re-fined as society in the East, and that the High School had been called just as good as Andover or Saint Paul's for Rob — but when it came to the question of Sue, it was probably better for her to go on East for a little finishing and if Sue's father had risen to be President of the First National Bank, there might be a year in Europe. And meanwhile the Middle Western woman had quietly become a fixture on the American social chart, a shadowy Titaness, a terror to editors, the hope of missionary societies and the prey of lecturers. . . . Was she fabulous? No, but she existed rather as a symptom of America's increasing cheapness than as an attitude of womankind. Her performances were listlessly sanctioned by men whose covert emotionalism she openly and more courageously expressed in an instinc-tive envy of all that was free, cool or unhaltered in life, in art and affairs. She was an emblem, a grotesque shape in hot black silk, screaming threats at naked children in a clear river, with her companionable ministers and reformers at heel. The collapse of American thought excused her forays; all that had been finely stalwart in the Bostonian age had vanished, the reckless courage and self-willed individualism of Emerson, Thoreau and Channing, the deliberate cultivation of research into the motives, not the manners of human action. The confusion of morals with manners, apparently inherent in the world that speaks English, had helped the mental lassitude of the Americans to destroy what was honourable in the Bostonian tradition, and from the remains of that tradition welled a perfume of decay, cants and meaningless phrases: " the nobility of democracy," " social purity " and the like. In the weak hands of the Alcotts individualism ceased to be a sacred burden, save when it showed itself as a vague and vaguer aspiration toward some prettiness still severe in outline, the grim nymph who navigates above the swinging soldiery of the Shaw memorial tablet in Boston's self. This nymph hovered upon shoals of women shuffling and cawing in congresses of the World's Fair in 1893. Here the Titaness of the midlands was hostess to her more restrained sisters of the East and West. The ungainly women of little towns sidled among the gowns of receptions and shyly fingered bows and laces of opulent robes. A gorgeous materialism had made a cavern for voices of the nation and the noises blended in a roar.

Ambrose Bierce had already testified a good memory of obscure French prose by noting in the *San Francisco Examiner* that applause is the echo of a platitude. The nation now hastened to applaud this prodigiousness of white stucco pinned to iron between Chicago's smoky breast and the blue water. Architects had paid a valiant compliment to the Beaux Arts, and mankind now gaped at studded domes and

classicized fronts in the best mood of that school infesting
Paris after the reign of the vulgar, useful Baron Hauss-
mann. French tourists shrugged in the dining-room of the
Hotel Richelieu. All this had done service at their own exposition of 1889. Could the Americans think of nothing
fresher? Why not vast wigwams? But there was a certain
cleverness in detail. The columns of the Fisheries Building amused with their capitals of twining eels and lobsters.
There was dignity in the mass of the Agricultural Building
with its Indian woman leaning on the challenging bull before the entrance. By night Edison's perfected bulbs
dripped glitter on the shivering lagoons. Rockets swam
across faint stars. The Midway's shows and bands roared
wonderfully. Edwin Booth could not give his promised
season of Shakespeare, because he died in June, but you
could hear the metallic, just soprano of Lillian Russell in
La Cigale or shudder as the colonel's daughter of " The
Girl I Left behind Me " intoned the Burial Service while
Apaches whooped outside the stockade and her father reserved a bullet to save his child from rape — an effect
which Henry George found most distasteful, for the parent
of the single tax could conceive art only as a vehicle for
" good and noble " purposes. But George was touched by
the Fair. He stood one night with Charles Nolan, watching
the crowds of the Midway, and dreamed aloud: the people
had done all this! It was " of the people, by the people, for
the people! " The lawyer argued: " No, most of the money
was subscribed by rich men. The people had nothing to do
with designing the buildings." The economist pulled his
beard and sighed. Anyhow, the people were enjoying it,
and his friend Altgeld would govern Illinois. Perhaps the
Kingdom of God was a little nearer. He strolled among
the crowds and scandalized a waiter at the Auditorium by
demanding for late supper cold stewed tomatoes, sugared,
while his host drank champagne. Materialism triumphed

around him; Grover Cleveland had offered William Whitney a place in the Cabinet; nobody had protested the sending of troops to Buffalo, last year, to curb the strike in the railroad shops; Edward McGlynn had gone back to the Church of Rome and the reconciliation was announced quietly, after the awful tumults of the priest's excommunication in 1886. But there was hope in Altgeld and the People's Party, even if Cleveland had gone over to capitalism and McGlynn's social criticism would henceforth be limited to the admonitions of a formal creed. The Prophet drifted through the show, shook hands with Mrs. Potter Palmer at the Women's Building into which she had somewhere driven a nail of precious metals, and then he vanished eastward, courting no notice.

But clamour filled the ears of ticket-sellers on the morning of June 22nd. That day all California seemed rushing westward, bound for the funeral of Leland Stanford, whom Henry George had denounced as an able thief. The immense man lay dead in Palo Alto suddenly. He had never been unpopular in his State. The easy casuistry which protected all the railroad-builders had peculiarly worked on his behalf, and he had been genial, truly kind. He tossed gold coin to newsboys on the streets of Washington; his dinners were royal; his stable thrilled sportsmen; he had given the State a complete university in the memory of his only child, and after that criticism swooned into a mere mutter. But no kindness woke in the being of Mrs. Ada Channing Walker, lately landed at San Francisco with her niece after an inspection of Japan. She wrote a denunciation of Stanford, not the financier, but the " winebibber, atheist and horse-racer," and sent it by messenger to the *Chronicle*, which failed to print it. Mrs. Walker persevered and in person visited the offices of journals. Editors were deaf. The man was unburied and flags of San Francisco flew at half-mast for him. Her shamed and frightened niece implored Mrs.

Walker to be still and then found an ally in a young Methodist preacher when her aunt decided to attend the funeral and call attention vocally to Stanford's defects. The preacher wrought powerfully and in some way deflected Mrs. Walker's zeal. She took a train for Chicago, and Leland Stanford was buried in peace. . . . He lies with his wife and son in a temple of slick grey stone under the patronage of a superb oak-tree. The tomb is guarded before by two male sphinxes of Semitic aspect and at the rear by two female sphinxes wearing Florentine necklaces. The right-hand sphinx is obviously insane and her eyes glare furiously at a barrier of foliage as if it hid some enemy. Beyond this silent corner of the park, lads with hair bleached by perpetual sunshine swirl in fast motors and profanely flaunt jerseys of cardinal red, as though death and judgment did not matter much.

Besides Mrs. Walker, battalions of the virtuous now appeared at the Fair. Congress after congress for the correction of mankind drew ladies to galleries. Walter Besant, an English writer, described literature as engaged in social tasks with a new sobriety and purpose. There were ripplings and shiverings while E. T. Gerry assured the Purity Congress that prostitution existed in the United States and that abominable practices among Romish choirboys had been rumoured. Susan Anthony and Frances Willard congratulated the new Anti-Saloon League. Celebrities gleamed in frocks with ruffled sleeves at receptions of the Woman's Club. Provincial gentlewomen might stare upon the gowns of Mrs. Potter Palmer or Mrs. Charles Henrotin and then shift their adoration to Mrs. Frances Hodgson Burnett, mother of " Little Lord Fauntleroy " and lately mother of " One I Knew the Best of All " in *Scribner's Magazine*, a graceful summary of her English childhood which fascinated William James and S. Weir Mitchell but found thin sales with her usual audience. So presently mothers trapped restless offspring and read to them the record of Mrs. Burnett's return to her stall in the sugar market with " Two Little Pilgrims," which tells how two quaint and fanciful children went to the beautiful World's Fair and were adopted by the kindest rich gentleman. Then there was the quiet, dry woman known as " Octave Thanet " who soon would assert that American women in crowds lost their manners. And always there was Frances Willard, whose shrine was in Chicago.

Women celebrated in other capacities might be seen. Amused journalists of New Orleans chatted with their city's leading procuress, who had brought her entire stock, suitably costumed, on a holiday to broaden their minds. And there was the aureate creature of whom Mark Twain lazily remarked that the average man would rather behold her nakedness than Ulysses Grant in his full dress uniform. Indeed, ladies wearing white ribbons besought the Mayor of Chicago to exclude painted women from the Fair's grounds, but uselessly. So in that city, on the night of July 5th, as it slumbered under the doubled protection of Mrs. Palmer and Miss Willard, there came the birth of an American folksong. The agent of a New York bank was roused and brought hastily to room 202 in a packed hotel. The room held a priest, some doctors, a handsome, scared lad from a small town in Iowa who blubbered that the lady just told him she was taking some headache medicine, and the bared body of a wonderful woman stretched on a bed in the muscular torments that follow a dose of strong poison. There was also a purse that enclosed a startling bankbook and some cards. The adolescent knew nothing. She had spoken to him on the Midway at the Fair. They let him go. The priest prayed and the body stirred until dawn. Delicate and just audible, voices filled the room and there came the scents of Jockey Club and heliotrope, the fluttering whisper of laces, the chuckled gossip of " The Black Crook's " dressing-room. . . . Kitty, did y'see Jim Fisk's sleigh with the silver bells yest'day? . . . Say, Kitty, who gave you the house in Twelfth Street? Honest, Kitty, I won't tell! . . . Kitty! Kitty, Ned Stokes shot Jimmy over at the Grand Central an' the p'lice are lookin' for Josie Mansfield! . . . These astral echoes floated over the fair body until it loathsomely stiffened on the bed. And then something slim and exquisite rose in a cloud from the sagging wreck. She stood preening the ruffles and the slanting hat in which Brady photographed her for the delight of bucks along Broadway in 1869. She hitched tighter to the famous ankles her striped Watteau stockings and her feet that once ran bare across bogs in County Clare now tripped in those ridiculous little shoes from which men drank champagne. Outside a misty door Kitty dawdled, a bit scared, uncertain in the gloom pierced by red shadows rolling up from Purgatory, and then a voice ineffably French murmured behind her: " *Ma toute belle!* " and Kitty turned to beam professionally on a delicious gentleman, smartly groomed once more, whose grin suggested release from some sharp agony. They looked and liked. The gallant blond fellow tucked under one arm a ghostly advance copy of M. Pierre Louys's *Songs of Bilitis,* not yet published, after turning down the page at . . . " *Mon dernier amant, ce sera toi, je le sais. Voici ma bouche, pour laquelle un peuple a pâli de désir.* . . ." and pretty Kitty went down the ordained steps with Guy de Maupassant chattering tenderly in her ear, and now the ribald sing:

> " In room Two Hundred and Two,
> The walls keep talking to you.
> Shall I tell you what they said? " . . .

And in New York a balance of more than three hundred thousand dollars acquired by a dancing-girl who didn't dance was split among her Irish kin. She was not yet forty.

In Constantine perhaps Pierre Louys was polishing off,
"*Se peut il que tout soit fini! Je n'ai pas encore vécu cinq
fois huit années . . . et déjà voici ce qu'll faut dire: On
n'aimera plus . . .*"

The Fair went on. Mr. John Pierpont Morgan stalked
through the palace of Fine Arts and brutally remarked of
the French exhibits that they seemed to have been picked by
a committee of chambermaids. Indeed, artists were disappointed with the French exhibits, and that disappointment
speaks in William Walton's official volume on the Fair's
art. Where were the Impressionists? These Monets,
Seurats and Renoirs cried up in the magazines weren't to be
seen. Mr. Brownell had been describing the new movements in *Scribner's*, but where were the symptoms of all
this fever? Instead, here was the full Academic tone and
scope — military pieces, the inevitable Madeleine Lemaire,
the inescapable Debat-Ponsan, the "Wasp's Nest" of
William Bouguereau, lent by Charles Yerkes, a financier
who had rightfully succeeded Bouguereau's first American
patron, the gambling procurer "Cash" Brown. Mrs. Grace
Ralston Lewis escorted party after party of rural folk
though the galleries and was disgusted because the Iowans
and Kansans would stop to stare at Edwin Weeks' "Last
Voyage," a dead Hindu rowed toward the burning ghat, in
the American section, when they should have hurried to
gaze at the Whistlers and Lord Leighton's "Garden of the
Hesperides." She could not interest them in her favourite
English painter, Ellen Terry's first husband, who had sent
over as a free gift to the United States one of his best pictures. It showed the tanned captain of an Eton crew clad
in an apron of misty shadow leading a naked but pretty
imbecile up a slope of rock toward nowhere. The picture
had already been displayed in America without popularity
or comment. It was called "Love and Life." Mrs. Lewis,
on her own admission, was then a rather sentimental person,

lately wed, and she thought well of " Love and Life," but her guests and visitors weren't enthralled. It wasn't the nudity of Love or Life that annoyed them. They simply didn't care for Art in the rendition of George Frederick Watts. She recalls small outcries before the "Temptation " of Claude Bourgonnier, a very buxom trollop lolling on the shoulder of an addled Saint Anthony, and before Rosset-Granger's " Jetsam," a dead lady wallowing in the backwash of a wave on some Bohemian seashore. But nobody protested " Love and Life."

All through the '80's had risen a discussion of " the nude " — that soft, then hard insinuating syllable that nearly rhymes with " lewd." The nude had been denounced by Anthony Comstock and, of course, had been mentioned in his amazing " Traps for the Young." Will Low and Kenyon Cox had written conjointly a defence of the nude in *Scribner's*, the sounding-box of art in the '90's. At the World's Fair the artists who essayed the nude announced by every concession of wind-blown drapery, floating vegetable matter and opportune posture that they considered a naked body most obscene. As usual the statues were more daring than the pictures and, as usual, nobody cared. Paul Bartlett's completely naked Ghost Dancer was admired and people merely chuckled over Rudolph Maison's enthusiastically naked Negro bouncing on a donkey. Comstock had declared that " nude paintings and statues are the decoration of infamous resorts, and the law-abiding American will never admit them to the sacred confines of his home," forgetting comfortably that the Greek Slave of Hiram Powers had been copied and distributed freely years before and that a statue of George Washington dressed in nothing but a blanket constantly faced the Capitol at Washington. Elbert Hubbard wagered that Comstock would appear at Chicago and make himself heard against the Fine Arts. Comstock lost the bet for the fantastic editor. But another

force moved. Mild paragraphs dotted the journals . . .
" a powerful organization of ladies " had protested the
sending of " Love and Life " to Grover Cleveland. The
papers were not specific. The ladies were " members of a
society to promote temperance," or " some members of a
semi-religious society headed by Miss Frances Willard of
Chicago." Incorrect versions blew about. The Young Women's Christian Association was blamed, and so were the
suffragists. Excitement broke out in the small artistic quarter of New York. A group of young artists, headed by William Sonntag, went from editor to editor, until James Gordon Bennett of the *Herald* told them blandly that he had
no intention of fighting women and they broke up in dis-
couragement. A pure and enlightened womanhood had won
without a struggle.

III

THE WORLD'S FAIR definitely set afire the suffragists. Without doubt and in spite of some ferocious squabbles, Mrs.
Potter Palmer and the Board of Lady Managers had shown
great competence. At receptions of the Woman's Club in
Chicago there had been a parade of quietly effective professional women — Jane Addams, Florence Hunt, Jane Logan
and the rest. Suffrage now woke with a roar. Bills to en-
franchise women were offered in New York and in other
eastern States. There were speechs and canvassings. The
Reverend John Buckley implored male voters to respect
female moral superiority by making sure that it wouldn't
be soiled and degraded by putting a bit of paper in a ballot
box. The Honourable George Hoar begged the men to let
female moral superiority purify politics by voting. Rebecca
Harding Davis remarked in Philadelphia that " silly, super-
ficial arguments " were being used on both sides, and declined to take part. The usual pointless insults were ex-

changed in drawing-rooms, and the usual number of intelligent gentlewomen were lied to and rebuffed by politicians at Albany. New York showed the excitement at its highest. The campaign faltered along and its written record displays all the reasons why, twenty years later, Inez Milholland remarked: " They raised enemies for themselves in the clubs and whisky distilleries with every breath," for the question of woman's moral superiority constantly took shape as a direct threat of what woman would do to all these barkeepers and rich men's clubs and the like, and in the midst of the mild little tumult a certain Rose Lipschowsky got up on a soap-box in Union Square to say violently: " Why don't all these ladies do something to help the Garment Workers' Union instead of saying how good and refined they are? " She was much applauded, got down from her soap-box and vanishes altogether, an unconscious symbol of what suffrage in the '90's omitted from its speeches and programs. It would be a long time yet before a woman would ask in print: " Are women people? " and it is in character that Alice Duer's career in prose began with the fable of an undecided nymph and a cynical owl. The suffragists of the '90's, if it's fair to quote the words of their representatives, were on another tack. They were not people; they were " women, trained by the essence of our natures to deeds of moral elevation, education and the work of God! " This moral superiority, Frances Willard wrote in 1892, had been a thousand times declared by the mouth of man. And so it had. But one sees curiously little about moral superiority in Constance Cary Harrison's novel, " A Bachelor Maid," written in the winter of 1893 with her customary smoothness. Mrs. Harrison's principal treasure was a hatred of fools. She interrupted work one afternoon to see some callers. One of them, a heavily moral young matron, observed about a girl of good family lately mother of an illegitimate baby: " She's behaved like a woman of the working-class! " Mrs. Harrison mildly gazed at this idiot and mildly drawled: " I believe that illegitimate babies are arranged for in just the same way in all classes, my dear! " and signalled Mrs. William Tod Helmuth to remove this creature from her sight. " A Bachelor Maid " says neither Yes nor No to suffrage. It is competent light satire — the professional suffragist of the tale is an ignoble fraud sketched from a specimen that floated close to Mrs. Harrison's hand; there is suitable demonstration that woman's place isn't always the home. This is merely clever journalism and it had no chance of much discussion, for *Harper's Magazine* was publishing " Trilby."

With " Trilby " there came a sudden exposition of American woman. Du Maurier's drawings had always been published in *Harper's* and the house had brought out " Peter Ibbetson " in 1891. This second novel began with the January number of 1893 and instantly came storm, cancellations of subscriptions, and an increase of circulation. In June a jeweller produced a scarfpin, Trilby's foot in gold or silver, and women wore the badge. The soul of James McNeill Whistler was riven by Du Maurier's sketch of himself. He protested aloud and the cartoonist let the portrait be suppressed when the novel was published. The critics saw that this was Thackeray in solution, but a craze had begun among women and now comedians in light opera asked each other: " Where's Mamie? . . . Upstairs reading ' Trilby '? " and feet and shoes were suddenly " Trilbies " while ladies in the beginning literary clubs debated Trilby's ethics and clergymen regretted to point out to fashionable parishes that Mr. Du Maurier was no Christian. Harper's Brothers paid royalties on edition after edition. Virgins posed as Trilby in her Greek gown in the tableaux of two winters. A bathsuit, a cigarette, a cigar and a restaurant were named for Du Maurier's marshmallow goddess. Suffrage got tangled with the question of nude art.

Trilby had something to do with woman's independence. Saint Gaudens said airily at a male dinner party: " Every other woman you meet thinks she could be an artist's model," and the hunchbacked Paul Leicester Ford wanted to know of the same group: " What would happen to an American if he'd written ' Trilby '? "

The question was unfair. But young John Ford Bemis was just then finding out what happens to an American novel in which conventional religion is mocked no more sharply that Du Maurier had mocked it in " Trilby." He had written on his uncle's farm in Georgia the story of a preacher named John Orme who took to reading history and then collapsed into agnosticism. He was driven from his church and sat enjoying Kant in a hut beside a swamp, after his wife had abandoned him in the name of Christ. She returned as a mob came to lynch him after the tumult of a camp-meeting near by. The pious chased the pair into the swamp and slaughtered them. Their bodies sank into the muck, the symbol of modern religion. All this was told nimbly and discreetly in the manner of Bret Harte. Mr. Bemis sent it to his mother's friend, Frank R. Stockton, for approval. Stockton advised: " You had best get the couple out of the swamp alive, but your conclusion is logical and right." He recommended the book to the *Century*. Richard Gilder wrote, when returning the manuscript, a kind, long letter explaining that the *Century's* large domestic circulation wouldn't receive this story placidly. *Lippincott's Magazine,* able to publish Oscar Wilde's " The Picture of Dorian Gray," was afraid of the " religious element " in the American book. For *Harper's Weekly*, Henry Mills Alden wrote: " Would it not be possible to mitigate the final scenes? Is it strictly necessary that Mrs. Orme should die with her husband? We have so many ladies on the list of our subscribers. . . ." Mr. Bemis came up to fight for his infant. Alden and Charles Dudley Warner

were firmly kind. Yes, to be sure, "Trilby" contained
agnosticism, an unhappy ending and some harlotry to boot,
but — Well, Mr. Bemis had an income. His novel could
wait. It is dismoded, now, but it had many merits for the
day and he retired from letters with that sense of the sewer
which will float among American writers for a long time
yet, perhaps. He didn't recognize that Paris is the Amneran
Heath of the American woman on which anything is likely
to happen, and that the legend of a naked woman beside the
Seine was safe from that certain censorship of the Titaness.

This question of American woman and letters seems to
have been much debated just then and Charles Nolan fell
foul of the shrewd Julian Ralph in an argument on a
steamer. Ralph assured him that editors were really bothered and often insulted by notes from women and when
the lawyer hooted the idea Ralph proved his point by collecting twenty-five specimens of abuse addressed to *Harper's,* the *Century* and, it seems, to *Lippincott's.* Three letters are dated from New York. The rest came from Ohio,
Illinois, Indiana and Kentucky. The main topics of ob-
jurgation are three. . . . A nice woman has been killed or
failed of marrying the right man in some story. Liquor,
including beer and claret has been drunk by otherwise respectable people or has been mentioned without assault
in an article. The story teaches nothing. In six of these
letters the name of Louisa Alcott is cited as a proper writer
and to one of them is signed the name of Frances Willard.
By way of minor complaint one learns that John Fox's "A
Cumberland Vendetta" has ungrammatical passages and
contains coarse language unsuited to growing boys, that
Lester Raynor's tale of the intriguing Mrs. Deepwater who
arranged her dinners by getting in one celebrity to meet
another is an insult to "Western womanhood," that it is
"disgusting and unmanly" to mention the Pope in an article containing the name of Edward McGlynn, author of

"The Pope in Politics," and that the words "breasts,"
"belly," "damn," "vomit," and "rape" are unfit for
Christian women to read. The one attack on "Trilby" is
signed by Ada Channing Walker, whose activities were now
ending. She had lately discovered that William Whitney
was a horse-racer and had written Grover Cleveland to
oust him from the Democratic Party without getting satisfaction. So she drew up a document on marriage for her
niece, advising her to marry only a man resembling "our
precious Saviour, Jesus Christ, in manners and appearance." Unable to do so, from lack of data, the girl mourned
her aunt two months and married a sugar broker, six feet
three inches long.

A trait binds these letters: they are dated directly on the
offence. Emotion took up a pen and wrote on the best
paper. There is not a trace of intellectual process. They
were annoyed; etiquette had been battered or an opinion
expressed that they didn't like. It is the voice of the porch
shaded by dusty maples along Grand Avenue in a hundred
towns, a resolute violence of the cheapest kind, without
breeding, without taste. And there comes, too, a hint of the
slow battle between the city and the small town. "You
people in New York" are doing thus and so. "I suppose,"
said Mrs. Janette B. Frobisher, "the society women in New
York like to read swear words, but ——" . . . And yet
in Bucyrus, Ohio, a copy of Zola's "Nana" went from
soft hand to soft hand until it came back to its owner in the
state of a worn Bible and slim fingers stained the pages of
a tall "Salammbô" opposite to the plate of Matho squatting with his head against the knees of the Princess, who
cried out: "Moloch, thou burnest me!" while the kisses
of the warrior, Gustave Flaubert said, seared her body,
more biting than flames. However, he was French. From
France, too, came the monotone of a querulous oboe, languidly reciting how sure pain was, how fleet light love in

Constantine or Nagasaki. He had joined Mrs. Humphry
Ward in rejecting the sacraments, but then he mourned so
prettily: " O Christ of those who weep, O calm white Virgin, O all adorable myths that nothing will replace, you
who make tears to run more gently, you who show your
smile at the edge of death's black trench, you alone give
courage to live on to childless mothers and sons motherless,
be ye blessed! And we who have for ever lost you kiss
while weeping the prints left by your tread as it moves
from us." So an untidy infant at play in a park owned and
managed by a fat squirrel named James G. Blaine concluded that Mr. Loti was a great ladies' man, probably one
of those who sometimes sang of their darling Clementine
at night behind red nipples of cigars, beside a moonlit cot-
tonwood, rustling over laughter and music of guitars. . . .

But if you were a proper editor, bred in the society of
Newark or of Hartford, you did not trifle with the Titaness
and for her sake you issued tales of women, by women, for
women, in which one discovers the strangest things about
that duel of the sexes, a deal discussed in the '90's. It
would be fun to know what Sarah Jewett, Agnes Repplier
or Margaret Deland thought of stories printed alongside
their work. The voice of Louisa Alcott echoes in these
tales: Alice Perrine on a trip to Boston found that her betrothed had once tried to kiss the pretty wife of a professor
during a dance. He is given no chance to explain. Tears
dribbled on a box which takes his ring back to him: Miss
Cornwall finds that her lover once wooed a girl who scorned
him. The other girl is now very sorry. Miss Cornwall,
allegedly fond of her swain, simply packs him off to his
former fancy. The gentleman gulps and goes to his doom.
Another Miss Cornwall finds her affianced once lived, ten
years before, in Rome, with " a woman." He is dispatched
to find and marry the girl, and " with bowed head, he faced
the long path of his duty." Charles Milton's lungs have

sent him to California, orange-growing, and he is very comfortable and prosperous. But his wife yearns for Boston, the scene of her girlhood, and on finding that out he simply sells the orange grove and takes her home, " for he had learned what he owed to her womanhood at last." And again you hear Louisa Alcott in tales of Aunt Semanthy and Cousin Hetty from the country who set the frivolous city folk to rights with advice and chicken broth, flatteries of the farm against the triumphant urban women whose photographs spotted the *New York Herald,* whose balls were detailed in a dozen journals of widest circulation.

Now too there appeared, sparsely, another fictional flattery of women, often written by men, in which young girls decide the winning of great football matches by sending some player a violet at the right second, in which maidens repel and crush a male animal in high lust by a simple stare of wonder, in which the female principal is risen above romance and becomes an opalescent cloud, dripping odours which had nothing to do with the processes of child-bearing at all . . . and concurrently in Chicago a living lawyer was consulted by a young woman of fashion about a marriage contract in which her husband would pledge himself not to consummate the marriage. He reported this to a friend of his calling in New York, and on March 9, 1898, found that the metropolitan lawyer had already been consulted about a dozen such contracts. A few months before, in England, George Bernard Shaw had inquired whether it was true that American women really liked to be worshipped on false pretences.

Did they? It has been argued that an extraordinary deference to women began in America with the sexual starvation of the colonial time. In 1709 some cynic named E. Lea wrote, on the margin of a " Venice Preserved," that " I did see in New York for 8 years together that any punk may marry her well who had not her calling too rank on

her face, so strong the men were to wive." And that phenomenon against prudery occurs in all colonized societies.
Scarcity excuses the offered article. E. Lea's notation simply records the obvious source of innumerable American,
Canadian and Australian families. But with the nineteenth
century that situation had altered; in the East old maids
were plentiful. As the century waned, all the European
ills had arrived. Prostitution had increased immensely.
Female workers in the industrial centres were abominably
paid although associations mostly organized by foreign
Jewesses had a little improved the condition in New York
and Chicago. The farmer's wife continued to raise welts
of muscle along her arms beside the sink and in the garden.
In the South, ladies of place smiled as Sphinxes smile when
told by Northern tourists that they lacked practical gifts,
and went on planning gowns to last three years, writing
sketches for newspapers and subtly urging their men out
of the stagnation then changing its colours. Everywhere,
the schoolteacher starved along on disgusting wages. But
for the woman of any means a terrific machine of flatteries
had been patented. Her social importance had climbed
higher and higher since the Civil War and in the following
twenty years of rank commerce. There was no longer any
talk of hosts in the great cities: social columns announced
the acts of hostesses. The men were too busy to bother.
The men were too busy to bother with their own homes, and
with the '90's they were suddenly informed of woman's
power. A spattering foam of satire flecked new comic weeklies — *Puck, Life, Judge, Truth.* Women, it seemed, were
bullying husbands and fathers for money to be spent on
frocks, French tenors, flowers for actresses and actors.
Women were listening to Oriental philosophers and reformers, sitting to expensive painters, running abroad to hunt
down titled Europeans, gouging man's eyes out with hatpins,
hiding his view of the stage at plays with vast hats, adorning

his house with costly gewgaws, making him damned miserable in all ways.

In 1895 the neurologist S. Weir Mitchell wrote to a dead man of his dead wife: " You are entirely responsible for Mrs. . . . 's condition. I say so on your own admissions to the effect that you have accustomed her to spend money on herself and your daughters without stint and met all her demands in the way of entertainment. I am tired of writing letters such as this, for the tendency of American men to leave the management of their homes and families to their wives without advice or supervision is growing malignant in its results. Mrs. . . . now feels herself deeply aggrieved by your interference and her condition is dangerous in the extreme. A meaningless and injudicious deference to her wishes has done the harm. . . . I advise a permanent separation." A meaningless deference to the wishes of Mrs. . . . had caused her to tear down a superb Georgian house while her husband was abroad and to order the erection of a French manor in white stone which hideously existed until it happened to burn ten years after the psychiatrist's advice.

Indeed it was a singularity of the Titaness that she had quite succumbed to all exterior ornaments of France and every summer saw her in augmenting swarms as she invaded the world's most successful shop, acquiring stereotyped clothes, furniture, attentions and parasites with that wide-eyed credulity which remains her great excuse and charm. Richard Harding Davis saw her browbeating bandmasters for American tunes, just as he had seen her romping and running races in staid English hotels, and brotherly gave her warning that relatives of a French husband would hold her beauty small and herself no better than the Indian squaw whose voice she possessed, whose dignity she has not yet assumed. But Mamma and the Girls were abroad to see the world, and it was theirs. Europe beheld them jamming past the guardians of secret, obscene galleries in Naples, set there to guard their famed innocence; they aimed cameras at William Hohenzollern, Donatello's simpering David and the Prince of Wales with equal zest. In spring they flooded New York's marmoreal hotels, waving steamer tickets from table to table and threatening to meet each other in London, and autumn saw them home again, radiant in fresh frocks, hats rejected by the prostitutes of Paris as too gaudy for their use. So Charles Dana Gibson portrayed his Mr. Pipp, bullied all across Europe by Mother and the Girls, these last a pair of goddesses, certain of admiration everywhere, miraculously sprung from ugliness. For the American Girl had been invented. The saponaceous *New York Herald* announced her as " better dressed, better mannered, more lovable and lovelier than any maiden of Europe," and now she glowed in coloured calendars, on the lids of candy boxes and the covers of magazines, more and more vividly as the decade wilted down. There came the Gibson Girl, the Christy Girl, the Gilbert Girl, and the paler, more subtle virgins of Henry Hutt, the slim patrician girls of Albert Wenzell — a parade of incredibly handsome, smartly dressed young things without existence anywhere. The beauty of two Englishwomen, Mary Mannering and Julia Marlowe, was set in rings of roses on pasteboard to show Flowers of the American Stage. The exquisite Julia Arthur, a Canadian of Irish parentage, was announced as " the supreme bloom of our national beauty " when she conquered the critics in " A Lady of Quality," which proved that the best way of ending an illicit love is to brain your paramour with a riding-crop. But Paul du Chaillu went hunting across New York for " those women that I see in your newspapers " and seems to have been slightly disappointed in the results of his chase. The commercial worth of these flatteries has been quite forgotten by critics, native and foreign, who have

chattered of a feminized society. " In America," wrote
Aline Gorren in 1899, " it is the business of the artist, the
shopkeeper and the publisher to show vain women an improved photograph of themselves." And to the improvement of that photograph had been added the suppression of
all other images. Adept lecturers promulgated the notion
of a native literature pruned for the benefit of the virgin
and the sedate matron, who were reading Alphonse Daudet's *Sapho,* D'Annunzio's " Triumph of Death," Rudyard
Kipling's " Light That Failed " and " Love o' Women."
It could be proved by Hamilton Wright Mabie that Tolstoy's " Resurrection " was admirable and worthy the attention of any lady, but that Stephen Crane's " George's
Mother " was " harsh and unnecessarily frank " even after
the phrase " for he had known women of the city's painted
legions " had been stricken from its third chapter. The
Titaness in the garments of Cybele must be placated as the
priests of the Great Mother were wont to do. William Winter would lash the playwrights in her behalf and at the first
night of " Arizona " Acton Davies would find himself surrounded by a band of ladies denouncing Augustus Thomas
for his picture of the sullen, bored officer's wife, tired of
the desert, ready to elope with a lover in whom she has no
belief. Even Pierre Berton's " Zaza " would be tagged
with a last scene showing the strumpet redeemed, successfully regnant as a great actress.

Then, and on March 1, 1900, a version of " Sappho "
was produced at the Casino theatre in New York. Clyde
Fitch had softened the tale carefully. Fanny Legrand was
no longer a woman on the edge of age, hunting a lover, but
a goddess, applauded as she came down a staircase, to music, by the guests of the masked ball. Miss Olgo Nethersole, the English actress who appeared as Fanny, had already pained William Winter by kissing actors on the

mouth in " Carmen," and now there rose a scandal when
she permitted her leading man, an excellent amateur photographer, to lug her bodily up winding steps to a theoretic
bedroom at the end of the first act. The curtain fell for a
minute, and then Jean Gaussin was shown descending in
the light of dawn to a twitter of zinc birds in the wings.
Horrible noises ensued. Miss Nethersole was bullied by
the press and arraigned in court for indecency. A committee of gentlewomen gathered at the house of Mrs. William Sonntag and hastily wrote a petition to the Mayor
of New York stating that " the version of this novel is in
no respect obscene and is in fact milder than the novel
itself, which has had free circulation in the United States.
Miss Nethersole's performance is entirely proper and restrained. . . . It is derogatory of the public intelligence
that a celebrated work of art should be altered or expurgated. . . . Since this prosecution has been asked in the
name of American women, we find it necessary to protest."
The petition was circulated for two days and signed by
suffragists, writers and women of the smart world. The
prosecution had already become silly. Miss Nethersole
was acquitted; the play went on. Ladies stormed the theatre. William Winter was horribly upset. But on April
4th a minor actor in the company received a note from the
head mistress of a school for girls in the Hudson valley, re-
questing him to remove his daughter, a child of eleven, " as
several mothers of several students have seen the play in
which you are appearing and they cannot consider Margaret a fit companion for their daughters in consequence.
. . ."

It is not alleged against the women of the Mauve Decade
that they invented cheap cruelty and low social pressures,
but they erected these basenesses into virtues by some defensive sense of rectitude, and a generation of sons was

reared in the shadow of the Titaness, aware of her power, protected by nothing from her shrill admonitions. Is it matter for such wonder among critics that only satire can describe this American of our time who drifts toward middle age without valour, charm or honour?

CHAPTER II

WASTED LAND

S IR RICHARD BURTON'S last American visitor was an intrepid lady who once had been a reporter in New York when the calling was held unfit for women and their summaries of balls, religious meetings or such things were sent by messenger to profane offices of Park Row. Burton began by being rude to Mrs. Beach. American writers, he remarked, were a pack of muffs; the publishers — particularly his own — and the critics made up another pack. He stormed at his guest until it proved that she came from California. His sympathy was then as tedious as his rudeness. Why was nothing written about the West? In some room of his intellectual warehouse he had stored a mass of facts in Western history and scandal. Mrs. Beach finally fled from the surge of questions and before she reached London, homeward-bound, the adventurer was dead — on October 13, 1890, leaving his translation of " The Scented Garden " in the clean hands of Isabel, his wife, who promptly burned it without pausing to think that he had already ruined the fame of two celebrated obscene works by simply rendering them into English. Her silliness caused a deal of trouble, but French booksellers profited by selling Le Jardin Parfumé to Americans who never would have heard of it save for Lady Burton's prudery.

Mrs. Beach gave her report of Burton on American affairs to the journals when she landed at New York and failed to sell her unabridged article. Eastern editors were then rather averse to printing rude observations on themselves, and Burton's comment came belated. The West was suddenly a subject in 1891. The *Century* brought out notes on primitive California and a tale of Hamlin Garland. Julian Ralph's careful reports of Western States and cities appeared in *Harper's*. Frederick Remington's sketches and the first of Owen Wister's stories found attention. The wave of interest lasted through 1892 with a froth of politics as the young People's Party began to boil and essays on the farmers of the midlands, on the railroads and rural banks were printed in the *Arena*, a magazine that seems to have had at least one devoted reader, Theodore Roosevelt. The wave sped among obituaries. Eminent people were dying in groups. Herman Melville, George Ernest Marie Boulanger, Charles Stewart Parnell, Edward Bulwer Lytton, author of "Lucile," James Russell Lowell, Cardinal Manning, the Duke of Clarence and Avondale, betrothed to a Princess of Teck who married somebody else, Edward Freeman, Walt Whitman, William Astor, Manoel Deodora da Fonseca, George William Curtis, and John Greenleaf Whittier all had vanished to appropriate music of the journals before incredible persons such as those who weep in theatres and build tombs invited clergymen to pray for the health of Alfred, Lord Tennyson. Prayers were offered in several American cities as September of 1892 ended. All the worst of Tennyson's poems were known by heart in the United States while Thomas Wentworth Higginson vainly tried to have the tidal verses of "Ulysses" taught in the public schools of Boston, asserting almost piteously that a poet should be known by his best work and not by his weakest. Notes on the failing man's condition dotted the Eastern newspapers. The illiterate West, however, prepared an escort.

At half past nine on the bright morning of October 5,

WASTED LAND

1892, a lad named John Sibert was helping his aunt to wash dishes in a house of Coffeyville, Kansas. He had arrived in the little city two days before and was leaving Coffeyville on the train at noon. Coffeyville had two topics, that week; the main street was torn up for new drains and somebody had told somebody else from saddle to saddle on the prairie that Bob Dalton had bragged he would raid his own town in broad daylight. At half past nine, then, John Sibert was helping to wash dishes diligently. Between that moment and the second of twenty-five minutes to ten, rifles crashed. John leaped down his aunt's steps and slid against a post, stopping his watch. Some lad ran past him yelling: "The Daltons are in !" and the word reached a clerk at the station. In a few minutes men in Omaha and Kansas City were shouting the news as the one word, "Dalton, Dalton, Dalton, Dalton . . ." clicked from the keys all through the midlands. John Sibert loped around a corner and suddenly faced two long, grave young men with rifles in their hands. He didn't know Bob and Emmett Dalton from any other strangers and he started to ask something. Bob drawled: "Keep away from here, bud, or you'll get hurt," and shoved the boy aside placidly, then placidly strolled along with Emmett, snapping his fingers and whistling through his teeth. At once a lad named Luke Baldwin hurried into sight and didn't pause when one of the brothers shouted to him. Bob Dalton killed him forthwith and the pair trotted from John Sibert's view. . . . The famous gang rode into town at half past nine. They left their horses in an alley and calmly strolled up to separate in the space before the town's two banks. Bob and Emmett plundered one bank. Grattan Dalton with the henchmen Bill Powers and Dick Broadwell [1] attended to the other. Citizens grabbed the rifles with which the antecinemic West did its serious shoot-

---

[1] Called sometimes "Jack of Diamonds" from the song which he sang constantly. The song now passes as a "Negro melody."

ing and the fight began. Bright spires of glass toppled from
frames of windows; smoke went in surges along the street
as men fired busily from porches or through doorways.
There are a hundred legends of what happened. Young
John Sibert knelt beside the dying boy in the alley behind
one bank and heard a man named Gump swearing in the
pain of a shattered hand. Presently Broadwell rode wildly
down the street with his hands gripped on the horn of his
great Mexican saddle and fell dead from his mount a little
way from the noisy town. Somebody killed Bill Powers.
Grattan Dalton ran down the sidewalk with blood on his
face and paused to rip the green handkerchief from his
throat in full range of the batteries before he turned at the
corner of a stable and fired back, killing the city's marshal
with a superb shot from the hip. His shoulder was riddled
so that he couldn't lift his rifle. He lurched from sight down
the alley toward the tethered horses. Bob Dalton strolled
into view, loading his rifle, and a hundred muzzles were
aimed at his blue shirt. One ball caught him above the
navel but he walked on and sat on a heap of stones beside
a barn, firing again. A man named Kloehr ran from cover
straight at the terrible rifle and shot the gang's captain in
the lungs, then whirled and sent a bullet through Grattan
Dalton's throat as the youngest brother crawled toward the
plunging horses. Firing stopped. Men hurried up and a
thick group formed around Bob Dalton in his carmine
puddle on the clay. The body heaved in its blood but he
kept yelling: " Ride! " Then someone howled and the
crowd saw Emmett Dalton struggling among the horses. He
was wounded four times when he got into his saddle and sat
huddled with his gloves clasped on his groin. Men lowered
their rifles, expecting him to fall, as men shot in the groin
do, generally. But all the brothers were valiant. He
spurred his horse down the alley and swung from the stir-

rups to seize Bob's arm. Politeness ended. Carey Seaman
blew in his side with a fast shot. The last Dalton slid across
his brother's body. It was now ten minutes to ten. Sightseers poured from trains before noon and the corpses of
Lord Tennyson's escort to Walhalla were photographed so
that it could be proved the Dalton gang was out of business
after five years of graceful, even endearing performance.
Unlike the James and Younger gangs, they didn't blow un-
armed children to rags nor did they kill their mistresses in
farewell as did the unlovable Tumlinson, once something
of a hero. They were amiable and rather mannerly bandits,
on the whole, and yet no ballad bears on their name. The
great tradition of Sturdevant, Murrel of " the mystic clan "
in Andrew Jackson's reign, Boone Helm, Billy the Kid and
Jesse James ended here in an alley on the crackling sound
of Carey Seaman's shotgun. Jay Gould died eight weeks
later in civilized New York, and in his bed.

The brothers had little notice in the East. Editors gave
them a paragraph surrounded by notes on Grover Cleveland's latest speech or President Harrison's hopes. The
West's main exhibit in October of 1892 was the dangerous
People's Party. It demanded the governmental ownership
of railroads and telegraphs, urged governmental banks for
the use of farmers and upheld the issue of silver currency
on terms making it almost the equal of gold. Not one of
these notions happened to be strictly new but speakers of
the young party assailed the railroads, their builders and
owners, and the party swiftly became a cyclone whirling
from Kansas or a scowling farmer in a cowboy's wide hat
stretching predatory hands toward Washington. The dignified little essays of Hamlin Garland and the rest in the
Arena were probably not read; the Populists naturally were
" crazy " when mentioned in the journals. Edwin Godkin
viewed them without sympathy. One editor who might

have broadly taken their side was Joseph Pulitzer, whose wrath against Collis Huntington and other lords of the railways had been repeatedly in print. But only a few newspapers in New England condescended to treat the People's Party as a positive effort in social criticism and when four senators and eleven congressmen were elected from States in which Democrats and Populists had fused, there was a waver of real panic among the rich, those sons of the Golden Ass hopeless of rose-leaves to make them men. Some alarmed gentlemen interrupted Mark Hanna on a busy afternoon at Cleveland and asked him if they'd better sell their holdings in railroads at once. Hanna said amiably: "You make me think of a lot of scared hens." In New York a great lady proposed to John Kendrick Bangs that all the Populists be tried for treason. The humorist asked what the Westerners had done and the matron magnificently answered: "Everything!"

The Democratic triumph returned to his chair in Congress a tall, harshly beautiful young man from Nebraska named William Jennings Bryan and in Illinois a pallid, unconsciously emotional North German lawyer, John Altgeld, was elected governor. His success troubled the considerable Tory element, for it was known that he had the oddest notions of prisons, courts and popular rights. Senator John Macauley Palmer of Illinois had also irritated some Eastern editors by a speech of July 7th. The old soldier drawled for thirty minutes, damning the use of armed detectives — he chose to call them bravos and ruffians — by Andrew Carnegie's steel plant at Homestead in Pennsylvania. Ten lives had been lost at Homestead in the ugly battle between strikers and detectives. General Palmer went the length of protesting "these private armies" and of insisting that Carnegie's workmen had the right of considering themselves permanently employed and of demanding reasonable pay for their drudgery. . . . Conservatives looked westward

with annoyance. Mr. Bryan was still unknown in the East
but Altgeld now replaced the People's Party as the demoniac
shape essential to American journalism.

In New York Ward McAllister's star reached its zenith.
He censored the lists of a famous ball and his importance
was trumpeted everywhere across the country. The career
that began with careful courtships of wealthy hosts now
concluded in the domination of great hostesses. The dandy
was solemnly reported in the *New York Herald*, the valet's
guide to celebrity, as writing his memoirs. The Four Hundred, the balls of some man named Bradley Martin, Pink
Teas and the attempt of youngsters to wear silken knee
breeches at dances — all these matters were copied from
paper to paper and delighted lumberjacks in Oregon. The
timid ostentations of a possible three thousand men and
women living in cramped, airless houses between two
polluted rivers were advertised as though an aristocracy
moved proudly through some customary ritual. Had it
been equally advertised that these people admired paintings by Alexandre Cabanel, who might have learned his
trade over again from Thomas Dewing, Edward Simmons
or Kenyon Cox and stuck up views of clean French peasants
flirting with a white horse, by Debat-Ponsan, nobody would
have understood. Perhaps if the cynical dealer in wines
who openly bragged of selling Algerian brews in French
bottles to the best clubs had written his thoughts to the press,
provincial editors might not have taken the Four Hundred
so seriously. But the Four Hundred had been created, now,
and New York was an extravagant shimmer that persisted
in the general imagination as a drunken planet while a disastrous, earthly pageant moved in the middle West with
John Altgeld for its standard-bearer. An antithesis of the
coarsest kind had been arranged, by journalism, and Altgeld appeared as a bearded prophet pointing up wrathfully
at a frieze of cruel, jewelled figures on a marble ledge,

creatures not mundane or merely silly but a set of brutal gods. It could hardly be known in Nebraska that a gentle minority in this society would not meet the plunderers, the railroad kings and the low politicians whose affairs were parables from 1892 to 1896. The West saw a solid rank of the plutocracy — Collis Huntington and Matthew Quay arm in arm with women for whom the tribal name of " Mrs. Astorbilt " was invented in 1893. What the East thought of the West is less and less important to know or to record. But journalism changed the pale governor of Illinois into a Maritsakro, a divinity of snakes risen from hell, through Chicago, who pardoned anarchists duller than Ward Mc-Allister out of prison, forbade Grover Cleveland to send troops into his State, and his demoniac quality lasted until his person was replaced by another, taller man.

Grover Cleveland entered the White House. President Harrison departed. The World's Fair began in thunders of music and flurries of rockets. Immediate trouble overtook the procession. A triumphant Democratic Party was split by instant quarrels. The government of British India suspended the free coinage of silver. American railroads stopped ordering new coaches for the traffic to the Fair from Mr. George Pullman's great company on the edge of Chicago. This gentleman was an amiable person enough who shaved his upper lip and wore a tuft of grizzled whisker on his slightly jutting chin. One day of May, 1893, he was showing some friends through his plant and happened to drop a paper. A wiry boy stepped from the unfinished bulk of a car and handed the paper back to his owner. Mr. Pullman smiled. The boy grinned. The grandee and a human item of his property met so and never saw each other again. The human item survives as a chemist of repute. His name can be Jim for this page. He was sixteen and his guardian uncle had let him come to Chicago from a tame farm in central Indiana. He boarded in Pullman, the model suburb approved by Frances Willard, as liquor was sold only to guests at the hotel, and the harlot had no booth. Young labourers went into the hideous city for diversion and returned to pure Pullman according to circumstance and temperament. Jim vanished from Pullman in June when the least valuable workmen were civilly discharged. News of a " financial depression " vaguely reached the human item, taking a holiday on his uncle's farm, telling envious young cousins in the barnyard how Buffalo Bill's elaborate hair flapped under his sombrero at the Coliseum and what Lillian Russell really looked like. Financial depression meant nothing much. Jim went back to Chicago and found that plants were hiring nobody. He was idle for five weeks and then, one of thousands, tramped off into the fields where hands would be wanted for the harvest. But the tanned men were not hiring many helpers.

In November, the item had learned that financial depression meant no drawers inside his frayed trousers and a constant, increasing wonder as to what the Congress was doing in Washington. The triumphant democracy fought over tariffs and tinkered with currency. Jim heard and read about silver standards and gold standards, issues of fresh bonds to meet the shortage of gold in the Treasury. The panic was real, now. Notices of failures and suicides, starvation among miners in Ohio and the work for their relief by William McKinley, prophecies of A. P. Gorman and Russell Sage were printed side by side. Jim beamed at brakemen on freight trains and intrigued for passage into Indiana. He reverted to agriculture in December.

In the harassed, lugubrious January of 1894, a solid, quiet financier at Cleveland in Ohio spent some afternoons strolling with an old friend along mean streets and letting bills pass quickly from his plump fingers into the hands of shabby men lined at corners who nudged each other, muttering: " Here's Mr. Hanna." No identity had yet been manufactured for the placid person by Alfred Henry Lewis and Homer Davenport. On January 28th he wrote to an attorney in New York: " The situation here is terrible. We are not in as bad shape as Chicago. H—— tells me that our friend B—— is in a bad way and likely to go into bankruptcy. Take enclosed to him and tell him to hang on." The unhappy B—— broke into tears at the sight of Mr. Hanna's abominable script on a cheque, and hung on.

The Senate and Congress wrangled over tariffs. David Hill damned the proposed income tax as unconstitutional. Populists accused conservatives of taking bribes to prevent the destruction of the McKinley tariff, and the journals announced a strange affair called the Army of the Commonweal, headed by General Coxey. Coxey and his lieutenant, Kelly, were bringing a mob of unemployed workmen eastward to make Grover Cleveland do something for them. Fights between Commonwealers and sheriffs happened in Oregon and California. Men discharged from halted work on railroads in Oregon joined the army. In Chicago scores and hundreds of workmen discharged by the Pullman Palace Car Company were joining the American Railroad Union. The Union consented to arbitrate its fight with the Great Northern railroad and won most of its wishes. The newspapers congratulated both parties and went on announcing the approach of Coxey's Army. Workmen in Chicago were anticipating the fictions of O. Henry and Anatole France, just then, by insulting policemen or smashing windows so as to be jailed, fed and warmed. . . . In March the item Jim set off for the tannery of a cousin in Nebraska. He already liked to potter with acids and materials. But when he reached the tannery it was shut and his cousin was desperately trying to raise loans to tide himself through the depression. Other small employers and great farmers in Nebraska were miserably conferring with the Bank. Jim faced about with six dollars in his pocket and began a free navigation eastward. The fringe of Kelly's division of Coxey's army picked him up at Omaha where Eugene Debs came to shake hands with Kelly, in a white necktie. The army, now a comic feature of memoirs, travelled on toward Saint Louis amid the sorrows of hens and the alarm of housewives. Jim swung his legs from the rear of a car and listened to a mixture of misery and bravado. But the curious humour of American workmen still operated among these unwashed. They were literate and mostly young. What could Grover Cleveland do for them? Or Congress? They deserted Kelly in swarms at Saint Louis. Jim made northward with a Dutch lad in a hospitable caboose and his companion presented him to a Dutch family in an unchronicled region outside Chicago where stolid folk named Annekje and Dirk grew vegetables.

Mr. Pullman and his workmen were now in full quarrel. Pullman had "nothing to arbitrate." The nation roused to a situation in Chicago, where twenty-four railroads centred and vast yards exchanged a thousand kinds of freight. Mr. Pullman was handsomely begged to submit his case to arbitration or simply to restore the wages of last year to his shrunken forces. It has since been explained that the manufacturer's close friends were against an arbitration. The American Railroad Union, the mayors of cities adjacent, Civic Federations and simple millionaires urged Pullman to come to terms. Far away Ambrose Bierce paused in his rattle of wit against the Southern Pacific Railway of California to remark that Mr. Pullman was a gentleman in the American definition only. "A gentleman," Bierce mentioned, "is a man who bathes and has never been in jail." He then resumed the heaving of liquid fire at the Southern Pacific, called the Octopus in the State whose capitol was its office. The Octopus had absorbed the Central Pacific and had decided that its debts in the sum of sixty million dollars ought to be slowly refunded, say at two per cent yearly for half a century. A bill to permit this emollient arrangement in favour of the Octopus was accordingly presented to Congress. . . . But outside Chicago the item Jim was tending vegetables in an embarrassment of adolescent pride. His Dutch hosts couldn't afford him. Nobody wanted to hire him in Chicago, where grown men were doing a day's work for a bowl of soup and a loud roaring in saloons followed each day's notice that Mr. Pullman wouldn't arbitrate. Then the whiskered paternalist discharged three members of a committee that pled with him while he fingered a black rubber ruler on his desk. Most of the workmen left struck in a body and the plant closed. Mark Hanna hammered a cigar to death in a club at Cleveland and said angrily: " What in God's name does Pullman think he's doing? " William McKinley sent his brother Abner and three lawyers of power to call on Pullman, who told them that the matter now rested with other powers than his. Abner McKinley, kind as his brother, turned and walked out of the manufacturer's house in a rage.

The parade of Coxey's army had ended in a pathetic scene at Washington, where Coxey and some of his attendants were arrested for walking on grass with intent to commit a demonstration below the bulbous dignity of the Capitol. But there was an uneasy stir in the warming air all around Chicago. A convention of the Railroad Union gave Pullman its opinion. Editors everywhere openly favoured the strikers. Pullman's aides were voluble in the newspapers. A week of June passed in suspense. Then the Union declared a sympathetic strike and Eugene Debs begged everybody to refrain from violence. The railroads were palsied on July 1st.

It was promptly said that managers of lines hired men to rip up tracks, burn freight and destroy switches so as to make the strikers unpopular. Marshals were sworn in. Men who would not strike were hammered on the head by somebody. Orators yelled in saloons. Useless injunctions forbade strikers to preach the strike to nonstriking. James Sovereign, grand master of the Knights of Labour, pondered on ordering his immense forces to strike also. Altgeld now reared and commanded Grover Cleveland to keep the Federal troops out of Chicago. Cleveland retorted that the mails must be guarded and the troops came on. Real violence exploded twice in two weeks. Men charged the guard at the Monon depot and were killed. Cars smouldered in the huge yard of the Chicago, Burlington and Quincy Railroad. The strike spread westward into seven States and Californians grinned at the attorneys and counsellors of the Octopus emerging from long conferences in its office.

Federal troops and militia camped on the margin of the lake at Chicago expecting anything. Agents of the railroads passed quietly through crowds in the hungry city offering five dollars a day for workmen at yards and stations. One of these picked up the item Jim, who was getting tired of this " battle between the producing classes and the money power of the country " in a phrase of Eugene Debs, and had tramped into Chicago hopeful of a train moving eastward to Indiana. Could he get a place as brakeman on such a train? The agent gave him a card with the name of some foreman on it and sent him off to report at an office in the yards. Scudding down an alley, the boy ran into a group of men, one of them wearing an engineer's cap. In the dusk the boy mistook that cap for a token of employment and called out asking where he could find this foreman. The word " Scab! " rose. The group converged and then left the atomic Jim blind and comfortably senseless in the gutter. Next morning a soldier found him crawling but unaware of motion, a bloody wretchedness that moved by habit. . . . On July 17th they began to arrest Eugene Debs for violating untenable injunctions. He submitted with his customary good nature. The strike collapsed. The sympathy that had followed it was rather dashed by the plundering of freight and ruin of property effected by men who may have been strikers. But there was a sharp protest, even in Tory newspapers, when Mr. Debs was sentenced in December to six months in prison. The phrase " government by injunction " had been invented. The *Springfield Republican*, the *New York Evening Post*, the *Evening Transcript* of Boston and a dozen other conservative journals struck at the sentence as a dangerous precedent. Mr. Debs went to jail but the Supreme Court at least admitted the right of workmen to strike peacefully. The strike at Chicago began to collapse in latter July and presently Mr. Pullman opened his plant. Wages and prices rose once more. The panic waned and vanished. But the middle West had been scared in its vitals. Its industries had been battered; the farmer had suffered, unequally according to location, and little towns had seen suicides of their bankers and merchants. There was no social parade to cure memory of a sharp impression, and Republican speakers were busily telling men that unsettled conditions, low tariffs, experiments in currency came of bad government. Other speakers were pointing out that a government pliant to the summons of railroads needed a bath. Altgeld was a hero in a stormy cloud to thousands who had never seen him. The commonplace journals professed to admire Cleveland's intervention, as they admired his candid threat to England in the next summer when he took up the Venezuelan quarrel and alarmed Edwin Godkin so that the editor wrote two essays against war, repeating everything that Thackeray had said on the subject without improving the satirist's simple statement of soldiers and murderers as interchangeable terms. These grand concerns soared over the item Jim on his uncle's farm while he read texts of chemistry. He still brushed his hair low on the right temple to cover three inches of blue scar, and lads swimming with him in a lazy creek admired a healed gash across his shoulders that seems to have been made by a knife. But his broken ankle mended and one night of May, 1895, he was tramping comfortably alongside the tracks, a mile from his uncle's farm, when a train slowed to a water tank and he saw "Pullman" in gilded paint high on a car's side. Simultaneously he stumbled on a provident half-brick. The contact of the brick with the name on the moonlit car naturally followed. Damage to property of a great corporation is thus reported long after date.

The Octopus came to glory in January of 1895. Its bill in Congress was defeated and now the Californians declared war on the amiable fish itself. Nobody denied that the Southern Pacific had advertised California terrifically in the East. The *Overland Monthly* hinted that politicians revolting against the Octopus did so in the hope of swift bribery. But Ambrose Bierce had gone to New York to carry on the battle from that vantage. Shares and bonds of a new railroad were sold and men of wealth gathered around the venture to protect it. Eastern magazines heartily applauded. The long war of the Californians seemed a success. The Octopus had cynically raised and lowered rates to suit the weather and the profit of crops. Ranchmen sent stuff to market behind mules rather than meet the startling expense of shipping fruit on the Southern Pacific. Joseph Pulitzer renewed his attacks on Collis Huntington in the *World*, dictating editorials from which his stenographers removed the oaths. A pleasant confusion existed in the Eastern mind between owners and promoters of the Western railroads and the military engineers, surveyors and draughtsmen who dragged and bullied the lines into being. The distinction between a Grenville Dodge, sweating in

the deserts, and a Collis Huntington, contemplating the results in an office, was finally clear for a moment, and is now
again forgotten.

The Octopus floated on conversations for some months.
Dr. Barrett Wendell amused a party at dinner in Cambridge by comparing Collis Huntington to Bronson Alcott.
The professor had a curious, arranged voice that may have
covered an intense shyness. He observed that the railroad
king and the philosopher were both Yankees from Connecticut, sons of small farmers. Both had been pedlars in their
boyhood. Suppose that Alcott had taken his pack into the
hidden West and discovered an ideal of service to humanity
to be expressed by shipping it and its goods for small sums
of cash, instead of lecturing to it on meaningless subjects?
In 1900 the professor shocked reverent people by his criticisms of Alcott and appalled a lady who met him shortly
after Huntington's funeral where the heavy scents of
flowers had stifled her. " But the smell of sulphur wasn't
noticeable? " Wendell inquired. It was accounted a heart-
less remark.

The assault on the railroads had continued, with rallies
and silences, from 1892 through 1895. Many Populist
speakers found themselves justified in their acts. Some
lines figure little in the piled clippings of the campaign.
James Hill was assailed less sharply than were the owners
of the Southern Pacific. Nothing much was alleged against
the great system now the Atchison, Topeka and Santa Fé
Railroad although it had critics here and there. Some of
this matter is unjust, of course, but the whole printed collection of logical attacks and useless tirades might excuse a
cynical comment, more invasive of American sentiment
than Barrett Wendell's gibe. What was offered in the '90's
was the spectacle of the plain people attacking themselves,
for the railroad builders were sons of the plain people,
nursed in the manners of small towns and of farms. But it

will not do to suggest that early studies in sophisticated milk or the pressure of a thumb on scales in a rural store had anything to do with the root of these accusations, true or false. For in 1896 an excellent voice recited that " the plain people, bred without guile at the knees of Christian women, alone can cleanse this land of tyranny."

Mark Hanna now impressed himself strongly on a number of Eastern politicians who came to Saint Louis in hot June. They seldom knew how to spell his name and often added a final " h." The man of affairs was not particularly visible. He cared nothing for oratory and himself was never eloquent. His position was simple. He proposed to get his friend McKinley nominated and to have him elected. McKinley would keep the tariff high where it was needed and wouldn't experiment with the international laws of banking. The little, religious candidate's political ideas were few. He had spoken manfully for reforms in civil service, for boards to arbitrate strikes, and he was honestly shocked by the manners of the Octopus. Having secured his nomination, Hanna retired quickly from sight in a mist of flying aides-de-camp. He expected the Democrats to nominate Richard Bland, a wordy friend of Free Silver who apparently believed in the supremacy of the United States to an amazing degree, for he is quoted as saying: " If America issues a currency that raises silver to be the equal of gold, the rest of the world will quickly follow our lead." Bland's mind had embraced Free Silver with the lust of a grammarian for a debatable verb. It was known that Altgeld had approved him in a general fashion. Hanna expected him to be nominated on July 1st but he sent some volunteer spies to report the tone of the crowd in the Coliseum at Chicago. The Republican impresario was surrounded by young midlanders, sons of his friends and sons of McKinley's friends. The Major was dear to them, and the core of the plutocracy's body-guard consisted of young lawyers, insurance

agents, postmasters and mere " business men," few of
whom had any near hope of being able to give their wives
a second servant. Four of this body-guard dropped their
affairs and went to Chicago. They provided themselves
with tickets and sat awaiting the nomination of " Silver
Dick " Bland. The Republican Convention had been, ex-
ternally, tame enough. This hot, moist assembly at once
developed symptoms of poisoning by strychnine, and the
spies discovered that they were minions of a superior Octopus, or of an armed ogre. . . . An emotion had been
subtly born in this wasted land beyond the notice of the
Eastern journals which now judged it so jauntily. Muscles
had ached too long beside restless kine and winters had
rimmed in men to talk, talk endlessly of the banks, the railroads and the glittering rich. Free Silver? It was just a
phrase. Their wives had fed the strays of Coxey's Army.
Middlemen had taken too much of their profits. Their sons
had come home penniless and frayed from closed factories
and offices. This emotion only wanted, now, a tragic hero.
Mark Hanna had drawled, at Saint Louis, that any handsome man with a taste for making speeches ought to try
politics. David Hill, who was ugly, made speeches immensely and the convention yelled with or against him when
he sneered at Free Silver. Eastern Democrats were hissed
by Populists in the galleries. The extraordinary A. P. Gorman was mentioned as a low bastard by a delegate from
Iowa. Altgeld was not well and his pallor startled one Republican watcher passing close to him as the crowd poured
out from a session of words and excitements. The convention tossed and sweltered. Richard Bland's fortune rocked
along in the welter. Then a tall, trim delegate walked
through a shout to the platform and his voice stilled the
crowd for forty minutes. Men rose everywhere. Mr.
Bryan, a very handsome man who liked to make speeches,
had the floor. Mark Hanna's spies ripped their path out

through the herd gone mad in adoration of this incarnate drum.

Mark Hanna was not the phlegmatic joss of caricatures. When he was told that ladies of small Nebraskan towns admired Mr. Bryan, he threw a cigar into a fire-place, briefly swore, and then resumed business. His position was less and less pleasant as the National Silver Party and the People's Party swung behind Mr. Bryant with rejoicings, and not with much cash. But in early August, asking no future favours, great Democratic personages at New York handed cheques of size to Hanna's inconspicuous messengers and one of them said quite wildly: " Tell Mr. Hanna I'll turn Protestant if he wants, so long as he licks this feller! " And then on the first cool air of September came news of an Independent Democratic Party in assembly at Indianapolis. These Gold Democrats nominated John Macauley Palmer, the critic of Andrew Carnegie, and men of the labour unions sent their good wishes to the old soldier. Eastern politicians were alarmed. Hanna was delighted. " The general," he said, " will get about a hundred thousand votes from Mr. Bryan." The general outdid the estimate.

It was now quite necessary to elect McKinley. The Major's little court at Canton, Ohio, pored over Democratic speeches. A tall young lawyer, Julius Whiting, wrote on September 3rd to a friend: " The best thing would be to convince the voters that this Silver humbug will bring on another panic." The impresario had already ordered that note in some pamphlets. He nodded when the letter from Canton was brought to him and said: " Make a placard out of that." So handbills headed " Free Silver Will Bring Another Panic " were liberally printed and went whirling along in boxes through the middle West. Printing had never been used to such effect or in such bulk as Hanna now used it. His lieutenant at Chicago, William Hahn, scoured the region for speakers. Volunteers from New York, even with notes of recommendation signed by Theodore Roosevelt and Cornelius Bliss, were declined in favour of drawling men who knew how to talk to farmers. Hanna sat as a comfortable shadow in the Major's car when the candidate went forth to speak, and gossiped with Herman Kohlsaat, who was present in a small, astonished group that heard McKinley decline to come to terms with the disreputable Matthew Quay. Hanna did not scold his candidate. Next day speakers were telling audiences in Illinois and Minnesota that Mr. McKinley had refused to promise Quay anything.

But the terrible drum of the Silver Knight sounded from city to city, and his beauty towered in the flare of torches while bands played *El Capitan*. Hanna had raised a drapery behind the Major of golden cornucopias and golden coins, harbingers of prosperity under a high tariff. Yet an emotion might be evoked against an emotion. So a train appeared, passing over shorn fields. Messengers hurried a day ahead of its coming. Men of the Grand Army brushed black hats and gilded badges, then marched down to await this train with its last platform smeared in flags. They stared up at generals, veterans of their war. Howard, the Christian soldier, gravely reminded them that the Major had hot coffee served to his men in trenches and camps. There was Sickles with his glorious moustache. Alger and Stewart leaned down to shake hands and blushing grandsons were pointed out to them. Bugles and cornets yelled old songs and set heels tramping so that dust shot up and eyes watered. What had been believed was true again, in the noise of bugles; Union was strength and to hell with the Democrats, at the sound of cornets. Ghosts rose and charged through the cold air, at this noise of voices and brass, and cheers followed the train away. But one dusk at a junction of Illinois, the young manager found the crowd cool to General Sickles and puzzled until a lad beckoned him around the station to another lighted train. Hanna took his cigar from his mouth and said blandly: "Don't you know that this is a blue Presbyterian district, son? All these women remember Sickles shot his wife's beau. Give 'em Howard." He smiled and climbed back into his own train. The crowd applauded General Howard. . . . After a while torn posters blew in the streets and the emotions sank away. Henry George cried: "Oh, what did it matter about Free Silver? It's too bad, too bad!" and went pacing up and down his rooms at Fort Hamilton in distress; the people had lost again! In the high, yellow dining-room of the Union League Club above Fifth Avenue, Theodore Roosevelt assured some men that Hanna had done remarkably well for an inexperienced person. One of his hearers choked and upset a glass.

II

ARCHITECTURE in America was still nothing but a malady. The tradition of fine building was ruptured and sterile before the Civil War. A mania for the grandiose began in the '70's and continued more and more fruitfully in the '90's. Congress gave itself a library such as nobody had ever seen. A pillbox of white marble with a conical cap was ordered to contain the mortal part of Ulysses Grant, and James Huneker met the general's spectre tramping up and down before his last home, chewing a cigar and swearing. Monsters of shingle crawled on suburban lawns. Even the reviving Georgian lines were frothed over with illegitimate detail. The wondrous rich now employed the power of fairy hands to raise Florentine fronts ending in manorial windows that excluded air in summer, light in winter. The Westerners could bring little that was worthy from the learned East and it is miraculous that the worst models were left on the Atlantic coast. But Easterners quite rightly complained, and

67

may still do so in all honesty, of the ugly Western cities. The West rather pathetically called attention to handsome marble banks and dignified public structures, behind masks of electric cable and pole. Its imperial aspirations bade America do a deal of building; hotels resembling ennobled bath-rooms without visible conveniences rose everywhere; in her " Van Cleve " Mary Watts has beautifully reported the banks approved by sons of German immigrants in the midland, and in " The Conquest of Canaan " Booth Tarkington comments on the rural German brewer's villa. These things were no worse than preposterous " suites " in New York, where, says Harry Leon Wilson, sedate French violinists were mellowed into playing ragtime at dinners of the barbarous Westerners then invading Manhattan.

It is only in " The Spenders " that a vision of the movement from West to East survives out of the '90's. For there was such a movement. The goal was New York. Boston and Philadelphia civilly refused to be interested in Western money, but New York was less coy, and politic young gentlemen in clothes from London or Brooks Brothers escorted daughters of mines and ranches to the horse shows or hastily explained to sons and brothers of ample Western ladies that nice women didn't go to see Anna Held, a girl of Polish origin whose carved shoulders and narcotic eyes informed schoolboys and their fathers nightly what a French courtesan would be like if she were facially able. Californian fruits and heiresses appeared seasonably in New York and were absorbed. It was assumed that all rich Westerners came wooing Eastern favour and since the Western cities were so crude and ugly it was not worth while to inspect them. To-day the Easterner slides in a motor past ranged villas in Pasadena and hears names of men who took leave to grow rich unnoticed by the *New York Herald*. He hears, too, legends of men who fantastically existed in this waste without Eastern noise: Henry, or Heinrich,

Miller ran errands for his thousand cowboys in San Francisco and once was kindly tipped by one of them for his trouble. He heard that a discharged clerk threatened to shoot him and sent the man a silver-mounted revolver with a pink ribbon bowed on its trigger. He shed tears on hearing that one of his favourite Poland sows was dead and a little later stood watching a drunken Mexican aim a rifle at his heart and lightly batted the muzzle aside with his hat, saying: " Do not be foolish," as the bullet killed a pony behind his shoulder. They told him how his compatriot Claus Spreckels had shocked men at a luncheon by saying that it was fine to be rich so that he could punish old enemies. Miller drawled: " I have no time to waste in having enemies," although he had certainly not been reading the verses of Emily Dickinson. He only once advertised himself in New York and then by an accident of taste. Miller got up during a performance of a silly play called " The Cowboy and the Lady," said " Chesus! " violently and stalked up an aisle muttering. Hundreds of soiled young men in rhapsodic hats would have told the New Yorkers that Miller could buy the theatre and burn it to express his disgust. No, his gross materialism did not lure the Easterner into this hidden world of opportunities and the midlander began to replace him as the banker of Western enterprise. Yet there had been a time when Bostonian merchants and chandlers came to lay aside their dignity, forgetting Stone Chapel and Brattle Street, and played the jolly faun in dance-halls of Dodge City, Cheyenne or Abilene. A tour through the West was rather the thing in the '70's. In the '90's sons of the tourists carelessly sold land bought by their fathers on advice of Mr. Ladd at Portland or Mr. Crocker at San Francisco for the price of an English drag in which their adorned wives were suitably reported watching polo at Westbury. In 1896 a silly beauty threw away her father's purchases outside Los Angeles against the advice of Joseph Choate. She and her urbane adviser are in dust. The land survives them, loaded with chromatic villas as the lawyer prophesied.

This altering society beyond the Mississippi begged for some great comedian to record its changes. But Owen Wister and Alfred Henry Lewis were busy with its past. Charles Lummis delved in New Mexico and Arizona. Kirk Munro told tales for boys. Mary Hallock Foote varied from sentimental romance to a sudden passage or two of bitter realism and critics neglected her to discuss something by Mrs. Humphry Ward or William Black. Stephen Crane flashed his short string of Western sketches through *Mc-Clure's* and the *Century*, refutations of melodrama in melodrama's terms. Doane Robinson and Vernall Webster seem to have vanished just as they began. The stencilled characters of Bret Harte returned thinly masked in the *Argonaut*, the *Wave* and the *Overland Monthly*. So in 1898 Harry Thurston Peck mourned: " I would give ten Mrs. Humphry Wards for one good, realistic novel about Denver or Seattle. Apparently Garland and this Edward " — he meant Edgar — " Howe are the only writers who take the West seriously. Crane's sketches are good as far as they go. . . . I am not slighting the writers whom you mention in your letter. They are all promising but they have not achieved anything so far — excepting Mr. Fernald — that warrants much excitement. The annoying feature of these stories is that the women are so badly studied. . . ." The critic saw the defect. Women of the Western stories were feeble outlines. But women on dusty ranches of New Mexico chewed red petals and spat false blood so as to be sent in haste to the lighted verandas and Eastern voices of Colorado Springs. Women shrieked when a shot split the plain's belly and a grey bowel seemed to writhe as rattles clicked less loudly and the snake died in gracious coils. Women pressed on soiled glass, while men slept, to wait some train's far pas-

70

sage through tremendous night, moving to remembered waters that would not sink in summer and leave a mockery upon baked earth. Then there were women stately as great cows, and grammarless, before whose eyes the legend of the West had been erected. They had borne children on jolting floors of wagons, washed clothes that stunk from a week in oiled saddles and had piled salt on wounds in brown flesh ripped by bullets. They knew well just what happened when some drover's wife came from the East and a squaw vanished, richer, to her tribe leaving complimentary bronze offspring on the porch. These coarse memories gave them a drowsy smile that roused and glowed when they rocked in deep verandas among old men who quarrelled as to whether Pat Garret should have answered Billy the Kid's question, " Quien es? " when the lean marshal fired across the moonlit bed at Sumner and the outlaw died at last. They were likely to swear terribly if the champagne came too warm to table, and Art, for them, was just a lacquered bowl to be filled with litchi nuts for grandchildren or the gilded clock that so gently ticked out their time in a son's house beside the rocks at Monterey. Perhaps the unforgotten kindness of their hands may raise them up a chronicler, else they are lost who were not ladies.

III

A VERY pretty lady went shopping with Frank Norris in Chinatown. The realist bought a pound of brown, dried fruits and puffed his breath into the bag as he strolled beside his friend, discussing San Francisco. The gaudy street was forgotten. He meditated: " Nobody seems to think out here. Don't you ever think it's hard to think in San Francisco? " But the bag exploded, just then, and the fruits rolled on the sloping walk. The lady laughed. Chinese babies ran giggling in blue silk to catch the spilled delights.

Norris laughted, too, and they went away to dine in a room on Russian Hill and later watched lights of Berkeley spread as golden lace on the bay's farther shore.

Every abomination of building stood in San Francisco. Tourists shuddered and fled into the Silver Dollar to drink heavily, then stayed on Nob Hill's crest while tiny cars were hauled up the steepness below them on subterranean cables that still chuckle like contented ghouls. Islands stirred restlessly when mist fled over the great bay. The hills were tawdry gold in summer — dry grass on rosy clay — and jade in winter. On all these slopes things loved as homes reeled together in a drunken kiss and marvellous plaster roses hung on wooden doorways. Meaningless turrets sprouted from ledges of tin roof that descended toward Market Street's uproar. None of this mattered. Crowds bawled at prize-fights; crowds idled on the cliff while obliging seals cavorted in a dazzle of spray on their theatrical rocks; crowds splashed and yelled in the huge Sutro baths. Old Joaquin Miller swore that he had to elbow through crowds of poets in his favourite bar when he came to town and lectured, with a white rose in his jacket, telling ladies that " musicians will one day ransack the stores of these Tartar and Indian musics for fresh rhythms and measures." The crowd was king in San Francisco. A sense of pleasure had been born here and here persisted, somehow, in pulsing sunlight and iced shadow of the streets. Sober Eastern æsthetes got enmeshed in the chatter of the brown Bohemian club and are known to have become frivolous among colours of its audacious posters in which men were, obviously, men. The courtly Ambrose Bierce once was seen escorting two magnificents of literary New York to the scene of a good recent murder and pointing out spots where blood had pooled. But he himself declared that murders in San Francisco had lost quality, and only a few killings of the '90's are memorable. If the high quality of slaughter had been maintained, Bierce would never have left San Francisco.

A friend printed " Tales of Soldiers and Civilians " for Bierce in 1891 and the wit noted in a preface that these stories had been declined by all the Eastern publishers. His art was candidly inhuman. The soldiers and civilians are merely subjects of wit and destruction. Character didn't interest the strange humorist, trained in England by the second Thomas Hood. He erected his mortuary filigrees with traceries from the style of Edgar Poe and remarked to an amateur critic: " If it scares you to read that one imaginary person killed another, why not take up knitting instead of reading? " But he faced the secret softness of the general critic and only journalism paid his way in this world. The book of 1891 has three hundred pages. Private Carter Druse helps to kill his father on page 17. Peyton Farquhar's spine snaps on page 30. A mother's brains are bubbling from her shattered skull on page 52. Men die of fright on pages 90, 198, 237. About page 270 the ghost of a lady lacking the middle toe of her right foot disposes of her murderer. Death dances intricately. A seemingly dead woman revives and chews the ear of a panther as it bites a hole in her throat. A decaying Rebel corpse drives his own sword into a Northern officer's heart. Captain Coulter, half naked and blackened by smoke of his cannon, cowers over the body of his Southern wife slain by his aim. But once death's dilettante became human. " A Son of the Gods " is his tribute to courage. The prose breaks into phrases of stately excitement when the rider on the white horse gallops to death, as though the artist rose and cheered him on. For Bierce's valour was authentic as his wit. If it is true that they shot him against a wall in Mexico, some literate member of the firing-party heard a last pungency and the old man buttoned his coat and faced the rifles, smiling.

But the crowds are not to be seen in Bierce's few tales of San Francisco. Then Chester Bailey Fernald sent a Chinese baby trotting through the streets with an adored cat, One Two, for whom idols in a hidden temple underground were urged to provide another tail. The city was a vapour behind this distinguished godson of Rudyard Kipling. The infant became a citizen of the *Century* and so did Fernald's brainless, human sailors in salty yarns of genuine flavour. Mr. Fernald's talent engaged an audience and then he steered away into dubious seas of pallid social comedy, leaving admirers of " The Monkey That Never Was " and " The Spirit in the Pipe " sitting aghast. Plainly he read Kipling but his whole management was in another scale and at his best he was master of a chilly pathos hardly American. . . . . The smiling city, though, had been just a backdrop in his theatre. The *Chap-book* appeared at Chicago, a symptom of a rash of little magazines. Suddenly San Francisco had the *Lark* well printed on tawny paper, edited by *Les Jeunes*. Gelett Burgess let his boneless homunculi, then called *Goups*, romp on margins of advertisements for coal and they peered gloomily around doors or swung over abysses in floorless rooms with a sinister dignity. They were not altogether domestic, then, and their father employed them in travesties of drear French art, those pictures of Eve in her old age borne along by prehistoric sons. Mr. Burgess produced an effect in black and white as a forecast of Masereel's fashionable effects now current. (The cleverness of the '90's was very much the cleverness of our moment. In the '90's you could agree with Charles Warner that the acting and singing of untrained Negroes was vivid and delightful. You could agree with Harry Peck that " the little grotesques of the comic supplement may one day be treasured and collected as types of a real art " and the theme has supplied matter of ten essays in the year 1924.) If Mr. Burgess once or twice leaned on Rudyard

Kipling, as in his " Ballad of the Effeminates," he was never much of a burden and he could juggle an idiocy with greater ease, perhaps, than any other humorist in verse save Guy Wetmore Carryl. He was abetted by Porter Garnett, who wrote a poem on Omar Khayyám that happens to be good and thus quite different from other such American poems. Bruce Porter contributed a graceful prose, characteristic as his shapely caravel for Robert Louis Stevenson in Portsmouth Square or his ventures in glass. Yone Noguchi's first verses were paraphrased. Ernest Peixotto designed covers. The magazine amused its readers and its owners for two years, then *Les Jeunes* signed its obituary on May 1, 1897, and the death certificate states that the *Lark* was born in a sunny studio far above the mingling vulgarities of the street. There it lived, a stranger to the crowd.

But crowds pile and their feet are heard in " Vandover and the Brute." Norris let his victim stand and ponder on them in the old Pavilion. They pass in noise outside the idler's windows while his pride collapses. They loiter and hurry in a constant being on Polk Street below the lair of McTeague. They pack close to the giant and his Trina in the smoky music-hall. An immense, common life appears and passes behind the bodies of the fool and his woman. Even the little girls who find Trina's smashed corpse trot in a chattering group. He could evoke a relentless sense of human movement around his sad comedians. And yet the city's robe of sunlight does not glow and there are no flowers at corners of the tangling streets. Only in " Blix " when the lovers idle at sunset or laugh in a restaurant is San Francisco gay. The moralist is there, beside the artist, and as time passed, the moralist won in some hidden battle. There came " The Octopus," a tremendous melodrama with Jehovah thundering at its close. " The Pit " was worse. The gambler in wheat and his tiresome wife run off to begin life anew, the last prudent fluctuation of a moving picture. Cheap people were delighted. This was comprehensible as " Uncle Tom's Cabin." The artist had become the bitter pamphleteer, still powerful, still adroit. Yet he had never been partisan to his time's disease. He had no duties in the politic club of reticent, tranquil gentlemen who had quite excused themselves from seeing God as a reckless satyr and seem to have chosen a sidereal lawn mower that smoothed landscapes for their careful feet and paths among " old books that time has criticized," comfortable topics, empty refinements all forgotten, now. At least he had been male. But he was not the poet of this city whose king of dandies sold Mumm's champagne — the city that laughed when a young athlete, a jeweller nowadays, led his own funeral of cabs with himself for subject in the first wandering vehicle. Ugly, vulgar, adored in her wallow beside the bay, she knows that her lovers return. Poets are not needed.

CHAPTER III

DEPRAVITY

THERE was a dinner at the Everett House in 1890 given for a youth from Illinois who sat in awe across from Elbert Hubbard's floating tie and hairs, beside Edgar Saltus. Just one remark can be recovered from that meal: someone mentioned Christianity and Saltus slowly said: "Has it appeared in America?" The stylist was beginning to drift from sight; his brother's death saddened him; his first marriage was a failure; his best work was done. He became a civil shadow. In 1913 a boy was startled into rigour on hearing a man say graciously in a doctor's antechamber: "I'm Mr. Edgar Saltus." He lived to remark that America was the hypocrite of nations and then he vanished.

The odd blending of smugness and hypocrisy with which Northern editors treat all Southern affairs was on hand in early spring of 1892. Spring blew from the heating Gulf up Louisiana; African voices thrilled in love's renewed excitements among fresh flowers; earth seemed a body sweating perfumes, bared not ignobly to the sun. This classic season was, for once, neglected because a governor would be chosen in April and the Lottery's candidate must be beaten at the polls. Northern reporters were appalled by the sight of gentlewomen slaving relentlessly in committees. The legend of Southern ladies as languidly maudlin creatures was still in force. An occasion had brought Mrs.

William Preston Johnson out to head the women of superior New Orleans. Edgar Farrar, Charles Parlange and Murphy Foster were speaking — and rather carefully — of the State's wealth, proving that the Lottery's annual dole to charities could be excused along with the Lottery. In its agony the machine offered an income of a million and more dollars to Louisiana for its safety. Now the Lottery's real master was John Morris, an uninteresting gambler from New York, who had foistered the thing on Louisiana, strongly maintaining it through several fights; but the decoration of the Lottery was General Beauregard, so adored by the farmers of his race that one of them recommended Robert Lee as an estimable person, saying: " I hear Gen'ral Beaur'gard speaks very well of him." The lesser glory of Jubal Early's assistance also belonged to the Lottery. So the reformers walked carefully; in that atmosphere of manners and sentiments they must be tactfully bold.

Congress had barred the mails to the Lottery in 1890, but express companies carried its tickets everywhere and paid its losses. Even in Boston a revel broke out among sophomores at Harvard when a lad won something in 1890. In New Orleans people of many tints lounged on corners, developing a set of superstitions in betting and buying chances. Did a fish seen in a dream mean 7 or 13? The Lottery was indubitably a nuisance; it drew idlers of all kinds into the city; Negroes wouldn't work on farms up the river for days before a drawing, and negroid legislators supported the Lottery in its difficulties with a solid loyalty. . . . General Beauregard's position was one of candid sense. He wasn't responsible if fools chose to waste their time and money on tickets. The reformers pled that the fools were an industrial annoyance. Most of the journals backed the Lottery. The polite battle waxed and had its place on front pages in the North — then lost the place.

Some wealthy ranchers, two of whom were certified as

literate by Harvard, decided to revive the obsolete practice of killing cattle-thieves in Wyoming without trial.
They were advised against this method of reform by the
veterans at Cheyenne who'd known Wild Bill Hickok and
could tell the real reason why Calamity Jane shot Darling
Bob McKay's sombrero from his head in 1872. But the
amateurs invaded Johnson County with force and arms,
twenty picked Texan cowboys who could shoot, a box of
dynamite and an English tourist anxious to see this quaint,
native pastime. Two lorn alleged thieves were trapped at a
far ranch and killed. Johnson County then besieged the
social critics, urging them to be hanged for murder. Reporters came hurrying. After an awful crash of journalism
three troops of amused cavalrymen rode down the olive
turf from Cheyenne and took charge of the amateurs,
whose zeal was entirely spent. They simply wished to be
out of Johnson County for ever. Californian earthquakes,
floods on the Mississippi, the rush of settlers into opened
land of Oklahoma and South Dakota, mixed with the end
of this comedy in the news, and Murphy Foster's election as
governor of Louisiana on April 18, 1892, was not much
noticed. The reformers had done their uncomfortable work
without appeals to the crucified Christ, blasphemous battle
hymns or any bloodshed not to be amended by a bandage
and some arnica. This phenomenon deserved attention and
more compliments than it got. The Lottery went into exile
without leaving its respectable defenders in the posture of
criminals; the spring now had its due.

Our model of social movements in America is the freeing
of the slaves by a process of religious excitements and
abominable orations delivered in biblical rhythms with
many quotations from sacred Jewish writings. The sincerity of both parties is never questioned. They enjoyed
the human pleasure of calling each other criminals against
the laws of God, tyrants, murderers, vandals and such other

names as the recurrent megalomania of the primitive American suggested. Delusions of grandeur overcame most of them. They invoked Christ with the freedom of mediæval kings in a brawl over the border. Realism began in 1861 with the usual spawning of profiteers and continued until Robert Lee's soldiers knelt in mud to hug his stirrups and Ulysses Grant gave the whole flock of triumphant valkyrs at the North a lesson in breeding. William Lloyd Garrison suspended the *Liberator* as his holy cause was now achieved. His admirers presented him with thirty thousand dollars. He went to Paris, as a good American should, and his son Wendell Phillips Garrison reports that his father's moral sensibilities were offended by the gory battle canvases at Versailles. But " he took real delight and lingered long in the art section of the Paris Exposition of 1867, of which he especially enjoyed the statuary where the intent was chaste." There is no report of his opinion on a marble group named *Soldat Americain Tuant Son Enemi*. But the biblical rhythms and the uses of megalomanics had been finely taught. Even George Augustus Sala could note that: " An oration with biblical quotations or phrases suggestive of the Bible's prose is useful in stirring them [the Americans] as nothing else would be. They have an uncultivated hunger for pathetics." His last thought is from Sismondi. His own thoughts are singularly scarce. The peculiar advantage of calling your opponent a transgressor against God is manifest in the oratory of the Gilded Age. The nineteenth century liked men to perform with voices and hands, actors in a romantic tragedy, while discussing economic and social issues. It wasn't until July of 1896 that a forgotten illustrator, Walter Appleton Clark, dropped a journal showing the styles in oratory at Chicago and proposed to a gathering of Bohemians in Buchignani's café that all orators be strangled at birth. He sent Buchignani from table to table with a long strip of tissue and on this

ballot thirty men voted for the strangling of orators save
one who scribbled: " Why not boil them in oil? " Below
that Jay Hambidge wrote: " Too expensive," and drew a
dynamically symmetrical coffin. This remote consideration
might not have been understood in the Coliseum at Chicago
where men would yell for half an hour after hearing an
orator melodiously shout: " You shall not press down upon
the brow of labour this crown of thorns — you shall not
crucify mankind upon a cross of gold! "

This uncultivated hunger for pathetics was easily fed.
On July 4, 1825, Charles Sprague stunned the Bostonians
by telling them: " Where you now sit, circled by all that
adorns and embellishes civilized life, the rank thistles
nodded in the wind and the wild fox dug his hole unscared."
If a eulogist of Sprague does not lie, many broke into tears
and shouts of applause. This stuff was printed in schoolbooks; children learned and recited it. Then came Wendell
Phillips, the summary of Mark Hanna's politician, a handsome man who liked to make speeches, the whip of the
Abolitionists. He had not one-tenth of Garrison's honest
ability and he was incapable of such a speech as Henry
Ward Beecher's defence of the Union in England. The
clergyman assumed that he was heard by reasoning men.
Phillips simply made orations. He stated that God chained
that age to the redemption of the slave. He wished to remark that Daniel Webster was dead, so he brought out:
" The unhappy statesman, defeated, heart-broken, sleeps
by the solemn waves of the Atlantic." All that was legiti-
mate in his method is shown in his orations for woman's
suffrage. His triumph was a discourse on Toussaint
L'Ouverture, a superior Negro whose taste in dress was
bad. Phillips concluded: " You think me a fanatic to-night,
for you read history, not with your eyes, but with your prejudices. But fifty years hence, when truth gets a hearing, the
Muse of History will put Phocion for the Greeks and Brutus

for the Roman, Hampden for England, Fayette for France, choose Washington as the bright, consummate flower of our earlier civilization, and John Brown the ripe fruit of our noonday [thunders of applause]; then, dipping her pen in the sunlight, will write in the clear blue, above them all, the name of the soldier, the statesman, the martyr, TOUS-SAINT L'OUVERTURE." The Muse of History's duty was to be performed on December 14, 1911. This peroration also went into the schoolbooks. So in 1891 it was natural enough that a living woman presented Frances Willard to an audience thus: " One day an angel will take a pen of diamond and dip its point in the sun's chosen rays. Then she will write, high above the proud titles of Joan of Arc, Florence Nightingale and Lucretia Mott, the name of our loving sister in Christ's work who is with us this evening." The mingling of simple assertion with sacred names was somehow licensed. They had been reared in that school. Miss Willard thanked the speaker and began her talk " holding a lovely bouquet of lilacs and sweet peas in her left hand."

But an opposition was created. Perhaps there had always been an opposition among the minor folk who seem more interesting in their casual acts than do these paraded great. A generation was passing out of sight. There was the elder Henry James, once called the Chinese Mandarin for his ceremonious manners, who wouldn't surrender his emotions to Alfred Tennyson and calmly wrote that Emerson no more satisfied his mind than did chattering old women. John McClure Daniel hated the tawdry hotels of the '50's and pitched *Les Misérables* into his stove at Richmond. John Esten Cooke admired Villon before the English announced him. And now old George Boker came back to Philadelphia from his tour as minister in Turkey and Russia. He was still handsome, long and courtly. He still gave cheques to helpless young artists and still insistently read

82

books in five languages. He was born in 1823. As a lad at Princeton he awed the other children with his coats and cravats, an appalling swell who gave suppers and quoted Dante in Italian. Boker was just a gentleman with a taste for verse, to be sure, but Lawrence Barrett revived his "Francesca da Rimini" and again it was applauded in England and America. The playwright came to New York for a performance and faced the changing times. A lady stalked up to him in the old Fifth Avenue Hotel and ordered him to have the wine-cups removed from a scene in his play. So he may have given some study to social conditions in America. In 1889 he had guests at dinner in Philadelphia and sat among them gracefully railing at "the moujik orators who quote the Bible. . . . In Russia they call them Village Christs." Then he contributed his mite against mythology, standing next day on Chestnut Street in his Russian furs, twirling his white moustaches. Petronius? Oh, Petronius was a second-rate writer, interesting to people who fancied Sodom and Gomorrha to be extinct communities. He lifted his hat to his young friend, in the manner of his times, and strolled away. He died in January of 1890.

Another astringent person went on with the opposition. Charles Dana, editor of the *New York Sun*, sent a novice to report Henry George. The boy was made imbecile and covered paper with words of which he now recalls only "lyrelike voice." This went into Dana's cell and came out with the editor's comment over its face: "You sound like Wendell Phillips reporting Saint John the Baptist. I asked you to see a Mr. Henry George." This was insufferable to a boy able to recite most of "Toussaint L'Ouverture." Dana was lectured for some minutes on style, composition and the beauties of eloquence, then the *Sun* lost a reporter. The rhapsodist went hurrying for sympathy to the office of *Puck* and showed Dana's cruel remark to Henry Cuyler Bunner. But the humorist was curiously cool after reading the description of Henry George, and limited his sympathy to saying: " Mr. Dana's wrong. I think it sounds like Hall Caine." Bunner's aversion to Hall Caine was already public. There could be no justice in the frivolous city. The profession of medicine had a recruit in the next week; but the *Sun* continued its lancing of swollen estimates. *Puck* mocked the politicians in its big, coloured cartoons that unkindly imitated the drawings of Gustave Doré's illustrated Bible. So *Puck* and the *Sun* were not wanted in conservative homes or in several clubs of New York, Boston and Philadelphia. Yet every club could take in the *New York Evening Post;* Edwin Godkin's paper must be counted a member of the opposition, for the editor objected to excesses of speech just as he objected to cuspidors or to a defective Civil Service.

Godkin once showed the weakness of American criticism. He himself was English and his enemies called him an imported snob. He had come to take wholly American positions in many matters, though, and once wrote an editorial in which Grover Cleveland was a " Moses, leading the army of political righteousness." It is to be supposed that this was just a figure and not an appeal to piety. A fight began in the Woman's Christian Temperance Union; the quarrel became publicly known. The rebel accused the sacred leader of gross egoism, saying: " In all her great work she has been but seeking a background for her personal exploits and a theatre for the exercise of her wonderful powers and accomplishments." A committee of four replied in words of Christian savour, telling the rebel that she had lost " the faith of her old comrades in her sincerity, the chaplet of their admiring love and the crown of leadership in the grandest body of women known in the world." The President's wonderful powers and accomplishments are admitted by the rebel as a matter of course; the Union, in crushing her, states with firmness that it is the grandest body

of women known in the world. These insolences amused
Godkin but he would not comment. " I suppose," he wrote
to a friend, " that we must defer to these religious or semi-
religious bodies in their overblown rhetoric." The position
is plain: the civilized editor assumed that any body of
speakers pleading what they called a religious or humane
cause had the right of effrontery. He could be very tart to
the Republicans for simply calling themselves " the Grand
Old Party," without reference to the known world. Yet in
the year of the quarrel among the Christian women, a religious gentlewoman, Rebecca Harding Davis, suddenly
halted a young martyr in a meeting of early feminists by
saying: " I don't see haloes over any of our heads, my
dear."

Mrs. Davis had fallen badly out of step with the new
school in social movement. She had no delusions of grandeur and she spoke of God in a pleasant fashion that was
respectful without patronage. It had never impressed her
that there was any crown of leadership to be seized. She
saw that Edwin Booth had his Madeira and waffles when he
came to dine with her in Philadelphia, and any guest could
begin his dinner with a dose of whisky if he liked. In the
early '90's a lad got remarkably drunk one night, smashed
furniture in a brothel and spent some hours in jail. He
found his mother's door technically locked in his face the
next morning, and went to refuge with Mrs. Davis, who considered his disorders and said briskly: " Go up and take a
bath while I get you some breakfast, you silly child! " She
fed him and packed him off to young Richard in New York,
with orders verbal that a job was to be found for him at
once. In 1894 she was taken with pity for the wasted virgins
on Cape Cod; so in February of 1895 the *Century* printed
an essay, " In the Grey Cabins of New England," that no
man of the time would have dared to write in such flat
candour. She once gave a shock in Boston by remarking,

before she was even married, that women desired men. She had noticed as much in her work among the labourers of mining towns. Now she did worse. . . . New England was full of decent girls who would grow old childless, morbid in a territory drained of men. It was all very well for Sarah Jewett and Mary Wilkins to write touchingly of them, but why in God's name didn't somebody do something for them? The Bostonians got up societies to improve the Russian lepers and to help the South take care of its Negroes. Here were these undedicate nuns at home. One clergyman had shipped thirty of them into barbaric Montana and they were easily married off. The West was full of cowboys and such things ready to assist in the production of babies. She rather stressed the babies in her pleasant prose.

Frances Willard was appalled. The pretty old maid had passed her rhapsodic period. She now simply awaited the time to rejoin her mother in another sphere. Her father seems to have been less important in her thought. While waiting she still sometimes gave addresses in schools for girls and ended by shaking a finger at them and saying: "Be good, girls, be good!" The small son of one of her neighbours in Evanston, outside Chicago, once ran downstairs from some monster that was noisy under the bed as he got off his undershirt and appeared, aged eight, in the parlour before Miss Willard, dressed in mere tears. Miss Willard kindly begged his mother not to punish him, as he didn't know that he had done anything wrong. In that same parlour she once stood counting over the bouquets given to her at a public meeting. She must have dropped one in the train. Couldn't Ned just run down to the station and see if anybody had found it? Far away, in a house on Gramercy Park, the rather intolerant Stephen Crane was remarking that Miss Willard's affair with Miss Willard should be stopped by the police. In the autumn of 1897 she met Rebecca Harding Davis in New York, and told her gently that

" membership in the greatest spiritual movement since our
Saviour's time " should be enough for the virgins of New
England. Mrs. Davis stood in silence that may have been
rapture or penitence, or perhaps the words " You silly
child! " formed behind her smile. In her old age at Marion
she remarked to a caller that Miss Willard's views seemed
somewhat extreme. . . . Miss Willard died in 1898. She
was five years older than Friedrich Nietzsche, who wrote:
" You have made danger your calling and in that is nothing
contemptible. Now of your calling you perish." They
shared the depravity of an extreme softness. The German
rebounded from study of his own nature into exaggerations
and harsh yells in praise of strength, building out of his
weakness a philosophic concept of persistent honour. But
thought was not the relentless pursuit of her own beliefs to
Miss Willard. She accepted a formula and called on God
to make it sacred. Her eventual vice was an enlargement
of the weak clause, " Lead us not into temptation," and the
civilization that she foresaw was a sterile meadow, danger-
less, sprinkled with folk wearing white ribbons. She was,
however, a pleasant person who excited devotion. One of
her disciples used to get herself through crises of propaganda by pausing to say: " Help me, God or Frances E.
Willard! " Help came from somewhere on the prayer and
she resumed her work.

II

IN a Christian country no book would be suppressed for
quoting the eloquence of reformers at six congresses favour-
ing purity held in the decade. Bits of this matter may be
found in " The Encyclopædia of Social Reform," edited by
William Dwight Porter Bliss, D.D. It is not recorded that
S. Weir Mitchell, J. West Roosevelt, William James,
William Graham Sumner or Arthur Hadley attended these

meetings. Mitchell went to one session at Baltimore and remarked to a friend that he'd never seen people enjoy themselves so. There is no further interest in the business of stimulating purity.

Nor is there any interest in Anthony Comstock's life during the '90's. He began the decade by bullying a shop-keeper in New York over the photograph of a naked statue. In 1895 George Barrie issued a handsome edition of *Crimes Célèbres*, by Alexandre Dumas, lush with illustrations. Comstock was urged to take action, and a Catholic lady gave him the set of books, calling notice to the libels on the Borgias, on the nuns who had Urbain Grandier burned, and other lewd details of the rubbish. Comstock wrote a censure but did nothing. He then persecuted a fleshly novel of the empty Gabriele D'Annunzio, concurrently raising a row because dealers in athletic goods would exhibit the elastic breech clouts worn by boys playing football. These, he said, hadn't been worn when he was a boy in the country. He ended the decade by starting a fight over a photograph in " A Gunner Aboard the *Yankee*," in which seekers may find a naked sailor, less than half an inch long. His friends prevented a ridiculous disturbance. . . . In an able man such a obsession would be pathetic, as it saddens one to watch Thomas Rowlandson's decline. Hogarth's successor found it easy to draw trousers. Even in his lovely sketch of Angelo's fencing-school, there are seen traces of this mania. He dallied with knee ribbons, invented grandiose comedies of dropsied gentlemen. Gillray replaced him in caricature. By 1800 Rowlandson's soldiers and sailors were just hand-some dolls ineffably trousered and skirts were becoming bifurcations. He rallied and fought hard; but an unfinished sketch is a mere trouser, a last luxury.

The flattery of the country-side appeared in America in the '40's. A noble farmer saves people of the wicked city in " Fashion." There followed a list of melodramas built with an eye to touring companies which would play them in rural opera houses. These shows included a pure farmer, a pure country girl, a villain from the city and an urban adventuress — that is, a woman in fine clothes who did evil that no good might come of it. There was also a silly old maid who chased all the men in the piece from the comic hired boy to the villain himself. She was or wasn't enjoyed by plain, unsought women watching her from leathern cushions in little theaters. The specific of these plays was simple: the country mice might have foibles or even stumble into sin but their hearts were in the right place. Much of the formula can be read in James Herne's plays, of which Clara Morris remarked that they had as much to do with New England as her corsets had with Eleanora Duse's hands, floating just then in " Camille," at the Fifth Avenue Theatre. . . . This was badly translated to Duse one night after she had thrilled the crowd by her scream, " *Armando mio!* " and people huddled into her dressing-room to gape at her, in a maroon wrapper, eating ice cream. The translation was ineffectual. Duse examined her hands slowly and said in bewilderment: " *Mais, je ne porte pas un corset sur mes mains!* " . . . Clara Morris was in the right of her assertion. " Shore Acres " was far the most honest of these plays. Henry George liked it, after seeing Herne behave so abominably in " Margaret Fleming," a dreadful concern to the pure as in its last act a virtuous woman adopted her husband's bastard, which was quite improper and unwarranted. The rural drama made money splendidly from 1870 to the end of the century, and the whole formula was repeated in " Way Down East," the final glory of the school.

" Way Down East " is a demonstration in illusion, and it explains how Mr. George Moore's way was made cloudy in America. For Harry Thurston Peck liked " Way Down East." He admitted that the melodrama at the old Broadway Theatre was trash; but he went again and again to see the pure country girl tricked by a false marriage, and the polished seducer slapped by the gallant young farmer, and the snowstorm, and the comic fellow who sang his song about a woollen string to the air of a bawdy Yankee ballad of the whaling days. The apologist of Zola, Sudermann and Frank Norris was seen sitting thralled at matinées. It was an idyll of some kind. It enchanted him as did the suave graces of Mr. Moore's prose. His flirtation with the novelist went on from book to book. Peck telephoned friends in Yonkers, a suburb of New York, to announce " Evelyn Innes " in 1898 and wrote two reviews of the romance.

This extraordinary story will be incomprehensible to the next generation and it should be explained that people such as Sir Owen Asher once really walked and talked. Lingering specimens are to be found living among awed Americans in Paris or in liberal Taormina. Sir Owen is an amateur of everything who undertakes to seduce Evelyn Innes, a pretty singer, by describing the philosophy of Omar Khayyám in parks and by telling her all about painting in the National Gallery, now a storehouse for the work of John Sargent, a fashionable artist of the '90's. Evelyn flies with him to Paris, where he explains Balzac's novels and cookery to her, then prepares to consummate the seduction by draping his frame in silk pyjamas and reading a bit of Théophile Gautier: " I am as pagan as Alkibiades or Phidias. I never gathered on Golgotha the flowers of the Passion, and the deep red stream which flowed from the side of the Crucified and made a red girdle round the world never bathed me in its tide. I believe earth to be as beautiful as heaven, and I think that precision of form is virtue." Evelyn puts up with this loon for some years; then her egoism discovers a pleasure in saving what she calls her soul and she goes into a convent.

Peck could enjoy Mr. Moore when he behaved in this

way among drawing-rooms, smart restaurants and bars. But when the novelist led his rakehelly gallants out of London and chattered of lust beside hedges or in rustic houses, the critic couldn't stand it at all. He scolded Mr. Moore maternally in angry reviews; he called him the greatest — he used such words — the greatest novelist since Thackeray, but begged him to keep sin inside city limits, where it belonged. " My Lord, Harry," said John Kendrick Bangs, " are you this man's press agent? " Peck was. He helped Mr. Moore to become an idol of American writers who went meekly pattering after his diabolic shepherd's crook wreathed in orchids. They have not been able to imitate his delicate, running sentences that escape monotony by the turn of a word, a gull's whirl in the fog, but they learned about women from him.

There was no pure American country-side before the Civil War. Most of our coarse balladry dates from that time. The barbarous, dramatic " Frankie and Johnny " was known on the Mississippi in the '50's and was chanted by Federal troops besieging Vicksburg in 1863; a copy of twelve stanzas was made by a young officer and is preserved.[1] " Susie Skinner," " The Little Fat Dutchman " and others came from Puritan New England to the West in the covered wagons. These songs have now a name in the muff's slang of our moment. They are " pro-sexual "; that is to say that they admit the existence of lust among men and women, as candidly as do the ballads of any country. So the cowboys sang " My Lulu " and the soldiers in barracks on the plains put a wailing chorus to the impropriety, an air of the bugles:

" Bang away, bang away, bang away, bugle!
What you goin' to do when the bugler's dead an' gone? "

---

[1] Mr. Emerson Hough dated this song from a murder at Natchez in the '40's.

These collapses into biblical franchise are man's realism asserting itself against sentimental decorum, as Mark Twain once asserted himself when a living critic assailed Mr. Irving Bacheller for making mention of a man's navel in a pleasant story. Clemens lifted a white eyebrow and drowsily asked: " Haven't you got one? " There were young boys in the room and the critic evaded a vulgar admission by changing the subject.

Clemens was of the superior rural class in Missouri. Manners of the inferior class amused an editor of Saint Louis in 1847. The rustics went to bed in the grand manner, then, even with a stranger in their midst: " the old man stripped unscrupulously and sought his share of the one collapsed-looking pillow, and the sons cavalierly followed his example, leaving the old woman, the gals, and the stranger to settle any question of delicacy that might arise." The risen question may be found in " The Drama in Pokerville "; the same volume contains a sketch that is simply an equivocation of an obscene word, and a true story, " The Death of Mike Fink," which has implications even less heartening to mythologists of a pure America. These books of the '40's were issued by a reputable firm in Philadelphia and were illustrated by Felix Darley, who in 1860 announced that he had never illustrated what he thought an immoral book. Obviously " Simon Suggs," " The Louisiana Swamp Doctor," " Yankee Yarns and Yankee Letters " were not held to be slanders on the countryfolk who gamble, brawl and carouse in their pages. They passed everywhere and are found stored in farm-houses. The young Wises, Staggs and Cabells grinned over them at Virginia Military Institute before they went out to be profusely shot in the holy war. Clemens read these adventures of pedlars and roaming preachers when he was a boy, and then in his gay winter of 1894 was frank as they were. He was amusing a crowd of men before the fire-place in The Players when

DEPRAVITY

Mr. Merritt Coulson asked him to criticize Henry Bunner's tale of a Northern Bishop rebuking the hysterical crowd at a Southern camp-meeting, "As One Having Authority," but the satirist refused to criticize and broke into jeers at the camp-meetings. His prudent mother never let him go near them, he said, and then told the story of a recruit in the Civil War unable to name his father, explaining: "Captain, sir, I guess I'm just a camp-meetin' baby." Mr. Coulson repeated this cynicism to John Hay, once Abraham Lincoln's secretary, in 1899. The diplomat chuckled and said: "Yes. Mr. Lincoln used to tell that one." In the same year a friend wrote to the diplomat apologizing for a song sung by an indiscreet young playwright at a dinner in Hay's honour. Hay answered in one of his short notes: "I heard that song when I was eight years old in Indiana. Yours, J. H. P. S. — He sang it badly."

After the Civil War the country-side began to purify itself in fiction and oratory. In 1891 its purity was extolled by a minor Populist speaker, Paul Suckow, who invaded New York and assured an audience in 14th Street that there was no such thing as impurity in Kansas. In 1896 the purity of the inner United States was proclaimed by both political parties jointly and severally. So some records of the year 1896 have been brought out from the one reliable source, the notes of doctors in counties chosen because they were then wholly agricultural, without any taint of the industrialism which is supposed to breed corruptions. In central Massachusetts a young doctor began his practice in February. In the course of the year he was invited to prevent six illegitimate births. Two of the girls married. He attended the birth of one child, and knows nothing of the other cases. He notes that the youth of the town in which he lived seemed to believe that decorum was regional; they were models of virtue in South Duckleberry and went over to sin in Ethansville, ten miles away. The county then held less than four thousand people. There was one brothel in the county seat. In upper New York a county of some three thousand people produced six illegitimate children in 1896. The physician ends: " As I understand that this communication is to be anonymous I feel free to add that ten births occurred within six months of weddings. Drinking has always been heavy here and continues to be so." In central Ohio there had been a vice crusade, as they are now called, led by an Episcopal clergyman, and no known prostitutes were in his county. In 1896 there were eight illegitimate children born. As there had been only three such accidents in 1895, the doctors of the county came to terms with the reformers and the trulls were allowed to return. There was only one illegitimate child born in 1897. In Indiana, four illegitimate births and two births of children to wives by common law. In Illinois, in a county that held less than four thousand people, seven illegitimate births. To these statistics may be added an adventure of a young surgeon, afterwards distinguished as a military medical officer, who was benighted riding in upper Kansas in November of 1896. He turned into a farm-house and found himself charged two dollars for admission to a dance of young farmers and blowzy girls, the maidservants of the region. These dances were events of Sunday night, an aftermath of the day's propriety and a respite from all costume. . . . In 1917 at the head-quarters of a division recruited from the midland States, this same surgeon patiently talked to groups of pastors, eager women and, once, to three Catholic priests with an escort of laymen. The deputations had a common purpose: they wanted to prevent the prevention of crippling diseases among the soldiery, in the name of God. A bored young adjutant steered the callers into the brown shell of an office and sometimes stood listening to the talk, as the impersonal surgeon repeated that military necessity could not admit their interpretation of God's laws. In one group there was a thin, dark woman weathered by years on some farm, who began to rock as the colonel argued, and suddenly cried out: " Oh, you're trying to make our good boys just as bad as those boys from the city, but the Lord Jesus won't let you! " She became beautiful in the cry, a saint of the grand abolition in cheap blue silk. The Lord Jesus was a bearded man in a white robe out of the picture beside the melodeon in Sunday School, a name to be invoked against something hotly nameless in her blood that stirred under trees of her father's farm when she was young and a lad held her hand.

III

PAUL DU CHAILLU stood with David Graham Phillips and another at the top of the steep front steps, still steep, of the Hotel Brevoort. The explorer had some skins of rare African monkeys over his arm and these wafted in the air of a warm spring night as he gesticulated. A victoria came to the curb below through the mauve light of lamps and Richard Harding Davis handed out a slim gentility whose voice melancholy even in laughter enchanted that decade. The young celebrities came up the treads; her glove was white on Davis's black sleeve. Du Chaillu gazed and then stood on his toes to watch the slimness move into the hall beside the tall man's shoulders. Couldn't one be presented? They nervously told him that his conversation, flowing strangely between two languages, might give offence. " Quoi? " the explorer gulped. " Une actrice vierge? " He lost his balance in the shock. An explorer, a realist, skins of monkeys and a spilth of cigarettes descended the steps rapidly in disorder and landed disparately on the sidewalk of Fifth Avenue. " Mais," said Du Chaillu, sitting up, " I am yet incrédule! "

The Americans of the '90's achieved a frame of mind

that was apparent even to small boys; when the ladies said
" actress," they meant something else. Virtuous women
were driven over the downs of Nantucket Island and pursued some harmless players who spent summers in the
village of Siasconset. They panted in lanes, bearing cameras, and asked children where the actresses lived. Gaunt
old Mrs. Gilbert, called Grandma in her world, once whirled
to snap: " Well, young woman, where did you learn your
manners? " at a large impertinence dogging her black
skirts. But the nation sat in gilded ulcerations of theaters
and gaped at the women on the other side of hot bulbs with
speculation. The decade became a little more liberal in
conversation and in print. Even that shy elf of Victorian
writing, the word " whore," came from its covert once or
twice, rendered as " w———," which deceived nobody but
gave everybody a sense of daring. Children were told that
it stood for " where " and didn't believe it. This liberalism
did not tend to realism. Translations of *Germinie Lacer-
teux* were failures and Stephen Crane's " Maggie " was almost a failure. Poor drabs faithfully presented were not
what the Americans craved. It is unjust to say that Americans like sordid fiction. The parade of French antimili-
tarist novels, the ferocious *Biribi* and the *Sous Offs* of
Lucien Descaves, were unheard of, save that one doctor of
divinity who read French declaimed against *Sous Offs* from
a smart pulpit in Boston. These *contes Zolatiques* offend
the theory of Plotinus, which is sacred in America: vice
must be shown adorned, thus inciting by its beauty to virtue,
one perfection recalling the other. So the megalomaniacs
sat and wondered about the pretty mimes whose names
float in the memoirs of James Lauren Ford, and matrons
would have been incredulous if they had known that the
grand courtesan of New York — hence, of America — was
a woman resembling an inferior cook, whose clothes were
ordered for her because she had no taste. They saw her;

she sometimes appeared on the stage. She was a Christian Scientist and suffered greatly from sciatica. Her charm was an exquisite voice that gave point to her humours, for it is sworn that she invented the phrase " a stuffed shirt," meaning a tremendous nobody. Her flat was jammed with facile, clever men when she gave suppers, the jaunty nothings who rolled dice for drinks in the old Metropôle, the writers of smart plays, cheap songs, forgotten reviews — pink Acton Davies, Paul Dresser, Clyde Fitch, who always seemed to lead his clothes into a room, and a luckless, charming man whose wife once crawled over the floor of their poor lodging in the pulsing woe of childbirth to open the door and find a messenger with roses and his card: " With love and loyalty, from Paul." But such a woman is not the courtesan desired by virtuous people, the seductress, she-who-lies-in-wait-for-husbands. The American cannot define vice but he wants a glitter; his delusion against realism craves that. He has been taught to believe in absolutes — grandeurs of lechery, prodigious wastes. So in the '90's his pastors heartily commended " The Sign of the Cross " with dark Corona Riccardo suitably undulating in gauze around a burly centurion in the midst of Nero's Rome, that suburb of the religious American mind where Nero exists as a purple obscenity leering from his box at edible white Christians on the sands below his perfected reputation.

Nero has always been popular among clergymen, to whom he represents the pure depravity; he did everything that he wished in the most expensive fashion. He began to be denounced in America along with the slaveholders. Bad historical painters of the nineteenth century enhanced him. Piloty showed him swaggering over ruins; Sigalon made him rather thin, scowling at a poisoned slave, a likeness of Mr. Calvin Coolidge; Siemeradski made him a point in a tumble of naked folk watching some Christians burn on flowery stakes. All these eulogies may be seen in a costly edition of Suetonius, issued by Gebbie of Philadelphia in 1889. The book sold amazingly; it is hardly expurgated. In 1890 came another edition of Suetonius, without a publisher's name, at one dollar, unexpurgated and illustrated by some Frenchman who admired Félicien Rops but who could not draw. Also in 1890 there is historical record of a parody on " Nearer, My God, to Thee," which begins: " Nero, my dog, has fleas." Novels representing Nero disagreeably were current, such as Dean Farrar's scholarly " Darkness and Dawn," probably the worst of his books. The emperor figured disgracefully in sermons; no pastor ever seems to have thought of saying: " This silly child." As only one-twentieth of the sermons annually delivered in the United States are printed, it may be assumed that some preacher once put in a word for the scared clown running in black streets while the soldiers yelled up a new emperor, whose servants begged his body from his enemies and spent two hundred thousand sesterces to burn it decently in the gold and white, not purple, robes he wore just last year at the feast of January. They were simple people, slaves and freedmen, and not literary. His old nurses and his first mistress carried the ashes to his family's tomb. If it hadn't been for all those trashy poets, they said, and his mother spoiling him so, why, he might have had a good, long reign and behaved himself. It is probable that they cried a good deal. But perfection of form is virtue, and the pastors carried out the instructions of Plotinus in the case of Nero. In 1892 a Reverend Earl J. Stimson circulated in the Middle West, lecturing, with magic lantern, on Nero " the Anti-christ." A leaflet announcing his performance insists that " He will conclusively prove to you that Nero sank below the most degraded inhabitants of Sodom and Gomorrha. See Genesis XIX, 5." Dr. Stimson also had for sale copies of a work on harlotry, " The Maiden Tribute to Babylon," by William Stead. " The Sign of the Cross " followed. So there must have been an understanding nudge from elbow to elbow in December of 1896 when the president of Princeton told the undergraduates that Oscar Wilde was the vilest sinner since Nero.

An amateur of demonology has collected all the notes on Wilde published in the United States before the scandal. Unless there was a private cult of admirers in the country, Wilde cannot have been a great figure to Americans in the early '90's. His books sold badly and his plays were just successful, not triumphant runs such as " The Sign of the Cross " or " Shore Acres." But the same amateur discovers that Wilde was mentioned by clergymen in at least nine hundred known sermons between 1895 and 1900. His social position improved from Sabbath to Sabbath. He was " the king of England's intellectual circles " in Denver, Colorado, and sober parishioners of Cleveland heard that no banquet was complete without his presence. English Kings were his least companions in this eloquence. He condescended to Edward II and James I. He walked with the purple Cæsars. The crown of leadership in the grandest body of sinners known in the world could not be his; he had never thrown Christians to lions. One rector even seems to have read " The Picture of Dorian Gray " in his excitement; he produced Wilde as beautiful, rich and young. Pastors might have explored *Biribi* or the milder *Sous Offs* and found that common prisoners and soldiers were not so remote from the dandy. Or they might have evoked from American legal or medical print a tawdry fellowship of tramps, clerks in haberdashery, mere farmers. A wretched schoolmistress of the year 1894 was left where her jailers stowed her. These vulgarians never followed the exquisite's shape on Sunday. He somehow was unique, a creature of perfumed alcoves, and Nero's house had a guest. They arranged a terrific setting around a simple medical fact, and sinister music blew as this romance flowed along. Trusting small boys asked their aunts why the pastor talked so about Mr. Wilde, and one of them was told that the poet ate babies, which was untrue. The megalomaniac instinct had full play and Wilde's future audience was assured. It even seems that cynical dealers in pornography heard the tumult; in 1899 an agent was selling at twenty dollars among undergraduates a set of photographs in a scarlet cover lettered, " The Sins of Oscar Wilde."

A long freshman who looked over the photographs in the spring of 1899 and naturally had read all Wilde's work at once, was found guilty of sketching respectably in the summer. It was already believed that one-tenth of an artist was something superior to a man of affairs. The boy's father couldn't protect him; he went drearily to Paris and in Paris stayed until his mother changed her mind in the spring of 1900. His stutter made him shy; he loathed his task and spent most of his time in such cafés as were haunted by Americans, ready to spend his handsome allowance on food and drink for anybody who understood the meaning of the word " biscuit." Early in 1900 he was sitting with the *New York Herald* and a bottle of white wine in what he remembers as the Café de la Régence when a bleating voice asked: " Have you a match? " The shabby, flabby face across his round table was dusted with some yellow powder or dried ointment on its brownish stains. Mr. Armstrong shoved matches over the marble and the tall man began to talk in slow, elaborate sentences, interrupting himself to call for a glass as a waiter passed. The boy watched his bottle empty itself and was amused enough to send for another whose net content ebbed, diminished to nothing. Some time during a third bottle a waiter dropped a friend's card at his elbow with a scribble on the pasteboard: " That is Oscar Wilde." Of course the young fellow blushed. Wilde instantly looked at his silver watch, exclaimed at the hour and rose. Then his theatrical habit

overcame him. He bowed and said: " I remove the embarrassment," which wasn't quite civil after two bottles but
may be excused as Art. The boy was incredulous. No, that
ugly lounger with a mouth full of decayed teeth and cheap
rings on his hands wasn't the " yellow lord of hell's corruptions." Besides, Wilde hadn't made an epigram. A few
nights later he found conviction in another café when Wilde
came into the place with a pair of simpering English lads,
all very drunk. He even made a sketch of the poet on the
back of a bill of fare. It isn't exhilarating. Still he wanted
to hear an epigram. One afternoon on the Pont de la Tour-
nelle he was pretending to paint the river in water colour
when he heard Wilde's voice in a duet with a French voice,
that of some middle-aged man who presently shook hands
with the dandy and left him by the parapet. . . . The big
youth struggled with a genuine fright. He saw a man, true
enough, in bad, plain clothes. But the whole megalomaniac
course of the nineteenth century was on trial, here, with its
Masters, seraphs of æsthetics, great sinners and great wits;
its abolitions of what it did not understand in the name of
God now effected a miracle. He was afraid of this stricken
posturer, the son of a silly woman who darkened her rooms
and read verses to guests in light of candles so that her
wrinkles wouldn't show. In a few years an older, more
learned man would be addressing Wilde in the manner of
that century as a fallen tower that once proudly shone in
the sun's eye, a ruin fair for ghouls to batten on, a great
silent talker making his bed in hell, and with other titles of
Celtic endearment. The boy wanted to run when Wilde
waved a hand and strolled up to him; but he might hear an
epigram, so he stayed. He thinks that Wilde had been
drinking; the voice was thick. The poet looked at his sketch
and launched into a defence of formal art. Water could
not be painted. The Greeks and the mediæval painters were
right in showing waves as mere jags and curves of line. And

then he aimed his cigarette at Notre Dame, purple in a sun-
less dusk, and hauled Old Paris from his historical band-
box. This river had rolled white corpses after Saint Bartholomew's Eve. Yonder had passed Catherine de Medici
with her glittering maids of dishonour picking their way to
mass among the dead. He turned out his elaborate imitation of Walter Pater's slow rhythms, and his audience was
very badly bored. There is a phrase of our slang that will
be forgotten too soon: " He did his stuff." Wilde did his
stuff for the young fellow who wanted an epigram. The
king Henry III minced along in a knot of slim gallants
crusted with pearls. All the fripperies were on show. Mr.
Armstrong softly stamped his cold feet and awaited that
sparkle of words, something about something being more
beautiful than the seven deadly sins, while the celebrated
fribbles of the sixteenth century paraded. Then Wilde
stopped sharply and rubbed his hands over his forehead.
Was there not a spring in the State of — of Arkansas, very
well recommended for rheumatism? Mr. Armstrong had
heard of Hot Springs. Yes, that was the name. Wilde said
something vague about fleeing like a wounded hart into
Arkansas, and was silent. Mr. Armstrong's feet were icy
and lamps brightened everywhere in the dim fronts along
the river. But no epigram had come. Wilde sneezed suddenly and said: " Thank you for listening . . . I am much
alone . . ." and the grace of that " much alone " is his best-
remembered phrase. Then by an indirection he did a service to the boy. Mr. Armstrong wrote to his mother that
he'd met Oscar Wilde, and was ordered home by cable
within five minutes of his letter's coming.

On March 12th a doctor paid William James a compliment, calling his researches " great," and the psychologist
turned on him, saying: " Great? I'm nothing but an as-
terisk! " Such reductions are horrible to the soft and to the
inflated who would rather hear some man say elegantly

and eloquently: " The unhappy statesman, defeated, heart-broken, sleeps by the solemn waves of the Atlantic," than be told that a politician is dead.

Wilde's art becomes too dusty. But he has his standing as a great sinner, and polite Frenchmen working in the vast cemetery above Paris show the way patiently when rapt Americans pant: " *Oo est le tawmbeau d'Oscar Wilde?* " This might amuse him in the hell to which his adorers have condemned him with full benefit of Clergy.

CHAPTER IV

DEAR HARP

THE FANCY of eternal damnation should be tenderly nursed by American writers on behalf of policemen who in general are dull, underpaid creatures and frequently fathers. As it appears that there are natures so feebly egoistic that they must be kept in order by an idea of God as an angry cat in wait for them beyond this being, the lot of the policemen should not be hardened by destroying the immoral support of a Babylonian myth. A decent casuistry should have prevented journalists of the last century's latter part from bragging that newspapers had made hell and purgatory ridiculous, hollow as the bragging was. For cartoons and ridicule have never damaged anything mainstayed by man's total unwillingness to separate the religious emotion from some ritual or from some set of legends. Artists of the Renascence mocked Saint Joseph, showing him as an angry cuckold scolding the stork in corners of pious scenes. Saint Joseph so comfortably survived the ridicule that in 1923 an American lady loitering beside his shrine in a French temple heard a decent woman address his idol thus: " Blessed Joseph, friend of the married, grant, if my husband is false to me, I may not know it or, if I find it out, that I may not give a damn " (*que je m'en fous*). She then tipped the saint one franc and went her way. Mysticism has its highly practical side; and the preservation of hell and purgatory is, at least, expedient un-

til by a process of increased pay or by imposing uniforms
the duties of policemen can be rendered alluring to the more
intelligent. The calling may then be recommended to
writers and other artists as likely to provide them with
healthy exercises, worldly experience — which would be
useful — and a social state of greater dignity than that at
present in their power of achievement.

As the class to which William and Henry James belonged
by birth sank from importance in the United States through
its lack of courage, there was an alteration toward the religious standards of the other James brothers, Jesse and
Frank, who intermittently attended church in Missouri between spells of brigandage and were accounted good Christians by their neighbours. In the mildly libertarian period
that preceded the Civil War a gentle agnosticism had been
plausibly prevalent among the civilized, and it was apparently possible to discuss religions in the drawing-rooms of
New York or Boston in philosophic, not in emotional terms.
Perhaps the slaughter of the young educated in the war impaired liberalism or perhaps the velocity of cheap evange-
lism, the apparitions of Dwight Moody and Frances Willard, made it less safe. Presently Robert Ingersoll was a
lonely figure, roving the cities and dispensing the raw material of the eighteenth century's rationalism with a slab of
tobacco in his pocket and a consummate sense of the showman's craft. Editors and critics, when he died, found it
evasively easy to say of Ingersoll that he had given out
nothing new, that his agnosticism — many called it atheism
— was a simple derivative from Paine and Voltaire, but he
more truly was a product of the Bostonian age, the tag end of
an intellectual stir that died out in the rank commerce and
collapsing dignity of the '70's and '80's. Among a people
who mistake a shallow amenity for civilization, the profane
lawyer was a little heroic, a solitary point of open protest,
navigating in a void. Certainly there existed the body of

thinking men for whom Mr. Irving Cobb would at last find
the name "innocent bystanders," but they preferred a
voiceless peace to the humiliation recited in an unprinted
letter of Mark Twain, in 1889. " A nice English boy came
to dinner on Thursday. Carelessly said that he did not believe in the Virgin Birth. Every lady in the room jumped
down his gullet and rent his garments from him." So in
1896 the thin Jeannette Gilder denied Stephen Crane's right
to express his disgust with Hebraic wraiths in " Black
Riders." It was timidly urged that free speech was any
man's privilege. " Not if it hurts people's feelings," said
the female critic; and the saying may be taken as the American's whole social posture before free thought at the century's ending. . . . Children of the '90's might hear religious discussion if they went idling in the haunts of the
vulgar and displaced. There were cool, gloomy academies
of sophisticated discourse up any alley in those days, deep
livery stables where the voices of Negro hostlers mixed an
oily languor with the harsh drawl of grooms as harness was
polished on sunny afternoons; the adolescent of the succeeding time has found freedom in smells of gasoline and wayward gin; in the '90's freedom was perfumed with saddle-
soap and leather, with rotted straw and dung.

But it was assumed that the Roman Catholics' feelings
were not important enough to be spared, and through the
'90's the sensitive American Catholic saw tippling, flirtatious choirs of monks on the stage in musical shows.
" Notre Dame " could be made into a play without softening the lust of Claude Frollo for the gipsy girl. John Rockefeller and his crew were caricatured in *Life* as the Pope and
a bevy of cardinals. The rather pretty parades and gesticulations of the sacred Catholic enchanters were already being aped in Protestant churches; but James Lane Allen could
have his say on the isolation of a nun in the *Century*, and
show his ignorance of nuns or their government. In 1894

the pastors were busy with Saint Bartholomew's Eve and
the fabulous experiments of the Borgias in distilling. The
Borgias, indeed, were almost Neronic in their popularity;
Roderick Lazuoli's family offered such a compound blessing of bastardy, lechery and murder to the attacking mind
that it was certain of an airing. In November of 1894
James, Cardinal Gibbons, poised some sugar over coffee of
an agnostic guest in Baltimore and said with dry bitterness:
" On my honour, there's not a drop of poison in the house."

Oddly the man who raised the pack against Rome in
1894 was a lean Irishman, Catholic and devout. He was a
capable prosecuting attorney who gave his aid to a commission appointed by the Senate to examine the morals of New
York City. This Lexow Committee began its sittings without the faith of the journals. How could a crowd of rural
politicians cope with Tammany Hall, entrenched in the affairs of New York for forty years, an undefeated organization? The journalists were cynical. But Mr. Goff was suddenly an uncanny prestidigitator in a dingy room thronged
with reporters, evoking strange beasts from a bottomless
hat. He summoned up Irish patrolmen who bullied contribution from bawds and gamblers, or took it from wretched
immigrants in lawful business who assumed humbly that
the Yankee police were like all police. The hog's share of
this income passed upward from official glove to glove and
vanished in a political haze over Tammany Hall. The scandal was superbly handled by the press; Harvey Scott sent a
reporter hurrying clear from the misty slope of Portland to
whip back news to the *Oregonian.* New York, the hussy,
was taken in sin again! Irish names sprinkled the lists of
outgoing steamers and one of these tourists died lately after
thirty years of exile in Algiers. All the beauties of a
moral reformation were now displayed. Brothels were dis-
mantled; the vapid contents found lodging in the tenements
and presently children along the Bowery were courteously

guiding sailors and other students of womanhood up dirty stairs in the certainty of fees for each client thus brought in. The writhings of vice before the Lexow Committee had their place in the news all summer, even with the great strike gripping the midlands and Altgeld hardly pitching his epigrams at Cleveland. Violent Irish leaders of labour helped the fight along. The American Protective Association was suddenly in action on the broadest scale, complaining that the Irish were making America a Papal state, that priests were allowed to ride without paying on trains in California, that Irish aldermen had attempted to fund parochial schools from the treasuries of cities, that a statue of Marquette, the Jesuit explorer, was erected in the Capitol at Washington. . . . The campaign came on with every card in the hand of Republican orators. A dozen Democratic governments of middling cities were upset; in New York a fused party elected a forgotten reformer mayor; Theodore Roosevelt was appointed to clean the police and by this carom the apprentice harlequin came bouncing back from obscurity to the bright, noisy centre of things, where he remained until flags were lowered for him, and old Joseph Ignatius Constantine Clarke said amiably that the crooked Irish of New York had made Roosevelt great. So the Irish and their Church were rebuked, and then in the summer of 1895 the steamers brought home groomed, plump men from Paris in time to chaffer for paving contracts and the repairs of municipal buildings. Familiar faces showed once more in the saloons along Fourteenth Street or on the steps of Tammany Hall. The " boys " were back. . . . Their heavy voices laughed again among the chattering women whose sleeves that year were hams of pallid colour in the paddock at Saratoga or on the verandas of the vast hotels where the bands played Victor Herbert's newest airs and the composer, Samuel Lover's grandson, passed from group to group making his pretty speeches to the actresses and con-

tractors in a queerly German accent. Richard Croker
walked at his gorilla's trot, swinging his long arms, from
horse to horse under the trees, and once appeared, as drags
and victorias bowled in from the course, dumbly sitting beside a famous harlot in her English cart, so scared of her
effulgence that his one remark was: " I think your check
rein's too tight, ma'am."

Croker's bearded face had been planted on the Tammany tiger's bicoloured body in cartoons of 1894, and bets
were made that he would leave the city after election. But
he understood completely the worthlessness of the superior
American in politics. Gentlemanly subscribers of the *Century*, the *Nation* and the *Arena* would never persist, effecting any permanent organized force. The fireworks of the
virtuous triumph in November meant just another awkward
period for the boys at the Hall, who must now get subtly to
work through friends and go to the trouble of securing contracts from the city by stealth, while this reformer was in
office. Croker endured in tranquillity and didn't seem to
know that he was a beaten villain. One morning he strolled
past awed pages into the high, sombre office of John McCall
at the New York Life Insurance Company, wearing an
odious purple necktie in honour of the financier. Perching
on a deep leather chair, he fixed his unmeaning gaze on the
ruddy president of this gigantic company and said: " Mc-
Call, I want you should lend Martin K. a hundred thousand
dollars." McCall explained that his company wouldn't
lend a gambling publican a hundred thousand dollars to
build a hotel. Crocker nodded and continued in his chair
while wriggling Brazilian bankers, begging priests and
agents filed to McCall's great desk. At intervals the lord of
Tammany repeated simply: " McCall, I want you should
lend Martin K. a hundred thousand dollars." The rules of
a huge life insurance company were not his affair; he had
pledged himself to find money for an ally, and a Democrat

of Irish descent would provide it. All day he sat, contentedly immovable in his necktie, and at dusk the wearied financier telephoned frantically to a plunging banker, asking him to make the loan. Croker paddled down the marbles of the hallway beside a young attorney and said, with an approval: " That McCall, now, he's stubborn." He had been impressed. In 1899 he turned on the streets of Washington and pointed out McCall to an acquaintance, saying: " That's Jawn McCall, there," and adding: " He's stubborn." His peasant's intelligence could respect stubborn refusal. He had risen from an Irish slum by stubbornness and may have recognized the trait as worth a little praise. But too much stiffness ended in annoying him. He laid contribution on a theatrical manager of the '90's and was refused. Croker patiently wrote and sent messages for a month. Then snow fell heavily. . . . The gutter and sidewalk before the showman's theatre were not cleaned until incense was offered to the boss in Fourteenth Street. His rise had taught Croker that successful government in the American democracy is merely a vile exchange of favours, and his abiding offence is that he demonstrated the fact. His story has been cleverly manipuated by two sentimental journalists but he remains an obscure, grey figure in description. He was not unkind, not debauched or aggressive, yet he had no savour, and men who knew him long find nothing much to say of the chief. Other Irish leaders of his time have left legends; Croker was merely the ruler of New York and fond of handsome horses.

II

SENSITIVE Irish-Americans in 1894 suffered considerably and their recollections of the year are sour indeed. A puddling of social nastiness ran under the political fight. A gentlewoman whose name was Irish as Kelly was forced to

take oath at a school not far from Ralph Waldo Emerson's
grave that she was really Unitarian, as she had represented
herself, before beginning to teach algebra to the young
Yankees. Returning from this humiliation to her lodgings,
she found a gang of Christian women rifling her trunk in
search of a nun's veil or penitential emblems. In a middling city infected by golf a family whose wealth had enriched the town for two generations was nervously requested not to appear at the new golf club laid out on land
donated to the game by the family itself! A committee of
Titanesses had ruled against the admission of Catholics.
There was a sudden show of the emerging American lady's
will; two liberal young women rose against the brutality
and there followed one of those guerrilla battles which no
native author has ever dared to describe, a succession of
calls and scenes, with embarrassed husbands and fathers
lured in and out of the vulgar absurdity. Finally the daughters of light faced the principal Titaness and threatened to
turn over the shabby facts to Democratic newspapers of
the place. In New York a committee of females and pastors
hunted down an intimate of Grover Cleveland and urged
him to secure the president's approval of a bill excluding
Catholics from West Point and Annapolis. These episodes
were Eastern and the persecutors in all instances belonged
to what is called respectable society in America.

Nonsense rioted for months, then slacked and was forgotten, no doubt, with the jokes of the year and its hats.
There was even a public revulsion, after the election; editors gravely deprecated religious intolerance in America.
Perhaps the Catholic advertiser and subscriber were already
worth some conciliation or perhaps the incurable sentimentalism of the American editor was working yeast. In the
latter '90's orders were given in offices of newspapers in
New York, Cleveland and Chicago that no matter derisive
of Catholics should be printed without strictest approval.

111

That process of immunity began through which, in our day,
a cardinal may issue pastoral letters against legislation, one
priest may murder another in a drunken row or an archbishop may order the police to interrupt a lawful public
assembly without more than the most passing comment in
the press, while a Protestant pastor cannot be slaughtered
beside his mistress, forge a cheque or manfully announce
his retirment from belief in the miraculous birth of Christ
without pages of condign publicity. Lately the city of New
York offered this disparity in a public contrast; a melodrama centring on a rape committed by a Protestant missionary was played for hundreds of nights without objection; meanwhile a corporation announced that its version
of *Notre Dame de Paris* had been suitably altered, " in deference to the religious feeling of thousands," so that
Dom Claude's libidinous qualities were transferred to his
brother. One lone review found the favouritism distressing.

There was no suspension of Protestant feeling against
the Catholic in the '90's whatever the journals said. The
published matter had fully informed pastors that their celi-
bate rivals now commanded the largest audience in America, and the rest of the decade is spotted with underhand
assaults of various Protestant groups on the ancient sect.
The gospellers sank to methods which outdid those of the
traditional Jesuit, as described by the smug English novelists of the century's middle. The quiet cardinal in Baltimore often had to act with speed to prevent some nuisance.
Thus in 1898, as the nation lumbered sideways into war,
with the heartiest approval of innumerable Christians who
signed petitions for blood and sent them to William Mc-
Kinley, Gibbons was denounced as an ally of Spain by a
powerful Baptist preacher still alive. Simultaneously the
same clergyman headed a mixed committee of Baptists
and Methodists which appeared in Washington demanding
that all Catholic chaplains be withdrawn from the battle-

ships. Roosevelt sent the committee out of his office at the War Department with one sentence, but he then passed into his military incarnation and the committee hung about in Washington bragging too loudly of an ally in the President's Cabinet. So a Protestant attorney of the New York Life Insurance Company, which had strongly backed McKinley in 1896, was suddenly at the White House. The President instantly sent his promise to John McCall. The zealots pestered Abner McKinley and dodged to and fro around Mark Hanna strolling with his train of attentive gentlemen through the old Raleigh's lobby. They were still in Washington when the fleet sailed, armed with Catholic chaplains, and then withdrew, certain that Rome had set its hands on the President. . . . The attorney found a case of the Orvieto favoured by Leo XIII at his house outside New York with the stamps of a wine-dealer in Baltimore. James, Cardinal Gibbons resumed work on that dreadful preface to " The Collegians " which so dismayed his relative, James Huneker. In the autumn it was rumoured that priests were not admitted to the hospital tents at Camp Wikoff; one day a buzz passed under the brown canvas, through smells of typhoid, and the titular pastor of Santa Maria in Trastavere walked slowly down the line of cots, pausing to speak to a red-haired Unitarian youth of Celtic expression and bestowing a blessing which, he said, would do the boy no harm. He had been told that priests were being kept out of the place. It was a great relief to find that untrue. He sauntered on. . . . As this serene personage rose in power, a certain sort of noisy political priest was less heard of in America. The Church took on a higher polish, a more mundane seeming. Its banal buildings spread; its universities increased their scope, and instruction improved yearly. There was naturally a sharp yell of approval when the cardinal was vilified at a public meeting of pastors in favour of Prohibition in the month that followed his placid death. His writing was spiritless; he made no profession of deep scholarship and once unfortunately alluded to Christian slaves in Cleopatra's gilded barge; but his management was perfect and his manners might be effectively studied by his less politic and less interesting successors. . . . If his sect forsakes the dignified urbanity which protects it from hot satire now expended frankly on other areas of decayed Christian philosophy in America, all its vulnerable surfaces, its superstitions and inconsequences will be opened to rational attack, and its ancillary service to the police will be much impaired.

III

DION BOUCICAULT died at New York in 1890, leaving four hundred plays or adaptations and a false legend of himself as creating the gay, rollicking Irishman of the theatre. He did not. The comic Irishman existed in the English theatre of the eighteenth century already wheedling his master out of drink or cash and already saying " Be jabers." Boucicault merely took a competent playwright's licence of arranging this creature on the scale of Charles Lever and Gerald Griffin's tales. It has been forgotten that he made use of his own handsome person and musical brogue in " The Colleen Bawn," " The Shaughran " and the other variations on Griffin's " Collegians." Primitive theatrical reviewers in the United States saw clearly what he had done. Lever was still popular and Griffin's book had its day. Poe's famous curse on " London Assurance " is the only historical estimate of Boucicault in America, but obscure critics, when the Irishman was a figure in New York and Washington before the Civil War, took high exception to his Ireland and sometimes to his acting.

The playwright himself was shrewdly observant. When he returned to America in 1876 he found the Irish in an

114

altered position and noted in a letter of 1877: "We are more popular in the theatre than ever. Young actors and singers commonly take Irish names for the benefit of the fashion. . . . In society a bitter prejudice has been stirred up by the unseemly conduct of some Irish political black-legs and, I should judge, by the constant immigration of humble people from Ireland. Mark Twain has made great fun of some rich Irishmen for palming themselves off [1] as French and what not. I have no complaint to make of my own reception. My old friends have been kind indeed and Mrs. Leslie [2] tells me that I am the object of envy among the Thespians for being a social lion, although I am no such thing. But I have heard a great deal too much of humiliating slights put upon Irish ladies at balls and there are rules against us at one of the best clubs in town. The Emmetts, I believe, are the one Irish family who have entrée everywhere." He must have continued hearing a great deal too much of slights put upon Irish ladies through the '80's. A little before his death a young fellow complained that his wife had been ignored at some seaside colony. Boucicault said morosely: "Go West, my friend, and change your name."

This prejudiced social atmosphere with its religious draughts had not existed for the Irishmen who followed Thomas Addis Emmett into exile. They melted easily into the westward movements of the '30's and '40's, shedding their habits from prairie to prairie so that families named O'Donnell, Connor and Delehanty are now discovered drowsing in Protestant pews of Texas and Kansas. The cultivated Irishman romantically disposed himself in a drapery of Thomas Moore's goods and found decent social lodging in New York, Baltimore and Washington. The phrase "a professional Irishman" had been invented before the

---

1 "The Gilded Age."
2 A rather literary lady who attempted a salon.

Civil War, apparently in the music halls of New York. Then there was an intermediary period with the Irish clotting in Eastern slums, Fell's Point and the Five Points, " the ignorant, the poor, the uninstructed Irishmen " of Henry Ward Beecher's description. Just here, however, the theatrical forces, politicians, actors and songmakers, found out the commercial advantages of flattering this alien. Oakey Hall, that entertaining mayor of New York who spoke French in public and criticized Gustave Flaubert, appeared before the people on Saint Patrick's Day in a green coat and ordered the Irish flag run up over City Hall. Tony Pastor hitched an Irish verse to his ballad, " The Upper and Lower Ten Thousand," and Johnnie Pendy introduced one into " The Queen of the Cannibal Islands." Alice Somers, Maude de Lasco, Joe Hurley, Harry Duval and Lou Boshell had always an Irish song ready for the gallery at Pastor's or Niblo's. An Irish dance and song were tricks of the great travelling minstrel shows, Bryant's, Delehanty and Hengler's and Carter's Zouaves. Augustin Daly warily investigated Irish feeling through a friendly priest before offering Clara Morris in " Madeleine Morel " with its scene in a church's nave, and the actress's amusing memoirs tell how the company waited for hisses from the gallery of the '70's.

But while the whole parasitic class, dependent on herds for place in office or income, wooed the Irishman, native mechanics and clerks began to resent him; he underbid them at all turns; he would work for less and live in worse quarters. There was at least one anti-Catholic — implicitly anti-Irish — secret order in the '70's, the United Order of American Mechanics. The American Protective Association appeared in 1886, and in 1894 it was understood that there was a third. The cheaper professional Irishmen met all this parade of enmity with cries and allegations of wrongs done the race and the faith. But meanwhile the

flattery continued with the abuse. The Irish were at once
established as tremendously funny, gay and charming people and concurrently were snubbed. So there was turmoil
at a literary dinner in 1896 when James Huneker contended
that the Irish were seldom gay and his lonely supporter was
Stephen Crane, who tried to make a difference between wit
and gaiety, then brought on another broil by asserting that
an Irishman could be a coward. He had now doubled Huneker's offence and the two were accused of abysmal affectation. This dummy figure of the Irishman had become
deeply sacred with Americans; in 1898 a group of young
journalists went hunting the first trooper to reach the blockhouse on San Juan Hill, assuring each other, said Acton
Davies, that he would be a red-haired Irishman and warmly
disappointed when he proved an ordinary American of German ancestry. . . . Nineteen years later, another group
of journalists went hunting a red-haired Irishman who
fired the first shot of the American Expeditionary force in
France. Some clever military commander will eventually
sense an occasion and provide the necessary type.

The dummy of the '90's was an infinitely pugnacious,
utterly common and merry animal, a fiction not yet done
with, satisfying still to Americans who profess that they like
an Irishman, and still know nothing about him. " Of all
the tricks," George Bernard Shaw wrote in 1896, " which
the Irish nation have played on the slow-witted Saxon, the
most outrageous is the palming off on him of the imaginary
Irishman of romance. The worst of it is that when a spurious type gets into literature, it strikes the imagination of
boys and girls. They form themselves by playing up to it;
and thus the unsubstantial fancies of the novelists and music-
hall song-writers of one generation are apt to become the unpleasant and mischievous realities of the next." But in the
United States, the natives, not the invading Celts, had produced the spurious type, and as the century ended, the

117

American of Irish race was quietly, uncomfortably trying to escape his destiny. He had prospered dizzily in a hundred capacities, and now found himself classed, in most cities, as something unwanted outside his shop, his contractor's office or his bar. Under the green froth of Saint Patrick's Day oratory there floated sentences of expostulation. " We are good as the best of native Americans. Let them blame us for the acts of a few politicians and rioters and we will answer that for every Irish rogue we will find one born and bred under the Stars and Stripes. . . . We can proudly boast that in every city in America where there is an Irish population are to be found cultured and dignified ladies and gentlemen." The strain rises, wistfully assertive, in the wearisome Irish and Catholic journals from which the clever writers inevitably vanished into offices of big newspapers.

The spokesman of the superior Irish in America had notably been John Boyle O'Reilly. He died only a few days before Dion Boucicault in 1890 but by the time that his mediocre monument was unveiled at Boston in 1896, there was little left of O'Reilly's reputation. He had met the American definition of a poet fully; ladies recited the vaguely radical stanzas of " In Bohemia " where recitation was encouraged and the pretty lyric of the roses was a legend on Christmas calendars, dusted with snowy mica and edged with shamrocks. " Moondyne," his Australian study, is now more active than his verse. A dozen unpretentious poets of the '90's outdid him — John Vance Cheney, Lizette Reese or, later, Arthur Colton. He had been a charming figure in Boston; he was honestly esteemed and his lectures kept the man's regal voice and manner in enough evidence to warrant reputation. There was no successor and throughout the '90's Irish letters in America were feebly represented by a few journalists, Katherine Conway, James Jeffrey Roche and the amusing Joseph Clarke who had his moment in 1898 when he replaced Henri Dumay as editor of the *Criterion*.

This mad review was founded by a retiring, gentle lady who somewhere discovered Dumay and brought him to New York. It was the association of a saint with a gambolling catamount. Dumay editorially pondered the intelligence of New York's social rulers and rhapsodized the little sanitary stops of a French dancer's dog. The young clever contributed in swarms. Perceval Pollard first was widely known through the *Criterion*. Rupert Hughes attacked the paper on its taste; Dumay noticed a good writer and engaged Mr. Hughes at once. His owner's interviews with the Frenchman became events and she finally paid the balance of his two years' salary to be rid of him. Clarke succeeded the roaming free lance, and the *Criterion* kept its tone of a French review of 1880 until the century ended and the magazine vanished into the leaden haze of the Decade of Muck. Like *Mlle. New York*, Vance Thompson's biweekly, the *Criterion* now has a devilish legend. It was engaging enough under Dumay and Clarke. Perceval Pollard and Rupert Hughes wrote soundly of books and music; why it was held " immoral " and refused by libraries is incomprehensible. But in those days it was also held eccentric for the artist, Alfred Brennan, to sign his letters with a French adverb, and a dinner of sculptors, all male, with erotic symbols in plaster on the table, has become one of the whispered orgies of Stanford White whereas the host and designer of the party was a sculptor who lived and died in a positive halo of marmoreal prettiness and domestic solidity. . . . Mr. Clarke was typical of these native Irish journalists; he had facility and a handsome breadth as an editorial writer; he dabbled in playmaking and versified fluently. He could not take O'Reilly's place, had he wished, and the '90's brought up no interpreter of the Irish in America.

A society which mistook amenity for civilization natu-

rally had a low rôle for this untidy intrusion of people who
spoke musical English and supposedly danced jigs. Pat
and Mike held endless colloquies in the comic weeklies;
the pig and goat watched through the shanty's door while a
fat shrew belaboured her man with a skillet. The rich contractor and his wife strung with diamonds pushed at the
social wall in cartoons and burlesques. A merry clown of
the principal metropolitan court squawked across a dinner
table to a lovely Miss Sullivan: " I suppose you're related to
John L.? " meaning the prizefighter of the day, and this
jape roused Joseph Choate, when he heard it, to saying:
" We may think the Irish vulgar, but God knows what they
think of us! " Perhaps it is safer to let the Irish speak, from
the recollections of a man then young and always shrewd.

" My father and grandfather had been the best surgeons
in X," says the deponent, " since the Mexican War. When
I was a kid in the '80's, there were factories built and the
edges of the city filled up with ' shanty Irish.' It never occurred to me, in those inocent days, that I was Irish. Father
and mother both were born in America. He had the medical
man's impatience of miraculous religions. My grandfather
was a grand old warhorse of the Daniel O'Connell period,
very courtly and gushing to the ladies. He always spoke of
the immigrant millhands as ' bog trotters ' and wondered
why they did not take farms instead of working in the plants.
. . . Everybody knew us in the city. It was about 1890
that trouble began for us. I was conscious of it as a boy is
conscious that something is wrong. My sisters came home
from school in England and the beaux began to call. The
oldest daughter engaged herself to the lad next door and
then trouble really began. His family would not swallow
any agreement that the presumptive children of this marriage should be raised in the faith. They were our warmest
friends. My father secretly sympathized with them, I imagine. But my poor, devout mother was in the extremity

of sorrow. . . . As a doctor I have had to see this situation
played through over and over again, and until the Church
takes a different position in the matter the Amerirish are
always going to be in difficulties. The business ended in my
sister and her boy eloping, much to father's amusement.
She now attends a Unitarian Mosque in Boston. . . . I
must describe Dr. Daniel O'D., the pastor of Saint Mary's.
It is not my antipathy to formal religions but my memory
of the priest that is speaking. Your soft-headed literary
gang has invented a Catholic priest on its own pattern and
doubtless he is satisfactory. Father Dan was a sour old
prude, an educated peasant from South Ireland who had
been a priest there before he came to the United States. He
hated a Protestant and he despised Protestant education.
Once he found me playing with some of my Nordic crowd
on our street and told me: ' Remember, Owen, that you'll
never see any of those lads in another world unless you
should offend God and be sent to hell.' Of course the old
man would go through ten blizzards to a death-bed or risk
getting himself in the papers to beg a Catholic boy out of
jail, and he got a hundred dollars a month out of my family
for his poor. But I dreaded him, and his sermons in Lent
scared me into a nervous misery although I was not in
the least a sensitive child. You can find how he talked about
hell and purgatory in Joyce's first novel. This godly man
came to see that my people hunted my sister down and made
her take all the proper Catholic steps. All our trouble came
of being bad Catholics and bad Irishmen, he said emphati-
cally, and too proud to associate with our own race. He was
not at all subservient to wealth, I should say. I suppose he
was entitled to his point of view. The Irish were the Irish
to him. He had no use for American institutions of any
kind. He continually denounced the public library in X
for keeping books ' that speak against us.' His kind justified some of the A. P. A. twaddle. I do not suppose that

121

there were many of them, but they did exist. He turned on me and said: ' And here's Owen that never plays with any good Catholic boys!' . . . You pagans cannot understand a young Catholic's awe of a priest. This was not just a big man in a black vest speaking, but the Church. There is no good in trying to explain how this one sentence, just a slap at my mother underhand, drove me into Irish patriotism. I turned my twelve-year-old back on all my Protestant friends and associated exclusively with the Irish. . . . The Amerirish in X who come back fondly to me in memory were the middling kind. They lived in a little colony of frame houses on three parallel streets back of Saint Mary's. The men were superior mechanics or shopkeepers or little lawyers. The Nordics held them at arm's length and treated them in a half-humorous, half-condescending way, as the middle-class American treats the Catholic Irishman. They had their defects, God knows! They were touchy and clannish and sentimental. Some of them flattered me for being the rich Dr. K.'s boy and some of them resented me tremendously. It is the weakness or the excessive sentiment of the Amerirish that no writer has spoken of that life in realistic terms. His book would be condemned and spat upon, but what an audience he would have! Well, ' the root is in their mother's heart and wrapped around their father's bones.' . . . Your literary fakers have neglected the extreme simplicity of the Irishwoman so as to talk blatherskite about ' Celtic poetry.' The Irishwoman born in Ireland is not gifted with much taste in dress or in household goods. I often think that the Amerirish girl develops into smartness and a fine sense of ornament because in her childhood she has to look at Mamma and the lithograph of His Holiness framed in bog oak on the parlour wall. . . . I can remember one of these good women saying to me in perfect sincerity: ' I wonder now why herself ' — meaning my mother — ' keeps the doctor's house so plain and him

with all the money in God's world.' The men often had
better taste than their wives, and the children differed from
the young Nordics in very little, except that they knew those
pure Americans looked down on them. Oh, yes, they did!
Over on the edge of town was Irish Hill, where the ' bog
trotters' lived, a stinking slum that started every epidemic
in X and sold its votes to the dirty German politician who
ran the Democratic machine in X. . . . Americans think
in generalities. One Irish name equalled a Catholic and
that equalled mud. Or if it was not Catholicism that was
the bane, it was the social connotation of Irish Hill. Your
anecdote of John McCall [3] illustrates the point. . . . A
realistic writer about the nice Irish in X would have to
harden his heart and transcribe such a scene as this. Here
is young Terence stalking up and down the parlour with
his chin quivering because those damn Republican kids at
High School have gone and elected Robert Wilbur Abbott
or Calvin Coolidge Jones captain of the baseball team and
here he'd been on the team three years, and — and — and
—— Over in the corner is Aunt Jane, who can remember
O'Connell speaking at Cork, and the fine handsome man
he was, telling Terry: ' Never mind, boy, them black per-
verts will find out in the next world! ' The truth being that
the Nordics were perfectly justified in electing Bob or Cal
instead of Terry. As for pretty Norah crying her eyes out
because she had not been asked to Sadie Smith's birthday
party, I decline to discuss that at all. The worst of which
was that the boys were frequently invited where the girls
were not. . . .

" I do not deny that among these people, kind and well-
meaning as they were, existed a lot of cheap Catholic
bigotry and prejudice against the Nordics not on the grounds

[3] A magnificent female at a dinner in Washington said to my father,
across McCall: " He's not at all Irish, is he? " McCall asked her sweetly:
" Did you expect me to bring a pig and a shillelagh with me? " She assured
him: " Oh, dear no! I don't suppose you even keep a pig, do you? "

123

of their social superiority but simply as Protestants. You see I am talking a good deal, more than you like maybe, about the religious side of the business, because that seems to me the important thing in the 1890's. These people were often unconscious of their too frequent vulgarity and they attributed all snubs as relative to their religious nonsense. It was particularly true of the women, as they did not mix with the Nordics in business or wait on them in shops. I can remember women who themselves were shrewd and even witty who had manufactured a Protestant just as your critics have manufactured their chemical Catholic, who is a great liberal because he dislikes Prohibition and plays cards on Sunday. This atmosphere was frequently bad for the children. It was likely to make them flatterers of the Nordic for the sake of social advantages and it made many lads into toughs. They were going to show those Republican sissies how a real Irishman went on! So they hung around the houses of ill fame in the railroad district, got into fights on small provocation and thought it pretty smart to be arrested once or twice. I must take leave to say here that the attitude of the Protestant ladies in X toward these people simply struck me as implacably mean and silly. Well, God is for men, and religion for women, as Conrad said. . . . My mother gave dances a great deal and she kindly served as a social wedge for some of the nice Irish families. The boys all danced well. The girls were often lumps. For dancing was not approved of in some of those households. I know that sounds absurd, but it is true. My secretary at this moment is a pretty girl born in a small town of south Ireland whose family disapproves of dancing — so much so that she and her brothers have invented a friend on whom they are calling at night when they want to go to a dance. Father Dan did not disapprove of dancing publicly, but he hated it and quarrelled over it with the other priest in X, a very progressive young American-born

German. Why is it that only Theodore Dreiser and young FitzGerald seem to know that there is an enormous Catholic German constituency in America? And, oh, my, how the Amerirish in X looked down on them and snubbed them! Just as the other day I sewed up his head for a young Italamerican who had been trying to impress the haughty Harps on his street. 'They treat me and my sister like we was Polacks,' he said. For, putting Catholicism aside, the Irish can be awful snobs. I remember sitting in one house at X, and it was one of the most cultivated homes, too, listening to the family pore over the names of every prominent Irish personage in America, from Augustin Daly to John L. Sullivan. I hate to drag in that dead duck, the inferiority complex, but the root of it was there. And to-day I know Amerirish who would have colic if they read 'A Portrait of the Artist' or 'Ulysses' but who brag about James Joyce. . . . As to the virtues of these people, it strikes me that their generosity to their kids when they were prosperous was a lovable thing. Nobody, unless it is the prosperous Hebrew, is kinder to his children than an Ameririshman. It is more of a virtue, as they do not brag of it. Then, barring their noisy quarrels among themselves, they were and are mannerly folk. They like to please. Why not? It is a pity that they overdo the thing so often and get the name of flatterers. I remember Frank Norris saying in 1899 that an Irish compliment landed like a falling house. There is also a basis for the rumour that Irishmen are witty. It is true that the most humourless creature in the world is a dull Irishman. The percentage of them is not small, either. Was not the humour of Dunne's Dooley papers the playing off of the stupid Hennessy against the sharp-witted Dooley? . . . When I was at college I knew two brothers, call them Dennis and Tom, the sons of a big Tammany contractor in New York, a terrible rascal and vulgar as a sewer. Dennis was immense. He had the cynicism of a French waiter at

eighteen. He loathed his family. He despised Americans.
He had an imaginary friend named Judkinson, a real-estate
dealer in Brooklyn, who was the quintessence of American
banality, an uncle of Mr. Sinclair Lewis's Babbitt. Denny
was the first American I ever heard quote Bernard Shaw.
There was a professional Irishman in our class. God permitted him to think himself a humorist and a gay dog among
the women. He aspired to no less than Anna Held, who
was the rage then. So he consulted Denny, as an expert in
such things. Denny gave him the best of advice. Bill went
down to New York and stepped up to the girl, as she was
getting into a cab outside Weber and Fields', with a hun-
dred-dollar bill wrapped around the stem of a rose. The
girl tucked the rose into that feather boa she wore so much,
then tore the bill into pieces and blew them in Bill's face.
He came yelling murder to Denny, who looked him over
and said: ' It's our national genius for treachery, you big
fool, and do you think you'll ever be anything but Hundred
Dollar Bill here until you graduate? ' Bill could not stand
being teased and left college, no loss to anybody. Your
Yankee habit of automatically laughing at an Irish joke destroyed Bill. He had no more wit than his shoe, but he told
jokes until the maddened bystanders ran from him. Just
this morning I heard my young daughter telling a swain on
the telephone: ' If you bring that funny Irishman back here,
I'll have dad dissect him.' The boy was well enough except
that he thought it his sacred duty to be funny. I remember
when I was studying in Paris, an Amerirish boy fixing himself on Booth Tarkington one night in a café and driving
him from table to table as he told him merry tales until
Mr. Tarkington got wedged in a corner and could not run
farther. He had the look of a man sitting beside his father's
coffin, and I have waited for the episode to bob up in one
of his stories. . . . Denny's young brother was in all ways
his opposite. He was a splendid athlete, pious and dull as

mud. But he was painfully sensitive about his father's reputation. He bristled whenever anybody said 'Tammany' or 'politician' in earshot of him. He suspected slights where none were intended, and thought himself unpopular when he was really admired. He changed his name, later, and lives in England, these days, avoiding Americans. As for Denny, he died at twenty-four in Paris. I helped the doctors take care of him. We were afraid to give him much morphine and once I tried to trick him with an injection of warm water. He grinned and whispered: 'National genius for treachery.' It was his contention that Shaw should have written 'genius for discovering treachery.' There were many Amerirish boys in college in my time, some of them good lads and well liked and some of them impossible. When these last were passed over in the elections of clubs and what not, they fell back on religious difference, or political prejudice. This 'black heart of Ireland,' is it anything but a lack of self-criticism? There was no religious prejudice at college and the young American is not politically excitable. . . . My own Scotch-sounding name and my agnosticism have always allowed me to hear what the Nordics think of the Celt without dilution. My Nordic wife malevolently insists that I stir the subject up. The Irish position in America has improved, of course, since I was a boy back in X. But what happened in X was the development of an Irish plutocracy against a larger Nordic plutocracy. Some of the best Irish families left X in order to be out of the social frost. One of those families changed its name. . . . That stunt was laughed at in the funny papers of those days but I have known intelligent Amerirish to do it with cold deliberation. 'What is the use,' one of them said to me, ' of having the children grow up with every damned matron on a hotel porch in summertime lifting her nose at them because their name is Kelly? ' . . . There were States in the 1890's where the Irish were

better treated, such as California, where enough Irishmen
had made themselves respected early to insure a kind of
counterweight for the bosses and that amateur Robespierre
whose name I forget just now, the Sand Lot man . . ."
(Dennis Kearney, a popular leader, once very noisy). " I
could say generally that the Irish were luckier where they
were fewest and the Nordics had a chance to know them
better. . . . As to American writing on the Irish, it has
always been bad and is bad to-day. It either flatters them
for possessing the ordinary virtues of decent people or it
turns them into comic supplements. Harold Frederic knew
a good deal about them but he used the common trick of
using their religious sincerity and nice manners as a club
on the Methodists. The rest of the writing in the 1890's
struck me as just damned rot. There are some clever
sketches of Irish city types in O. Henry's things. Dunne
picked up his Dooley smartly, although I see no overpower-
ing humour in calling the Spanish prime minister a Spanish
onion. I remember a writer named Charles O'Keefe who
did some grim little stories well but there was not many of
them." (Naturally: O'Keefe died at the age of twenty-
two.) " Such a writer as Seumas McManus simply made
capital of his background. He was a mighty pleasant lecturer and told an Irish story well. As for the professional
Amerirish writers who go around proving that a chief of
police should not arrest a fellow member of the Knights of
Columbus and slobbering about Catholic blood spilled on
American fields, they are simply *agents provocateurs* of the
Ku Klux Klan. Who ever heard of a Mason refusing to
arrest another Mason or a Presbyterian shedding tears on
a platform about Presbyterian blood shed in the Argonne?
It is against such slop that I wish some realistic writer, and
he would almost have to be an Irishman, would come up.
It is time for them to be done hunting poor compliments, or
treacheries either. Their muscle and their humours are

about all the Irish have really been allowed to show in America. I love them too much to be patient of such waste. So unless somebody else does it, I may hire a collaborator and do it myself. My life is well insured and if the worst comes to the worst I can run to Hawaii when they mob me, and cultivate pineapples on my plantation."

Yet the compliments, poor as they have been, perhaps came as a tribute from the writers who saw in this vain, charming, baffled folk a certain brotherhood to their own prosperous adversity, facing a society not " implacably mean and silly " but perpetually childish in its concepts of all art. They have flattered the Irish, surely, misting them in drear humours, drearier romances. But they stand in like case whose food is bought by the mere muscle of narration, an artisanship in gaiety, until the illusion of pleasure that supports all artists is sucked away and they see themselves as tired, as amused attendants in a glittering charnel where lamps shed no warmth.

CHAPTER V

THE UNHOLY HOST

THERE was a little revolt of one against the process of education at Vanderbilt University in the spring of 1891. The rebel was the son of a clergyman in Georgia, densely shocked when a professor gave him translations from Haeckel and a classmate advised him to read the perfumed insufficiency of Ernest Renan's life of Jesus. Rebellion carried him through a quarrel with a young instructor and into the office of the chancellor, a Virginian gentleman named Landon Cabell Garland. The boy stammered out expostulations; biology, agnosticism and the sinfulness of the French language bubbled together in his head and, being a Georgian, he had committed an oration before the old mathematician said in his thin, aged drawl: "Men never amount to much until they outgrow their fathers' notions, sir." The rebellion of 1891 ended with the injection of that thought among boiling prejudices. There came a stillness in Tennessee. The boy mumbled something and stumbled out of the room, whipped by twelve words from a drowsy magician in a chair beside a window.

The chancellor vanished from his university and died in 1895 just as Robert Grant told readers of *Scribner's Magazine* that an American existed in self-righteous commonness of spirit who sat at home in his shirt-sleeves, reading the newspapers, and was "graceless, ascetic and unimaginative in the name of God." Newspapers neglected Mr. Grant's discovery and printed very little about Landon Cabell Garland. He had no " news value " — Julian Ralph invented the phrase in 1892 although it would be long before it became sacred. Improving journalism had won to a complete knowledge of its audience at last and swept obliging rays across the form of John L. Sullivan, whose neck was seventeen inches in circumference, or dabbled the glory of a whole column on William Waldorf Astor, a man of means who fled the social grossness of New York and wrote a number of tales to celebrate his tenancy of an English castle. His tales are now known only to eclectic amateurs. These " figures of earth " were comprehensible, editors saw, to the graceless, ascetic and unimaginative American. And what news value had Landon Cabell Garland, born in 1810, celebrity in mathematics by 1840, professor of chemistry, astronomy or any such sere art that needed teaching in the South, president of a railroad in the war time and defender of liberal education everywhere he passed? He wasn't news value. Joseph Leidy, dying in 1891, the foremost of American natural historians, stepfather of the Smithsonian Institute, was not news value, but any rogue who announced his faith in his mother's Bible and his unaltered trust in the plain people whom he fleeced or cajoled for votes was news value, and is to-day. The notions of his father were sufficient to the graceless and shirt-sleeved, in the name of God, and the passing of that faint, scattered aristocracy spiritual which once disturbed his complacency was not to be lamented. He had his newspapers. The asceticism of growing dullness held him to this fodder, and the arts abetted his feeding.

The arts, disguised as a young writer, now sardonically reminiscent, sat facing Edward Drinker Cope in the palæontologist's favourite restaurant, at Philadelphia. The arts were a little bored, listening to the strange, handsome Quaker debate a skull just sent from diggings in the West.

Henry Fairfield Osborn had one opinion, Cope had another and the listening arts yawned into an empty glass, eventually so bored that they must ask Cope what was the good of palæontology? The professor fingered his jaunty waxed moustaches and began to simmer, then boiled over: " Friend, thee — you do not ask the poet to write bills of lading or the painter to whitewash fences. Do you expect the abstracted scientist to invent a patent churn? " He spoke, and presently the journals casually mentioned that he was dead, in 1897, in his house overflowing with papers and specimens of his long exploit in speculative history.

" In a way," says the man who insulted him, " I was excusable. Like most young Americans of that time I was all for art with a capital A, and I suppose my idea of a scientist was Thomas Alva Edison. The American idea of science was already so inæsthetic that Sinclair Lewis could have written ' Dr. Arrowsmith ' with perfect propriety in 1897. Æsthetic, if you please, was an essay by Arthur Symons or a statue by Saint Gaudens. By the way, I am he who wrote to *Harper's* that the editors ought to be shot for printing Owen Wister's ' Em'ly ' in the same number with Walter Pater's ' Apollo in Picardy.' Æsthetic, I repeat, was something graceful and smooth and so distinct that you didn't have to think about it twice. Science was certainly not æsthetic. If Bertrand Russell had called an Einstein of the period an ' explorer in æsthetic' someone like Edmund Gosse would have fairly cartooned him all over the magazines. I don't suppose that people such as Cope cared a damn about the neglect of their work by the critics and I don't suppose that Richard Swann Lull, Francis Tondorf, Edward Maurer or Ellsworth Huntington care to-day what the critics think of them. My sensation, when Professor Cope flared up, was simply one of outrage that a grubber among fossils should dare to put himself in the same class with George Moore and Rudyard Kipling. . . . Back of this disorderly theory of æsthetic I think you will find the holy shade of James Russell Lowell. The learned man of the golden '90's was someone like Lowell who knew a great deal about all the right books and talked about them gracefully. I choose Lowell as the best of his kind, for you may tear him in pieces as much as you like but you will have to admit his erudition and his consistency of mind. Lowell, and his gang, represented æsthetic. The Copes and Sumners and Francis Amasa Walkers represented some dull nonsense about skeletons and wages and ' mores.' As far as we were concerned they might just as well be trying to invent patent churns as not. . . . I took Sumner's course at New Haven, under protest, and, of course, I respected him without knowing why I respected him. He was a prodigious personality, something cold and massive and autocratic. He came stalking into the classroom with a sort of ' Be damned to you ' air, and even when he said something tremendously good he drawled it out in his New Jersey whine with so little emphasis that it wasted itself. I remember perfectly his famous lecture on the expurgation of history, the one in which he said that Ethan Allen probably did not say: ' Open, in the name of the Continental Congress and the great Jehovah ' but did say: ' Open up here, you god-damned son of a bitch! ' But he never ' pointed up ' his good things as Barrett Wendell did and it was only years afterward that I began to appreciate Sumner at all. I find in my notes: ' When two religions appeared in the primitive community the one favoured by respectable cattle thieves was practised as religion and the other was called illicit medicine or black magic ' but that did not impress me at the time and neither did his blistering discourses on the crowd mind. He sat there in 1895 and demonstrated the difference between morals and manners as no American has demonstrated it before or since, and whatever his biographer may say, he did shock his students terrifically when he cut loose

133

against protective tariffs or pointed out that dress was the mother of decency, not decency of dress. What was his subject, after all, but this ' ape grown rusty at climbing who yet feels himself to be a symbol and the frail representative of Omnipotence in a place that is not home '? The old fiend made it pretty plain that his opinion of the ape was rather a low one, too, just as ' Folkways ' shows you what he thought of literature. We respected him, and admired him, as I say, however little we appreciated him. If he had been seriously threatened with expulsion from Yale in 1899 when he blew up imperialism, there would have been an academic revolution. His mind may have been a little narrow, but he laid the foundations of social science in the United States and his neglect in the republic of letters, American department, has been shameful."

Dear sir, the republic of letters, in all its departments, can do nothing with a Sumner. He belongs on the high place over against the politic Jerusalem. It is said that from this windy eminence nations are seen as coloured sands poured carelessly through hands of inattentive demons and the haughty arts, themselves, viewed from above, are merely tiny emblems of man's protest against brevity and weakness, his poor revenge on God. This hill is no place for a good republican of letters, although now and then one steals off to join the unholy host around the accursed fires up there. But it is safer to sit discussing whether a sound style shouldn't resemble the running tone of conversation among civilized people — ourselves, in short. Our fathers' notions are warm around us. We do not care that, from the hill, we seem just lice, clinging to folds of a stale blanket.

II

ROBERT LOUIS STEVENSON went not fully after the Lord as did Thomas his father, but wore a velvet coat, spent his shillings among venal girls and announced himself an atheist. While he was worrying his proud father remarkably in Edinburgh a quite commonplace farmer in middle Ohio asked the law to keep his only son from denying the regional god and spending his nights with a gallant widow of the Fourieriste persuasion. The law replied: " This court cannot issue a frivolous order limiting any sane man in the free use of his faculties "; but the decision is possibly irrelevant in a case to be tried under the laws of the literary republic. Stevenson, then, rebelled and finally went the length of running away to California after a married woman whose husband courteously stepped from his corner of the forming triangle and walked off into legend.

Assuming the literary republican's viewpoint, all this is rather fearsome. As an episode under the laws of Ohio, or seen from the high place by Anatole France, there isn't much in it, except the good breeding of Mrs. Stevenson's first husband. The poet had used his faculties, for some years, as freely as his finances allowed. These practices were abhorrent to the odd, parochial Lord of Edinburgh, a creation something in the nature of an angry grocer, and even when his rebellion was done with, the poet never reconciled himself to the tartan bully.

His ample, light intelligence had been trained in the theatrical manners of decayed Calvinism, a version of the Christian philosophy which, in those days, excluded morality, the law of the individual, and dealt totally in manners, the laws of the herd. Stevenson had seen through this apparatus, but he could not discard it. His intellect was not legitimately rebellious at all, and the wistful apology of " The House of Eld " is the whole statement of his case. So the high place was not for him; but his levity impressed timid, bookish folk as red rashness, and for fourteen years a moving syrup of appreciation supported the gay invalid on its sweetness. His subjects were inoffensive — murder and more murder, fratricidal hate and madness, blood lust and piracy in seven forms. His prose chimes gently on, delicately echoing a hundred classic musics, gently dwindles from the recollection as do all imitations, and is now impressive only to people who think that a good prose is written to be read aloud. But this theatre delighted the times: Vice and Virtue fought a duel in a frozen garden by candlelight, and Lord Rosebery was fascinated; the pirate ship sailed to a jolly tune and children watched the rain through nursery windows. . . . Only now and then an awkward sense of life intruded in the show, a sombre undertone welled up from somewhere and gave you Herrick, still disgraced in his own mind, staring at the white figurehead on the Presbyterian reef or the last paragraphs of " The Beach of Falesá," but generally the show was well in hand, one range of effects suited to peers and schoolboys and another conciliating the literary republicans: the castaway of " Falesá " will turn his talk into rhythmic prose or Herrick will score a phrase of the Fifth Symphony on the wall in Tahiti and scribble to his sweetheart: " Think of me at the last, here, on a bright beach, the sky and sea immoderately blue, and the great breakers roaring outside upon a barrier reef where a little isle sits, green with palms. . . ."

His decadence was just that of a man who has worked too hard in his apprenticeship and cannot escape from the schooling. Only it happened that this classical simulation was in high favour in the '80's, and that a hundred younger writers were pounding about among the *prosateurs* of the seventeenth and eighteenth centuries in search of some such medium for themselves. Hadn't George Saintsbury urged them to be *écrivains artistes?* Another set of decadents succeeded the humdrum, harmless people who aped Dickens and George Eliot, and Oscar Wilde appeared. The yellow and lavender carouse of the early '90's brought Stevenson into high relief. Good republicans saw that he was even more meritorious than he had seemed in the '80's. His name was suddenly invoked, as an image of chastity, against this terrible crew whose products agitated William Watson and scared the producers themselves. They advertised yesterday's mistress and to-morrow's satiety in verses wildly graceful as a painted Easter egg, and the whole business now suggests a college glee club rigorously intoning:

> " Gentleman rankers out on a spree,
> Damned from here to Eternity.
> God ha' mercy on such as we!
> Baa! Yah! Baa! . . ."

Some of these men were talented. Arthur Symons was a specimen of thermal conductivity in letters, through which the ideas of French artists passed into English perception with little damage. Lionel Johnson was an admirable critic up to the point of his rigid intellectual dishonesty. Aubrey Beardsley was a decorator so superior that his " Salomé " convinced people that Oscar Wilde had written a tragedy of the name, just as Oliver Herford's illustrations in some tales of the declining Joel Chandler Harris made American children of the '90's believe that they enjoyed " Aaron in the Wildwoods " and " Little Mr. Thimblefinger." But the whole temper of the crowd was toward a species of languid exhibitionism that makes one grin.

> " I cried for madder music and for stronger wine,
> But when the feast is finished and the lamps expire,
> Then falls thy shadow, Cynara! the night is thine;
> And I am desolate and sick of an old passion,
>   Yea, hungry for the lips of my desire;
> I have been faithful to thee, Cynara! in my fashion. . . ."

The delaying melody charms for a second, and then the staleness of the phrases overcomes any pleasure in the orchestration. All this is still found momentous, by correct

English criticism, and perhaps it is, if one can manage the straitly literary view. The audience rustled in embarrassment while the glee club sang. Biology was intruding in letters. Then the end came with a theatrical violence. Stevenson died in December of 1894; six months later Oscar Wilde was on trial for pæderasty in London. Some intolerable person announced that the dandy had made a new Thermopylæ of infamy; haberdashers in verse, men of fashion ran off to the Continent. Wilde blubbered as the crowd jeered him on his way to prison, and a voice came grimly out of Scotland: " How pure and clear our Stevenson's genius seems beside this ' art for art's sake ' which the public now sees in its true colours at last! "

In the United States, the romancer had only one strong academic support up to his death. Brander Matthews had showed a limited enthusiasm, tempered by admissions of Stevenson's incurable Calvinism. But for four years the English paraded in force. Stevenson was mourned honestly, sentimentally and politically by the right people: Edmund Gosse, James Barrie, Sidney Colvin, Ian Maclaren, Lord Rosebery, Conan Doyle, Anthony Hope, William Archer, Walter Raleigh, Arthur Pinero, William Watson and a number of forgotten greatnesses were all in print. The silences of Henry James, Rudyard Kipling, Thomas Hardy and George Meredith were nugatory, and George Moore's rudeness of 1886 was forgotten, if ever read. Under this manifestation the shapes of two acute publishers and an affable literary executor were dimly busy, and in the political eulogies the violet shadow of Oscar Wilde is amusingly visible, the more so that his name was never mentioned. The American result began to show in 1897, or showed itself to Harry Thurston Peck, Anthon professor of classical literature at Columbia College, editor of the *Bookman*. " I," he wrote, " am the last person in the world to deprecate poor Mr. Stevenson's posthumous vogue. He was a romantic writer of the greatest qualities, and while I cannot help preferring the realists, good romance gets under my skin very easily. But I cannot help feeling that these eulogies of Mr. Stevenson are going too far; and I greatly dislike the ' solar plexus jab ' that I see in some of them, aimed not only at Wilde but at Messrs. Hardy, Moore and Kipling who all have burned a little incense at the altar of Aphrodite Pandemos, if you know who the lady is. For one, I am not sure that Mr. Stevenson's abstention from those tragedies and mishaps due to passionate influences in our human life was altogether the admirable trait that it is declared to be, by some of his friends. But then Mr. Barrett Wendell has rallied me on my ' morbid enthusiasm for amorous modern fiction ' and I suppose that should put me in the corner where I belong. Furthermore, I dislike the personal element in much that is being written about Mr. Stevenson. It is natural that his friends should say the best for him, but why say anything of his ' pure, unsullied Scottish faith '? He was a free thinker, although not an atheist, in the manner of Mr. Howells and Mr. Crane. And why say that his life was an ' example to the young,' unless we are in for a very unexpected wave of liberalism in education? I have never heard that he indulged himself in stupid debaucheries but he was a gay blade in his green days and once was absolutely alienated from his father, who was of the unco guid description. How silly it would be to contemn Mr. Stevenson because he had a mistress or two in his youth, but how silly it is, on the other hand, to dress him up as Christian hero who ne'er brought the blush to maiden's cheek! I fear," the professor mused, " that his friends are overdoing it. . . . Well, I took your MS. to Mr. [James] O'Neill. He seemed interested in the subject and promised to read the play himself. He seems to be a shrewd, quick-witted man, and not half so conceited as I had been told by some of his acquaintances. My impressions of him are not worth a red cent because one of my toes was sore and Mr. O'Neill's little boy came and stood on it while we talked. . . ." [1]

But the stunning parade of the English grandees was too much for the increasing type of academic instructor, forced into being by the expansion of the universities. In 1898 the flippant Guy Wetmore Carryl remarked that American colleges were the back yards of English criticism, and in 1898 two professorlings rounded on John Jay Chapman when the essayist attacked Stevenson as a derivative writer, quoting long paragraphs from Edmund Gosse and Walter Raleigh in their lectures. In 1899 the Vailima prayers were quoted at Princeton's theological seminary; and in 1900 the prose was introduced in five schools and colleges. . . . The comedy appeared in its fullest value to Mr. Charles Mason Maurice, an amateur who stuttered out his compliments to Stevenson at Saranac in 1888, adding those of his English teacher in a Chicago high school, and was answered gaily: " Eh, lad, I like your good word better. Professors are puir bodies when it comes to a tale."

Stevenson, here, is merely an emblem of the intellectual battle of the '90's in the United States. That battle, so far as it affected creative æsthetic, was won by the pack described in William Dean Howells' defence of " Maggie," those " many foolish people who cannot discriminate between the material and treatment in art, and think that beauty is inseparable from daintiness and prettiness . . ."; in the contemplative æsthetic of science and speculative history, the battle was an indeterminate muddle of fogged personalities, and in that haze the memorable beings of William Graham Sumner, William James and Barrett Wendell appear more clearly than the rest. But Wendell himself is rather an emblem than a man, vibrant point of protest against the vulgarization of American life, a realist in politics, a refugee among the dead in letters. He swayed before

---

[1] His correspondent had dramatized " The Master of Ballantrae."

the dressed beef of his classroom and tried to illuminate it by chanting bars of the Elizabethan music in his amazing colonial English, or crackled with a wit that survives him: " Charles II was no more immoral than a cab-driver, or than some of yourselves, but his tastes were expensively administered unto and his loves were public as those of a fox terrier. . . . The modern theatre's only excuse is that it sends the milkman home in a good temper. . . . A writer in *Scribner's Magazine* tells us that good taste is universal in France. Good taste is not even universal in heaven." His method was not unlike that of little Arthur Wheeler, who faced the football-players of the Iron Age at Yale and lectured on European history, puncturing legends with a succession of groaning sniffs. . . . " Lord Nelson now arrived at Naples, where Lady Hamilton greeted him. Her experience of men was great and Nelson's intelligence was that " — sniff — " of a sailor. . . . Byron tore himself from the countess and set out for Greece. Even countesses become irksome and Byron had always understood " — sniff — " the advantages of combining his domestic mishaps with a little advertisement. . . . The Duke of Wellington, being " — sniff — " an Englishman, believed in letting his allies have a fair share of trouble in any undertaking. . . . If Napoleon's ambition to spread French culture in the Orient was reprehensible, that of the English to enlighten India has somehow escaped the attention of English " — sniff — " historians." But Wendell had the advantage of his topic: he was teaching " English literature," his epigrams, his unconscious forays against modernism, his saline comments on political affairs all stood out in the tissue of the one subject popular with the lazy undergraduate. Expanding universities now offered ten courses in English literature to one in science, and of this massive gift in cultivation about two-thirds were devoted to the study of fiction. Thus the sophomore of 1900, and 1920, could pillow his brain on " Treasure Island "; it had been conceded to his sloth that he should not be vexed with " Manners and Fashion " or asked to follow the lucidity of " Evidence as to Man's Place in Nature "; it was certainly not suggested that the rich style of " Principles of Psychology " was worth his while. These things belonged to " science." The beauties of fact became more and more imperceptible, and the young poet who affronted Edward Cope was excused by an atmosphere in whose slackened oxygen the duel of brothers by candlelight in the frozen garden and the orchestral snivellings of Tschaikowsky stood for perfected art.

III

HARRY THURSTON PECK was a Yankee gentleman whose fractious brilliance as an undergraduate had startled the little faculty of Columbia College. He was no friend to strict accuracy, but it was early plain that he could think, and in the middle '80's he began to write. He wrote Tennysonian verses, a book for children, tabulated the Semitic legends of creation, edited Latin grammars and reviewed novels for the newspapers. In the '90's his name, with its suggestion of frivolity, dodged here and there in magazines and journals. Columbia, itself, was regarded as somewhat libertine by other universities. It had no dominating religious tradition; it was assembled in godless New York; its professors appeared in smart restaurants, and published mundane " vignettes of Manhattan." The eccentricity of owning a professor named Hjalmar Hjorth Boyesen alone was considerable, and to have Professor Peck trace the permutations of " Ta-Ra-Ra-Boom De Ay " in a popular magazine utterly finished the place in the mind of one Bostonian educator, already unmercifully busy with the business of criticism.

THE UNHOLY HOST

Peck's interest in the world around him expressed itself anyhow. Everything took his eye — the life of street cars, the size of sleeves and the religious fervour of crowds attending unrehearsed ballets of football and baseball. He dashed off letters of twelve lines, as John Hay so often did, to tell an invalid friend in Colorado some anecdote. One learns that a tender young millionaire applied to Joseph Choate for counsel when a married woman was chasing him around Newport. " Tell her," said the lawyer; " ' Madam, I have no time for a liaison, but I am willing to oblige you, if you promise that our adultery is not to be of a serious nature.' " Or one sees the professor listening to a debate on the strike at Chicago among Mr. Henry Holt, Edwin Godkin and Richard Watson Gilder in a club, then listening to the same opinions from a group of workmen in a Sixth Avenue street car and so pondering: " It was very interesting, and the most amusing part of it was that a young fellow who was doing most of the talking looked so exactly like Godkin. Their grammar was awful, but they talked with great point and good sense. How much thought that we admire in the best magazines is commonplace to any sensible man, after all! Even the symbols and images that we admire in poetry are often but childish dreams and similes dressed up in a style." Or Stanford White had flung himself moodily into a group at Martin's, cursing softly and ordering white mint mixed with brandy, to soothe his discomfort when a great lady asked him to roof her ballroom in glass and silver. Or Brander Matthews had taken Peck to see a play, and how pretty Ida Conquest was in it! He added her to an imaginary seraglio inhabited by Clara Morris, Bijou Heron and Isabel Irving, " not one of whom," the professor added, " has ever met me, but has been respectfully adored from a safe distance." Things were not always so cheerful. Up came Sarah Grand's terrible novel, " The Heavenly Twins," which proved that there shouldn't be one law for men and

another for women, and told how a girl went mad, contract-
ing syphilis from a husband related to Ouida's guardsmen.
The professor tried to talk of this book to some Western
ladies who announced themselves suffragists and " They
simply froze me alive. The woman's rights movement will
never get along very far until women get down off the high
horse and become rational in such matters. Mrs. Grand's
book is important to their cause, and in stating their approval of her program, then refusing to argue the matter,
they show the weakness of their repeated declaration of
strict equality between the sexes. I often think that the
evasiveness of American women on such topics tends to do
harm to our young men. The boy who sniggers and blushes
when he is translating Catullus in the classroom must be the
son of a prude. . . ." And the devil tempted him to say
in his essay on Grover Cleveland that the President had been
accused of gross indecencies in his first campaign. Abusive
letters poured in on Peck for weeks after the essay was
printed: " Well, why shouldn't I have said so? The Republicans called him a drunkard, a lecher, and I can remember
men who knew the addresses of all his illegitimate children!
Everybody knows of these vilifications. Mrs. Cleveland
must know of them and so does the Cleveland cat, if there
is one. Why leave that part of the story out? What fools
these mortals be! " The devil tempted him yet again. He
strolled up and down a narrow drawing-room in lower
Madison Avenue, expounding " The Songs of Bilitis " to a
group of learned ladies who nervously read some of the
Lesbian biography when Peck had left them, and then
burned it in a fire-place adorned with little crabs and stars
in English tile. They forgave him, and went in a fluttering
clump of cloaks edged with swansdown to see " The Sunken
Bell " when Charles Meltzer translated the heavy German
fantasy and Edward Sothern played it, submitting to this

sadness for the professor's sake; he said it would do them good. But mostly the world was cheerful around the cheerful man, supping with the De Rezskés in their court of French parasites and jockeys, with Charles Meltzer scolding the big Edouard for a false note in " Faust." The establishment of the *Bookman* gave him fresh importance. His taste kept the magazine from the pretentious heaviness that marked earlier literary reviews; in fact, there was nothing heavy about Peck. His coat had a flower; some of his waistcoats, even in the faded sheen of photographs, were illustrious of their kind. " Scholar, and wit, and something of a child."

In forty preserved letters, dated from 1889 to 1901, there are not half a dozen discussions of books. He sometimes made a little epitaph, or gave out an interesting portrait. " I liked Miss Woolson's stories better before she fell under the spell of Henry James. She was, by nature, a pleasing romantic writer of a sentimental turn. Her ' Horace Chase ' is a funny mixture of realism and romance, but there are very good scenes in it. She caught the tone of masculine conversation very well. . . . Mr. James is impressed with her ' Dorothy,' I hear, through a mutual friend, as it is a theme that he means to tackle one of these days.[2] . . ." " Henry George's funeral was most impressive. Poor people filed past the body for hours. He lay in state with his son's bust of him above the casket with several Catholic priests and ministers always there, standing close to the body. His obituaries have surprised me in their omissions. George was a humorist. He told a story splendidly and fairly sparkled with good things. He was not one of the sour, ' intense ' radical brethren, but in all ways a genial, open-minded little man. He will be greatly missed in the socialistic world, although he had lost standing in recent

[2] " The Wings of the Dove," perhaps?

years by refusing to embrace communism as a long-lost brother. His single tax was enough for him; he never looked for a world where all our ambitions and impulses would be submitted to the will of our next-door neighbour. It was possible to disagree with Mr. George and yet to respect his disinterested goodness of heart. . . ." . . . " Yes, I sadly assent to your condemnation of the new Bangs book. The truth about [John Kendrick] Bangs is that he is not really a humorist at all. He is a cultivated, serious man who is at his best in little sketches of manners. He can write a pat review of any book and is very well read. But he began by writing humorous anecdotes and verses, and on he goes. There is always a sound idea in his things, but he stretches them out so that it irritates me, for one. . . ." " Mr. [Frank] Norris has taken a place with Doubleday, McClure. He is a most interesting personality, a silent, moody boy who never seems glum, although he can be obstreperous in an argument. He adores Zola, Stevenson, Kipling and the middle ages, the queerest combination imaginable. I think that you can see his feeling for Stevenson in ' Moran of the Lady Letty.' . . . He is a handsome fellow; his face suggests photographs of Hawthorne or of some classic actor.[3] Now why should you fall into the delusion of likening a man's character to his fiction? Is Ambrose Bierce a murderer because he writes about murders? Is Mr. James an infanticide because he wrote ' The Other House '? I never met a less blood-boultered Banquo than poor little Mr. Crane. He is inoffensive as a lamb, and Mr. Norris is extremely like him in manner, albeit he has none, or too little, of Mr. Crane's humour. The author of the terrible ' McTeague ' is a pleasant, cultivated young gentleman, inclined to be obstreperous — and humourless

---

[3] " He was not exactly humourless but he didn't show much humour in conversation. . . . His face suggested an old-time tragedian . . . Edwin Booth, perhaps. . . . He had Booth's eyes. . . ." — *Jesse Lynch Williams.*

— in arguments on realism, but in every other respect a very pleasant boy. . . . Your letter inclines me to the belief that there is not too little imagination in the world but too much of it. . . ."

His mind was a goldfish everlastingly drawn by some bright object to glass of its tank, then swirling off in fright to shelter in weeds. He had read a paper on Nietzsche to a fugitive literary club in 1885 and ten years later he began an acute, plausible description of the heroic poet's content — then broke off on some interior alarm and dismissed the madman to the mercy of God in the ringing cant of a cheap evangelist. Ingersoll's faded dialectic scared him. Howells must be scolded, a little, for his pessimism. He looked with a quaint, wistful interest at the stout dogma of the Roman Church, so secure among the changes and attritions of the Protestant sects. You may watch the intelligence grappling with some fiction, represented in the detached, remote manner of the French realists whom he unconsciously adored. Ideas do not seem to shock him; he surveys and describes the artist with the clarity of Edward Cope moving around a fossil monster; then the Puritan drums beat all at once in his head and the emotionalism of the American comes tumbling out in undramatized, ridiculous sentences. His father's notions triumph suddenly, and he frantically asserts the human dignity. There have been no evidences of man's place in nature; criticism ceases in a burst of frightened eloquence. George Moore must be slapped for his extrasphaltine adulteries. The huge indignations of Zola were preferable to Flaubert's cool suspension of identities. Immeasurably read, informed and shrewd, capable of much, he remained superstitious in the midst of his urbanities, and was at last ruined by a superstition — that wholly ignominious notion of his fathers, still earnestly maintained, that a man's sexual adventures disqualified his intellectual value.

THE MAUVE DECADE

There was in the '90's a distinguished but scattering and, of course, ineffective effort toward a primary sophistication in American letters. Survivors of this movement, such as Vance Thompson, John Barry and the publisher of the *Chap Book* must have grinned, and James Huneker groaned aloud, when the new sophisticates of 1916 solemnly disclosed the works of Rimbaud, Laforgue, Vielé-Griffin and the designs of Toulouse-Lautrec, Forain and Cheret to a renovated public, when it was again decided that Felicien Rops had been overestimated, that Pierre Louys was merely beauty's ghoul and that Pierre Loti was a trifle thin. Wholesale thefts from Peck's paper on Stephane Mallarmé and quotations from Richard Hovey's translation of "Herodiade," without mention of Hovey, figured in the revival. Aline Gorren's study of Rimbaud was, naturally, not so much used as that of Arthur Symons. The process of recolonization, evident in the latter '90's, implicitly established English critical prints as the best source of American critical writing. Even in 1925 it was possible for American essayists to approve a British essayist's approval of:

> " We'll to the woods no more,
> The laurels all are cut. . . ."

without any mention of the French derivation of A. E. Housman's pretty lines. The triangular movement of the '50's, really, has been restored and the American habit of the '90's is cast aside. In the last decade of the nineteenth century there had been a very plain tendency, not at all unhealthy, to cut across the maternal intervention and to take ideas undiluted from Paris without awaiting the passage through an intermediary province. Peck's importance in the movement is clear.

In the summer of 1896 New York had a shortlived paper, *Tattle*, which roused enough attention to give an accidental impetus to the *Daily Tatler* published first on November

148

7th, by the young firm of Stone & Kimball. *Tattle* had given space to gossip about authors, during its brief run,[4] but it had mostly been news of courtesans, insinuating paragraphs on the mores of prizefighters and the like. Stone & Kimball's daily was quite literary, and placidly impertinent.

The *Daily Tatler* is good fun. The owners let it live for thirteen days, then killed it because it was too much trouble. People were amused by Edwin Emerson's diary, in which the wit appears as Samuel Pepys, reborn, trying to ride a new " chariott made of two wheels," meeting Master Oliver Herford, Karl Bitter, Lincoln Steffens, David Gray, Samuel McClure at suppers, mistaking somebody at the horseshow for Master Gibson, the pamphleteering artist. The simulation of the Pepysian dialect is clever, and the trick pleased the times. John Barry's theatrical reviews inform you that " The Sign of the Cross," recommended by bishops and other theatrical reviewers, was a cheap affair, and that Maurice Barrymore was a poor actor. There is other evidence to this effect. James Barrie's arrival in New York is mentioned in a faintly sour manner, and irreverences multiply from page to page: " It was undoubtedly very wrong of Mr. Mosher to reprint Mr. [Andrew] Lang's little book. To print any book of Mr. Lang's is wrong, but to do it without paying Mr. Lang any money, or, more important still, any attention, is worse than wrong, it's discourteous." . . . " Sir Walter Besant, whom many people will remember as the author of a number of volumes, is writing a parlour play." . . . " Mr. J. B. Gilder's description of the Barrie dinner, to which he was one of the six invited guests (not in-

---

[4] *Tattle*, apparently, lasted from May until September. There is no file in the Congressional, New York or Boston libraries. It was on sale in New York and Chicago without a publisher's name. Names were not used at all, except in the sporting notes. It seems to have been a witless business, but it was extremely careful to keep within the laws. The number dated July 19th has an historic importance: the loathsome phrase " It's naughty but it's nice " occurs on the second page.

cluding other reporters), is one of the nicest things we ever read. . . ."

But the unsigned verses are ruder than the prose. Here is Thomas Bailey Aldrich, adversely seen:

" Dandy Tommy, spick and span,
Struts before the Gilder clan.

All the Gilder clan bow down
To the beau of Boston town.

What though, like a lady's waist,
All his lines are overlaced?

What though, from a shallow brain,
Smooth inanities he strain?

In his emptiness content,
He achieves his ten per cent.

And secure in magazines,
Rules all rhymesters in their teens. . . ."

The Gilders seem to have been disliked in the office of the *Daily Tatler*, for they appear five times in the thirteen numbers of the review. There are pasquinades on George Woodberry, Brander Matthews, F. Hopkinson Smith, and the rudenesses addressed to Elbert Hubbard and to various publishers. But the general tone is amiable enough, even in an editorial discussion of the battle in Boston, where an insipidly frivolous Bacchante by MacMonnies had scandalized trustees of the Public Library, and the row satirized by Robert Grant in " The Chippendales " was progressing. There are highly competent reviews of " The Country of the Pointed Firs," " The Cat and the Cherub," " The Other House," " George's Mother," " The Little Regiment " and a silly depreciation of " A Shropshire Lad." You hear of forgotten monthlies, *Cosmopolis* and *Le Magazine Interna-*

tional. Richard and Henrietta Hovey talked of the French poets. Many of Hovey's verses are printed, for the first time, the fleetly famous " Barney M'Gee " among them. George Barnard is civilly scolded for planting fig leaves on his statues. Sadakichi Hartmann's unremembered " Tragedy in a New York Flat " is shudderingly admired for its brutal realism. . . . There is too much about " brutal realism " in the *Daily Tatler.* . . . And Mr. Hartmann appears as a contributor in the next to the last number. Harry Thurston Peck is mentioned only once, as writing the whole contents of the *Bookman.* On November 10th the editors refused an article attacking Peck for his partial praise of Nietzsche, ending their rejection with a curious sentence: " We are the last people on earth to condemn Mr. Peck for his interest in European literature."

Peck's position may be judged through an autograph of a conventional female author of the period, perhaps too lately dead for mention here: " He takes," she reflected, " so much unnecessary trouble in dragging out the foreign writers." The true colonial spirit had revived in the lady, for she had once been something of an enthusiast for Tolstoy, Daudet and Turgeniev in the '80's when Howells, Henry James and Eugene Schuyler were making pleas for French and Russian fiction. But Peck had just rejected her poem on Robert Louis Stevenson, and possibly that had tinged her considerations of the professor.

He did drag out foreign authors, even some such as Petronius and Alkiphron who were not alive to trouble the colonial clique. Heathenish names sprinkled his casual reviews — Krafft-Ebing, Hugues Le Roux, De Joux, and in 1899 Remy de Gourmont, " a clever casuist." He was the first writer in English to describe George Moore with any sympathy and the first American who treated Huysmans, Mallarmé, Prevost, Sudermann and Hauptmann to more than a passing paragraph of uneasy regard. It is not a brilliant criticism, but it is alert and, until the Puritan ghost woke, levelly kind. His was the loudest voice in the forlorn group of American critics who took literature as something not inevitably conditioned by English opinion. His apostolate for Zola was continuous. He staggered a literary dinner of 1898 by saying: " Balzac, Shakespeare's equal and in psychology Shakespeare's superior," and later printed the opinion in *Munsey's Magazine*. His sudden heresies sent out ripples through one collection of literary autographs. Was there really an American who thought, in 1899, that another age would account the English scientists of the nineteenth century the strongest claim of English literature to remembrance? He said something of the kind, or was so understood in March of 1899. He, with Brander Matthews, Vance Thompson, Richard Hovey and the conjoint Stone & Kimball did what they could, in varying ways, for the European continent in letters. His reward was natural; in 1899 a sedulously Bostonian voice in the University of Chicago told a class of attentive students that they could not do worse than to follow Professor Peck's " garish " tastes.

He stands, then, in the muddle of the '90's as the superior American who wanted to be mundane, definitely sophisticated in the better sense, and who honestly strove to be liberal. Liberal he was, up to the point of admitting that a novelist might display the animal called man in the impartial mood of Huxley discussing crayfish. He could not attain a final position: ideas shocked him. Guy Wetmore Carryl's verbal epigram, " It takes two to make one seduction," distressed the apologist of Zola, so that he is remembered scolding the poet in a corner for half an hour. The urbane gentleman might become on any cross draught of emotion the lad in Wallingford, Connecticut, who cried over Longfellow's poems. The moralistic training had been too thorough. An idea was not, at the last, black ink on white paper, a thing to be dismissed with raillery. His demolition of Nordau took on the terms of an emotional flurry, sound as it was in its main contentions. He could perceive the social parable in Stephen Crane's "The Monster" where other critics, silly as the folk of Whilomville, saw only a "horrible" story, and he prophesied long glory for George Douglas when "The House with the Green Shutters" was issued in 1900. Douglas was already dead, but the professor did not know that, praising the boy's "resolute grip of situations that would be infinitely grotesque in the hands of a weaker writer." And yet it shocked him to hear young Carryl say that it needed two bodies to make one seduction! The obvious, to the end, could palsy this fine intelligence, even after he had come out as analytic champion of "Nana" and "Sappho" and had slung ice water on the range of English fiction, likening his adored Thackeray to a cynical old grandfather, calling the modern English novel a "bungling blotch of pruderies and false psychology" in a private letter of 1905 and at the same time issuing praises of Trollope, Tennyson and Longfellow. A hypocrite? No, he was an American.

After 1900 this mentality seems to divide itself. He rejoiced on paper over the worst "uplifting" novels of the calamitous decade between 1900 and 1910; students eyed the flowered coat facing an unacademic prettiness at luncheon in Claremont above the sweep of the Hudson and his classes were startled by erotic witticisms hardly gay while conservatives of the Columbian faculty were dazed by Professor Peck's essays on perfumes and the charm of women for men. Scandal flared; reporters were sent hurrying among painted stuff of theatres for notes on a strayed professor; in Cambridge an authority recalled to his giggling sophomores that enthusiasm for the light girls of Zola and Daudet; the graceless, ascetic and unimaginative American was aware of Harry Thurston Peck at last, a figure whirling in headlines of the journals. " The crowd," said William Sumner, " likes to see realistic representations of life, yet it also likes to see in the drama that ridicule of the cultured classes which seems like a victory over them." The name of a dull farce, " Peck's Bad Boy," was useful to merry folk of the newspapers. " Vice," said a person in a pulpit, " has lured this brilliant man from the path of truth." No definition of truth was supplied. The triumph of his father's notions was complete, and a crackling echo from poor lodgings in Connecticut came as an anticlimax.

IV

THE DULCET Henry Adams, idling before his dead wife's monument in the necropolis beyond Washington, reflected much on the stagnation of the United States, more and more ruled by crowds, desperately indifferent to things spiritual. His mind was now preparing to supply a false philosophic contour for history and some critic not staggered by the historian's family name may one day amuse us by showing how a man painfully deprived of a charming wife begins to discover the sexlessness of American literature, then becomes the chivalrous rhapsodist of the mediæval Virgin. " The Education of Henry Adams " decorously omits the education of Henry Adams, just as it describes the whisky of shabby, provincial Adam Badeau and gracefully leaves out the Scotch and soda flooding perpetually around one of the proper friends so lovingly recited in the languid, amiable prose. The Puritan aristocrat in this much followed God: he dealt lightly with persons of quality. The Count Cassini is the mannerly, if rather unscrupulous, Russian minister, and never the ribald commentator on American society who vanished from Washington in a puff of lurid gossip under Theodore Roosevelt. John Hay's triumph of

1901 is suitably declared, the apparition of one's friend in the grand rôle of international negotiator, but John Hay's poker game with the English press in the spring of 1898, with the sinking fund of the State Department as chips at the little diplomat's elbow, is less memorable. One learns that the sudden show of Germany in the Orient threw England and the United States into accord, thus gratifying a member of the Adams family extremely. The decencies and moralities are all observed. The world revolves in full dress around the reticent Bostonian, and the '90's make a fine show. You will idly look down the index of the " Education " for such names as Coxey, Altgeld, Garland, Bland. The machinery of the comic opera in 1896 has no interest for the student of force. Mark Hanna is a shadow. William Jennings Bryan, the logical pendent of such figures as Charles Sumner and Wendell Phillips, has no existence, and the wisdom of the '90's apparently bored the idle witness. He gently regretted that he had never met Josiah Willard Gibbs, but he found Langley useful, conveniently located in Washington to answer questions while Professor Gibbs stayed in New Haven, at work. Psychology began to interest him and he makes us irritably aware that a department of psychology had developed at Harvard, but William James remains a dot in a group of professors, somewhere seen. Sociology occupied him, later, but William Sumner never came within his perceptual area. The education of Henry Adams was an exclusive affair, and magnificently futile. . . . One, having achieved impersonality without detachment, protested nothing, except the rudeness of John Randolph to one's ancestors. One did not mind the progressive cowardice of one's class. One observed the ugliness of chaos — chaos is always ugly to a moralist who demands rules, answers, codes and restrictions for his personal comfort. But the combative spirit of one's Puritan forbears had passed out of one, and one ended, with the rest of the Yankee hegemony, as a pleasing figurine on the intellectual shelf.

And yet to be a moralist, asking that humanity disentangle its unguessed motives and align itself to a program, a philosophic system, is not so bad as to go bawling in newspapers and magazines about the perils of the cigarette and bicycle for women, to spend ink in protesting French novels, the size of sleeves, the use of rouge. In discussing this minor morality — Sumner's " mores " — the literary republicans went a length to justify the sociologist's jeer: ". . . the literary products are nearest to the mores. . . . They lack all progress, or advance only temporarily from worse to better literary forms." The minor moralist is nothing but an item in the mores of his period; he records and perpetuates superstitions of the society which he dreads. It is impossible that he should stand aside from the social customs that surround him, take his two steps up the hill against Jerusalem and see, behind his moment, a long fluctuation of human absurdities, laws once sacred grown disreputable and tabus overthrown. He challenges no belief, imposes no new value on the human groups about him, and ends nowhere. He cannot be a realist, and he peculiarly hates that last turn of disillusioned romanticism which shows us stars flattened into tarnished tin, love yawning, ambition staled among its victories. So for the minor moralist of the aspiring decade that tried so hard to be purple, imperially grand, and ended in a compromised, ridiculous tint, there is no hope. He brought out a pale chatter in essays about " the temple of our American democracy," " the corruption of our financial life," " the falling ideals of our womanhood " and whatever he meant by all that is now too tedious for an attempt at discovery. The discussion of society is limited to a few papers of Howells, Robert Grant, Hamlin Garland and E. S. Martin who could assemble ideas and utter their protests in an intelligible prose. The theorists who followed the lovable Henry George had, anyhow, a form and a belief. Elsewhere is vagueness and a rustling of waste paper. " Our social thinking," as Edwin Godkin said, " is growing more verbose and less dignified every day. . . ." In this void, naturally, the editors who had followed William Lloyd Garrison's habit of a personal tone came to profit and success: Godkin and Dana in the East, William Nelson and William Allen White in the midlands and Harvey Scott of the *Oregonian* were more and more admired. Editorials of superior provincial newspapers — the *Springfield Republican*, the *New Bedford Mercury*, the *Detroit Free Press*, the *Cincinnati Enquirer* — are quite as good as the solemn pettiness of essayists in the monthly magazines and the cultural reviews. Here, the American respect for journalism justifies itself; and the journalists, in varying shades of ability, did sometimes dare to flout " some great decorum, some fetish of a government, some ephemeral trade, or war, or man."

In this maze of intellectual timidities William Sumner emerges as a cold, ponderous groper, an Episcopal clergyman who threw off his silk and became deliberately an analyst of society, and the last libertarian of the nineteenth century in the United States. He was born so early in the century that he conceived the practice of free speech as an inalienable right of the American citizen, and education not as a species of social drill for the sons of pretentious women, but as education, an argument between the instructor and the instructed. His mind was essentially slow, unlike the flashing intelligence of William James; he wrote from first to last without grace or delicacy. In " Folkways " ideas are hidden around the bulk of a clumsy oratorical protasis and definitions must be exhumed as fossils from the marsh of swollen paragraphs. His mind freed itself slowly from conventions and inhibitions of his class, and that it never en-

tirely freed itself is plain enough in his biography; but he
took the one stride that separated him from other American
sociologists of the period: he was able, finally, to assume an
exterior view of all societies; and in the '90's the professor
of political science at Yale College became a stormy identity on the edge of controversies, consulted by capitalists
while he denounced their fetish, the protective tariff, quoted,
without quotation points, in the feeble radical weeklies and
journals while he openly preferred free capitalism to the
paternalisms offered in some or another disguise. He had
fought his way into authority, wrestling with the moralistic
governors of Yale who dreaded his use of irreligious and
rational texts; he would now fight anything from a bastard
notion of currency to the government of the United States
or, more powerful, the pruderies of a timid student. He
appeared as the declared enemy of restrictive legislations,
educational fig leaves and fluffy little white dogs, for which
he had a distinguished aversion, as he had for anything
frail, decorative and futile. He was the first real sociologist
of his country, the first critic to protest the literature of
financial success which, from 1870 onward, increased with
the increasing vulgarity of the literate American, and the
first American educator to approach the topic of decency
without evasive words.

In 1897 his godson, William Sumner Dennison, who had
never met the professor, came to New Haven and made his
respectful call on this alarming sponsor. They got along
smoothly for twenty minutes, and then the young doctor
mentioned Mark Hanna, or rather the Mark Hanna then
advertised by caricatures and libels. "Nonsense," the sociologist grumbled, "the first impulse in this country is
always to lambaste a successful politician by calling him a
dissipated man. It is the most effective method of blackening his reputation. You could attack his political ideas, but
people have no thought about political ideas. They only

understand a social personality — a man's manners or his vicious habits. Americans have no political ideas; they follow leaders who attract them or who know how to manage them. The kind of political leaders they like are human circuses." [5] He talked along. The American's stolidity came in question. Dr. Dennison was fresh from watching a revolution in South Africa. No, the professor objected, the new American was not stolid. He was emotional, shallowly emotional, easily whipped into an excitement. It took twenty years, he drawled, to start the Civil War, but the next great war could be started impromptu. He didn't like that. Emotionalism was " antisocial." . . . There seemed to be no growth of " independent thought " in the United States. The discussion of public events was puerile. When you had looked through the *North American Review* and the *Nation,* there was little else to read. Oh, someone had given him an amusing book on " the tribal customs of children." He tossed William Allen White's " Court of Boyville " to his godson and then gravely dismissed his caller with a stiff old-fashioned bow.

Meanwhile the cheapening of the American was going on comfortably. The silly woman of 1892 who wanted the Populists tried for treason was now a general type. Altgeld and the Silver Knight had scared the conservatives. The mob was divided into two herds, both subscribing to the imbecile communism of herds. In 1899 the pompous idea of an American empire, with booted subalterns and barrack rooms, with ballads, in the Philippines, delighted journalists, and congressmen quoted " The White Man's Burden " in Washington. There was the usual fracas about moral duty which can always be used to cover a combined movement of interested politicians. Sumner roused, and then roared against this weary imitation of British imperialism.

[5] This one sentence is synthesized from a letter written that evening, but the other statements, naturally, rely on Dr. Dennison's memory.

Followed the modern academic comedy; a pair of fatuous rich men in the corporation of Yale wanted the heretic shut up. But it was difficult to shut up a Sumner. The rumour of his expulsion came on. Two men of affairs charged eastward from San Francisco to protest. There was a twittering in other universities and a ripple of comment in the press, but Sumner remained intact and rumbling out objections to the flimsy legislations under Theodore Roosevelt which tried to correct the open coarseness of capitalistic method and thus drove it into subtleties. This legend of his expulsion is now firm among radicals and has been published, but he survived a situation that no professor could survive to-day in universities where individualism is dreaded as nothing else, wherein manufactures of patent drama, business schools and courses for the propagation of fine embroidery are established on the order of the moneyed, with professors shipped about as little white dogs in wicker cells, the price marking the label. Sumner's ghost was heard, for a moment in the spring of 1917, when William Phelps shouted down the jeering boys who had interrupted old David Jordan in a rambling plea for peace, but the libertarian echo was perhaps the last. What Richard Harding Davis protested long ago in a romantic yarn has placidly happened, and governors of universities fall into their natural place behind the golden calf, bearing shovels.

Sumner is most articulate in " Folkways," the first grand essay on the nature of human societies ever written by an American but in many libraries left to the safety of the " reserved " shelf so that young idealists need not read the origins of cheap patriotism, the victimization of man by his own clothes and customs. There is no reason to call the attention of girls reared on " The Courtship of Miles Standish " to a gross form of Puritan wooing called " bundling."
. . . This mind, immense and clumsy, with traces of the moralist, moved in his last text to regions uncomfortable

for the merely literary and his synthesis has no standing among critics, save as a source of unmarked quotation. The book is a ghost. . . . Sumner himself seemed a little ghostly in his last years, a bulky, stern figure moving in heavy robes of an academic procession, or listening in the rear of a huge lecture hall while Richard Lull chivalrously deplored the extinction of the sabre-toothed tiger and the amiable little eohippus, or described the strange domesticity of the amœba. Indeed, the old man seemed most at home in dim, high spaces of that museum where man is but one form of many that live and have lived, where beasts stuffed and strung on wires are ranged to show another age what once stirred and drew its breath in freedom.

CHAPTER VI

THE AMERICAN MAGAZINES

SLIM, often ailing, wrapped in gay, soft robes, Egeria used to sit beside these windows, above the quiet little park. . . . The long room seems modern, unlike the taste of the '90's? Yes, but this hard, white paint was laid on in 1887 by a workman whom Napoléon Sarony found for Egeria's husband. There is Sarony's photograph of Egeria behind the seven-branched candlestick. But of course women used to crop their hair in those days! Nothing is newfangled; the fashion was called *la recluse* and you can see it in old albums of French actresses. No, the great candlestick was not bought yesterday in Grand Street. Once, in the brutal winter of 1882, when New York's slums were flooded with Jewish families, refugees from Russia, Egeria and her mother were shopping on Fourteenth Street, in falling snow, and a woman big with child lurched against the girl's sealskin cloak, then slipped down on the iced pavement while her rabble of frightened children tried to lift her and a bearded father groaned. Egeria's mother made out with her few words of Russian that they had no home, no food, no hope. She packed the tribe into the coupé and loaded them off to a private hospital, cashing a cheque, in passing, at the Fifth Avenue Hotel. . . . A while later there was a grand dinner, here, and old John Skidmore was exchanging thunderous witticisms with Mayo Hazeltine of the *Sun,* when the butler stooped at Egeria's

shoulder to whisper that a Miss Lazarus was in the library,
" a very odd-looking person," and the girl came up to see
a pallid woman curiously shrouded in dull, red velvet. The
father of the rescued family, said Emma Lazarus, was a
brassworker, and this candlestick was his first making in
the new country, an offering to the benefactress. " May it
light great happiness in this house," the poet said, and lifted
her hands for a moment, and went away.

The room is modern, if you like. In the '90's ladies deplored the Russian trinkets and Hungarian embroideries.
It was " eccentric " and not French, or " cosy." The Negro
in the silver frame? That is Edward Gill, a tenor who sang
in drawing-rooms of liberal people. He was a fad of 1892
and 1893. Edouard de Rezské ordered him to Paris for
training, but he vanished, and his patrons never knew what
became of him. Alfred Brennan did the little sketch. Brennan? He was Joseph Pennell's rival, and only Mr. Pennell
has praised him since he died. You'll find a good deal of
his work in the *Century*. He sketched himself for Egeria
and signed the picture, " A. B. *ætat* 600 from being an artist in America." . . . Oh, yes, they used to talk so, even
back in 1895! Poets and story-tellers stamped up and
down this room, cursing the magazines by which they had
to live, and asked questions about Paris. Wasn't it cheaper
to live, over there? And that atmosphere, didn't your mind
work more freely in it? And, and—— The chryselephan-
tine image beckoned and they raised hands to test the wind
toward exile.

The black-eyed woman in the oval frame? That is
Scalchi. She sang here, often, and her fees must always be
presented in bunches of Parma violets. Underneath her is
Henry Cuyler Bunner, the editor of *Puck* until he died in
1896 and Harry Leon Wilson succeeded him. You'll find
his " Short Sixes " in the bookcase. Yes, it was he who
wrote:

" It was an old, old, old lady
And a boy who was half past three . . ."

A humorist who sinks into sentiment sinks very deeply.
Think what Mark Twain did to Jeanne D'Arc. . . . Those
are some of the correspondents in Cuba, on July 3, 1898.
That is Frank Norris leaning on the tree. That's Richard
Harding Davis shaving over the bucket. The man without
a shirt may be Ralph Paine or Arthur Lee; they looked
alike. Yes, Frank Norris came here, once, with his pretty
wife. Egeria thought him charming, and not humourless
at all. You'll find the suppressed first issue of " Mc-
Teague " in the bookcase, with that reference to little August's personal moisture. . . . No, the bearded man is not
Joseph Conrad, although the likeness is staggering. That
is Wright Prescott Edgerton, the military mathematician,
who spent ten years craftily digging in mazes of red tape to
humanize West Point and had the pleasure of hearing a
president of the United States take the credit of his endless
work. He was the son-in-law of Mrs. William Tod Helmuth,
the famous doctor's wife, a primordial suffragist who once
told Joseph Choate in Paris: " You see that I can pick the
winning horse at the Grand Prix, and order a dinner so as
to satisfy even you, and take my children all over Europe
without a servant or a courier, but I can't vote and your
illiterate coachman can! " There is Joseph Conrad, across
the room, in the faded snapshot. Brede Place, Sussex, September of 1899. That is Moreton Frewen with his hat under
his arm beside Mrs. Stephen Crane. Yes, the man in
gaiters is Henry James. After the photograph was taken
Egeria and Conrad strolled out into the country, talking in
French. She admired some passage — she forgets which
one — in " The Nigger of the Narcissus." That must have
taken effort? The dark little man shrugged and tossed his
glass into his eye. " Ah, madame, we are always so much

praised for things that we do without thinking and the really difficult affairs are passed over! " He agreed with her that the high art of fiction was to find a detachment. It was not necessary to be inhuman, or mocking, but a detachment was necessary. What else had Flaubert, Anatole France, Stendhal and Turgeniev? Dostoyevsky? Oh, that amateur! She was slightly shocked.

The other snapshot? That is Guy Wetmore Carryl whose variations on La Fontaine in *Harper's* amused everybody. He was a good deal dreaded for his tongue, but Egeria thinks he was a soft-hearted boy enough. He came, hysterically white, and stood, there, at the fire-place, cursing the magazines that wouldn't buy his story of a young rake in Paris, ready for suicide, but relieved by news of his rich father's death in barbarous America. He stood and raved. But, said Egeria, filling one of the green cups with kümmel, did you expect them to buy a realism? Carryl banged his hands suddenly on the mantelshelf and said: " I'll make it worse and make 'em buy it! " You will find it in his volume of Parisian sketches, neatly dressed out in the formula of Robert Louis Stevenson. The Americans of the '90's were discovering that you can tell any story if you tell it lightly. . . . Yes, the slaves of the magazines came here, and raved, and sometimes put their heads among the trinkets of the mantel and wept. Egeria reached for the kümmel in its purple flask, or for the cheque-book in the rosewood table, as there might be a wife in Brooklyn, or up in Harlem. . . . Look in the big tulipwood box with silver handles. These are all literary autographs. What have you there? . . . " Of course the magazines will print stories by Rudyard Kipling about horizontal women and locomotor ataxia, but if an American tries——" Put it back, and don't read the signature. That refrain gets monotonous in this, and in another huge collection. What's that? . . . " My natural disgust with your American public which so ardently sup-

ports the fiction of Mr. Hardy and —— " Be discreet!
Never look at a grandee in his undress, especially when he
seems to be talking of money. His published opinions on
commercial writers are those that we must believe. He was
a little annoyed to see that *Scribner's* would make a serial
of George Meredith's " The Amazing Marriage " and that
Hardy's " Jude the Obscure " was running in *Harper's*.
Authors should never write letters without a friend watching the pen. . . . But see how gracefully Mary Wilkins
answered a congratulation on " Jane Field " when it was a
serial in *Harper's* in 1892. And Owen Wister, you see, dep-
recates Egeria's opinion that his grim little affair, " The
Promised Land," is the only readable tale in *Harper's* for
April of 1894. He calls attention to a story by Grace King
printed just after his, and calls it " excellent," and so it is.
Miss King's stories of Louisiana were better, in all ways,
than Cable's repetitious novels. But close the box. It has
explosive contents. No, wait! In that blue envelope are
two notes from Lamb House, Rye. It had been hoped that
Mr. James would send some trifle to two funds for the care
of artists' children; in each case he sent orders for fifty
pounds . . . " and my little donation — may I ask so
much? — is to be permanently anonymous—— " Now,
shut the box. No, shut it! Let us be reticent and generous
as the authors of the '90's weren't, when writing about each
other.

The man with such fine eyes? Egeria never knew him.
That is Richard Watson Gilder of the *Century*, a pleasant,
shy, accessible man. Egeria's riffraff of young poets always
liked him, even when he irritated them. In 1896 he partly
bought a tale from one boy and then boggled at " the bullet
had left a little blue mark over the brown nipple." The boy
protested that the nipple was male, hence not lascivious; he
even picked up the *Century* for April and showed Mr.
Gilder that André Castaigne had unblushingly represented

the male nipple in illustrations of Allan Marquand's article on the Olympian Games, revived that year, but Mr. Gilder was firm, and the tale was printed in *McClure's Magazine*. . . . Do not laugh, Faustine! There is a certain pride and, beyond that, a certain principle in such a squabble. In 1925 the sentence, " She took one glance at her daughter's pink dampness poised on the edge of the bathtub," was stricken out of a tale printed in a magazine which, at the same time, was editorially imploring writers to be less prudish, less " hopelessly enslaved to the totems of the national respectability." Curious, too, that you may print the word " brothel " in the conservative *Saturday Evening Post*, but not in a monthly which, again, editorially resents " Mr. Lorimer's maidenly exclusion." Mr. Gilder is no more comic than many editors of this year. He had his blindnesses and his inhibitions, but one considerable merit: he liked oddities in Americana, and he realized, and said, that " it is necessary to keep this public constantly informed in history. In the United States we have a steadily increasing number of citizens anxious to be historically educated. . . . The *Century* means to keep up a supply of historical information to meet this demand. Does our attitude seem unwarranted when a public man commits such a gross error in a speech before a literary society as a reference to ' slaves contesting in the games at old Olympia '? Macaulay's eternal schoolboy knew that the contestants must be ' free sons of free sires.' . . . I think that this species of ignorance excuses Mr. Johnson and myself for making historical topics something of a specialty in the *Century*." [1] So in the *Century* between 1890 and 1901 you find S. Weir Mitchell's historical tales " The Adventures of François " (the French Revolution seen through the eyes of a thief), " Hugh

---

[1] Unprinted. His correspondent had objected that Professor Marquand's article on the Olympian Games was superfluous. Since 1920 the error about slaves appearing in the games has been printed at least four times.

Wynne " and " The Red City," which did nobody any harm
and are quite as readable to-day as novels of dolorous
young women yearning in the midlands for great careers.
But if you wish to know anything of Dr. Mitchell read his
" Characteristics " of 1892. There is a copy in the bookcase: " To the most patient of patients, this little collection
of causeries in the style of the great critic whom we both
admire. . . ." They both admired Sainte-Beuve. The
novel puzzled readers, and some critics, because it had no
plot. He admired Sainte-Beuve, sound Burgundy, fine
women and fine manners. In " Characteristics " out come
his distaste for paper collars, raucous advertising, " business men " without hobbies or avocations to make them
bearable, and millionaires in the stripe of Jay Gould. The
neurologist's Pharaonic beard and strange, clear eyes were
little seen in New York; he preferred his scholarly group in
Philadelphia, where the art of dining was still understood,
to the cramped fetor of New York. . . . Yes, the *Century*
stuck to its historical program, and printed articles on the
tune called " The Arkansas Traveller," or on the capture
of the last slave ship before the Civil War, as well as William
Sloane's life of Napoleon, Benjamin Ide Wheeler's study of
Alexander. Paul Leicester Ford's polite papers on George
Washington and Benjamin Franklin were once considered
irreverent and even a little shocking. . . . It was in 1899,
of course, while Ford was prudently discussing Franklin's
lapine qualities, that a young author was suspended from
a particular club in New York for telling the vouched anecdote of Abraham Lincoln's answer to an oratorical caller
who sympathized with his labours. The President heard
him through and then, in his pure, homely way, said: " Yes,
I don't even get time to shave or ———" However, the anecdote belongs to what a teacher of literature has called " the
manure pile of civilization." . . . So Paul Ford's mild
essays on the Revolutionary great were not esteemed in

some circles, on account of that lack of holy rapture which Thackeray's daughter found also lacking in William James's notes on religion. Greatness, Faustine, was greatness in the '90's. . . . Well, you'll find this historical and natural strain in the *Century* — notes of old-fashioned life in Maryland, jottings of Harry Stilwell Edwards on the Georgian farmers of his youth, a denial of the legend about the white-haired grandsire ringing a crack into the Liberty Bell on July 4, 1776, and, in the early years of the decade, matter on the slums of cities, on relief of the poor, on innumerable reforms. The fiction? Not so good. For one Chester Bailey Fernald you'll find a dozen forgotten people who dealt in a mildly moral tale of rural life or in something about a girl who wasn't sure she wanted to marry a man, and did or didn't. Of course the *Century* printed Mrs. Humphry Ward's best novel, " Sir George Tressady." Marion Crawford's " Casa Braccio " is pleasant. But the *Century's* strength was its critical side. No, the best fiction of the time is found in *Harper's* and *McClure's*. But you'll find something familiar on a page of the *Century*, in January of 1898. Read: " The maid softly put the baby into the room. She pinched him and he began to cry. ' Oh, pitiful Kwannon! Nothing? ' The sword fell dully to the floor. The stream between her breasts darkened and stopped. Her head drooped slowly forward." Do not shrug, Faustine! " Madame Butterfly " was a simple, artless person before she was betrayed in Puccini's heavy music and clad in a tradition of yowling Italian tenors, and, being so simple, one wonders why the editors stuck her in the same volume with James Whitcomb Riley's agonizing " Rubáiyát of Doc Sifers," simplicity gone stale.

This " Rubáiyát " haunted everybody in the '90's. Elihu Vedder had given it a forward push by his illustrations. — Elihu Vedder? He was an excellent draughtsman of the time, much admired by Edwin Markham, Ella

Wheeler Wilcox and other poets. He lived, though respectably, at Capri and is kindly remembered. — The " Rubáiyát " fairly romped in magazines and newspapers. It was imitated, apostrophized and parodied. They found some escape from the muddled aimlessness of ordinary theology in thinking that God was a good fellow and 'twould all be well, that they could take the cash and let the credit go and that the world would last a long, long time, and they might as well go to hear the Bostonians in " Robin Hood." This hedonism was involved with the rising passion for urbanity, champagne and Anna Held, beside them singing in the wilderness. People came all the way from Brooklyn to hear an imported author declaim, in Martin's restaurant:

" O Thou who man of baser earth didst make
And ev'n with paradise devised the snake,
For all the sin wherewith the face of man
Is blackened man's forgiveness give — and take —— "

He would then sink on the table as though the Central Will had smitten him for his impudence, and the simple Americans were amazed. The craze increased; Elbert Hubbard printed the verses in diverse bindings of limp, soft leather. The parodists and imitators went ahead. There were " Rubáiyáts " of everything, kitchen stoves, motor cars, bicycles, and the industry increased after 1900, until Mr. Oliver Herford slew it by offering Omar's intellectual content in " The Rubáiyát of a Persian Kitten." Always lucky with his kittens, he made this one unusually good as he tucked his nose on a pane and mused on that inverted bowl they call the sky, or puzzled over the complex vagaries of his ball, the rug and the window shade. His philosophy was as sound as that of the original Persian. The flow of " Rubáiyáts " diminished, and then stopped. . . . But perhaps the craze was a nervous symptom of mental growth, a fleet glance out of so much bawling optimism at things in-

soluble. There was a wistfulness in verse, toward 1900; a
young poet sang to your godmother:

> " When all the brooks have run away,
>   And the sea has left its place,
> And the dead earth to night and day
>   Turns round a stony face,
>
> " Let other planets hold the strife
>   And burden now it bears,
> The toil of ages, lifting life
>   Up those unnumbered stairs,
>
> " Out of that death no eye has seen
>   To something far and high;
> But underneath that stair, Faustine,
>   How melancholy lie
>
> " The broken shards, the left behind,
>   The frustrate and unfit,
> Who sought the infinite and kind,
>   And found the infinite. . . ."

Come along, child. Egeria is late at her concert. Shall
we change this Bokhara rug into the usual flying carpet and
be off to a room roofed in blue wood, above a cove in California, and sit there watching waves tangle sleepily through
naked spires of rock, and hear how Clyde Fitch made thin-
nish epigrams in a Turkish bath? But you must not expect
to be told that Fitch was a dramatist, or even a good playwright; Americans of the '90's were not fools, my dear, and
they knew that Fitch was simply clever. And you can hear,
too, what Paul du Chaillu unprintably but not unkindly
said of Richard Harding Davis, and what Henry Bunner
unprintably and most unkindly said of editors who removed
brandy flasks and garters from his tales, and how Henry

171

James raised a small shrug, saying " I — ah — regret the malaise of transportation which . . . has detained me," meaning that his cab was slow. Or shall we slide down to Baltimore, where the cocktails will be admirable, and you can coo rhapsodically over furniture rubbed by slaves before the word " antique " was sinister, and hear how sedulous William Osler was at the deathbed of a favourite pupil? Or to Cleveland's edge, to hear how abominably Mark Hanna spoke when circumstances forced him to make speeches, and how youngsters in elder Tennessee drove out to call on Mary Murfree, lame and witty in her veranda at Murfreesboro? — She? She fooled the early '80's by writing such stiff, little, compressed stories that everybody took " Charles Egbert Craddock " for a man. Yes, several Americans were writing highly compressed short stories before Guy de Maupassant had written anything save love letters — Thomas Bailey Aldrich, Ambrose Bierce, and more — but it is always safest to accept the English verdict on the American short story, Faustine, just as it is safest to agree with nine English and American critics who copy George Moore's cheap remark about Howells imitating Henry James. . . . And in Cleveland you can hear, too, how mocking-birds raved to the moon above a long porch while Miss Ada and Miss Willie fluttered white frocks among the beaux, and the moon was inevitably the moon in Tennessee. Yes, and how grandees of New Orleans writhed when George Cable postulated that a great family in Louisiana could exist in duplicate editions, differently bound. Or shall we merely take a cab, and go up to tea in Beekman Place? These old Canadian ladies keep the poised, slow voice of their youth when they were taught to speak distinctly, and to say something when they spoke. You can hear how Frances Willard was once a jolly, human person in thundering Chicago before the Spirit moved her, and how drunken strikers were clumsily gallant to pretty women of a company playing " Lady Windermere's Fan " at Ogden in 1894, and how the players saw fires break out in the uneasy town, and troops filling the streets, in smoky dawn. Poor Faustine, you'll live so much longer in a country where nobody under the age of fifty can converse! No, dear, a girl who enters a room yelling: " For God's sake, give me a drink! " has not made an entrance, but just a noise. Or shall we build, here, a monstrous alcove blackened by all the magazines of the '90's? Pile up the *North American Reviews* and — here — take these flat *Pucks* for a footstool, and light your cigarette, Faustine.

Now you're surrounded by an amassed competence of journalism, some wit and an enormity of tiresome fiction. These are the magazines that wouldn't print Ambrose Bierce's " Killedat Resaca " or " The Occurrence at Owl Creek Bridge " because they were " grim," but brought out fathoms of verse on the Cathedral of Chartres, that lodestone of the American soul, on nymphs and fauns and Grant's Tomb, and anthems to Emile Friant, Gérôme, Vibert, Madeline Lemaire, to Neapolitan stone-cutters called sculptors in the name of international courtesy, essays on English death masks and quaint Scotch inns. Meanwhile the literary supplement of the *Detroit Free Press* risked " The Record of Badalia Herodsfoot," a forgotten weekly brought in " The Damnation of Theron Ware "; " The Red Badge of Courage " was a serial in newspapers; " The Turn of the Screw " scared people who understood it in the very new *Collier's,* and " The Market Place," refused as " cynical " by monthlies, was calmly published in the renovated *Saturday Evening Post,* as was Crane's last good tale, " The Second Generation," which not unreasonably suggested that a soldier in Cuba could have been a cowardly cad, thus alarming an editor who, in ten months, would print Henry Cabot Lodge's waspish attacks on that army. But then, this is the period in which Frank Stockton remarked that one letter of protest from some damned nobody would raise more hell in a magazine's office than ten letters of praise from intelligent people, and that remains quite true, Faustine. It was in the '90's that a power of *Scribner's*, buying a nice story about a dog, said with the composed gaiety of a stylist: "This is what happens to literature when it deserts the well-beaten track of adultery." For, Faustine, the literary republic had already created a special æsthetic of adultery. Didn't Voltaire say that marriage is the only adventure possible to cowards and does it not follow that adultery is the last pass of romance to literary republicans? True, it is the dullest amusement known to mankind but it already had its literary code, in 1896, when Charles Mason Maurice offered *Scribner's* a short novel, the tale of an adulterous couple so searingly bored after two days, in Buffalo, that they went home to their proper partners and forgot each other. But *Scribner's* literary adviser thought this "unreal and brutal," which must mean that he wanted adultery in its literary, or ideal, form, ending in repentance, forgiveness or double death, preferably by drowning. . . . No, Faustine, young writers of the '90's were aware that life and the notions of editors clashed. Some of them raged, some shrugged and put letters of rejection in drawers, where they persist, and sat at literary banquets listening to praises of "Anna Karenina" or little witticisms on the charms of "Aphorodité" uttered by men who—— Well, what of it? But, eventually, Mr. Saltus left that observation on hypocrisy wandering in the air. . . . When *Harper's*, in 1894, brought out Brander Matthews' "Vignettes of Manhattan" the general limit of sophistication permitted the American writer had been reached with the professor's gentlemanly admissions against optimism. The stories were considered slightly "French" in tone. This means that Mr. Matthews showed a pregnant woman watching her paramour's funeral and a wastrel dining with an old friend at Delmonico's, enjoying an admirable dinner, then retiring into his shadows of the street. One story, " A Summer Midnight," was praised by O. Henry in 1900, and you may see its formula worked again and again in his tales. But this was about the limit permitted the natives. . . . No, it's not an indefensible attitude, wholly, because " Whilomville Stories " and Mrs. Deland's gently Puritan " Old Chester Tales " did rouse female squeakings when they were read aloud on verandas in the susceptible midlands and suburbs. One of Henry James' unprinted letters is a tart defence of "' Europe ' " written to a lady in this alleged metropolis. There isn't the least doubt that the Americans would, and do, accept a touch of grimness or dryness from the English author when they resent it from the native. Thomas Hardy's " Tess " and " Jude the Obscure " were never so insolently and vulgarly attacked in the United States as they were in his own country. In those *Critics*, there, you can see Jeannette Gilder writing well on Hardy. They say that she had an absolute concept of the critic's duty. She resented and disliked some subjects inordinately, but when she came to write reviews of the offensive books she composed her mind and was more manly and mannerly in her appraisals than were some of the journalistic reviewers. . . . But " Vignettes of Manhattan " was the margin of sophistication allowed the natives, and at the end of the decade two writers, whose names you needn't know, gave a last shrug and walked away from letters into life " rather," says one, " than to be told to read Stevenson and Barrie, and to do likewise, when I went to lunch with X . . . and to get Emerson bunged on my nose when I tried to sell something to Y. . . ." The phrase " bunged on my nose " lacks elegance, Faustine, but immensely describes a certain editorial manner of speech. So, if you'll look through these magazines, child, you'll see a number of diverting methods

by which authors escaped the necessity of removing all
critical ideas from tales. Mark Twain had discovered —
was it unconsciously? — in " Huckleberry Finn " that the
personality of a child could be used to project realistic
views and pictures of a society, and that trick begins to
appear in the latter '90's, more and more. No, never use
a girl as the point of projection, dear! Girls are still tradi-
tionally supposed to be idiots.

There were other modes of escape from the bloodless
regimen. Romance — no, you won't find much valid romantic writing in the '90's. You'll find, in the old *Harper's
Round Table*, an entirely simple story for boys by Howard
Pyle, " Men of Iron," which never stops its movement from
first to last. Pyle had a painter's eye for shapes and colours,
and the oddest trick of jerking in some bit of mood that
would be called profound psychological insight in one of
the elected " great writers." Thus, his scared page, caught
in the grim Lord Mackworth's garden, stands thinking that
he can make a square of some pebbles at his feet with just
one push of a toe, and that is the sort of thing, Faustine, that
is deliriously praised in a Dostoyevsky or Conrad. One remembers a mad Negro in a tale of Virginia Boyle, screaming that the butterflies have come back as sparks dance up
from a blazing cabin, and the man abandoned on the moonlit cliff in " Prisoners of Hope," staring after a canoe on
the river, as the rowers sing. Buried in *St. Nicholas*, you'll
find John Bennett's " Master Skylark," half artifice, half
sentiment, which children followed from month to month,
doting on Gaston Carew's ferocious, unmoral swagger, but
not caring a rap about Master Skylark who smelled as
though he'd been playing in Mrs. Frances Hodgson Burnett's nursery, until he got home-sick and became real, asking the red-haired queen, after his song had pleased her, to
send him home. For the only defined sentiment that children really have, my dear, is that sense of home which,

176

basely, begins as a love of petting not to be had on the playground and the street. Perhaps " Master Skylark " is nothing much, or here entangled with memories of grapes that nodded, as one read, blackening on whitewashed stakes, of the pennyroyal which is peculiar incense of Ohio's summer and of voices, now not heard, that called me in to supper through the flowers. No, there was not much sound romance, but a deal of that romance which is too surely an escape from decorous realities. Yes, householding novelists ran backward to caper among the broodmares of Henri Quatre and to dally with home life in the Parc aux Cerfs. Those rowdy French kings, you see, had achieved what Henry James called " the detached impersonality of legend " and nobody minded their nasty doings, any more than Americans minded when Mark Twain discussed that Regent of France, dear friend of Florian, Duc de Puysange, whose historian was lately singed for some realistic details of his subject's manners.

Yes, James knew that antiquity gives detachment and sterilizes much. This was demonstrated in 1896 when Petronius, Arbiter Elegantiarum, made his grand tour of the modern world, appearing languid and ironic in an ivory litter, borne on shoulders of Bithynian slaves. Wilde had crashed, the milliner of classicism, who tried in sonorous, empty poems to revoke hard contours and attitudes of the Hellenic time about which, dear, we know so comfortably little. Now came Petronius Arbiter, to whom his biographer attributed that third-rate work of fiction " Satyricon " still popular among members of societies for suppressing things, although the poet Petronius has one good line: " It was fear that first made gods on earth," a fact discovered freshly nineteen hundred years later. Petronius isn't agreeable in the first chapters of " Quo Vadis " but then you may see how the earnest Pole, who thought he was writing a moral tale, fell victim to that inner sensuous education which forbids honest men to believe in the unstable, altering fictions known as sins. Sin, said one American of the '90's, is disloyalty to one's own beliefs and purposes, and that definition, Faustine, has its grain of sense. But his Catholic biographer bent lower and lower before the patrician, abandoning the heroine and her tiresome lover and the grey choir of Christians while he coloured Petronius, the resolute hedonist who yawns away things that he cannot believe, who boldly prefers the detached contemplation of beauty and the enjoyment of his senses to superstition and tedium. The figure cannot become real, because it is nothing but an argument and a decoration, but the oddest flutter of applause broke out in this America. Petronius was all over the place and the novel was discussed, analysed and quoted in the most virtuous circles with funny, pathetic mentions of the arbiter's death to slow music among paper blossoms. Even you, child, have seen the vogues of novels that express some hidden resentment, or longing of sensitive people, and acquire the merit of an universal mood. This Petronius seemed to be carried in his ivory litter through the market place of the image-makers and editors, and his voice came lazily in a courteous drawl through saffron curtains, saying: " I cannot care a great deal for your meritorious confections. I, who am the detachment of a final, appraising taste, have never been taken in by cheap moralities, although I have nodded to moralists whom I conceived to be men of honour and courage. . . . Yes, I like this grim poem, here, which has no buyers and hides in a trunk, of the man poisoned by idleness and self-distrust. . . . Yes, this is something! How clearly the pedlar's breath comes up in pumping bubbles through the Pacific, and how the crowds move! Neither is this image of the Chevalier of Pensieri Vanni despicable with its air of joking softly at respectabilities and its unstressed narrative grace. I like this scared recruit, wild-eyed in the battle of

Chancellorsville, and I like him rather better than the hypocritical young preacher with one eye on the Irish girl who
seems, Mr. Frederic, to be paste. I can be more at home
in the country of pointed firs, among simple wives and old
maids of a barren region, sir, than with your Catholic
priests made up to show the Protestants how cheap they
are, for you do not seem to see, Frederic, for all your wit
and force, that both parties to your argument are a little
low and that your preacher's wife will survive in the mind
as the best, most human figure of your tale. I, who am detachment, am not inhumane. But I applaud your force. I
can amuse myself with these rhythmic outcries against the
Jew god and these epigrams in rhymeless verse, and the
noise damning ' Black Riders ' seems to me the voice of
your nation's malady, its lack of poise in the face of novelty.
. . . The poets need not press near me. What have I to do
with all this twitter-twatter about Pleiades and cathedrals
and persons named Omar? I am not unaware of the quiet
lady in Baltimore with her definite sincerities or of John
Cheney's honest sentiments and metrical clevernesses; such
things are not for me, but for my fairhaired Eunice to read
in her garden; her eyes dampen more easily than do mine.
And your rural balladmongers make me curiously ill at
ease, capering around the old swimming-hole and babbling
of sin. All this stinks of enforced adolescence, and I see a
mark or so of suffering on your faces, as though chains un-
derlie your clothes. . . . Put me down, Bithynians! . . .
Gelos, bring the editors of the magazines, to whom all these
writers are mortgaged. . . . Put the litter down there, by
the tall new statue of the two natures wrestling in man.
. . . Surely this is the best sculptor of your ten years, and
of the next twenty-five! Yet I see in your prints that he is
more praised because his wrestlers have been commended
among the Gauls than for his merits as an artist. Strange,
this art has not advanced since some nameless Egyptian

made the image of the Lady Takuishit that stands in the museum at Athens. . . . Are these the editors? Men of Athens, I do perceive that in all things ye are too superstitious — I beg your pardon, I was inadvertently quoting from an acquaintance, a writer of some parts. But I see that your superstitions are disgusting. And yet," he drawled, rubbing verbena on his temples, " I am not without sympathy for you, knowing that most writers and readers of your quaint nation conceive the arts of fiction as merest entertainment, on the easiest terms, and that your critics constantly fall into that belief. Will not the year 1925 be luminous with the critical saying, ' Writers whom the great public does not take to its heart, finally, are not good writers '? *Mehercle!* This will be said as a covert gibe at the garrulous poet soon to be scolded for his tale of a girl whose inner being, Americans, seems to be unimpaired by what you call debaucheries, and who, in that, is like a thousand people I have known. . . .

" Your superstitions interest me, almost pathologically. You of the *Century* and *Scribner's* load numbers with essays by Jacob Riis and Oscar Craig on the perils of the slums, and yet you shy from a stern little novel about those perils. Your essayists hint the dangers of transmitted diseases and then four of you, editorially, shiver when Ibsen's ' Ghosts ' is played. I have never been able to see the difference between an act of imagination which takes the form of fact, and fact. This is my pagan blindness. Most of you talk of grave and serious views of life and beg the writers to take serious views of life. But I have not time to listen to your notions of what serious views may be!

" I can praise this in your magazines: your journalistic sides are excellent. I like this article of John Corbin on the Jewish theatres of New York's East Side, these sketches of the labouring man by Wyckoff, these notes on hotels, or newspapers and businesses by Williams, Steffens and more.

These, your historians will find valuable. The representation is adequate. One sees the birth of aviation in *McClure's* and jottings of the primitive shadow play in *Scribner's* and descriptions, too, of the universities where the boys who badgered Richard Harding Davis for autographs in 1890 will be yawping over 'Billy Baxter's Letters' in 1900, trash by a drummer, written for drummers. And that decline of the superior class's tastes, gentlemen, you will be attributing to the rise of cheap magazines but you will not admit that this feeble fiction which you print, these aimless tales of shadowy women and lifeless men and these tenuous 'society' dialogues have anything to do with that decline. . . . There your two natures struggle in the marble, and you do not see it! You see merely that it is best to be safe from objections of women in small towns, and meanwhile you fight among yourselves for tales of Rudyard Kipling who taunts your native writers with his primary sophistications and half ironies until three of them get astonishingly drunk at Martin's, when the Englishman is sick to death, and pray that he dies. . . . Yes, yes, I know all that! These are ' furrin goods, fotched in,' as the mountain folk say in your South, and the foreign setting excuses them to your critics! In 1922 one of your judges will be suavely complimenting an English novel which encloses a scene of a naked wench and her lover in bed, and, on the next day, insulting the native author of a small compliment to the lady of Cythera. I know all that!

"But I do not excuse you! Samuel McClure and his two expert henchmen can stand aside. You uttered bilge — I use the least offensive word in deference to Miss Gilder — bilge about improving the public taste, and then you did what you could to weaken it by inviting writers to ' see the pleasant side of things.' Your letters of advice to young artists on ' moderation ' and ' pessimism ' stand with your signatures! I have heard less said against McClure and

his staff, and I see their hospitality to experimental writing.
. . . Style, Mr. Brownell, will not always be subject to
dicta of the admirable Matthew Arnold. . . . I have heard,
too, McClure, your dry answer to the meddler in 1896 who
protested the size of cheques given to young writers without a name. ' The boys have to eat.' That pleases me who
have never believed that residence in gutters is healthy for
poets. But I agree with one of your reputable critics that a
taste for drawing-rooms has spoiled more poets than ever
did a taste for gutters. . . . In the gutter, truly, men see
things that may become shapes of free beauty, skirts that
swirl, arguments of dogs and boys in love, starlights on
broken glass and dung that is a jewel in the shade beside a
tree. All this is not so visible from drawing-rooms, and
your neat pages smelled, gentlemen, too much of orris and
laces sprinkled with popular scents. I miss, in your accepted work, the ferocious movement and swift colour of
the world, and the plebeian life which will remain the one
thing that your nation has to give a man of taste. Who wants
to be told what Robert said to Clara under gaslights of your
parlours, or under the globes that will light your sons? I
can like the feline pace of Howells in ' The Story of a
Play ' or his sketch of the Kentons, and much in ' Wheels of
Chance,' where his last paragraph touches modern impressionism, but these tales have nothing to do with your superior society, and the social comedy of your time is dusty
nonsense. . . . Henry Mills Alden? Oh, so that is you!
Mr. Alden, in 1894 you excused yourself to a young writer
for refusing two tales so mild that they appeared in *Lippincott's* without a word removed, by saying that simple folk
would be shocked at their contents. So? You remember?
. . . After that I find against you that you cut out the line:
' A painted girl glanced at him as he moved away,' from a
printed story. It is true that you had no objection when

Richard Harding Davis amiably discussed the painted women of Paris, but that, again, is the foreign scene. And I hear of you always making little changes of homely words, such as ' breasts ' and ' belly ' and ' spittle ' and ' sweat,' until your name gets to be rather a joke, and a source of that nervous irritation, that feeling of being treated as a naughty child, which accounts for the bawdry, the animal surcharge in letters of American writers that will stagger one or two explorers in the correspondence of your time. And then, in 1899, you write that ' our large circulation among unsophisticated people ' prevents your acceptance of a story which will appear two months later in *Munsey's.* You preceded Henri Bergson in some of his philosophic contentions, and that fact has been neglected, and you wrote with taste and spirit on things Greek. Did you never notice, in those drinking-cups of the Athenian time, that the boldly elegant outlines of pensive goddesses and athletes are no less bold, and elegant, than the line that marks the satyr's subumbilical activity? You were, I hear, fond of quoting that bit about seeing life steadily and whole. Mr. Alden, your care for the susceptible, unsophisticated plebs, was it — I do not ask, Was it quite sincere? because your excuse has become classic among American editors. But was it quite — I do not wish to offend you. But, before you died, your acquaintance, Mr. Wister, gathered up his sketches from *Harper's* and mixed them in a story that is still popular among the plebs. In 1918 a surgeon tending the mashed foot of a common sergeant, wounded in your next," the patrician yawned, " holy war, saw that the fellow had ' The Virginian ' beside the pillow and asked what he found in the story. ' Why,' said the unsophisticated creature, ' the plot is ' — I defer to you again, Miss Gilder — ' but this cowboy in the book, he's alive from the waist down.' The compliment from the lowly, Mr. Alden, seems to have been won by Mr. Wister admitting that his cowboy joked about the paternity of babies, sang rowdy songs and had seen dawn through various windows, not through a bridal veil. Perhaps the serenity of the satyr in the Greek cup, Mr. Alden, is the healthiest thing. . . . Gelos, get home to the insula and bid the fair-haired Eunice wait for me in the gardens, beside the pool rimmed in copper. Tell her to wear her thinnest gauze of Cos, and to spread moistened violets on her breasts. You must excuse the word, Mr. Alden. . . . Yes — 'see life steadily and see it whole.' Perhaps another generation will have a revenge on yours for these excisions of the lifelike mention and the little word. I, who yawned when Tigellinus covered the shores of Agrippa's pond with a thousand naked women, will be bored enough with novels in which one printed ghost possesses a positive battalion of printed female ghosts. I have always preferred a selective faculty. . . . Your nation has attempted this distinction between emotions of the bridebed and those of the lupanar. But in your decade the humorous weeklies took a certain licence and were quite skittish with jokes about chorus girls and old men applauding the ballet. The chorus girl and the flirtatious woman even appeared in those humorous pages of your superior magazines, from which explorers will draw up an endless stream of sorrow and mortification in a few more years. . . . I deprecate the reputation of your nation as being one of humorists. Is not a plain story by John Bangs, perhaps 'The Mayor's Lamps,' or Arthur Colton's half sad 'Tobin's Monument' more amusing than all this delirium of punning on the word 'lobster' and this meaningless huddle of dialogues between 'He' and 'She'? I look back with more favour at Henry Bunner, aiming little mudballs at vulgar crazes in the pages of *Puck*, jeering at the cant of Hall Caine and Marie Corelli, and stating his resentment of foul religious hysterias. However, you are a nation of humorists, and the dog, as the

Jews say, goes back to his vomit. Mr. Hapgood of *Collier's* will protest, as your time ends, and much good that will do! No, humorists you are. . . .

"Why, sirs, I find myself brought down to making compliments on the simplest that you do! I find it strange that your women are so much braver than your men in dusting the myth of greatness. How admirably Rebecca Harding Davis speaks, here, of her meal at Nathaniel Hawthorne's, and of her outcry when Emerson and Alcott praised their holy war and she had to tell them of camps fringed with shoddy merchants, ringed with corruptions! How delicately gay Hawthorne's daughter is, telling of Alcott's transformation after his Louisa began to make money! And here is Clara Morris, in 1899, saying kind things of John Wilkes Booth and James Fisk. . . . And here is Aline Gorren, in *Scribner's*, discussing French poets and foreign manners without that lackey's respect, Mr. Burlingame, which destroys so many of the writers who describe European painters for your magazine, although your service to the plastic arts is memorable. . . . Yes, I find myself praising the simplicities of your magazines, sirs, and not their advertised splendours. I do not care for these English poets named Aldington, or is it Lang? and English novels by these Merrimans and things, in no way better than those of Nelson Page, and generally not so good. I am irreverent to essays by George McClean Harper on French writers whom he tries to put through the paces of a Sunday school, as I believe you call those assemblies of wretched children held once a week for the sake of making them loathe your God. Such unpretending stories as 'Red Rock' interest me more than criticism of Balzac written by a male schoolmarm, as I think you call them. Yes, all your magazines can find these competent tales which may be nothing permanent, but which do not make one retch — pardon, Mr. Alden — as does some of your criticism. . . .

185

" And in your capacities as public critics," the patrician drawled, " you were timid beyond thought. You, McClure, and you, Walker, of the *Cosmopolitan,* were more liberal to the Westerner and the radical than the rest. I, as a libertarian, caring not an as, the least of our Roman coins, for your Bryans, Altgelds and your single tax, still see the evasive fashion in which the superior magazines discussed all that. You, Godkin, will one day be regretfully censured for your parochialisms by your friend Oswald Villard. The *North American Review* was more patient in its dealings with the new movements, and kinder, than you were in the *Nation.* But this is the usual thing. I have never," he said wearily, " found much intelligent political criticism on my tours in the modern world, as you call this place where nearly everything is old, and little comely. . . . Lift me, Bithynians! I have done. In short," Petronius yawned, " what you offered to your people was not a leadership but a politic conservatism, and as for the writers, what they mostly gave was a pruned mediocrity. — Yes, yes! I heard the cry out of all these leaves. Artists winced in their recovered silence. This Howells once told a dull boy at a wedding feast that writers often wrote proud stories of their lives, but that artists seldom did. Artists are men who know that they must fail. They look up from the finished page and know it is not finished, for beyond the desk is a sexless, colourless statue without eyes that does not even grin at their defeat. Then they may run to whimper on some woman's knees, or nurse their sense of bruised inadequacy as best they can. . . ."

Wake up, Faustine! The arbiter is gone. Give me a cigarette. There is Egeria's cane tapping the stairs. Straighten your hat, my dear.

CHAPTER VII

FIGURES OF EARTH

IT was late August of 1899 and Theodore Roosevelt, governor of New York, was concerned with a question of trousers. The burly gentleman sat, writing to a friend, and stewed the matter. He had to ride at the head of the State's militia in this parade that was coming, and there was no costume for a governor's appearance on such occasions. Well, perhaps a frock-coat and grey pantaloons made the best way out of it. It wasn't much of a dress, and the garb called for a silk hat, too. He would look a riding-master! But it couldn't be helped. . . . He sat in Albany, writing, and it may be that grossening muscles twitched around his mouth; the flat, not ugly face was already hardening into broad lines that made it, later, a writhing mask when he broke out in arguments and oratory. He had come some distance upward — or along — with a gathering strength of showmanship in store, armed with a memory that helped him over political stiles, and through his banging speeches. For, some living people say, he laughed loudly at a banquet in 1895 where John Kendrick Bangs, amusing the guests, said that " all theatrical press agents belong to a club of which Ananias is the honorary president." Whether he recalled the little witticism or not is permanently unimportant. The memory is strange: in " The Bostonians " a dozen sentences from cheap, forgotten authors whose stuff Henry James read on the beach of Newport, and an epigram of Thomas Wentworth Higginson, appear transmuted in the slow, inimitable medium projected by that scrupulous mind. Here, then, sat Roosevelt, vexed on this question of trousers and coat, the heir of a political situation arranged quietly by Mark Hanna between sandwiches at Saint Louis in 1896. Yes, the nation had invoked capitalism to save it from oratory, and now oratory would have to be noisy, appealing to the rabble and the newspapers in its forays against capitalism. This figure in warm clay, with its female tact and childish tempers and its sense for crowds, now swells a signature across the note-paper and gives to printed record its consideration of the subject of trousers and coat in the coming parade.

The parade was first planned to pass upward along Fifth Avenue and then to wheel westward along Fifty-ninth Street. . . . Westward! . . . Odd, how all dying things turn to this West, the region of questions? So mourners on the Nile consigned the mummied citizen to the mercies of the West and soldiers of the recent muddy muss in upper France "went West" to join Hiawatha, King Arthur and the ecstatic nun Petronilla who saw God descending from the West in the shape of a fish-hook to lift her virgin soul into bliss. The great parade with its President and admiral and heroic soldiers would pass and mingle with these legends.

The whole nineteenth century had been rotten with the disease of greatness and its wretched successor seems unwilling to get rid of this malady. Greatness, to be sure, has existed ever since fear first made gods in this world and men invoked them to witness the twin vulgarities of success and failure. "To have had our little quality" isn't enough and there come the passion for a following flicker of heads that turn in the smoke of restaurants, the monthly necessity of a visit to the photographer, that willingness to flood admirers with correspondence, to be seen at banquets, to fuss

188

a trifle about a costume in the great parade. . . . The
nineteenth century had been prolific of parades and ached
in its last ten years with news of them. Earthen figures sat
in carriages or on horses and, granted an apex of greatness,
lay in hearses and paraded while troops with reversed
muskets lined gutters and sweated, being base creatures,
in their uniforms. . . . A tall young Philadelphian saw
much of this tinselled movement and will have, one day, a
second value. He was expensively hired to tell the world
about Nicholas Romanov setting the crown of Russia askew
on his thick head in a torpor of incense and in such a reflected dazzle of golden cloth that Richard Harding Davis's
eyes reddened. Ladies, that night in Moscow, went hunting
lotions from hotel to hotel jammed with Americans, all for
R. H. D. His life was spent in a hurry from show to show
and names were tagged to sights: " Sarah Bernhardt " —
a woman whose Empire bonnet is drawn down to her
painted eyebrows, lying in a phaeton banked with white
roses that glides through the flower battle in Paris. Nurse-
maids and virgins stare after the great courtesan with
frightened admiring eyes — or, being our mother's son,
we think the eyes were frightened. " Julia Ward Howe "
— an old, stooping woman declaiming " The Battle Hymn
of the Republic " in a drawing-room of Commonwealth
Avenue, in dying Boston. " Oscar Wilde " — a tall man
pent into a tight coat at luncheon in London who tries to trip
him into criticizing a French painter and then sits sulking
when the American is not tripped. After some years an
English doctor comes to a hotel in Paris and asks if Mr.
Davis can let him have a few hundred francs for Oscar
Wilde " the great dramatist," and gets mauve bills stuffed
in an envelope. " William Dean Howells " — a quiet,
grey little man who denied genius altogether, whose talk
wandered easily from the colours of Venice to the making,
in primitive Ohio, of a terrible sweetmeat known as " peach

leather," who, alone in the literary republic, had the courage to ask mercy for the anarchists officially murdered in
Chicago. . . . His dislike of assassination was instinctive.
He once stood at a reception listening while a female
humorist destroyed the arts of Thomas Hardy, George
Moore and Henry James and suddenly he began to tell
anecdote after anecdote of his alarmed provincialism when
he first came from Boston to New York. At the twentieth
recital of his tremours and bewilderments, the lady bulkily
withdrew her humours into another room. Her public greatness had been subtly rebuked, without a word addressed to
her. " Queen Victoria " — a turtle-shaped person nodding
in a huge carriage down the streets of London at her Jubilee,
a little figure drowsy under a parasol at Ascot in the Royal
Enclosure with a tall Hindu servant constantly picking up
the scarf that droops from her shoulders. . . . The gowns
at Ascot seem monotonous and badly worn, and parading
celebrities have a look of caged animals. Mr. Davis yawns
a little. He cannot manage to be wholly taken in by this
Europe, and he winces, in the land of sportsmanship, when
big policemen swim out, hand over hand, in a yelling crowd
at the Derby, to rescue a bookmaker, half naked and bloody,
from disappointed creditors. " Carnot " — something in
a black and silver catafalque with Casimir-Perier walking
behind its wheels, unguarded. A stand collapses at the corner of the Rue Castiglione and Mr. Davis winces when the
French soldiery scuttle from the crackling noise. Greasy
papers float on the asphalt after the long funeral has passed.
Mr. Henry James, otherwise delighted with " About Paris,"
is vexed by those greasy papers and gently scolds Davis at
dinner in London. " Réjane " — an ugly, graceful woman
screaming and weeping in an artist's garden when she is
shown Aubrey Beardsley's poster of her face with its Cyth-
erean grin. Mr. Davis leaves the scene in his unprinted
notes and, later, tells it on a condition of silence, for Réjane

is then still alive and one does not tell unkind stories about women. "Yvette Guilbert" — tall, red-haired, strolls down the stage at a daylit rehearsal at the Ambassadeurs. Other actresses smile civilly with half-closed eyes and men stir as though a whip had touched them. "William McKinley" — men link their hands and make a long aisle through the swarm of the inaugural ball in Washington. The little President goes by, with his pretty, invalid wife on his arm. "Alexandre Dumas" — a dark, small-eyed man who sits during an inane speech at the Institute, staring up at women in the gallery. Mr. Davis is impressed by the grace of manner and the air of tired reserve. . . . He has an odd feeling for manner. Is there not an element of vulgar fraud surrounding Aristide Bruant, the "new Villon" in his café where guests are pillaged for copies of songs and photographs of the people's champion? But Bruant sings:

> "Christ aux yeux doux
> Qu'es mort pour nous,
> Chauff' la terre oùs —
> Qu'on fait leur trou!
> Pierreuses,
> Trotteuses,
> A' marchent l'soir,
> Quand y fait noir,
> Sur le trottoir . . ."

and he sings well. But isn't he putting some of this on? Other, older and more cultivated Americans will accept Bruant at his own stated pretensions and write grave paragraphs on him in *Scribner's* and *Harper's*. The new Villon will die and his greatness will have been forgotten by journalists who write his obituaries in American newspapers. "Franz Joseph" — a stagnant old thing in a chair, watching the procession of Hungarian nobles in outrageously wonderful clothes parading on Saint Stephen's day in Buda

Pesth. "Theodore Roosevelt" — the burly figure of earth with its blue neckerchief hurries ahead of Davis in the hot olive woods at Las Guasimas and stands in a prodigy of sunlight below the hills outside Santiago de Cuba, talking a good deal to reporters. . . . Then great ladies, backing the war in South Africa, chatter in verandas at Capetown, and the astonishing nineteenth century ends its list of parades and consequences. Mr. Davis has not criticized its last decade, but he has seen the greatness and parades, and they remain, glitteringly stored in his swift, smooth sketches and long reports.

Another tall young American had missed all the sights and figures, although he had early seen greatness and had even smelled it, for the dimness that picked up a child of four from the nursery's floor in Saint Cyr smelled of tobacco, and that is all that Charles Maurice recalls of Gustave Flaubert. However, the smiling "Monsieur Guy" who taught him French tennis at Arcachon was naturally clear in his mind, and among his multitudinous rejected manuscripts is one saying that he thought Guy de Maupassant dull in many things. Chicago's smoky air tormented the boy's lungs; he stood with Stevenson's face haloed in straggling furs before him in the lane at Saranac and eight years later saw, for a wet second, a yellow skeleton in waterproof fighting an umbrella on steps of a chapel in Mentone, and recognized Aubrey Beardsley. . . . But this was his last greatness until doctors pronounced his lungs able to stand unselected airs and he cautiously spent a month in Buffalo with his sister, in 1899. There was no greatness around there, but he went out to call on Elbert Hubbard in East Aurora.

"I admit the dramatic manner and the necktie but I must say that he seemed shrewd. He talked about a number of people very adroitly, saying things which have been said since their deaths by biographers and critics of high degree.

. . . Just as I was leaving he asked me, very suddenly, what I thought of Rudyard Kipling. There was only one attitude for a young American in 1899 as to Kipling. Mr. Hubbard listened and then he remarked: ' I wonder what you will be thinking of him in twenty years. Come and tell me if we are both alive.' . . ."

For nine years the nigromancer's coloured shadows danced out of his pot, and literary republicans watched the parade in maddened speculation. Some of them saw this: the American public, considered a nervous virgin by its guardians, was avidly buying a fiction in which everything not permitted to the native writers was done and said openly, and gave no offence.[1]

Why, certainly! Rudyard Kipling wished to mention the shapelessness of a pregnant Cockney woman, howling in a street with naked breasts. It interested him to relate Love O'Women's locomotor ataxia, which, says a character in the tale, comes from being called Love O'Women, and to send the dying man back to a mistress in a brothel for the sake of a theatrical death. The subalterns flirted with married women, drank their whisky and soda, gambled and blew their brains out with some detail in lonely bungalows. The nigromancer brought a raving shadow down to roll a dead man's head and the crown of an Himalayan empire on

[1] I suggest that some historian of criticism in the United States amuse himself by comparing reviews of " The Light That Failed," to those of " McTeague," or the many discussions of " The Record of Badalia Herodsfoot " to those of " Maggie " and " George's Mother." Shifting from Kipling to the brilliant, luckless George Douglas, compare reviews of " The House with the Green Shutters " to adverse notices of " McTeague " and " George's Mother." The reader not interested in fiction must excuse this missionary foot-note. Douglas's novel is, psychologically, an act of revenge on the environment of his boyhood. He was illegitimate, the son of a maidservant in a small Scotch village, and the characters of his story are fairly hated into life. The story involves debauchery, cancer, cowardice and, at the end, parricide — marred by a suggestion taken from " Oliver Twist," which was one of Douglas's books in his dreary childhood. But the story was reviewed respectfully by American critics who simply sent " George's Mother " and " McTeague " to the literary hell.

a journalist's table in the middle of night. Georgie Porgie's forsaken Burmese woman sobbed below his house beside the river. A drunken workman flooded the platform of an English station with his spew. Merry lads at an English school buried a cat under a floor and let its stench revenge them on a disliked master. Lalun, of the world's most ancient profession, jested with her lovers in the gay room on the city wall and had the approval of Mr. Theodore Childs, who, elsewhere, saw, regretfully, that American writers were attempting to introduce " depraved women, subjects for pity but not for literature," into the national fiction. The reporter passed through Indian slums and hauled out shadows of white women sold to the Hindu; Vice, draped in jewels, salaamed from her doorway. Salty words cropped everywhere on the verbal structure of the spreading illusion. Cheers for the sergeant's weddin'! Give 'em one cheer more. Grey gun 'orses to the lando, an' a rogue is married to an 'ore! But he talked as directly, as personally, as William Lloyd Garrison had talked to subscribers of the *Liberator* or as William Allen White was now talking to subscribers of the *Gazette*, in Emporia, Kansas. The little friend of all the world, sitting next to you on the bench in the barber's shop, was not even so impersonal as George Ade, telling of the preacher who flew his kite or the fool killer's meditation at the county fair in " Fables in Slang." This excusing presence, the speaking voice, so inaudible in the bewildering sharp anecdotes of Stephen Crane, or in the slow, grave narration of " McTeague," was at their ears. The Americans, under conduct of the sophisticated Methodist, went out for to admire and to see the world, and couldn't stop it if they tried. And then — rapture! — he told stories of America! and told them with none of that detached superciliousness of " The Bostonians," either! The millionaire's private car lunged from Los Angeles to Bos-

ton, with that quite American note of pleasure at the record
made, when the trip is finished. Eugene Debs and all those
unsettling characters were rebuked in " The Walking Delegate," parabolically, and force and speed were sincerely
admired as Henry Adams, sardonically, reverenced the
dynamo in Paris. It was too good to be true. Here was
somebody willing to take the American's side against European condescension and to brag with him of machinery, and
to hold the balance level, in " An Error in the Fourth Di-
mension," between Yankee impulse and British stolidity.
He had become a national fact; before 1896 he was mentioned and quoted in, at least, five hundred tales and essays
in the magazines. Criticism, or what there was of it, consented to everything, after some shiverings, and read " Cap-
tains Courageous " with the warm thrill that rises in the
American author when he sees ten words of amiable patronage by a French journalist follow his name in a Parisian
review of the third consideration. The mania grew; " The
White Man's Burden " pleased imperialists, and then
" Kim " commenced its devolution in *McClure's*. A great
writer had been created. This was his longest, his most
elaborately written work. Then, with a sort of gasp, the
critics, and that indefinite film of literary amateurs which
exists even in America, saw that here, in the gorgeous, infinitely piled fabrics of the legend, was just Dick, the Boy
Detective, inevitably successful from first to last, and the
illusion of ten years shredded upward. Then anger of disappointed sentimentalists snapped into fire; critics wheeled
with the smartness of Mulvaney's squad at drill. Amnon
loathed his Tamar, and farewell the nigromancer! But
there remained the great writer of the '90's, and a coroner's
jury of idolaters either called the live corpse names —
" cheap journalist," " press agent of Empire," " inspired
hack," and the pleasing like — or heaped wreaths. " Ten

years ago," Harris Merton Lyon said in 1907, " they were
all saying KIPLING, and now they say, Kipling — oh,
yes! "

But the nigromancer's smokes had coloured, falling here
and there on manuscript, much printed excellence. That
final literary analyst will pluck out phrase after phrase,
whole sentences and derived paragraphs from the work of
men who have shrugged Rudyard Kipling into a remote vulgarity, that imaginary limbo from which authors return
as annoying spectres. He has his lien on the goods of wiser
writers, of men more speculative as to the awkward and in-
soluble; whole novels have been spun on plots which stand,
in his earlier sketches, as outlines and anecdotes. The collapsing, drugged measures of the dreamed adventure in
" The Brushwood Boy," have suggested long passages in
modern impressionism. His delicate notices of noise have
been complacently adopted by those, the terribly superior,
who so often will take a plot or an image from anybody,
who write " A Connecticut Yankee in King Arthur's Court "
for a second time in terms of William Morris plus Henry
James, or tranquilly rescore the classic music of: " There
are no fields of amaranth on this side of the grave; there are
no voices, O Rhodope, that are not soon mute, however
tuneful; there is no name, with whatever emphasis of passionate love repeated, of which the echo is not faint at
last. . . ." The rhetorical address, so thoroughly criticized when Harry Leon Wilson said that King Solomon
composed somewhat in the crisp style of Mr. Kipling, the
directness of narrative — from him to them — and the obvious smartness of epithet were copied promptly, but the
evasive, frequently beautiful statements in colour and sound
have too plainly haunted sensitive artists, and the nigromancer's tacit revenge will be, simply, a record of derivations and an acknowledgment of many inventions.

He had met the unspoken, half conscious wish of Americans for an entertainment which would reverse the formulas of Louisa May Alcott. This primary sophistication admitted, by not denying, that champagne, music halls and good cigars were not evil. He had, by an accident of birth and travel, enlarged the literary map. Fans of descending vision opened from his tales; the society of Simla, an evening in Topaz, Colorado, and the marriage of a princeling in Ghokral Seetarun flashed, in temporary outline, on eyes of readers in American towns growing weekly more hideous. A plane in the world showed with one expert paragraph that displays the wives of engineers and chandlers, dependent on the safety of steamers. A massive catalogue in mere geographical reference existed, and increased with every volume of the tales. The effect, necessarily, was that of implicit romance to people whose day passed in a quarrel with the cook, a conference with the book-keeper at the office, a call from the high-school superintendent and the disintegrating excitements of six-handed euchre or a meeting of the lodge after dinner. His status as apologist of Empire, the schoolboy's patriotism and the fact, not immediately visible, that he reported but seldom analysed his tremendous cast — all those objections were worthless. They saw the spinning earth, and saw it through rigidities of a temperament that defended them; unyielding wires protected the children from the wolves. Sin, with some lenities against concepts of Dwight Moody and Frances Willard, was still sin, and God, addressed so vehemently, was clearly God.

Under the stir and chromatic rippling of the general narrative, came the claim on that " uncultivated hunger for pathetics." The pathos ranged from candid appeals to the pity of children, which is perhaps more common than affection for children, to the simplicities of a statement in misery. He had, and had in better control than any other writer of the times, a sense of the point at which an explosion of sentiment may be allowed to crash on the reader. It is singularly idle to talk, here, of his intentions, for his intentions are only to be stated by those prodigies in criticism who begin reviews by saying: " This writer means ———— " Who knows, pending the discovery of some admission, what Henry James intended in that last wrenched paragraph of " The Beast in the Jungle " or if he wished his audience to sympathize with the ignoble Julia Bride? There is nothing in this range of narrative comparable to " Riders to the Sea," or an understatement so mutely graceful as Jurgen, turning from his grandmother's corner of the Christian heaven. But the broken lullaby of the childless woman in " Without Benefit of Clergy " and the lama's sudden outcry before the Gates of Learning in " Kim " remain touching, until some alteration of the human mood dismisses them to that museum whose principal exhibit is the death of Little Nell. And, even in his excesses, the journalist never committed such a thing as the last chapter of Pierre Loti's " Matelot," the literary onion, as vulgar as possible, arranged by dressing a sailor's mother in her best clothes and sending her to meet news of his death in the Orient, then invoking Christ and the saints to help her out of Loti's situation, applauded in America and England as " irony." . . . This pathos in its variable quality was an additional claim of Rudyard Kipling on his enslaved population; and in this capitalist of story-telling, the Americans of the '90's had their wish. He was, in much, themselves; but, in much, an artist of extraordinary forces, he whirled before them a vision, a gleaming newspaper whose columns enclosed anecdotes of red-coated Irishmen, tougher than those of their own fiction, mundane women, notes on ships and engines, rachitic splendours of a millionaire's private car and green country-sides in the England then dominating their perplexed desire for some decoration. Is it absurd to guess that this reiterated, constant advertisement of the East, the thread of imperial thinking, and the unlimited suggestion of dominion over isles and forests, influenced plump men in Washington after Dewey had won his little battle in Manila Bay and the Orient, that immense and empty mystery of all literature, had been entered by American troops?

Well, Theodore Roosevelt pondered his costume for the great parade and, after some weeks, somewhere in New York, put on a black coat, a pair of grey trousers and the other necessities of a cool morning. He dressed. Troops and admirals, presidents and senators, got themselves clad for high occasion. The city dressed itself from end to end. . . . An unimportant creature, here apologetic, was sternly removed from bed and had to think of trousers in a sleepy tangle of wonders about this parade. His consciousness began, once, when the grandfather who knew Sitting Bull lifted him and someone brushed down dust thickened on panes by those hot storms that smear windows in the valley of the Missouri with grey, baked powders. A parade wonderfully moved for him under blowing cottonwoods; striding giants of dust marched past the leaves and, below them, fans of plumage rippled, faces were scarred with streaks of green and red and squaws were blanketed lumps on the dragging slopes of travois behind ponies of the tribe. One naked little girl was an oily statue with a red rag about her stiff black hair, serene on a white horse, and an old chief rode with strings of shivering wampum and bright shells swaying on his stark ribs. The last of a great tribe moved so, glowed so, between two lines of troopers in blue coats. Covered wagons, stamped " U. S. A." in scarlet on the cloth of jolting hoods, spaced the parade. " Blackfeet, sonny. Going up to the new reservation." They passed along, endlessly to his awe, and a tanned trooper swung his horse over the low iron rails, to whirl down from one stirrup and catch up his hat blown among geraniums flattened by the wind. Then the colour of a guidon flared; a bugle yelled far up the street, and the dust closed down. " Time for little boys to be in bed." The World's Fair was a silver fish of wax on an elastic cord and it vanished, tragically, down the maw of an enormous English mastiff in Saint Paul where veils of thin colours shook at night and shed fugitive tones on the prodigiousness of snow that heaped the yard. The Northern Lights, and the sharp lights of Chicago seen sleepily through rain, join to lights of farms seen on so many nights as trains brought his bewildered unimportance from East to West, in a confusion between the tall grandfather mysteriously ruined in " the cattle war " and the other grandfather who sometimes drew little pictures on margins of fat law books or played a violin in jade dusk, crooning out "Lord Ronald " on sorcerous strings that merely yapped, when privately investigated. This unimportance lived in chronic bewilderments of aunts. Impalpable, perhaps sinister, creatures were always somewhere on the dark edge of conversations, Populists, Pierre Loti, Richard Harding Davis, Little Lord Fauntleroy, Major McKinley, Henry James and Grover Cleveland who, at least, was adequately visible in coloured cartoons of *Puck*. Boys in blue shirts ran, bawling: " Hey! Coxey's army's comin' ! " once, and once, incredibly, the Missouri rose and flooded a cellar so that the more Western grandmother stood wringing her thin hands on steps, lamenting preserves and jellies all afloat around a tub in which the negligible creature navigated, very wet, wet as he got to be, sitting on a grand stand opposite a white, dripping thing which was Grant's Tomb, with President McKinley very miserable above the soaked procession, bending suddenly out as a horse slipped. Even the great submitted to rains of that decade. General Miles was something tall, sliding his uniform out of the moist grace of a military cloak in a hallway at West Point, not then a bastard operatic Valhalla of cement and stone.

Bewilderments multiplied, with a cold internal shrinking as the unimportance was led along tremulous floors of a train to be seen by Mr. Hanna, a person imagined as the brother of the fearful Hanno in " Salammbô " who bathed his leprosy in blood. Mr. Hanna, though, seemed placid in his stateroom with a gang of standing gentlemen, somehow suggesting amorous dogs, who watched the hands which had played on the emotionalism of a nation as though it were a piano's keyboard. The hands stopped their movement among cards on a table and the voice said anxiously: " But you've got some other children, Beer? " Relieved, he picked up his cards again, and the train came to Washington. A Mr. Hay stooped to shake hands and left an impregnable belief that he was a decent, although elderly, person. The unimportance yawned at a piece of metal shaped as a cloaked woman who was Mrs. Henry Adams, in a cemetery, and, as she was dead, very dull to consider. . . . Frances Willard was also dead. A woman came screaming into the peace of the Ohio garden: " Girls! Girls! She's gone! " The sky had fallen, somewhere! " Run down to the barns, dear. Miss Willard's dead and poor Kate was so fond of her! " The negligible identity, sure that this corpse must be in the flat town beyond the orchard, roamed between two pastures and examined empty plots in the cemetery, a very friendly one, where a mason made the sound of a marmoreal castanet, chipping lies on stones. . . . Now he had to get into his best trousers and go to the parade, and the silver morning was sharp around him; the Hudson sparkled beside the pulsing train, and earthen figures packed the streets. Long draperies of flags and streaks of restless bunting dangled before brown fronts of that Fifth Avenue. Here was the Plaza Hotel with a charming bronze lioness on a pedestal in the midst of the lobby. He had to stop looking at this glory to shake hands with Mr. Henderson, who criticized music in the *Sun*, but whose hair was different, much shorter, than that of Mr. Meltzer, who criticized music, too, and sat in Bronson Howard's veranda on Nantucket Island, consulting him about the graver arts. A long room overlooked the square, not then defaced by a high metal woman waving her stupidity at the gilded image of Sherman, and flags memorably shook above bronze cliffs of hotels on the eastern side of the street. This was Central Park, northward, and a red house like the castle in " Ivanhoe " to the south, and blue policemen shoved crowds about. The parade would happen in an hour. Meantime a pretty aunt laughed excitedly and gentlemen helped themselves to glasses filled with hissing yellow liquid from a gaudy bottle close to the huge, ormolu piano.

Somewhere down the street's thundering voices, officers were holding folk into the crossways and a victoria's horses were ordered back, back from the open space of Fifth Avenue. The curved woman in her scarf of blue feathers rose on a seat and screeched prayers to a policeman. Oh, but she must — must get across! Men recognized the goddess of the crowd and began to yell: " Let Anna get across! Let her by! " A young soldier in dirty brown khaki sprang on a step of the carriage and the crowd howled. They opened a lane for Anna Held and she crossed Fifth Avenue, laughing and blowing kisses to the herd.

The parade was coming. A flashing lady stopped strumming the piano and a rim of people swayed on the sidewalks. A bright dust of confetti, endless snakes of tinted paper began to float from hotels that watched the street. Voices of congratulation came bubbling in these rooms. Why, you could see everything from here! And this was the greatest parade since the Civil War! Greatness! . . . Brass of parading bandsmen flashed and columns wheeled,

turning at the red house to the·south. Balconies and windows showered down confetti, and roses were blown. The
very generous dropped bottles of champagne and the paper
streamers slid in facile twists and wreaths on the white and
grey of uniforms. Cadets down from West Point seemed
curious birds that wheeled and strode in oblong flocks. The
little admiral was a blue and gold blot in a carriage. The
President, and the plump senator from Ohio, and all these
great were tiny images of black and flesh in the buff shells
of carriages in a whirling rain of paper ribbons, flowers
and flakes of the incessant confetti blown everlastingly,
twinkling from high blue of the sky. How they roared!
Theodore Roosevelt! The increasing yell came up from
the street. A dark horse showed and slowly paced until it
turned where now the gilded general stares down the silly
city. A blue streamer, infinitely descending from above,
curled all around his coat and he shook it from the hat that
he kept lifting. Theodore Roosevelt! The figure on its
charger passed, and a roar went plunging before him while
the bands shocked ears and drunken soldiers straggled out
of line, and these dead great, remembered with a grin, went
filing by.

APPENDIX

One anecdote printed in this collection rests on a sentence in a letter of Abner McKinley to my father, dated October 4, 1896, and on a recollection of having heard Mr. McKinley discuss his interview with George Pullman. I find no suggestion in any official life of President McKinley that he sent his brother as a private ambassador to Pullman in 1894. There were such private messengers, dispatched by powerful politicians or financiers. Henry Miller, Cornelius Bliss and others tried to bring Pullman down to the safe ground of arbitration, and I see no discrepancy between President McKinley's published character and the idea of this private effort. However, Mr. Abner McKinley's daughter is alive to correct the statement if it is wrong.

On the announcement of this book a number of kind people sent me letters of literary folk of the '90's, for my use, and seemed anxious to see these treasures printed. I greatly enjoyed reading the letters, and have not printed them. Why? In the first chapter of this trivial work occurs the anecdote of Mr. Patrick Keogh's little journey in the company of Louisa May Alcott to the house of Dr. Lawrence, where he was washed, fed elaborately and given five dollars. Mr. Keogh recollects " some more women " in the female doctor's house. One of these shadows on May 3, 1888, wrote: " I wonder what became of the darling little red-haired Mick whom she adopted last winter? " Behold the

204

literary sentimentalist at work! Miss Alcott brings a pretty Irish child into her friend's house; ergo, adoption. The same lady put on paper a version of Paul du Chaillu's tumble down the steps of the Brevoort, in Chapter 3, which belongs in the higher regions of romantic writing, and her version of Frances Willard's rebuke to Rebecca Harding Davis — she admired Miss Willard — takes a page of notepaper to unfold itself. But Miss Willard's actual remark, as reported by two quite unliterary ladies and corrected by Mrs. Davis, was, as herein recorded, very brief.

This book, as far as possible, relies for its descriptions of literary people, on the testimony of bystanders neither inimical nor devoted to the person in question. Mr. George Warden Sims, naturally, has the most vivid recollections of Bronson Alcott's fingers digging into his small shoulder at Emerson's funeral and of Miss Alcott's outcry. Miss Alcott's opinion of " Huckleberry Finn " is taken from an unprinted letter to Frances Hedges Butler. Alcott's relation to Emerson was once cleverly discussed by William James Stillman and the opinions of Barret Wendell, Rose Hawthorne Lathrop, E. C. Towne and others were long since printed. He appears to have been one of the complacently self-deluded characters of that era. After a thorough examination of his printed remains I can see nothing original in them, and his charm, no doubt existent, must have been that " sweetness " which also hung about Donald Mitchell. I call attention to Thomas Wentworth Higginson's defensive essay, however, and by way of epitaph print one sentence of a letter from Sarah Dix, the war worker, dated January 29, 1863. ". . . Mr. Alcott was offered a post here " (in Washington) " at Mr. Emerson's instance but the latter wrote to me that Mr. A. has other projects, but I have not heard what those projects are from Miss A. or from this philosophic gentleman when he took the poor girl home in such conditions as to rouse the worst fears of her friends and their bitterest protests. . . ." Finally, I have my own recollections of hearing Thomas Bailey Aldrich in a state of reminiscence on the topic of Alcott: the pathos of Mr. Aldrich is that he did not write as he talked.

I cannot expect, for reasons of an obvious kind, that a man who was shut out of his mother's house after a wild night in his nineteenth year or another who smuggled the remains of his employer's mistress from Chicago on July 6, 1893, at a cost of five hundred dollars in fees, bribes and tips, should sign their names to public statements. The discretion of three lawyers and ten doctors has supplied me with data for which they, also, cannot be thanked, publicly, save in this ill-contrived fashion. My specific obligations to Mr. Charles Clery Nolan for the use of his autographs, Wildiana and his monstrous collections of American religious eloquence are sufficiently visible, as is my indebtedness to Grace Ralston Lewis for her notes on the World's Fair. People who recall John Wise's undervalued book, "The End of an Era," will not have forgotten his account of the cadets of the Virginia Military Institute at the battle of Newmarket and the deaths of Sergeant Cabell and Jacquelin Stanard. Curiously, a copy of "The Louisiana Swamp Doctor," one of the paper-backed satires mentioned in Chapter 3, was found in a second-hand shop in Saint Louis, in 1923, inscribed: "V. M. I. 1863, belongs to J. B. Stanard." So I have assumed that this class of fiction was commonplace in Virginia as it was in Ohio.

Reading through the proof of this book, I find myself wondering if I have opened the characters of the dead great to any malevolent insinuation. I hope not. Chester Arthur's indignant remark about his private life was made to a female writer who intruded on him at Saratoga and demanded his views on alcohol. No life of Grant mentions the several attempts toward procuring his signature to warnings against alcohol and tobacco, but the children of the avenging Ti-

taness who stormed Mt. MacGregor vouch for the horrid
performance. I don't know whether the Mrs. Walker who
headed the committee that asked Dana to suppress Carmencita is the Ada Channing Walker elsewhere described.
Mrs. Walker's niece was in school until 1892 and was not
yet following her aunt's fantastic trail. It may be well to
add that titles of books, such as " All the Brothers Were
Valiant " and " Many Inventions," are used in my text
without quotations on an assumption that they will be recognized. Persons interested in spiritualism need not apply to
me for any news of James Huneker's interview with General
Grant before the tomb on Riverside Drive and my information as to the meeting of Guy de Maupassant and Kitty Kane
on the steps of Purgatory belongs in the class of conjecture
along with the book of Revelations.

I am indebted, for documents and information, among
the dead to Mrs. William Tod Helmuth, Caroline Secor
Ames, Colonel Robert Thornburgh, U.S.M.C., Sir William
Young, Richard Harding Davis, John Kendrick Bangs,
Emerson Hough, James Huneker, George Walbridge Per-
kins, Abner McKinley, Henry Fosdick Morgan and to Wil-
liam Collins Beer; among the living to " Egeria," Laura
Spencer MacGillivray, Adeline Gibbs Penrose, Frances
Hedges Butler, Helen Kimball Slosson, Caroline Gunther,
Marion Gillespie Bemis, Grace Ralston Lewis, Aline Fran-
kau Bernstein, Helen Arthur, Ada Weber and Bird Housum,
Jesse Lynch Williams, Harry Leon Wilson, Rupert Hughes,
Joel Elias Spingarn, William Sumner Dennison, Charles
Mason Maurice, George Warden Sims, Patrick Keogh,
Amos Cliff Armstrong, Metcalf Beach, François Grivault,
Chester Beckley and to sixteen others who, for prudential
reasons, cannot be named.

STEPHEN CRANE

A STUDY IN AMERICAN LETTERS

FOR

ROBERT HOUSUM

INTRODUCTION BY
Joseph Conrad

O N a rainy day of March of the year 1923, listening to the author of this biography telling me of his earnest labors for the memory of a man who was certainly unique in his generation, I exclaimed to myself with wonder: " And so it has come to pass after all — this thing which I did not expect to see! " In truth I had never expected the biography of Stephen Crane to appear in my lifetime. My immense pleasure was affected by the devastating touch of time which like a muddy flood covers under a mass of daily trivialities things of value: moments of affectionate communion with kindred spirits, words spoken with the careless freedom of perfect confidence, the deepest emotions of joy and sorrow — together with such things of merely historical importance as the recollection of dates, for instance. After hearing from Mr. Beer of his difficulties in fixing certain dates in the history of Stephen Crane's life I discovered that I was unable to remember with any kind of precision the initial date of our friendship. Indeed life is but a dream — especially for those of us who have never kept a diary or possessed a notebook in their lives.

In this extremity I had recourse to another friend of Stephen Crane, who had appreciated him intuitively almost as soon as I did myself and who is a woman of excellent memory. My wife's recollection is that Crane and I met in

London in October 1897, and that he came to see us for the first time in our Essex home in the following November.

I have mentioned in a short paper written two years ago that it was Mr. S. S. Pawling, partner in the publishing firm of Mr. Heinemann, who brought us together. It was done at Stephen Crane's own desire.

I was told by Mr. Pawling that when asked whom he wanted to meet Crane mentioned two names, of which one was of a notable journalist (who had written some novels) whom he knew in America, I believe, and the other was mine. At that time the only facts we knew about each other were that we both had the same publisher in England. The only other fact I knew about Stephen Crane was that he was quite a young man. I had of course read his *Red Badge of Courage*, of which people were writing and talking at that time. I certainly did not know that he had the slightest notion of my existence, or that he had seen a single line (there were not many of them then) of my writing. I can safely say that I earned this precious friendship by something like ten months of strenuous work with my pen. It took me just that time to write *The Nigger of the Narcissus* working at what I always considered a very high pressure. It was on the ground of the authorship of that book that Crane wanted to meet me. Nothing could have been more flattering than to discover that the author of *The Red Badge of Courage* appreciated my effort to present a group of men held together by a common loyalty and a common perplexity in a struggle not with human enemies but with the hostile conditions testing their faithfulness to the conditions of their own calling.

Apart from the imaginative analysis of his own temperament tried by the emotions of a battlefield Stephen Crane dealt in his book with the psychology of the mass — the army; while I — in mine — had been dealing with the same subject on a much smaller scale and in more specialized conditions — the crew of a merchant ship, brought to the test of what I may venture to call the moral problem of conduct. This may be thought a very remote connection between these two works, and the idea may seem too far-fetched to be mentioned here; but that was my undoubted feeling at the time. It is a fact that I considered Crane, by virtue of his creative experience with *The Red Badge of Courage*, as eminently fit to pronounce a judgment on my first consciously planned attempt to render the truth of a phase of life in the terms of my own temperament with all the sincerity of which I was capable.

I had, of course, my own opinion as to what I had done; but I doubted whether anything of my ambitiously comprehensive aim would be understood. I was wrong there; but my doubt was excusable since I myself would have been hard put to it if requested to give my complex intentions the form of a concise and definite statement. In that period of misgivings which so often follows an accomplished task I would often ask myself who in the world could be interested in such a thing. It was after reading *The Red Badge*, which came into my hands directly after its publication in England, that I said to myself: " Here's a man who may understand — if he ever sees the book; though of course that would not mean that he would like it." I do not mean to say that I looked towards the author of *The Red Badge* as the only man in the world. It would have been stupid and ungrateful. I had the moral support of one or two intimate friends and the solid fact of Mr. W. H. Henley's acceptance of my tale for serial publication in the *New Review* to give me confidence, while I awaited the larger verdict.

It seems to me that in trying to recall my memories of Stephen Crane I have been talking so far only about myself; but that is unavoidable, since this introduction, which I am privileged to write, can only trace what is left on earth of our personal intercourse, which was even more short and fleeting than it may appear from the record of dates, October 1897 — May 1900. And out of that beggarly tale of months must be deducted the time of his absence from England during the Spanish-American War and of his visit to the United States shortly before the beginning of his last illness. Even when he was in England our intercourse was not so close and frequent as the warmth of our friendship would have wished it to be. We both lived in the country and, though not very far from each other, in different counties. I had my work to do, always in conditions which made it a matter of urgency. He had his own tasks and his own visions to attend to. I do not think that he had more friendships to claim him than I, but he certainly had more acquaintances and more calls on his time.

This was only natural. It must be remembered that as an author he was my senior, as I used to remind him now and then with affected humility which always provoked his smiles. He had a quiet smile that charmed and frightened one. It made you pause by something revelatory it cast over his whole physiognomy, not like a ray but like a shadow. I often asked myself what it could be, that quality that checked one's carefree mood, and now I think I have had my answer. It was the smile of a man who knows that his time will not be long on this earth.

I would not for a moment wish to convey the impression of melancholy in connection with my memories of Stephen Crane. I saw his smile first over the tablecloth in a restaurant. We shook hands with intense gravity and a direct stare at each other, after the manner of two children told to make friends. It was under the encouraging gaze of Sidney Pawling, who, a much bigger man than either of us and possessed of a deep voice, looked like a grown-up person entertaining two strange small boys — protecting and slightly anxious as to the experiment. He knew very little of either of us. I was a new author and Crane was a new

INTRODUCTION

arrival. It was the meeting of *The Red Badge* and *The
Nigger* in the presence of their publisher; but as far as our
personalities went we were three strangers breaking bread
together for the first time. Yet it was as pleasantly easy a
meal as any I can remember. Crane talked in his characteristic deliberate manner about Greece, at war. I had
already sensed the man's intense earnestness underlying his
quiet surface. Every time he raised his eyes that secret
quality (for his voice was careless) of his soul was betrayed
in a clear flash. Most of the true Stephen Crane was in his
eyes, most of his strength at any rate, though it was apparent
also in his other features, as for instance in the structure of
his forehead, the deep solid arches under the fair eyebrows.

Some people saw traces of weakness in the lower part of
his face. What I could see there was a hint of the delicacy
of sentiment, of the inborn fineness of nature which this
man, whose life had been anything but a stroll through a
rose-garden, had managed to preserve like a sacred heritage. I say heritage, not acquisition, for it was not and could
not have been acquired. One could depend on it on all occasions; whereas the cultivated kind is apt to show ugly gaps
under very slight provocation. The coarseness of the pro-
fessedly delicate must be very amusing to the misanthrope.
But Crane was no enemy of his kind. That sort of thing did
not amuse him. As to his own temper, it was proof against
anger and scorn, as I can testify, having seen him both
angry and scornful, always quietly, on fitting occasions.
Contempt and indignation never broke the surface of his
moderation, simply because he had no surface. He was all
through of the same material, incapable of affectation of
any kind, of any pitiful failure of generosity for the sake of
personal advantage, or even from sheer exasperation, which
must find its relief.

Many people imagined him a fiery individuality. Certainly he was not cold-blooded. But his was an equable

glow, morally and temperamentally. I would have said the same of his creative power (I have seen him sit down before a blank sheet of paper, dip his pen, write the first line at once, and go on without haste and without pause for a couple of hours), had he not confided to me that his mentality did flag at times. I do not think it was anything more than every writer is familiar with at times. Another man would have talked of his " failing inspiration." It is very characteristic of Crane that I have never heard him use that word when talking about his work.

His phraseology was generally of a very modest cast. That unique and exquisite faculty, which Edward Garnet, another of his friends, found in his writing, " of disclosing an individual scene by an odd simile " was not apparent in his conversation. It was interesting of course, but its charm consisted mainly in the freshness of his impressions set off by an acute simplicity of view and expressed with an amusing deliberation. Superabundance of words was not his failing when communing with those whom he liked and felt he could trust. With the other kind of " friends " he followed the method of a sort of suspended silence. On a certain occasion (it was at Brede Place) after two amazingly conceited idiots had gone away I said to him: " Stevie, you brood like a distant thundercloud." He had retired early to the other end of the room, and from there had sent out, now and then, a few words, more like the heavy drops of rain that precede the storm than growls of thunder. Poor Crane, if he could look black enough at times, never thundered; though I have no doubt he could have been dangerous if he had liked. There always seemed to be something (not timidity) which restrained him, not from within but, I could not help fancying, from outside, with an effect as of a whispered *memento mori* in the ear of a reveler not lost to the sense of grace.

INTRODUCTION

That of course was a later impression. It must be stated clearly that I know very little of Stephen Crane's life. We did not feel the need to tell each other formally the story of our lives That did not prevent us from being very intimate and also very open with each other from the first. Our affection would have been " everlasting," as he himself qualified it, had not the jealous death intervened with her cruel capriciousness by striking down the younger man. Our intimacy was really too close to admit of indiscretions; not that he did not speak amusingly of his experiences and of his hardships, and warmly of the men that helped him in his early days, like Mr. Hamlin Garland for instance, or men kindly encouraging to him, like Mr. Howells. Many other names he used to utter lovingly have been forgotten by me after so many years.

It is a fact that I heard more of his adventures than of his trials, privations, and difficulties. I know he had many. He was the least recriminatory of men (though one of the most sensitive, I should say), but, in any case, nothing I could have learned would have shaken the independent judgment I had formed for myself of his trustworthiness as a man and a friend. Though the word is discredited now and may sound pretentious, I will say that there was in Crane a strain of chivalry which made him safe to trust with one's life. To be recognizably a man of honor carries no immunity against human weaknesses, but comports more rigid limitations in personal relations than the status of an " honorable man," however recognizable that too may be. Some men are " honorable " by courtesy, others by the office they hold, or simply by belonging to some popular assembly, the election to which is not generally secured by a dignified accuracy of statement and a scrupulous regard for the feelings of others. Many remain honorable (because of their great circumspection in the conduct of their affairs) without holding within themselves any of these restraints which are inherent in the character of a man of honor, however weak or luckless he may be.

I do not know everything about the strength of Crane's circumspection, but I am not afraid of what the biography which follows may disclose to us; though I am convinced that it will be free from hypocritical reservations. I think I have understood Stephen Crane, and from my too short acquaintance with his biographer I am confident he will receive the most humane and sympathetic treatment. What I discovered very early in our acquaintance was that Crane had not the face of a lucky man. That certitude came to me at our first meeting while I sat opposite him listening to his simple tales of Greece, while M. S. Pawling presided at the initiatory feast — friendly and debonair, looking solidly anchored in the stream of life, and very reassuring, like a big, prosperous ship to the sides of which we two in our tossing little barks could hook on for safety. He was interested in the tales too; and the best proof of it is that when he looked at his watch and jumped up, saying: " I must leave you two now," it was very near four o'clock. Nearly a whole afternoon wasted, for an English business man.

No such consideration of waste or duty agitated Crane and myself. The sympathy that, even in regard of the very few years allotted to our friendship, may be said to have sprung up instantaneously between us was the most undemonstrative case of that sort in the last century. We not only did not tell each other of it (which would have been missish) but even without entering formally into a previous agreement to remain together we went out and began to walk side by side in the manner of two tramps without home, occupation, or care for the next night's shelter. We certainly paid no heed to direction. The first thing I noticed were the Green Park railings, when to my remark that he had seen no war before he went to Greece Crane made answer:

INTRODUCTION

" No. But the *Red Badge* is all right." I assured him that I never had doubted it; and, since the title of the work had been pronounced for the first time, feeling I must do something to show I had read it, I said shyly: " I like your General." He knew at once what I was alluding to, but said not a word. Nothing could have been more tramp-like than our silent pacing, elbow to elbow, till, after we had left Hyde Park Corner behind us, Crane uttered with his quiet earnestness the words: " I like your young man — I can just see him." Nothing could have been more characteristic of the depth of our three-hour-old intimacy than that each of us should have selected for praise the merest by-the-way vignette of a minor character.

This was positively the only allusion we made that afternoon to our immortal works. Indeed, we talked very little of them at any time, and then always selecting some minor point for particular mention; which, after all, is not a bad way of showing an affectionate appreciation of a piece of work done by a friend. A stranger would have expected more, but, in a manner of speaking, Crane and I had never been strangers. We took each other's work for granted from the very first, I mean from the moment we had exchanged those laudatory remarks alongside the Green Park railings. Henceforth mutual recognition kept to that standard. It consisted often of an approving grunt, sometimes of the mention of some picked-out paragraph, or of a line or only of a few words that had caught our fancy and would, for a time, be applied more or less aptly to the turns of our careless or even serious talks.

Thus, for instance, there was a time when I persecuted poor Crane with the words " barbarously abrupt." They occur in that marvelous story *The Open Boat* and are applied by him to the waves of the sea (as seen by men tossing in a small dinghy) with an inspired audacity of epithet which was one of Crane's gifts that gave me most delight.

How amazingly apt these words are where they stand, anybody can see by looking at that story, which is altogether a
big thing and has remained an object of my confirmed admiration. I was always telling Crane that this or that was
"barbarously abrupt," or begging him not to be so "barbarously abrupt" himself, with a keen enjoyment of the
incongruity; for no human being could be less abrupt than
Crane. As to his humanity (in contradistinction to bar-
barity), it was a shining thing without a flaw. It is possible
that he may have grown at length weary of my little joke,
but he invariably received it with a smile, thus proving his
consistent humanity toward his kind. But, after all, he, too,
liked that story of his, of four men in a very small boat,
which by the deep and simple humanity of presentation
seems somehow to illustrate the essentials of life itself, like
a symbolic tale. It opens with a phrase that anybody could
have uttered, but which, in relation to what is to follow, ac-
quires the poignancy of a meaning almost universal. Once,
much later in our acquaintance, I made use of it to him. He
came on a flying visit to Pent Farm, where we were living
then. I noticed that he looked harassed. I, too, was feeling
for the moment as if things were getting too much for me.
He lay on the couch and I sat on a chair opposite. After a
longish silence in which we both could have felt how uncertain was the issue of life envisaged as a deadly adventure
in which we were both engaged like two men trying to keep
afloat in a small boat, I said suddenly across the width of the
mantelpiece:

"None of them knew the color of the sky."

He raised himself sharply. The words had struck him as
familiar, though I believe he failed to place them at first.
"Don't you know that quotation?" I asked. (These words
form the opening sentence of his tale.) The startled expression passed off his face. "Oh, yes," he said quietly,
and lay down again. Truth to say, it was a time when

neither he nor I had the leisure to look up idly at the sky. The waves just then were too " barbarously abrupt."

I do not mean to say that it was always so. Now and then we were permitted to snatch a glance at the color of the sky. But it is a fact that in the history of our essentially undemonstrative friendship (which is nearly as difficult to recapture as a dream) that first long afternoon is the most carefree instant, and the only one that had a character of enchantment about it. It was spread out over a large portion of central London. After the Green Park the next thing I remember is the Kensington Gardens, where under the lofty and historical trees I was vouchsafed a glimpse of the low mesquit brush overspreading the plum-colored infinities of the great Texas plains. Then after a long tramp amongst an orderly multitude of grimy brick houses — from which the only things I carried off were the impressions of the colored rocks of Mexico (or was it Arizona?) , and my first knowledge of a locality called the Painted Desert — there came suddenly Oxford Street. I don't know whether the inhabitants of London were keeping indoors or had gone into the country that afternoon, but I don't remember seeing any people in the streets except for a figure, now and then, unreal, flitting by, obviously negligible. The wheeled traffic, too, was stopped; yet, it seems, not entirely, because I remember Crane seizing my arm and jerking me back on the pavement with the calm remark: " You will get run over." I love to think that the dear fellow had saved my life and it seemed to amuse him. As to London's enormous volume of business, all I know is that one A B C shop had remained open. We went through the depressing ceremony of having tea there; but our interest in each other mitigated its inherent horrors and gave me a good idea of Crane's stoicism. At least I suppose we had tea, otherwise they would not have let us sit there so long. To be left alone was all we wanted. Neither of us had then a club to entertain the other in. It will give a good notion of our indomitable optimism (on that afternoon) when I say that it was there, in those dismal surroundings, we reached the conclusion that though the world had grown old and weary, yet the scheme of creation remained as obscure as ever, and (from our own particular point of view) there was still much that was interesting to expect from gods and men.

As if intoxicated by this draft of hope we rolled out of that A B C. shop, but I kept my head sufficiently to guess what was coming and to send a warning telegram to my wife in our Essex home. Crane then was, I believe, staying temporarily in London. But he seemed to have no care in the world; and so we resumed our tramping — east and north and south again, steering through uncharted mazes the streets, forgetting to think of dinner but taking a rest here and there, till we found ourselves, standing in the middle of Piccadilly Circus, blinking at the lights like two authentic night-birds. By that time we had been (in Tottenham Court Road) joined by Balzac. How he came in I have no idea. Crane was not given to literary curiosities of that kind. Somebody he knew, or something he had read, must have attracted lately his attention to Balzac. And now suddenly at ten o'clock in the evening he demanded insistently to be told in particular detail all about the *Comédie Humaine*, its contents, its scope, its plan, and its general significance, together with a critical description of Balzac's style. I told him hastily that it was just black on white; and for the rest, I said, he would have to wait till we got across to Monico and had eaten some supper. I hoped he would forget Balzac and his *Comédie*. But not a bit of it; and I had no option but to hold forth over the remnants of a meal, in the rush of hundreds of waiters and the clatter of tons of crockery, caring not what I said (for what could Stephen want with Balzac?), in the comfortable assurance that the Monstrous Shade, even if led by some strange caprice to haunt the long

room of Monico's, did not know enough English to understand a single word I said. I wonder what Crane made of it
all. He did not look bored, and it was eleven o'clock before
we parted at the foot of that monumentally heavy abode of
frivolity, the Pavilion, with just a handshake and a good-
night — no more — without making any arrangements for
meeting again, as though we had lived in the same town from
childhood and were sure to run across each other next day.

It struck me directly I left him that we had not even exchanged addresses; but I was not uneasy. Sure enough, before the month was out there arrived a postcard (from
Ravensbrook) asking whether he might come to see us. He
came, was received as an old friend, and before the end of
the day conquered my wife's sympathy, as undemonstrative
and sincere as his own quiet friendliness. The friendship
that sprang up between them was confirmed by the interest
Crane displayed in our first child, a boy who came on the
scene not quite two months afterwards. How strong was that
interest on the part of Stephen Crane and his wife in the boy
is evidenced by the fact that at the age of six weeks he was
invited to come for a long visit to Ravensbrook. He was in
fact impatiently expected there. He arrived in state, bringing with him not only his parents but also a young aunt, and
was welcomed like a prince. This visit, during which I
suffered from a sense of temporary extinction, is commemo-
rated by a group photograph taken by an artist summoned
with his engine (regardless of expense) to Ravensbrook.
Though the likenesses are not bad it is a very awful thing.
Nobody looks like him or herself in it. The best yet are the
Crane dogs, a very important part of the establishment and
quite conscious of it, belonging apparently to some order of
outlandish poodles, amazingly sedate and yet the most restless animals I have ever met. They pervaded, populated,
and filled the whole house. Whichever way one looked at
any time, down the passage, up the stairs, into the drawing-

room, there was always a dog in sight. Had I been asked on the first day how many there were I would have guessed about thirty. As a matter of fact there were only three, but I think they never sat down, except in Crane's study, where they had their entrée at all hours.

A scratching would be heard at the door, Crane would drop his pen with alacrity to throw it open — and the dogs would enter sedately in single file, taking a lot of time about it, too. Then the room would resound for a while with grunts, sniffs, yawns, heavy flops, followed by as much perhaps as three whole minutes of silence. Then the dogs would get up, one after another, never all together, and direct their footsteps to the door in an impressive and ominous manner. The first arrival waited considerately for the others before trying to attract attention by means of scratching on the bottom panel. Then, never before, Crane would raise his head, go meekly to the door — and the procession would file out at the slowest possible pace. The recurrent sedateness of the proceedings, the utter unconsciousness of the dogs, dear Stephen's absurd gravity while playing his part in those ceremonies, without ever a muscle of his face moving, were irresistibly, exasperatingly funny. I tried to preserve my gravity (or at least to keep calm), with fair success. Only one afternoon on the fifth or sixth repetition I could not help bursting into a loud interminable laugh and then the dear fellow asked me in all innocence what was the matter. I managed to conceal my nervous irritation from him and he never learned the secret of that laugh in which there was a beginning of hysteria.

If the definition that man is a laughing animal be true then Crane was neither one nor the other; indeed, he was but a hurried visitor on this earth on which he had so little reason to be joyous. I might say that I never heard him laugh except in connection with the baby. He loved children; but his friendship with our child was of the kind that put our mutual sentiment, by comparison, somewhere within the arctic region. The two could not be compared; at least I have never detected Crane stretched full length and sustained on his elbows on a grass plot, in order to gaze at me; on the other hand this was his usual attitude of communion with the small child — with him who was called *the Boy*, and whose destiny it was to see more war before he came of age than the author of *The Red Badge* had time to see in all the allotted days of his life. In the gravity of its disposition the baby came quite up to Crane; yet those two would sometimes find something to laugh at in each other. Then there would be silence, and glancing out of the low window of my room I would see them, very still, staring at each other with a solemn understanding that needed no words or perhaps was beyond words altogether. I could not object on any ground to their profound intimacy, but I do not see why Crane should have developed such an unreasonable suspicion as to my paternal efficiency. He seemed to be everlastingly taking the boy's part. I could not see that the baby was being oppressed, hectored over, or in any way deprived of its rights, or ever wounded in its feelings by me; but Crane seemed always to nurse some vague unexpressed grievance as to my conduct. I was inconsiderate. For instance — why could I not get a dog for the boy? One day he made me quite a scene about it. He seemed to imply I should drop everything and go look for a dog. I sat under the storm and said nothing. At last he cried: " Hang it all, a boy ought to have a dog." It was an appeal to first principles, but for an answer I pointed at the window and said: " Behold the boy." . . . He was sitting on a rug spread on the grass, with his little red stocking-cap very much over one eye (a fact of which he seemed unaware), and propped round with many pillows on account of his propensity to roll over on his side helplessly. My answer was irresistible. This is one of the few occasions on which I heard Stephen

Crane laugh outright. He dropped his preaching on the dog theme and went out to the boy while I went on with my work. But he was strangely incorrigible. When he came back after an hour or so, his first words were: " Joseph, I will teach your boy to ride." I closed with the offer at once — but it was not to be. He was not given the time.

The happiest mental picture my wife and I preserve of Crane is on the occasion of our first visit to Brede Place when he rode to meet us at the park gate. He looked at his best on horseback. On that day he must have been feeling well. As usual, he was happy in the saddle. As he went on trotting by the side of the open trap I said to him: " If you give the boy your seat I will be perfectly satisfied." I knew this would please him; and indeed his face remained wreathed in smiles all the way to the front door. He looked about him at that bit of the world, down the green slopes and up the brown fields, with an appreciative serenity and the confident bearing of a man who is feeling very sure of the present and of the future. All because he was looking at life from the saddle, with a good morning's work behind him. Nothing more is needed to give a man a blessed moment of illusion. The more I think of that morning, the more I believe it was just that: that it had really been given me to see Crane perfectly happy for a couple of hours; and that it was under this spell that, directly we arrived, he led me impatiently to the room in which he worked when at Brede. After we got there he said to me: " Joseph, I will give you something." I had no idea what it would be, till I saw him sit down to write an inscription in a very slim volume. He presented it to me with averted head. It was *The Black Riders*. He had never spoken to me of his verse before. It was while holding the book in my hand that I learned that they were written years before in America. I expressed my appreciation of them that afternoon in the usual half a dozen, or dozen, words which we allowed ourselves when

completely pleased with each other's work. When the
pleasure was not so complete, the words would be many.
And that was a great waste of breath and time. I must confess that we were no critics, I mean temperamentally.
Crane was even less of a critic than myself. Criticism is
very much a matter of a vocabulary, very consciously used;
with us it was the intonation that mattered. The tone of a
grunt could convey an infinity of meaning between us.

The articulate literary conscience at our elbow was
Edward Garnett. He, of course, was worth listening to.
His analytical appreciation (or appreciative analysis) of
Crane's art, in the London *Academy* of 17th December,
1898,[1] goes to the root of the matter with Edward's almost
uncanny insight, and a well-balanced sympathy with the
blind, pathetic striving of the artist towards a complete
realization of his individual gift. How highly Edward
Garnett rated Crane's gift is recorded in the conclusions of
that admirable and, within the limits of its space, masterly
article of some two columns, where at the end are set down
such affirmative phrases as: " The chief impressionist of
the age . . . Mr. Crane's talent is unique " . . . and
where he hails him as " the creator of fresh rhythms and
phrases," while the very last words state confidently that:
" Undoubtedly, of the young school it is Mr. Crane who is
the genius — the others have their talents."

My part here being not that of critic but of private friend,
all I will say is that I agreed warmly at the time with that
article which from the quoted phrases might be supposed a
merely enthusiastic pronouncement, but on reading will be
found to be based on that calm sagacity which Edward
Garnett, for all his fiery zeal in the cause of letters, could
always summon for the judgment of matters emotional —

---

[1] Extended and republished in the volume *Friday Nights*. New York:
Alfred A. Knopf; 1922.

as all response to the various forms of art must be in the main. I had occasion to reread it last year in its expanded form in a collection of literary essays of great, now almost historical, interest in the record of American and English imaginative literature. I found there a passage or two, not bearing precisely on Crane's work but giving a view of his temperament, on which of course his art was based; and of the conditions moral and material under which he had to put forth his creative faculties and his power of steady composition. On those matters, as a man who had the opportunity to look at Crane's life in England, I wish to offer a few remarks before closing my contribution to the memory of my friend.

I do not know that he was ever dunned for money and had to work under a threat of legal proceedings. I don't think he was ever dunned in the sense in which such a phrase is used about a spendthrift unscrupulous in incurring debts. No doubt he was sometimes pressed for money. He lived by his pen, and the prices he obtained were not great. Personally he was not extravagant; and I will not quarrel with him for not choosing to live in a garret. The tenancy of Brede Place was held by him at a nominal rent. That glorious old place was not restored then, and the greatest part of it was uninhabitable. The Cranes had furnished in a modest way six or seven of the least dilapidated rooms, which even then looked bare and half-empty. Certainly there was a horse, and at one time even two, but that luxury was not so very expensive at that time. One man looked after them. Riding was the only exercise open to Crane; and if he did work so hard, surely he was entitled to some relaxation, if only for the preservation of his unique talent.

His greatest extravagance was hospitality, of which I, too, had my share; often in the company, I am sorry to say, of men who after sitting at his board chose to speak of him and of his wife slightingly. Having some rudimentary sense of decency, their behavior while actually under the Cranes' roof often produced on me a disagreeable impression. Once I ventured to say to him: " You are too good-natured, Stephen." He gave me one of his quiet smiles, that seemed to hint so poignantly at the vanity of all things, and after a period of silence remarked: " I am glad those Indians are gone." He was surrounded by men who, secretly envious, hostile to the real quality of his genius (and a little afraid of it), were also in antagonism with the essential fineness of his nature. But enough of them. *Pulvis et umbra sunt.* I mean even those that may be alive yet. They were ever hardly anything else; one would have forgotten them if it were not for the legend (if one may dignify perfidious and contemptible gossip by that name) they created in order to satisfy that same obscure instinct of base humanity, which in the past would often bring against any exceptional man the charge of consorting with the devil. It was just as vague, just as senseless, and in its implications just as lying as the mediæval kind. I have heard one of these " friends " hint before several other Philistines that Crane could not write his tales without getting drunk!

Putting aside the gross palpable stupidity of such a statement — which the creature gave out as an instance of the artistic temperament — I am in a position to disclose what may have been the foundation of this piece of gossip. I have seen repeatedly Crane at work. A small jug of still smaller ale would be brought into the study at about ten o'clock; Crane would pour out some of it into a glass and settle himself at the long table at which he used to write in Brede Place. I would take a book and settle myself at the other end of the same table, with my back to him; and for two hours or so not a sound would be heard in that room. At the end of that time Crane would say suddenly: " I won't do any more now, Joseph." He would have covered three of his large sheets with his regular, legible, perfectly controlled handwriting, with no more than half a dozen erasures — mostly single words — in the whole lot. It seemed to me always a perfect miracle in the way of mastery over material and expression. Most of the ale would be still in the glass, and how flat by that time I don't like to think! The most amusing part was to see Crane, as if moved by some obscure sense of duty, drain the last drop of that untempting remnant before we left the room to stroll to and fro in front of the house while waiting for lunch. Such is the origin of some of these gleeful whispers making up the Crane legend of " unrestrained temperament." I have known various sorts of temperaments — some perfidious and some lying — but " unrestrained temperament " is mere parrot talk. It has no meaning. But it was suggestive. It was founded on Crane's visits to town, during which I more than once met him there. We used to spend afternoons and evenings together and I did not see any of his supposed revels in progress; nor yet have I ever detected any after effects of them on any occasion. Neither have I ever seen anybody who would own to having been a partner in those excesses — if only to the extent of standing by charitably — which would have been a noble part to play. I dare say all those " excesses " amounted to very little more than the one in which he asked me to join him in the following letter. It is the only note I have kept from the very few which we exchanged. The reader will see why it is one of my most carefully preserved possessions.

RAVENSBROOK.

OXTED.

17 March. (1899)

" MY DEAR CONRAD: I am enclosing you a bit of MS. under the supposition that you might like to keep it in remembrance of my warm and endless friendship for you. I am still hoping that you will consent to Stokes' invitation to come to the Savage on Saturday night. Cannot you endure it? Give my affectionate remembrances to Mrs. Conrad and my love to the boy.

Yours always,

STEPHEN CRANE.

P.S. You must accept says Cora — and I — our invitation to come home with me on Sat. night.

I joined him. We had a very amusing time with the Savages. Afterwards Crane refused to go home till the last train. Evidence of what somebody has called his "unrestrained temperament," no doubt. So we went and sat at Gatti's, I believe, unless it was in a Bodega which existed then in that neighborhood, and talked. I have a vivid memory of this awful debauch because it was on that evening that Crane told me of a subject for a story — a very exceptional thing for him to do. He called it "The Predecessor." I could not recall now by what capricious turns and odd associations of thought he reached the enthusiastic conclusion that it would make a good play, and that we must do it together. He wanted me to share in a certain success — "a dead-sure thing," he said. His was an unrestrainedly generous temperament. But let that pass. I must have been specially predisposed, because I caught the infection at once. There and then we began to build up the masterpiece, interrupting each other eagerly, for, I don't know how it was, the air around us had suddenly grown thick with felicitous suggestions. We carried on this collaboration as far as the railway time-table would let us, and then made a break for the last train. Afterwards we did talk of our collaboration now and then, but no attempt at it was ever made. Crane had other stories to write; I was immersed deeply in *Lord Jim*, of which I had to keep up the installments in *Blackwood*; difficulties in presenting the subject on the stage rose one after another before our experience. The general subject consisted in a man personating his " predecessor " (who had died) in the hope of winning a girl's heart. The scenes were to include a ranch at the foot of the Rocky Mountains, I remember, and the action I fear would have been frankly melodramatic. Crane insisted that one of the situations should present the man and the girl on a boundless plain standing by their dead ponies after a furious ride (a truly Crane touch). I made some objections. A boundless plain in the light of a sunset could be got into a back-cloth, I admitted; but I doubted whether we could induce the management of any London theater to deposit two stuffed horses on its stage.

Recalling now those earnestly fantastic discussions it occurs to me that Crane and I must have been unconsciously penetrated by a prophetic sense of the technique and of the very spirit of film-plays, of which even the name was unknown then to the world. But if gifted with prophetic sense we must have been strangely ignorant of ourselves, since it must be obvious to anyone who has read a page of our writings that a collaboration between us two could never come to anything in the end — could never even have been begun. The project was merely the expression of our affection for each other. We were fascinated for a moment by the will-of-the-wisp of close artistic communion. It would in no case have led us into a bog. I flatter myself we both had too much regard for each other's gifts not to be clear-eyed about them. We would not have followed the lure very far. At the same time it cannot be denied that there were profound, if not extensive, similitudes in our temperaments which could create for a moment that fascinating illusion. It is not to be regretted, for it had, at any rate, given us some of the most light-hearted moments in the clear but sober atmosphere of our intimacy. From the force of circumstances there could not be much sunshine in it. " None of them saw

the color of the sky! " And alas! it stood already written
that it was the younger man who would fail to make a landing through the surf. So I am glad to have that episode to
remember, a brotherly serio-comic interlude, played under the shadow of coming events. But I would not have
alluded to it at all if it had not come out in the course of my
most interesting talk with the author of this biography that
Crane had thought it worth while to mention it in his correspondence, whether seriously or humorously, I know not.
So here it is without the charm which it had for me but
which cannot be reproduced in the mere relation of its outward characteristics: a clear gleam on us two, succeeded by
the Spanish-American War into which Crane disappeared
like a willful man walking away into the depths of an
ominous twilight.

The cloudy afternoon when we two went rushing all over
London together was for him the beginning of the end. The
problem was to find sixty pounds that day, before the sun
set, before dinner, before the " six forty " train to Oxted, at
once, that instant — lest peace should be declared and the
opportunity of seeing a war be missed. I had not sixty
pounds to lend him. Sixty shillings was nearer my mark.
We tried various offices but had no luck, or rather we had
the usual luck of money-hunting enterprises. The man was
either gone out to see about a dog, or would take no interest
in the Spanish-American War. In one place the man wanted
to know what was the hurry. He would have liked to have
forty-eight hours to think the matter over. As we came
downstairs Crane's white-faced excitement frightened me.
Finally it occurred to me to take him to Messrs. William
Blackwood & Sons' London office. There he was received
in a most friendly way. Presently I escorted him to Charing
Cross, where he took the train for home with the assurance
that he would have the means to start " for the war " next
day. That is the reason I cannot to this day read his tale

The Price of the Harness without a pang. It has done nothing more deadly than pay his debt to Messrs. Blackwood; yet now and then I feel as though that afternoon I had led him by the hand to his doom. But, indeed, I was only the blind agent of the fate that had him in her grip! Nothing could have held him back. He was ready to swim the ocean.

Thirteen years afterwards I made use, half consciously, of the shadow of the primary idea of the " Predecessor," in one of my short tales which were serialized in the *Metropolitan Magazine*. But in that tale the dead man in the background is not a Predecessor but merely an assistant on a lonely plantation; and instead of the ranch, the mountains, and the plains, there is a cloud-capped island, a bird-haunted reef, and the sea. All this the mere distorted shadow of what we two used to talk about in a fantastic mood; but now and then, as I wrote, I had the feeling that he had the right to come and look over my shoulder. But he never came. I received no suggestions from him, subtly conveyed without words. There will never be any collaboration for us now. But I wonder, were he alive, whether he would be pleased with the tale. I don't know. Perhaps not. Or perhaps, after picking up the volume with that detached air I remember so well, and turning over page after page in silence, he would suddenly read aloud a line or two and then, looking straight into my eyes as was his wont on such occasions, say with all the intense earnestness of affection that was in him: " I — like — that, Joseph."

JOSEPH CONRAD

CHAPTER I

SUNNY BLUE

T HE BIRTH of his fourteenth child so distracted Jonathan Townley Crane, D.D., that a letter went unfinished until the next day, when he neatly changed its date from November 1 to November 2, 1871 and concluded: " I was interrupted yesterday and did not send this to the Post Office. Mrs. Crane sends her regards. The new baby is a boy and we have named him Stephen for his ancestor who signed the Declaration."

This naming of the new baby must have been important in the gentle, elderly man's mind. Master Edmund Crane, aged thirteen, took the letter to the post and tumbled on the steep front steps of 14 Mulberry Place, Newark, New Jersey, dreadfully bruising his knee. So Jonathan Crane wrote, a week later: " Mrs. Crane is still alarmed for Ed's knee which continues painful but the baby is very good and quiet. We have named him Stephen because it is an old name in the Crane family." And the family was old in the State of New Jersey, largely lettered on grants of land and the documents of two wars; there were Cranes in the colony when Anne was Queen of England; the Crane who figured in the Continental Congress had his coat armor painted on the flaps of his saddle-bag. Plainly, the good and quiet baby was named with care.

He was good and quiet and frail. In the spring of 1872 Jonathan Crane halted a sermon in the Central Methodist

Church with a blunt statement that Stephen was ill and needed him. There were eight older children living, but Stephen had arrived in this surprising and belated fashion. Sermons and the writing of controversial pamphlets were suspended when Stephen took cold. He took cold with regularity, and his first appearances in the solid society of Mulberry Place were made as an attachment to a monstrous red silk handkerchief which he liked immensely as a plaything and dropped into the aisle of his father's church, cutting the drift of a sermon with wails until somebody brought it back and his parent could go on talking slowly of the necessity of foreign missions and the danger of frivolous amusements to the youth of his sect.

Jonathan Crane came of Presbyterian stock, but it appears that, as an undergraduate of Princeton, he was disturbed about a point in Presbyterian dogma: did the souls of unbaptized infants go to hell? It seemed hardly just. Methodism offered an escape from the problem and gave his controversial abilities fuller scope. He delighted in argument but argument must be kept within the bounds of breeding. Once some cruder Christian flung at him in debate: " Brother Cane never forgets that he is a gentleman! " and Jonathan Crane retorted: " Why should I, sir? "

He wrote a good, severe prose, and some of his ideas remain interesting. He had, like Somerset Maugham, deep doubts as to the intentions of missionaries. The Word must be spread, but " by all means the candidates for the post of missionary should be strictly examined as to their motives in undertaking these duties. We hear grave reports of some who domineer and oppress these childish intellects committed to their care and it can not be doubted that some of our brethren seek to exalt their own station and that some are more interested to clothe the naked bodies of the heathen than to enlighten their minds." And he had doubts about the sanctity of small towns: " I am much more concerned that we should live truthfully and kindly here than that we should be busy in condemning the luxuries and sins of New York City." And he had doubts about the Christian Temperance Union League when four ladies from Ohio came to consult his wife on the subject in 1873: "Mrs. Crane is much impressed by this project. I do not think it exactly practical . . . but they mean very well. Little Stephen has a bad cold this week."

Stephen had become the pet of the family. Only his mother could brush the fair, soft hair which curled a little and he was always shown to callers at the plain brick house. In 1873 young Richard Watson Gilder brought a Miss Rutherford to see Mrs. Crane, and Stephen fell in love with the girl. He was discovered as an ornament of her red skirt when Mr. Gilder was squiring her round the corner of Market Street. Enchanted by the conquest, she came back the next day with a toy for the baby, but Stephen sat disdainfully in a corner and wouldn't look. Whenever Miss Rutherford wore red, though, he was hers completely.

The family taught him his letters and he showed a bright interest in the career of his biggest brother, Jonathan Townley Crane, Junior, cub reporter of the *Newark Advertiser*. Mrs. Crane was the domestic dictionary and Townley would ask her how to spell adjectives of his articles. The baby attended the process and becomes a personage with his first recorded question. He was making symbols on a piece of paper in good imitation of the journalist and lifted up his voice to ask: " Ma, how do you spell *O*? "

In 1874 Dr. Crane's time at the church in Newark was up; the family moved to Bloomington on the Raritan across from Bound Brook, and Stephen was held on a white horse which he remembered twenty years later as a savage beast. But it was no part of Mrs. Crane's theory that a child of hers should be afraid of anything. He was told to stay on the horse and not to be scared. Somebody threw a ball of hard rubber too swiftly into his delicate hands with thin bones; Mrs. Crane wiped his sapphire eyes and told him that he mustn't cry. She took him to the religious frolics at Ocean Grove, where he saw the waves from the beach and had an atrocious dream of black riders on black horses charging at him from the long surf up the shore and so woke screaming, night after night. But, always, he must not cry.

His brothers took him to bathe in the Raritan from a sandbar that jutted into the clear river near the house, although both Miss Frances Willard and Anthony Comstock had lately assured the world that it was a disgusting and unchristian thing for any boy to be seen in an undressed condition outside his own home. However, he was taken to swim in spite of the joint edict, and his brothers were delighted by his ambition. He was left paddling in the shallows, but he wouldn't stay there. He must get out where Will or Ed was splashing and somebody would fish him out just as his head disappeared. Stevie came up strangling but not afraid. He missed the river, it seems, when the Cranes spent a year in Paterson, and made a manful effort to climb down into the Hudson from a pier of Jersey City when his father was preaching there in 1877. The straggling port and a return to Paterson disagreed with him and there is a legend that some doctor advised Jonathan Crane to find duties in high air. So in 1879 the man of sixty left his native state and took charge of Methodism in Port Jervis, over the border.

Port Jervis was then a pretty town, splashed in white houses about the hills that were making northwestern New York known as a game-preserve. Stephen improved and could be sent to school on his eighth birthday. He could read and write and was already learned in the moral adventures of Goody Twoshoes. The school at once annoyed him. Here he was debased and hemmed in by a pack of infants aged five and six. Humiliation dragged him forward and " they tell me that I got through two grades in six weeks which sounds like the lie of a fond mother at a teaparty but I do remember that I got ahead very fast and that father was pleased with me. He used to take me driving with him to little places near Port Jervis where he was going to preach or bury somebody. Once we got mixed up in an Irish funeral near a place named Slate Hill. Everybody was drunk and father was scandalized. . . . He was so simple and good that I often think he didn't know much of anything about humanity. Will, one of my brothers, gave me a toy gun and I tried to shoot a cow with it over at Middletown when father was preaching there and that upset him wonderfully. He liked all kinds of animals and never drove a horse faster than two yards an hour even if some Christian was dying elsewhere. But it is a big job to be presiding elder in a Methodist Conference. He worked himself to death, my people thought."

Jonathan Crane had worked long and hard. He had once been president of the Pennington Seminary and was fond of boys, who, he said, " should be handled with great kindness and care as they have often notions about justice in conduct far beyond their years." So he was much distressed when a lad named nothing less than Samuel Weller wrote from Newark to say that he had been discharged from the shop of a good Methodist for denying hell. The old man took his daughter Agnes down to Newark and hunted other work for Samuel Weller, caught cold on the way back to Port Jervis, and died suddenly, having preached the day before.

He died and terror closed on his last child. People came from everywhere to lament Jonathan Crane. Some country wife stood in the kitchen and sang long hymns. Townley and George and Will and Edmund were in black clothes; his mother sat in the darkened parlor surrounded by whispering women and, somehow, one of Stephen's hands brushed

239

the cold silver handle of the coffin; the full horror of Christian death smashed on the lank child's consciousness. " We tell kids that heaven is just across the gaping grave and all that bosh and then we scare them to glue with flowers and white sheets and hymns. We ought to be crucified for it! . . . I have forgotten nothing about this, not a damned iota, not a shred."

There followed penitential confusions. Mrs. Crane lived for some months in Roseville, outside Newark, and Stephen endured scarlet fever in a boarding-house, but his mother had learned to like Port Jervis, and Stephen had been well there. So he was brought back to the hills and played games patterned on *Black Dick of the Pony Express* and *The Terror of the Sagebrush* with other children. It was a good time — " a bully time " — afterwards. He could make up a game more quickly than the rest of the gang, and brother Edmund gave him a quarter to get his long curls cropped, against Mrs. Crane's orders. She made for him mittens of the brightest red and he had red-topped boots in winter when snow thickened on the paths after sumach's bloody flare had died from the hills. He was very well and happy. Wind whipped up color in his pointed face, and his mother let him go racing in the wake of grown men whose heels rang sharply on frozen earth, running past the house toward the wild glow of fires that reddened the whole night.

II

THE TACTFUL Matthew Arnold, on pilgrimage among us in 1883, told William Forester that Americans should get done with the Civil War as a topic; it was a bore. The surgeon answered: " But so many of us fought in it." The critic playfully retorted: " That's no excuse. War is seldom fruitful or important." He then gave Dr. Forester a signed copy of his note on the translation of Homer's *Iliad*, a poem dealing with the siege of Troy, and went somewhere else. As he recedes in the Victorian mist, it sometimes seems that Matthew Arnold was singularly obtuse, for war happens to be a department of æsthetic available, as is religion, to everybody.

The Civil War ceased physically in 1865 and its political end may be reasonably expected about the year 3000. As heroic legend its history has been curious and remains un- written because of that spiritual censorship which strictly forbids the telling of truth about any American record until the material of such an essay is scattered and gone. How did the men who scorched their youth and scarred their bodies think of those four years, before the easy sentiment of senility clouded down? One knows that in 1868 General Custer's wife noted: " My husband's troopers seem to have absolutely no unkind feeling toward the Secessionists at all and they never talk about their triumphs and exploits. They are always teasing each other about how badly they fought and how many times they ran away. It is distressing to see and hear how little exalted their views are." And one knows that in 1869 at a banquet of the Grand Army a man lifted his glass and toasted: " Everyone that ran at Shiloh, like I did! "

The distress of Mrs. Custer and the boredom of Matthew Arnold meet to supply a conjecture. The war did become a bore to foreigners and literary critics and the common man's attitude toward the myth of a pure, courageous host bent on the Lord's work was truly shocking. The swift cynicism of the American which is the basis of our popular thought rounded promptly on romantic views of the Rebellion. Duval, the leading ballad singer of New York, was hissed from the stage in June of 1865 when he tried to please an audience speckled with soldiers by chanting: *Home Have Come Our Boys in Blue.* The gunbearing animals shouted: " Dry up! " and " Sing something funny! " A pamphlet

241

without signature was issued in Philadelphia before 1866 began and, along with a wholly accurate account of the war's two last months, buyers were invited to believe that General Grant told masculine stories to his staff and that General Sheridan drank whisky before all men out of a silver flask. Both rumors have unofficially persisted to this day. There were songs current attributing mistresses to the popular Northern generals, doubtless due to an adolescent habit of making heroes in all things strenuous, and a New York publisher found that John Esten Cooke's frankly Southern novels, *Surry of Eagle's Nest* and *Mohun* sold most readily in the North although Cooke had not one flattering word to say of the Union forces, and the Virginian himself wrote that " I am surprised by the number of handsome letters that come to hand from former soldiers of the enemy."

The war left almost nothing printed that the literate peasants and clerks who fought would recognize as the truth of their acts. In Cooke's *Mohun* one finds a rather vivid picture of collapsing Richmond with its intrigues, its profiteers, and its frantic pleasures, but the mind of the Virginian gentleman, trained on Lever and Dickens, shrank from the detail of the battlefield, and his tales merely build a Pantheon for the South with central niches rightly reserved to the figures of Lee and Stonewall Jackson. He was honest and not too extravagant, but he was no realist. There is no Northern fiction worth a glance, and narrative reminiscences such as Warren Goss's *Recollections of a Private* were rare. Goss, the best of the narrators, was remorselessly pruned by his publisher even though his book succeeded among boys and soldiers on the ground of its frankness.

The realists sat on fences and the steps of stores in the sprawled depth of the nation and made a topic of the war when political campaigns and labor held no thrill. They might be flogged by acute orators into the ready ferocity of election days and Grand Army rallies, but in 1870 James

Russell Lowell found that stories of the battleline " obscene and horrible " were being told before young boys by the commonplace veterans of Cambridge, Massachusetts, and it is pretty evident that the realists on shady corners preferred war in form. A lad growing up in Ohio saw two men not yet middle-aged come to blows about the rightful ownership of a pair of boots lost in the baking trenches before Vicksburg, and a queerly sensitive child in upper New York may have heard and seen equal ironies. " An American," the sulphurous John Skidmore wrote in 1880, " has only three subjects — his work, the Rebellion and women. Owing to our freedom of speech he can only talk about the first subject in the company of ladies and Mr. Lowell is right in saying that our national conversation is dull as the ladies are most averse to hearing anything truthful about the war." The realists, one imagines, were restricted to the fence and the cornfield. But in 1883 a Miss Olive Brett came upon Stephen Crane digging her small nephew from the sands at Ocean Grove and was told that Johnny was a corpse foolishly planted by the burial squad while he still had a canteen full of whisky on him and that Stephen was his provident comrade retrieving supplies. This is not a child's fancy of battle; Stephen had been listening to some realist; Miss Brett was properly horrified and directly spanked him.

Now, Stephen's brother William is remembered by men who knew him as an undergraduate at Wesleyan as an expert in the strategy of Chancellorsville and Gettysburg. His brother Edmund yearly gave the boy volume after volume of Harry Castleman's " Frank " series. There were *Frank on a Gunboat* and *Frank on the Red River* and *Frank at Mobile Bay* — unpretentious and straightforward tales about a boy in the war written, apparently, for boys. There is no known biography of Harry Castleman, but this oddity makes him interesting. Stephen adored these works. Mrs.

Crane let him look at the monstrous flat tomes of the Harper's history of the Rebellion with their crude and romantic pictures, and on rainy days, when the pictures palled, he poured all the buttons from his mother's store into battalions and regiments that marched and countermarched about his bony knees in an endless conflict, incomprehensible to the family. It was a private war.

There were other books, of course. When he was ten his sister Agnes gave him *Sir Wilfrid's Seven Flights*, a thing printed for children by the moral Routledge, but certainly the least moral book ever issued by his house with that aim, as the hero is a rake and all his adventures end in some frustrated scene. Sir Wilfrid sees El Dorado buried in its own golden sand and flings back the gift of eternal wisdom rather than live forever with the revived Rhodope in her kingdom beneath the pyramids. Stephen liked it and a paragraph of the stiff, ornate prose Tom Hood claimed to have written came to the surface of his thought eighteen years later. *Sir Wilfrid's Seven Flights* must have affected him badly; in the summer of 1882 the kind Miss Brett tried to read him *A Christmas Carol* by Charles Dickens and Stephen went to sleep.

In 1883 Mrs. Crane moved to a small house in Asbury Park, New Jersey. Asbury Park was advertised widely in the nation as a resort quite free from sin, but there was some mistake about that since Stephen was riding the retired circus pony his brother Townley had found for him along a road behind the seaside town in May of 1884 and he saw a white girl stabbed by her Negro lover on the edge of a roadmaker's camp. He galloped the pony home and said nothing to Mrs. Crane although he was sweating with fright.

A strain of secrecy had developed in the slim boy or he knew that his mother's health was failing. Mary Crane had passed sixty now, and no longer insisted that Stephen must

be brave. She worried in the other extreme and told friends:
" Stevie is like the wind in Scripture. He bloweth whither
he listeth." He rode the pony into the ocean, to the admiration of other children, and clung to its bare back while it
did tricks. He also pulled a somewhat older boy, Wallis
McHarg, out of the surf and then told Wallis he would
punch his jaw if the rescued dared to tell Mrs. Crane they
had been swimming on Sunday.

" My mother was a very religious woman but I don't
think that she was as narrow as most of her friends or her
family — " She was Mary Helen Peck, the child and sister
of famous Methodist preachers; " My brothers tell me that
she got herself into trouble before I was old enough to follow proceedings by taking care of a girl who had an accidental baby. Inopportune babies are not part of Methodist
ritual but mother was always more of a Christian than a
Methodist and she kept this girl at our house in Asbury until she found a home somewhere. Mother's friends were
mostly women and they had the famous feminine aversion
to that kind of baby. It is funny that women's interest in
babies trickles clean off the mat if they have never met papa
socially. . . . After my father died, mother lived in and
for religion. We had very little money. Mother wrote
articles for Methodist papers and reported for the [New
York] *Tribune* and the [Philadelphia] *Press*. Every August she went down to Ocean Grove and reported proceedings at the Methodist holy show there. . . . My brother
Will used to try to argue with her on religious subjects such
as hell but he always gave it up. Don't understand that
mother was bitter or mean but it hurt her that any of us
should be slipping from Grace and giving up eternal damnation or salvation or those things. You could argue just as
well with a wave. . . . She was always starting off when
she felt well enough to some big prayer meeting or experience meeting and she spoke very well. Her voice was

something like Ellen Terry's but deeper. She spoke as
slowly as a big clock ticks and her effects were impromptu.
. . . It is in me to think that she did some good work for
the public schools. One of my sisters was a teacher and
mother tried for years to get women placed on the school
boards and to see that whisky was not sold to boys under
age. . . . I used to like church and prayer meetings when
I was a kid but that cooled off and when I was thirteen or
about that, my brother Will told me not to believe in Hell
after my uncle had been boring me about the lake of fire
and the rest of the sideshows. . . . Once when I was fourteen an organ grinder on the beach at Asbury gave me a nice
long drink out of a nice red bottle for picking up his hat
for him. I felt ecstatic walking home and then I was an Emperor and some Rajahs and Baron de Blowitz all at the
same time. I had been sulky all morning and now I was
perfectly willing to go to a prayer meeting and Mother was
tickled to death. And, mind you, all because this nefarious
Florentine gave me a red drink out of a bottle. I have frequently wondered how much mothers ever know about their
sons, after all. She would not have found it much of a
joke. . . ."

She was a woman of intense pride. She had been educated more thoroughly than were most American girls of
her period, and her dignity on the platform of meetings is
remembered. Her last years were stimulated by a project:
the sale of alcohol to children in New Jersey had become a
scandal and she proposed to stop it. It seems that her work
was effective and that the women of other sects admired
her. She has been somewhat wildly described as a religious
maniac, but what is known of her shows a fine mind trained
in a formula.

But the child of her age was to have everything and be
everything. She worried over him when he had troubles
with algebra at school and his brilliance in other studies de-

lighted her. For he was brilliant; the sensitive brain absorbed and recorded swiftly; he seemed to learn without
effort and his memory of words was prodigious. A boy of
fourteen who can use *irascible, pyrotechnic, impartial,* and
memorial correctly in an impromptu essay written for a
prize of a quarter between two hot games of baseball is not
as other American boys of fourteen. He had a passion for
outlandish words and even invented one, a verb, *higgle.*
It appears that to higgle is to behave in the manner of a
school-teacher. . . .

Baseball was now more important than verbs. The game
had crystallized by advertisement and professional playing into the national sport and nuisance. Stephen's thin
fingers began to thicken at the knuckles. Being fifteen he
wrote to Wallis McHarg that he was going to be a professional ball-player. " But ma says it's not a serious occupation and Will says I have to go to college first." Wallis,
aged sixteen, was sympathetic but wrote from Chicago that
Stephen had better go to college. There was an alternative
measure. Why should not Wallis and Stephen enlist in the
army? That would end all difficulties with mothers and so
forth. But baseball had driven out war from Stephen's
imagination and he hung about taller boys playing on the
beach and endured the fate of umpires willingly if he might
be let in for an inning. Before he was sent off to boarding-
school he had a sort of small fame in Asbury Park and
thereabouts: no one could pitch a ball that he would not
catch barehanded.

Baseball made him eminent in the Hudson River Institute
at Claverack, New York. He arrived there in February of
1887 with six pipes which he smoked with some uneasiness
and several volumes of Harry Castleman's romances. The
school was in high repute at the time and was semi-military,
but, curiously, the child who had once been fascinated by
the image of war could not drill well. He had turned into a

wiry lad whose mouth rose at the corners in a charming, remembered grin when he was amused. Some of the boys
thought him sullen because he seldom talked, but baseball
answered for the social defect and there was enough muscle
on his long arms to get him safely through an immense
fight in the spring of 1888. The fight began with Stephen's
assertion that Lord Tennyson's poems were " swill." He
lost a bit of a front tooth in making good his opinion.

His schooldays were to stay in mind with fragrance although " I never learned anything there. American private
schools are not as bad as our public schools, perhaps, but
there is no great difference. I tried to learn French because
my mother thought it important but no foreign language
will ever be my friend. . . . But heaven was sunny blue
and no rain fell on the diamond when I was playing baseball. I was very happy, there."

The summer of 1888 was happy with a new excitement.
He went to work for his brother Townley, collecting items
for Townley's press bureau at Asbury Park. The Jersey
shore was populous now, and fresh colonies sprang up
along the endless beach. So a calamitous bicycle replaced
the pony and Stephen plowed along hot roads, hunting
news of arrivals and departures and the small excitements
of clambakes and sailing parties. A matron from Elizabeth
was told then that " our papers " would be glad to know
how long she was stopping at Avon-by-the-Sea and the *Philadelphia Press* accepted half a column on the history of a
traveled merry-go-round which had come all the way from
San Francisco to please the children of Asbury Park. The
half-column contains seven split infinitives. No earthly
criticism could or ever did make Stephen Crane respect an
infinitive. But he was now a reporter and the boys at
Claverack were impressed by accounts of a gloveless prizefight seen secretly in a barn behind Atlantic City.

He met odd people; he saw, in the riff-raff of cheap en-

tertainers and idlers, those amazing types who are still so
feebly represented in American fiction, the attendants on
shooting-galleries and carrousels, the mercenary pilgrims
of a tiny circus that broke up at Asbury. Stephen begged
five dollars from his mother to start a lost cowboy back to
Wyoming and the man gave him a real revolver alleged to
have slain six Indians. A private education was in progress; it became plain that the world was a wide place filled
with creatures who didn't conform to the rules prescribed
for boys. And a Canadian lady, nameless in the record,
gave him a paper-bound copy of Count Tolstoi's *Sevastopol*.

In February of 1890 a young civil engineer, Porter
Cheney, was convalescent after typhoid in the house of a
relative at Easton, Pennsylvania, where Lafayette College
supplied what excitement there was. Cheney spent his afternoons in a poolroom behind a tobacco-store and a lean,
fair boy played pool very badly against him while they
talked about camping trips in the New York hills and about
books. Cheney took his companion for some remarkable
lounger who had no duties anywhere. At times the boy fell
abstracted and stood trying to balance a cue on the small
tip of his arched nose, without much success. He burned
cigarettes between the fingers of his left hand, seldom putting them to his mouth, and asserted that Count Tolstoi was
the world's foremost writer. There was a lesser fellow
named Flaubert who had written a novel much too long
called *Salammbô*. We are annually told that *Salammbô*
is a firework which failed to explode, but one wonders if
that failure was complete. Those catalogues of jewels,
tribes, gods, and those terminal paragraphs in which the
view is switched so swiftly from one shape to a thousand,
from death to a setting sun or the sound of something far
away? If imitation is flattery, the dead firework has been
flattered. Well, he had read *Salammbô* and did not think
very well of the Carthaginian Princess, but this was better

writing than the English could do. No, he didn't like Robert Louis Stevenson and he didn't know anything about Henry James. The engineer was impressed, somehow, and described this lad to his sister in several letters. The faculty of Lafayette remembered Stephen as a tow-headed, pleasant boy who preferred boxing to study. Stephen took home the pin of a fraternity, Delta Upsilon, and in June of 1890 captained a mixed team of lads and grown men against a like team from Atlantic City. The score was 9 to 0 in Stephen's favor.

Summer of 1890 held other significant details in American civilization. Anthony Comstock, agent of the Society for the Suppression of Vice, invaded the shop of Eugene Caret, a new art-dealer on Broadway, and bade him take from a show-window the photograph of a statue by Rodin. Monsieur Caret was so scared that he sold his stock and retired from New York City by the next liner. He was later bewildered to hear that the Metropolitan Museum had bought a copy of *L'Age d'Airan* and that it was public to any stare, without a figleaf, in the main court of the Museum. In July Miss Frances Willard committed written mayhem on the person of Richard Watson Gilder for allowing the word " rape " to be printed in the *Century* because a magazine meant to be read by " Christian women " had no right to soil their eyes with such immundicities. Mr. Gilder carefully assured the great reformer that the American public was not wholly composed of susceptible Christian women, but he got back no answer. Frances Willard had spoken and that was enough. In August the editor of the *Atlantic Monthly* informed a young man in Topeka, Kansas, that " New York has now become the capital of art and letters in the United States." The issue of *Scribner's* for August contained " A Walk Up the Avenue " by Richard Harding Davis, already known as the author of *Gallagher*.

Herewith Davis mounted into celebrity as gracefully as he might have swung his fine body in its handsome dress to the cushions of a waiting cab. He rode, a figure of pleasant sophistication and fresh good humor, among passengers who lacked those qualities precisely, and boys laboring with manuscript looked up and saw a star.

Townley Crane got for Stephen the post of correspondent to the *New York Tribune* in the town of Syracuse, and Syracuse University was pleasant enough after Mrs. Crane consented to a change from engineering to " belles-lettres." Stephen wanted to be a writer and his mother was willing. He must be good and always independent, always honest. She wrote these orders in one of her last letters. There was little left for Mary Crane but a trip to a congress of women in Boston, a few days of illness, and a painless end in a hospital. Stephen would make for her kindness a small monument and would miss her silently.

He lounged at Syracuse in the back room of a restaurant and other freshmen were impressed by a classmate who sold sketches to the *Detroit Free Press* and who assured them that the police court was the most interesting place in Syracuse. He got notice from the faculty by telling a professor that he disagreed with Saint Paul's theory of sin and seriously shocked the wife of another authority by declining to meet Miss Frances Willard at her house for the reason that he thought Miss Willard a fool. A boy who had no reverence for sacred characters must have been notable in a Methodist university, and spring made him famous. The baseball team had never had such a shortstop and, after a vehement argument, never so young a captain. It is legendary that he was offered a place on a great professional team, but it is certain that his friends all knew Crane was going to be a writer. Writing, he said, over coffee and cigarettes in the restaurant, was a business like any other.

One trained one's mind to observe and a man should be able to say something " worth while " about any event. American writers were not " sincere " and American magazines were " no good." As for college, it was a darned nuisance and he was glad to be done with all things academic in June of 1891.

CHAPTER II

ROMANTIC MOVEMENTS

THERE was an old house on Twelfth Street which belonged, in 1891, to a rowdy Italian merchant who
had adorned its big spaces to please an Irish dancer,
and the union of such talent had produced a wonderful,
gay result of gilded chairs and flaming tapestries in a drawing-room that glowed, by night, under the jets of a monstrous chandelier. The flag of Ireland was effected in
colored tiles above the fireplace, and elsewhere the house
was quite as remarkable. But in September of 1891 this
polychromatic paradise was rented to an invalid lady whose
companion was an unsuccessful contralto, trained in Europe, a tall darkly pretty girl named Helen Trent.

Miss Trent left Avon, New Jersey, in the first week of
September and came to rejoin the ailing Mrs. Potter. She
found waiting a telegram from Avon: Stephen Crane was
sorry that he had not seen Miss Trent to say good-by. Miss
Trent had an idea that this might be a silent boy who played
baseball on the beach at Avon, but she knew nothing of
him and was busy, nursing her friend's asthma and slowly
packing for a journey to Switzerland. Then on the 10th a
servant brought word that Mr. Crane was calling and she
went down to find a fair, untidy youth in black clothes,
whose eyes seemed brown in the glory of the chandelier.

She thought him handsome, shy, and dull. The call went

on for warm, indifferent hours while she tried to talk and he stared. Then he startled her. Had she seen Hamlin Garland, the new writer from the West, while he lectured at Avon? [1] She had not, but she asked what the Westerner looked like.

" Oh," Crane said, " like a nice Jesus Christ."

This was not in the conversational area of the year 1891. The next morning Miss Trent had from Crane a letter of a dozen sheets, written at the old Fifth Avenue Hotel. He was suddenly informative; his brother Will had a baby named Helen; he was a reporter, himself; what was Miss Trent's favorite color? Did she like flowers and was she fond of dogs? He came, that night, to have these important questions answered and kept coming, as the girl was pleased by his slow talk of camping trips in Sullivan County and of curious people met on the Jersey coast. Then, one evening, he brought a terribly bruised and plastered eye. He had been sitting in a saloon of the Bowery and a thrown bottle had landed on him. The accident did not amuse Miss Trent and she at once retired into the attitude of girls who find themselves comfortably older than admiring boys. Crane had already revealed some shocking opinions: a Negro could be handsome, even without the " classic profile " demanded by a world soaked in the art of Leighton and Poynter; American religion was " mildewed "; he found Buddhism interesting; he saw no reason why a young actress with a cottage at Avon couldn't go swimming at dawn, when the beach was empty, without a bathsuit. Miss Trent took the emphatic posture of American gentlewomen and forbade him to go near the Bowery. She had sung in charitable concerts there and it was a slum as vile as anything in Paris or Munich. It was not " nice " of Crane to go there. (The middle-aged lady who then was Helen Trent recalls her use of the word.) She spoke until Crane's lean body reared in

[1] See *A Son of the Middle Border.*

his chair and he exploded with: " Hully gee! " The Bowery
was the only interesting place in New York. Nobody had
written anything " sincere " about its people. He was going
to write a book some time soon about the Bowery and it was
going to be a sincere book and he must see how these people
lived and what they thought. Miss Trent broke in with protests. She was, for the hour, the composite portrait of all
well-bred young women who have tried to explain proper
art and letters to American artists. Why must he write any
such book? Who wanted to read about such people? That
Ferdinand Brunetière had lately stated: " The first temple
of the young creative mind is the abyss " was not within
her knowledge, nor within Crane's. So they wrangled unhappily and Crane walked out of the house, at last, leaving
the word *hypocrite* in air. But he mailed a note, dated from
the ferry to Jersey City: " I shall come back tomorrow night
and we can start all over again. Yours sincerely, Stephen
Crane."

So they argued and she sat playing Chopin for him at the
black piano while he leaned on its side and sometimes
hummed a barytone accompaniment to the wild bars. . . .
He was enmeshed, one may guess, in an adventure that fell
as fantastic on the mind of nineteen years spent in the lazy
pleasantness of small towns and the placid medley of
Asbury Park's crowded summer. The music pealed and
chanted in this gaudy chamber where " great folds of lace
swept down in orderly cascades . . . the colossal chandelier, gleaming like a Siamese head-dress . . . caught subtle flashes from the gilt and tempestuous silk." He had seen
handsome rooms, of course, in Newark and in Syracuse,
but he had never seen Latin profusion joined to Celtic vulgarity with a lovely girl in the pooled lights and colors, singing songs in the French that he could not read or understand. He was not unconscious, though, of the theatrical
base in all this, for when she took him up to her guardian's

boudoir of shrieking velvets and enamels, he asked: " When will the stage hands take it away? "

There seemed to be no cause for mention of her betrothed young surgeon, studying at Guy's Hospital in London, and Miss Trent was not wearing an engagement ring while she drove with Crane in the warm night through Central Park or when he took her to a play at Wallack's Theater. They did not talk of books after a quarrel on the merits of Robert Louis Stevenson, but she sewed a button on his coat and tried to make him brush the fair, limp hair back from the width of his forehead and he lighted her cigarettes although he did not then approve of these for a lady. He was hoping for a place on the *Herald* and day after day he came to town and night after night he lounged on the piano, hearing the music of Chopin.

LAKEVIEW, N. J.
September 18, '91.

Dear Miss Trent:

I have found out something that you should know at once and will be up this evening to tell you.

Yours, S. C.

He came in solemnly excited. Did her guardian know that this house belonged to the very evil Mr. X and that the Italian had furnished it for a " person "? Well, Mrs. Potter should take her away at once; people might not understand that the house was merely rented. . . . Miss Trent woke up, honestly surprised and touched, with a lover on her hands. She thanked Crane and sent him away and next evening she was not at home. But the morning mail brought an undated scrawl on a leaf from a yellow notebook:

" Your window was lighted all last night but they said you were not in. I stood and looked at your window until a policeman came and made me go away. But I came back and looked until my head was just a sponge of lights. Please do not treat me like this. Nothing else counts but that."

It frightened her. He came on the evening of September 20th while she was dressing to dine with friends in Sixtieth Street. Rain had fallen and Crane went out to find a hansom, then drove with her up the long channel of Fifth Avenue where white stone just patched the solid face of dim, chocolate buildings that rose above a pavement always blue under the lamps that sent, perhaps, jogging pulses of light on her bare arms. She remembers him quite silent as the hansom moved and when she came home late at night, he had left another note:

"You have the most beautiful arms I ever saw. You never should have to wear dresses with sleeves. If I could keep your arms nothing else would count. It would not matter if there was nothing else to hope for in the world or if there was no more world. In dreams, don't you ever fall and fall but not be afraid of anything because somebody safe is with you? I shall be here tomorrow. I must get back to Ed's house, now."

So he went off on the dreary trip to his brother Edmund's house at Lakeview, outside Paterson, where he was teaching lads of the neighborhood to play tearing football on Saturdays and writing furiously through nights in an attic turned to a study for his use. He came back, on September 21st, and Miss Trent strolled nervously into the florid drawing-room to tell him that she was to be married in London, soon. Crane gave a quick gasp and lifted both hands to his face. Then he spun and walked out of the house, permanently. In January of 1900, when an Englishman pointed out the celebrated Stephen Crane, she saw him across the flare of a London theater without knowing why he was celebrated. But in *The Black Riders*, on the eleventh page:

257

STEPHEN CRANE

" Should the wide world roll away,
Leaving black terror,
Limitless night,
Nor God, nor man, nor place to stand,
Would be to me essential,
If thou and thy white arms were there,
And the fall to doom a long way."

II

ANOTHER romantic movement had accomplished itself
while Crane grew up. Three days before he was born, sheriffs came to the house of William Marcy Tweed, in New
York, and tenderly put under arrest the tall, obese stevedore
who had stolen from the city one hundred and fifty million
dollars. His fall was largely the act of a disgusted Irish
gambler, and gelatinous grandees of New York sat in some
confusion while the trial was forced along by a young Yankee lawyer. Many of the city's foremost men had privately
done Tweed's bidding and had publicly shaken his gouty
fingers while he lolled in his carriage at the curb of Wall
Street. But Tweed's fall advertised radiantly the wealth
and rascality of the plundered town's ruling strata, and tiny
journals inland printed with due exaggeration the list of his
pleasures and palaces. The tawdry seaport was suddenly
Babylon in the mouths of rural preachers, and dealers in
pornography now shifted the scene of revels from Boston
or Philadelphia to New York. The city's population swelled
between 1871 and 1873 by a hundred thousand and of this
earned increment it was known that hundreds were people
of means who now gazed in real awe at the stiff, timid native
aristocrats. New York took on, in the nation's eye, the combined aspect of an eating-house and a gilded lupanar irresistible to the peasant mind. There followed a gradual
welding of the parochial rich with a fresh plutocracy ready

to outdo the pomps of the first Belmont, and soon the child of this match was a glittering amalgam which, toward 1890, complied with the custom of all adolescents and fell in love with itself.

Metropolitan society of the nineteenth century's last decade had a color of compound paradox. It was metropolitan only in location; it viewed with amazing disdain the aristocracies of other cities and instead of drawing in their wealth and fashion it ignored them. It was plainly a society of capital for it permitted family after family once eminent to sink from its midst unable to endure the monetary strain of entertainment. Yet it clung with ferocity to Washington Irving's pleasant myth of a Knickerbocker lordship while the descendants of the real patroons quietly took themselves elsewhere or fell into humdrum obscurity as the high world became a grocer's window filled with quarrelsome fruit. Money talked so loudly that small satirists of *Puck* and *Life* were not deceived by the grand gesticulations of the aged Ward McAllister and the younger Berry Wall. The man in the street knew that descent had the least possible part in this feckless, handsome show. But the whole movement was ruled by a sickly æstheticism: these vulgarians went laboring and stumbling after a dim ideal. They hunted grace.

This grace was altogether external and pictorial. A movement somewhat similar was afoot in France and England, the available models, where capitalism wooed a real aristocracy and wedded it effectively with all the blessings of journalism on the tinseled bed. In meek rapture from afar the ruling women of New York could observe the impatient gayeties of the Prince of Wales and might imitate with feeble discretion the balls of Madame de Sagan. " Anglomania " was nothing more than a rather wavering effort to improve the American picture. Now antiquaries found a market for chairs of stale oak and tapestries that might be

Gobelins were carted to new country houses — some of which, strangely, were discovered to have long been owned by their possessors. Meanwhile gold service flashed at dinners given to successive French painters who pronounced American women the loveliest of earth. In 1896 it was seen with delight that eighty ladies appeared crowned with jewels in the boxes of the Opera and in 1897 one of them offered to remit the rents of certain cottages beside her park on Long Island if they would let her replace the tin of roofs with English thatch. But the American winds blew the thatch away. . . .

Men were seldom powerful in this scented herd, but there did tower one commanding female shape. Documents well display the alert and vigorous Caroline, wife and then widow of William Astor, a woman truly charitable who could conceive a gay and liberal grouping of her allies. She so far ruled the manifold fluctuations of her tribe that when old McAllister mentioned " our social leader " housewives of the midlands knew just who was meant. If rivals did not concede that she was absolute, the baser world did, and she addressed herself in the third person to editors of newspapers. It was reported that she was subtle, wise in the mysteries of arts and crafts, and it is true that she would verbally singe a committee for the stupid adornment of a public hall, but she would not permit the same committee to consult John La Farge because the colorist was a " professional painter." She liked to laugh, but she made known her surprise that her son should go to dine with Mark Twain. She was an admirer of Ouida and read *Moths* five times, so she must have been literate, yet, hearing that Miss Alice Duer had begun to publish poems, she cried: " But the girl's not at all plain! " and seated in London beside Harold Frederic she found the novelist amusing, so was moved to ask who were his friends.

" Mostly writers and artists."

" Indeed," said Mrs. Astor, after a musing period, " that must be very strange! "

She lived on until she could be described in a popular romance as an old, old lady drowsing on a golden throne, but when she died and appraisers were busy with her goods, an astonished public read that the chairs of her ballroom might have been owned by anyone and that the carpet of her famous, dreaded staircase, threadbare and faded, had no more a value.

If all critical elements are carefully shorn from a society by the will of its rulers, it can remain comfortably in love with its own flesh, and it did. The smart world of New York's great decade failed to discover in the patronage of its superiors the last flavor of aristocratic contempt. In those bright rooms, agitated for weeks by the assertion, without exhibition, of fresh rosebuds pinned to the garters of young beauty, where were hung pictures by Rembrandt alongside the trash of Marcus Stone and Debat-Ponsin, the native artists, the native critics had no place. It was understood that they existed, probably somewhere in the shadowy void where vague hordes were known to be crying out for the abolition of wine, wealth, and unwedded love. But a great lady phrased the objection of her group quite neatly in 1897 to a traveling Briton: " On the whole, Sir William, don't you think that reformers and writers always make things unpleasant? " And a little later William Dean Howells was driven to muse: " It sometimes seems to me that the wealthy class of New York fights shy of the writer and artist just as a schoolboy is timid before an older man. This was not true of Boston. Mrs. James Fields and a dozen other intelligent women were more than hospitable. . . . A young writer in New York may be given tea and a bun by his publisher's wife but the city is not hospitable to talents unless they come from Europe. Nor is the European artist always welcome. . . . You asked me last year what the rich New Yorker reads. He reads the newspapers." Precisely. If the Narcissus read anything, it read the newspapers, and its whole notion of things came from that unsubstantial, flashy medium. The paradox was perfect: a society bragged of its isolate refinement, and its ideas were those of the street. So in 1903 an acidulous Russian Ambassador noted that New York's high world was " *une servante qui porte assez gauchement les robes de sa dame* " and the same Count Cassini also wrote that the matrons of the city had not heard of the printing press save as an instrument to list " their stupid names."

Who doubts that such an attitude was profoundly influential? The wealthy class of the nation's largest city was a natural mark for imitation. The capital of arts and letters had no welcome for the artist, native or foreign, unless he had been stamped by the press, its guide, as an eminence. He was permitted to exist upon such terms as he could make with his environment, and a realm of cheap lodgings, cheap restaurants, and cheap journals lay ready to provide that environment unless he had cash in pocket to keep him elsewhere. For another romantic movement was afoot: the romance of journalism as the school of letters was well established now, and the delusion brought boys scurrying to the offices of the New York papers in droves. Had not Richard Harding Davis, Julian Ralph, Edward Townsend, and, more brilliantly still, Rudyard Kipling emerged from that battering apprenticeship? So journalism took hold of the national fiction and for a decade fiercely attuned it to the key of commonplace perceptions and to the flattery of an inferior city.

The tone of the press, in the decade of this history, was flattering to all things visible in New York save administration as contrived by the Democratic party. Spasmodically, in the cramped critical departments of the *Sun* or the *Herald*, a Mayo Hazeltine or Charles Meltzer might cry against some popular novel or deride the cult of suave goddesses shoved forward by the Frohmans and Palmers in banal rotation on the stages of Broadway. Everybody could see, though, that these were the gruntings of discontented and sour critics. The word *critic* itself was rather shunned. The word *reviewer* was brought into being; it was a milder, more pleasant generality. One reviewed the spectacle of the city's superb existence and was thrilled by such immensities of life and color. Manhattan became a crowned woman in the frescoes of new hotels and if James Huneker, in the pages of a perky monthly called *Mdlle. New York*, chose to hint that Manhattan really resembled a customshouse clerk, why, his magazine had its reward and did not live long. If the *Arena* kept insisting that the public schools were abominable and that the public libraries were maladministered antiques, the audience of Flower's dull ravings was mostly made up of school-teachers and reformers. Meanwhile the show was good. Victor Herbert's increased orchestras made silky melody in theaters where shoulders were naked at last, after a long discussion of a gentlewoman's right to dress as she pleased. Each autumn the groomed horses trotted in the New Madison Square Garden, after football games had filled New York with roarings and with the sight of youth pouring down to the festival with chrysanthemums in its coat of tawny English cloth. Each winter the Opera dazzled provincials and some people listened to the voices of the de Reszkés, of the soft-eyed Schalchi, of the patrician Emma Eames. These things were popular and therefore good and the newspapers reported them in affable detail never smirched by realism. The Sunday supplement was invented and suburban householders could see in hazy photographs the very bathrooms of the obliging rich who also let heaped gifts at the weddings of their daughters appear for the contemplation of brides who were not American beauties plucked by European noblemen from the profitable stem. All brides were ravishing and all weddings gorgeous in that strange decade, just as all parades of militia and all civic ceremonies were " inspiring sights." The Narcissus tilted a mirror to his visage and beamed with condescension on an envious land.

It is plain that this pervasive flattery must have been, in some part, due to ignorance and to a lack of any valuing sense. But that its root was the congenital cowardice of the educated American there can be no doubt at all. A movement in counterpoint was sounding in the magazines, new and old. The whole history of the decade's mild revolt against the quality of American life is bound for display in the slick paper of the *Century, Harper's, Scribner's, McClure's,* and the *Cosmopolitan,* revived under John Walker to startle editors by its mad varieties. Revolt showed first in the illustrations which swung out of the inane traditional woodcuts and dreary imitations of Maclise into the stony veracities of Howard Pyle and the smooth skill of Joseph Pennell and of Radford Brennan, Pennell's superior in draftsmanship, his inferior in assemblage. People suddenly looked like people, it was said, and if the general taste hung to the domestic pleasantness of Charles Gibson and Howard Christy, there were other hands at work. Here was Abbey's feathery line. Here were Low, Linson, Sonntag, Castaigne, and the earlier Maxfield Parrish. Peter Newell and A. B. Frost made farces of the respectable commoner's clothes, and his face took on a satiric emptiness under their touch. Here, little noticed, were the photographic exactitudes of Ernest Peixotto and Jay Hambidge. Taste moved forward boldly and a children's monthly, *St. Nicholas,* offered derivations from the art of Georges Seurat to a public which, like that of his own country, had never heard of him.

In this pictorial progress the *Century* had taken the lead and it now led on in a new venture. There began to be a mild, most courteous analysis of the American scene and Richard Gilder bravely introduced, through his magazine, essayists and historians whose work was not devised to flatter any element of the nation. He had already made himself responsible for an impartial history of the Civil War and he was a man of defined political tendencies. The cloudy stir to be christened " the reform movement " found an ally in him and he conciliated intellectual groups by critical matter far outside the general taste. But the charming intelligence of the man was haunted by some barren theory of good form. He would allow the honorable studies of Walter Wyckoff, those first visions of the American laborer, to pass from his desk to the office of *Scribner's* because *The Workers* seemed flamboyant and he shrank from Josiah Flynt's sketches in crime because their subjects were " sordid." It is uncanny that Gilder, first of the native editors, should have recognized the talent of Jack London, as he did. The success of *McClure's Magazine*, with its profanity, its bad poems, and its vivacity, passed his understanding, but he made of the *Century* a stable, enduring creature and its life is not yet spent.

These editorial powers, with their growing public, knew that eyes were turned to the artistic whirlpool of the European world. They saw that publishers found profit in translations of Zola. Some plane of the United States was soothed and saddened by Loti's wailing grace. There was an outcry against unwholesome foreign fiction, and even Rudyard Kipling, already sacred, was now and then attacked. But in the midst of these noises Howells and his local rival, Mayo Hazeltine, praised Russian writing and implored their admirers to read Thomas Hardy. Was there, then, something viable in the mode that Hazeltine had named " stark realism "? There might be and one can follow, in that decade, two parallel motions. There was the glib, smoothly moving fiction of the reportorial school and there was a minor realism by permission, under surveillance. This realism was hedged and neatly confined both by editorial policy and by the temper of its friends. Howells was its father and it stayed well within his orbit, daring little and effecting not much more than a break with the moralities and prettiness of that precedent fiction which has left the single name of Bret Harte, an artist of whom it has been surprisingly discovered since his death that he imitated Dickens, quite as though Harte's critics while he lived had not noticed the habit. Harte's influence, too, survived in this quasi-realism. The neat pattern of his product had stamped itself too heavily in the editorial brain, where it persists. But intermittently arrived in print stories of commonplace people, and the public welcomed this placid observation of sempstresses soured by age, of bored country women, of dirty stokers in Pennsylvania mills. The observation was commonplace as were the themes. Here were dignity and sincerity, with Hamlin Garland's Western sketches and Sarah Jewett's acid etchings to add some genuine, memorable achievements in brief narrative.

Yet here came a boy whose visual sense was unique in American writing and whose mind by some inner process had stripped itself of all respect for those prevalent theories which have cursed the national fiction. He was already an ironist, already able to plant his impressions with force, and reckless of the consequent shock to a public softened by long nursing at the hands of limited men. Upon what section of the visible scene would he commence his sardonic operations? Perhaps it was simple recoil from the lukewarm current of letters, or perhaps it was a deeper curiosity that took Stephen Crane headlong and resolute into the slums.

CHAPTER III

MAGGIE:
A GIRL OF THE STREETS

NEW YORK was proud of the Bowery precisely as
a child is proud of a burned thumb, and the fame
of the long, tawdry street grew by rumors of incredible debauchery until in 1890 one Ahearn, a publican,
found it worth his while to post youths in the Grand Central
Station who offered arriving men to " Show you the Bowery
for a dollar, mister? " with the understanding that trips
through the glamorous sink would end in supper at Ahearn's
saloon, where ruffians duly arranged battles among the
tables and prizefighters were bred. But there was nothing
fictitious in the poverty of the region, and the soberly industrious Continental Jews who would finally tame the
quarter by mere numbers were still in a passive minority.
The name " Bowery " had been made inclusive: all adjoin-
ing streets, alleys, and squares held Bowery boys and
Bowery girls in popular report. The alleys, too, were plentiful and buildings of wood crazily leaned above fissures
black by night, as part of the Democratic revenues rose
from the profit of lighting and cleaning small lanes which
were never lighted and so seldom cleaned that corpses often
were unearthed in piles of rubbish months after their relatives had given up a hunt for some vanished entity. The
Bowery's self had an honest average of three saloons to the

block and its nightly glitter raked the eye with raw tones of green and red in the glazed doors of these solacing haunts. Laborious prostitutes strolled from sunset to dawn on selected beats and many moved westward from the economy of lodgings on Third Avenue to the public halls of Broadway and Fourteenth Street.

The Bowery, though, was funny. Comedians aped its dress on the stage of Koster and Bial's improper vaudeville and speakers at banquets recited Bowery jokes. There was no other slum in America so settled of speech and habit. It was supposed that the Bowery invented words. In 1890 the word *jay* was current as a Bowery coinage in contemptuous reference. The word was actually from the South, of course, and its original employment was the sentence: " Naked as a jaybird," much used by begging tramps who spent the warm season in the North. Patches of English slang floated in the talk of the district and blossomed as native when reporters drew on this reservoir of unchaste diction. Stephen Crane found " on the turf " a convenient evasion of " prostitute," for instance, and was accused of inventing a meaning known in London before 1870. But the Bowery language was humorous, as are a dozen dialects in which the fierce, defensive cynicism of the illiterate American takes on color and shape. There was a choppy rhythm in the speech from which the sound of *th* had been drawn away. Many vowels were washed over so briskly that it took experience to tell whether they had been pronounced at all by some hasty group of lads hanging for a breath together while the policeman's back was turned. For the Bowery was full of youth that lived without license to draw pay and the poor preyed comfortably on the poor.

In January of 1892 Wallis McHarg came to New York, ready to sail for Germany and the study of medicine. He found Crane's address by way of the *New York Herald's* office and invaded a house of far East 23rd Street where

MAGGIE: A GIRL OF THE STREETS

Crane was sharing the big bedroom of some young actor.[1]
At once Wallis must be shown the Bowery, and Crane led
his friend down its reaches with a happy air of proprietor-
ship. Here was the saloon where he had got a black eye.
This was the dance-hall wrecked by a gang of sailors from
the Brooklyn Navy Yard who had been wrongfully expelled.
There was a notorious procurer and that girl was supposed
to be the daughter of a wealthy family somewhere uptown
who came here for the curious pleasure of attracting suitors
and then making them quarrel while she went to refuge in
the shadow of some policeman. Then Crane abruptly said:
" I want you to read my book."

McHarg had no pretensions in letters. He was the very
practical son of a roaming family, not much given to reading. He took the pile of manuscript to his room at the Gilsey
House and looked through its neat, tall writing with bewilderment. No character had a name in the short story of
a girl seduced by a bartender, and the use of " God damn! "
struck him as impossibly accurate. Here was something
strange, new, and outlandish. Next day he told Crane that
nobody would print such a story and that the people should
have names. And when had Crane written this?

" I wrote it in two days before Christmas," said Crane,
coolly, and then admitted that his brother William also
thought the people must have names. The lawyer had seen
the defect of the experiment. These characters stirring in
a stupid mist and almost without physical being would confuse readers. They were " the girl," " the girl's mother,"
her brother, her lover, and out of this original framework
something remains. The " woman of experience and audacity " was never thereafter christened.

McHarg went off to Germany appalled and thrilled. He
had read the curt, compressed tales of the Wyoming Valley
which Crane sent him in clippings from the *New York*

[1] Probably William Riley Hatch.

Tribune, but he had never taken " Stevie " seriously as an author bound to be famous. Now the younger boy had done something that was at least extraordinary and would create noise if anybody published it. Late in February he had a note, dateless and without address. Brother William had named the book. It was now " Maggie: A Girl of the Street," and in a postscript: " The *Herald* fired me last week."

Crane's shadowy term with the *New York Herald* exactly prophesied his whole career as a journalist. He could not report. Apparently he did not even try to report. Of what use to any newspaper was an impression of impatient horses kicking " grey ice of the gutter into silvery angles that hurtled and clicked on frozen stone " when the boy had been sent to get the facts of a large and important fire? The stamping horses hitched to the engine and the stolid movement of a young fireman stepping back from a falling wall, these things took his eye and went on paper. The name of the building's owner, its number on the street, and the question of its insurance simply wafted from the brain behind the plunging blue eyes. Nor could a city editor accept an interview with a prominent alderman when that dignitary, under charges of corruption, " sat like a rural soup tureen in his chair and said, ' Aw! ' sadly whenever ash from his cigar bounced on his vest of blood and black." It is not now to be proved that the *Herald* discharged Crane. He was probably taken to task for some fantasy on an alderman or an actress and dismissed himself.

But a boy of twenty, loose in the world filled with improvident and hopeful other boys, would not much care, and *Maggie* was ready for high inspection. Crane got himself a note of introduction from his brother Townley and appeared at the offices of the *Century.* Richard Watson Gilder knew all the Cranes and knew that this must be young Stephen before he read the note. " He was thin and his blue eyes seemed enormous. He sat wrapped in a grey ulster much too big for him, talking very slowly about his family with whom I had lost touch," Gilder wrote, later. " I saw that his manuscript was not long and gave him an appointment for the next day."

Gilder had a bad evening with *Maggie*. The novel is almost unknown to Americans. It begins: " A very little boy stood upon a heap of gravel for the honour of Rum Alley. He was throwing stones at howling urchins from Devil's Row who were circling madly about the heap and pelting him. His small body was writhing in the delivery of great, crimson oaths. . . . From a window of an apartment house that upreared its form from amid squat, ignorant stables, there leaned a curious woman. . . . The engineer of a passive tugboat hung lazily to a railing and watched. Over on the Island, a worm of yellow convicts came from the shadow of a grey ominous building and crawled slowly along the river's brink. . . ." The calm world watches Jimmie Johnson fight and then he goes home to his drunken mother, with his drunken father. His sister Maggie upbraids him: " Yeh knows it puts mudder out when yehs comes home half dead, an' it's like we'll all get a poundin'." To this unsentimental address Jimmie answers: " Ah, what de hell! Shut up or I'll smack yer mout', see? "

These children grow up in the shade of fear. Their mother is an incessant drinker who bullies them. Jimmie becomes a truck-driver invested by habit with an awful contempt for everything, especially those strings of street cars that followed his truck " like intent bugs." He has some respect for heavy fire engines: " They had been known to overturn street cars. Those leaping horses, striking sparks from the cobbles in their forward lunge, were creatures to be ineffably admired. The clang of the gong pierced his breast like a noise of remembered war." He attends meetings in missions where the hearers, hopeful only of free soup, confuse the preacher with Christ. He "menaced mankind at the intersection of streets . . . dreaming blood-red dreams at the passing of pretty women." He seduces a pair of women, himself, who " caused him considerable annoyance by breaking forth simultaneously, at fateful intervals, into wailings about support, marriage and infants. . . . Nevertheless, he had, on a certain starlit evening, said wonderingly and quite reverently: ' Deh moon looks like hell, don't it? ' "

His sister Maggie is a pretty girl — Crane did not describe her — who goes to work for a Jew in a collar factory at five dollars a week rather than go on the streets. She is wooed by Pete, an opulent young bartender who hasn't the slightest thought of marrying her and does not when he wearies of her stupid prettiness and goes back to a more experienced mistress. Jimmie has vague fancies that his own position should not permit him to be too stern with Maggie — there are his own informal brides — but all his ideas are cribbed by the conservatism of his breed. He allows his mother to turn Maggie out and in a chapter unforgettable the feeble child goes drifting across New York, trying to speak to busy men, and halts in the profound shadow of the river's edge. Word being brought that " Mag's dead " her mother finishes supper before breaking into due lamentations and, urged on by friends, concludes the story with the cry: " Oh, yes, I'll fergive her! I'll fergive her! " and the first ironic novel ever written by an American thus crisply ends.

On his own admission, made in 1904, this book gave Richard Gilder a fearful shock. It seemed to him daring and filled with good touches but it was " cruel." There was no visible sentiment. These creatures of an environment had no tenderness and no restraint of action to excuse their callosity, and next day Gilder sat pointing out excessive adjectives and slaughtered infinitives to the shy boy, who finally cut him short with an untactful question: " You mean that the story's too honest? "

Being a gentleman as well as an editor Gilder gave his courteous little nod and *Maggie* was carried away from him in a pocket of the gray ulster. It may have consoled Crane, on March 23, 1892, that Gilder saw nothing obscene in the story. There is no animal detail in the seduction of Maggie Johnson and the profanity of the novel was simply the " damns " and " curse yehs " of the Bowery's emotion lamely piling out. But Crane here had his first experience, without guessing, of a dualism which faces all American writers. In two years more Gilder would be bidding his friends to read the English Arthur Morrison's *Tales of Mean Streets* and would be aiding the Tenement Commission to clean up the slums of New York. But that a story of those slums, told without apology, should appear in the *Century* of 1892 was unthinkable. In 1904 he was asked why Morrison's " Child of the Jago " did not offend him when *Maggie* still seemed a breach of taste, and he made response: " But Mr. Morrison's an Englishman! " as if some permission of God rested on the Briton that his truculent realisms should be found inoffensive. The attitude might be comic if it were still not spinal in American editors of the year 1923.

Maggie roamed the offices of various magazines in March and April until Crane locked her up in a box at his brother Edmund's house in New Jersey and got to work on sketches which he might sell to the *New York Tribune*. He was now a freelance reporter, one of hundreds who haunted Park Row daily, trying to sell interviews with notables, articles investigatory and descriptive. The *Tribune* was a good market; he was known favorably in the office, and the paper had printed his work since 1888. Now he began to have a little reputation in all the offices, before summer. His adjectives were oddly placed and his brusque paragraphs stayed in the mind. To say that an injured street-sweeper "flattened his face toward heaven and sent up a jet of violet, fastidious curses," was certainly too elaborate for the journalism of 1892, but men buying material for the *Sun* and *Tribune* would remember even when they had chopped it from an account of an accident in Twenty-third Street.

Meanwhile the boy was engaged in a private game. He was being independent, as his mother had ordered him to be, and small pay, cheap rooms, casual food were part of the sport. If he sat by night on a bench in Union Square with John Northern Hilliard or Acton Davies wondering when a check might drop from somewhere, there was pleasure in that and Hilliard could tell him stories about the West. If the check was too long in coming, he could get on a train and go to Lakeview, where he spent aimless evenings with pretty girls singing popular songs around a piano. In May he wandered through Syracuse and glanced at the class of 1894, then spent a week at Port Jervis with William Crane. But on May 26th some check had been too long delayed and he wrote to Acton Davies that he must have five dollars before he went to Lakeview or Edmund Crane's front door and his baby would be his next meal. The baby and the door survived. In June he admitted that he had sat on his brother's back steps and compiled a mental dictionary of oaths. In July he was in Asbury Park once more, sending off sketches to the *Tribune* and helping Townley Crane gather notes of a very busy season.

The season was also busy in the *Tribune's* offices. Whitelaw Reid was candidate for Vice-president on the Republican ticket and the early campaign went badly although William McKinley had been brought east to speak on protection of industries from New Hampshire to Virginia. Reid's newspaper shows the strain of operation on behalf of a losing issue. Every meeting of workers that showed favor to the Republican party was reported in fullest detail.

MAGGIE: A GIRL OF THE STREETS

It was understood that the Grand Army of the Republic inclined toward Harrison and Reid and the Army's encampments fill page on page of the paper. Various societies of the laboring class, as it began to be called, had outings and holidays on the Jersey shore. Reports of these doings, then, were waited on eagerly in Park Row.

Meanwhile Crane lounged about Asbury and Avon and played baseball rather less than formerly. Some of his old friends thought he looked unwell that summer, and his silences were prolonged. He was a little criticized for an article on Asbury Park in which the respectable fathers of respectable families were sweepingly mentioned as beings " with a watch chain and about three children apiece." Then, one day, his brother went to a funeral in Newark and left the impressionist to chronicle a parade. These good men lugged banners praising Harrison and Reid, and Crane, looking at the motion of this spectacle, forgot that Reid owned the *New York Tribune.* He merely saw a number of sweating persons who mostly worked with their hands, marching on behalf of capital, and the thing amused him. All parades were silly, anyhow, and this was too silly. The men shambled in dust and sunlight for his eye. There was a doubled oversight both at the press bureau in Asbury and in the office of the paper on Park Row. Next week complaints arrived at the *Tribune's* door in every mail. The paragraph, printed obscurely and in only one edition, was too much read. Crane had fallen foul of the American commoner's inalienable right to be reported respectfully, no matter how tawdry or foolish his communal manifestations may appear. Somebody [2] in Park Row sent Townley Crane a heated message and Stephen retired to Port Jervis, to ride a horse in peace. The emotions of Townley Crane are now inscrutable.

But *Maggie* was haunting her maker. In November,

[2] Whitelaw Reid was not responsible.

275

Crane borrowed one thousand dollars from his brother William and went to New York with the revised manuscript. He had a definite scheme: cheap publishing houses then often put out paper-bound novels at the author's expense, and since the higher criticism would have none of *Maggie*, let her be seen on the news-stands. Few of his friends had read the manuscript and he knew, now, that Stephen Crane was nobody at all in the city of New York: " I hunted a long time for some perfectly commonplace name . . . I think that I asked [Post] Wheeler what he thought was the stupidest name in the world. He suggested Johnson or Smith and Johnston Smith went on the ugly yellow cover of the book by mistake. You see, I was going to wait until all the world was pyrotechnic about Johnston Smith's ' Maggie ' and then I was going to flop down like a trapeze performer from the wire and, coming forward with all the modest grace of a consumptive nun, say, I am he, friends! . . . The bill for printing eleven hundred copies was $869 and Appleton's tell me that the printer must have made about $700 out of me. . . . A firm of religious and medical printers did me the dirt. You may take this as proferred evidence of my imbecility. Will made me get the thing copyrighted. I had not even that much sense."

He was obliged to sign a statement that he was twenty-one years old before this vanished firm would take the contract. They refused their name for the title-page, in any case.[3] But *Maggie* was now born in mustard paper with the price " 50 cents " on the right-hand upper corner of the cover and the talent of Johnston Smith might be seen by the world if Stephen Crane could get somebody to expose it for sale. So the book was offered to the shops which in that year were quietly selling flat, large copies of Émile Zola's *La Terre* and *Potbouillie* to schoolboys. But nobody would take *Maggie* save Brentano's, which took a dozen

[3] The name of this firm seems to be lost forever.

copies and returned ten of them. The news-stands didn't want such a book. By the end of January 1893 Crane had got rid of a hundred *Maggies* and on one of these, sold in 1922 for two hundred and fifty dollars, is the inscription: " Miss Wortzmann. This story will not edify or improve you and may not even interest you but I owe your papa $1.30 for tobacco. S. Crane." So *Maggie* lay in yellow piles in the corners of his room and Crane went into that period of starvation so much admired in the history of artists by comfortable critics, sure of next week's bread.

His family knew nothing about this. When he dropped down to Edmund's house at Lakeview he was as usual, ready to play games with his small nieces and likely to write all night, coming to breakfast when the small household was at lunch. The secrecy of a boy was heavy in him; he had the icy courage of a sensitive nature which has taught itself to be brave; Edmund was under orders never to lend him more than five cents at a time. But one night there was not enough in his pocket to get him to Lakeview and he tramped through the mud of a country road, dazed with emptiness, with the sense of a great bundle pressing on his back. Then some man said from frosty shadow: " You seem to be in a pretty bad way, boy," and took hold of his arm. Crane mumbled that he was ill and they tramped toward Lakeview together, the countryman drawling out some wandering yarn, until Crane saw the lamps of his brother's house. The farmer shook hands with him and trudged away, his face unseen, to become the twelfth chapter of *The Red Badge of Courage*.

Crane's courage afterwards seemed to him simple silliness. Two of his brothers believed in his talent, and their homes were his. He could have given himself quarters with William or Edmund and stayed as a pensioner until, somehow, he had established himself with a public. But Crane's independence had a bent almost savage and ungracious. He would not tell his family anything about gloomy days in the old building of the Art Students' League in East Twenty-third Street and there was a new biting horror; he could not write now. Not only could he not write enough wooden descriptions of fires and strikes in Brooklyn — temporarily the home of strikes — to pay his meals, but he could write nothing that pleased his own judgment. All words seemed false and awkward. One day in February he came to Edmund's office in New York and said, drearily: " I'll trouble you for five cents, Ed," and on the first of March he answered an advertisement in the *Herald* and became clerk in a wholesale house on Bleecker Street for one week, precisely.

The external Stephen Crane of this passage was a silent boy who might be spurred on to amuse the crowd in a lamentable restaurant of lowest Lexington Avenue. Here the waiters wiped spoons in the leather pockets of fouled aprons and here Crane might rouse himself to say that Mark Twain's *Yankee in King Arthur's Court* was " inappropriate as a drunken bride." The quality of his talk was tinctured always by adjectives strange and prolonged. His boarding-house was a respectable hypocrite of a place. An ancient egg had a " snarling smell." The feather on the Sunday hat of a pretty chambermaid was " quivering invitation."

This pretty chambermaid was named Jennie Creegan, and all the crew of hapless youths whose beds she made called her Bunny. She sat on trunks, chewing gum " like a slim, reminiscing cow " and told tales of the Bowery. Crane had borrowed of her some phrases of *Maggie* and she tried to read the book when he gave her a copy but the words were too hard. One day she collected an armful of *Maggies* from Crane's quarters and used them to light a fire. The ironist grinned and helped her to lug the dusty books downstairs.

MAGGIE: A GIRL OF THE STREETS

Hamlin Garland appeared in this fog as the rescuing angel. Crane was surrounded by other boys, some younger than himself, who partly understood that *Maggie* was a rare performance. When anyone praised him with intelligence, he might flush and beam, but nobody in authority had yet said good words of *Maggie* and perhaps his confidence was slipping when Mr. Garland wrote to him inviting a call. The handsome Westerner was living not too comfortably in Harlem and Crane tramped the four miles between their rooms for the first visit. Mr. Garland was startled by the boy's admission that he would give away his literary future for thirty dollars and began work with an instant, practical kindness. So a copy of *Maggie* was sent to William Dean Howells. Sketches were mailed to O. B. Flower of the *Arena* and Flower promptly bought *An Omnibus Babe* for twenty-five dollars. The adviser understood something of markets. He recommended Crane to the *Press*, fed him beefsteak, and loaned him dollars. This was no springtide of fortune, but it was something solid after a winter of freezing doubts, and the *Press* had literary pretensions second just to those of the glittering and eclectic *Sun*. To Garland there was already a tragic vesture on this lean, sallow boy, who had played baseball with him at Avon eighteen months before. The palpitating eyes were somber; the tearing intensity of the brain was clear to his experience. He might laugh a little when Crane hummed tuneless anthems in praise of food but, to his scrutiny, Crane was a shape of pathos.

Crane's appearance misled people. He had heavy shoulders and a pair of meager hips that made clothes fit him badly even when he dressed with care. His eyes discolored easily and, after a night of work or indifferent poker, he seemed always ill. Women invariably thought him handsome; men, with some exceptions, thought his face too long and his mouth too flexible. But even in the summer of 1893

279

after weeks of good diet at Edmund Crane's house he left an impression of starved neglect on strangers. As this narrative must be, in part, the demolition of a romantic myth, it should be pointed out that Crane was actually muscular and his body was an enduring machine that could carry him through a good deal of fatigue, as long as he was given plenteous sleep. But his exterior was, somehow, fantastic and already, in March of 1893, he was pointed out to a Southerner, Ford Bemis, as an eccentric who spent all his time in dives of the Bowery and was the outcast son of an Episcopal bishop. It should be pointed out, too, that Crane had a degree of the grand innocence in his character. Walking across Union Square with Elbert Hubbard and Acton Davies, he would deliberately stop to talk to an interesting tramp or some elderly painted woman and would hold his circumspect, annoyed companions still until the wearisome string of lies had been rolled out. " He had," said Hubbard, " no sense of propriety." The publisher's own exterior was that of a professional Bohemian from the novels of Mürger, but he was circumspect in the highest degree and Crane's simmering curiosity frightened him.

Meanwhile William Dean Howells had gone sedately mad over *Maggie* and was trying to persuade Henry Harper to have the book issued with more dignity. Harper declined, but Howells asked Crane to dine with him and the impressionist appeared — in John Hilliard's best suit — to get a dose of praise administered by the first critic of the land. Howells happened to be master of a small art that is not forgotten: he could stand in a crowd and make compliments without embarrassing the beneficiary or annoying the witnesses. He presented Crane to his other guests with: " Here is a writer who has sprung into life fully armed," and followed that music by saying, while Mark Twain was under discussion: " Mr. Crane can do things that Clemens can't." Then, after dinner, he took down the volume of Emily

Dickinson's poems and read some aloud. So it must have been an evening of amazements for Crane, in a borrowed suit of clothes. The one man in America who had properly praised Tolstoi had also praised him and he had heard a new sort of verse, better than *The Charge of the Light Brigade* and *The Burial of Moses,* but he did not stop to let his mind bask in all this; he walked over to the Bowery and spent the rest of the night watching drunken Negroes play poker in the rear room of a saloon.

Then he was suddenly absorbed in some kind of research. He raided piles of old magazines in the studio of Corwin Knapp Linson and complained to the illustrator that nobody had written anything worth reading about the Civil War. He dropped in, one Sunday, at the house of Mrs. Armstrong — once the Miss Brett who had spanked him for burying her nephew — and borrowed the *Century's Battles and Leaders* after her father had assured him that these were accurate. One afternoon he was idle in the rooms of William Dallgren, watching Dallgren sketch Acton Davies, when Davies tossed him Émile Zola's *La Débâcle,* in a translation. Davies was a round youth who doted on Zola and when Crane slung the book aside he was annoyed.

" I suppose you could have done it better? "

" Certainly," said Crane.

On April 2nd he sent back *Battles and Leaders of the Civil War* to Mrs. Armstrong with a note: " Thank you very much for letting me keep these so long. I have spent ten nights writing a story of the war on my own responsibility but I am not sure that my facts are real and the books won't tell me what I want to know so I must do it all over again, I guess." This is the birth notice of *The Red Badge of Courage.*

His mind had gone swinging back to war in the recoil from failure in realities. *Maggie* was not absolute reporting. He had invented its small plot, and only two incidents of the story were from the life — the fight in the saloon and the destruction of Maggie's lambrequin by her mother. But he was in full flight from the codes of naturalism. . . . Flight took him inevitably to his first passion. He had made games of battle when he was a child. He was always playing mentally and all the force of imagination dragged at him in his very genuine despair of methods to release the hiding vigor of his brain. He could stand through nights in a blizzard of late March to write *Men in the Storm* or sleep in a Bowery shelter to get at the truth of *An Experiment in Misery,* but the emotions of a boy in battle he must find for himself, in himself, and the birth of the book was travail incomprehensible to men who have never hunted in themselves passions and the flood of acts to which they are alien. However, there had been a boy who went confidently off to make war on a world and a city. He had been beaten to shelter and had lurched up a lane in darkness on the arm of some stranger. He had been praised for his daring while his novel, like a retreating army, lay in unsold heaps and the maker of images was sure of his own clay.

But *Maggie* was riding his neck. Howells saw no reason why the book should not be sold: " To this hour," he said in 1913, " I cannot understand the attitude of the dealers. I saw several of them personally and tried to interest Mr. Brentano. If Crane had cared to try that trick he might have disposed of ' Maggie' through certain stores which had the reputation of selling obscene paperbacks. I suppose that the profanity of his masterpiece would have appealed to High School boys. But he did not descend to the method and, on my suggestion, mailed copies to Dr. Parkhurst and another minister who were then interested in the condition of the slums. Neither acknowledged the gift and Crane told me, afterwards, that a Roman Catholic notable wrote that ' Maggie' was an insult to the Irish. I shall never understand what was found offensive in the little tragedy."

MAGGIE: A GIRL OF THE STREETS

Howells might not understand, but as late as 1921 *Maggie* was described as " flippant and unfeeling " by a reviewer and it is plain that sardonic observation of seduction, drunkenness, and fatuous plebeians would not wash down the throats of booksellers in 1893. The book came headlong against an American mode in fiction. These characters were poor and so should have been treated more kindly. Even in the championship of Howells one sees a slanting attitude: the book was a " little tragedy " and the pity of Maggie's case appears more sharply in his three essays than any other feature of the story. But he was a champion and he shocked friends by his praise of this grimness. . . . The Howells of 1893 had altered somewhat from the nervous friend who scolded Mark Twain for writing " she combed me all to hell." He had emerged from the warm fogs of Bostonian eminence and was living among men whose theory of things possible differed broadly from that of his former group. He had been lightly bidden to sit still and talk while Saint-Gaudens finished the model of a quite naked woman who went on chewing gum as though she were fully clad. He was standing beside Stanford White on the deck of a ferry when some stoker fell from the stern of a tug and was smashed by its screw to pulp that left on the waters a lacquer of bloody oil. The architect yelled: " Oh, poor devil! " and then brought down both palms on the rail of the ferry with another cry: " My God! What color! " Thus, one sees in the realist's later novels a weak and brief concession of the absolute: a man might thrash another with a cowhide whip and then vomit in repugnance; the good and kindly might in *New Leaf Mills* come off second best in a peculiar world; his ethical optimism sometimes waned into admission of things senseless, chill, and real.

But neither Howells nor anybody else could sell *Maggie*. Edward Marshall of the *Press* tried to persuade his paper to make a serial of it and in May 1893 Crane had some hope of a hundred dollars and a chance to hear what " Men of Sense " would think. There existed a collection of humans who were " men of sense " as differing from mere men. They were people not shocked by trifles who were willing to believe that he meant what he said. Marshall, not much older than himself, was a man of sense and Crane took heed when the young editor told him that his adjectives were often too heavy and that his coined adverbs were frequently difficult. So a sketch to be called *The Reluctant Voyagers,* for which Corwin Linson made illustrations with Crane as a model, shows fewer adjectives, fewer adverbs, and greater ease. But nobody bought it. Nor did anybody buy, immediately, *The Pace of Youth,* which includes: " In the darkness stretched the vast purple expanse of the ocean, and the deep indigo sky above was peopled with yellow stars. Occasionally out upon the waters a whirling mass of froth suddenly flashed into view, like a great ghostly robe appearing, and then vanished, leaving the sea in its darkness, whence came those bass tones of the water's unknown emotion. . . . High in the sky soared an unassuming moon faintly silver." Not knowing that two eminent novelists of another land would at last honor his prose by adopting it, Crane had no consolation and no cash for *The Pace of Youth* in 1893.

In June he turned over three hundred copies of *Maggie* to Mrs. Armstrong for safekeeping: " Sometime or other somebody or other might buy some," and went to Edmund's house. He came downstairs often and read bits of his manuscript aloud to his brother. *The Red Badge of Courage* was being slowly examined and partly rewritten. Edmund Crane could write pure English and his young brother made test of a clear intelligence. The man of business objected frequently, to sentences without verbs and to adjectives that had got loose from all mooring, but he was excited by the battle, having himself started off to war at the age of seven.

Stephen Crane was not taking much advice. In September shooting had begun at Port Jervis and on the first of October he was feeling "bully. Am going camping in Sullivan [County] with some other bobcats." In that company he spent three weeks, but on some date of the month's last week he arrived in New York with a valise and a slight cold and the price of a pair of shoes in his pocket.

Having bought new shoes he used his last five-cent piece to descend on Edward Marshall in the office of the *Press* through a cold rainstorm that soaked his clothes. The two young men had a singular regard for each other. Marshall was a writer of some skill and not a flattering reporter of New York. His dismissal from the *Press* had been demanded more than once by annoyed and powerful men and he had not been dismissed, although no influence kept him in place. When Crane passed beyond the point of casual amity, his feeling became fixed and savage. He liked Marshall and trusted him as simply as he now asked for a job. Marshall sat on the corner of a desk, swinging his watchchain around a finger for a minute, and then answered: "No. I'll take all the special articles you can do, Stevie, but you are made for better things. Don't waste your time."

Instead of asking for five dollars, Crane walked out of the office and started uptown through the rain. He tramped with two-thirds of *The Red Badge of Courage* in his valise from the tip of the city's tongue to East Twenty-third Street and stumbled into the rooms of Frederick Gordon in the Art Students' League building, a wildly fashioned barrack "which squatted, slumbering and old, between two exalted commercial structures which would have had to bend afar down to perceive it. . . . The northward march of the city's progress had happened not to overturn this aged structure, and it huddled there, lost and forgotten, while the cloud-veering towers strode on." Gordon, after a look at the shivering creature, got him out of his clothes and into bed. The artist's room was big enough for another cot and Crane stayed on after a week's violent illness. His cooking added infamy to his host's life and he placidly told an arriving Englishman, Holmes Bassett, that Mrs. Humphry Ward must be an idiot. Her celebrated novel, *Robert Elsmere*, was a lot of higgling rubbish and so was most English writing.

Bassett had called on Gordon by mistake and was already embarrassed, talking to an utter stranger dressed in an undershirt who looked deplorably ill. This critical blast blew him from his feet, and as he had met Mrs. Ward in London, he was shocked. So he went off to the Holland House and then came back, after ten days, to hunt up this irreverent character and take him to a prizefight at Madison Square Garden. Corbett was to give an exhibition and all the world was going. . . . The occasion became historic, suddenly. Crane dined at the Holland House with a man wearing a monocle and sat beside Bassett near the ringside while the smoky height of the great oval cavern filled with men. Presently Mark Twain appeared in a box with Robert Reid and the ruddy Stanford White. There rose a considerable stir. Clemens was in the papers, fighting ruin after the collapse of his printing scheme, and a comber of sentiment splashed toward the tall figure, sheathed in furs, while the people of cheap seats whistled, here and there, recognizing the clown of innumerable lectures with his whitened hair and the beauty of his beginning age. Crane sat staring at " the divine amateur " in silence and on some question said: " I only like one of his books." Which one? " *Life on the Mississippi.*"

Corbett boxed. Clemens was led in state by Stanford White to the prizefighter's dressing-room. Crane went off to his borrowed bed and a christening took place in a house near the Players' Club on Gramercy Park. There was a

Hungarian band playing. Mark Twain came at 10.45 and Richard Harding Davis followed him. Walter Damrosch made music on a piano while a tenor sang and people began to discuss what names they would choose if they could have the matter adjusted. Then Davis wanted to know what name Clemens would have liked had he been a woman? The humorist dallied with the matter, then decided on " Petunia Bloggs." The joke went around the room. Queerly, Stanford White wanted to be called Evelina. Then they began to christen famous people who were else-where. The Prince of Wales became " Lily " by allusive process. Ellen Terry was suddenly " Roderick Dhu " — it is not remembered why — and Davis asked for a new name for Henry James.

" Oh," said Clemens, " call him Henrietta Maria."

This jape was in London six months later, but Crane, a few blocks to the north of its making, was far from well. He took more cold and Gordon had to nurse him in the windy building of three entrances where young fellows hunted each other with candles by night to borrow twenty cents against the morning's breakfast. Bassett, no Bohemian, sometimes took Crane out to dine and was pulled along the Bowery, with his monocle. This glass delighted Crane and he liked to play with its round when there was nothing else for his fingers to caress. He must have something to fondle or he wasn't comfortable. Smoking seemed to mean just an object between his fingers and a dead cigarette was quite as good as one burning until he noticed the extinction and threw the thing away. He hated champagne because it made him dizzy after two glasses, but a white German wine rather pleased him, and meanwhile he told Bassett all about bears, horses, dogs, and sailing boats. His opinions squirted out in shocking jets on a conservative who was, at the time, devout. Marriage, Crane said, was a base trick on women, who were hunted animals anyhow. A wedding was a legal ceremony, if ceremony there must be, and of all sects the Episcopal Church was the biggest inanity. Men had been allowed to pervert the teachings of Christ and Buddha into formulas and there was no such thing as sin "except in Sunday schools." Bassett went off to see an uncle in Ottawa with an impression of wild radicalism afoot on East Twenty-third Street. But *Maggie* came to him by the next mail inscribed: "This work is a mud-puddle, I am told on the best authority. Wade in and have a swim." So he learned that his acquaintance was a writer for the first time.

In February Crane took *The Red Badge of Courage* to a typist and left it for copy, finished and ready for anybody to read. Typewriting then was still expensive, but thirty dollars seem heavy for the short book. Having paid fifteen of the fee, he got half the manuscript back and went up into Harlem to see Hamlin Garland. After one look Garland lent another fifteen dollars and the whole treasury was out of pawn. On the 24th of February Crane wrote to Bassett: "I have just sold another book and my friends think it is pretty good and that some publisher ought to bring it out when it has been shown as a serial. It is a war-story and the syndicate people think that several papers could use it." He had sold *The Red Badge of Courage* to Irving Bacheller's young syndicate for less than a hundred dollars.

CHAPTER IV

FAME AND PREJUDICE

S TEPHEN CRANE'S scarce letters are not often interesting. They have a formal running tone, now and then lifted by a phrase. Sometimes he exploded into an utterly informal and prolonged expression. These vital papers must have been dashed down at the end of a mood. They are seldom dated, seldom headed, and recipients say that they were usually addressed haphazard. Thus, on some date of late November 1894, and obviously from Port Jervis, comes: " If you hear that I have been hanged by the neck till dead on the highest hill of Orange County you may as well know that it was for killing a man who is really a pug — No, by the legs of Jehovah! I will not insult any dog by comparing this damned woman to it. There is a feminine mule up here who has roused all the bloodthirst in me and I don't know where it will end. She has no more brain than a pig and all she does is to sit in her kitchen and grunt. But every when she grunts something dies howling. It may be a girl's reputation or a political party or the Baptist Church but it stops in its tracks and dies. Sunday I took a 13 yr. old child out driving in a buggy. Monday this mule addresses me in front of the barber's and says, ' You was drivin' Frances out yesterday ' and grunted. At once all present knew that Frances and I should be hanged on twin gallows for red sins. No man is strong enough to attack this mummy because she is a nice woman. She looks like a dried bean and she has no sense, but she is a nice woman. Right now she is aiming all her artillery at Cornelia's [1] new hat. I have been deprived by heaven of any knowledge of hats but it seems to be a very kindly hat with some blue flowers on one side and a ribbon on the other. But we rustle in terror because this maggot goes to and fro grunting about it. If this woman lived in Hester Street some son or brother of a hat would go bulging up to her and say, ' Ah, wot deh hell! ' and she would have no teeth any more, right there. She is just like those hunks of women who squat on porches of hotels in summer and wherever their eye lights there blood rises. Now, my friend, there is a big joke in all this. This lady in her righteousness is just the grave of a stale lust and every boy in town knows it. She accepted ruin at the hands of a farmer when we were all 10 or 11. But she is a nice woman and all her views of all things belong on the tables of Moses. No man has power to contradict her. We are all cowards anyhow. Bacheller thinks I had best start for Nevada as soon as possible, maybe before Christmas, but I should like to be with the family, of course." Then, in a postscript: " Somebody has written clean from California about The Red Badge."

The story, cut into lengths convenient for the *Philadelphia Press*, had surprised him by the number of letters that came showering through the Bacheller Syndicate. Another surprise was less pleasing. Bacheller took him down to Philadelphia and the whole staff of the *Press* had swarmed up to congratulate him. There were old soldiers among the printers and their words had been very warm. Excitement or something more tangible gave him an attack of dyspepsia and this was new, painful, and lasting. He was used to colds, sore throats, and chilblains, but dyspepsia seemed unlawful, especially as it recurred. In

[1] Mrs. William Crane.

1894, too, the heat of New York's summer had suddenly been " fog, like a Turkish bath's steam chamber, with the whole dressed city panting and scratching in its weight." A trip to Scranton with Corwin Linson was a relief. They reported and sketched the mining town for Bacheller with a prospect of another article on deep-sea diving, but the sea change did not come and Crane was much at Port Jervis in the later summer. In Port Jervis he evolved a social theory that Elbert Hubbard bought for the *Philistine* together with an essay on charities in the New York slums. Hubbard lost these papers on a train and Crane never replaced them, but the social theory remains, in a letter of Hubbard.

The world was full of old, plain, and dull ladies who sat about on porches and were omnipotent. Nobody could argue with them; they ruled the universe; they blighted the scene. This bestial force came from the education of all Americans by female school-teachers. Men were sent to school under the power of dull, limited women, and learned to cringe from them. The habit was so stamped in males that they never dared to argue with any woman and so there should be more male teachers. The article on the slums included some criticisms of Tolstoi, still Crane's literary god although *The Kreutzer Sonata* bored him so that he could not finish it — the thing was " an old maid's picnic." He seems to have distrusted any novel favored by elderly women, clergymen, or Frank R. Stockton, an author of the time, harmless, amusing, and much petted by the minor critics.

In 1894 he was enraged by Mrs. Frances Hodgson Burnett's *Little Lord Fauntleroy* and encountering two small boys who had been tricked out by their mothers in imitation of Reginald Birch's too faithful illustrations, in long curls and lace collars, he coolly gave the sufferers money to have their hair cut. This act of altruism took place about September 1st in the city of Albany and Crane carefully told his alarmed hostess what he thought of *Lord Fauntleroy.* His opinions of books never altered greatly. In 1899 he wrote: " No thanks. If the Whilomville stories seem like Little Lord Fauntleroy to you you are demented and I know that you are joking, besides. See here, my friend, no kid except a sick little girl would like Lord Fauntleroy unless to look at Birch's pictures for it. The pictures are all right."

This innocuous romance was printed in 1886 and its results sullied the lives of many small boys born in the decade following that date. Crane's rage was rooted in his dislike of sentimentalized children. Mrs. Burnett's shrewd bit of writing tells how one Cedric Errol, the grandson of an aged and gouty Earl, reformed his ancestor and soothed the life of an English countryside. Crane had heard, somewhere, Matthew Arnold's " sweetness and light" and he tacked the phrase to *Little Lord Fauntleroy.* As he seldom read books, an annoying novel left a scar in his mind, unhealed to his end. His impressions of Chicago in January of 1895 were stained by a procession of Lord Fauntleroys met on a corner beside a church. That any young male should be draped in lace and velvet and made to wear long curls!

Bacheller was sending him west to write sketches with a free hand, as long as he finished the trip in Mexico, and Crane's course is hard to follow. Most of his letters have been lost and the sketches appeared out of order. He had, though, three immediate wishes. He must see a cowboy ride. He wanted to be in a blizzard of the plains. He must look at the Mississippi because Elbert Hubbard had persuaded him to read *Huckleberry Finn* and 143 East Twenty-third Street had heard his grunt of disgust over the lame conclusion of Mark Twain's masterpiece. Didn't the genius know any better? A baby could have improved the end of *Huckleberry Finn*! The boys stopped being boys and were dolls. So, as in the mind of Arnold Bennett, *Life on the Mississippi* was always Twain's best book. It is not known that he saw much of the Mississippi, but he had his two other wishes. He saw cowboys ride and visited a ranch near the border of Nevada, where somebody gave him or sold him some silver spurs. He changed trains once at a dreary junction town where was a hotel of a dreadful blue that fascinated him. His thirst for blues ran to shades of cold electric tones and this blue was a lugubrious, fainter tinge. In a hotel painted so loathsomely, some dire action must take place and after four years he made it seem so. But in Lincoln, Nebraska, on February 13th, he pushed himself into an irony by trying to stop a fight in a drinking-place. It appears that a very tall man was pounding a rather small one and Crane shoved himself between them. "But thus I offended a local custom. These men fought each other every night. Their friends expected it and I was a darned nuisance with my Eastern scruples and all that. So first everybody cursed me fully and then they took me off to a judge who told me that I was an imbecile and let me go; it was very saddening. Whenever I try to do right, it don't."

A blizzard was raging at Lincoln, but he found warm weather in Little Rock, Arkansas, and hurried off to look at Hot Springs. There he broke a tooth on a dried persimmon's stone and saw five funerals. "It rained funerals on me. I was soaked with lamentations and the hope of widows." New Orleans was a pictorial disappointment, while Creole food gave him more dyspepsia, but when he reached San Antonio, he fell in love with that maligned city and with Texas. . . . All the adolescence in him frothed to a head. His letters from San Antonio are almost childish. A wonderful Greek cook broiled pompano. Here was the monument to the defenders of the Alamo with its legend: "Thermopylæ had its messenger of defeat; the

Alamo had none "; and that, he wrote to Hilliard, boomed
in his ears like the clashing of war-bronze. Every night
here was the blaze of East Houston Street, in spring, with
parading men in real sombreros and the lace of veils flung
across Mexican eyes. Persons with parenthetic mustaches
sat in saloons filled with antlers and lied about old duels. A
red-haired man swung his elbow against Crane's arm to get
a revolver from his belt and aim it at an enemy, before the
bartender threw a seidel and spoiled the show. He pulled
a small girl out of the soapy little river that wriggles
through the town and she told him for his trouble to go to
hell.

One day he was lingering on the Alamo Plaza and distressed sounds hit his ear. He saw a sixteen-year-old boy,
as tall as himself, sitting on the edge of the gutter, sobbing.
Young Edward Grover had come southwest from Chicago
to begin life freshly as a cowboy with a birthday gift of
sixty dollars in his pocket. Now the pocket was empty and
the officers of Fort Sam Houston would not let him become
a recruit. Crane marched this wretch into a restaurant, fed
him thoroughly, and took him straight to the railroad station. At Saint Louis the home-going runaway met an uncle
who could telegraph back funds to Crane. Six days later
Grover had a note:

Dear Deadeye Dick:

Thanks for sending back my money so fast. The hotel
trun me out, as my friends of the Bowery say and I was
living in the Mex diggings with a push of sheep men till my
boss in New York wired me money.

Now, old man, take some advice from a tough jay from
back East. You say your family is all right and nobody
bothers you. Well, it struck me that you are too young a
kid [2] and too handsome to be free and easy around where a

---

[2] Crane used the word long before it was popular in fiction.

lot of bad boys and girls will take your pennies. So better stay home and grow a mustache before you rush out into the red universe any more.

Yours sincerely,

STEPHEN CRANE

In that Mexican lodging-house he met a blushless rogue who, peddling illicit drink to the thirsty soldiery of Leon Springs in 1917, called himself Keenan. This man had charms; he was a Bowery boy who had wandered away from police and friends. He told Crane a tale of shooting down some Mexicans who tried to drive his sheep from a waterhole. The slaughter was a simple gesture of carelessness, for at once he sold his sheep to them and retired from the pass. Crane sent him, in 1897, a copy of the *Century Magazine* with *A Man and Some Others* and Keenan hated Crane ever after for spoiling the point of the story.

The enchantment of Texas was partly equine. He rode a mule in the Painted Desert of Arizona, but again, in Mexico, there were all sorts of horses and a little bay that carried him through a real adventure faithfully reported in *Horses — One Dash.* . . . Crane and a Mexican guide, Miguel Itorbide, were benighted in a village suddenly invaded by a fashionable bandit, Ramon Colorado, and his followers. Diaz, the President-dictator of Mexico, did not discourage a certain easy freedom in rural administration and small groups of banditry went cheerfully about their business within a hundred miles of the capital. Colorado heard that an American was lodged in the village and determined to absorb any money or luxuries that Crane might have with him. Then, exactly as in the story, a train of peripatetic harlots arrived on their way to some rejoicing in Mexico City and Colorado went to inspect. Crane and his guide crept from the hut and raced across the plain on their horses with Colorado's gang half a mile behind them. The pale

295

uniforms of the rurales, the mounted constabulary of the district, came to solve the difficulty and a lieutenant sat cursing Colorado while the bandit tried to apologize for having annoyed a friend of the government. This business was delicious to Crane. . . . He had watched terrific brawls while, dressed in his worst clothes, he sat in Bowery dives and lodging-houses, but he had never been so closely threatened and the detail of his emotions pumps through *Horses — One Dash* in a clear ripple of self-examination, sardonic always.

Let it be stated that the mistress of this boy's mind was fear. His search in æsthetic was governed by terror as that of tamer men is governed by the desire of women. *Maggie* had represented the terror of an environment tinged by social judgment. In all the Mexican and Texan sketches appears, as in *The Red Badge of Courage,* a vision of man's identity faced by its end, by incomprehensible death. One gets the solid courage of the marshal of Yellow Sky who shoves annihilation from him by a simple statement; the rogue of *A Man and Some Others* dies easily because he is bound by contract to defend his flock. In the true story *Horses* and the fanciful *Five White Mice* one sees Crane himself, recording his own pulse before a shadow which he refused to kneel and worship. He could be afraid, and afraid with all the quivering imagination of an artist — here stood the great death and here, mentally or in flesh, stood he. But his recording of the state is never more than civilly sympathetic. The boy of *Five White Mice* stands with a drunkard on each hand and the cloudy group of Mexicans before him, speculating on his friend's attitude after the slaughter. " The other Kid would mourn his death. He would be preternaturally correct for some weeks, and recite the tale without swearing. But it would not bore him. For the sake of his dead comrade he would be glad to be preternaturally correct and to recite the tale without swear-

ing." Then the tortured thought veers off to a memory of a
summer hayfield and to the wonder of a distant crooning
stream. And then he steps forward and the great death steps
back. The Mexicans retire up the dim street. Nothing has
happened. The emotion has projected its intensity against
nonsense, against a posture of some loungers. It is the last
point in futility, the hurtle of mighty cords on an unhearing
ear. . . . That this work was outside the mood of his time
and his nation everybody knows.

Notoriety now jumped on him while he tramped the
streets of Mexico City with his waistcoat pockets filled with
opals given him by Charles Gardner, an American engineer,
invalid after smallpox in the brilliant, lazy town where
Crane saw, for the first time, the Latin consent to public
pleasures. " You can sit at a table in front of a Café — a
real café — and drink cool drinks. Nobody comes up and
says, Stop! The Yankees and the Englishmen get drunk
sometimes and make noises at the circus but the Mexicans
make noises just at the bullfights." The bullfights were disgusting to him because horses were killed there, an unthinkable sacrilege. Mr. Gardner, reading the *New York Herald*,
saw that an absurd book of poems had appeared and asked
across a table: " Is this poet Stephen Crane related to you? "
" I'm him," said Crane.

A fog rests on the birth of *Black Riders*, sold to Copeland
and Day of Boston in 1894. Crane was careless about dates.
His own judgment: " I wrote the things in February of
1893," cannot be true because he had not then dined with
William Dean Howells and had not heard the critic read
Emily Dickinson's verses aloud. The testimony of Hamlin
Garland and John Northern Hilliard must be correct and
the startling lines were written some time after the first of
April 1893. Some of them were read by John Barry at a
public meeting of literary persons in March of 1894, with-
out applause. They came into Crane's head while he was

depressed one night and it seemed, almost, that somebody dictated them to him. The whole manuscript was twice lost, once by Crane himself in an elevated railway car and once by a friend who left the shabby papers somewhere and had to ransack New York for them. They existed in the autumn of 1894 as proof sheets which Frederick Gordon had in his pocket while he helped Crane gather facts in the crowds watching bulletins of the mayoral election which temporarily took New York's affairs from the orderly pillage of Tammany Hall into the sloppy ineffectiveness of the Reform party's hands. Copeland and Day issued *Black Riders* with a clever design by Gordon for the cover of the handsome little book, which came out in April of 1895, and, with two favorable reviews in objection, the reading nation was told at once that Stephen Crane was mad.

The nation had been offered unrhymed sonnets of Anna Brackett and that Walt Whitman wrote long poems without rhymes was an established fact. The English even liked Whitman's concoctions. But *Black Riders and Other Lines* was the work of some pert maniac and opinions to the contrary in the *Bookman* and the *Lotos* had no weight. Here was simple insanity finely printed:

> Charity, thou art a lie,
> A toy of women,
> A pleasure of certain men.
> In the presence of justice,
> Lo, the walls of the temple
> Are visible
> Through thy form of sudden shadows.

That was rude and pretty bad. Worse came:

> I saw a man pursuing the horizon;
> Round and round they sped.
> I was disturbed at this:
> I accosted the man.

FAME AND PREJUDICE

" It is futile," I said,
" You can never — "
" You lie," he cried,
And ran on.

Two or three angels
Came near to the earth.
They saw a fat church.
Little streams of black people
Came and went continually.
And the angels were puzzled
To know why the people went thus,
And why they stayed so long within.

If I should cast off this tattered coat,
And go free into the mighty sky;
If I should find nothing there
But a vast blue,
Echoless, ignorant, —
What then?

God lay dead in heaven;
Angels sang the hymn of the end;
Purple winds went moaning,
Their wings drip-dripping
With blood
That fell upon the earth.
It, groaning thing,
Turned black and sank.
Then from the far caverns
Of dead sins
Came monsters livid with desire.
They fought,
Wrangled over the world,
A morsel.

299

But of all the sadness this was sad, —
A woman's arms tried to shield
The head of a sleeping man
From the jaws of the final beast.

In the Bowery he had seen a young streetwalker cover the head of a drunken procurer with her body while the fellow's assailants were trying to stamp his face to pieces. Crane ran to bring help and the police arrested the girl for cursing. (The exact morality of the Irish police amused Crane considerably.)

A man feared that he might find an assassin;
Another that he might find a victim.
One was more wise than the other.

I walked in a desert.
And I cried,
" Ah, God, take me from this place! "
A voice said, " It is no desert."
I cried, " Well, but —
The sand, the heat, the vacant horizon."
A voice said, " It is no desert."

A man's perception of beauty in disastrous circumstances should have been phrased with more prolix sentiment in 1895. But Richard Watson Gilder and others found pleasure in:

Places among the stars,
Soft garden near the sun,
Keep your distant beauty;
Shed no beam upon my weak heart.
Since she is here
In a place of blackness,
Not your golden days

FAME AND PREJUDICE

Nor your silver nights
Can call me to you.
Since she is here
In a place of blackness,
Here I stay and wait.

But the vision of the world as a rudderless ship " going ridiculous voyages, making quaint progress, turning as with serious purpose before stupid winds," had no claim on a public which was reading Fitzgerald's quatrains just then with a delighted sense of ethical exploration. Omar Khayyám might suit the awakened hedonism of a nation still taught to recite the stuff of Longfellow, but *Black Riders* suited nobody. The poems were bombast and drivel and obscene and that was completely all there was to the matter. But Crane was now somebody and he had expected this blast before he dedicated the book to Hamlin Garland. His friends, with some exceptions in the shapes of Hilliard, Gordon, Linson, and Hubbard, had openly told him he was an affected ass. So, arriving in New York in May, he took condolences serenely and said: " Some of the pills are pretty darned dumb, anyhow. But I meant what I said," and being asked if he admired Stéphane Mallarmé answered: " I don't know much about Irish authors."

He was made welcome at the new Lantern Club of journalists and editors in a crazy added story on the roof of an old building near Brooklyn Bridge. Irving Bacheller, Thomas Masson, Edward Marshall, Willis Hawkins, Richard Gilder, John Langdon Heaton — whose wife was " the most sensible woman in New York " to Crane — and some others lunched there almost daily. Crane shook hands with Richard Harding Davis for the first time, gave the best choice of his Mexican opals to Corwin Linson, then let the others vanish among " the Wild Indians " of the Art Students' League Building, save one kept carefully for his

301

niece, Helen, his brother William's daughter, who lost it later at school in Switzerland. Then he went up with his silver spurs and some woven blankets to Hartwood, a hamlet of Sullivan County, easily reached from Port Jervis. There Edmund Crane had taken charge of some undeveloped property and had a simple house where Crane lay grinning over the reviews of *Black Riders* and taught his nieces to play fan-tan.

Ripley Hitchcock bought *The Red Badge of Courage* for Appleton's in December of 1894, but Crane's trip to Mexico had delayed correction of the proofs and the book did not appear until October 3, 1895. Hitchcock was a man of extraordinary shrewdness. He could see the merits of *The Red Badge of Courage* and of such transient dullness as the forgotten *David Harum* with equal speed. He nicely predicted the success of *The Red Badge* in August of 1895 and saw the prediction come off by the first of January. The success has become a legend in American publishing. It is still commonly stated that the book did not sell until the English reviews in January lifted it to notice. The facts, as taken from amalgamated statements, are these: All or nearly all the American reviews were enthusiastic and booksellers in New York bought large numbers of copies. But from Crane's hand on December 24, 1895: " Mr. Hitchcock tells me that the book does not sell much in New York. It has gone to about 4500, though, and many of them have been sent west." At one bookshop, Leggett's, only two copies had been sold by the 10th of January. . . . Then, in middle January, the city began to buy *The Red Badge of Courage* and the sale mounted so swiftly that Edgar Saltus, who in October wrote that Crane had outdone Zola, Tolstoi, and Kipling in a breath was now, on February 6th, moved to write to Charles Devlin: " A man sometimes yearns for the power to write vulgar inanity and sell it by the cart-load to fools. I hear that Stephen Crane has made twenty thousand dollars out of his trash." Devlin called the exquisite's attention to his former praise of the book and their interesting correspondence untimely ceased.

The history of a triumph is always dull. The unfavorable reaction to Crane's masterpiece is better worth study. Copies of *The Red Badge* were returned to Brentano's store in New York because the book held no " love-story " and it was sometimes returned because it was too grim. Two specimens of the first issue are scattered with bitter notes in the tremulous handwriting of some veteran who wrote: " Insulting," " unpatriotic," " damned nonsense " abreast of each sentence describing the young soldier's fears in the blank wildness of his flight from the first day's battle. A clergyman in Illinois, George Stephen Crane, who had served in a regiment at Chancellorsville, was assailed by letters from old friends either praising his memory or damning him for betraying confidences made at that less sentimental moment when his comrades were in retreat from the Southern army. Crane himself had letters profoundly pointing out that the boy's return to camp with his damaged head and his acceptance of his friend's belief that the bloodstains come from a wound taken in battle make up a nasty comment on the hero. Irony, says Carl Van Vechten, should always be carefully underlined in an American novel. And there is no notice, save that of William Dean Howells, printed in 1895, which mentions the ironies chasing themselves through *The Red Badge*. That critics of the day should note: " Mr. Crane's interesting novel contains no strictures on the cruel uselessness of war " was to be expected. Merely to expose is never enough for the prim intelligences posted as guides to the American public. Then, as now, their vision of the artist in letters is the cloudy image of a poet in solemn posture on some sanitary stage, dealing out commonplace evidence of man's imperfection and urging on the universal good.

STEPHEN CRANE

The comedic element of *The Red Badge* probably had little notice at the time. But very soon certain episodes were imitated. Within a year the business of the lad who turns over his letter of farewell to Henry before the battle appeared in adaptation twice. The quarrels of the two boys could be fitted into other scenes and were, promptly. . . . The biographer has been reproached for pointing out, elsewhere, that Alan Seeger's graceful poem, still current, with its line: " I have a rendezvous with death," was suggested by the tenth chapter of Crane's novel, but Seeger's admiration of the book was known to his friends. The flowery advance of the banners has been precisely imitated in English and America war-tales to the number of three hundred and ten times. The finish of the tenth chapter, the finding of the dead man in the wood, the row between the regiment's commander and the disgusted general and the description of the fires by night have been used ceaselessly. Crane's effect on Anglo-American prose has never been questioned by critics of any competence and his clear departure from the traditions of written English startled his day. There were vigorous catcalls and brayings, of course. It was passionately urged that no decent youth should describe emotions in terms of colors, that his grammar was wildly molded to the needs of a point. But he was indisputably famous at the age of twenty-four, by reason of a book written, or designed, before his twenty-second birthday.

The act fell on academic culture as noisily as though a broken drumstick smote a plane of limp velvet. Crane had letters of praise from Bliss Perry, William Graham Sumner, and Brander Matthews, but recognition of living art had no place in the universities of the decade and Barrett Wendell, pausing in the consideration of Restoration comedy at Harvard, told one of his students that the book was sensational trash, then resumed his sour brilliance. So far as penetrable, smart society knew nothing of any such novel, for the Englishman already quoted in this history's second chapter vainly hunted in 1897 for somebody of New York's grandiose flock to make him known to Crane and at a dinner of forty found only one couple — the late Frederick Whitridge and his wife — who had ever heard of the author. But Boston rolled in its shrines and the new writer was asked swiftly to appear. He was pointed out to visitors at a football game in Cambridge, in latter November, and stood shyly for a few minutes in the famous drawing-room of Mrs. Fields.

Elbert Hubbard gave a dinner for him on December 19th in Buffalo and Crane stammered out something which, in the memory of Claude Bragdon, the dinner's master of ceremonies, was hardly a speech. Some of the guests took the party as an elaborate joke on Crane, who must be rather mad or a posturer, but excitement was growing in the vague kingdom of arts and the blaze of the English reviews lighted up January. Harold Frederic's letter to the *New York Times* was carefully arranged so that Henry James might know how little Frederic thought of his judgments — James having recommended Heinemann's new publication in Frederic's presence — but this war of two expatriates had no meaning in America and Crane was pleased by a note from Frederic while he rode his new horse, Peanuts, about Hartwood. The magazines were suddenly on his track and to *McClure's* went the whole collection of Texan and Mexican stories. Meanwhile Ripley Hitchcock was urging that *Maggie* be altered and published and Crane's old friend Harry Thompson wanted *George's Mother* for Edward Arnold as soon as it should be finished. The crowd at the Lantern Club wanted him to write a tale with a newspaperman as hero, of course, and people came driving compliments at him from every quarter. One of these was Richard Harding Davis, who did not particularly like Crane, but who chose to make himself an agent of the younger man's reputation. The air was full of projects: he should write a political novel; he should write a play with Clyde Fitch. "It seems that I can do any damn thing I want to but be let alone," he wrote in February, but walking with a friend up Broadway, elation swelled. It was pleasant to stroll to dinner at Mouquin's and to be a success.

II

WEIR MITCHELL was a practising, experienced neurologist as well as a narrator of modest historical tales. He once put on paper a speculation: "The phenomena of envy are very much more marked among artists than in other professions. Invariably or nearly so, these take the form of gossiping stories about the personal character of a successful writer and the stories always show the same trend: the successful man is given to heavy indulgence in alcohol or to irregular use of drugs. The point is most interesting when one considers that artists are perpetually demanding for themselves the license of conduct which they deplore in print." These two methods of subterranean attack were in full use against Crane before March of 1896.

He had a trick of using small formulas in conversation and now, when he was pressed to write some story which seemed too dull or too fantastic he began to say: "Oh, I'd have to get too drunk to write that." That this was hardly circumspect is plain and part of Crane's legend became fixed: he was obliged to get drunk before he could write at all. This had no currency among his friends, but it was probably gospel in the bars of Mouquin's restaurant and of Louis Martin's café. The fiction of a successful man aided in his success by alcohol is very flattering to the less successful.

Here appears the shape of a forgotten and vanished being whose name was Thomas McCumber. He was very tall, very handsome, and usually very tipsy in the popular bars between the years 1895 and 1904, when he died in a hospital of paresis. His card bore the word *Photographer* in one corner and he once lived at the old Gilsey House for some months of 1896. He also once lived at a boarding-house in East Nineteenth Street where James Huneker knew him casually as a clever talker. It is faintly recalled that Crane had a nodding acquaintance with this man and did not seem to like him. He was described by O. Henry as " an infernal nuisance," but he was genial and he talked, apparently, in an amusing fashion. On a definite date, then, February 22, 1896, he made himself responsible for the statement that Crane took morphine.

In March of 1896 Crane seems to have been conscious that he was under fire. His last note to Wallis McHarg, dated from Hartwood, says: " When people see a banker taking a glass of beer in a café, they say, There is Smith. When they behold a writer taking a glass of beer, they say, Send for the police! No great law of nature can be proved from this but it pretty often hits me that people are ingenious blockheads. I have been to Washington about a book on political society for Mr. McClure but I came straight back." His further letters to McHarg are lost, but in another he mentioned that some lying story had upset his friends and that a man hardly known to him was to blame.

The rumor of morphine had already reached Ripley Hitchcock and he diplomatically asked Crane's views on the taking of drugs. Crane did not approve. His liberalism had certain inset features. The ordinary prejudices of formal codes simply washed down from his mind, but drug-taking was a habit of fools and he had seen the dreary end of it on the East Side. A man of sense would not take drugs, and two years later he repeated the opinion to James Huneker.

" As soon," said Harding Davis, " as Mr. Crane's success

began there were ugly stories set in circulation about his private life. When he died his friends found it necessary to issue a denial that he took drugs. The yarn was absurd on its very face but it was told constantly. . . . I was never intimate with Crane but his best friends assured me that the story was false and they were not men to lie. He had a decided prejudice against drugtaking which I heard him express frequently at dinners and at the Lanthorn Club. But appearances were against him. He smoked constantly and he was very sallow and very thin. To see him through the smoke of a restaurant and to be told that he ate morphine would not have surprised me. But I know a great deal about the signs of the drug habit and Mr. Crane had none of them. Neither did it seem to me that he drank excessively. I remember that he disliked champagne, for instance, and as far as my memory serves me, he mostly stuck to dark beer. I know nothing about his relations with women and the story told about him in connection with some actress or artist's model was untrue to my knowledge."

The story yields up these facts. Crane was sitting with Acton Davies and Clyde Fitch in Mouquin's restaurant one night near the first of 1896 and a woman of some notoriety came up to ask Crane for a loan. This person had a number of titles and was sometimes married, informally or formally, but her actual name seems to have been Doris Watts. Crane had met her in 1895 as the titular wife of an acquaintance and she now appealed to him for a loan of fifty dollars. So he borrowed a blank check from Clyde Fitch and gave an amount not known. Acton Davies warned him that he would never be repaid. Crane's own statement of the sequel was dictated in November of 1899 and was also made orally to two friends. The woman, then known as Mrs. Bowen, began to worry him with letters asking for more funds on the plea that she was destitute and wanted to " reform." . . . He had a recklessly generous attitude toward women of all sorts and perhaps he was touched. He seems to have sent her several small checks which came to a total of a hundred and fifty dollars or thereabouts. But she wrote to him incessantly and at last threatened to come to Hartwood. This was a light variety of blackmail, of course, and Crane came to New York to have done with it. She was not sufficiently destitute to have dismissed her maid, a Negress, who let Crane into her rooms on West Forty-eighth Street. " I leaned on the door and told her to drop this nonsense. There was one of those horrors called Turkish corners in the room with a shield stuck full of knives. She lost her temper and grabbed a knife from the shield. It flew over my shoulder and stuck into the wood beside my ear and quivered so that I can still hear the noise." The disconsolate heroine then swooned, by rote, into the arms of her maid, and Crane went away, hatless. He borrowed a cap from a friend whose studio was in Thirtieth Street and retired to Hartwood.

The story was abroad by July and its general form was that Crane had seduced and then abandoned some girl of respectable parentage. The story naturally varied: she was a trusting artist's model; a country girl; a virgin actress. In July, Willis Clarke, a young fellow who was trying fiction, asked his brother, starting for New York, to make inquiries about Stephen Crane. In the old Cairo restaurant Clarke's brother was told that Crane was notoriously the father of a child by an unhappy girl who now was loose on the town. The Cairo was an excellent springboard for such information, as, with the exception of the Haymarket on Sixth Avenue, it was probably the rowdiest large night resort in New York at the time.

However, Crane was fair game for any legend. Hadn't he published a book of affected poems, one of which denied a Commandment? *Appleton's* had issued the slightly revised *Maggie* in June and it was plainly a shocking work although the reviews were civil. Besides, reporting for the *Press* the opening of a music-hall called the Broadway Gardens, he had already been published as the hero of a fight with a policeman who had bullied a girl about her business in the rear of the hall. . . . Crane was boyishly proud of the incident and discussed it with his brothers. He made a vehement attempt to destroy the policeman totally and was locked up all night but dismissed by some sensible judge in the morning. . . . A distinct flavor of *Maggie* mingled in the gossip and some of his admirers were seriously told that in order to write of her fate he had seduced a Bowery beauty and then thrown her to the wolves. All this compounded silliness was stirring, and in August the drowning core of the fable herself appeared in the offices of a young attorney with four letters from Crane as evidence that he owed her support. But all the letters began and ended formally and the checks were described as "loans." The attorney refused the case. She then attempted to have a warrant issued for Crane's arrest but was denied. A paragraph on August 23rd reports: "A young woman well known to habitués of the gayer restaurants along Broadway yesterday applied for a bench warrant to right the 'wrongs' done her by a prominent young writer of sensational fiction. The application was denied as her evidence did not seem sufficient and the lady left the court room on the arm of a gentleman whose buttonhole of lilies of the valley had already interested onlookers."

It is impossible, now, to retrace the jigging route of this scandal. It blew here and there fragrantly and entered the offices of the *Century*, where lay the manuscript of *A Man and Some Others*, sold to the magazine by Paul Reynolds. In early autumn the literary agent was hastily sent for by the editor, who demanded: "What does Crane mean by getting into such a mess when he's sold a story to *us*?"

The world of journals, though, had no space for the spite

of a pretty drab against an eccentric author. Front pages must be cleared for the whirling news of a great duel between two voices — the barytone roar of William Jennings Bryan and the milder basso of William McKinley. It was now understood that some numerical incantation known as the silver standard would either make everybody sixteen times richer or would ruin the United States. Few minds were strong enough to comprehend the reasoning of this process, but a plain case of the people against the wicked rich had been made out, and as Mr. Bryan had already chosen the role of buffoon in the arid comedy of American religion, he had the support of countless women in the midland, where they have always been quietly powerful in our politics, so the Nebraskan was shown in posters as a mailed knight spearing the fat dragon of plutocracy, and Democratic bankers were secretly heaving funds into the hands of Mark Hanna, the fat dragon's visible jockey. It was the battle of a noise against a timid, dully honorable man in hidden armor, but the nation shook in genuine hysteria until election day, when Ohio contributed another of her characteristic sons to the Presidential gallery and Hanna, worn out by exertion, lighted his cigars in capitalistic peace. . . . Crane was shooting along the colored hills with his brother and the charming setter, Chester, and stopping to ask: " Will, isn't that cloud green?. . . But they wouldn't believe it if I put it in a book."

CHAPTER V

FILIBUSTERING

HE loved babies, horses, oceans, or anything that offered an enigmatic surface to his thought. This comes strongly to view in a letter of 1895, when he was reading the criticism of Henry James: " What, though, does the man mean by disinterested contemplation? It won't wash. If you care enough about a thing to study it, you are interested and have stopped being disinterested. That's so, is it not? Well, Q.E.D.. It clamours in my skull that there is no such thing as disinterested contemplation except that empty as a beerpail look that a babe turns on you and shrivels you to grass with. Does anybody know how a child thinks? The horrible thing about a kid is that it makes no excuses, none at all. They are much like breakers on a beach. They do something and that is all there is in it." So he put them under a detached observation and played with them by the hour. The detachment was so perfect that his tales of childhood in the town of Whilomville were called cruel when they appeared. But he had an absolute sentiment for children and on November 12, 1896, he wrote to a Miss Catherine Harris: " Thank you very much for your letter on Maggie. I will try to answer your questions properly and politely. Mrs. Howells was right in telling you that I have spent a great deal of time on the East Side and that I have no opinion of missions. That — to you — may not be a valid answer since perhaps

312

you have been informed that I am not very friendly to Christianity as seen around town. I do not think that much can be done with the Bowery as long as the . . . [blurred] . . . are in their present state of conceit. A person who thinks himself superior to the rest of us because he has no job and no pride and no clean clothes is as badly conceited as Lillian Russell. [1] In a story of mine called ' An Experiment in Misery ' I tried to make plain that the root of Bowery life is a sort of cowardice. Perhaps I mean a lack of ambition or to willingly be knocked flat and accept the licking. The missions for children are another thing and if you will have Mr. Rockefeller give me a hundred street cars and some money I will load all the babes off to some pink world where cows can lick their noses and they will never see their families any more. My good friend Edward Townsend — have you read his ' Daughter of the Tenements '? — has another opinion of the Bowery and it is certain to be better than mine. I had no other purpose in writing ' Maggie ' than to show people to people as they seem to me. [2] If that be evil, make the most of it."

Then, on November 29th, writing from Jacksonville, Florida, to his brother William, a horse rises in the directions for his will and precedes the appointment of his literary executors — Howells, Garland, Willis Hawkins, and Ripley Hitchcock. William Crane was to be his sole executor and to receive a third of the estate, Edmund Crane was to have another third, and the remainder was divided between his two other brothers. But the horse, Peanuts:". . . my saddle horse I would not like to have sold. I would prefer that he be kept in easy service at Hartwood and have him cared for as much as possible by Ed himself or by somebody whom it is absolutely certain would not maltreat him

[1] Crane singularly disliked this actress, for reasons unknown.
[2] " You abuse me for objectivity, calling it indifference to good and evil. . . . It's my task simply to show people as they are." — Anton Chekhov.

. . . and all I can add now is my love to you and Cornelia and all the babies."

Filibustering was much the fashion in the years 1895 and 1896. The condition of Cuba was now so acutely revolutionary that European papers were wondering why the Cleveland administration didn't interfere, just as in two years they would be indignant that the McKinley administration had interfered. A century of inartistic government tinted with sadism had wearied Cuba. Thirty thousand men were admittedly in revolt and thousands more were under suspicion. Enterprising ships passed carefully from the ragged coast of Florida, laden with cartridges and guns, to meet signals of the insurrectionists flashed from the rim of the tormented island. The Bacheller Syndicate had sent Crane in a hurry southward with a belt full of gold, and his ambition was to see real war. He also took along for revision the manuscript of *The Third Violet*, which tells how a young impressionist painter wooed a wealthy beauty, in dire fear of her all the while, and won her in a drawing-room where a colossal chandelier cast malign lights, as if a piece of prose could fulfill a buried wish of his twentieth year. But Jacksonville bored him, on first view, and he was alone who liked to have people always around him: " The town looks like soiled pasteboard that some lunatic babies have been playing with. The same old women are sitting on the hotel porches saying how well the climate suits them and hurling the same lances with their eyes to begin bloodshed. . . . I went down the shore some distance yesterday and watched the combers come counting in. Sometimes their addition changes to multiplication and the music is confounded, like a war of drummerboys." He had thrown a dinner-party into gay convulsions lately by insisting that music was " addition without pain," but the mathematical basis of music was not much discussed in 1896 and Crane could not quote Leibnitz in support of his view, as he had never heard of Leibnitz, but the remark stuck in the memory of James Huneker, who thereafter insisted that Crane was an intuitive natural philosopher. Meanwhile the " war of drummerboys " did not console him for the absence of friends and he desperately tried to finish *Peace and War*, as he called it. But Tolstoi's endless panorama annoyed him. " He could have done the whole business in one third of the time and made it just as wonderful. It goes on and on like Texas."

Complete darkness covers him then until December 29th, when the small and elderly steamer *Commodore* dropped down the river from Jacksonville commanded by a strapping young Irish shipmaster, Edward Murphy, and containing, besides cased guns and a ton of cartridges, a large party of Cuban insurrectionists headed by one Delgado. Crane's instinctive aversion to sheer theatrical points would not let him believe that a plot had been arranged to frustrate the cruise of the *Commodore*, but threats were shouted at her crew in Spanish while she lay at the pier taking on coal, and a Cuban student, Juan Broch, on his way northward, heard two men saying: " It is all fixed. She will sink," in Castilian while he lingered on the dock after bidding good-by to a friend. Jacksonville was a nest of Cuban interests. Ralph D. Paine reports in *Roads of Adventure* the location of the Cuban patriotic committee, and the Spanish secret service may well have been busy with the *Commodore*. The Spanish diplomatic powers at Washington had been protesting all autumn against the open sailing of filibustering ships from American ports. In a general embarrassment, the United States navy patrolled the coast, and Spanish gunboats were watchful. The *Commodore* went down-stream and met a squall as she passed from the St. John's River into pure salt water. Crane thought the ship no more seaworthy than an ice-house although she had been lately examined for reinsurance, and that she should begin to fill abreast of St. Augustine was not strange, but his last impression of the engine room stayed deeply in his mind, with the fixity of all scenes in which the red he so loved was the commanding tone: " Water was swirling to and fro with the roll of the ship, fuming greasily around the half strangled machinery that still attempted to perform its duty. Steam arose from the water, and through its clouds shone the red glare of the dying fires. As for the stokers, death might have been with silence in this room. . . ."

The seasick Cubans lost their heads even before Captain Murphy turned the *Commodore* toward the shore. Their leader, Delgado, lost his temper and the jarring noise of quarrels rubbed on Crane's nerves. No one had slept for a day and a night and Crane was already ill before the ship began to founder. He watched her as she " shifted and settled as calmly as an animal curls down in the bush-grass " while he crouched beside the injured captain in a ten-foot dinghy, the last of the three boats to leave the heel-ing side of the steamer that disappeared noiselessly. " She might," he said, " have blown up to celebrate the New Year but she did not. She calmly left us orphans." The orphans were Captain Murphy, the ship's cook, Montgomery, an oiler, William Higgins, and Crane. Now, none of them knew the color of the sky.

The Open Boat is Crane's report of this wandering and Ralph Paine's statement shows that the sketch was cor-rected by Captain Murphy's memory. They rowed and the wind helped them toward their general aim, the point of Mosquito Inlet with its lighthouse and station. Murphy was helpless against the water-jar in the stern and Crane changed places with the oiler, Higgins, constantly. . . . They talked of food. " Canton flannel gulls flew near and far. Sometimes they sat down on the sea, near patches of brown seaweed that rolled over the waves with a movement like carpets on a line in a gale. The birds sat comfortably

in groups and were envied by some in the dinghy. . . .
One came and evidently decided to alight on the top of the
captain's head." Incorrigible, Crane's humor forbade him
to neglect the absurd sight of Murphy timidly waving a
hand to keep this gull from his soaked hair. Crests tumbled
spray into the boat and the point of the lighthouse danced
to view when the dinghy rose on the " jagged " waves. . . .
A work of art progressed while his back ached with the
work of the oar. Then followed woe; they were seen from
the beach; men waved — then night came without rescue
and a shark circled the drifting boat with a luminous wake.
. . . " When it occurs to a man that nature does not regard
him as important . . . he at first wishes to throw bricks
at the temple and he hates deeply the fact that there are no
bricks and no temples. Any visible expression of nature
would surely be pelleted with his jeers. Then, if there be
no tangible thing to hoot, he feels, perhaps, the desire to
confront a personification and indulge in pleas . . . saying, ' Yes, but I love myself.' " . . . Dawn came and they
turned the dinghy to the bobbing shore knowing they must
swim after its inevitable upset. So they swam in a gripping
current and Crane was flung clear across the floating boat by
a comber. But even in that iced, stupendous motion he must
see the water-flask bouncing gayly while he thrashed. They
got ashore, somehow, and a wave smashed the spine of the
oiler, Higgins, so that " a still and dripping shape was
carried slowly up the beach and the land's welcome for it
could be only the different and sinister hospitality of the
grave."

He was not well, suffering from some intestinal trouble,
when the *Commodore* sailed and now he had spent fifty
hours almost sleepless, drenched with water, imperfectly
fed on diluted whisky and biscuit. It is the opinion of his
brother that health never returned and he certainly did himself no good by tramping and riding through the swamps

317

below Jacksonville for weeks after the disaster. Rumors of
very secret small expeditions kept the town wakeful and
the navy was now most active off shore, sweeping plumes of
searchlight across the skies at night. The tug *Three Friends*
was the villain of the Spanish government now, and Crane
might yearn for Cuba and wish that filibustering could be
handed over to the adept management of a trust, but he
could not get to the island, and the war between Greece and
Turkey swung to view with all the promise of a fine testing-
ground. " I am going to Greece for the *Journal*," he wrote,
" and if the Red Badge is not all right I shall sell out my
claim on literature and take up orange growing."

He was not without vanity and to be told, as he was constantly, that his book was mere fancy did not please him.
To be told that he had imitated Zola's *La Débâcle* probably
pleased him less, as he disliked most of Zola's work. Even
Nana, that secret favorite of the American Puritan, bored
him by its length although he found Nana herself amusing
and, with his fatal lack of circumspection, informed a
woman that "this girl in Zola is a real streetwalker. I
mean, she does not fool around making excuses for her
career. You must pardon me if I cannot agree that every
painted woman on the streets of New York was brought
there by some evil man. Nana, in the story, is honest. . . .
Zola is a sincere writer but — is he much good? He hangs
one thing to another and his story goes along but I find him
pretty tiresome."

Effecting this irreverence casually he took orders from
William Randolph Hearst and went off to England with a
bad cold, having told Clyde Fitch that he would go on with
their play when he came back from Greece. . . . The play
had been a dozen times discussed and Fitch was impressed
by the theme proposed. But the two brains fell from each
other on an obvious point. There was to be this village in
the Virginia of 1864 and the contentious armies would

318

sweep in and out; a frightened young sentry would kill his
best friend in the dark; a man would be afraid to touch a
fallen body under orders to find papers in its pockets. Yes,
said Fitch, but, now, about a heroine? Crane saw no woman
concerned in this affair. They argued in the vapor of Mouquin's while men came up to borrow money from their
generosity, helpless in the face of any claim by an old acquaintance, but the mind back of Fitch's rather wistful
mask of a French dandy was conventional. A play without
a " love interest " would never do. With all the playwright's atmospheric intelligence he was not daring outside
small devices. His plays, alert, topical, and vivid ran always in due form. He consented to the usual and never
shook off the habit of the theater even after success had
piled about his anæmic body treasures of delicate furniture, of marmoreal surfaces shown against the lushness of
purple velvet, of rare wines he could not use or relish in the
slow starvation that rose from his earlier struggles to end
his industry, his passions of gratitude, and his respectful
service to lovely women with pallid golden hair. . . . A
curious miasma seemed to flow on all these Americans of
that century's last decade. Their lungs broke and slew
them. They were slaughtered by their brothers or by crazy
musicians. Fame had picked up a dagger and made use of
it at random, but no bores died young.

Crane's sketch of his arrival in London shows his defect
as an artist for popular use. He lacked the easy sentimentalism which so graces the notes of other American writers
who get to London, but he saw a cab horse gravely slide
down wet asphalt and was suddenly convinced that a man
in a top hat might be human. He had silently distrusted top
hats on Americans although their use was spreading and
" there now exist many young men who consider that they
could not successfully conduct their lives without this furniture. To speak generally I should say that the headgear

319

then supplies them with a kind of ferocity of indifference.
. . . Philosophy should always know that indifference is a
militant thing." He also saw the newest novel of Hall Caine
advertised on posters and startled William Heinemann by
asking his English publisher if England read Hall Caine's
works. Crane may have shared the purely American delusion that cheap novels are only read in the United States.

London contained, just then, dozens of American correspondents and he could at once meet Harold Frederic, principal agent of the *New York Times* in England and, in
1897, the author of *The Damnation of Theron Ware*, the
sole courageous or truthful novel ever written by an American on the subject of religion. Frederic's fictions had
changed, as their maker changed, from simple romanticism
to a sort of shrewd, rough realistic tone and *Theron Ware*
had for Crane the precise appeal of familiarity. He
thought, privately, that " it could have been written a
darned lot better," but he liked the story of the wavering
young Methodist preacher who was bullied by sour old men
of his stagnant church and learned to like pleasure at the
hands of some crude hedonists who discharge their wisdom
on Theron Ware as encyclopedic lumps, terribly prophesy-
ing the American novel of this moment. . . . Frederic's
style suggests the man's diverse personality. He was
shrewd, witty, and assertive to a degree. Even a dear friend
would leave admissions that Frederic was not " finely
fibred " and people who met him toward the end of a rather
vexed life seldom much liked him, while his kindnesses to
folk without importance and his desperate loyalties are as
well remembered. He made many useful quips which survive in transmutations and borrowings. " Mr. Matthew
Arnold plainly believes that Columbus should have been
hanged in chains for the crime of discovering America.
. . . In the United States it is considered sinful to drink
champagne and eat lobster after midnight. Up to that hour

it is a matter only of digestion. . . . Actresses are events which may take place in the most respectable family circles." His mind swung from balanced and liberal surveys to vehement prejudice, and the one letter available to this study displays: " Mr. Edward Garnett [3] would be an El Dorado to an American publisher of the superior class. He seems to be able to scent a new talent in fiction from a thousand miles and as a critic he possesses both sincerity and distinction of manner. He should be made known to Americans. . . . ' The Red Badge of Courage ' has probably been successful in the U. S. more because it is a Civil War story than because it is a brilliant study of an individual. . . . Henry James is an effeminate old donkey who lives with a herd of other donkeys around him and insists on being treated as if he were the Pope. He has licked dust from the floor of every third rate hostess in England. . . . Mr. James recommended Mr. Crane's novel before me in the house of our one mutual acquaintance and I was deterred from reading it for some days for that reason. With his usual lack of sense or generosity he described the book as an imitation of Zola's ' The Downfall ' which it resembles as much as I do Miss Ellen Terry." His encounters with Henry James were infrequent but dreadful to people who preferred that the older man's gauzy periphery of sentiments and perceptual tenderness should remain unbruised. In 1895, for instance, Frederic listened while the novelist outlined a charming tour of cathedral towns to an American lady and then advised her to look through the slums of Liverpool and Manchester as well. . . . The florid, tall man haunted Ireland in hope of seeing a revolution start, but when a row began between peasants of his favorite fishing village and the British constabulary, he intervened. He abominated all the capacities of Oscar Wilde, but when the grand fakir was on trial, at last, refused to

[3] He had no personal acquaintance with Mr. Garnett.

allow exaggerations to be sent to his newspaper and turned loudly on a group of gossips in a club with: " Why do you sit and lie about the poor devil when he's done for? " He had a war always threatening with any exquisite and some of his rudenesses were wondrous. " Your new book held me spellbound," he told a writer of thinly charming essays who started to return thanks and was halted by: " Yes, I rode clear past my station. The guard had to wake me up at the next one." Such wit belongs in the snuffbox of Talleyrand. But Frederic had an honest, quite unaffected admiration for Crane and led him into the Savage on March 26th as though, says a witness, he had invented the boy.

They appeared together at a luncheon given for Crane by Richard Harding Davis on March 28th in the Savoy and there Crane was presented to James Barrie, Justin Mc-Carthy, Anthony Hope, and some more. Frederic followed his new friend to Dover and said good-by on April 1st, giving him into the keeping of Henry Sanford Bennett, a Canadian, on his way to Greece also. Bennett spoke French and guided Crane through Paris on April 2nd, making discoveries about the silent American that ended with a flash of Crane's disgust in Notre Dame where some procession was passing toward the altar in color and music. Bennett was watching this ceremony when Crane pulled his arm and broke out: " I can't stand that nonsense! " Color, music, and the traditional pathos of mass made no excuse to his nature for theatrical display. He looked with indifference at a review of cavalry but made Bennett talk to a trooper for him about horses in the French service and ask if the man had been at Gravelotte in 1870. " He took," said Bennett, " not the slightest interest in any of the show places except the Luxembourg gardens and I had to help him talk to some French children there."

Paris never properly impressed Crane, who spent his time on the way to Greece trying to master some phrases of

French, suddenly worried because this war must be fought in strange tongues and he could speak only English. At Basel he mailed a letter: " I now know that I am an imbecile of rank. If nobody shoots me and I get back alive through those Indians in London I will stay home until there is a nice war in Mexico where it does not matter what you talk so long as you can curse immoderately. Willie Hearst has made a bad bargain." . . . He was right. Part of his prompt and flat failure as a war correspondent lay in his helplessness. He must rely on guides and interpreters throughout the brief campaign. The *New York Journal* and the *Westminster Gazette* had made a bad bargain. Even his sense of the comic straggled out under the blight and he could not well enjoy Athens with its masses of tourists who had come to see a real war comfortably. Notes of clear impression mingle with his reporting, but his whole raid into Greece was a series of irritations and he wrote: " I guess that I expected some sublime force to lift me in air and let me watch. Well, no! Like trying to see a bum vaudeville show from behind a fat man who wiggles. I have not been well either."

He was not well and, given a practical nature, he would have resigned his post in Paris. Perpetual indigestion bothered him and he found the Greek food abominable. Meanwhile the Crown Prince Constantine had begun practice of his specialty by running away from combat, to the disgust of all Greece, and Crane arrived at Velestinos eight hours after the beginning of the great engagement that finished the war. He had gone plunging along the line of emptied hilltowns and villages that lay between Velestinos and Volo and came hurrying back with other stragglers to find Richard Harding Davis and John Bass the only American correspondents on the scene of the long duel between the ill-officered Greek infantrymen and the agile Turkish force that peppered the trenches from an elevation. The

323

war was lost, Davis accurately declared, in the cafés of Athens, and like Crane the expert raged at the command of the willing soldiers by dandies so ineffective. Davis went swiftly off to London, and Crane, worn out, suffering from attacks of bowel trouble, strolled about Athens with Julian Ralph, who marveled finding that the impressionist knew nothing of Greek architecture and could not distinguish types of columns on the Acropolis.

Crane had no sense of line. His few attempts to draw a human shape are not even in proportion and the whole mass of his impressions, transcribed so brilliantly from a visible scene, are truly " impressions " and not careful photographs. He seldom mentions contour in his quick passages of description. He saw the frenzied peasants rushing down the mountain into Volo: " It was a freshet that might sear the face of the tall, quiet mountain; it might draw a livid line across the land, this downpour of fear with a thousand homes adrift in the current — men, women, babes, animals. From it there arose a constant babble of tongues, shrill, broken, and sometimes choking, as from men drowning. Many made gestures, painting their agonies on the air with fingers that twirled swiftly. The blue bay with its pointed ships, and the white town lay below them, distant, flat, serene." The people of his tales have very seldom more than a suggestion of body. A man has " indomitable whiskers " or some clothes. The lad in *The Red Badge of Courage*, late in the book, has a bronzed throat. The pretty girl of *The Third Violet* is simply something the artist would like to paint — a trick of entry that Crane left to some thousands of writers. Since his art has lately been often likened to that of Anton Chekhov with inevitable comments by American critics as to his " able imitations " of the Russian, whose works were not, while Crane lived, known outside Russia, there is an interest in the parallel, but Crane never so elaborated his pictures of people as did Chekhov in *The*

324

Steppes, and his fullest description of a being is that of his brother's setter, Chester, appearing as Stanley in *The Third Violet*. The contour of man had no particular spell for him and when he was asked to describe Gertrude Kingston, the English actress who was his choice as the prettiest woman on the London stage, he said: " Well, she's got black hair and a nose," which left James Huneker unenlightened.

These habits didn't prevent his enjoyment of prolix or exact art. He valiantly argued with Julian Ralph in Athens that *The Portrait of a Lady* was a masterpiece. Tolstoi's *Anna Karenina* was " too long because he has to stop and preach but it's a bully book." He adored Tolstoi the superb and ruthless artist, but for Tolstoi the emotional pedagogue, the pilgrim of redemption, he had no use. No fact so clearly sets Crane apart from Americans of his day and shows the course of his damnation by that criticism which still, for all the changing tone of these last years, most resembles a wavering lady in a dark crinoline, prudently girdled with chaste iron. Scratch an American critic, says the astute Julian Street, and you find a Yankee schoolmarm. To that instructive gentlewoman Crane appeared as a rowdy little boy who brought dead mice to school, a lurid and irregular child who upset the other children and then ran off before he could be taught on some filibustering game of his own making to leave a boy's cry trailing its shrill beauty against the stupid night.

In tumultuous Athens, though, Crane was ill of a mild dysentery and was nursed by a fair, affable woman, older than himself, Cora Taylor, who had fallen in love with him at Jacksonville and had come after him to Greece. So writing from Paris on September 2nd, he told Sanford Bennett: " Frederic and Mr. Heinemann have been urging me to stay in England for a time. So my wife — after practicing nine days I can write that without a jump — and I will be hunting a house or an attic in London pretty soon."

CHAPTER VI

LONDON TO CUBA

AN AMERICAN writer is safest abroad when he has somewhere left in storage his entire critical sense and has for the voyage replaced it by an emotional willingness comparable to the felicity of a noticed puppy. He may then roam in his destined character giving neither pleasure nor offense to men who will accept his admirations and hear his raptures as mature women might accept the flowers and phrases of some harmless schoolboy. On the Continent he will be, mostly, the child of the world's milch cow, but in England he must be wary as are boorish relations of whose manners something too much is known.

Crane's extreme dislike of Robert Louis Stevenson got him in trouble at William Heinemann's table early in October when he recklessly or absently assured two of the dead Scot's correspondents that Stevenson bored him. All through his first English winter he was forever meeting filaments of that monstrous reputation then being groomed for the American market by adoring hands. It had been well and naturally established in England that " R. L. S." was an American idol, and a transatlantic who didn't admire may have seemed vastly affected. On October 12th Crane wrote: " I believe in ghosts. Mr. Stevenson has not passed away far enough. He is all around town."

There was another spook, in better flesh, whose reputation was not, in 1897, amenable to grooming. Literary London was shaken or amused by the rumor of memoirs being written in Reading Gaol by Oscar Wilde, and Henry Harland, once an editor of the *Yellow Book*, assured Crane that terrible things might be expected to happen if the collapsed dandy found a publisher for his book of memories. Crane again was bored. Only some passages of Wilde's plays had any interest for him, and the poet in his view was just a sentimental neurotic who should be shipped for treatment to S. Weir Mitchell " or some other doctor who knows all about that kind of thing." He would later be shocked and nauseated by the sight of Wilde's blotched and powdered face bleating compliments at him in the smoke of the Café Procope, but now his refusal to discuss Oscar as a splendid sinner irritated Harland sharply. A pet criminal is always sacred, but Wilde had acquired a curious dignity because his case was restricted, in conversation, to small and liberal circles. In Crane's disgusted commentary: " Wilde was a mildewed chump. He has a disease and they all gas about him as though there was a hell and he came up out of it. . . . Mr. Yeats is the only man I have met who talks of Wilde with any sense. The others talk like a lot of little girls at a Sunday School party when a kid says a wicked word in a corner." Perhaps it was Crane's misfortune to be a little more modern in 1897 than was necessary. Or perhaps a young man who had sat in tramp's clothes by night in Union Square listening to darkened chatter of real tramps might not be so thrilled over the neurosis of an Irish poet. His indifference to the purple legend was disheartening. He failed of taking Oscar Wilde seriously or sadly and that, too, was held to be an affectation.

There was no tumult in the high world of letters English because Stephen Crane had rented a villa named Ravensbrook at Oxted in Surrey and proposed to make a stay. He was even snubbed with a vehemence that still bewilders the witnesses by George Meredith on the steps of a club before

Crane had spoken to the celebrity. Algernon Charles Swinburne asked him to tea at Putney and, discovering that Crane neither read nor talked French, entertained the American by translating bits of a sixteenth-century manuscript to him. Extremely sensitive to courtesies of men older than himself, Crane was still somewhat wearied by this cultivated afternoon and spent the evening tramping with Robert Barr through a slum not then well advertised in fiction, the Limehouse now illustrious and now, as then, very dull indeed.

He was so sensitive to attentions of people more ancient than Stephen Crane that the trait lends itself to psychiatric description. Many of his letters were written to two ladies fifteen years ahead of him, on whom he lavished luncheons in his prosperous spring of 1896. . . . They were both dyspeptic. He would turn from the prettiest girl in a crowded room to chat with an elderly lady. Favors of middle-aged folk had some special meaning for the final child of a long family, used to petting and scolding from brothers and sisters who had been longer living. When he was seventeen he doted on a Canadian gentlewoman with seven infants. At twenty-six he was ordered by James Huneker to read Balzac and only the contrary opinion of another authority stopped him. And now he was ordered by Harold Frederic to write a novel about his trip to Greece and, in November of 1897, he began it. Mr. Frederic thought he should, so he would. But *Active Service* somehow began itself slowly and lagged on his desk at Oxted while he took up other tales and finished *The Monster* one day in early December, having spent a whole week of interrupted evenings on the long story, which shows every strength and every weakness of his armory. Harold Frederic strolled over from Robert Barr's house at Woldingham, within sight of the dank villa grown already detestable to

Crane, and with Sanford Bennett made an audience for the reading aloud of the fantasy.

The Monster is a study of popular stupidity. The foremost doctor of Whilomville restores to life a vain Negro hostler who has rescued his small son from a burning house. Dr. Trescott's sentiment keeps alive this fellow, now an idiot and faceless. The sentimentality of Whilomville has acclaimed Henry Johnson a hero and a martyr while he was thought dying. Now the kindly and aimless monster terrifies first the Negroes who are paid to lodge him, then a children's party, then his former mistress, the belle of Watermelon Alley. The town swings against the surgeon who has kept Henry Johnson in being and the subject passes in vocal exhibition through the gossip of the barber's shop and through the kitchen wherein Martha Goodwin, a woman who was nothing but the mausoleum of a dead passion, gives judgment on the world's affairs and helps forward all local troubles by a series of sniffs. The sermon on useless pity completes itself with the picture of Dr. Trescott counting unused teacups on his wife's neglected table. Sentimentality has clubbed sentiment to death in Whilomville. *The Monster* suffers from a defect of exuberance; Crane's passion for recording fatuous conversations reaches a height twice in the narrative. The chatter in the barber's shop would not again be equaled for sheer emptiness until James Joyce wrote his *Portrait of the Artist as a Young Man*, but it is dangerous to lay emptiness before emptiness without pointing out the vacuum and Crane's satire is implicit. To the taste of 1897, *The Monster* was plainly a horrible tale of a man who had no face and, when Paul Reynolds offered it to the *Century* it was refused with speed, an editor explaining to the puzzled agent: " We couldn't publish that thing with half the expectant mothers in America on our subscription list! " Even to Harold Frederic the story was offensive and he told Crane to throw it away. The other half of the audience, Mr. Bennett, promptly gave proof of the power of impressionism, deftly handled, as a mode in fiction. He was for years troubled by a memory of the Negro's shattered visage and, picking up the tale after Crane died, was surprised to find that all his horror had been excited by the simple statement: " He had no face."

Crane thrashed up and down the room waiting for luncheon and arguing passionately while he tapped the butt of his Mexican revolver on furniture. What was wrong with people, anyhow? Here was a lot of ink on white paper and a story " with some sense in it." Why be frightened? His hopeless failure to catch the emotional viewpoint of average readers or, for that matter, of average writers came flashing up. " Men of sense " would not care if Henry Johnson had a face or no. The argument blazed. Mr. Bennett sat listening to the battle that lasted all through luncheon and ended in explosion. Frederic turned his guns on *The Nigger of the Narcissus*, and Crane, crashing down the revolver fatally on a dessert plate, yelled: " You and I and Kipling couldn't have written the Nigger! " Thus are these artists.

It has been worth while to detail this abstract quarrel since Crane was swiftly reported in New York as Harold Frederic's slave and subject. They were not seen so on November 30th by an American lawyer who called at Oxted. Next day he wrote to his wife: " Mr. [John] Stokes gave me a note of introduction to Mr. Crane and he was very pleasant in a quiet, boyish way when I got to his house. It surprised me how little he uses slang when his books are full of it and how young he is. Mrs. Crane asked me to stay for lunch. She is a southerner and very nice. I should imagine her to be six or seven years older than Mr. Crane with big blue eyes and reddish hair. Mr. Frederic, the *New*

York Times correspondent came in the middle of the lunch with five other men and it was very embarrassing for Mrs. Crane as they were not expected. Mr. Frederic is not at all agreeable. He is funny in a sarcastic way about politics and people but he kept interrupting everybody else and was downright rude to Mr. Crane several times. They made Mr. Crane shoot with his revolver after lunch and he is a very fine shot. Some children came over from the next house to watch and Mrs. Crane made biscuit for tea. She is a wonderful cook."

By December a visible strain came on Crane's purse and Cora Crane's cookery. He wrote to Acton Davies: " Will you see if X and Y could let me have what they borrowed last May? I took X's note for $300 and Y owes me about $250. I hate to press nice fellows but it costs more to live over here than I was led to believe and some of these Comanche braves seem to think I am running a free lunch counter. Seven men have been staying over Sunday." So the plump little dramatic reporter ran Crane's errand in New York and failed to collect from men who hardly knew Crane and meanwhile parties of seven or, once, nine men came dropping down to convenient Oxted for Sundays of talk and poker. More game pies and claret must be sent for and, on December 3rd, he wrote: " I have been staying at this hotel " — it was Brown's, in Dover Street — " two days so as to finish some work. Cora just now wires me that she has got rid of some people who have been boarding with us for three days, so I can go home."

He was, in short, pillaged by people who found his chromatic talk and his wife's biscuit admirable while his helpless good nature couldn't or didn't repel visitors scarcely agreeable. At tea in John Hay's house he told the Ambassador, after being congratulated on his success: " I wish success paid me a salary, sir," with a grin. In a few minutes the grin must have faded. A Countess asked him

about his parents and when she heard that his father had
been a Methodist pastor broke into laughter of some quality
offensive to Hay and probably searing to Crane, who thereafter recorded that Lady Cardigan had no more manners
than a streetwalker. This was, outside a small group of
intimates, his last truthful statement as to his family in England and a few days later he told a lady dining beside him
in the house of Hoyt De Fries that his father was a Presbyterian Cardinal.

" Oh," said she, " do Dissenters have cardinals in the
States? "

The English unconsciousness of American habits and
customs did not annoy him but it entertained him largely
and he got an amusement out of wholesale lies: " They will
believe anything wild or impossible you tell them and then
if you say your brother has a bathtub in his house they —
ever so politely — call you a perjured falsifier of facts. I
told a seemingly sane man at Mrs. Garnett's that I got my
artistic education on the Bowery and he said, ' Oh, really?
So they have a school of fine arts there? ' I had, you see,
just told Mrs. Garnett while this mummy listened all about
the Bowery — in so far as I could tell a woman about the
Bowery — but that made no difference to this John Bull.
Now I am going to wave the starry flag of freedom a little "
(he was writing to Huneker) " even if you contemn the
practice in one who knows not Balzac and Dostoywhat'shis-
name. You Indians have been wasting wind in telling me
how ' Unintrusive ' and ' DELICATE ' I would find English manners. I don't. It has not been the habit of people
to meet at Mr. Howells or Mr. Phillips or Mrs. Sonntages
to let fall my hand and begin to quickly ask me how much
money I make and from which French realist I shall steal
my next book. For it has been proven to me fully and carefully by authority that all my books are stolen from the
French. They stand me against walls with a teacup in my

hand and tell me how I have stolen all my things from De Maupassant, Zola, Loti and the bloke who wrote — I forget the book. I find nothing 'unintrusive' or 'delicate' in these goings on. The simple rustic villagers of Port Jervis have as good manners as some of the flower of England's literary set."

It was not believed in England that he was truly ill informed in letters and he tired of explaining that some books of criticism and a few paper-backed copies of Flaubert and de Maupassant in translation were his acquaintances, casually made, with the French nineteenth century. He had never read Stendhal's *La Chartreuse de Parme*, and Henry Harland's insistence that he *must* have read it before writing *The Red Badge of Courage* finally angered him. The journalists at the Savage were willing to take him as an amusing companion and the taverns of London were more interesting than drawing-rooms where " everybody knows everybody else's business in the superlative degree and everybody reads everybody's books mainly — unless I am blind — to be at once able to tell everybody else how bad they are. Politics and literature have got wonderfully boiled into a kind of chowder. I feel like a clam."

Winter brought bad colds and a trip to Harold Frederic's pet Irish fishing village. On February 5th he dined with Frederic and Charles Griswold, an American tourist, at Richmond. To this matrix of a pleasant evening was suddenly added a nobleman then in alliance with a lady never certain as to her nationality, understood to be the honored subject of verses in the *Yellow Book* and reputed chaste though seldom sober. The party came back to Mr. Griswold's rooms in London and Madame Zipango (the name is certainly international) was imitating Yvette Guilbert when Henry James appeared to pay his young compatriot a call. The correct and the incorrect swam together in a frightful collision. Crane withdrew the elderly novelist to a corner and talked style until the fantastic woman poured champagne in the top hat of Henry James. Her noble lover had gone to sleep. Frederic was amused. The wretched host of this group was too young and too frightened to do anything preventive and Crane, coldly tactful, got the handsome creature out of the hotel, then came back to aid in the restoration of the abused hat.

Crane did not find this funny. In the next week he wrote: " I agree with you that Mr. James has ridiculous traits and lately I have seen him make a holy show of himself in a situation that — on my honour — would have been simple to an ordinary man. But it seems impossible to dislike him. He is so kind to everybody. . . ."

He was so kind. From the sacred fount of his self-adoration there yet welled on gifted folk those pools of tender correspondence and those courtesies a trifle tedious, one hears, but rendered with such grace. Ada Rehan might vexedly call him " my dear snob " across a luncheon-table, but she would repent for weeks that bit of premeditated, natural frankness. Another actress, in a forgetful breath, assured him that she found his friend Paul Bourget's novels vulgar and then shook as the deep voice stammered: " Vul— " to begin some sentence of pained expostulation that ended in mere syllables of affront. He was no longer a man. Henry James was a colored and complicated ritual that demanded of spectators a reverence unfailingly accorded. People who swooned under the burden of his final method sat and sat in pleasure while that astonishing egotism bared in slow phrases its detached and charming appreciation of its own singular skill. He had written plays incoherent and banal in exquisite English for the simple and admitted purpose of making money " as much and as soon as possible," and his votaries shuddered when the plebeians hooted *Guy Domville* from the stage. He committed in reviews consummate silliness such as his famous statement

of tears shed over the butchered children of Rudyard Kipling's *Drums of the Fore and Aft* with its added comment
on the dreadful dirtiness of the dead drummers. The sob
balanced the snobbery and nobody jeered, save one remote
and logical American. Critics mired themselves in verbal
anguish over his successive novels. This plain and limited old bachelor commanded the world to respect him and
the world obeyed. He was so kind.

Life waned for this man in his absurd and wonderful
position, the patron of a cult. His books were so little read
in America that he could be mentioned as "the late Henry
James" in 1898 at a public banquet without exciting laughter. Americans invading England found, to their horror or
secret relief, that nobody seemed to read his books in the
territory assigned to his renown. But to no other writer in
the Anglo-American field were attached such bristling ad-
herents! He was holy and impeccable to the gaze of innumerable talented folk. Mrs. Humphry Ward fell speech-
less and scarlet when it was said, in her presence, that Mr.
James had derived his tale *Paste* from de Maupassant, and
another votary still living ordered from his house a heretic
who chose to argue that the Master's preoccupation with refinements was a vulgar habit. He was prim and circumspect, as befitted the child grown old who was ordered at the
age of seven to compose a note of apology for appearing
barefoot on the porch of a seaside villa before callers, and
he was the pet of cynical voluptuaries. He was a provincial
sentimentalist touted by worshippers as the last flower of
European culture while he recoiled in amazement from the
profound civilization of Havelock Ellis, who would and,
"so successfully delicate in his attack on the matter of these
abominations that one reads, I may say, almost painlessly,"
did write of sexual deflections and gross social phenomena
without any sign of shock. This fading life of Henry James
had passed in a series of recoils. Civilization, in his sight,

seems to have been not the overthrow of empty inhibitions but an exaltation of limits. He had fled — and who blames him? — from a society that became, in his dreams, a tentacled beast ready always to overpower his individual trend, but he remained a Bostonian by every implication of his rare and scrupulous art. Even when in *The Turn of the Screw* he attempted to tell the story of " abominations " he must produce it with ghosts for sinners and the corrupted bodies must be those of children impossible and lovely as the babes of his predecessor Hawthorne. This master of groomed circumstance had found out a sunny garden where poisons blew as perfumes too heavy for a refined sense and crimes were shadows, not clouds, that swept across his shaved and watered turf.

Destiny now jolted the European sod beneath the feet of loitering transatlantics. On the night of February 15th the battleship *Maine* was blown up in the harbor of Havana and in two days it was known that treachery was suspected by the American government. The world's press went mad with all the brilliance of its eternal parochialism and any student in popular misinformation may gather material of delicious merits from the abiding files. Henry James was distressed by the " seeming inaccuracy of the Parisian, or indeed of all the Continental reports " and Stephen Crane was bored at once to hear that " American troops always run at the first shot and there is no such thing as the U. S. Navy. These matters were clearly proven to me last night at the Savage by a Mr. Wyndham who once met General Grant. I have vainly tried to tell some good men and true that Cuba is not on friendly terms with California but they will have it that one gets on a tug at San Francisco to go to Havana."

He took the end of the *Maine* so calmly that some of his friends were appalled. The quality of his nature forbade outcries after an event and his " fatalism " seems rather to have been a severe reticence in the sight of disasters. The American colony in London grew hysteric and John Stokes reproached Crane with his coolness while the English press assumed an indignant tone and in Paris *La Patrie* invented a formula of objections. Were the compatriots of Cervantes and Velasquez to be accused of sinking a warship in time of peace? Some emotional incantation, now unknown, summoned up Velasquez and Cervantes as the Castor and Pollux of the moment in aid of Spain. These artists were invoked ceaselessly and jumped the Channel. . . . All at once Americans discovered themselves to be the dogs of the universe. This issue was confused by the report of the commission which investigated the sinking of the *Maine* and with a certainty neither graceful nor diplomatic experts French, English, and German in the capitals of those lands asserted that the commission lied in all its findings. Dislike of the United States turned journals formerly loud in their insistence that the United States should intervene on behalf of Cuba. Alternately Spain was a tottering lady to be defended from the assaults of a brutal ruffian or a proud power capable of sweeping American fleets and troops from the map with one gesture. The press of America was silly in its brashness and the press of Europe was silly from contempt long hoarded in its editorial brain. The spectacle was repeated, of course, later, but its vividness in 1898 bewildered the Yankee and roused the Southerner. In Europe the nose of the golden calf was slapped with such violence that the poor beast began, not without primitive reasons, to turn and canter lowing homeward. On March 10th landlords in Paris were quaintly worried by the flight of Americans from a city in which they were daily insulted and the proprietors of hotels addressed themselves in some agitation to the newspapers. Tinkling harshly, the dollar rolled away from the scene of its worship and cynics were diverted by the minatory sound. . . . The American's one value was in motion, and vulgar, acutely sensitive to that noise, Joseph Chamberlain advised: "Care should be taken that the American financial authorities do not take offense."

Another excitement shook London in the middle of March. Paying huge prices for stalls the smart world went in its best coat to see a benefit arranged for Nellie Farren, crippled and penniless in her discarded age. Magnificents who had refused to contribute a pound to her comfort now blubbered duly in boxes while the little paralytic was borne on the stage to croak her thanks. Henry Irving kindly recited *The Dream of Eugene Aram* and Ellen Terry loosed the enchantment of her voice as Ophelia. Marie Tempest sang a ballad from *The Geisha* and a whole train of celebrated actresses deployed their graces before Crane, whose evening dress was painfully tight, he wrote, but " Oscar Hammerstein couldn't get people to make bigger fools of themselves. Except Willie Hearst nobody understands the popular mind as well as Oscar. I see no difference between the *Journal* and Hammerstein's roofgarden. You get the blonde with the tincan in her gullet and the comic speaker and the song about mother's wayward boy in both shows. I must affiliate with Hammerstein. Mr. Conrad and I are writing a new kind of play."

But, in Washington, the Senator from Vermont had read his dry, emotionless report on the condition of Cuba and in a bar of Broadway some man lowered his glass with the wavering sentence: " Gentlemen, remember the *Maine!* " Imperfect history tells us only that he had a red mustache, but war was now inevitable and, for once, his court turned unbelieving eyes on Mark Hanna when he grunted that Spain could be licked in six months. The Assistant Secretary of the Navy paused before resigning his post to frustrate the revealed wish of some fifty Methodist and Baptist preachers in self-appointed committee that all Roman Catholic chaplains be withdrawn from ships sent to action, then went off to gather a regiment of cavalry. With parade and consequence promptly recorded in the social columns hundreds of well-washed New Yorkers offered their services to their country and bloody squadrons sailed in print from Cadiz to ravage the American seaboard with guns of a caliber not yet found. . . . Whether the nation was preparing to avenge the *Maine* or to free Cuba was quite uncertain in the nation's mind, but somebody was going to suffer and Crane wrote: " This war will be fought in English. I can at least swear in Spanish and it will be more comfortable all around. But I have not decided on going yet."

He was ill. After a cerebral hemorrhage Harold Frederic was dying, so consciously that he lifted aside a corner of the handkerchief partly veiling his distorted face to wink at callers who told him he would soon be well again. And, dying, the hedonist accepted Christian Science treatment to please a devoted woman who was made a scandal in the press with all the usual vulgarities attendant on an erratic and published man's vanishing. He had taken close hold on Crane's affection, though, and the younger American lingered. Then, suddenly, he left a note at Sanford Bennett's rooms: " Sorry not to have seen you. I have raised the wind and sail tomorrow. Nothing I can do for Harold. Barr will look after him. Write me at Hartwood, N. Y., care of Edmund Crane. Shall get myself taken in the Navy if possible." He was so swiftly out of England that guests came down to Oxted and were surprised to find him gone. Only after he sailed the *World* cabled to secure his services and he did not present himself at the office in New York until a naval recruiting bureau had declined his body. Then he was off to Key West, where Sampson's fleet pivoted on the mangy little city filled with journalists, harlots, and mosquitoes, who all found a nightly meeting-place in the gambling-hell. Thence came to Robert Barr a letter postmarked May 23rd: " You should see the jay who runs the

339

table here. He is straight out of a dime novel, moustache and all, with bunches of diamonds like cheap chandeliers on each hand. Now I owe Harold an apology for laughing when he said they would tear me in pieces the minute my back was turned. Hi, Harold! I apologize! Did you know me for a morphine eater? A man who has known me ten years tells me that all my books are written while I am drenched with morphine. The joke is on me."

But the gambling-hell was delightful and he took notes of its owner's conversation. The man knew easily, he said, nine hundred distinct oaths. When he told bawdy tales the ceiling changed color and his sarcasm was so theatrically effective that it appears too theatrical in *Moonlight on the Snow*. This character must be made use of in the play and Crane's character was blighted more deeply while he lounged, pointed out to strangers, in the smoky rooms already hot with tropical spring. He missed the fleet's bombardment of Matanzas, but once the flagship carried him so closely by the breakers lazily flapping crystal foam on the island's sands that he could see a naked child tossing its hands in welcome from the shore.

CHAPTER VII

CHANGE

THAT irrelevant baby becomes a convenient symbol of Crane's doubled nature. He still wanted to push his growing frailty against the random gestures of society's bad behavior. He would be in the middle of matters with which, as an artist, he found himself concerned. Sense and the warnings of friends should have kept him away from Cuba, but his curiosity took him there quite inevitably. The man had not yet learned certain high values of posture: as a superior writer he should have sentimentalized his position, retiring gravely into an attitude, but the elaborate fustian of his profession had no charm for him at the age of twenty-six and here was this comprehensible war to be heard in English with many of his comrades impatient at Key West or dodging in dispatch boats after Sampson's fleet as it swept along the island's northern coast. So he appeared and won three hundred dollars from the estimable gambler in intervals of slow cruising on the tug *Three Friends* with a bundle of manuscript and the worst equipment for a campaign ever seen.

He was at once wonderfully disliked by some men who here saw Stevie Crane for the first time. Travel and reputation had not made him less reserved and he gave no proper account of his stay in England. England was all right. He had met some bully people. No, he hadn't seen much of Rudyard Kipling and while he found James Barrie a nice

341

fellow he did not praise the new favorite's work. There was a prompt impression of chilly listlessness and to a young gentleman who told him how greatly he resembled Robert Louis Stevenson Crane straightway answered: " I hope I outgrow it," and that, too, was not diplomatic. Old friends thought him little changed and his poker was as bad as ever.

The war now halted while Europe took care to revise its opinion of the American navy after Dewey massacred a feeble collection of Spanish gunboats in Manila Bay. Lord Salisbury paraphrased for the Primrose League, on May 4th, some ideas of Friedrich Nietzsche as to dying states and the rights of the stronger nations. Crane grinned a good deal over the new tone in dispatches from abroad and went one day quickly to look at the sandy camping-place appointed for troop gathering at Tampa in the rising temperature of May's last weeks. There he cast an eye on volunteer regiments assembling and disgusted correspondents by one of his usual failures in enthusiasm. The volunteers had forsaken their business and already underwent the hardships of the soldier without complaint. This was plainly noble of the volunteers, but Crane affronted a group by asking: " Don't the militia take an oath to defend the country anyhow? " and only Frederic Remington joined him in this negative state of mind while the woes of the militia were telegraphed daily to journals which either suppressed the details or began, as no battles occupied front pages, to make a cause against the laborious Alger, Secretary of War, who was following the routine of his task and giving proper orders never strictly obeyed. Crane gave a lad from Wisconsin, discharged for heart trouble without any means of leaving Tampa, the necessary fifty dollars for his fare, then went back to Key West and the dispatch boat's motion on a sea now troubled by mythical Spanish keels. Admiral Cervera's swift squadron had eluded Commodore Schley and lay serene in the harbor of Santiago, but Admiral Camara's monstrous armament was roaming in the sophisticated press of New York and old ladies of Nantucket Island were agitated by glimpses of smoke on the horizon.

"The sailormen of Sampson's big canoe," Crane wrote from the *Three Friends* on June 2nd, " ought to make us all ashamed of our trade. The papers come aboard the flagship and who, I ask, want to see this goulash of legendary lies and solemn rumours? We do, we the cynics of Fleet Street and Park Row, the Rudyards, the lords of the popular mind. The Jackies just look at all this manure and say, Well — and go on polishing brass. Davis and I tried to make them excited by donations of headlines and they said, Well — and peeled more onions. It is now the fashion of all hotel porches at Tampa and Key West to run Davis down because he has declined a captaincy in the army in order to keep his contract with his paper. The teaparty has to have a topic."

Other topics being scarce, he revised a story called *Vashti in the Dark* which tells how a young Methodist preacher from the South killed himself after discovering that his wife had been ravished by a Negro in a forest at night. To Acton Davies, who typed the manuscript, this was one of Crane's best tales, but no magazine ever bought it and Crane burned it in one of his rare fits of pique. Now he was struck by a title for a novel — "The Merry Go Round." This would be the adventures of a wandering carrousel in the Southwest and along the Atlantic shore. Projects boiled in him while the tug rocked and was nearly mangled by the U. S. S. *Machias* one hot night. James Pinker, his English agent, was paying forty pounds for each thousand words of his prose, so there might be a trip around the world, because " a Polish friend of mine who is an unancient mariner says I would be dippy over Polynesia." Meanwhile he lounged and wondered, with crescent boredom, how to make an end of *Active Service,* and out of that contemplation rose a remark on a postcard: " A reporter is no hero for a novel."

He came to the decision at the wrong second of journalistic history. In Tampa some reporters were doing the heroic thing. The process of vision had brought revolt, and offices in New York were bothered by facts, facts of all sorts, written and wired from the buzzing luxury of the hotel where ladies following chastely that odd camp danced under colored lights. Windy patriotism and romance were collapsing into hot veracity. The men of the press saw a willing army ill fed, badly dressed for a climate grown tormenting, and made ready for transport in ships hardly fitted to carry uncritical cattle. John Jacob Astor was offering to pay, since the government wouldn't, for a decent supply of water and many eyes saw the beginning of a crime on men rendered defenseless by discipline. The nation had engaged in a sentimental war and whooped at home for news of bloodshed. The symbol of Tampa was a rocking-chair in cartoons and already Major-General Shafter was complaining of his health to the attachés of Germany and Great Britain. Back from Florida spread a humming noise of discontent. The regular army was worthless. The war ought to be turned over to the volunteer officers directly. Everything was wrong. The papers said so.

On June 10th six hundred Marines landed from a bevy of gunboats on the eastern bank of Guantanamo's charming bay below Santiago, and the dispatch tug shed Crane with the force, enchanted by the glow of a burning village whence a fiery light was thrown upon some palms and " made them into enormous crimson feathers." The Marines in tawny linen uniforms camped on a flat plateau that interrupted this steep shore, and Crane talked all night long to a surgeon named Gibbs about consumptions while trenches were dug. Men were annoyed by the active Cuban land-crabs scuttling on their faces as they slept. Next afternoon, while they bathed in squads from the littered beach,

344

firing began suddenly and Cuban scouts brought word that the guerrillas were the marksmen. Naked Marines and dressed Marines shot for an hour against the dense, lustrous green of the jungle and night came with vehemence while Crane lugged water up the hill, canteens rattling by the dozen from shoulders that already shivered. The surgeon gave him quinine and advised flight. The *Three Friends* had sailed to Jamaica, but Gibbs wanted the sick man to take shelter on the *Marblehead* or some other gunboat. . . . No. He had come to see this war and the correspondents of the dispatch boat had let him stay to see it. Volleys scattered on the plateau where men sprawled in hot blackness and Crane crouched part of the doleful time beside the signalman who waved slow lanterns sending word to the *Marblehead* how things went on this knob. The lights drew fire from the brush that on three sides flowed near the poor entrenchments and the guerrillas conversed between shots in the song of the local wood-dove. Then a ball struck the surgeon Gibbs and he began audibly to die in the crowded darkness while other wounded men cried out. Crane lay listening. . . . " Every wave, vibration, of his anguish beat upon my senses. He was long past groaning. There was only the bitter strife for air which pulsed out into the night in a clear, penetrating whistle with intervals of terrible silence in which I held my own breath in the common unconscious aspiration to help. I thought this man would never die. Ultimately he died." The next noon, when Ralph Paine landed from the returned tug with a flask of whisky, Crane had an illusion of his tall friend as Harold Frederic in a fur coat, and neither whisky nor fresh food cleared the thought from his brain for hours. Perhaps one does not jam the color of life on a feverish intelligence stoked with quinine harmlessly. He had no belief in ghosts and arguments on the immortality of the soul were dull to him as Presidential speeches, but now people began to remind him of the dead. Caspar Whitney was like his father and he soon startled Harding Davis by telling the big man he was a corpse seen at Velestinos.

On June 14th the parties of Marines advanced into the jungle and swept the Spanish sharpshooters before them, burning a blockhouse and its heliograph with a water-tank named Cuzco from a village that had been. The *Dolphin* shelled the woods ahead of the column, and Crane was vexed by another illusion, transmuted in *War Memories* to a mere comparison. He was shooting with his brothers at Hartwood and the bursting shells were setters that roused birds. He ran errands for the lieutenant in charge of this fantastic sport and got official notice of his coolness under fire. Then the *Three Friends* carried him off from four days' piled strain to Port Antonio and, he hoped, to fine meals. But the resources of the small neutral port were scanty and the chemist had only one toothbrush in stock. " This town," he wrote, " is disgustingly ill appointed."

He made a tour around the Spanish outposts and saw, guided by half-clad Cuban scouts, the squadron of Cervera anchored in the round bay of Santiago as he cowered in the brush above the packed town wherein yellow fever had sprouted. It was a ride of almost forty miles, coming and going through danger, but " I did not discover my condition until we were well through the Spanish lines and . . . then I discovered I was a dead man. The nervous force having evaporated I was a mere corpse. My limbs were of dough and my spinal cord burned within me as if it were a red hot wire." But he must tramp the beach at Daiquiri and watch the troops land from transports commanded mostly by insolent or cowardly civilians who flouted the signals of General Shafter's orders and sailed tranquilly out to the supreme safety of open water with medicines and necessary equipment in the holds of the shipping hired at such colossal rates by the government. The tragedy of the Santiago campaign had well begun and confusions heaped themselves on heat while Crane investigated the American regular officers, those curios of a system which immured boys for four years in a military monastery, sent them to duties in petty forts and barren towns of the vanished frontier, and then produced their weariness for a public which at once expected of them diplomacies, social censorship, and the suave attitudes of a society that exiled and disregarded them until the instant of its need.

The commanding officer of this little army was a fat invalid who reposed on a cot and whined about his health. In gayer hours he told anecdotes that shocked both Richard Harding Davis and Acton Davies by the flavor of medical information contained in his style. Apparently the man was too sickly or too careless for any exercise of will and after the neatness of the landing Major General Shafter simply vanished from the beautiful beach while his veteran subordinates did what they could to make life better and brighter for twelve thousand men sweating in shirts of thick wool and in a temperature wavering between eighty and a hundred degrees. Dismounted cavalrymen and the hard infantrymen called sometimes " doughboys " bathed their mosquito-bites in salt water wondering why the commissariat was already short of tobacco. . . . From the camp of the First Volunteer Cavalry arose the pulsating voice of Theodore Roosevelt demanding food and clean drink for that amazing regiment of tramps, actors, cowboys, expert bartenders, millionaires, and football-players. From the camp of the journalists rose the anguish of the *World's* chief correspondent as Crane didn't turn in his highly paid prose for the cable to jerk in edited sentences to New York. The terrible infant was loose among the regiments delighted with so much to see and hear.

He saw almost nothing of the battle known at Las Guasimas on June 24th, a tortuous raid through two converging trails carried out by Wheeler's brigade. As usual, Richard Harding Davis had the best of that news. The thing envied as " the Davis luck " was rather a very swift, shrewd judgment of possibilities and Davis followed Roosevelt while unseen Spaniards in the metallic prettiness of the foliage killed some Rough Riders. Crane ran three miles to overtake Young's dismounted troopers on the other trail and presently ran back six miles to Siboney without stopping to survey the end of this action. His friend Edward Marshall had been shot through the body, so the war lost all charm while Crane tried to get help from the *Journal's* staff at the beach. Then he guided some sailors with a cot for the wounded man and walked beside this improvisation to Siboney again. That night he could not eat but he shocked Henry Carey and Acton Davies by saying it must be interesting to be shot. He had noticed that men struck in the chest ran ahead for a while before falling. Abdominal wounds crumpled the recipient. Davies was in the last miseries of sunburn. His rotundity always appeared to be coated with pink celluloid and he was now the tint of boiling lobster speckled by huge blisters. Crane stopped pouring linseed oil on the misplaced dramatic reporter's shoulders and mused: " You'd look bully if a shell hit you, ol' man. Like a squashed peony." The comparison was not kind and Davies took alarm. Crane seemed to want to be hit and talked academically of locations on his person for a bullet's entry.

He certainly went about the business of risking a wound with extraordinary and scientific zeal. Brigades pushed on in the riotous jungle and stretched thinly on July 1st before lizard-shaped crests upholding the villages of El Caney and San Juan. These hills were a necessity to the Spanish defense. Santiago could be shelled at leisure of the invaders if the range of steep slopes and delusive plateaus fell to the Americans. General Vara del Rey bravely commanded the

force at El Caney and there he was killed in a ferocious
little battle that lasted for nine hours. The San Juan fight
was less venomous but more trying. Regiments sat in hollows or hasty trenches while the Spanish fire came sputtering downhill and the road rearward was a muddle of
wounded men, advancing columns, and, for a while, of
struggling horses as the few guns were brought up to shell
the enemy's position. Intolerable heat, windless and constant, lay on this episode as Crane walked to and fro in a
gray, conspicuous English waterproof, afraid to shed the
coat because he might lose it. When he appeared with
James Hare strolling along the line of Wheeler's brigade at
noon, the cavalrymen lifted their heads and begged him to
wear furs if he wasn't hot enough.

Crane brooded, staring up the hill, and stooped once or
twice to look at the holes made by bullets landing near his
feet in the bleached grass of the slope. He wandered close
to a depression that didn't greatly shelter Leonard Wood
and Richard Harding Davis. It seemed to Davis that the
pale coat drew shots. Yellow sand flickered from the trench
and soldiers called to Crane, swearing uncomfortably. His
speculation became interminable and the Spanish officer
who paraded the defending trenches with a walking-stick
once visibly aimed it at the artist. This unknown warrior
pleased Crane immensely and many other reporters tried
afterwards to find the man's rank or name. But his pleasure
in the spectacle was interrupted by Davis, who yelled to him
and bade him lie down. " Crane jumped," Davis reported,
" as if he was waking from a nap and looked at me, astonished by my voice, perhaps. He flattened out on the grass
and crawled back behind a small hillock. But pretty soon
he rose on his knees and then stood up once more, absorbed
in watching. I called out as sarcastically as I could that
Colonel Wood and I were not impressed by his courage
and he blushed scarlet before he lay down. He did not stay

long after that but helped a wounded man back to the battery at El Poso. . . ." The third point of the narrative was omitted by Davis. Colonel Wood moved away and Crane got up for the second time. Davis also rose, stepped over some prostrate soldiers, and caught Crane by the shoulders, forcing him down. A bullet knocked off Davis's hat and the leather of his field-glass was chipped by another ball. Then Crane went to play his game elsewhere and drank some coffee at the reporters' camp behind a battery that slung shells toward the Spanish blockhouse. He came back as the soldiers struggled up the hill and was seen trying to hammer back a loose heel of his shoe while the American flag was swung over the conquered village. Night and desolation smothered the battlefield while officers wrangled as to the safety of holding the crest and Leonard Wood reverted to his primary profession in the hospital, undermanned, packed with dying youth. Another step had been taken in the publicity of Theodore Roosevelt. Santiago was lost, although nobody quite understood so, and a corporal shot through both arms sat up in a corner of the stinking tent reserved to fevers, singing *The Star Spangled Banner* with irony, at the top of his voice.

Chill winds belied the date and rain fell in long showers on the camps now stretched twelve miles from the beach to the taken hills. Days passed and Crane found that life without doses of whisky and quinine was mere haze. He lurched off to see refugees from the city straggle into El Caney and to watch a surgeon operate on wounded Spanish soldiers in the chapel. He saw Richmond Hobson come between the regiments standing hatless in honor of his release and watched the hero of the *Merrimac* bow profusely as men pressed around him, but this welcome was his last sight of the idle army waiting outside Santiago. Crane was now a figure of irresponsible sickness. His friends tried to feed him and kept him sometimes quiet but he wandered on a pony from place to place in the lines and lamented that he had missed the destruction of Cervera's fleet on July 3rd. He had gone to Jamaica with the dispatch boat for a bath and some decent food. When the *Three Friends* brought him back, there were Sampson's gray ships in their usual place and the invincible Spanish squadron was already beginning to rust with tropical swiftness on the beach.

All sorts of fever had broken out in the American camp. Crane was apparently no more ill than were a dozen other reporters and photographers. People who spoke to him often thought him merely drunk. Then suddenly he was very plainly delirious all one night and Sylvester Scovel hauled him down to a ship loading with sick in Daiquiri. Crane was in a state of alternate vapor and lucidity. He sat on Scovel's pony chatting to Henry Carey and George Rhea gayly and then began to beg for pickles. Fever had dowered him with two yearnings — orange ice-cream soda and sour pickles. Rhea saw the wreck taken aboard the transport and Crane was ordered to isolate himself as a case of yellow fever. He lay on a rug, aft, and was fed casually on stewed tomatoes. Cuba vanished from him in an opalescent languor while wounded Negroes chanted jubilee as the ship sailed westward.

He had not yellow fever, actually, but the accumulated fatigue of twenty mad days had smitten him. It can only be a theory but Crane had long shown symptoms of intestinal consumption. Improperly or too coarsely fed, he was ill and in Cuba he had relied on stimulants from July 1st to July 7th. In order to meet the procession of the *Merrimac's* crew at San Juan Hill he swallowed half the content of Carey's brandy-flask, and as soon as his brain drank in the show, he let himself flop in the grass, asleep at once. Scovel and Rhea tried to feed him, but everything save soft fruit was an abomination. He could not even ride the Jamaican polo pony and men who had heard of his marvelous horse-

351

manship saw the gaunt adventurer tumble from the saddle. Crane made his body a testing-ground for all sensations of living and for this most unliterary habit he paid, in the useful language of melodrama, the price.

A representative gathering of Americans now saw the physical bill of their emotional war. Cuba was freed. The transport floated to the pier at Old Point Comfort and Crane was allowed to go ashore directly. The hotels of the resort were jammed with women — wives of naval and military officers, fashionable ladies from New York, curious tourists, or anxious waiters. On the veranda of Chamberlain's Hotel he bowed to Mrs. Bolton Chaffee, who had dined at Oxted three months before. She did not know the wraith in soiled khaki, hatless and unshaven, and her small grandson was scared to tears, but after recognition she tried to get Crane to bed. No. He sat smoking on the arm of her chair and drawled sarcasms. Here is what he wanted to see: " The verandah was crowded with women in light, charming summer dresses and with spruce officers from the fortress. It was like a bank of flowers. It filled me with awe. . . . Across the narrow street on the verandah of another hotel was a similar bank of flowers. Two companies of volunteers dug a lane through the great crowd of the street and kept a way, and then through this lane there passed a curious procession. I had never known that they looked like that. Such a gang of dirty, ragged, emaciated, half starved and bandaged cripples I had never seen. . . . Then there were many stretchers, slow moving. When the crowd began to pass the hotel the banks of flowers made a noise which could make one tremble . . . something beyond either a moan or a sob. Anyhow the sound of women weeping was in it — The sound of women weeping."

Of course he went back to see the orderly, almost bloodless taking of Porto Rico and accepted the surrender of a rural village in which he was found the next morning drill-

ing children on the principal street. Mrs. Chaffee was seen
with him at Old Point, so naturally it was reported in New
York that Crane had eloped with the wife of General Chaffee and was living in adulterous splendor at San Francisco.
General Chaffee had no wife possible for this purpose, but
Crane wrote to Mrs. Bolton Chaffee: " You must be careful
about feeding runaway dogs. Mr. Bemis informs me that
you and I are sinners and that we have flown to San Francisco. They have promoted you to the rank of Mrs. Briga-
dier General Chaffee. Perhaps it is not known to you — and
it has not long been known to me — that my name in New
York is synonymous with mud. Give my regards to your
husband and tell him the cigars made many correspondents
happier. My friends will pile a mountain of lies on me but
they will smoke my cigars as freely as I smoke theirs. That
is cynicism."

Accused promptly of cynical coldness as to the war, his
·real mood was the usual indifference to cheap sentiment
tied with amazingly frank admission of his liking for certain exhibits. He was mute on Theodore Roosevelt's conduct as a commander in battle and positively lyric as to his
care for the Rough Riders: " Say, this fellow worked for his
troopers like a cider press. He tried to feed them. He
helped build latrines. He cursed the quartermasters
and the — ' dogs ' — on the transports to get quinine and
grub for them. Let him be a politician if he likes. He was
a gentleman, down there." Admiral Sampson's coolness of
manner did not distress him, as it did other correspondents.
But the commanders had scant interest for him. The men,
the utterly commonplace privates and recruits, absorbed
him. " Yes, yes, I know that it has been wonderfully proven
how that the doughboys and the Jackies know nothing of
manorial architecture and Pierre Loti. They care not if the
journal of the sisters De Goncourt is never published at all.
Velasquez? No. Cervantes? No. United intellects of su-

perior lands bade them be licked to the glory of Cervantes and Velasquez. I don't know why. I shall never know why. But there is an excellence of human conduct independent of Cervantes and Velasquez. The Spaniards who lay dead in El Caney knew something of it. Our men knew something of it. Mob-courage? — mob-courage. The mob has no courage. That is the chatter of clubs and writers. Pray go stand with your back to deadly fire from a painted drop for a pantomime and wave signals for half an hour without wincing and then talk of mob-courage. Imperialism? All right. The White Man's Burden? What in hell did Private Jones and Seaman Smith know of it? Stop being sarcastic. A year hasn't diminished by one inch my respect for the men. I shall never see another war. I don't care if Buller drives all the Boers up Egypt's fattest pyramid. The men were all right."

His own posture in *War Memories* is that of a nervous and embarrassed spectator at an imbecile and ill-rehearsed show, but he chooses no such attitude for the soldiers in *The Price of the Harness* or elsewhere in the sketches of the little campaign. There was lacking in Crane that profound and diffused sentimentalism that turns an individual reaction into a universal woe. It was impossible for a being who had lived in the Bowery by night and watched the ferocious diversions of San Antonio's Mexican quarter to whimper over mud and sweat and pain. War was ridiculous but men went to war. He accepts the visible with small protest. . . . "What were we doing there at all? There was no definition. There was no use in quoting Tolstoy. There was no Napoleon to say the right thing and lend a gilded finish to the occasion. It galled one's mind at times. But there we were." It seemed best to accept the situation with calm raillery, to notice that a dying man could vex his friends by peevishness, and that "the sun threw orange lances over enamelled, broad leaves."

He now fell in love with Havana and so sat writing there when he should have gone back to England. Some shadowy person named "Wells," not to be confused with H. G. Wells, had informed the woman anxious in Surrey of Crane's adultery with the mythical general's lady. A theme had occurred to him. The past was wooing Crane more vividly than it did in his first years. Havana, lazy and filthy, suggested a tale of old days. Suppose that a young sailor was cast up naked on the shore of Cuba and became the lover of a Spanish lady in the colored, lascivious city? But he could get no clear account of Cuban history and Spanish was unreadable. The story was abandoned and he finished *Active Service* before starting north, then threw the last chapters aside and wrote them afresh. In October he got to New York after a stay in Washington, where again he considered Congress from its gallery and again it bewildered him. He was presented to some Senator who told him gravely about the failures of the war and the discomforts undergone by a nephew in the Rough Riders. "I understand, now, that Congressmen and Senators all rolled in august pain by night and sat weeping by day over our lot. This warhorse told me so. He told me that he visited the War Department hourly on July First. I asked him what good that did and he said it showed his interest in the campaign. Nobody would believe in him. I can't believe in him but it is true that I saw him."

New York received him with a faint but noted noise. His arrival was announced. Crane exposed himself in Cuba no more recklessly than did Edward Marshall, H. T. Whigham, or George Rhea, but he had been officially mentioned and Harding Davis had already before the public his article on the correspondents. Frederic Stokes was anxious for a novel and accepted another book of verses. Editors were offering higher rates. Paul Reynolds could sell *The Blue Hotel* for as much as three hundred dollars, a price almost

as high as those accorded to Davis or Kipling. But Crane
was off to Hartwood at once and his brothers were appalled
by a condition suddenly manifest. The man was ill and
restless. He rode and shot with vigor, but listlessness had
come on him. People at Port Jervis crowded to hear him
talk or to tell him stories he should write and he played
long games with his nieces. Yet something had happened.
The vitality of manner was gone; he slept endlessly; he put
off necessary visits to New York. He was too tired to
breathe, he wrote, and when William Dean Howells gave
a luncheon for him at Delmonico's he sat silently respectful
among older men, eating nothing, turning the stem of a
wineglass in his yellow fingers. The grandees of criticism
had been assembled — Mayo Hazeltine, probably the most
powerful reviewer of the decade, and Marrion Wilcox, who
was concluding an attempt to get facts from the war's beginning legend and soon rather shocked the world by his
history's impartial discussion of the Spanish side. The
luncheon was a failure and Crane fell asleep on a couch in
his admirer's house that afternoon without apology. He
was twenty-seven and had given up adding a year to his age
while Howells was amused by his references to " my youth "
and " when I was young." In the operation of his mind he
was now an elderly, settled character of many responsibilities who needed a house in the country and had thoughts
of buying a ranch in Texas. Once sensitively keen to hear
what people were saying about his work, it left him cool to
know that President McKinley had spoken favorably of
The Little Regiment. But the President had been a soldier.
" He would know if the stuff was real or not, even," Crane
drawled, " if he can't write good English."

On November 23rd he strolled into Delmonico's bar with
Huneker, and the critic nodded to Thomas McCumber, who
was idle at a table. The pair drank cocktails and went off
to dine somewhere, at the Everett House or in some German

restaurant where talk might be unbridled and the frothing outpour of Huneker's conversation need not shock ladies. But at Delmonico's tongues were busy. Somebody knew Crane by sight and a discussion began. Was it true that he'd tried to get himself killed in Cuba? McCumber pulled himself into the chatter, uninvited. It was true, he said. Some incredulous stranger argued the point. Why should a famous young writer try to kill himself? The gigantic photographer grew noisy and men coming in for dinner stopped to listen. Crane was dying of nameless and disgusting diseases and everybody knew it. A reporter protested and the giant wanted to fight him. Richard Harding Davis had come in alone and was quietly ordering dinner in a corner of the room. After a moment he shouldered through the fringe at the bar and commanded McCumber to be still. McCumber didn't obey. He repeated his indictment with additions, towering and swaying above Davis's evening dress while an alarmed waiter pulled at his coat. The smaller man wearied and twenty or thirty people were witnesses of a suppression by force. Davis, blushing furiously, towed the big gossip out of the place and came back with his customary dignity and a cut lip to ask such men as he knew to forget the affair. . . . All penalties of the popular writer have now been paid by Davis. A general damnation has included his alert sketches of London and Paris and the satiric portrait of Captain Macklin, the military cad. The mind displayed was, perhaps, conventional but the man had a persisting quality most remarkable. He would praise and advertise his rivals and his betters with pen and voice. He lauded his successor, Gouverneur Morris, and distributed the first book of James Huneker to friends who didn't want to read it and could not understand what it meant. He called attention to Crane's reports of the Cuban war and afterwards, when he was obliged to explain who Crane had been, spent hours in description of the man who always, clearly, somehow shocked and puzzled him. Crane was " a strange genius " but that genius should not be neglected. This oddity of temperament got him into trouble when Stanford White was murdered by some inconsequent fellow in a quarrel over a trumpery woman who then was shown at the trial tricked out as a schoolgirl. The legal proceedings were so cynical in their appeal that the New York press recorded them with real unwillingness. The dead architect's mild sensualities were sprayed with slime so completely that the reviving courage of his friends has not yet established the hollowness of the attack. Here and there journalists and writers feebly denied that White was Nero recrudescent. He was a jolly, harmless pagan who possessed an enormous enthusiasm for art, art in all kinds. He was now reviled by men who had dined at his expense the week before his death and artists fled from the remains of their patron with that speed begotten in cowards by a scandal involving lust. Davis was not intimate with the monster but this strange sense of justice flashed out in a published praise of White. The man had been kind, talented, and generous, slain by a drunken fool. The brave reporter shouted against the world his outraged theory of fair play and his books were forthwith dumped from a public library in New Jersey while lads were warned by the headmaster of a famous school to beware *Soldiers of Fortune* and *The Princess Aline* as foul emanations of a depraved romancer. Only in an English-speaking country was such a folly possible and only an American could know the consequences of the act. It leaves him lonely in the tale of the national letters.

II

THE ALLIANCE of Crane and James Huneker began casually and without much warmth on Crane's part but in the autumn of 1898 they walked and dined together frequently. A change was apparent in Crane. . . . His earlier friends were scattering. Corwin Linson went abroad in October and John Willard Raught, another young painter, was gone too. John Northern Hilliard had become an editor in Rochester. Hamlin Garland was much in the West and Edward Townsend was often traveling. The men of the Lantern Club were bully fellows and he could entertain himself with the garrulous wit of Acton Davies, but discontent had set in and he found himself thinking of England while he hunted a house in New York. Lounging at tea with a lady in December this came to expression. " Englishmen aren't shocked as easily as we are. You can have an idea in England without being sent to court for it."

His ideas and opinions had not given Edward Garnett, Harold Frederic, or Ford Maddox Hueffer any moments of uneasiness. He sometimes appalled Robert Barr, who was conservatively minded, but Stephen Crane's cynicisms have by this year paled into common sense. His objection to the Mosaic deity, of course, did not belong to his decade of careful avoidance. It is known that he startled by an aristocratic habit of calling peasants in America peasants. He derided the sacred petting of all Irishmen. His description of pity as " a virtue almost useless in ninety-nine cases out of a hundred . . ." seemed affectation in 1896. His political thinking is obscured but the violence of his rages with social and religious limitation is recalled. He had no patience with doctrines that sank individuals into the mass and defined their mental path. " Frances Willard," he told Miss Harris, " is one of those wonderful people who can tell right from wrong for everybody from the polar cap to the equator. Perhaps it never struck her that people differ from her. I have loved myself passionately now and then but Miss Willard's affair with Miss Willard should be stopped by the police." At some time he " was a Socialist for two weeks but when a couple of Socialists assured me I had no right to think differently from any other Socialist and then quarreled with each other about what Socialism meant, I ran away."

His views on women alarmed some of his friends. Against the current of the nineties he was both chivalrous and realistic. He had got himself in jail by protecting a streetwalker from a bullying policeman but " most street-walkers would be ' demimondianes ' " — so spelled — " if they had money. Lots of women are just naturally unchaste and all you jays know it," yet the faint tinge of Puritanism lay in him. He was perpetually nervous when gentlewomen smoked before him and a man who would accept a woman's prolonged fidelity without offering her marriage was, in some way not explained, censorable. He projected in *The Monster* and *Active Service* finely compressed sketches of disagreeable middle-aged women, but a pretty girl was too much for his detachment and only a frantic admirer would join Elbert Hubbard in calling Crane a profound student of the female mind. The heiress of *The Third Violet* takes on rank life when she throws herself at the head of the timid, obtuse Hawker, but elsewhere, like the novel, she is something never quite finished. There was no androgynous streak in Crane and perhaps without that embarrassing trace no man writes well of women until age has calloused him to the wonder of a body unlike his own. However, some of his random annotations were disliked and he lightly expressed rather unusual thoughts, for his time. It was not circumspect in an American to suggest that women knew " the joys of cruelty." Margharita and her mother in *The Clan of No-Name* were too frank for many readers. He once wrote the story of an artist's model who married into a small town, but the tale froze editors while it amused James Huneker and it has disappeared.

Crane was lingering, hesitant, with sour comment reach-

ing him as to his habits and customs. " There must," said
Huneker, " have been people who hated the boy monumentally. Three or four times when he had been spending
the whole evening with Ryder and myself I would be told
in the morning how drunk and disorderly he had been the
night before by men who had not seen him. For a mild and
melancholy kid he certainly had fallen completely into the
garbage can of gossip. . . . The charm of his talk defies
description. It was all adjectives and adverbs. He spoke
of his friend Conrad as the devout speak of the B. V. M.
Harold Frederic's case was dragging through the papers
still and the bourgeois in Park Row used to bore Crane
about it a good deal. He was a great individualist and he
resented the twaddle about suicide intensely as he knew
that Frederic could not have recovered anyhow. I saw him
last about Christmas time. . . ." After Christmas he
reached decision suddenly. He would go back to England
and stay there. So he rode on the frosty highways around
Hartwood with his brother and once his horse fell with him
at a turn. Then he sailed on the *Manitou* in the first week of
January. . . . Perhaps with some regrets. That New
York, that acreage of brown stone and shoddy stucco was
altering and imperial tones of marble shone everywhere as
hotel after hotel opened to dazzle rustics with frescoes and
satin chairs. Little pleasures faded in the crash of new display but he might recall long breakfasts in hot summer
under the striped awning of the Vienna Bakery beside white
Grace Church and the wet bodies of prizefighters lurching
in the smoke of Harry Hill's queer restaurant where light-
weights fought while men dined. . . . Music of that decade was the rolling of hansoms and he who so loved shimmering tones of light might remember the damp sheen of
cabs on Broadway. There had been the young talk of the
Hotel Griffon and the Bœuf à la Mode and the fresh voice
of the Wild Indians in their barrack on Twenty-third Street.

STEPHEN CRANE

He would not forget a murmurous park with a pair of white arms beside him as he was driven around and around through warm night, and in an alien valley he would be sick again for the sight of tall towers and the noise of hurrying wheels.

CHAPTER VIII

THE LAST

WRITING to Edward Garnett on January 10, 1899, Cora Crane showed a knowledge of her husband's situation in two sentences: "His great difficulty is a lack of that machine-like application which makes a man work steadily. I hope that the perfect quiet of Brede Place and the freedom from a lot of dear good people, who take his mind from his work, will let him show the world a book that will live. . . ." Nine men, breathing or extinct, have claimed that they first mentioned Brede to Stephen Crane, but to Mr. Garnett belongs the credit of a sensible suggestion made in November of 1897. The critic advised Crane to find a house somewhere less easy of access. He talked of Brede as an available ruin and Mrs. Crane went to investigate while Crane enjoyed Cuba. So, on January 16th, they drove from Hastings through twilight and Crane saw his next home by the pleasing glow of lamps. The house, begun in the fourteenth century, was wonderfully dilapidated and an owl had built a nest on a beam of the paneled hall. He was charmed by the faint sound of water spilling under the bridge and by his wife's delight in this solidified romance: "It is a pretty fine affair," he wrote to Sanford Bennett, "and Cora believes that Sir Walter Scott designed it for her. They began one wing in 1378 and somebody kidded it with heavy ar-

363

tillery in Cromwell's time. We shall move in as soon as we can. I enclose 10 pounds. Do I owe you more than that? "

Brede was a relief after Oxted and Crane's stored goods were sent from Hartwood. Mexican blankets hung red and white on the walls of a little room above the gateway and furniture was somehow bought for ten chambers. The butler, Heather, appeared and undertook by stern discomposures to correct his master's habit of running downstairs coatless to meet guests. Maurice Hewlett was shocked on calling to find Crane in muddy boots when the ride that excused such articles had been taken before breakfast. Henry James came from Rye to inspect and was pained to hear Sanford Bennett call Crane " Baron Brede." An abrasion of tradition and privilege had occurred by no known intention. To Crane his manor was a playhouse and to some of his friends — or acquaintances — it was a sanctity invaded, carelessly, by an irreverent whose claret they would gladly still consume while they sighed in London over his bad form. A literary clergyman arriving to ask a hundred signed copies of *Bowery Tales* in the name of a charitable bazaar was peculiarly outraged by the sight of Crane in a gray flannel shirt rolling dice with strange adjurations on the hall's depressed floor. It is recorded that these dice were " not of the ordinary colour and must be American," and that, at tea, there were small, flat " hot rolls which Mrs. Crane insistently called biscuit although they were not biscuit but agreeable." Oh, England!

Crane worked and " the dear, good people " did not get at him unless they were summoned. He was reading a great deal. His individuality did not regard itself as a completed labor of God, at twenty-seven, and chance had dropped him among critical folk who knew things. His reverence, when one finds the quality coming to view, was latterly on the drift away from men who could do things and expending itself on men who knew things, on Huneker and on the

Garnetts, whose progenitor "bossed the British Museum and talked about old man Caxton as if they had been at school together." The advantage of a little pedantry had been pointed out to Crane by Ripley Hitchcock and by Hamlin Garland, whose books he borrowed and probably never returned since his one absolute vice was a habit of not sending books back. He returned money when he thought of it with long apologies for his remissness but books he simply took and kept. So in one week of March 1899, he read a volume on Greek vases, Turgenev's *Smoke*, Du Maurier's *Peter Ibbetson* (he didn't like it), *Cashel Byron's Profession*, *Literature and Dogma*, *In the Cage*, presented to him by Henry James with an elaborate and almost affectionate inscription, in French. History, save as the background of battles, he had never much explored until now and its fascination was plain in Sussex with walls so ancient shedding dampness on him and the ghost of William the Conqueror troubling his wife's dreams. He even read May's constitutional history of England and survived without trouble the involuted dreariness of its manner. Huneker still wanted him to read Balzac, but Mr. Conrad had told him all about Balzac and he held himself excused.

With spring Brede was gayer. He had pledged a series of articles on great battles and fancied he would enjoy the work. *Harper's Magazine* wanted him to continue the stories of Whilomville. *Active Service* was finished and in print. Half a dozen tales had been sold and he could cheerfully lend a hundred pounds without taking a note. So he saw more people and the butler hired more servants to support his dignity properly. In April Crane discovered several housemaids washing the battalion of dogs necessary to life and wondered at Heather's ability. " My man," he wrote, " can hire me a pair of maids while I ride to Rye and back. If I went to Russia I should come home and find Parliament in buttons and Marie Corelli in the kitchen."

But the maids were useful to wash Sponge and his consort Flannel and the solemn Russian poodles who were so indiscreet when they called on Henry James at Rye. Young ladies played absurd games in the hall with young authors after dinner and Crane watched nascent flirtations devotedly, although his wife refused him lamps with red shades.

He had come under scientific eyes and Mark Barr [1] caught his passion for red. The walls of the study must be made soothing by paint of a shade between vermilion and claret, the color of fresh sumach on the hills around Port Jervis. This red meant comfort, thrilling excitement, or desire, according to the mood. When some eventual psychologist has cleared from the investigation of such manias the guesses now clinging to them, Crane's work will be a chart of illustration. Writers in all degrees have indulged in favorite colors. Grays and soft blues abound in the stanzas of Verlaine. Henry James had a positive, but not crude, affection for clean floods of light and for brown dusks of interior. William Morris would halt an address to stare at certain shades of orange or dull green, a woman once noticed, and resume Socialism when some memory was slaked in his brain. In Crane's work one sees milder manias. Purple was sinister and repugnant. Grayish blue and strong yellow were pleasant. Above everything comes the notice of lamps seen in the dark. . . . "Down an alley there were sombre curtains of purple and black, on which the street lamps dully glittered like embroidered flowers. . . ." When Mrs. Chaffee played for him some phrases of Debussy the swift notes were "windows in a train at night going over the edge of a plain. . . ." A kindness of Moreton Frewen was "a searchlight on a hungry boat at sea . . ." and the foolish, persisting air whistled by American troops in Cuba was "a jumble of Chinese lanterns in a

1 Mr. Barr is an American chemist.

fog." Half Crane's achievement in letters was his astonishing ease of visual description, and seemingly simple statements have a haunting effect of complete justice to a scene. Nothing could be better than the two lights of *The Open Boat* which were the " furniture of the world," to his racked eyes.

The Open Boat appeared in the autumn of 1898 and American critics received these tales with the calm cordiality and the lack of criticism that maddens. One review alone rises from the banal level of the list. Rupert Hughes wrote of the new book with a sensitive appreciation and a considerable analysis of the methods employed. The other reviews were kind and flat. Crane exploded in a fluff of angry words before the sympathetic Edward Garnett. Some day he might make Americans forget *The Red Badge*! He wanted to know what certain American reviewers would have to say, in the next year, of *The Blue Hotel* but nobody said anything very discriminating and Mark Twain thought it a grisly business. The Lincoln of our letters was never pleased by grimness in the fiction of other writers and Crane, told of this censure, simply grinned.

American failure to recognize Crane's short stories was not so sweeping as it may have seemed to him. His nation's tribute to Crane has been the compliment of conscious or unconscious theft and if only the inferior war-time episodes of *The Little Regiment* were broadly popular, *The Blue Hotel, Death and the Child, A Desertion,* and *The Five White Mice* have been much honored in a ghostly fashion. He swayed clean from the national orbit. Where Ambrose Bierce failed by clinging to the tradition of Poe, Crane failed by a blank abandonment of the form still sacred with editors and critics, the truncated novel produced by Harte and de Maupassant. He was interested to sketch curtly colored cross-roads on the map of existence and that map had for him no sure or solacing pattern. His vision of the

world is jabbed into *The Blue Hotel* by a symbol atrocious
to the soft and, one supposes, distressing to the pious. A
panicky and tipsy Swede is knifed in a Nebraskan saloon
by a mild little gambler who, in Crane's speech, is merely
the apex of a human movement, an adverb in the meaningless sentence. But the corpse of the Swede, " alone in the
saloon, had its eyes fixed upon a dreadful legend that dwelt
atop the cash-machine: ' This registers the amount of your
purchase ' . . ." and Crane, indifferent to his childish public, did not stop to brandish paragraphs of comment on the
futility of such a bargain. Thus in *Wise Men* the two charming Kids back a fat old bartender against a trained runner
in a footrace, for no reason, and their champion wins. Accident dominates an inchoate society. In the weaker *Twelve
O'Clock* an idle argument about a cuckoo-clock brings
death on two men and the cuckoo pokes out its inhuman
head to squawk twelve times over the heaped slaughter.
Once it begins, this human movement proceeds with all the
vigor of a holy war but there is no cause to justify the hopes
and terrors, the pompous stir of man's nonsensical activity
under nature's bland survey. Rewards are as accidental as
calamities. In *Active Service* the war-correspondent gets
his sweetheart by merit of being the chance rescuer of her
parents and through no virtue whatever. In *The Clan of No-
Name,* one of Crane's poorest efforts, one still sees the dull
Mr. Smith win Margharita simply because her lover is dead
under the machete in Cuba. Even in *The Red Badge of
Courage* the boy is allowed his moment of glory as the army
staggers off the field in retreat. It needs no critical power
to know that this perpetual refutation of endeavor is a thing
disconcerting to the general, a caviar of pebbles. Edgar
Saltus, setting forth in a polished and most literary style his
derived philosophy of negations, was a figure more comfortable to the times, especially as he piled such a treasure
of lewd facts in the lives of Czars and rowdy, luxurious

Cæsars, a treat to housewives and that sort of critic for whom art is not art unless the toys of art be shown. Add to Crane's matter the manner described by Richard Gilder — privately — as grim flippancy, and the reason of his failure is plain enough. In *The Bride Comes to Yellow Sky*, his own favorite, he shows the drunken Wilson lurching through streets of barred and silent houses, death in his hand, then makes the man absurd in the universe by mention of his shirt from a Bowery sweatshop and of his boots with the red tops dear to little boys in snowy winter. He forbids primitive emotional relish to break out. The adobe house scarred by the cowboy's bullets rebukes his magnificence with its immobile dignity. The town is Wilson's plaything, but he, threshing his revolvers, is the plaything of a sardonic, casual fortune. Man is just man, even in the hour of courage when Crane lets him be, homely and awkward still, an image of endurance not without honor, not, in the end, without beauty. It should be remembered that in his decade's critical vocabulary " ironic " was a reproachful adjective.

One Cuban night Acton Davies [2] was moaning for his dear Broadway. He wanted such and such dishes at his pet restaurant, such wines, and a lustrous lady to sit across from him. Crane cut short the dream by saying: " Why don't you just say you want a good meal and a girl and be done with it? " That salvage, somewhat brutal, of the real from the sentimental obliquity was the right token of Crane's offense against the spirit of his day.

Brede Place warmed and Crane wrote through silent nights, lying abed until noon. Harold Frederic's lovely orphans played on the lawn and bruised their fingers in the

---

[2] This is directly quoted from a letter of Mr. Davies dated July 2, 1898. The story was at once twisted to suit the mythology of Stephen Crane and has been printed as Crane's statement: " If I were on Broadway tonight all I'd want would be a bottle of whiskey and a woman." I regret the obligations of veracity in spoiling so neat an epigram.

old falconry. Mrs. Richie, from Kentucky, and her handsome daughters were privileged guests. Robert Barr, H. G. Wells, A. E. W. Mason came and went. England was mildly concerned with the Boers but Crane heard that three regiments and some cavalry would chasten these yokels. This prophecy was made at Rye while Mrs. Humphry Ward poured tea for Henry James. Crane thought the lady pleasant but duller than a President and he had doubts as to the Boers. " People tell me that the South Africans and the Japanese can shoot like the devil and then tell me a couple of Guard regiments could whip them in a week. When a Yankee says such things he is bragging but I guess an Englishman is just lugging the truth from some dark cave."

A party escorted his niece Helen to Paris and there waited while Crane took the girl on to her school at Lausanne. Money still passed through his fingers without stopping and he had to borrow to get back to Paris. But now he was scared and working furiously: his wife must be secured for the future. He must try to repay his brothers the loans they had never mentioned. He would not live beyond thirty-one, he thought, and serenely drawled that guess to Karl Harriman when Robert Barr brought the young American down to Brede. " I never thought I'd live long," he said, " and I'm not much account any more." The mental tensity that had supported his first writing now was gone with health. Everything relaxed. He still rode Hengist or Horsa at a gallop along lanes and carried pots to the flower-show where Henry James helped Edith Richie to sell love-potions in a booth and enchanted Crane by a sentence that had easily thirty clauses and nine parentheses. He sometimes drove the trap whose wheels were painted in the somber colors of the Crane armor — although he wouldn't explain the choice when he was asked. Pride of race was one of his secrets and he shrank from snobbery as he shrank from talk of his health. . . . What did he think of death? With Robert Barr he had wasted a night in burlesque incantations to bring Harold Frederic back and, Barr wrote, " Stephen put me to bed about dawn but we did not evoke anything except one of his dogs." Brooding suited him less than did endless discussions of everything in the stone kitchen while July storms showed wet haycocks on the slope by flares of lightning and Mr. Mason's eyeglass was a violet round to catch his stare. Death? Here was humanity. Why bother? And he could dash off a tale about a haycock just to show Barr and Harriman how the thing was done.

His manners were not silken but he had always inoffensively gone through proper parties in New York or London. Lady Randolph Churchill thought him somewhat formal and other hostesses were surprised to hear that Crane was in any way Bohemian. He could be diplomatic when he chose; one of his guests recalls the nimbleness with which Crane manipulated conversations to spare the feelings of a man lately divorced. His natural informality was not a parade of what is called the artist's freedom as in England he found himself more at ease among intelligences than in America: " I once horrified Elbert Hubbard and his household by telling the story of an old negress in Minetta Lane I met when I was working for Ed Marshall on the *Press*. This old black devil was taking a bath in a wash-boiler when I walked into her flat and she called, ' Chile, I'se all disdressed.' That anecdote slew its thousands at Hubbard's and got me in much trouble. I shall never know why. They acted as though I had read one of Zola's loudest roars. Over here I have told it in front of seven or eight mothers of families and I assure you nothing happened. Nothing at all." He told the anecdote to Maurice Hewlett who responded: " Ah? She meant that she was distressed? I see," and the response possibly explains why no friendship

371

ripened between Crane and the author of *Richard Yea and Nay*.

Crane liked people for obscure reasons and his open dislikes were so few that inevitably he collected both bores and boors. In moments of frightful tedium he occasionally rounded on someone with gibes too subtle for thick skins. A journalist appeared at Brede and paralyzed all present by his overbearing rudeness for three days. On the fourth morning he lodged a complaint about a servant who hadn't brought something to his room and Crane drawled: " Perhaps she has patrician instincts," but the journalist stayed on until, through James Pinker, Mrs. Crane managed to dismiss him. Once in July Crane broke out to his literary agent: " If you don't tell some of these lice that Cora and I aren't running a hotel I'll have to advertise the fact in the *Times*! " and then cleared his dwelling by taking off five youngsters to the Henley regatta. " How," he asked Sanford Bennett, " does it come to pass that anybody in England thinks he can come and stay with me before I've asked him and patronize my wife's housekeeping? " He wrote to Elbert Hubbard: " I must have Egyptian blood in me. Mummies rise from the tomb and come to pay me calls that last for days."

Summer was pleasant, though, and he got slowly through the Whilomville series, but finding that the Great Battles wearied him, simply finished them off as he could in dry recitals of fact not anywhere florid but never enriched. One or two of the histories — such as Bunker Hill — have an interest but nothing went well with Crane when he wrenched his talent from its bent. In *Active Service* he had attempted a popular novel and had failed as he failed in popular reporting. The story lacks all the devices of its brand. Crane could not take his journalist seriously either in his professional aspect or as a lover. Fitfully the book glows

THE LAST

— the lights of Broadway are jewels of a giantess, the poker
game is a real game, the moment when the correspondent
wanders in darkness beyond the Greek lines is wonderfully
rendered, but *Active Service* dropped far below Crane's
standard and some of his friends were indignant for the
contemptuous portrait of a newspaperman. Some wrote to
him their outrage with the poem in *War is Kind* when the
verses were printed.

> A newspaper is a court
> Where every one is kindly and unfairly tried
> By a squalor of honest men.
> A newspaper is a market
> Where wisdom sells its freedom
> And melons are crowned by the crowd. . . .
> A newspaper is a symbol;
> It is fetless life's chronicle,
> A collection of loud tales
> Concentrating eternal stupidities,
> That in remote ages lived unhaltered,
> Roaming through a fenceless world.

The gray book of poems again bewildered reviewers. He
was still writing unrhymed lines and his sentiments were
still unusual. The first poem was somehow cryptic, or silly.
They were not sure. " Mr. Crane's sense of humour," a
Bostonian had to say, " is of a mystifying kind. He deliberately shows us the horrors of war and then entitles his
work 'War is Kind.' " It wouldn't do.

> Do not weep, maiden, for war is kind.
> Because your lover threw wild hands towards the sky
> And the affrighted steed ran on alone,
> Do not weep.
> War is kind.

Hoarse, booming drums of the regiment,
Little souls who thirst for fight,
These men were born to drill and die.
The unexplained glory flies above them,
Great is the battle-god, great, and his kingdom —
A field where a thousand corpses lie. . . .

All the best poems of this second attack on formal versi-
fication are known to date from 1895, 1896, and 1897.
Several were written while Crane and Captain Murphy
lamented the *Commodore* in Jacksonville. Some experiments in rhythm go along excellently, but the love-poems
are not fired by the spirit of the earlier work and only here
and there is the tone of amusement memorable.

" Have you ever made a just man? "
" Oh, I have made three," answered God,
"But two of them are dead,
And the third —
Listen! Listen!
And you will hear the thud of his defeat."

A man said to the universe:
" Sir, I exist."
" However," replied the universe,
" The fact has not created in me
A sense of obligation."

Very plainly rises his own patrician instinct before the
spectacle of some triumphant vulgarian in a nest of spoils
once the goods of better men.

. . . The outcry of old beauty
Whored by pimping merchants
To submission before wine and chatter. . . .

If anything is to be gained by analysis of *War is Kind*,
the book shows less agitation. The man of 1898 has got

done with musing on sexual adventure as " sin " and his young quarrel with a Jewish tribal divinity is over. Sin had become for Crane any act of disloyalty to the given purpose. " Men have never much deserved Christ and Buddha," he wrote, " because they went to work and changed the teaching of generosity into a teaching of roars and threats. I can not be shown that God bends on us any definable stare, like a sergeant at muster, and his laughter would be bully to hear out in nothingness." As for his theory of love, one sees in the verses a knowledge of sentimentalized desire as a tumult not in proportion to the cause. He was an amorist and young. The interest was enormous, candid and not complex. One thinks of him as a thoroughly romantic lover who had not made many exactions in love and probably knew precious little of women. He could finely record the duel between the stupid George and his narrow, devoted mother, because he could coarsen his own figure and that of his parent, making Mary Crane a scolding woman of the tenements and himself a dull young workman, but the duel of desire was too tremulously moving for discernment and his erotic verse drops into the banal.

III

CRANE seldom brought forth an opinion of a contemporary unless he was sure of his hearers but sometimes he was driven to expression and often he gave offense. The man was generous, almost crazily generous in his judgment up to a point, then out poured his distaste for the dramatized personality and those minor arts of exhibition so dear to most writers. Luckless in all things, he chose to say " an author is a man licensed by public opinion to act like a chorus girl at supper," when he was leaving the Savage Club after an evening with Mark Twain wooing adoration in the foreground. The retirement of Thomas Hardy struck him as "all right" and Mr. Kipling's notable absence from the drawing-rooms was "the man's own business." These views were harmless but, and before the wrong audience, he drawled that he could write in a circle all around Mariott Watson. Vastly pleased by the startling *McTeague* of Frank Norris he yet pronounced the book too moral and that sensible objection was whispered along as proof of his conceit. He also said there was too much "I" in W. E. Henley's *Invictus* and preferred the poet's less popular stanzas.

He was conceited in streaks. An eminent writer who is proud of mastering the revolver and publicly wishes he could write verse as well as he plays poker (Mr. William Crane denies that his brother could play poker even reasonably well) is courting comment. Now and then fits of pride came on Crane and in one of these he announced that *The Bride Comes to Yellow Sky* was a whole heap better than anybody had said in print. Sometimes he seemed to be drinking in flatteries from very trivial people and then he was coolly indifferent to pleasant words from beings in critical place. An air of ingratitude blew often in his drawl. His independence was dear to Crane and he exploded in August of 1899: "It seems that I am the only person who had nothing to do with bringing myself before the public!" Indeed, on his side of the question it should be said that too many gentlemen of the late nineties had "brought Stephen Crane before the public" and the manner of that production remains hopelessly dark after long investigation. He wrote: "I am, I think, sufficiently grateful to men who really did things for me and in particular to Mr. Garland who, as you know, gave me sound advice about 'The Red Badge.' But just what is it to the credit of A and B that they bought things from me? I mean, what is my obligation to them? They saw a profit to their papers in buying my stuff and we break even. If it comes to that sultry point, why shouldn't they be grateful to me? "

But the ingratitude of authors to publishers, critics, and editors is a notorious thing and safety lies in letting the balance tilt toward the appraising power. Crane further erred in writing: " Why should I be grateful for an utterly bad piece of criticism that leaves out everything good in ' George's Mother ' and mentions just the things I would like to write over again if that was honest? "

He would not rewrite. He was careless in reading proof and for some of his books he never read proof at all. Ripley Hitchcock begged him to think over *The Third Violet*, as Crane admitted many scenes were too compressed, but the story had appeared as a serial and it was " dishonest " to change the thing now that it had been offered to readers. He restored only a few paragraphs of *The Red Badge* for its final form, so an opening description of the two armies as watchful beasts which so pleased Mr. Garland is forever lost. Sketches dashed off in a few hours were issued with all their imperfections just as first seen in the *Press* and the *World*. Enormous holes appear in his egotism, and his failure in grooming himself for the general gaze is a thing too curious.

> A little ink more or less!
> It surely can't matter?
> Even the sky and the opulent sea,
> The plains and the hills, aloof,
> Hear the uproar of all these books.
> But it is only a little ink more or less.

People came to Brede Place in the autumn of 1899 in numbers fatally large for the bank account. An insurrection occurred one morning in September and the household was cut down. By strenuous devices Crane swept the manor

for a visit of Mr. and Mrs. Conrad and then was over-
whelmed with guests invited or self-invited in the month's
last week. Certain friends had license to come and go as
they pleased. He was always glad to see Mrs. Richie and
her daughters, Robert Barr, Mark Barr, H. G. Wells, and
A. E. W. Mason. He wrote: " John Stokes and George
Lynch have the kindness to let Cora know when they are
coming but would to God that some of the other Indians
would write and ask." . . . A paradox established itself.
To some of his English friends Brede seemed a Bohemian
stronghold while roaming Americans thought Stephen
Crane in severe evening dress surrounded by formal gowns
and black coats a most unhallowed spactacle, the Bohemian
turned snob. Mark Barr suggested that hollows of the hall's
flooring had once been filled with rushes and for a week or
so rushes littered the place, painfully impressing Henry
James as a parody of baronial state. A village blacksmith
hammered iron holders for candles and the beams had their
ancient light again. Its ghosts were invited back to Brede
and its master of the moment, reading the Whilomville tales
aloud to his young circle, coughed gently as mists of October
leaked through his ruinous dwelling in the most romantic
way. Processions of dogs followed him when he rode
Hengist or drove Horsa off to Rye, and the white Powder
Puff got her tail caught under a door, on Crane's birthday.
An offspring of Sponge and Flannel was selected for the
use of Master Borys Conrad and the Russian poodles shed
gloom by their presence at teas when literary ladies came
to ask questions about Crane's ethics. . . . All this went
on while Mr. Conrad and Mr. Garnett were wondering
about the gaunt man's lungs and his wife spent afternoons
guarding his privacy in the red study. He had read with
appreciation Knut Hamsun's *Hunger* when Karl Harriman
brought the book to Brede in summer, but appetite ceased
and Mrs. Crane had agitated conferences with friends as

to Switzerland and the Black Forest. He would not see
doctors although he smoked less and less. Miss Edith Richie
carefully poured doses of Scotch whisky into a sea of soda
and is still indignant: " Cora and I would mix his highballs
for Stephen. There would be about a tablespoonful of
Scotch at the bottom of the glass and I have heard men who
were drinking five times as much say, ' He is drinking himself to death.' He would light a cigarette and then let it go
out in his fingers and, when he noticed that, light another
and men said, ' He is smoking too much. . . .' " He sat so
with that faintly colored beverage turning in his hand and
listened to random talk. Now and then a rocket of adjectives mounted but he was becoming very silent and his
voice went slowly while he praised the new Western sketches
of Owen Wister and Alfred Henry Lewis.

He could still be excited by a discovery. Somebody
urged him to read Anatole France and he went mad over
The Procurator of Judæa, that picture of the aged Pilate
trying to remember any such person as Jesus of Nazareth.
He detailed his high opinion of Monsieur France to Henry
James and to Edmund Gosse quite as though they had never
heard of the Frenchman. He besought William Heinemann
to buy the next novel of Frank Norris. Unliterary in his
conduct, Crane was yet a man of letters although he
chattered slang when talk became too exquisite of an evening at the Savage or in the waste spaces of the Reform
Club. He had even critical views a little prophetic: " I
should say that Mr. Wells will write better and better when
he sticks to characters altogether and does not so much concern himself with narrative. I may be wrong but it seems to
me that he has a genius for writing of underclass people
more honestly than Charles Dickens. . . . I will bet all
my marbles and my best top that Walter Besant is forgotten
in twenty years. . . . Every one tells me that Mr. Stevenson was a fine fellow but nothing on earth could move me to

change my belief that most of his work was insincere."

He would forgive all other crimes if a writer seemed to him honest in his scheme and for that reason he championed artists dead or living who were never important. His generosity gushed on half a dozen commonplace realists who "tried to write honestly about things." They did not get very far but they must care for their work and that was the point of honor. Æsthetic must be the application of emotional weight and to Crane it was plain enough that the arts were merely departments of the intelligent treasure in humanity. Once Mark Barr was talking of a research in higher mathematics and ended: "You see, I cared so much."

Crane broke out, "That's it, Mark! Now that you've said it always remember it. You can never do anything good æsthetically — and you can never do anything with anything that's any good except æsthetically — unless it has at one time meant something important to you."

In the same spirit he wrote to a youth who wasn't sure whether his genius would find better expression in sculpture or fiction: "You might be one of the people who have picked on a defenceless art as a means of telling how much certain things have meant, or mean to you, but did you ever think that this world is full of artists in alligator growing and the promulgation of mixed vegetables? Mr. James was recently quoting a piece from some French poet [3] who shows Narcissus seeing in himself the motion of all time. An artist, I think, is nothing but a powerful memory that can move itself at will through certain experiences sideways and every artist must be in some things powerless as a dead snake." Blessed in simile, did any writer ever limit the power of his vision by such a figure? Perhaps the secret of Crane's charm for many men lay in his rebuke of the artist's swollen vanity. He wrote to his intimate Hilliard: ". . .

[3] Obviously André Gide.

380

For I understand that a man is born into the world with his own pair of eyes, and he is not at all responsible for his vision — he is merely responsible for his quality of personal honesty. To keep close to this personal honesty is my supreme ambition. . . ."

Himself Crane recognized his lucklessness and lightly mentioned it to Willis Clarke when his admirer called at Brede in late November. Ripley Hitchcock had given the young fellow a note of introduction and Crane interrupted work to see him. Lamps were already lighted and Mr. Clarke's eye was caught by a photograph of Hall Caine framed on the wall with a legend below the familiar black cloak: "Christ on the Mountains of Man." Mr. Clarke wanted to write down their talk in shorthand and Crane was listlessly amused. He spoke of his parents at some length and then of *Maggie*, but his attention veered. He began to ask questions about Texas and about baseball teams in the Middle West. Mr. Clarke brought him round by saying: "It's hard luck that you and Mr. Kipling began to write at the same time."

"Yes. I'm just a dry twig on the edge of the bonfire," said Crane.

Chance had erected him as a slim, inscrutable statue before the running opal and fierce light of a talent then shimmering so changefully in the lettered air. It was just his luck.

IV

CHRISTMAS must be gay. He was homesick. He filled Brede with youth and his wife cooked passionately. There were theatricals and the ghosts of Brede romped visibly. The dog Sponge became a father on New Year's Eve and Crane lifted his glass to the oncoming months with: " Let's drink to the twentieth century — in spite of your objection, Mark," he added to Mr. Barr, who had scientifically assured him that the century was not yet begun on January 1, 1900. But they danced through the night and guests trailed up to the rooms of the turret where C. Lewis Hind and other hardy souls had to sleep on cots. A man came back for a forgotten cigarette-case and saw Crane at one of his oddities, humming with his face close to the strings of a violin. His guest strolled up to speak to the dreamer and Crane fainted suddenly against his shoulder.

Alarm had commenced among his friends. Robert Barr was urging a voyage to South Africa in salt air. Some days after the New Year, Crane spoke of Texas to James Pinker. He had been very well down there and living was cheap. Moreton Frewen advised the south of France. People were not willing to say so, but they saw all signs of consumption. Crane listened to nothing and worked at highest speed, inviting folk to keep " Cora from seeing spooks." One night there was long poker and next afternoon he led a party of unshaven friends to a tavern in Rye where they idled under the stare of a most civilized person in a shadowy corner. Crane recalled his errand in the town as dusk fell. He must take back a manuscript to Henry James. The civilized being lifted from obscurity a voice of cultivated distress. Mr. James would not see a stranger save on appointment.

" Oh, sir," said Crane, " I know that the duel is not practiced in this country but I am prepared to waive that for your benefit."

The votary faded out and Crane was commanded to bring his friends into Lamb House, where ladies were dressed to dine. The Jamesian servants, so dreaded by the master, brushed off tweed coats and dinner went graciously forward. James played a joke on a matron who denounced prizefights. He had seen one, he said amid shudders, and slowly detailed the sweating muscles and the bestial faces of the crowd, all viewed, it turned out, on the decent screen of a crude moving-picture show. . . . Sometimes he seems to have stared with a strange wistfulness across the parapet of his seclusion. He must ask Mr. Hueffer's thoughts on the peasants about Rye and he must hear from Crane how cowboys lived and, if their livid emotion deserved that verb, loved. A little later he would weary an ailing millionaire at Hyères for the facts of his pauper boyhood. How did a person who so well knew French happen to have been a farmhand at thirteen? How was it allowed? Was — er — was there no resource? No, no grandfather had flourished in the Illinois of his friend's childhood to dispense millions among a dozen descendants and make it certain that nobody need worry about money or have to know coarse and humble people. " Oh," said the novelist of the finer grain, " horrible! Damnable! " . . . What did he think of the tired guest at his table who had " lived with violence " and was " so truly gifted " and " so very lovable " and " had the mannerisms of a Mile End Roader " and " was of the most charming sensitiveness " in his somewhat diverse and troubled expressions? He sent to Stephen Crane, unasked, five manuscripts and invited an opinion, so he must have respected something in the weary impressionist. Being very old he said: " I loved him. . . ." and that, perhaps, was a convenient synthesis for a mind wanting to understand but not approving the vivid wayfarer.

On January 20th Crane drifted into Mr. Pinker's office and reclaimed two tales mailed the day before from Brede. They weren't good enough, he said. His agent asked how the New Year's party had gone and Crane drawled: " I've heard it was a Babylonian orgy."

A confused impression followed. People were told that Crane had shut Brede and was gone to New York or to the Continent, and Robert Barr wrote, on January 24th, to an American: " Mrs. Crane is so incensed by the nonsense talked about the New Year party at Brede that Stevie is taking her home. England has been kind to Stevie in many ways but some of his cherished friends have said things too carelessly about his most generous but not too formal hospitality and I have heard some gossip that must wound him deeply. His skin is very thin and he is subject to a kind of jealousy that knows how to hurt him worst. His present plan is to take some land in Texas and live in the open air but, between ourselves, it is all over with the boy. He may last two years but I can not bring myself to hope for more than that. . . . He sails on the first of the month."

He did not sail. The mood lasted an evening after his explosion of disgust. Only a few people knew that he had thought of quitting England. The rumor started and died. He had begun a fantastic novel, *The O'Ruddy,* and was sketching in the last somber flood of his prose as *War Memories.*

Meanwhile in America readers of *Harper's Magazine* were delighted and repelled by the Whilomville stories. For the first time since Mark Twain's demigod floated with his lazy slave on the Mississippi, the national child stepped forward and yelped among the maples and swinging gates of a little town, unmoral, unadorned, and far from sweet. This creature lied and bragged and shocked ladies dreadfully. Crane's detachment wasted no loving words on Jimmie Trescott, Willie Dalzell, and the petted daughter of the painter who blindly gave his brat five dollars and so desolated the land. Midway in the series is a pure tragedy. Jimmie took his share of picnic to the lake in a tin pail and all the children made him suffer for no reason. He was hooted and cast out because of this tin pail. It is the epic of democracies and Crane's enchantment with the idiocy of communal thought had its last fling. But the stories were not popular among mothers trained on Mrs. Burnett's patent food, and male critics only were loud in praise. It was left for Booth Tarkington to prove the justice of Crane's performance and with gallantry to remind the public of his predecessor's exploit. Crane handles the children as he handled mature beings. There is the same gravity and the same lack of all respect for ordinary values. As usual not one adventure of Jimmie Trescott is a success. Everything turns out badly, down to the frustration of the Christmas tree for whose glittering sake he joins an alien Sunday school. So biographical memory preserves soft female out-cries against this cruel raid in the pink and white realm of childhood. . . . He had no luck at all. Surely in æsthetic mathematicians are most fortunate, raising their spells for the keen few in a tent of crystal fictions. Painters and makers of sounds have prompt appeal to a single sense and may thereby profit, but this written word must sink in a dark water of all senses mingled, rousing strange brutes of some forgotten dream, brushing to nervous life old preju-dice submerged and shadowy in the mind that reads. Re-ward? No man of honor may demand felicity buttressed on ease in a world so subject to mere chance, but in the final dust vainglory cannot thrill.

Friends wanted to send him as a correspondent for the *Morning Post* to Saint Helena but one day of March his mouth filled suddenly with blood while he petted a dog at luncheon and nobody had much hope, after doctors had shaken their heads. He rallied in April and was jubilant over the birth of twin nephews, one to be named Stephen Crane and destined to short life. People must come to Brede and amuse a frantic woman who paced the hall, try-ing to be affable still and bidding callers be sure to come again, reproaching herself for so much entertainment. Henry James, full of solicitudes, hurried to London when papers wrongly announced that Dr. Trudeau, the famous specialist of Saranac, was lodged in the city grown gloomy, as nothing went well with English armies in South Africa. Terrific fevers of the malady swept the man's fancy back to bright sands of New Jersey and he lay reading bits of his father's sermons. Once he was worried because Sanford Bennett recalled some words of Ford Hueffer and he sent after the Canadian a last note: " You must not be offended by Mr. Hueffer's manner. He patronizes Mr. James. He patronizes Mr. Conrad. Of course he patronizes me and he will patronize Almighty God when they meet but God will get used to it, for Hueffer is all right. . . ."

Robert Barr must finish *The O'Ruddy*, and the Scotchman came to get orders for the jolly satire on old Ireland. Mrs. Crane thought of Germany after May entered Sussex and borrowed money broadcast for the useless journey. He was carried down to Dover and laughed when the dog Sponge clawed wallpaper in a room of the old Lord Warden. There Eugénie and the dead Prince Imperial had waited to welcome the last Napoleon into exile and, being told so, Crane stared at the Victorian adornments, whispering: " Hope she liked the carpet." Men came down out of a London surging with news of victories in South Africa. Ill himself, Joseph Conrad dragged to Dover and watched the blue eyes rove to a sail that fled above gray water outside the window. Grace of indifference thickened. He did not care which world held him or if the multi-colored dice of a new being would flash beyond this towering shadow of the void. Out there? He didn't care, stroking his dog.

His niece joined him in hired chambers at Badenweiler and sun glowed in his wife's hair while he dictated orders for the gay novel and sometimes patted her white arms. On the fourth day of June he was very eager. Letters must go to his brothers and to John Hilliard. Sponge hopped around the bed and must be teased for a while. Then it was night and the tired woman fell asleep, to be wakened before dawn by the little dog's vain howling in the dark.

APPENDIX

Stephen Crane is buried at Elizabeth, New Jersey, and a tablet to his memory is now in the Free Library of Newark. Mr. Max Herzberg of the Newark *Evening News* was one of the movers for this memorial and to Mr. Herzberg I am much indebted for the use of certain papers collected by him in his personal researches as to Crane. I must at once acknowledge an even greater indebtedness to Mr. Willis Clarke for his generosity toward me. In 1903 Mr. Clarke began to collect copies of letters and facts for a life of Stephen Crane, but was so baffled by conflicting statements that he dropped the work. His shorthand report of an interview with Crane at Brede is quoted in Chapters i, iii, and iv and vii of this book. He was also the donor of letters from Mrs. Bolton Chaffee, Julian Ralph, Robert Barr, Acton Davies, and Henry Davies Hume, and of a passage in the diary of the late Charles Cary Griswold. The mythology encountered by Mr. Clarke may interest readers who have been struck by a note of apology in this most imperfect study. Mr. Clarke was informed by people who had met Crane and admired him that he was the illegitimate son of Grover Cleveland, the outcast child of an eminent family in New York, an Australian sailor, a German actor, and an ex-convict. He was gravely assured that the several published statements about Crane in journals, the *Bookman, Leslie's Weekly,* and *Scribner's Maga-*

zine, were industrious camouflage devised by the late Ripley Hitchcock on behalf of Appleton's. My own contact with the legendary Crane revealed other jewels of rumor. I have, with regret, rejected the tales of Crane's love-affair with the lamented Sarah Bernhardt, of his duel in New Orleans, of his attempt to burn James Gordon Bennett's yacht, of his marriage to Australian, English, Spanish, and African dancers, of his ninety-thousand-dollar cablegram to the New York *Journal,* of his death of delirium tremens in Paris, and of his murder by an actress still living who happened at the time of his death to be in Chicago. With less pain I have rejected anecdotes of Crane which were in print during his childhood as anecdotes of Mark Twain, Thomas Hood, Abraham Lincoln, and Andrew Jackson. There have also been visited upon me stories of his gayeties which are, with probably as much truth, told in regard to Bill Nye, Eugene Field, Clyde Fitch, and other celebrities still extant.

It was suggested to me by Mr. Huneker that Crane's picturesque exterior offered a field for the imagination of some contemporaries and that " they turned a little Flaubert into a big Verlaine." The injustice of that romancing was great, however, and inevitably I have concluded that a considerable spite followed him after his success. Else why did three unsigned letters reach me when Mr. Christopher Morley printed my wish for correspondence in the New York *Evening Post?* All three votaries of romantic biography had charges to make and the charges were couched in excellent English.

Some of Crane's friends erred in their mention of him after death. Elbert Hubbard's paper in the *Philistine* contained equivocal statements, and Robert Barr's " qualities that lent themselves to misapprehension " is not a fortunate phrase. An article printed as an obituary of Stephen Crane in a New York paper of June 6, 1900 took pains to clear

him of the charge of drug-taking and probably settled that
charge in the popular mind he so distrusted. Three estimates likened him to Edgar Allan Poe, who is still, after
scrupulous examination, held to have been a drunken madman by the generality of readers. Without doubt I shall be
accused of " whitewashing " Crane, and by choice I retort
beforehand that a man is entitled to his own identity, not
to a cheap shell of gossip. If my assumption that the re-
issue of *Maggie* roused silly conjectures is incorrect, it is
in one instance well supported. Mr. William Crane tells
me that after *Maggie* appeared in 1896 several ladies of
Port Jervis solemnly consulted him as to the propriety of
receiving Stephen Crane in their homes. . . . The American nineties present a singular mingling of poltroonery
and bravado in the treatment of sexual and alcoholic matters public or private. You behold young men singing Hovey's pretty " Stein Song " and you hear the last despairing
outcries of Frances Willard, who wanted her world to be
Christian and in loud addresses assured it that Christ's
kindness to the woman taken in adultery was not an example
to be imitated " in our modern day." The author of *The
Black Riders, Maggie*, and *George's Mother* was plainly
an object of suspicion, and America never comes of age. A
fellow who defends streetwalkers in night resorts and lends
money to courtesans is naturally " immoral." His intimates took Crane for a man of honest and liberal views and
their indignation with the figure created for him by fiction
persists. . . . I take vast pleasure in issuing on behalf of
a dead and generous man a firm denial of an attack on
Crane in *The Derelict* by Richard Harding Davis. Illustrations of the story happened to resemble Crane somewhat
and Mr. Davis suffered a deal of comment for which he was
not responsible.

This book is probably filled with errors, but my variations from partial biographies have been made on the tes-

timony of Crane's few letters. With genuine regret I have
differed from Mr. Hamlin Garland's account of the birth of
The Red Badge, which, in his recollection, was first shown
to him in 1893 and in the month of February. Crane's own
statement and the memory of other friends place the writing
rather later. I can only suggest that the first rapid draft
was the manuscript brought to Mr. Garland in Harlem and
that the finished product was shown in the following winter.
But Crane's carelessness was astonishing. Belonging to the
vainest of professions, he took no trouble to annotate himself for history, and that carelessness remains a part of his
charm for those who knew him. Many of his last letters
were written in a singular blue ink that turned purple when
dry and has now faded beyond process of revival. I have
been unable to verify Crane's career as a reporter on the
Herald, and some amusing episodes have been omitted for
lack of proof. Also there have been removed from his letters some hasty estimates of living people in England and
America. Crane himself had no great idea of his judgment
as to character on first sight, as he took Mr. George Bernard
Shaw for a " clerical person " and Mr. Frank Harris for an
actor. It would have been pleasant to print his admiration
of certain ladies who received him in England, but the
wives of authors are entitled to such privacy as is left in
the world.

For their kindness in aiding me this book should be dedicated to a number of people. If I have not effected a portrait of the Stephen Crane known to them, that is because,
in his words, " an expression of life can always elude us."
Excuse me a little. Another may do better. My thanks are
offered, among the unconcerned dead, to: James Gibbons
Huneker, Charles Edward Devlin, Wallis McHarg, Clyde
Fitch, James Pinker, Acton Davies, and to Edmund Crane;
among the living to William Howe Crane, Edith Crane,
Vera Sidmore, Hamlin Garland, Mark Barr, Edith Richie

APPENDIX

Jones, Corwin Knapp Linson, Frederic Gordon, Edward Garnett, Karl Edwin Harriman, Vincent Starrett,[1] Paul Reynolds, Richard Brett Armstrong, Sarah McHarg, Victoria Sonntag, John Langdon Heaton, Edward Sanford Bennett, Charles Gardner 2nd, Claude Bragdon, Irving Bacheller, Jesse Lynch Williams, Henry T. Carey, John Northern Hilliard, John Willard Raught, Helen Marie Campbell, Caroline Gunther, Eileen Bassett Dufriche, Joseph and Jessie Conrad.

[1] Mr. Starrett's *Bibliography* contains all my information as to Crane's unpublished work.

HANNA

A NOTE TO
LEWIS MUMFORD

In the summer of 1910 a friend invited me to his father's house at Watch Hill and there I became the awkward cavalier of his sister, a young matron whose beauty was so extraordinary and musical that it persisted as a sounding nimbus about her even when she was shaking sand from the diapers of her small son upon the enchanted beach or pretending gallantly to enjoy a waltz with me. The book which I am dedicating to you was unconsciously begun, one night, while I defended her, on a gentle signal of her fan, in the veranda beyond a ballroom, between lanterns and moonlight. For the yacht of a certain Mr. Dives rode at anchor in the bay, and Dives himself, a pinnacle of creamy English flannels splashed with a tie in the colors of some Harvard club, sulked at the lady's feet, yearning to dance with her. He was dull; he was fifty years old; he attempted a flirtation in tones of a badly maintained boyishness, and the fan informed me that I must be useful, here. So we talked, and it happened that Mark Hanna was mentioned and Mr. Dives kicked alive a curiosity about the great adventurer in government.

He had found Mr. Hanna puzzling. Once they were lunching with some common friend in a hotel when the richest of Americans passed the table and nodded to the Senator from Ohio. Mr. Dives was thrilled. He was the

sort of rich man to whom richer men are sacred and he had
wanted to meet the grander Dives at once. But Mr. Hanna
said that the gaunt financier was not worth meeting.
" Why," Mr. Dives cried, " he's worth two hundred millions! " Mark Hanna grunted, " Yes, and what the hell else
is he worth? "

Mr. Dives did not understand that question. He recited
it to us carefully, the moonlight soaking his white coat and
his stupid face. I am glad to report that the beautiful lady
did not have to dance with this oaf. The music stopped in
the ballroom, and, next morning, his yacht twinkled past
the beach in a glory of brass and canvas, bearing Mr. Dives
off to Newport. Maybe someone else patiently told him,
somewhere, what Mark Hanna meant, but I doubt that he
really comprehended it, and he must have died in the satisfaction of feeling that a profound loss to the world was oc-
curring in the separation of himself from his millions of
hereditary dollars. He had made me think of Mark Hanna,
though, in a new way and the discussions of Mr. Herbert
Croly's book on Hanna in 1912 commenced my education
in the legend of this man's singular force. I don't mean
the public discussions; the capital biography was exposed
on the lacteal quagmire of American criticism and sank
therein through a scum of tepid reviews. But it was my
luck to hear the work tried by a jury of experts, men whose
names figured in its chapters, and, listening to them, this
familiar image of Marcus Hanna changed for me and was
enriched.

He was familiar to me and an awful nuisance of my
childhood, although I saw him just twice, once on a train
bound to Washington and once as he came stiffly walking down a driveway with little Quentin Roosevelt stick-
ing to his cane, a white moth of starched clothes chanting
out a tale about a pet rat's foul misconduct. But Mr.
Hanna annoyed me endlessly. He was a substance in Wash-

ington or Cleveland which my father had to see, a sort of joss or rune. I conceived him as silent in a shrine, and my father as a messenger hunting oracles. A voice would command over the telephone or a telegram would come, and then the cab was at the door and Mr. Beer was gone to catch the last express for Washington. An upbringing in the political seraglio is like any other; one's father's business is an awful bother; much of my father's business from 1896 to 1904 was Mr. Marcus Alonzo Hanna, and in proof of that I tender to your interest the footnotes and appendix of this book.

This prefatory note was made necessary by the quaint conduct of a veteran publicist and a younger author of fiction in April of this year. The first of five articles compressed from the full text of my study was available to the public on April 11th in an issue of *The Saturday Evening Post*. The veteran publicist, on April 12th, wrote to a friend in Chicago asserting that " Beer has begun to whitewash Mark Hanna in the *Post*. Ruth Hanna (McCormick) paid him fifty thousand dollars for his stuff and gave him the material. . . ." On April 18th the author of fiction had a much higher figure for Mrs. McCormick's generosity toward me and, in the latest quotations, her fee has reached terms quite imperial. So I am forced to deny, on behalf of Marcus Hanna's daughter, that she has ever seen me, written to me, paid me one penny, or caused any information as to her father's life to reach me. About the whitewashing of Mark Hanna, let someone do that who is willing at the same time to whitewash the American people as it existed in the latter nineteenth century — No, he must do more. He must clean from his account of mankind that unconquered essential of our being which makes us bid for a place beyond our fellows; he must prove that we act and fail driven by some sweeter impulse than the search for power. I prefer Hanna to another subject as I might

397

A NOTE TO LEWIS MUMFORD

negligibly prefer Grunewald to Botticelli, any Egyptian stonemason to Donatello, Hawthorne to Poe, or Faraday to Henry Ford.

But this is not a biography. You know very well that the biography of an artist is at least a plausible adventure; if he has the strength to speak his mind at all, he tells you much about himself. A politician's art is a long wrestling with the most dangerous of materials, ourselves. He lives as a demonstration of the one great modern saying: " It is life, not the individual, that is conscienceless." He puts out his will, not as he would but as he can, and his art is one of concessions, of oblique gestures and perpetual ironics. Search for his conscience and you must pluck it from a hundred battered shards of distorting mirror. He eludes you, and your justice to him is a demand, finally, that his skill and his force be applauded. Try to paint him out and he fades from your perception. You sketch — you strive — you almost reach conclusions, and then you sit at last humiliated by a shadow.

Thomas Beer

Siasconset, July 4th, 1929

CHAPTER I

THE YEAR 1865

A DARK man who smelled of brandy came up through a bright theater in Washington and shot Abraham Lincoln from behind. He then threw himself nine feet down to the stage and for a moment was a clear apparition to the people seated above the President as he shifted a dagger to his right hand, brandished it, and vanished. His pistol's small explosion was not heard at all by many in the galleries. When Mrs. Lincoln's shrieks began they thought at first that Mr. Lincoln had been stabbed, and an old preacher named Hugh Jones stood, shouting in Welsh, " He that took up the sword has perished by the sword! " He was half mad since the death of a third son in battle, and now he mumbled revengeful verses from Ezekiel and the song of Deborah while his scared daughter pulled him down the stairs through a commencing panic. In the cool street he lurched against her, silent. He lived six months, but did not speak again.

Even as men were thrusting Charles Taft in his blue surgeon's dress over the torn flag and gilded rail into the President's box it was shouted in the theater that this disappearing shape had been John Wilkes Booth. His last appearance in melodrama impressed the random young actor heartily; he paused to slash a musician who met him behind the scenes and then stunned the simple lad holding his horse for him in an alley with a blow of his dagger's handle. On the morning of April 15th, 1865, the mob's hot logic answered his performance in like kind. Mr. Lincoln was scarcely dead when a crowd of hundreds swelled into the white lobby of the Burnet House at Cincinnati, hunting Junius Brutus Booth, and the innocent tragedian lay hidden in a friend's room for days until he could be smuggled out of town. Toward noon a pretty girl on Broadway in New York was mistaken for Roberta Norwood by a gang of street boys who penned her against the rails of Trinity churchyard bawling, " Actress! Actress! " Policemen and a naval officer, a Mr. Dewey, rescued her after a real fight. All afternoon a committee of the pious rode through Pittsburgh trying to get signatures on a petition which demanded the closing of every theater in the state of Pennsylvania. That night the mayor of Boston posted guards before the playhouses of his city, and in Cleveland a negro boy who polished brass at the Academy of Music was set on by warm patriots and cruelly hammered.

Mr. John Ellsler, lessee of the Academy, had taken his famous company down to Columbus for a season. He was a reticent, rather stately actor, deft in comedy of the dry kind and competent in everything. He had lifted the whole condition of the theater in the middle West, refusing employment to celebrated drunken stars who entertained audiences by clinging to scenery as they mouthed their lines, often mistaking footlights for an exit. Mr. Ellsler's stock company was a model of drilled conduct; no scandal emerged from it and none entered it. Gentlemen lounged in, between the acts, to chat with the clever manager and to be presented to whatever notable player was being supported by Mr. Ellsler's troupe, to Edwin Booth, to Miss Western or Mr. Couldock. Ralph Waldo Emerson stood in the wings, one night of 1859, watching the Mephistopheles of a farcical ballet shot upward through a trap in a puff of red fire, and the actresses, led by Ellsler's wife, came forward to curtsy in modest reverence before the smiling philosopher.

But now Mr. Ellsler saw a display of ferocious diabolics. His players got the news of Booth's identification at noon of April 15th. They simply did not believe it. Why, this could never be Wilkie Booth! Just awhile ago the mailbox of the Academy was jammed with notes on the most scented paper, addressed to J. Wilkes Booth, Esquire, by ladies fascinated as he stalked in pale robes close to the boxes in *The Marble Heart,* since Mr. Booth repaired his lack of height by displaying his authentic beauty to the populace at close range. It could not be Wilkie Booth. He was too gay and kind and gentle. Mrs. Ellsler wept and little Clara Morris, the hungry child who played everything from Romeo's page to Hamlet's mother, was still weeping on Sunday afternoon when one of Mr. Ellsler's civilian friends found the miserable company keeping its nerves together by a lame rehearsal.

They were a city besieged. When Mr. Thomas Beer walked into the gray place, Ellsler darted at him, begging for news. Was Booth taken? What was being said in the streets? Was the profession to be suppressed? All these people packed around the burly young lawyer from the town of Bucyrus and heaved questions on him. It was a real peril, long forgotten. At the great mass meeting before the capitol in Columbus some man wise enough to be reckless asked the mob's compassion for the shamed players yonder in the theater. A growl stirred, deepening, and the crowd swayed until someone started a thin cheer and the dangerous moment passed. " And verily," says Clara Morris in her memoirs, " we were grateful! " But on Sunday Ellsler had nothing to be grateful for. He handed his friend a telegram from the mayor of Cleveland warning him that it might not be safe to bring back the company to the Academy of Music next week. His restraint broke. He raved, pitching Shaksperian sentences at empty maroon chairs of the orchestra.

This was the end of the profession in America! They would be vagabonds once more, preyed on by moral pamphleteers and sour pastors, shut from society and given the worst rooms in poor hotels! But he would not give up, by heaven! He would take his people back to Cleveland and open the Academy on Tuesday, as he had advertised! Come wind, come wrack! Let the Clevelanders whom he had served all these years lynch him in the streets!

Mr. Beer saw nothing comic in this state of mind, and reported it to a grandson grimly as something hideous he had seen in the year 1865. A terrific emotional machinery had been licensed in America since 1859 and the cool lawyer once had been its victim when he objected to some words of a vindictive orator who was damning Abraham Lincoln for offering to buy the slaves in Kentucky. He had been snubbed and cut on the streets. He had learned, in bewilderment, that all logic and all kindness were lost in this rhythmic billowing of organized hates. The windows of the tiny rural newspaper's office where his dry and sane editorials were sometimes published had been stoned by night, and a benevolent soldier had warned him that the partisans were talking rope. He had experienced the profound æsthetic of a wild drive in a heeling buggy through night and storm, which made him sensitive to the music of *The Erl King*, afterwards, and, in the year 1865, he faced, as gravely as possible, his ruin at the law, because he was a Democrat, and social blizzards because a drunken actor had killed the President. So, having lived for years among people ready to go mad on order, he saw no reason to laugh at John Ellsler's fears.

But, as it happened, the mob's mood did not last. For some days actors were insulted in restaurants and on the street. When Ellsler's company opened the Academy on

Tuesday night, the journals of Cleveland reported a full house and warm welcome home for " The Favorites." A very old gentleman recalls mild hisses in the gallery as the curtain rose, but the potency of the emotional machine was now aimed elsewhere: the body of Abraham Lincoln was parading the United States. On Wednesday carpenters began to lay the floor of a funeral pavilion in the Square, close to the Perry monument, and Juliet Araminta Smith probably saw a final demonstration against actors that same night.

The Smiths have left no trace on the history of Cleveland unless some venerable gentlewomen recollect a meek, pretty little Mrs. Smith who made children's clothes in the spring of 1865. She brought Juliet Araminta and Orion James to Cleveland in January, on account of economic conditions in central Illinois. Her father frankly told her he couldn't keep Nate Smith's offspring in food and copper-toed shoes, even if it was nobody's fault that Nate had been drafted into the Army. It was too bad, of course, but Orion Holt's farm would not support Mrs. Smith and her children, as well as her nine younger brothers and sisters.

So Mrs. Smith wrote to Cousin Jennie, who sewed in Cleveland, and Cousin Jennie promised plenty of work. Cleveland was growing rich; steamboats and foundries increased; ladies could afford the amplest mourning. The Smiths came eastward and resided, obscurely but agreeably, in one room of a boarding-house. And after young Orion Smith, who was almost eleven, got his job at two dollars a week in the warehouse of Robert Hanna and Company, they lived luxuriously and often had oysters for supper.

The oysters established Mr. Marcus Alonzo Hanna in the mind of Juliet Araminta, who was nine, as a benevolent jinni. She became addicted to oysters and always went with Orion to the fishmonger's shop to revere the salesman who counted oysters into the tin pail. As Mr. Mark Hanna had given Orion his job, because Orion was a soldier's son, her warm and confiding nature caused Juliet Araminta to think that this grandee should be thanked. His munificence rained oysters on her. She accordingly penetrated the warehouse in River Street and presented herself to Mr. Mark. He made the kindly mistake of tendering Juliet a heart-shaped lump of maple sugar out of the tin box on his desk. After that he was seldom without Juliet.

She helped him to escort customers and callers through his firm's premises. She dirtied her pantalettes on the docks of Hanna and Company. She ran diligently with notes addressed to " Angostura & Bitters, Gin Avenue " or to " Doe & Roe, Mud Street " and came tearfully back to tell Mr. Mark that policemen assured her there were no such firms and no such streets in Cleveland. Mr. Mark, refreshed by an hour of Juliet's absence, fed her more maple sugar and pulled her hair.

But it was certain that he loved her. He called her Sawdust and told her that the government should mint her yellow curls to redeem Mr. Lincoln's greenbacks when the war was over. He slew a monstrous rat which threatened her on the docks with one blow of his walking-stick. He — this was glory perpetual along her street — he even once drove her home behind his black horse Howard, with Orion clinging awed on the back of the buggy. And it was no good for Orion to keep saying that a Mrs. Marcus Alonzo Hanna already existed. Juliet Araminta knew better. She was Mr. Mark's beloved and he was hers and when the nasty war stopped they would be married, and they would eat oysters and maple sugar every day. So, walking down to the station on the night of April 25th between Orion and her timid mother, she wished that Mr. Mark could see her in the full dignity of her new best dress, as she was sure that she looked perfection.

404

Be sure that she did, for she was very pretty at the age of nine and her mother had composed a costume for her from a plate in the French fashion magazine. This costume survives — a tunic of stiff red silk nobly embroidered in vast roses of hard white cord. Under this were four starched petticoats, a shirt of some kind, a pair of cambric pantaloons edged with pink lace, and a girdle of canvas. Under all that was the rosy substance of Juliet Araminta in a condition of rapture. Somebody sensible had killed the odious Mr. Lincoln who drafted papa into the Army, and that had ended the war, and she was going to the railway station to meet papa. Her views of the war and the Army and Mr. Lincoln were harsh; it was all an uncomfortable boiling of tears and belated letters and mamma walking the floor at nights. Juliet Araminta glanced at the funeral pavilion in the Square and dared Orion to go and spit on it. But there was a policeman watching and they had to hurry, else the train would come in and Private Nathan Smith would arrive from the wars unwelcomed.

Private Nathan Smith was discharged from hospital at Georgetown on April 22nd, 1865, after two and a half years of service, with three fingers gone from his left hand and no prospects whatever. But he was still only twenty-eight years old — boys married young in the fifties — and he landed cheerfully in the smoke of the raw station, seeming taller than ever to Juliet Araminta, as he was thin and pallid. The family made a group commonplace in the month of April 1865: a tired woman crying on a tired man's breast, and two children hopping about in their best clothes.

He must be fed directly; he had been fifteen hours on this train without even a sandwich. The family wandered into what must have been rather a low eating-place near the station, as she recalls that it was lighted by oil lamps and that her mother told her not to look at some ladies in bright dresses who were keeping late hours in one corner. There

was sawdust on the floor, near a bar, and when the trouble
began, this sawdust flew everywhere. Juliet's father thrust
her behind him, against the wall, and she put her hands
tightly on her eyes. It was going to be worse than the riots
at home in Illinois when the marshals rode through a crowd
protesting the draft, and men had their scalps slashed open
by blows of the rawhide whips. There was the same dull
and thick sound of voices from the jostle at the bar and —
clearly remembered, this! — the wail of an old fellow who
kept saying, " I am not an actor! I am an elocutionist,
gentlemen! " He said it over and over as they pulled him
down on the floor. A waiter ran yelling into the street.
Women shrieked, of course, and Private Smith roared uselessly, his left hand still in bandages. But when other voices
came into her hearing Juliet Araminta knew that everything was all right and took her hands from her eyes. He
had come in time! Warned by love's echoes, sounding out
her terror, he had flown through the night to aid her. It was
not that the waiter had brought in anybody he could find
on the street. It was love.

He was standing inside the door, bawling orders at the
crowd, just as if the angry men were stevedores on the docks
of Hanna and Company. Juliet Araminta peeped around
her father's legs and admired him. His silk hat was probably tilted back and sideways on his round head. His
whiskers swept in auburn beauty from ear to ear under his
pink, shaved chin with its wide dimple. His large brown
eyes sparkled yellow as he shouted. In one fragile, long
hand he kept a cigar alight by little twitches of his delicate
fingers. Behind him a naval officer, perhaps his brother
Howard, and some civilians were mere and meaningless
shadows to Juliet Araminta. Here was her Mr. Mark! She
recalls nothing of the process by which Mr. Marcus Alonzo
Hanna quieted the men who had been willing to mob an
old stray because he talked like an actor. It is not unlikely

that some people in the bar were afraid of Robert Hanna's nephew, the husband of a daughter of the towering Daniel Rhodes. An eminent citizen, in those days, had certain habits of command, and at young Hanna's back was the prestige of a great wholesale grocery and shipping business; the steamboats of his firm ranged the Lakes; every roustabout on the docks knew Mark Hanna by sight and knew that he was not afraid to toss a tipsy stevedore off the deck of the *Northern Light* into the river. The men shied from him. Someone dusted the victim of applied emotionalism and got him through the doors into the safe darkness. Mr. Mark tossed a dollar on the bar, being already a sound diplomat, and was turning to leave the place when Mrs. Nathan Smith did all that a lady in an interesting condition was obliged to do after a public excitement in those days, and swooned on the floor.

Juliet Araminta's evening culminated in a pure bliss of sensations as she sat on Mr. Mark's knees in a real cab and his whiskers caressed her neck. He talked pleasantly to the simple family and ordered the cab to halt at some club or hotel when he found that Private Smith was still supperless. Waiters came running with sandwiches and coffee; Orion James and Juliet Araminta were fed ice cream. It was eleven o'clock when Mr. Mark lifted her up the steps of the boarding-house and twelve o'clock struck before she was in bed. She had never known there was such an hour as that.

Two hours later Jack and Will Garrett roused from a nervous nap in a shed on their father's farm near Port Royal, Virginia. They had not really slept; they were watching out the night beside the farm's precious horses, one of these a " present from General Grant," brought home after the surrender at Appomattox. All afternoon the handsome, curious stranger who called himself Boyd and his silly young friend had been trying to buy the

407

horses for a trip to the South. The Garrett boys mistrusted him and they had locked the door of the frail tobacco house when he and his companion went in there to sleep, for they could not risk losing the horses. Now they nudged each other. A familiar, increasing rhythm had brought them wide awake: a column of horse was pelting through the moist night. . . . It was a detail of Yankee cavalry coming closer down the lane from town. They must have known precisely each echoing detail of the business — the thud of boots dismounting, the chatter of carbines cocked briskly and the separating noise of heels in the dooryard, before Lieutenant Baker hammered on the kitchen door and the boys heard their scared old father answering him. Then it was too much for Jack. He dragged on his gray jacket and loped up the new grass, breaking through the ring of bluecoats on the porch. . . .

A little later and any negro crossing those flat fields heard the crack of Boston Corbett's pistol and saw flames spin up from the burning tobacco house. Soon a shifting audience collected along the roadway — negroes and white folks who had come running to help put out the fire. But the troopers would not let them inside the yard. They could stare across the fence at the boy in manacles who sat against a tree, whistling to keep from tears. That was young Herold. Mr. Booth was a shape under a blanket on the porch, voiceless. Now and then the handsome schoolmistress who boarded with the Garretts bent down and wetted his face with her handkerchief. He achieved, here, a fine drama of silence and complete futility. The sun rose. He died.

Juliet Araminta was not enough impressed by the morning's news to recollect it. Something local and pressing had her full attention. A telegram came before breakfast. Orion sped forth and told all his acquaintances that he was going to California on a ship and danced disgracefully. Mrs. Smith wept, of course, and Private Smith rubbed his chin while his daughter plangently wanted to know what had happened. She was not told, and things became a muddle until presently she was allowed to guide her father down to River Street to call on Mr. Mark.

There was a lot of talk. A clerk went out with a green slip of paper and returned with many bills. Private Smith painfully wrote his name on a note for five hundred dollars, without interest, payable in five years after date, and then wiped his eyes. Mr. Mark stood Juliet Araminta on his desk and drew a pencil around the coast of the United States on his map, from New York down past Florida, on below Cuba — it was south of Cuba that this child saw her still-born sister buried in the warmer seas — and so straight on to the Isthmus of Panama.

" If there was a canal through here, Sawdust, you could sail right up to San Francisco."

The Smiths spoke of this sentence often, after 1880, but it made Nathan Smith chuckle in the year 1865, and he told his daughter as they walked homeward that Mr. Hanna was just joking. There had been some crazy stuff in the newspapers about cutting a canal through Nicaragua or Panama. But it stood to reason that you couldn't cut a canal through mountains. And she was now to be extra good and help mamma pack. They were all going down on a German steamer with Cousin Jim Holt from New York to Nicaragua and across to the Pacific slope. Cousin Jim had made the trip three times and knew the ropes. Nothing to be scared about (he was trembling with the thrill of it, himself) — and they would live on Cousin Jim's land near a town named Santa Clara.

Juliet Araminta had no notions of distance or geography and was much pleased until it was dusk next day in the thunderous railroad's station and a distress came to her in the noise of Cousin Jennie's snivelling. But here was Mr. Mark. The slim female with him wore black splendors in token of mourning for Mr. Lincoln and glittered everywhere with jet so that she seemed a cloudy wonder from some journal of fashion. She smiled, though, and Juliet Araminta had no time to be jealous of Mrs. Marcus Alonzo Hanna. There was a basket filled with fruit and sandwiches and a smaller basket filled with garments cut, it mysteriously seemed, for a mere baby. Mrs. Smith wept gratefully. Orion James began to snuffle as Mr. Mark handed him up the steps of the tall coach. . . . She knew, now, that she was being taken from him, forever, and Juliet Araminta wailed for hours and fell asleep with her nose pressed to a pane of the lumbering car.

They woke her and told her to look out. It was dead night where the train was stilled on a siding among wet fields. But there was no darkness to hide the rain and the women huddled under wide shawls or umbrellas. Huge bonfires tinged the world; men and boys were feeding fence-rails into the flames. Then an engine neared, with bayonets of guards flashing from the tender and streamers of wet crape swinging curiously. And then all the women began singing *Rock of Ages* as the train came by. She saw a lighted coach brilliant with flowers, and some officer's white gloves, and she started to cry again, without knowing why. So Lincoln passed her.

II

AMONG the important towns of eastern Ohio in Andrew Jackson's time was New Lisbon, not a big place, but a thrifty center of farms and trade, dominated by a Quaker named Benjamin Hanna. He and his sons owned good land, the largest store in the county, shares in a flour mill, and much else. Their prestige was enormous in the region; sometimes Benjamin Hanna was called " Squire " in bills and documents. The pioneer societies had not yet come to

410

value themselves for homeliness, and in New Lisbon as elsewhere, they tried to reproduce the civil formulas and habits of their kinsmen in Pennsylvania, Connecticut, and Vermont. Wandering painters and primitive masters of the daguerreotype report the Hanna tribe in its best clothes for us. The hard Quaker's wife wrote invitations for a son's wedding in a grand, sweeping hand, and, since Benjamin Hanna traded eastward to Pittsburgh or acted as forwarding agent of mills and shops in Philadelphia, his establishment had its mild elegances in the way of handsome silver, miniatures, and pretty trash.

The cleverest and most sensitive of Benjamin Hanna's sons was Leonard, a long young man whose frail hands got him the nickname " Miss " when he was a boy. He had been elaborately educated for medicine and came back to New Lisbon to practice after refining years in Philadelphia. But a fall from his horse damaged his spine. He lapsed into the mass of the family and did as his father and brothers did, although he was always called Dr. Hanna. He dabbled a bit in politics, speaking in debates on primitive abolition and prohibition, trying to rouse sentiment against the Mexican war and forcing his tribe to back small ventures in civic improvement. For the family, when it acted as a body, had great force. It was much admired. The Hannas were tall, imposing men with large eyes, gray or brown, and resounding voices. It was said that you could hear them having an argument or singing a hymn for the space of two miles.

They helped New Lisbon to ruin itself, with the best intentions. A canal was planned which would join the community by water to Pittsburgh and the Lakes. Rather distrustful of the oncoming railroads, the Hannas threw their weight behind the project of the canal, and threw two hundred thousand dollars into its construction. It failed, after a long struggle; the section west of New Lisbon blocked

411

from bad engineering; banks caved in; a tunnel through a swale of rock cost immensely. Marcus Alonzo Hanna, Dr. Leonard's eldest son, must have lived as a baby in the sound of the word " canal." Meanwhile the new railroads were built at a distance from the worried town, and this was the end of New Lisbon's importance. People drifted away; the little cultivated layer of lawyers and clerks went hunting jobs in towns along the railways. One Hanna retreated to Pittsburgh. In 1852 Leonard and Robert Hanna took what money they had left, made an alliance with a shrewd trader named Hiram Garretson, and moved to Cleveland.

In this partnership the nervous, handsome doctor supplied the imagination. Supposedly the firm of Hanna, Garretson and Company was a wholesale grocery. It had that character for a few months, anyhow. But in 1853 Dr. Hanna went off, to rest his nerves, on a sailing vessel up the Lakes and watched something inspiring to a clever man. Hundreds of settlements sent out canoes or dories to the leisurely sloop asking if there was molasses for sale, or a spare steel blade, or a bottle of calomel, or an awl. Dr. Hanna saw a commercial light. He returned to Cleveland and there commenced a period of discussions between the Hanna brothers, often within earshot of young Marcus Alonzo. Robert Hanna was the natural conservative; Leonard was adventurous. In the end the ailing doctor won and soon the firm of Hanna, Garretson and Company had steamboats on the Lakes, dealing out supplies of all kinds, shedding passengers at the developing ports. The ships ran up to wild Minnesota and came back again with pig-iron, salted fish, timber, and skins. When the Hannas of Cleveland backed Abraham Lincoln in the election of 1860, they were eminent men, known everywhere throughout the basin of the Lakes.

But this basin of the Lakes, at the beginning of the Civil War, was an unasserted territory, and long after the war

was finished the trade of the Lakes meant little in the everlasting brag of American commerce. Certain families and
combinations on the Lakes advanced with a sort of stealth
into the literary or journalistic perception of the United
States. Indeed, the literary were long in judging what battle
had done to commerce. The war deflected all routes of
American trade; New York was to become definitely a metropolis; the Confederate cruisers interrupted with decision
the advance of American interest in the Caribbean; the
appalling importance of the Mississippi was discovered just
when the traffic of the Mississippi was suspended for three
years. Robert and Leonard Hanna had no place in the catalogues of wealthy Americans drawn up by the hacks of the
seaboard cities in the years before Lincoln's election, and
their support of Mr. Lincoln's campaign is not mentioned
in the many hundred sheets of raw propaganda which record that fierce episode in emotional politics.

Marcus Alonzo cast his first vote for Mr. Lincoln in 1860.
He was born at New Lisbon in September of 1837 and left
the failing town unwillingly in 1852 because he was already engaged to marry a pretty girl there. His parents
allowed him to consider himself engaged, at any rate, and
tactfully permitted the affair to drag itself into staleness for
three years, since the eldest son was stubborn as the freckles
on his flat face. Among several shaky legends of Mark
Hanna's boyhood one is certainly true: he had an astonishing stubbornness. When he was suspended from the Western Reserve University in the spring of 1857 for faking the
programs of a solemn Junior Exhibition and successfully
distributing his burlesque imitation among parents and professors, his father ordered Marcus to apologize to his
mother and Marcus would not do so. But the lady was
rather pleased and boasted of her son's refusal in her old
age. She was from Vermont, and she despised men who
" gave in."

Mrs. Leonard Hanna probably affected her son's whole
life. Her own name was Samantha Converse. Generations
of Huguenot and English ancestors supplied her traditions.
Her parents came in their own carriage from Vermont to
Ohio with some family silver and a deal of stiff pride. She
was a cultivated person, but not sentimentally so, for she
regarded the sweet ballads of the fifties and sixties as nonsensical and terrified people in the theaters of Cleveland by
genteel but audible snorts of contempt when passion gushed
too heavily on the other side of the footlights. She did not
regard poverty as an unfortunate condition, but as a disgrace. She gave royally to charities, but she did it, says a
lady who knew her well, with an air of simple scorn for
people who needed charity. " Any reasonable man," she
would say, " can make a living. . . ." Her eldest son
adored this lady and often did just what she told him to do,
in any unimportant matter of business or society.

In 1861 she confronted him on an important point and
beat down his will. He had voted for Mr. Lincoln and his
natural place, he thought, was in Mr. Lincoln's armies. But
Samantha Hanna knew that her husband was dying, whether
his sons understood it or not. Only Mark comprehended the
spreading and complicated affairs of Hanna, Garretson and
Company. After he was suspended from college he went
to work for his father. He wore and was slightly proud of
his jumper and overalls when he handled boxes at the warehouse. He saw customers, mastered double entry book-
keeping, acted as purser on trips of the Hanna steamboats,
and ranged as primordial traveling salesman through Indiana and Illinois. His uncle Robert did not see Mark as
the model of a business man. " You shake your head," said
the dying Mark Hanna to William Osler, " just like my
uncle Rob. . . ." Uncle Robert's head shook frequently,
it seems. Mark was too much interested in picnics at Rocky
River or in the affairs of the Ydrad Boat Club. Money spun

through those slim fingers inherited from his father. He had no respect for office hours. He danced until the bands stopped. His parents did not worry. Mark never drank and when he slept he slept in Prospect Street, at home. He might not be the model of a wholesale grocer, but he was a good son.

It was onerous to be a good son in the spring of 1861, when the solid society of Cleveland was laid open by Mr. Lincoln's call for volunteers. A fair half of the city's grandees were Democrats. Mr. Lincoln, to them, was an amiable freak who had been rushed into office by the mob. The Hanna family was Republican, loudly, and Dr. Hanna had even made a few speeches in the campaign. He fainted on election day, from excitement, and was insensible for hours. Marcus now faced his mother, one might say, over his father's body. There was no private fortune; Leonard Hanna's income was his share of the firm's business. Someone must watch the family's interest and keep unimaginative Robert Hanna wide awake. So there were long discussions, weary scenes. The argument lasted for two months. Then Howard, the second son, went off to the war and Marcus Alonzo stayed at home.

He then became pathetically conspicuous as his friends got back to Cleveland on leave or furlough. He made himself a committee of one for their entertainment; his mother's carriage was abroad at all hours supporting healthy young officers hither and thither. He gave dinners or swept together parties of twenty or thirty for the play. He was to have given a supper on the night of his father's death, in 1862. Among poor folk it was known that Mr. Mark Hanna, down at the warehouse, would go a length to find a job for a soldier's son. If there was no job with Hanna and Company, there would be a note of recommendation to another firm and a couple of dollars for the boy.

His pride had been hurt, but circumstances arranged a

compensation. He met the compensation at a bazaar in the
spring of 1862, when she had just returned as a finished
product from a school in New York to her parents in Franklin Avenue. Her name was Charlotte Augusta Rhodes and
she was very handsome, slim and straight. Marcus Alonzo's
consideration of her qualities made him forgive her for being a Democrat's daughter, but her father, Mr. Daniel
Rhodes, did not intend his favorite child to compensate any
damned black Republican puppy for not being a soldier in
the idiotic war, or words to that effect, and his position in
the matter was put as strongly as possible.

A romance in the Victorian form now progressed. Mr.
Rhodes was unspeakably rich, for the times, entrenched in
the coal and iron business and fortified by a natural icon-
oclasm of temper. One of his legendary remarks is that
he respected nobody for being wealthy or respectable. But
it is also legendary that he barked without often biting;
socially the leader of Cleveland's Democratic faction, he
was popular among Republicans and his charities were
numerous. Ladies invaded his office timidly, hunting gifts
for the Sanitary Commission, and got big checks with a
lecture on the asininity of freeing the no-account niggers.
He adored his daughter, and as it grew plain that Charlotte
Augusta had fallen in love with Marcus Alonzo it grew
plain that Mr. Rhodes had not. He had every excuse. He
was a cousin of Stephen Douglas, who had been defeated by
Mr. Lincoln, and was not Marcus Alonzo one of Mr. Lincoln's condemned screechers for freedom? . . . Charlotte
Augusta languished and shed tears. In one of her father's
more violent states of mind she dispatched notes to her
Marcus by a gardener's red-headed brat named Asa Barnes,
and Marcus Alonzo set the boy up as a junior capitalist by
paying him a dollar a note for a month of 1863. When Mr.
Rhodes cooled down, the wretched child was living far be-

yond his means, and the withdrawal of revenue ruined him at the candy shop.

The society surrounding this battle was polite. A very strong transfusion of Connecticut took place in the early history of Cleveland. Men of business, in the sixties, wore tall hats made in Connecticut and many had diplomas from Yale College framed on walls of their offices. They took in culture from the same round of lecturers which served their kin at Hartford and New Haven. When Henry Ward Beecher came to lecture on The Beautiful, boring Mark Hanna to slumber, the orator shook hands with people he had known as children in Litchfield and kissed their daughters. Erastus Gaylord's mansion or the house in which Mrs. Leonard Hanna lived on Prospect Street might quite as well have been set on Whitney Avenue in New Haven. A wash of immigrants was sweeping up against this Yankee layer of the city's builders, for Cleveland " boomed " after 1861, but the manners were still those of grave, conditioned Connecticut and the affairs of Charlotte Augusta and Marcus Alonzo were whispered, not unduly aired. Everybody knew what was going on, though, and ladies in skirts of seven layers interested themselves in the sad case of the good-looking Hanna boy. They sighed entreaties upon Daniel Rhodes when he appeared at evening parties where glasses were piled in bright pyramids on tables of real mahogany and eighteen kinds of cake affronted the digestion besides bowls of punch. It is said that Mr. Rhodes had no peace. He began to wilt in the spring of 1864. When Marcus Alonzo went off with his regiment of militia to defend Washington from Jubal Early's raid it was admitted that an engagement did exist and, on September 27th, 1864, Marcus Alonzo and Charlotte Augusta were united at Saint John's Church. Mr. Rhodes relieved his emotions by boxing the ears of Asa Barnes when he found the plebeian kid

417

climbing through a window to behold the cakes and bouquets of the wedding feast.

III

THIS sober quality of Cleveland kept the city from a howling festivity when the funeral train brought Mr. Lincoln's body to lie in state for a few hours on April 27th of 1865. The titanic Amasa Stone deprecated an outpouring of women in white gowns to meet the train, and less tremendous citizens spoke against display. Crowds slowly filed under the mortuary pavilion in the Square and the legend " *Extinctus amabitur idem* " on the pennants drooping from a ceiling sprinkled with hideous rosettes and stars was admired by those capable of translating it. Elsewhere cities and towns enriched by the war showed what they could do by way of public grief. Mr. Lincoln had come eastward to his first inaugural through communities in which a fortune, a factory, or illuminating gas were undreamed. His body now retired below arches of evergreen twined with silken banners and shimmering at night with colored globes. Ladies clad in fresh white robes posed mournfully near the tracks in choirs of thirty and fifty. Canvas pillars offered such painted consolation as " Go To Thy Rest," or " Ours The Cross, Yours The Crown." A certain new millionaire of Chicago made himself permanently famous among journalists by sending a basket filled with champagne bottles and roses to Mrs. Lincoln — she was not on the train — with his card. In Chicago, too, a photographer named Halstead had for sale at the station a bogus view of Mr. Lincoln rising among clouds into the embrace of Jesus Christ. . . . The train rolled down to Springfield between incessant bonfires and illumined stations. At last he was entombed in a placid valley, close to a soothing brook.

THE YEAR 1865

War had favored the cities of the North, although the first historians of the struggle got as far as they could from admitting the nature of the change. They talked mistily of a prosperity caused by the opening of new mines in the West or of free farmlands parceled out under the Homestead Act of 1862. Two or three forthright essayists in religious papers or magazines did say what was true. Something definite and simple had taken place, and yet only a few were ready to admit that the war itself had built factories, enlarged mills, increased railroads and telegraphic services. All trades and crafts had been put to its service, and the labor unions had forced a steady lifting of wages from 1862 to 1865. War tariffs protected industries scarcely existent in 1860 until they bloomed and asserted themselves in unions and associations. A pair of German girls who made roses for milliners in New York before the war sold a business and a trademark in 1866 for a hundred thousand dollars. A whole range of new, eminent families had been created from the rawest materials by the necessities of women's clothing; metal buttons and clasps, corsets, and such unmentionable matters as the cheap lace of drawers thrust up a thousand proprietors and workmen into the beauties of affluence. While millions flooded in official checks from the Treasury on the blanket-weavers and gunsmiths, the civilians paid their hundreds to these protégés of the tariff and the Confederate cruisers. It was a boom, timed to the pulsations of cannon and rifles on the Virginian border.

But the farmers had not enjoyed the fullest benefits of the war. Many rural opera-houses are dated from the sixties, and one who actually chooses to explore rural journalism of Lincoln's presidency will discover that pastors sometimes deplored the spread of fastidious costume among women of the plain people, but there were not enough novelties of the shop and playhouse loosed among the farms to

419

distract mothers from a strict and discomforting attention
to the casualty lists. Sons not allured by the recruiting office
were often lured away by high wages in the munition plants
or by the riot of sudden gain in the oilfields of Pennsylvania.
Population of the villages decreased and farms were abandoned in many regions.[1] The prices paid for grain, meat,
and hides were high, but the cost of hired men rose incessantly. Women of substance plowed and reaped in the
fields alongside their half-grown sons in 1863. And education slowed; a master would enlist or a mistress of some
petty schoolhouse marry, and the bothered school-board
was likely enough to let the school stay shut until the children were nuisances indoors when snow fell and mothers
remembered that book learning was a valuable thing.
Many families migrated into the towns near Pittsburgh or
into the city itself because their children must be schooled.
"The horrors of war," says a veteran, " in my family were
not those of the field, but of ordinary household life. My
father and my older brothers came home on furlough occasionally, but it was not until I was discharged from service in 1863 as physically unfit that my mother had any one
to contribute steady help in her round of tasks and to help
her control the lively small children. A modern woman
would have taken to her bed and enjoyed a case of nervous
prostration. . . . She was scarcely forty years old in 1865
but she had the appearance of a woman of sixty. . . . She
worked all day, and at night, from sheer benevolence, she
held a sort of school for the neighboring children old
enough to stay up after dark. . . . It is no wonder that she

[1] A letter of my great-grandfather to my maternal grandfather, dated
August 2nd, 1864, mentions good farmland near Cincinnati sold for sixty
dollars an acre " because no help is to be had." Farms were abandoned in
western New York, on Long Island, and in the region north of Gettysburg.
An acquaintance of my family bought two hundred acres to the north of
Springfield, Illinois, in 1864, for one thousand dollars, the price including
two years' back taxes. According to Senator Grimes, in 1864, twenty thousand acres had been abandoned in the states of Iowa and Nebraska.

used to say, ' The slaves could have been bought for a billion dollars but nobody will ever know what the Rebellion cost.' . . ."

Nor did these people wholly misunderstand what was happening in the cities and at their capital. The United States was already an uncomfortable topic with foreign essayists; its very peasants who tilled the fields and did what the European peasant had done in illiterate peace for a thousand years could read and write. Cavour pondered that it would be interesting to see the effect of their literacy on their wars and politics. The literate peasants, then, did not enjoy the war too well and knew that it was making money for the cities. The discontents and treasonous grumblings which passed through Ohio, Indiana, and Illinois were protests, not only against the war, but against the city's expanding glitter, and the return of the soldiers in 1865 brought, often, merely the ease of added muscle power. For the boys came home with tales of New York and Washington. They had seen gayeties and luxuries, mixed with urban types in camp, and heard all kinds of unsettling things. It was well that Mr. Lincoln had spoken so kindly of the plain people, for in 1865 the rustics must have learned rather sharply that they were pretty plain.

Yet this rural population derived an intangible benefit from the wretched performance at Ford's Theater on April 14th, 1865. A true folk-hero had been born to them, an obscure man of the plain people who rose to speak equally with kings and to slay monsters. Mr. Lincoln did not rest in his tomb outside Springfield. Very soon his memory was a phantom of rectitude fairly towering while emotional rhetoricians and jobbers ripped his party into quarrelsome bits. His legend was invoked against " the money changers in the temple of Liberty " and " the Pharisees of the Senate " or the divorced woman who dictated patronage from her drawing-room near the Capitol. He was dead; he could do nothing about the soft-handed men of the Eastern cities who had gripped affairs in Washington; he had the profound power, therefore, of King Arthur and Saint Joan. That he might have shown himself shifting and incapable in the problems which hampered his successors became an unthinkable contention. Lincoln would never have done wrong, because he was dead. Since 1900 he has slowly become a man again, but for thirty years he was something else. His figure mingled with that of another gentle bearded dealer in parables, a friend of the humble and outcast, once murdered on Good Friday; the mood of some pastors and journalistic poets in the weeks following his death grew to be an establishment in oratory, sacred and profane: Lincoln was a form of Christ. The cool political humorist and strategist vanished under a softer outline, and his orations with their haunting Biblical music were declaimed on Memorial Day to audiences truly reverent, hushed and tearful.[2]

This cult, like all such reverences, must do its harm. Forty years after Lincoln was murdered Harry Thurston Peck timidly implied in a defense of Chester Arthur that Lincoln's social example acted to the hurt of politicians who didn't happen to be born in log cabins or given to receiving callers with feet in woolen socks spread on a chair. Lincoln's life offered itself to the touchy rural mind in a

---

[2] On the appearance of this paragraph, somewhat shortened, in *The Saturday Evening Post,* in April, a gentleman teaching American history in a huge Western university at once wrote to me: " You are like all these other Bolsheviki who are trying to degrade the character of Abraham Lincoln and make him appear an ordinary man. Lincoln was the greatest man born in the world since our Savior, *if it is fair to call him a man at all. . . .*" A dozen other letters in a more temperate tone protested my " irreverence " to Mr. Lincoln. Mr. Rutledge Watson of San Francisco wrote to assure me, on the other side, that as a small boy in Kansas he was taught to mention Mr. Lincoln in his nightly prayers, saying, " Make me as good as President Lincoln." My grandfather once halted a witness before him in a case of manslaughter who swore by " Christ and Abe Lincoln." Mr. Lewis's *Myths After Lincoln,* issued in May of this year, was very grudgingly reviewed. It is plain that the historical interests of Mr. Lincoln are still jeopardized by his emotional values.

double capacity: he rose from obscurity to domination and he was as homely as I am. To the cheaper egoist in the bustle of a county campaign this came with soothing emphasis as a form of self-defense: Lincoln was plain as I am, so the cultured man — the smart city fellow — is wrong. And this defensive machinery was used by clever men, sometimes wholly dishonest, as leverage in the brawl between the city and the farm from 1865 to 1928. It was really in the year 1928 that the formula reached its highest utility in political blackguardism, when a Republican speaker, a clergyman, addressed a rural audience with the aphorism: " Remember that a country boy is born with the right principles, but a city boy is likely to be bad from the day of his birth. . . ."

In the amusing domain of legislative manipulation, too, the cult worked against the rural population to its infinite damage. Mr. Lincoln had four times signed acts of Congress which, as things fell out, set governmental policies inimical to the plain people in motion and all these policies were later twisted into the fuse of the grand political crash of 1896. Guiltless, so far as is known, of aiding any rogue by premeditation, Lincoln made himself the friend of rogues, the smart men who, more openly than in our times, haunted the economic scene of the United States to the end of the nineteenth century.

The adjective " smart " in earlier New England was not a complete compliment, but was reserved for the inventor of the wooden nutmeg and his imitators. A " smart man " was a horse-trader or a clock-peddler, a licensed trickster excused for his humors in a world where the humor of the eighteenth century was still admired. As the nation expanded, some of this primitive meaning sloughed away from the word, although it was offensive enough to cause an action in libel, in Ohio, in 1858. Lincoln is called " smart " in old newspapers, with a sense of mere shrewdness, before his elevation. And yet, persistently, there was something a little wrong with a smart man; the elder meaning hung around the adjective as the Civil War began.

On Mr. Lincoln's call for volunteers a number of smart men responded to the signal, but without military intentions. A silent " Yo, ho, ho! " rang from mind to mind. They came from everywhere, from apprenticeships in those inns where drovers met, high on the Hudson, or from tours as salesmen of candy or patent medicine in country fairs. Many of them knew the South rather better than did the new President and saw that this would be a war of some dimensions. They were ready, in a fashion, to make it their holy war.

Bull Run was hardly fought when a minor genius named Belknap arrived at the War Department with a large bill for packing sixty-odd dead Yankees in ice and transporting them to their grieved kin. A methodical clerk referred the account to regimental adjutants and found that there were no such soldiers dead. Mr. Belknap vanishes and his petty speculation is followed by the graver adroitness of men who fully knew what they were after. Light history has selected the name of Jim Fisk from this battalion, acting on the wise and always the popular theory of blackening a black sheep to make gray sheep paler. As Mr. Fisk ultimately was killed in a fuss over a courtesan his general reputation does not matter, and he left no acute descendants to specialize in the destruction of testimony against him. But, when one considers the mildness of his wartime exploits, he seems a weak choice. So many smart men were so much smarter and in such widths of roguery. They enjoyed that quality known to Italians of the Renascence as *virtù*, arranging their fortunes without regard to the safety of the Union. Congressional reports, records of Federal courts and the harried Court of Claims, the documents of the Adjutant General, and a hundred military orders exhibit their arrangements.

Twenty officers were disgraced and a pair of Congressmen damaged within eighteen months of the war's beginning, but the smart men continued. Rifles thrown away as unfit for real service by ordnance officers in the East were sold to General Frémont in the West. An expedition was dispatched to the Mississippi in rotten hulls for which the government often paid nine hundred dollars a day. Bayonets of polished pewter, tents of porous shoddy, coffee made of pulse and sorghum, carbines that exploded on the drill ground, blankets so long stored in Boston that water would not soak them to the thickness of a coin, and many other versions of the wooden nutmeg were offered to the Army between 1861 and 1864.

Often nothing could be done. The actual vendor vanished in a cloud of agents and guileless middlemen, or agitated legislators raved usefully when the name of some respected citizen was read out in the meetings of a Congressional committee. Sometimes the cases wound up in a tangle of smart lawyers and angry, inexpert judges. A few smart men were consigned to military prisons or common jails. It was the son of a famous philanthropist who was begged out of a dungeon by Henry Ward Beecher after the bright lad forged a presidential proclamation so as to influence the gambling in the gold room of the Stock Exchange at New York. . . . As one reads the testimony in these affairs Mr. Lincoln's suspension of the Habeas Corpus has an appearance of pure governmental necessity. But nothing could control this adept army of thieves, often so stately in their social placing, as it wrought from the rear. A Fisk is singled out and remembered in the mess; once the names of Wormser, Justice, Vanderbilt, and Simons smelled quite as evilly as did Fisk's sales of mouldy blankets on behalf of two estimable patriots in the city of Boston.

A natural irony followed the apparition of this scattered but most active battalion. When weariness and rural discontent solidified pungently in 1864 and Mr. Lincoln's own family thought he would not be elected a second time, the Republican party discovered in its ranks a number of paying guests, converts to Mr. Lincoln's principles, highly willing to see the war prolong itself. The names of convinced gentlemen interested in the making of sound munitions are to be seen on Republican lists alongside those of men who had been advertised in cases of fraudulent practice on the government. It is entirely true, of course, that successes in the field and the virile efforts of Lincoln's actual friends defeated General McClellan, but it is also true that the costs of the wild campaign were partly borne by men in every degree of shadiness and that Lincoln's party did not disclaim their aid. A political faction invented for the uses of a humane cause thus rapidly became, let us say, both practical and mundane. Smartness entered its being; after 1864 the crazy Western schism was a party of the smart man and of the East.

But the smart men were not all urban or Eastern. In 1863 louts rode through Ohio asking farmers if they had any " crowbait " for the army, and a Federal judge at Cincinnati lost his temper as he tried to explain to some hearty yeomen that they must not doctor up dying horses for sale to the cavalry and artillery. One of General Pleasanton's officers, in that year, presented his commander an affidavit reciting that three mounts just brought to the camp had been sold by himself as useless before John Brown was hanged. In December of 1864 Charles Francis Adams scornfully wrote to his father about the Treasurer's report: " He does not state one principle in sound finance, but he makes a stately onslaught upon ' speculators in gold.' Why not also on those in flour and pork? " Waves of cynical talk passed through regiments in which half the soldiers and their officers came from farms. Tricks of the city's smart men may not have been fully understood among the tents, but they did understand about horses and grain and pork, and a sense of betrayal can be found in the letters of sailors as well. An obscene variation of *John Brown's Body* sung in Farragut's fleet mentions wives and sweethearts lured away by the homekeeping profiteer " while we go sailing on. . . ." The tedium of war produced a recoil sometimes fatal to the cordial sentiment necessary to the war itself. " My one interesting experience with deserters," Colonel John McCook wrote to a friend in 1900, " was with two fine boys from Mr. Lincoln's own county. A sergeant caught them leaving camp in civilian dress and brought them to me. They told me honestly that their mother and sisters were practically destitute and were obliged to ' go out ' as hired help by the day. They claimed that men at home were getting rich by ' sharking ' on provisions for the Army. . . . I got to work through Anson " — General Anson McCook — " and had the matter referred straight to Mr. Lincoln. He looked after them. . . . He has been criticized for his leniency toward deserters. But I believe he knew what lay behind many of these cases. Mr. [Norman] Hapgood does not seem to realize the extent of guilt among dealers in provisions, etc., at that time. The writers seem to neglect this whole phase of the war. . . ." [3]

This phase was not so striking as the battles in which all instruments of civilization were used belligerently for the

[3] John J. McCook to William C. Beer, June 26th, 1900. It is probably now necessary to inform readers that the " fighting McCooks " were celebrities of the Civil War. The family was distinguished for its piety and physical charm. His men called John McCook " Stunning John " and " Beauty." In 1902 he was standing on Pennsylvania Avenue in Washington when an alcoholized person handed him a dollar bill, saying, " Beauty, here's some money I stole out of your tent in '62, God damn it! I ain't felt easy in my conscience since! "

first time. Potencies of the railroad, the balloon, the iron
ship, the machine gun, the telegraph, were declared. Europe had been astonished at us, with much reason. But the
war's interior effect on American manners had no immediate students and certain modern writers seem to fancy
that a period of corrupt legislation, fantastic morals in public affairs, and ethical sloth commenced only with the end
of the war, as if Booth's bullet had released seven devils on
the nation. Yet the Gilded Age set in with 1861; no phenomenon appeared after Mr. Lincoln's death that was not
plain by the close of 1862, and of many concurrent phenomena during his presidency he, himself, was the innocent
producer.

Mr. Lincoln, as is known, was obliged to sign acts of Congress under which an immense quantity of fiat currency was
issued. These " greenbacks " were sure to be dangerous.
Even the opportunist Thaddeus Stevens fought rather shyly
for the passage of the bill creating them in 1862. The
tempted government issued more and more of the things. In
1864 this fluctuating material had come almost to the sum
of four hundred and fifty million dollars. Gold and silver
were unseen objects; the public heard of speculation in
metal moneys, but the coins had vanished. In 1865 some
of his command, wanting to give Major William McKinley
a respectful token, pooled their greenbacks and bought a
five-dollar gold piece from a jeweler. Ladies wore coins
dangling from bracelets, and young children wondered why
the pretty gold stamped with eagles was called " money "
when it clearly wasn't a paper bill. But from the paper
bills arose a superstition in finance; the greenbacks were
" Lincoln's greenbacks " as soon as wise men tried to get
rid of them and, until 1896, this superstition twisted in and
out of the plain people's mind a frozen conviction of the
American nation's powers in money-making.

The greenback was not dear to Mr. Lincoln. He may

have been no financier, but he is said to have viewed the fiat money with distrust. Yet, in other instances, he played the hand of the smart men cheerfully. It cannot be forgotten that he was naturally an expansionist. He had lived most of his life in the current of the Western migrations; the pioneer and the settler, always tending westward, were commonplaces of his social thought. The United States was a curio among nations in that it could colonize within its own borders. Normans and Bretons were not advised, in the forties, to leave home in covered wagons and plant themselves in Provence; Russians removed to Siberia only under severest compulsion; the cockney went to Wales and Scotland for a holiday and scuttled home. But to the American expansion was a vivid factor of existence. It was even a patriotic duty, and Mr. Lincoln wanted to see the West colonized, as did everybody else. There is no evidence in any way denying that he took the swift increase of Western population for a benefit to his country, and he abetted it by his signature of the Homestead Act of 1862 and by two most dangerous acts creating railroad corporations with singular rewards and powers.

Nothing seems so harmless as the Homestead Act, granting settlers Western land if they would cultivate it for five years. Lincoln and Andrew Johnson thought westward to a prodigious vacancy in 1862. Through this arable desert would pass the two railroads — the Union Pacific and the Central Pacific — forming a spine for commerce and help to the colonists. Naturally, the railroads must be subsidized and they might, also, be granted some of this endless public land. Everything seemed natural while Congressmen and Senators argued a little as to terms. Four very smart men of Yankee stock smiled encouragement from the background of an enterprise which had, too, a color of military necessity. But the lean and pensive Senator John Sherman rubbed his beard and wondered, in silence, if trouble might not come of this. Nobody shouted, "Look out!" although there had been trouble in 1858 and 1859 over a subsidized railroad that was to have made Texas a garden and a pasture. The dignity of the Senate was offended by mad rows over the character of the road's directors and the uses to which they had put the granted lands. Now, John Sherman saw, here came this new bill granting strips of land ten miles deep on each side of the tracks and six thousand dollars in government bonds for each mile finished. Mr. Sherman shivered. But he was a strong Administration man and his shudders did not pass outward in protest. In 1864 he shuddered afresh as the directors needed more help and got it — bonds and more bonds of the United States — although the rails, somehow, were not being laid. And a hazy bill creating the Northern Pacific Railroad, with land grants and privileges, was stuffed through the Senate in a hurry. "These two bills," Sherman wrote in 1895, " prove that it is not wise, during a war, to provide measures for a time of peace. . . ."

Upon these acts a mountain of bright casuistry heaped itself and Mr. Lincoln's name was used, as it grew sacred, to warrant the governmental policies they engendered. What was worse and more pervasive was a certain frame of mind infecting principled men: the government came to be a source of help for private enterprise, of subsidies and candid gifts. It was not Lincoln's fault, but he had armed the smart battalion against his plain people and, in a sort, had made the West a victim of the East. Well, it needed a trained prophet to see beyond what John Sherman feared, and Mr. Lincoln was a prophet only in the popular style.

He was thinking about the West on the last morning of his life. Schuyler Colfax came to discuss the tour he had planned through the mountains to the Pacific coast. The President talked earnestly, deep in his chair. He must get the disbanded regiments and the new immigrants headed to the West, where mines and railroads needed them. Gold and silver would pour eastward, destroying the national debt. The seaboard cities must not be packed with cheap labor, bringing down wages when the mechanics were getting good pay. Colfax was to tell the Westerners that Mr. Lincoln had their interests at heart, and Colfax thrilled. He went away to chat about the President's foresight in Willard's Hotel at a lunch of officers and civilians and came back at night to talk some more.

The gaunt man rocked in his chair and drawled until it was eight o'clock. Mrs. Lincoln walked into the room, with her fan and brilliant shawl, to remind the President that he had promised to see the play at Ford's Theater. Oh, so he had! Well, Mr. Colfax could drop in tomorrow morning. He bowed himself away. . . . The President's carriage was waiting below dim pillars in the pleasant night. Soon the people in Ford's Theater rose and applauded as Mr. Lincoln strolled into his box. . . .

CHAPTER II

THE BULLETHEADED GENERALS

MR. HANNA, young or old, was not given to reading books. He went to sleep, even, over the political studies current in his last years which showed him up for a monstrous rogue, and once was found snoring in a hammock, an ear crumpled on a challenge to the Standard Oil Company. But he had a tendency often seen in men of an extraverted intelligence: he sometimes liked to read history. A caller entered his rooms at the Arlington Hotel in 1901 and saw the Senator pondering a great volume of Maspéro, his hands flattened on the pages, lost somewhere in Egypt or Assyria. Perhaps the pictures absorbed him and he was staring at a view of the Pharaoh or the Sār poised in a chariot, casting gold among reverent soldiers. He looked up, after a while, and said suddenly, " Isn't it funny, Jackling, that money and machinery came into the world at the same time? "

His life had been so bound to these two forces that he must have thought them endless partners in the story of man. Everything in Mark Hanna's early time had hung to the new machines. It was because wheels rolled too far from New Lisbon that his father brought him to Cleveland, and his family's success before 1860 had grown as the steamboats paddled money to the offices of Hanna, Garretson and Company. His whole triumph in affairs and politics was conditioned on the wheels and screws delivering

432

purchased commodities, scattering out his agents and his propaganda; he throve by the effects of speed. It might be said that his legend is that of a man who realized the full force of manipulated transportation. He had been born with the railroad's first exhibited potency in American life. He died just as that potency began to be threatened by new machines.

The disaster to America caused by machinery was inscrutable to young Hanna. But the machine clattered under the prelude of the Civil War so certainly that Herman Melville caught the sound and wrote it down in *The Confidence Man*. Obsolescent slavery was defeated by the machine, and it is not badly argued by Oswald Spengler that mere fuel — coal — was the actual victor behind Grant's troops. Latter-day slavery, he says, was " a threshold phase of our machine industry, an organization of 'living' energy, which began with man-fuel, but presently passed over to coal-fuel; and slavery came to be considered immoral only when coal had established itself. Looked at from this angle, the victory of the North in the American Civil War (1865) meant the economic victory of the concentrated energy of coal over the simple energy of the muscles. . . ." [1]

That is well enough for the speculative historian and the European. For the American, whose history is so short that he can watch its flexures and accidents within spaces of a decade, there is another victory to be mentioned: coal and the railroad and precious metal in the West were three Fates winding out an end of the fine provincial America. Compact social bodies too small to bear defection wilted as " the dream of the plains defeated the dream of the sea "; the romantic motive which perpetually imposes itself upon the economic in this business of migrations shimmered before the men of New England and Pennsylvania,

[1] *The Decline of the West*, Volume II, page 488.

drawing them inland after 1849, not outward on the waters
to maintain a liaison of culture with Europe. War accelerated this destruction of the provincial lines. And who saw
it? . . . One man at least, it seems.

In March of 1862 legislators, profiteers, and officers
smoking at Willard's Hotel in Washington might admire
a tall, trim gentleman who strolled past their chairs. He
was not old, but his hair seemed almost white, and straight
eyebrows showed gray above his dark blue eyes. Some
knew the face or remembered that they had seen it en-
graved in books, and John Hay walked nervously after this
magnificent along Pennsylvania Avenue one day, trying
to be brave enough to speak to Nathaniel Hawthorne, who
had tired of the rumors and the telegrams and had come
down from Concord to see what this war was like.

His thoughts were soon printed in *The Atlantic Monthly*
as a languid essay, musical with disdain for the mob in
Willard's Hotel, where " you are mixed up with office
seekers, wire pullers, inventors, artists, poets, prosers,
clerks, diplomatists, mail contractors, railway directors,
until your own identity is lost among them. . . . You
adopt the universal habit of the place and call for a mint
julep, a whisky skin, a gin cocktail, a brandy smash or a
glass of Pure Old Rye. . . ." The feebleness of modern
topers depressed him as he glanced at venerables in frilled
shirts swilling Bourbon by the horn. All these mild diluted
drinks were tame beside those eight inches of liquid fury!
Old times and glories passed in this conglomerate of vulgarities. But he seemed merely to be describing General
McClellan's camp, or the prisoners in the roundhouse at
Harper's Ferry, a " heap of unwashed human bodies " or
the *Monitor* at anchor, a sort of iron rat-trap. Nothing is
stressed save this flashing taunt to his friends at Concord
who had likened the calamitous John Brown's gallows to
the Cross, and his own intellectual satisfaction in seeing

Brown hanged for a fool is underscored by an apologetic footnote. But he saw a good deal: the iron rat-trap meant the finish of naval warfare in the adorable grand manner. He pondered for a sentence on future duels of submarines. He saw that something might well come of the poor Southern white when slavery was abolished. And as to the future of the Union, revealed to him in the smoke of Willard's Hotel, why, " one bullet headed general will succeed another in the presidential chair; and veterans will hold the offices, at home and abroad, and sit in Congress and the state legislatures, and fill all the avenues of public life. . . ."

He was really writing a dry little dirge for New England. These railway directors and mail contractors were enemies of that close order which had produced Nathaniel Hawthorne. The nation spread and its several integrities were thinned or slaughtered as troops hurried to the East by rail. Soon the same rails would slide away young men from the decadent villages of his province to the West; it was " the downfall of the Bostonian Empire " that appeared in the smoke at Willard's, and with Boston fell Virginia. . . . But, for Mr. Hawthorne, his own territory had been all America. He was not much interested in this large, raw, collection of states that claimed his devotion only to " an airy mode of law " and had no symbol but a flag. He was not worried about the bulletheaded generals who would rule this hazy space. Something good might come of them. They were Force. "It may substitute something more real and genuine, instead of the many shams on which men heretofore have founded their claims to public regard. . . ."

He had always seen into shams. Boys at college fancied a mystery behind his stare and christened him Oberon as much for this as for his beauty. And now he perfected the strangeness of his life by dying, with his province, as if in protest against the oncoming miscellany. He grew weaker, thinner, smiling at the doctors who could not say what was wrong. Mr. Hawthorne was simply selecting the right conclusion to a grave fantasy about a being who had stared from the shadows of a bewitched wood at man's hypocrisy and man's vain emotions. He vanished. Oberon withdrew, as was most right, while a dog howled below his window among the silent hills, in a cool midnight. . . .

Four years and a day from Mr. Hawthorne's death a Republican convention in Chicago began to fulfill his prophecies. General Ulysses Grant was nominated for the presidency in a roar. There could be no other candidate. And then the delegates behaved unbecomingly toward New England; the expanding nation yawned at the wishes of its intellectual nurse, and Bostonians learned from their newspapers that the West, this region beyond Buffalo, wanted a Western vice president. There is an old lady living who can recollect raucous delegates yelling, " Take yer damn' codfish home! " when the names of Henry Wilson, of Massachusetts, and Hannibal Hamlin, of Maine, were proposed. On a fifth ballot the gay Schuyler Colfax was nominated and the Republican convention of 1868 dispersed, by railway.

It had not been well reported, and the facts of the discord between East and West are mostly traditional. But it is true than an unled, formless resentment of New England's postures washed the West during the war. The feeling may be judged by six letters of a Mrs. Dix, an ordinary female of the more cultivated kind who worked in Washington's hospitals in 1863 and 1864. Just one person from Boston way seemed a human being to this lady out of Illinois; she loved Louisa May Alcott. But the wives of the cotton-spinning Congressmen annoyed her, reading tracts to sick men in the wards and " squealing " when some tortured invalid brought out an oath; and so did the Yankee Senators, iced and done up in tight black bindings, patronizing

Mrs. Lincoln at evening parties. She could not bear them!
" We " — she meant Ben in the cavalry and Geordie in the
Navy — " are fighting for Union, and all they want is to
see the Rebels humiliated! . . . I hope never to hear the
name of Massachusetts again when this ordeal is over.
. . ." The Yankees had shoved the nation into hell and
now they were sniffling at the Westerners, who did most
of the fighting. The rise of Grant and Sherman was a victory of the West. Who won the war? The West! . . .
Mrs. Dix died soon after Grant was nominated at Chicago,
perhaps in a state of revengeful contentment. Grant would
show 'em!

Something of this resentment was working in Marcus
Alonzo Hanna on July 3rd, 1868, when he wrote:

" Dear Cap: Lillian just remembered to tell us that you
brought those firecrackers for the best baby in Ohio. Dan
says to tell you that you are a gentleman. Mr. Rhodes was
just putting up a high fence at dinner. He does not want
to see Pendleton nominated against Grant. I hope they put
up somebody from Mass. or New York, so we can all turn
out and lick him. I am awfully sorry about the sheep.
" M. A. Hanna." ²

The document has its mysteries. Who was Cap, and what
happened to the sheep? The second sentence is mendacity.
Master Daniel Rhodes Hanna said nothing of the kind, at
the age of eighteen months. The rest is simple: Mr. Daniel
Rhodes has been bluffing at dinner about affairs of the

---

² This autograph has an odd history. It was found in an old novel in a
Washington shop and brought to Mr. Hanna in 1902 to be authenticated.
He was just then busy with his negotiations in the coal strike and was giving
instructions as to some telegram to his secretary, Mr. Dover. Turning the
paper over, he noted on its back, " Wiring Morgan, McCrea, Depew this
date," and then apologized for damaging the memento, saying, " I am awfully
sorry. . . ." He contended that his use of " awfully " was common in Cleveland in his youth.

Democratic Convention, which seemed to be ready to pick
George Pendleton, of Ohio, against Ulysses Grant, of Ohio.
As a capital financier Mr. Rhodes likes nothing less. " Gentleman George " heads the " soft money " faction of the
Democrats and wants to pay the government's debts, foreign and domestic, in greenbacks, the inconvertible paper
currency born of necessity in 1862 and now crumbling in
all cash-drawers and pockets. Mr. Hanna, whose son, you
see, is " the best baby in Ohio," hopes that the Democrats
will nominate some ghastly Easterner, so that the state's
loyalties will not be divided between two older native sons.

Mark Hanna had learned things in finance since 1865.
A little after his marriage the oil fever took him and he
built a refinery for petroleum. That was not enough for
a clever fellow, who thought well of himself as a business
man, and he built the *Lac La Belle,* the swiftest and smart-
est of Lake steamers, using his own money for the venture.
But the refinery burned and the steamer sank, uninsured,
and one morning in 1867 young Mr. Hanna, just convalescent from typhoid, found himself a pauper.

His daughter brought her diminished husband home to
Mr. Daniel Rhodes, who viciously teased Marcus Alonzo
and planned to make use of him. The teasing would be
abominable form in our times, but Mrs. Hanna's brother,
James Rhodes, lived to assert that " men joked each other
about business losses at that time as if they were country
boys having a fight over a stolen ball. . . ." The old
Democrat had his joke with Mark Hanna, but, meanwhile,
a wonderful perambulator rolled on Franklin Avenue,
containing Master Daniel Rhodes Hanna, although his
grandfather admitted no concern with the perambulator's
contents. He " put up a tall fence " about babies; they
didn't interest him, even Charlotte Augusta's brand. But
when Charles Nolan came from Washington to get the
signature of Mr. Rhodes on a contract, he waited three

days in the big man's office and, getting tired of hard furniture at Rhodes, Card and Company's, took himself to the magnate's house. Mr. Rhodes came down from the nursery, snapped his name four times on a paper, and hurried up to resume intensive studies of croup, leaving the caller to be entertained by his son-in-law, an agreeable creature whose name Mr. Nolan did not catch. . . . Yet, in 1888, a burly man whose whiskers now were mere strips of red fur close to his ears stared at Mr. Nolan a time in a hotel at Chicago and then shouted: " Hi, Mr. Nolan! " Mark Hanna's memory worked so; he had remembered a striking person for twenty-one years.

This memory and some other capabilities were put to use in April of 1867, when the renovated firm of Rhodes and Company was announced, with George Warmington, Robert Rhodes, and Marcus Hanna as partners. Daniel Rhodes retired. His son and his son-in-law were to assume his place in the business. Thus, in his thirtieth year, Mark Hanna neatly shifted from dealing in wholesale groceries to dealing in coal and iron, and this was his occupation for the rest of his life in business. He was to be Mr. Hanna, of Rhodes and Company, until the famous firm became M. A. Hanna and Company.

In 1868 his enthusiasm for Grant was natural. Mr. Hanna knew that American paper currency was degraded; Canadians sulkily accepted a dollar at thirty-five cents in the Lake ports, and all dealings of Rhodes and Company in Canada were hampered by the exchange. He must have well understood what General James Garfield, of Ohio, meant, in Congress, on the fifteenth of May. " We are cut off," said the Congressman, " from the money currents of the world. Our currency resembles rather the waters of an artificial lake, which lie in stagnation or rise to full banks at the caprice of the gatekeeper. Gold and silver abhor a depreciated paper money and will not keep company with it. If our currency be more abundant than business demands, not a dollar of it can go abroad; if deficient not a dollar in gold will come in to supply the lack. There is no legislation on earth wise enough to adjust such a currency to the wants of the country. . . ."

That seems clear enough? It made sense to a Mark Hanna in 1868, but it was idiotic gabble to farmers and small editors everywhere in the United States. They could not differentiate business, which is local, from finance, which, after the eighteenth century, had become international. In a nation boasting of its extraordinary financial acuteness there were so few actual financiers that members of banking firms in Wall Street caught up the soft-money heresy and were prepared to back Gentleman George. Sitting near Wall Street was Mr. James Pierpont Morgan, a tall Yankee who had once refused to be a professor of mathematics at Göttingen, keeping the ledgers of his firm in a deliberate double system, one set of books for American money and one set for real money — the sacred token of finance, gold; his cold eyes could examine what his house was supposed to be worth, and turn secretly to what it was worth. To this man General Garfield's words were platitudinous, to a fair portion of interior America they were fantastic. A sentiment had promptly gathered on the greenbacks; they were now " Lincoln's greenbacks." There was a lot of them. They filled the function of money. Of course the government could pay its debts in paper! Anyhow, it was the capitalist and the foreigner who wanted the government to redeem its bonds in gold . . . so to hell with the capitalist and the foreigner! An orator named Chidsey outlined this concept of the nation's case to a crowd in Shobonier, Illinois, in the spring of 1868, saying, " If Europe wants none of our greenbacks, we can blow them on Europe from the cannon's mouth! " That settled it.

Among Mr. Chidsey's hearers was a sickly young lawyer

from over in Minnesota who was trying to collect a bill for a client. War had filled Cushman Davis with fevers and made him prematurely bald. Endless lethargies possessed him and he struggled, even in court, with a passion for sleep. But Mr. Chidsey's oration exasperated him and he shouted from the crowd that the United States could not thrash all Europe. The crowd hissed. Mr. Davis went back to Minnesota, pensive, and, as Senator Davis wrote in 1896: "Here is that Balaam" (Mr. William Jennings Bryan) "telling people just what this jackass was telling them in 1868 and they are believing it. Verily, verily, men are fools when they fall into a superstition about money!"[3]

Ulysses Grant had no such superstition. He had lived through wretched times before the war when the "wildcat" money of banks along the Mississippi fluctuated weekly and might be worthless overnight. He stood boldly in 1868 for the unpopular proposition. "The United States is only one nation among many," he told a small girl, "and its money must be the kind that other nations will accept. You will understand this when you are older." Miss Prudence Watson was proud of the General's communication, but she had to grow up in a country which tried to ignore Grant's little dictum. In 1868 she saw her own brothers out parading for Horatio Seymour, the Democratic candidate, and heard orators bawling that the Republicans were trying to enslave the farmer to the capitalist. Miss Watson's understanding of the word "capitalist" was vague, but she knew that the Corinthian decorations at the top of the veranda's pillars were capitals and worked out her own definition: a capitalist, she reasoned quite correctly, was a man who sat on the top of a narrow post. . . .

From their shaky perches some smart men looked down unfavorably on the agreeable George Pendleton when Democracy convened in Tammany Hall at New York on July

[3] To James P. Holt, September 2nd, 1896.

4th, 1868. This hall was not so far from their offices; something could be done at short range, in the private name of Democratic bondholders and bankers. Money talked to itself and then addressed the convention's machinery. These forces came together into the life of Mr. Pendleton. After many ballots the delegation of his own state swung against the pleasing man, and Horatio Seymour, aghast, was nominated to head a ticket in which he did not believe. A "hard money" Democrat was nominated on a "soft money" platform. The straddle ended any hope of winning; farmers deserted the Easterner to vote in swarms for the man from Ohio. Next March, as per prophetic schedule, the first of Mr. Hawthorne's bulletheaded generals entered the White House.

II

PENDLETON's vogue had been an expression in the most compact terms of the nation's isolation and he had prospered until such time as the smart men saw his implicit dangers. But he had not amused his opponents; intrigue disposed of him, not laughter. The perils of fiat money were explained in America, and broadly, before 1860, but a heavy tithe of the nation's educated men had been taken between Sumter and Appomattox; the cultivated Americans had supported this war, and their mentalities did not survive their bodies. Really, you cannot kill off a medley of poets, engineers, journalists, undergraduates, and sharp young clerks or sterilize them against further ideas by the supreme heat of military experience without damaging the critical life of a nation; and you cannot sever a colony from its several mothers while it is still in the nursing period without damaging its political equilibrium. . . . In the forties and fifties the American had been incessantly stimulated by Europe. His poets, his two real novelists, his lecturers, had expounded Europe to him, if he read books. European heroes and charlatans visited his cities. But after 1860 he moved more and more swiftly into his present condition of " the stripped European." The many and truly informing contacts of simple commerce had been interrupted; in the swirl of his own current emotional adventure he lost all touch with the resolved emotional adventures of foreign arts and political facts. He would face Europe, from this point onward, in the mood of Mark Twain or of Henry James, trying to find it funny and producing just the nervous giggle of a lad thrust into a drawing-room among indifferent older folk, or accepting Europe's own valuations of itself with a fatuous respect. That this miscomprehension affected his understanding of finance began to be plain in 1868. The neurosis had formed; the nation was now in the state of an unconscious invalid who thinks himself wholesome because he eats, walks, and begets. It would need the crash of sensations to assure him that he was shut off by a film of ignorant defenses from the wisdom of mankind, which is not so small. Meanwhile he had money and machinery, and these contented his muscles as playthings. They do so still, some say.

A society of the positively neurotic waited to welcome Ulysses Grant in Washington. Many of these sufferers were soldiers who had served under the taciturn general; others had taken malaria under McClellan in the Virginia swamps. For years their nerves were kept at a certain palpitating pitch, and now they drank and gamed to keep up the tension of nights in camp along the Potomac. They alarmed ladies at dinner by twitchings and bursts of tearfulness over nothing. " Shell shock " had not been invented then, and the ladies did not imagine that a recurrent sense of the inane, war's least comfortable acquirement, was disturbing some giant in broadcloth between the baked shad and the roast duck. One member of Congress always left the House when Gettysburg was mentioned; another could not sleep in a dark room. Nothing seemed amiss with the whiskered men in loose velvet jackets who wore a tea rose in imitation of the Duc de Morny and swallowed champagne before luncheon in Willard's Hotel or drank six of the famous brandy cocktails at the Saint Nicholas in New York on their way to the stock exchange. Their grandsons, after 1919, were just as gay companions, with the whole vocabulary of the neurologist ready to explain their malady. It was the pay-day of a vast military exploit. Only, at the end of the sixties, men were not supposed to have nerves, and there was no talk about neuroses.

Anything for a thrill, though! They turned to ferocious amusements of finance and legislation, and roared in Congress when James Blaine told Roscoe Conkling that he was a dunghill, a singed cat, a whining puppy and some other things. Their taste in oratory had been formed by the sickening, rhythmic vituperations that preceded the war, and their logic had not been increased by fifty months of subjection to mere command. It did not bruise their sense of proportion to hear Abraham Lincoln and the " dead of a thousand fields " summoned up against a bill to deflate the currency, and they did not mind — it was exciting! — if an orator asked God to strike dead the Postmaster General who hadn't given someone's pet orderly an office in Iowa. They must be amused. Our historians primly tell us that " they joined in the mad scramble for worldly success." Perhaps historians may yet discover that success is just a form of amusement, mostly sacred to those who have not brains enough to attain it.

But as for the smart men whose interest in the war had been the costly shipping of soldiers and mail or the sale of munitions, and damn the quality, to the bewildered government, they were now in smoothest function as a medium between the American and his country, ready to explain its possibilities. They had money and machinery at their disposal and useful examples for their argument. The star of Empire, they said, glittered in the West. It was already a traditional saying; expansion was an old catchword. In the fifties there had been little difficulties about grants of land in the territories, but the Homestead Act and the donations to the railroads had countered that precedent. Hotels and boarding-houses in Washington now jammed with people eager to have the government run a railway across their acres, or appropriate ten millions to build a governmental school on their mountain, or widen their river. The popular mind had grown used to the government's benevolences, and smart men would surely not discourage this state of things. The expansionist mania, really, was washing back upon itself; the individual neurosis of the pioneer, his profound belief in future wealth, now mingled with the other neuroses in the East and made the smart man happy.

Huge tracts of Western land passed into the keeping of gentlemen who had rooms and pretty ladies at the disposal of excited Westerners wanting something done at Washington. Everybody was opening the country up. It was a pastime. The pioneers came eastward with charts of their possessions, and the smart battalion at the Saint Nicholas and the Willard entertained them suitably with promises and champagne, a drink popular among Englishmen and Americans because its gaseous nature recalls the ginger beer or soda water of infantile revelries. Confidence in the government was the note of the smart battalion's discourse to the returning pioneer; all that had been done for the Union Pacific and the Northern Pacific could be done again, and ought to be done. Now, as to expenses. . . . There was a deal of whispering about a man in Washington, who. . . . Soon every Western settlement had its sour loungers, aware of the best bars and hotels in New York and the capital, but bitter forever against the East. They had gone to meet the sunrise and came home shrivelled. They knew all about the damned capitalists of the Saint Nicholas bar, at least. Some of the capitalists locked away deeds to thousands of Western acres and waited for the country's movement to manure this unearned increment. While waiting they roundly applauded the Honorable Roscoe Conkling when he passionately argued, before Federal courts, that the Fourteenth Amendment of the Constitution forbade a mere state to regulate rates of railroads passing through its territories. Mr. Conkling could prove by sheer force of oratory that states should not regulate anything. The less regulation you had, the better. Was not the country being opened up? Even Mr. James Blaine agreed that the country was being opened up. It went on being opened up until the panic of 1873 halted the practice.

This society, not at all unlike the society surrounding another President from Ohio fifty-two years later, welcomed Ulysses Grant in 1869. Amusement-hunters, power-seekers, and orators swarmed on the guileless, tired soldier. He was no fool, but his weariness was clear even to the young daughter of William Lloyd Garrison when she saw him at Washington in 1866. That he became the subject of a game is common history, and the game was safe until such time as his stubborn temper roused and his suspicion leaped at his plausible friends. But he was tired and he wanted to be entertained; he had been poor all his days and he had a simple reverence for wealth. Rich people who could dine him in gilded private parlors on steamboats, where colored windows projected sheen on rattling silver and cut-glass goblets, circled the President, with various intentions. Handsome Congressmen who understood a horse, and Ben Butler, who understood the plebeian mind, rose and fell in his favor for eight years. He might buck out of their grooming hands and veto a bill to increase the inconvertible currency; he might sign a bill setting a date for the resumption of payments in real money of the government's debts. He might listen to reformers and establish a commission for the improvement of the Civil Service. He would decide three times to withdraw the soldiers from the racked South and let a conquered people disentangle itself from its miseries by its own will. But, for six days in the week, the smart men had him dazzled. He was tired.

Failure and war had eaten out of this man any essential will; he had been nothing for years, a drudge in a crude community, and then he had been exhausted by an incredible tension of command. " Let us have peace," was not just a political expression, but a personal and immediate prayer. He wanted no more trouble. It was easier to take advice from his friends, and it was soothing to have such pretty things given to him, horses and bonds and jeweled pins. Let the Senators and Congressmen make the appointments to the Civil Service; if the Cabinet made trouble, get another cabinet. Let him have peace!

His presidency will provide gossip for a dozen more biographies. The society about him can be dissected into a hundred layers of scandal. His failures were notorious from the first month of his vacillating reign. But, beyond the orators and the journalists, this general had a special audience, and it saw him not unjustly. He was Grant. He was not the President or the military commander to this legion, but a man. Historians cannot be taught to remember steadily the force of the human aspect on a people. You can pick Grant's effect from any volume of the *Photographic History of the Civil War*. . . . See, here is a circular bench under dusty pines. A group of officers and correspondents gabble in the sunlight. Orderlies and messengers are dimmer upon tall horses beneath the boughs. And here, somehow lonely on the bench, is a hard, lounging body, a plain hat drawn over a bearded face, a cigar, and a

pair of dirty boots. This is Grant, familiar to the men
watching him as Bill or Ed or Jason waiting outside the
smithy at home for a colt to be shod. Everything since dug
up by destructive analysts in the case of Grant was a commonplace of his camp. His men knew that he had hauled
wood for a living in Missouri, but that did not disturb them.
If his staff pumped ideas into him, what of it? A man ought
to listen to his friends. He was supposed to drink two
quarts of whisky a day. His men were not concerned. He
was no figure to be increased by religious lights, and verbal
gestures were not expected of him. He was no Liberator.
He was their neighbor. He had only to pause beside a cot
in the hospital below Vicksburg, saying, " I bet that hurts,"
to a lad with a smashed arm, in order to have the fealty of
a whole county in Iowa. So criticism of the President was
immaterial to this grand army. They might curse him for a
fool and even vote the Democratic ticket, but he was still
Grant.

He gained by an unspoken contrast with his background
of noisy creatures on paper stilts. The word " great "
flooded the press; great orators, great editors, great railroads, great thieves, and great strumpets were on every
page of the newspapers. Mark Twain became a great humorist, as he once said, between two lectures. The rapidity
of creation stunned, and the presidential sphinx, who had
really done something, seemed larger in this smear of
shams. And there was nothing else to look at, now. The
giants vanished or waned as querulous freaks. Thaddeus
Stevens died. Wendell Phillips had gone crazy over fads,
such as female suffrage and prohibition. Sumner was lost
in his obsessions, wanting the English flag washed off the
American continent, quarreling tiresomely with Grant over
the annexation of Santo Domingo or bullyragging the
President to get the fantastic item of two billion dollars for

" indirect damages " inserted among the *Alabama* claims. Ben Butler wallowed between the parties, grossly impudent and jolly. Roscoe Conkling leaned on a mantelshelf of yellow marble, now and then adjusting the famous curls on his advertised brow, and aspirants for his favor waited a gesture of Kate Chase's round fan before approaching the chief of the spoilsmen with some request or a new slander of James Blaine. This is the chart of the Gilded Age, a fierce assumption of greatness in a circumfluent weariness. Everyone was tired and wanted to be entertained.

Thus the first bulletheaded general becomes an emblem of his nation in that time. He was himself a victim in the comedy of the expansionist mania; his merits, which were solid as the merits of many men, had been diluted, expanded in all directions; the force so excellent in the drilling of a raw regiment exploded vainly. He did small things very well, as President, and wanted to do large things. But he strayed among his projects, as the expanding nation strayed, and his result was a network of incomplete roads towards a proper government, and the demolition of any respect for its rulers that survived in the United States.

Out in Cleveland young Mr. Hanna found that he couldn't interest his friends in politics. " Your newspapers," old Senator Hanna said, in 1900, " used to gas about the great excitement of some election or other. And then we had to hire livery hacks to get the voters to come and vote! " It was his first political lesson. He made himself inconvenient and obstreperous trying to get the Republican voters to attend a caucus or put off a trip to the marshes to shoot ducks on election day. The increase of Cleveland had brought into the city numbers of shabby laborers or immigrants whose votes were already manipulated in 1864, ordered by small bosses or put up for sale. Mr. Hanna profusely objected to the machinery of his party all through Grant's first term. In 1873 he bolted, with other Republicans, and helped to elect a reputable Democrat mayor of Cleveland. He kept fussing about this lackadaisical habit of his friends in regard to the affairs of the city and the state. It took time for cynicism to enter him. He was an Ohio man and a Cleveland man, locally absorbed. He would not see that it was absurd to be interested in a caucus or in the bad lighting of Euclid Avenue; his wife teased him and his friends called him a bore. Let the professionals handle politics and be damned to them. Politics was a dirty game. Nobody dissented at a banquet when Mark Twain put out his unprinted witticism: "There is a Congressman — I mean a son of a bitch — But why do I repeat myself?"[4] It was not until 1880 that Mr. Hanna shrugged and consented, and perhaps the experience of hearing himself called a rich busybody at a meeting of reformers was the conclusion of his first political mood. He knew, by that time, that machinery ruled in politics and that the machinery was companionably to be oiled by money. This image itself appeared in cartoons, in the time of Grant. All was appropriate. Factories vomited cheap furniture and cheaper machines on the country, and the vital machinery of cities cast up cheap men into place. Behind this apparatus was a point of reality: one might quietly rule in politics without being a politician. One might be an engineer.

III

In 1872 there was a stir and a flutter from Washington. The nation now learned why John Sherman had shuddered in 1864 over the act insuring the Union Pacific Railroad. It came to be said that the mighty construction company known as the Crédit Mobilier had distributed shares of its stock

[4] This was current before 1879. Mr. Clemens dated it about 1876.

among national legislators. Commissioners were appointed to discover what exactly had happened and the facts twinkled into view. Mr. Oakes Ames, a Congressman from Massachusetts, the son of poor but honest parents, was the main witness before the delving commissions. Mr. Ames spoke freely and indignantly and his statements crawled abroad to bite heels. A controlling group of stockholders dominated the Union Pacific and the Crédit Mobilier. As the construction company built the railroad, the railroad paid its friend in cash and stocks. Unpleasant bystanders asserted that the actual cost of building was about one half of what the Crédit charged for its work. It was shown that the Crédit had been paid more than ninety-three million dollars, while the costs could not be run to more than fifty-three millions. Skeptics alleged that the road had truly cost only about twenty-eight millions. Anyhow, stock of the Crédit was a " diamond mine." Mr. Oakes Ames said so himself. He was allowed to know what he was talking about.

The investigation was an affair of two stories. On the lower floor the committee discovered that certain Congressmen and Senators had taken or had bought stock at par from Mr. Ames. In the second story people accustomed to finance had an esoteric sensation. For, mile by mile, the government of the United States kept its contract with the Union Pacific by turning over securities to the road's officers. It was this load of bonds that really paid for the construction of the Union Pacific, on which, said the builders, they had " risked their every penny " and " staked their personal honor." And now the Government must wait until 1895 for the maturity of the railroad's debt. Engineers, surveyors, and workmen had risked their lives to build the line, but there had been no real risk of anybody's fortune in the deal. The government was the cow and the smart men filled their pails. The fact was there, and very

451

clearly to be inferred in the reports of the Poland and Wilson committees.[5]

Congress meekly voted that a Senator and two Representatives be censured, and casuists defended the legislators minutely through every turn of the business. It is true that no bills affecting the railroad were before Congress when the stock was distributed by Mr. Ames, and Mr. Ames assured the world he was just procuring a friendly influence against the evil-speakers and blackmailers who might threaten his scheme. People laughed over the word " blackmailers," and yet there was a glitter of realism in that statement, for the blackmailing of corporations had begun in the United States as soon as there was talk, in the fifties, of controlling railroads and contractors. However, Mr. Ames settled his case by going home to Massachusetts and dying. His notebook had done its worst to several careers, as he kept accurate count of the legislators who would pay for the stock presently, but hadn't paid him when the scandal broke. A blow glanced off and ruined Schuyler Colfax, who tried to show that a dividend received from Mr. Ames was a contribution to his campaign in 1868 given by one Nesbitt, chief of the " Paper Ring." Congressmen who returned stock and dividends to Mr. Ames, on second thought, defeated by their example the case of the casuists who kept it. " It was fishy," said one of these former, Allison of Iowa, in 1895, " and you can see what they were after, now.

---

[5] It will surprise anybody reading the journalistic comment of the period to find how seldom this second phase of the matter is mentioned, even in the partisan Democratic sheets. Possibly the method of giving out the reports tended to hide the real issue. Most of the denunciation was wasted on the so-called corruption of Congress. An interesting attitude will be found in *The Last Quarter Century in the United States* by Benjamin Andrews. Andrews was socially in touch with people who could inform him properly, but for a moralist and a reformer he is curiously mild in his recital. Mr. Myers in his study of the great American fortunes seems certainly to be more correct. Mr. Charles C. Nolan, who knew Mr. Poland, told me in 1926 that the investigator put the cost of the construction at about thirty-eight million dollars.

Ames and Huntington wanted to get rid of the debt to the government. They were looking a long way ahead." He spoke as the grandees of the Southern Pacific Railroad were attempting to put off the payment of their huge debts to the public, and the public was resisting the attempt with unusual success. Perhaps Mr. Ames had not looked so far ahead as 1895. He was a very smart man, though, and sprung of the plain people, who, Mr. Herbert Hoover tells us, are the backbone of the country.

This scandal was still piling its gossip in the summer of 1873 when a wide uneasiness troubled the expansionist financiers. Times were bad in Europe, after a panic in April at Vienna. Jay Cooke had to admit that bonds of the Northern Pacific Railroad sold slowly, as Europe would not buy. Europe bought less and less through the late summer, and bright lads in the brokerages now discovered that American finance was not free of Europe at all. Meanwhile sober investors wondered about the government of the Western railroads and a few journals talked, gently, of inflation and unsound prosperity. Then, in seven hours of September 19th, 1873, the whole expansionist bubble descended in water. Nature co-operated handsomely with business; rain fell a dozen times on frantic brokers lurching along Wall Street. Spectators huddled under porticos and umbrellas, staring at the wet show. Jay Cooke had failed, it was known on the eighteenth, but this show of the nineteenth was not wholly due to the collapse of Cooke or of Hatch and Company, although both houses ruined smaller banks and brokers as they fell. The image of the card castle is not accurate. This was real panic, for stocks of excellent value followed the descending railroad shares, thrown away without reason. The almighty American business man became a tremulous sheep in the drenching storm. Everything slumped, racketed, and dropped. Certificates of stock were found lying in the gutter by boys, abandoned — in one case, at least — by men who were solvent. The Exchange closed. People sat on curbs, mumbling to each other. There was nothing left.

And now men who had lived on stimulus since 1861 exacted a last thrill: suicide was constant in the newspapers. Mr. Edward Stokes, who had lately murdered Jim Fisk, sent word from prison that he was glad to be in out of the rain. " A horrible levity," Mrs. Henry Ward Beecher noted, " seems to prevail among the afflicted. . . ." The more fashionable pastors steered away from calling their flocks frivolous or superstitious, but mentioned that God's hand seemed to be on the nation. Mr. Jay Gould quietly swept thousands of shares into his control at very reasonable prices, and many sons of stockbrokers left school and went to work.

At the end of 1873 more than a third of the railroads in the United States were being nursed by receivers. The burden of the panic fell, of course, on the West, as the ruin of grand banks in New York brought on the ruin of the rural bankers. Much of the trouble was simply neurotic.[6] A state of mind succeeded a state of mind; inflation was the mother of timidity. In the spring of 1874, farms of ninety acres could not be mortgaged for a hundred dollars, and the charlatans were wailing to Grant for more money. Congress, in April, sent an act calling for an increase of the inconvertible currency to four hundred million dollars, and the cliques assured Grant that unless he approved this stupidity the Republican party in the West was ruined. But the President put his veto on the folly, and it cannot be decided, now, whether the new scandals among his odd friends or his veto did most to revive the Democratic party in the elections of 1874.

[6] A client of my grandfather, for instance, withdrew all his funds from solid banks in Ohio, sold his land, and kept more than two hundred thousand dollars in cash in his house for some years.

Business would not revive. The soft coal mines of Ohio and Pennsylvania had been suggesting gold mines until Black Friday. Now scared little concerns combined or drearily summoned creditors to appoint a receiver. Railroads curtailed orders, under stress of economy, and engineers joked about using coals twice over in the yards, as prudent wives used tea or coffee grounds. An association of miners sent its awkward delegates to implore decent wages, but the delegates could report only one friendly listener to the new union. Mr. Hanna, of Rhodes and Company, would hear them out and do what he could for them.

Mr. Hanna, much hooted at by conservatives, had organized an association of operators. Not being talkative he explained his purposes badly to his friends. He had no fancy name for his scheme, but he believed in what is now called collective bargaining. A strike was a nuisance to him, and nothing good, that he could see, had ever come of poor wages and discontent. He listened civilly to the delegates and promised to aid their association if they would promise to use strikes as a last means of getting attention. But he was to be baffled by the weak operators as he tried to keep things smooth in Wayne and Stark counties, called then " the Massillon district." Master Daniel Hanna's first lessons in finance were to be discussions of coal and wages around the dinner-table. Flushed gentlemen expounded the villainies of the Eastern markets, the horrible terms exacted by cautious managers of railroads, and the general awfulness of everything. Statistics rose in air and battered the boy's head. And then, or later, he learned that his father saw a fraud in all this twaddle of insecurity and bad times. " He held that some corporations and large industrial concerns were deliberately bleeding their workmen as a matter of selfish economy. I have heard the same opinion expressed in regard to the panic of 1873 by other men who were in a position to be acquainted with the facts. . . .

But the conditions in the soft coal business at the time were really very bad. It was impossible for Mr. Hanna to keep the rate of pay up. Several of the small operators were on the verge of ruin. . . ." [7]

In these three years of extreme depression Mr. Marcus Hanna began to be apparent to his rivals, for he was a salesman of Rhodes and Company's coal before anything else. He committed seeming miracles. It would be known that a large contract awaited someone in Chicago or Duluth; agents would hustle to the point of demand and meet Mark Hanna coming home with the contract in his pocket. He seemed to smell a chance for a big sale from Cleveland; he shot off to Saint Louis or was met in the streets of Winnipeg. He got there first. And, although it then was thought absurd, he went in for advertising. On his command Rhodes and Company issued leaflets and pamphlets, some written by the literary James Ford Rhodes, which circulated the offices of railroads and factories. It was advertising by indirection. The firm of Rhodes and Company seemed merely to be giving news of the coal-fields to the world.

The private news was saddening enough. Business went on, but prices stayed low and declined in 1875. In the early spring of 1876 the frightened operators reduced wages to sixty-five cents a ton in the Massillon district, over Mr. Hanna's warning, and the union could not keep the men from striking. Only one mine of Rhodes and Company was alive in the middle of April. When Mr. Warmington brought down some new non-union laborers from Cleveland one morning, he was mobbed and would have been killed had not two strikers saved him. A genuine disorder broke out instantly and the sheriff appealed to Governor Rutherford Hayes for troops. The grave veteran at Columbus hesitated and then sent a company of militia to the mines. Twenty-four hours passed. Then strikers set afire two mines of

[7] Daniel Hanna to Henry Adler, November 24th, 1905.

Rhodes and Company, and the militiamen made arrests. A man was shot, of course, and the timid babbled about anarchy in Cleveland. Mr. Hanna limped into his house and threw his hat the length of the hallway, alarming his son by the remark, " God damn militia, anyhow! " This salty sentiment, often repeated by Americans, was Mr. Hanna's first attack of profanity before his son, but excusable. He found himself, as chief of the operators' association, charged with the sickly job of seeing that twenty-three half-starved proletarians were properly punished by the law.

It was not easy to find a lawyer who would defend the miners before an antagonized audience at Canton in June. Some picturesque happenings in Pennsylvania had alarmed readers of newspapers. The " Molly Maguires " terrorized miners around Mauch Chunk, freely assaulting bosses and foremen, sometimes murdering these delegates of authority. There was awful talk of a general conspiracy of labor, perhaps arranged by the Pope or by Russian nihilists. So Major William McKinley's friends begged him to let the case at Canton alone when they heard that he would plead for the miners. He had a great deal to lose. He was being talked up for a seat in Congress and he was popular with the nicest people in his district. But Major McKinley had the unbelievable stubbornness of the mild, pliant man. He elected to defend the miners and take his chance.

His clients at first considered the volunteer a spy sent to entrap them. He was some dapper little devil who would sell them to Rhodes and Company; he was too handsome, too well dressed, too polite. It cost him a box of cigars and large bulks of chewing-tobacco to soothe the prisoners. They talked, at last, won over by his charming voice, a rather monotonous, easy voice with something of the pastor in its tones. People always talked to him, when they liked him, as though he were a professional confessor. " What a priest," said Monsignor Ireland, " he might have made! "

His success, in this case, was due to what he had got out of his witnesses beforehand. When he went into court in June, he was fairly sure of getting the men discharged and his legendary appeal against the brutality of capitalism is not even good legend, although it remains a pretty picture, with Mark Hanna shedding tears in the foreground. Major McKinley won his case on the facts.

Mr. Hanna did not enjoy the occasion. He was never vindictive against small people, and the miners were small people in his mind. About this time he let loose his first famous epigram: " Up to his neck a man is only worth the price of a day's labor." This puzzled or offended men who somehow or other tried to believe that one man was as good as another, in some way inexplicable. A man, below his brains, might be just a machine of muscles and worth no more than his neighbor, but it was not a comfortable witticism. In our times it would be called un-American. Mr. Hanna, if he sat in the court at all, was probably relieved to see the soiled machines of skin and muscle let out of their box, but nothing gave him much pleasure in June of 1876; he was suffering abominably with hives on his tender ankles. When he took young Dan to the great Centennial at Philadelphia in July, he was still smeared with sulphur ointment and leaning on a cane. The small boy deplored his father's habit of sitting down on benches in Machinery Hall in contradiction of Daniel's right to hours in the society of an elegant camel attached to the Exposition. It was very hard to get Mr. Hanna away from the machines, anyhow, since he understood what made the wheels go round and the valves open. He talked too busily to clerks and exhibitors, writing down prices and grunting arguments. Once, when Daniel was importunate for camels, the wearied father saw a man in a red fez and said, " Go and ask Abou Ben Adhem if his tribe's increased any." He was then left alone with some humming and clicking interest for a while before Daniel came back to report that Abou Ben Adhem had no tribe. By that time Mr. Hanna was ready to be a good parent and take his son to the camel.

When he was old, in April of 1903, Mr. Hanna leaned on his cane in the midst of political splendors at Saint Louis, where a majestic exposition was to be dedicated. All around him were emblems of power named Theodore Roosevelt, Benjamin Odell, or Senator or General. The machinery of intrigue clicked behind all these shapes. A faction was welding Odell to the President; a faction wanted Mark Hanna for President; a faction wanted Mr. Hanna to cast down Roosevelt and make someone else President. The machines whirred. Experts and reporters watched the show. And then a red-faced, clumsy personage rose on the platform, and the multitude began a lengthening shout which would not die away. They cheered Grover Cleveland, twice President, so hated by half of his party that his name was hissed at banquets of the proper Democrats, who swore by William Bryan. This roar astounded men. It outdid the roaring for Mr. Roosevelt; it was the apology of a people to a courageous man. Mr. Roosevelt stared. The Republican powers and dignitaries whispered lies to him that night, sputtering that Wall Street was backing Cleveland for a third term. But the noise went on, and it was seen that Mr. Hanna was quivering, his mouth tightened in amusement. They wondered if he was laughing at Mr. Roosevelt's humiliation. A friend led him aside when he came limping down from the platform. But he had been remote to the intrigue and the roar for a moment. He was thinking of a quotation that suited Mr. Cleveland's triumph. Lo, he thought, Ben Adhem's name leads all the rest. And that made him think of Dan and the fellow in the red fez, and the days in Philadelphia. Hey, what a grand show the old Centennial had been!

For Mr. Hanna, outside his office, was a simple person.

He was not by much different from any well-paid clerk or lawyer who led a son under the Centennial's domes of harsh stained glass. His tastes were plain. He gave his guests champagne and drank water. He doted on stewed corn and rice puddings. He liked a popular play or a good lecture. But he knew each line in whole acts of Shakspere and detested the eloquence of Henry Ward Beecher and Robert Ingersoll. He would play whist a full night without a stake and condescended to euchre if ladies preferred that imbecile pastime. Except that he was a daring pioneer of industrialism and could remember anything that once had interested him, he was the mental cousin of any prosperous midlander who afforded a trip to the Centennial. He resented the patronage of the East, just as they did, and he felt the same way about the massacre of General Custer's troops week before last on the Little Big Horn, and he was still ashamed of Grant for accepting Secretary Belknap's resignation back in March when Congress impeached Belknap for selling privileges at the trading-posts in Indian territory. He may have thought Samuel Tilden would beat General Rutherford Hayes for the presidency in the fall. The Republican party was in awful shape, everywhere. Hayes would never have been nominated if it had been possible to make Blaine and Conkling heal their quarrel at the convention. Mr. Hanna was little wiser, politically, in 1876, than anybody else. He was like the rest of the crowd. His strong cigars were costly, and be sure that his wife had the best rooms in the hotel. If officers of the Pennsylvania Railroad or men from Duluth and Milwaukee saw the heavy man in the press, be sure that they came to shake hands with M. A. Hanna, of Rhodes and Company. But Mr. Hanna was still nobody at Philadelphia in 1876.

THE BULLETHEADED GENERALS

IV

WAR did not make Rutherford Hayes neurotic although his hair and his long, square beard turned gray when he was commander of the Twenty-third Ohio. He didn't understand nerves and he despised excesses. Young officers were politely lectured when they drank too much, but he was indulgent to the enlisted men because they were less educated and had no responsibilities. He liked a soldier to be decorous, if he could, and was delighted with William McKinley's rise. The ironmaster's son was a proper little officer, and aware of his responsibilities.

General Hayes had never been a failure and evaded no responsibility. When he was shot through an arm he lay on the ground before his troops and directed the fire; when an electoral commission assured him that he was President of the United States he took on the job. It worried him the rest of his life to be uncertain if he had been fairly elected in that brazen row when both parties bribed and lied so furiously that the public believed neither side at last, and sat in peace all winter while the case was decided and General Hayes inaugurated. He was then badgered, bullied, insulted by newspapers, legislators and office-seekers throughout his term of office. One gapes at the mass of published but truthless information available on Rutherford Hayes from 1877 to 1881. But the salvation of this Yankee gentleman was that he was a Yankee gentleman, although born in Delaware, Ohio. New England returned to power with Rutherford Hayes, although Yankee journals did not claim him and he was vilified in Boston as he was in California.

He was not one of your fanciful Yankees. He admired Emerson's platitudes, but sometimes could not understand the drifting prose of his pet philosopher; life was a thing of considered rules to the second bulletheaded general; his passion was for conduct, not for speculation. Vagueness

461

didn't please him. He distrusted minds which moved from
side to side of a question. James Garfield's cleverness
seemed a want of moral principle. But he was not a dull
man. As a young lawyer he had undertaken, with a prophetic psychology, to defend a murderess on the grounds
that her ugliness and her sense of inferiority had shoved her
out of contact with humanity. He talked to people with an
alert sympathy until they annoyed him by their perpetual
unreason. Then he looked at them as though they were dis-
obedient kids, and gave them up. Mr. Hawthorne would
have understood him directly, had they met, for the romancer often talked with such Yankees — stiff, tall, cool —
when they brought ships into Salem through a January gale
and reported at the customs-house with ice caked in their
beards. It was this old strain, scrupulous, hard, and precise
in its functioning, that made Hayes loathed by the supple
spoilsmen who lived on gifts of office to their followers. He
had not been President two weeks when a breach showed
between the Executive Mansion and Capitol Hill, nor was
it ever filled in with any help from General Hayes. He had
a vanity, but it was not wide enough to hold much oil in the
shape of flatteries dispensed by Roscoe Conkling: he did
like to be called General.

Actually, much of what Hayes did was to carry out the
good intentions of Ulysses Grant. Grant had been wanting,
at the last, to withdraw troops from Louisiana and South
Carolina. Hayes did it and the carpet-bagger governments
of both states collapsed at once, freeing the whole South
from military controls. A third of the Republican legislators now cursed the President, who had undone the victory
of the Union on the glorious fields of etc., etc., etc. Grant
steadily disliked the inconvertible paper currency and had
favored the Resumption Bill of 1875, which set a date for
the redemption of the greenbacks in gold. Hayes and his
placid Secretary of the Treasury, John Sherman, accumu-

lated gold in 1878 by an issue of bonds and resumed the payment of gold for currency in January of 1879, while Greenbackers and Democrats howled, literally, in public meetings that this meant ruin, and severe rural patriots upbraided Sherman for letting foreign bankers buy the bonds. But no new panic came; people turned in hoarded gold pieces for bills at the Treasury. Nor was the stiff general afraid to face Roscoe Conkling, the oratorical giant. He made use of his executive powers to clean out a polite gang of Conkling's friends from the New York customs-house. It was not a wholly just performance, but they had been irritating and impudent, certain of Conkling's supreme protection. General Hayes ordered them out of there, as if he were ordering the chevrons off a refractory sergeant's sleeve. The Congress refused to back him, of course, when he wanted to revive the Civil Service Commission, and would not grant him funds.

Washington became a new kind of comic spectacle. The rush of Congressmen leaving the House after the reading of a presidential veto in 1879 was likened by Cushman Davis to the flight of bats from hell. Hayes was incomprehensible to the men hardened by the Gilded Age's acids. He sent poets, scholars, and cultivated lawyers who quaintly spoke several of those foreign languages to Europe as ambassadors and ministers. He made no use of patronage to secure himself a personal machine. One of his Cabinet was a former Rebel, David Key. He appointed unreconciled Confederate ladies postmistresses in Southern towns on the recommendation of Democrats. " He seems," said Murat Halstead, " to have no feeling whatever for the popular thing! " He was, it proved, quite ready to veto a bill shutting out Chinese immigrants from the United States because it dishonored an American treaty with China, and then he patiently observed in his journal that it was the popular thing to burn him in effigy beyond the Rocky Mountains.

HANNA

It was the nation's luck to have this temperament in office on the night of July 20th, 1877, when Mr. Hawthorne, startled by noises, abandoned a conversation with Pushkin and Miss Jane Austen in the literary heaven to stare down from a golden casement at a web of pink, pulsing irregularly on the map of the United States. The roadways of the machine were ablaze; burning ties and coaches made heaping buds of flame. The great strike had come at last. Black Friday fulfilled itself when the pay of railroad workers was reduced yet again and the men struck " because there was nothing else to do," one of them said. . . . Junctions and roundhouses were seized. The ties burned in six states. Perishable stuff rotted in warehouses and express companies. Cities had no ice and no milk. There was open rioting in Martinsburg, Reading, and Scranton. Militiamen would not shoot into the swaying masses that hooted them. Nineteen were killed in Chicago. Pittsburgh was an insanity of lights and smoke as strikers shoved blazing oil-cars into the huge roundhouse or fired machine-shops. Men lugged stolen mattresses and leaking cans of sirup or frivolous kid slippers from the looted stores up those steep hills to their shacks. It was Wagnerian — a revolt of the dirty dwarfs against the gods at Newport. Sewing-machines were tossed from halted trucks into the crowd.[8] Champagne puzzled the finders of a case and they used it to wash their hot faces, delighted by the fuzzy impact, not knowing it was wine. . . . At Cleveland it was chattered that two thousand men armed with revolvers were waiting to plunder Euclid Avenue. In New England it was observed by Mr. Henry Cabot Lodge that owners of mills began suddenly to raise wages, finding sharply that they could afford to do what had

[8] My mother was a witness of the first phase of the strike. She was taken from Pittsburgh on the last train to leave the city and saw the sewing-machines in progress up the hills. The detail is mentioned in reports of the strike. One of the surviving strikers is responsible for the tale of the champagne.

464

been impossible a week before. . . . Ten thousand miners struck in Pennsylvania. It was a huge and exasperated stirring of the betrayed.

General Hayes wrote three idle proclamations and sent out regular troops. One of his own kinsmen was among the militia besieged in the roundhouse at Philadelphia, but he does not excite himself over that in his journal. The regulars paraded in cities, took charge of junctions, and stood guard among smoldering cars in yards. An ordinary revulsion aided the troops. " We were ashamed of ourselves," says a man who was sixteen when he helped to loot shops in Pittsburgh; " we saw that this had not done any good, but had made people sore at laboring men. . . . we went back to work as soon as we could. Lots of men went out west that fall. They bummed along the lines or rode in freight cars. It was said that you could live better out west. I have since met a good many men who have done well for themselves in California who were roundhouse boys with me in 1877. . . ." By the first of August the strike was over. On August 5th the President wrote in his journal: " The strikes have been put down by force; but now for the real remedy. Can't something be done by education of the strikers, by judicious control of the capitalists, by wise general policy to end or diminish the evil? The railroad strikers, as a rule, are good men, sober, intelligent and industrious. . . ." But in the newspapers the strikers were demons waving axes and torches. In New York a great pastor whose salary was known to be twenty thousand dollars a year was persuaded to say, at a meeting of the indignant and comfortable, that a workman could raise a family on five dollars a week, although Henry Ward Beecher was not fool enough to say that workmen ought to enjoy this income. As it was, he had said too much, and there was laughter. People live who joined in the titter. Americans of those days still had humor and they might not have heard a presidential candidate putting forward the existence of the electric ice-box as a proof of his party's integrity, without laughing a little.

The strike was over, but it had sharply shown that something was ruptured in the being of the United States. Mass employment had swelled in time to the increase of all machines. It was only in small brick works or petty shops that owners now saw their men at all. Mark Hanna strolling out on the dock of Rhodes and Company, a cigar in his teeth, to listen to the firm's foremen stating a grievance as he sat on a barrel, which stained his trousers, was a survival of an elder order, a wholesome singularity left over from a tradition. Laborers, since the war, had grown used to feeling that the boss or the company was remote, unfriendly, an entity designed to keep wages down. There was a conspiracy of wealth against the masses, a dozen brittle parties of reform affirmed. The machine, spreading everywhere, had spread with it the dingy shack, the smoky flats. Mass thinking codified its simplicities and found a point against which its anger with its own weakness must be projected. This was Wall Street's doing. Wall Street was now to be the emblem of oppression.

General Hayes was badly placed to do anything about the judicious control of capitalism. The powerful legislators were openly his enemies. Quiet people and reformers packed his table at the White House and the number at his wineless evening parties grew, but the great figures of Washington did not condescend to the President. Congressman McKinley was a favorite caller, sometimes squiring Mrs. Hayes to lectures on foreign missions, but the journal says nothing of Roscoe Conkling and James Blaine. Congress passed, over the President's veto, the Bland-Allison Act of 1878, forcing the Treasury to issue at least twenty-four million dollars annually in full face of the fact that silver would not rise to par and that its depreciation had begun. Congress did everything it could to make itself loathed by Ruth-

erford Hayes. His last act as President in 1881 was to veto
a monstrous thing named the Refunding Bill. He then shook
hands with Senators who had insulted him in speeches, with
Congressmen who had jeered at his beautiful wife for her
modest little addresses on temperance; and so he went home
to Fremont, where he was glad to see that his new country-
house in its grove of fine trees had a low, plain, old-fashioned look. He had not wanted to be President a second
time; it was such a slavish, exacting job. And, he told his
friend William Dean Howells, you had to deal with such
extraordinary people. They seemed to have no principles
at all. They were like unruly cattle.

Mr. Hanna hoped to see John Sherman nominated in
June of 1880 at Chicago. The Secretary of the Treasury
had two merits at least that made Mark Hanna think well
of him: he was from Ohio and he really knew what business
was all about. But Mr. Sherman had two vices in the reck-
oning of the Republican party's leaders: he was not any
more a good showman than Rutherford Hayes had been and
he was critical of fellow politicians. Had he not called a
Senator an ignoramus to his face and publicly, even though
he asked the man to dine afterwards? He was still pensive,
he was proud, and he annoyed the smart men by his tendencies toward a reformed Civil Service. He jested sourly
about New York's financial heroes. He refused to meet Jay
Gould at a dinner in 1879. He was not on smooth terms
with James Blaine, and Roscoe Conkling despised him for
a friend of Hayes.

Roscoe Conkling now reached maximum. The superb
showman was truly able. His narcotic oratory was backed
by a soothing tact in private relations; he could stun the
public by three hours of pointless invective, and get his way
with a caucus by bland courtesies. He had the kind of sarcasm which covers a shortage of real wit, and the effrontery
of a practiced harlot. All this equipment was mottled and

disfigured by the most humorless egoism. He liked power; he had power and he did nothing with his power save to consolidate his hold on the politics of New York and to place Congressmen under obligations. Would he see John Sherman nominated? " This," he said, " would be fatal. . . ." Assertions of the sort were his daily offering in Republican councils. He addressed ten men across a table as though a thousand gazed at his curls and his gestures. He would suspend the reading of trivial notes to a committee while a page brought him water and resume his unimportant suggestions in the case of an Indian reservation after frowning in silence over the delay. It was right, in his mind, to assert that Sherman's nomination would be fatal, as though that meant anything outside the Republican party. For he had the charlatan's most valued gift in public life: he created excitements out of nothing and made simpletons believe that his causes were real issues. Sherman was unobjectionable to the party, but he was not that which Mr. Conkling liked to see in movement toward the White House. What could be played against him? Of course, there was Grant.

Grant landed at San Francisco from his voyage around the world and came eastward in a glory of applause. He was still Grant. Smart men arranged processions and banquets in the cities, but they needed none of that out in the country, where the special audience of this general gathered by the weathered stations at any hour of night in hope of seeing just his private car pass by. Cowboys raced their ponies alongside the tracks. Miners put burning boughs together, after dark, below the numerals of some old regiment carved white upon a hillside and hoped that Grant would look that way. The cheers were screams, and celebrating shots cracked the ears of children in the crowds swept together by this name. Here came Grant, and the noise of the welcome was soothing to Mr. Conkling after his dose of Hayes. He gathered the smart men behind him and appeared at Chicago with three hundred and eight votes of the Republican Convention pledged to Grant. They were Eastern votes, for the most part. Out on the prairies veterans hated Conkling, not altogether justly, as Grant's evil adviser in times past, and farmers knew him to be a pet of the railroads. They would take Blaine or Sherman before they would take Grant with Conkling's hand on his collar. Mr. Conkling did not know this.

His own insolence now spoiled the rhetorician's chances of a nimble victory. In his pounding speech, nominating Grant, he sneered at Sherman and Blaine. He was applauded for twenty-five minutes, or Grant was applauded. But he was answered by General James Garfield, of Ohio, nominating John Sherman, and something happened. This convention's numbers were mixed with a younger variety of politician. Garfield's speech was not wholly new in style — he had to say that God was preparing the outcome of the nominations — but he talked on amiably and courteously, without sneering, and the young men, sick of allusions to Appomattox and to envy's poisoned chalice sat up, listening. Once someone shouted, " We want Garfield! " and cheers disturbed the speaker. Mr. Conkling sank in his chair, staring at this unpleasant symptom of a change in public taste. When he sensed that he was watched he turned his stare to the galleries and kept it aimed there when the roar began as Garfield stopped.

On the thirty-sixth ballot Garfield's sudden following had risen to three hundred ninety-nine votes and he was nominated. Mr. Conkling's faction was handed the nomination for the vice presidency and chose Chester Arthur, of New York. The maudlin convention broke up. Mr. Conkling retired to New York in a state of mind and openly sulked. His language for some weeks is legendary and cannot be proved, but he talked too freely and an edge of the ridiculous entered his situation. He had personally been hit in full sight of the party by an expression of the party's will, after a fierce, maintained contest. It was stiff. Polite messengers and intermediaries could not budge him to meet Garfield. Chester Arthur had to persuade him to make any speeches in the campaign and Mr. Arthur, not caring to be defeated even for the vice presidency, lost patience with his patron at a dinner in Delmonico's. " I hope you understand," he said, " that if the Republican party is defeated, we are defeated with it! " The inner party of smart intrigue must not be allowed to go down. So Roscoe Conkling consented to appear as a loyal Republican. He collected a group of names and loaded them into a private car, summoning other great folk to meet him in Cleveland, whence the whole crowd of dignitaries would be lugged to Warsaw, Ohio, and would exhibit its devotion to General Garfield in the candidate's own state.

Mr. M. A. Hanna of Cleveland had demonstrated to the Republican leaders of Ohio that he was valuable in campaigns. The basis of campaigns was shyly kept in the background, owing to an old conventional sentiment which denied that money had anything to do with Americans around election day. Cabs and hacks took lazy voters to the polls and someone had to pay for that, and for bunting, posters, and brass bands. But there was never much chatter about the campaign funds except the rude words of the losing party. Still, someone had to collect for the local committees, and Mr. Hanna, genially persuasive, had been useful in 1876. He roamed northern Ohio, smoking cigars, and collected. It was a weary job and it had no dignity. It was like the function of some trusted priest in the Middle Ages, arranging the loans of Holy Church to the Jews and Italian bankers. It was business to be done quietly, by a solid man. As a reward, in 1880, Mr. Hanna was allowed some fuss and feathers. He understood transportation, to be sure, and that would make him useful on the trip to Warsaw. He went along to see that all these persons of great name were comfortable.

It was a fine mass-meeting. The crowd yelled for Grant when he mounted the platform and gaped as Roscoe Conkling expended five minutes in empty music of his noble voice. Logan, Cameron, and the rest were pointed out to children. Mr. Hanna smoked and admired the great or maybe wondered if they were worth the price of a day's labor from the neck down, or up. He was not conspicuous, unless one looked at his eyes; nobody paid attention to his emotions when it was whispered among the reporters and understrappers that the party would go straight back to Cleveland, ignoring General Garfield in his pretty house at Mentor. Mr. Conkling's loyalty to his party had limits. He would not meet the candidate or be reconciled to him. He would leave Ohio without acknowledging Garfield as chief of the Republicans. . . . The great filed down from the platform and were transported to the house of a state senator for luncheon. Mr. Hanna stayed outside with the small fry and listened to the indignant buzz in the dooryard. His friend Charles Foster lost sight of him for five minutes. Mr. Hanna had walked into the dining-room and bowed to Ulysses Grant.

" General, it has been arranged that we return to Cleveland by way of Mentor, and if you propose to stop there and see General Garfield, we shall have to start in a very short time."

Roscoe Conkling scowled. He had brought Grant into Ohio as a condescending favor to the party and now this plump imbecile with the brown eyes was going to drag him to Mentor, to the house of his enemy. It would seem a reconciliation, an admission of fealty to Garfield! But he could not speak; he did not dare to command Grant.

" We will stop at Mentor," said Grant.

Mr. Hanna came beaming out and told Charles Foster

471

what he had done. The crowd at Mentor went mad for Grant, and the great men stood about on the candidate's veranda for the world to see, then vanished from Ohio. Mr. Hanna set dutifully to work collecting Republican funds. He did not know that his small ruse worked the damnation of Roscoe Conkling. He had oiled the heels of the charlatan for a fall.

Conkling's egotism now spun him into a reverse of his position. He boasted of his aid extended to Garfield's campaign in " the West " as well as in New York. He spoke of the new President's obligations to him, and the simple creatures of the metropolis expected to hear of a cabinet picked by Garfield on Mr. Conkling's orders. Had not Garfield invited Mr. Conkling to his home in Ohio and told him that he was in his debt? But there was chuckling in New York itself. John Logan had turned loose a version of the scene in Warsaw; it was known that some friend of Garfield had challenged Grant to ignore the candidate and that Grant, not Conkling, had caused the party to call at Mentor.[9] Even Mr. Conkling's prim, industrious ally Senator Thomas Platt was not so sure that General Garfield would be biddable. Spring came; battle came. General Garfield made James Blaine his Secretary of State. General Garfield appointed a Secretary of the Treasury without Mr. Conkling's consent. Mr. Conkling forced an odious scene in Garfield's apartment at the Riggs House, and cold spread even in his own clique as the news of his language got abroad. Garfield coolly retorted by appointing an enemy of Conkling's machine collector of customs at New York. Mr. Conkling's rhetoric became a continuing thunder. He wagged his curls and vaticinated before a committee of conciliation, imitating sentences from the Bible, threatening to expose a disgraceful letter written by Garfield. He exposed it, and it was nothing but a hint for campaign funds sent to an official.

[9] See Appendix, Notes to Chapter II.

Committees and orators worked between the President and the Senator for days, but Conkling's anger sent his conceit floating upward. He would have the President humiliate all his enemies in New York and nothing less; Garfield must eat dirt. The two men met for a last time in a lady's drawing-room, bowed to each other below a chandelier while watchers gulped, and were blocked from each other's sight by a movement of resolute friends as Conkling seemed about to speak. On May 16th, 1881, Mr. Conkling and the mild Mr. Platt resigned their places in the Senate, as a gesture of outrage, knowing that the Senate would confirm Garfield's collector of the port of New York. The legislature of their state would, surely, elect them back to the Senate. . . . But the legislature wouldn't. Conkling was done for.

So was Grant. He soon gave the use of his name and his money to a smart man who had a scheme for a bank, and the smart man finished off the money. But the name was good. Poets and critics, sunflowers of emotion, turned to Grant again when it was known that he was dying, valiantly writing his memoirs in hope of paying his debts. Sympathy was a fountain. But his special audience had never turned from Grant and did not have to show its sympathy by calling at his house on the mountain. It knew Grant. He was doing the right thing for his folks. The farmers clubbed dollars and sent subscriptions for " the General's book " to Grant's publisher. . . . Clumsy coats and tanned faces appeared in the streets of New York on the day of his funeral. Rutherford Hayes nodded to men of his old regiment as he was driven past them on the curbs. Mr. Hanna lent veterans the money for their fare to New York and back. Soldiers and their grave children came to look at this burying-ground, where Grant was. And, after years, they came to New York once more on the windy day when Grant's white tomb was consecrated, with foreign soldiers parading before William McKinley and the Hudson dark with ships. Some of us who were children then, heard all around us the murmur of a man's name. They were talking of Grant, of this picture in a schoolbook. Because we have seen machineries creating sentiment for Presidents without honor, actors and empty sportsmen, we can grin at sentiment. But we dare not grin backward at this sentiment a man created for himself. He was Grant. The name, as they spoke, had the sound of a drum briefly pulsing, and no other name has sounded so, in this long time. There are illusions of the dead so firm and hard that they cannot be dissevered from their causes. He was Grant, to them, and that meaning was recorded in the mention of his name, the curt admission of their faith in him.

CHAPTER III

THE HUMAN MACHINE

WITHOUT notice in Eastern newspapers, on April 1st, 1873, Mrs. William McKinley began to alter American history. She gave birth to a second daughter and had a bad time of it. Her mother died while the pretty little lady was still in bed, and it seemed that Major McKinley's wife would never be well again, after the new baby vanished in August. She would sit for hours in a darkened room, holding Katie on her lap, weeping in silence. Katie was not allowed out of her sight, unless the major took the child for a drive, and poor Katie left just one childish saying to sting in the memory of her uncle, Abner McKinley. He found her swinging on the gate and invited her to take a walk with him. " No, I mustn't go out of the yard or God'll punish mamma some more. . . ." Then Katie died in June of 1876. God, revealed to Ida McKinley in the chatter of old women, had punished her some more. Presently the literal children of Canton told each other, across fences, that Mrs. McKinley had fits. A form of epilepsy showed; the handsome young Congressman was pitied at home and in Washington. A cloud of sympathy settled on William McKinley with the beginnings of his public life.

His buoyant manner changed. He became a soft-spoken, watchful nurse in his own house and a worried guest if he was in company without his charge. About 1880 there was

475

something worse. " Please," said the major to a pretty girl, " don't walk into the yard with me. Ida might see you. . . ." For a year or so the fading invalid thought herself neglected. When the major came down from President Garfield's funeral in the autumn of 1881, he mentioned a handsome lady seen at Cleveland, and his brothers were witnesses of a frantic scene, cut by an epileptic attack. The phase ended. She was a gentlewoman, and the wife of a personage. Public business might be interrupted by Mrs. McKinley's messages to the Representative, the Governor of Ohio, or, at last, the President of the United States asking his opinion of a scrap of silk for a new frock or the flowers of a bonnet, but Mrs. McKinley behaved herself as well as she could. She had a certain bright intelligence and was sometimes witty enough to amuse John Hay.

McKinley ascended into the headlines of newspapers with this burden, and it was genuine, wasting his time, hurting his health, and wearying his friends so that they canonized him before he was forty years old. A man who loved tramping in any weather and who broke wild colts for his neighbors was reduced to driving a bit, when Mrs. McKinley wanted some air, or to strolling through Canton with a bowl of blanc-mange sent to an ailing child.

She loved children, although she might cry if a child came to sit on her knees. In 1892 a Mrs. Saxton lectured on the work of Presbyterian missions in a church at Columbus and Mrs. McKinley seized upon her when she was through her talk, asking if they might not be relatives (her own name was Ida Saxton), and then insisting that the missionary come home with her to meet the Governor. She ended by dining with the two and telling them all about India. " It was a curious experience. They seemed positively fascinated by my stories. I have never been a good talker and have always known my deficiencies in conversation. It startled me to have them hanging on my account of my work in the hospitals. . . . Mrs. McKinley said, ' Oh, how wonderful to be like Lady Dufferin and help all those poor children and their mothers! ' I did not know of her losses and did not understand how keenly my talk about the Indian children must have hurt her. . . . She began to cry when I left and begged me to come back some other day. When we met afterwards in Washington, in 1899, she fairly implored me to see what could be done by the Presbyterian board of foreign missions for the children in the Philippines. . . ." Other people had like experiences. The women and children of the Orient lured McKinley's wife. He was murdered. She shivered through winters in Canton, cowering above fires and hot pipes, and wailed to friends that, if she had any strength left, she would go out and teach the babies in the Philippines. And the major had planned to take a trip through the Orient. And now she would never see all that. . . . Out there, perhaps, had been a paradise of colors and warm flowers, with Katie and baby Ida born again, brown and naked for her kisses, waiting to be brought up as Christian ladies. . . .

The major had been thriftily reared, being the son of an ironmaster who had a large family, and he rose through politics on a notion sacred to thrifty provincials. It was the tobacco-growing Connecticut farmer who demanded a tariff on tobacco from Sumatra, and the rural American ironmasters were noisy, primitive agitators for a tariff on iron and steel. Major McKinley was not amused when Winfield Hancock, the Democratic candidate of 1880, called protective tariff a " local issue." He said, " The protective tariff is a great combination of local issues. We can not neglect the force of so many local issues in judging the nation's great need of protection for its industries and produce. . . ." [1] He believed heartily that these amalgamated local issues made a demand on the government and that bet-

---

[1] Unprinted autograph, addressed to J. C. Parton, December 30th, 1889.

ter wages for the laboring man would result from a high protective tariff. Many of his speeches in Congress are plausible and well made; his voice was charming and the adroitness gained by constantly tending a nervous, fanciful woman helped him with irritable opponents; he nursed his subject along and grew famous as the champion of the tariff.

Tariff is a method of deliberated stealing from foreigners — that is, from a class of human beings in which the native has no sentimental interest. It is an old institution among men, but men have always shown their small faith in the lawfulness of tariffs by admiring smugglers, just as Americans of our time show their disregard of the ignoble Prohibition laws by tolerating sellers of alcohol. In the nineteenth century this theft, called a tariff, was sentimentalized by honorable men just as honorable men excuse a mother who steals for her young. Madison's catchy phrase "infant industries" echoed comfortably and, as William McKinley could justly complain in Congress, Europe was given to playing the hog against American necessities on occasion. Chicago burned, and prices of paints and metals rose too suddenly in Europe. A manufactory of cathedral glass in Missouri was destroyed; the value of European glass was suspiciously rising within a week. This game went on, and to oppose such jockeying by legal pillage did not seem wrong. McKinley's attitude was no more narrow than that of Thomas Reed, an educated, traveled, clever man. The protectionists were sincere enough — are sincere enough — but their final vision of a world's economics is small. They limit their concept within the art of successful government.

Successful government, up to the year 1929, is any kind of domination which assures a particular flattery to the most powerful factions of a state. The collective egoism of a landholding minority or a landless majority or a party of moral reform, backed by rich industrials, is soothed by the enunciation of principles which tend to flatter it. Physical comfort and the humiliation of another faction are practically the alternate offers of the artist in successful government; a full dinner-pail, " the highest standard of living ever known in the world," protection from workmen rendered careless by strong drink on Monday morning, and such benefits unforgettable are tendered and accepted. Anything will go in common times. But an uncommon period, when more than one powerful faction has to be placated, calls for someone able to suggest the grand art of government. And the period extending from the panic of 1873 to the end of the century was uncommon in the United States.

Mr. McKinley's merits in the eyes of an examining tactician were many. He had good looks, a good voice, and good manners, with an amusing trace of the country boy about him to conciliate the plain people. This last was valuable. The real tacticians in politics were now learning their job. They began to transmute Fernando Wood's epigram on pandering to the moral sense of communities, and, as the plain people grew defiantly proud of being plain, they pandered to this pride whenever it was possible from 1880 to 1928. Garfield was not advertised as a finished expert in currency and economics, but as a lad who had led horses barefoot along the tow-paths of canals. Grover Cleveland's rough simplicity and early poverty were duly expounded. It was difficult to exalt Benjamin Harrison as a son of the plain people, but wasn't he the grandson of a pioneer hero? . . . The plain people, curtly, had become a faction so powerful that even dull Eastern observers faintly recognized the point and some of Major McKinley's earliest followers were politicians in Connecticut and Rhode Island. This " shadow of Lincoln " was the thing demanded by the West. " I am unable to see," said Professor William Sumner, drawling to students at Yale College in 1888, " that a boyhood spent in poverty among simple people peculiarly qualifies a man for political preferment, but such seems to be the general argument. . . ."

As for the rest of McKinley, he was fond of red carnations, lilacs, and the music of brass bands. He was a Methodist, but not convinced that a guilty soul suffered eternally for its misdeeds in this world. Might it not be extinguished, sent into oblivion? He was uncertain on the topic of perpetual franchises for street railways. But he approved the classified Civil Service and he spoke up handsomely for arbitration in case of strikes or disputes between common carriers. He had no time for reading, what with politics and nursing, and said wistfully to his Vice President in 1901: " You make me envious. You've been able to get so much out of books. . . ." His memory was well trained, and this does him credit, for it had once been weak.[2] He liked his town and loved to dawdle around a farm.

He was adored, but this adoration prophesied the downfall of American character in the next generation. To be adored for negatives is not so well. The children of pioneers overvalued the conciliator, the very pleasant neighbor, everybody's friend. McKinley had the strength of certain opinions; he could be stubborn. Beyond him drearily appeared the caricature of the modern American; the jellyfish of satire, amiably afloat in a society of like mediocrities, agreeable to everything, the " good fellow " of the golfclub and the office.

But the adoration of McKinley was genuine. In 1928 a shrewd and *rusé* old gentleman of Cleveland amazed some youngsters by telling them that William McKinley was the

---

[2] My grandfather judged several cases in which McKinley was concerned. One of these the major lost by simply forgetting what a witness had said before him. He notably improved, afterwards. Mr. Abner McKinley said that the concentrated stare which annoyed people was really an effort of attention. Mr. McKinley looked straight at you and steadily, to the point of seeming rude.

only person he had ever known who suggested the possible personality of Jesus Christ; on the day of the President's funeral, in 1901, guests and uncomfortable servants in the alley of the old Manhattan Hotel stood watching a man, accounted brutal in finance and politics, who had just crumbled against a wall, sobbing in a roar of pain as the hush of the street told him that the service at Canton had begun. The major was adored, early in his career. " My opponents in Congress," said Thomas Reed, " go at me tooth and nail, but they always apologize to William when they are going to call him names. . . ."

At the Republican convention of 1888 an accident displayed Major McKinley favorably to Marcus Hanna. A distinct faction, made up of men from every part of the country, approached him with a suggestion that he let himself be nominated. McKinley refused and bluntly.[3] He had come there pledged to support John Sherman and he would support John Sherman. Much whispering indicated that Joseph Foraker, in charge of the Ohio delegation, was willing to shift grounds and join the Blaine faction. The Eastern leaders were willing to try a trick. If a " stampede " for McKinley could be started, his own state's delegation would be driven to sharing the movement. John Sherman would be removed from the list, and a deadlock arranged in favor of Blaine. But McKinley halted the attempt by declining to hear himself mentioned as a candidate; he interrupted the roll-call of states when his name was shouted from the delegation of Connecticut and succinctly denied that he was in the running. The nomination was thrown to Benjamin Harrison, and Marcus Hanna contented himself by reflecting, " Well, Harrison was born in Ohio, anyhow! "

[3] " I heard Mr. McKinley use violent profanity only once in his life. It was when he refused to be nominated by the Platt crowd at the convention of '88. . . ." Charles Foster to William C. Beer, November 15th, 1901.

481

HANNA

Mr. Hanna's admiration of Major McKinley was profuse. He appreciated men who stuck to a losing bargain, for he kept his contracts even if they were only oral, and delivered coal at the promised figure to customers at a loss. He would accept a back-drop painted for the Euclid Avenue Opera House ten feet too short for the height of the stage because he had given the dimensions to the painter and could not complain. He detested people who did not stick to a bargain, once made. The major's rectitude impressed him at just the right time, for he was quarreling with Joseph Benson Foraker.

Foraker and Mark Hanna were made to quarrel. The rich man from Cleveland accepted political theatricalities as so much chaff. There had to be processions, all these speeches, and " a lot of gas " about precedence. It amused him. He liked a phrase much used in conversation by Rutherford Hayes, " the hurrah boys." Mr. Foraker accepted the chaff as something else. He felt that a bit of parade and circumstance was becoming to him, at this time, as Governor of Ohio and as Joseph Benson Foraker. He was imposingly designed; he spoke with force and certainty; he had regulated the Republican machine of lower Ohio to an extraordinary smoothness of operation. Mr. Hanna's lack of dignity annoyed him. He was sharply disgusted when the millionaire failed to arrange proper rooms for him in the hotel at Chicago, and when Hanna obliged some Negro delegates from the South by taking over their tickets to the gallery of the convention at a price, he was outraged. Mr. Hanna was not behaving as a sound politician should.

On his side, Mr. Hanna was tired of the handsome Governor's attitudes. He had shed a deal of money on Foraker's campaigns and the Governor inconveniently had not done just the right thing about a job promised to one of Mr. Hanna's deserving campaigners. And, on June 8th, 1888, the Governor had let it be known that he disapproved a plan of Grover Cleveland. The President wished to restore the captured Confederate battle flags to the South, but his action brought on a shower of partisan protests. Mr. Hanna admired Grover Cleveland and he liked Southerners. When he met Mr. Foraker at Chicago, he tactlessly told him that his gesture of June 8th was " stale " and might damage John Sherman's candidacy, remarking these things before half a dozen men, one of them a stranger to Mr. Foraker. The quarrel swelled in a flare of suspicion, and the alliance of Hanna and Foraker ended with the last day of the convention of 1888.

Mr. Hanna was nobody in particular in the hotels at Chicago. He did not stand about bars, and few of the delegates met him. Charles Nolan heard him indicated in a crowd as the head of Hanna and Company in Cleveland, the man who owned the Euclid Avenue Opera House. But people were not interested in this stout and quiet person sitting with Benjamin Butterworth or Charles Foster in lobbies and restaurants. Mr. Hanna was now an actual millionaire, the possessor of his own business, the director of street railways developed from some ramshackle properties of his wife's dead father, the president of a bank, concerned in a ship-building company, partner in three rolling-mills, and nurse of the Republican party's finances in Cleveland. But he was not conspicuous; he was technically not in politics at all. He spent money on politicians. There was a difference, in 1888, which has since disappeared. Anyhow, the East dominated this convention. Reporters and sightseers were keen to talk to Mr. Platt of New York and Mr. Quay of Pennsylvania, the unbreakable bosses, who had knocked down John Sherman and got rid of Allison's promising little boom. So Hanna was nobody in particular at Chicago in 1888.[4]

[4] Mr. Hanna's remarks on Foraker's criticism of Cleveland are not mentioned in Senator Foraker's memoirs or in Mr. Croly's biography of Mr.

II

BENJAMIN MONTGOMERY, chief of telegraph service in the White House, had callers in his small office on a night in the autumn of 1902. A great strike in the coal-fields made this dim little chamber the most important point of the United States. Privileged correspondents and an agent of John Pierpont Morgan were talking to Colonel Montgomery as they awaited the end of a dinner-party elsewhere in the banal residence. Montgomery was a gently oozing spring of information on the Civil War, and this night he was reviving the siege of Petersburg when an apparition grew in the smoky door, and all these men in dinner jackets started. It was an old man, who seemed ten feet tall, towering in a wet ulster, and a soft black hat with the device of the Grand Army. He had got into the Executive Mansion, they could not find out how, and he would not leave it without speaking to Mr. Roosevelt, he would not say why. There he was, an immovable substance, an awkward fact. The President was at dinner? All right. He would wait. He stood just outside the door and inimically considered the official and the journalists, patently distrusting the lot of them. He did not take his hat off when Mr. Roosevelt came limping through the hall to write a telegram, but watched the President finish the message and then said, " I seen in the papers where you hurt yer leg, colonel."

Mr. Roosevelt spun and stared. There began the strangest conversation. The old man spoke slowly as a plow moves through rocky ground. He had come on east to thank the President for giving his son a " gover'ment " job. This

---

Hanna. But the matter is touched on in a letter of Charles Foster, who may have been present; and Mr. Charles Clery Nolan, who was present, is a living witness. A piece of gossip about a quarrel between Mr. Foraker and Mrs. Hanna over the Confederate flags seems plainly to be a mixed version of the alleged scene between the Forakers and Mrs. Grover Cleveland at a reception in Philadelphia.

Jim or Bill had been shot in Cuba and needed something
quiet to work at, and this was one of Bill's or Jim's children. A minor apparition, three feet long, edged around
the columnar ulster. The President snatched a carnation
from Colonel Montgomery's coat and knelt painfully on the
floor, talking to the child while he fastened the flower in its
clothes. Then he looked up at the specter and asked if it was
a Republican.

" I used to be a Republican when it was Lincoln an'
Grant an' Hayes an' Garfield. Then I was a Demmucrat
some. I was a Populist in '92 and I was for Bryan in 1896.
An' now I'm for you, colonel."

The President stood up. One of his hands helplessly felt
the silk of his evening coat. His eyes squeezed shut behind
his glasses. For once he had no answer to a compliment.
He bowed and limped away, the veteran watching him. But
when the old man spoke, it was in a level tone of sad censure.

" Lincoln would never have wore them clothes."

" Why, my friend," said Colonel Montgomery, " I can
show you a dozen pictures of Mr. Lincoln in evening
dress! "

But the Westerner knew better. His Lincoln was now
firm in his mind and the mind of his likes out there, a friend
of the plain people who scorned the silk-stocking crowd.
Without heat he told the gentleman, " You're a damn
liar," and then he vanished, with Jim's or Bill's child hanging to his fingers. . . . A bit later one of the reporters
showed Mr. Roosevelt a note of the scene, but the President
shook his head, saying, " No, as a favor to me, Dunn," and
there was no pretty anecdote in next Sunday's paper.

This apparition had told the story of a certain rural
mind. He voted for the heroes of his war while they lasted
and then he had been a Democrat because he could not vote
for smart Jim Blaine, the trafficker with railroads; then

Populism gave him a cause without a hero, and then Mr. Bryan was the hero of his cause in 1896. This was how he thought about things in a world without telephones, a world in which news was the county's newspaper or the babble along the road from the telegraph station when someone great died or a river flooded. He was a colonist, within his own country, unaware that he hurt his country's finances with manias and heresies, sure he was doing something fine for the United States out here on the prairies. He might have understood just the last sentence in William Sumner's arraignment of the colonial idea. " The notion is that colonies are glory. The truth is that colonies are burdens — unless they are plundered, and then they are enemies." This last he would have realized; he had been plundered. He was the enemy of the East, where all his good money, taken by the railroads, went to join the interest on his mortgage. It cannot be judged, now, whether he hated the railroads with their rates for shipping grain worse than he hated the mortgage. Let the son of such a man speak for him. This is Mr. William Dunn McCready, born in 1874 in southern Nebraska in a house four miles from town, half a mile from the next house, youngest of eight children and five sons. He first saw a metal faucet on a train taking him to Omaha for the funeral of an uncle, in 1884.

" There must have been faucets and similar appliances in our town, but I presume they were in the houses of our banker and the man who had the store. I was never admitted to those glorified precincts. The banker had a telephone put in about 1886. I can remember the profound sensation of the event. . . . I must try to convince you that our district was victimized by a kind of swindling that increased the hard times of 1891 and 1892. The railroad overcharged for everything. You know that it was cheaper to burn corn for fuel in 1888 and 1889 than to try to ship it. We were absolutely at the mercy of the railroads and the express companies. The performance of the Octopus [5] in California is always treated as an individual kind of high piracy in conventional books. What else did the middle Western states get, may one ask?

" Another form of swindling was that used by some store-keepers in such small communities. I know that a lot of sentimentalism has been expended on the dear old whim-sical fellow who has a general store by some of our writers of rural hokum. But the storekeeper was frequently a hard-fisted cheat. In 1890, when the McKinley tariff bill passed Congress, this smart Heinie in our town put up all prices ' on aggount of the dariff.' It was then that our banker came to the rescue. He told this robber baron to put the prices down or he would open an opposition store. Of course the storekeeper dropped his prices instanter. But it gave him an awful black eye with the community. He sold out to my uncle in 1891 and left town.[6]

" It was natural that our county went Populist in 1891 and 1892. I want to say for my father that he was about the only person who understood the fall of prices between 1885 and 1890. This was on account of his mania for geog-raphy. He comprehended that there were such places as Russia and the Argentine Republic. He would tell neigh-bors at calamity meetings that if Yurrupeans could get grain from South America and Rooshia for less than we sold it they would naturally buy it. But I swear that he was the only person I knew who did understand that. I am not saying we were a lot of fools. But the world was shut out from us and to a degree you people cannot get, even from the best descriptions in Willa Cather and *The Grand-mothers*. My dear old man did know a little about external conditions affecting the price of crops. On the other hand

[5] The Southern Pacific Railroad.

[6] Other storekeepers did the like in 1890. There are instances in Iowa, Ohio, Illinois, and Massachusetts known to me. Democrats were accused of this trick as propaganda unfavorable to the McKinley tariff.

he could not be made to understand that fiat money was not real money, any more than I could until your father banged it into my head at Saint Paul. He had been used to paper currency ever since he was a boy back in the fifties. If the government said a thing was money, it darned well was money. The Populists perfectly believed that in 1892, at the time of the convention in Omaha. They were so simple about anything financial that it is cruel for historians to laugh at them. Their delusion was this proposition: If the government will issue a lot of greenbacks per capita to the population of the United States, there will be more money in circulation and our crops will sell for more. If you tried to explain that this money was a drug in Europe and could not go abroad to purchase goods, they just did not get it. Europe was too far away. The Free Silver craze was part of the same delusion. I think I might say that they did not understand the depreciating quality of money at all, or so few of them understood it that it came to the same thing.

" May I add that the historians do not seem to realize the extent of the Free Silver advertising? It is funny to me that when this silver propaganda was so widespread and so openly shoved at us by men who were in the employ of the silver-miners nobody remarks the purely mercenary motive underlying the whole game. The silver-miners had a product to sell and they were trying to keep it sold by making up a bogus moral issue out of it. Because the suffering of the farm belt was intense and it really had been browbeaten and smacked behind by the railroad kings, it does not follow that Free Silver was anything but a financial hocus-pocus worked up by interested men. Bland, Bryan and Company were agents of the silver-miners, no matter how they stated the case to their consciences. The way the business is sentimentalized is what astonishes me. . . ."

In 1890 a remarkable instrument called the Sherman Purchase Act passed under President Harrison's pen and became law. Four million five hundred thousand ounces of silver bullion were to be purchased monthly and the Treasury was to issue against this gift to the silver-miners notes redeemable in coin at the discretion of the Secretary of the Treasury. This meant that the nation was to purchase approximately nine-tenths of the nation's monthly output of silver and that the Treasury could not refuse, since these notes were legal tender, to redeem them in gold if it was required to do so. Here was subsidy, in short. The silver-miners were secured from any loss by the people of the United States, and the people of the West were gravely informed by orators that this astonishing performance in pure capitalism was a method of giving the farmer a plentiful, assured currency.

The friends of silver did not discuss one or two facts. Silver was depreciating everywhere in the world, as they knew; all important countries of Europe were now using gold as the standard of value in finance. They knew this, as they knew that they were getting a subsidy for the silver mines and causing danger to the currency. But the act was signed and bankers began hoarding gold. Europe must be paid in gold, of course. . . . A bulk of silver dollars accumulated in the Treasury. Loans for small factories tightened at once. Little industries of the midlands were caught. In April of 1891 young Bill McCready came in from feeding the pigs and found the women petting one of his brothers. Nick had walked all the way down from Omaha when a factory closed, throwing sixty men out of work.

Many sons now came home to all these farms. If they were proud, they had come home on a visit; if they were honest, they had just come home. Democrats said it was the McKinley tariff and the banker said it was the Silver Purchase Act. But neither legislation produced the drought of 1891. That autumn one of the McCready boys took his long legs into the Army, the last resort in those days, and one of them tramped off down south to look for something to do in warm country, and Bill went up to a cousin in Saint Paul, on borrowed money, and found himself a job as an office boy at four dollars a week. This family of kind people split, under the mallet of his sacred majesty, hazard, and was never drawn together again.

Among callers at the office where Bill worked was a big young man of affairs, Mr. William Collins Beer, western agent of the National Surety Company. He would rave against the Silver Purchase Act by the hour or discuss it logically to any length. Mr. Beer was such an abominable mathematician that he had been decently discharged from West Point in 1883 after a battle with calculus. He could never add sums in his checkbook certainly, but he understood the movement of money. The office boy gaped, listening to Mr. Beer's prophecies of a panic. Having been born after 1873, Bill was not aware of panics. He had a secret thirst for mad, exciting things. He tried out older people asking them what had happened in 1873. One evening in June of 1892 he asked an amiable, stout man sitting beside him in the gallery of the Republican Convention at Minneapolis if he remembered anything curious in 1873.

The gentleman remembered all about it, and talked in short, undecorated sentences, saying " by God " a good deal. He spoke of suicides, ruined banks, and battered businesses, and the gang of clerks sitting with Bill listened to his stories instead of attending to the speeches which flowed down on the floor of the hall. This assemblage was distinguished and very dull, and the stout stranger seemed more amusing to these lads who had come over from Saint Paul to hear marvels. The only entertainment was Governor William McKinley of Ohio, president of the convention, who blandly conducted proceedings with a palm-leaf fan. Bill and his friends admired this personification of a statesman. The stout gentleman with the brown eyes admired Mr. McKinley, too, and told them many anecdotes of the Governor's kindness to all kinds of people. And what did they think of Thomas B. Reed?

They thought nothing of him. The fat, famous Speaker of the House of Representatives was no hero in the West. Out here he paid for his habit of being wittily rude to raw Congressmen. He was a smart man, the boys told the stranger, but. . . . Yes, the stranger argued, but what is it you have against him? Aw, said the nobodies, he's stuck up! They were all chattering their opinions, while the stout gentleman watched them with his brown eyes. People would talk to him torrentially and then wonder why they had talked, or what he had said to them, discovering at last that he had seldom opened his lips except to put a cigar between his teeth.

Mr. Hanna was gathering opinions. He had nominal headquarters of a McKinley movement at a hotel in Minneapolis, and there, on June 10th, 1892, he declined to combine his idol's admirers with those of Mr. Reed, although he was promised the Secretaryship of the Treasury for Mr. McKinley as a fee for helping Reed to the nomination. But he knew — he had been listening to the delegates — that this listless, discouraged convention would nominate Benjamin Harrison once more. He made no fight for his candidate, then, but was interested to idle in the gallery with these boys and to drive back with them to a respectable German beer-hall in Saint Paul. They liked him. He told them he was in the coal business, before he paid for the cabs and the beer and vanished. But, says Mr. McCready, " if anybody had told me what Mr. Hanna's name was . . . it would have meant absolutely nothing to me. I never heard of Mark Hanna from any source until the Hearst papers began cursing him in the spring of 1896. . . ."

Really, he was so located as to be unheard of. The Eastern newspapers discovered Chicago early enough in its his-

tory, but Cleveland remained unknown. Its rich folk were
not scandalous or showy; its politics had not the violent
quality essential to American fame. Easterners knew that
a street named Euclid Avenue existed, and actors knew that
Cleveland was a good town in their profession. Mr. Henry
Adler, for instance, was advancing on Cleveland in 1884
simply because it was a good town for the show business.
He was connected with the theater, in those days, only by
some pink ribbons and emotions, but he happened to be
reading a French technical magazine which contained
prints of theatrical machinery, and the stout man who
picked up the magazine for him asked to have legends under the plans translated. Mr. Adler was obliging, and discovered with interest that Mr. Hanna owned the Euclid
Avenue Opera House. As the young traveler was moving
to a seat in Mr. Hanna's theater because of the dazzling
lady who would tonight ravish Cleveland, he talked to Mr.
Hanna cordially and told him all about the lady. Mr.
Hanna must have said to himself, " You poor little fool! "
but he went on asking questions about theaters in France.
When the train reached Cleveland, he invited Mr. Adler to
dine at his house before the play.

In the hall of the big dwelling a small girl was uproari-
ously pretending to be a dog. Mrs. Hanna alarmed the
guest by showing signs of tearfulness. There had been another terrible editorial in the *Leader*! Mr. Hanna read
whatever his enemy Mr. Cowles had written about him that
day, grunted softly, and made the newspaper into a roll
which he tossed to his youngest child. Miss Ruth Hanna fell
on it and worried it.

" Marcus! You're not going to let her eat that ink! "

" Well, old lady," said Mr. Hanna, " it's the same kind
of ink we use on the *Herald*."

Gentlemen now swarmed into the house and a couple
more arrived when the crowd was seated. Mrs. Hanna told

Mr. Adler, shy at her right, that she never knew how many there would be for any meal; Mr. Hanna loved company. Yet, the new-comer asked, were they all in the theatrical business? Mrs. Hanna explained that her husband was interested in coal and iron, and owned the *Herald* as well as the opera-house, and was managing a street railway.

" But," she said, " you're from New York. I suppose the only man you've ever heard of in Cleveland is Johnny Rockefeller."

Down the table they were talking of actors. A florid, jolly boy announced that he didn't like Henry Irving. This Irving was a player who established a character with the audience by ten minutes of lucid and graceful performance and then, just when you didn't expect it, allowed his art to change into something richer and so strange. He gargled, hurtled, writhed, and yawped through some passage of simple emotion. He made Shylock a gibbering neurasthenic at one side of the stage and took him off at the other side as a nobly dignified English gentleman; he appeared as King Arthur in armor designed by Burne-Jones and declaimed for ten minutes so intensely that nobody knew what he was saying at all, but applauded him in a daze of apprehension lest they should not do the right thing. He became a fetich of the latter nineteenth century and was supposed to have contributed something to the pooled culture of England and America. Young Daniel Hanna did not like this actor, he said, because he was not like a human being.

"Don't you be a fool, Dan," Mr. Hanna grunted. " Why, you don't want a tragedian to act like a human being, do you? There wouldn't be any fun in that! "

But he judged comedians differently and watched them from his box in the Euclid Avenue Opera House with the attention he gave to a machine's first movement in a rolling-mill or to the conversation of his youngest child. Joseph Jefferson, William Florence, James Lewis, and the younger men as they rose were valued and discussed. His mouth would stiffen in contempt if a salty scene was allowed to drop into foolery; Mr. Hanna became an ugly, disapproving mask suspended above the public, scowling at the stage. When disapprobation was final, he began to rub an ear with a fist, and his emotion might take him out for a cigar in the lobby. If a play went sour, he was precisely the disappointed boy.

Actors loved him, because he complimented their profession by understanding it. He knew the mechanics of the game — how a fast exit was made and how one fell without breaking one's knees or smote down a villain without bruising one's knuckles. There were also big suppers at his club and occasional generous loans. He was not so familiar toward actresses. That night in 1884 he was taken into the dressing-room of Mr. Adler's bright lady, but stood silent, perhaps not sure that he was privileged in beholding her.

He became a habit of Henry Adler, idle, rich, and melancholy, as cultivated Jews so often were in that period of American society. When his lady led the boy to Cleveland he would drop in at the offices of Hanna and Company and sit for an hour beside Mark Hanna's desk while shipping men, naval architects, customers for coal and iron, and little officials of the swelling city filed in and out. He discovered why his broker in New York had never heard of the mighty Mr. Hanna. This was a lord of the Great Lakes. The formula of his father's success served Mr. Hanna. His iron ships rolled up to Milwaukee and Duluth to fetch back ore for the mills at Cleveland in gross quantity. He had allies in all the ports, men held to him by affection without contracts. But a hundred miles from the edge of the Lakes, Mr. Hanna ceased to be. He was blotted out in the mere size of America, and in New York he was unknown. Mr. Adler saw him walk through a crowd of bankers and business men one crowded night at Delmonico's with his youngest brother, Leonard, witout getting a nod. That was in 1888.

He had the fascination of a constant surprise for the clever idler. He knew so much; he knew nothing. An English tourist suggested that the United States would still be colonies of England if the Stamp Act had not been passed. Hanna thought and shook his head. No, the colonies and England would have quarreled in the nineteenth century as soon as the question of immigration from European countries commenced to be important. And his memory had picked up the system of Indian government with which to floor this same tourist in the same talk. And then he didn't know what the letters M.F.H. meant, or what the Reichstag was. He did not know the name of any eminent painter then alive, except James Whistler, but he spoke shrewdly and tartly about pictures sometimes, for his mechanical sense made Mr. Hanna keen on lines and curves. " He was certainly," Mr. Adler wrote in 1904, " one of the best and worst informed men I have ever known. . . ."

Just before Christmas in 1889 Mr. Adler's lady played in Cleveland and her victim walked into the office of Hanna and Company, and into a confusion of clerks around a weeping charwoman at whom Mr. Hanna was fairly roaring. To one side of this mess stood a beautiful little personage in a frock-coat who was trying to soothe Mr. Hanna. The rich man's eyes were yellow in anger and he would not stop shouting even when the Honorable William McKinley said, deeply, " Hanna, I'm ashamed of you! " Yesterday the major had been playing with a gold piece which he kept in his purse because his men gave it to him at the end of the war. He had left it on Hanna's desk when the millionaire took him away to dinner. And now where was it? Mr. Hanna did not care what she had done with it. He wasn't going to put her in jail. But, he shouted, she was to get back that " same, identical God-damn " coin from her husband or the saloon or the grocer, or, by God, he would find out who her priest was and tell him on her! . . . About then the gold piece rattled on Mr. Hanna's desk from the woman's hand. She slumped on her knees, inelegantly, and howled for pardon. Mr. Hanna stepped back from the suppliant and began to rub his ear. " Aw, get out of here! I'm not going to hurt you! "

Presently Mr. Adler was taking supper at The Players in New York with Lawrence Barrett and mentioned that one of the actors in the poor melodrama by Mr. Oscar Wilde in which Mr. Barrett was appearing looked like Marcus Hanna of Cleveland. The cold, superior tragedian positively warmed to an austere beam. He put his elbows on the table and talked about Hanna for an hour, saying that Mr. Hanna knew more of machinery than many engineers. " He's a human machine himself," the player said, " with a heart of gold." And then, on Mr. Adler's next visit to Cleveland, he saw the human machine at its function. Mr. Hanna sat on the floor of his office with Howard and Leonard Hanna perched behind him on his desk, all watching the model of a dynamo as it tried to lift a weight hitched to a tiny crane. There was an engineer to discuss things with the nervous inventor, but Mark Hanna gave judgment. He had nodded to Mr. Adler as if he had seen him yesterday, when his admirer came in. Then he went on studying his toy. . . . Would this thing do, or wouldn't it? . . . It wouldn't. His big head fell back. He looked at the inventor and said, " Not for me! "

He probably rejected Thomas Reed in the same fashion. He liked Mr. Reed, but Mr. Reed was not for him. He brought Mr. Reed out into Ohio to speak in William McKinley's campaign of 1891 and Reed was charmed by an evening party at Mr. Hanna's house. Cleveland gave the celebrity a good time, but rural Ohio did not like his speeches. The people laughed and applauded, and were not won to him.[7] There was nothing Lincolnian about Reed, obese, dapper, and sarcastic. He wasn't too friendly when they came up to shake hands after meetings. He was an Eastern product.

The swoop of American affairs between 1890 and 1896 made Mr. Hanna believe that no Easterner would do. In 1890 came the Silver Purchase Act. In 1891 business slackened. In 1892 here was the People's party in convention assembled crying out for government ownership of railroads and telegraphs, and for more silver to keep plenty of money floating into rural banks. The " soft money " heresy of 1868 had come alive again in this new form. Silver was the friend of the lowly and agricultural; silver was something clean and radiant, while gold was a red devil friendly to the rich of Wall Street. Gold was England's weapon against the United States. Gold was all wrong and silver was all right. Gold belonged to the capitalistic East, and silver was mined in the free and democratic West. . . . The Populists wanted other things. Explore the pamphlets and the lumbering speeches and you find the popular election of senators, the restriction of immigration, the subsidized farmer, the income tax, the regulation of rates for common carriers. You find everything, if you look, that had been stirring in the minds of reformers since the Civil War. Emotional politicians are seldom original; Mr. William Jennings Bryan, speaking rhythmic pieces at county fairs and religious festivals, heard all this chatter close to the soil, and listened attentively, his wits absorbed in the task of becoming a great orator.

---

[7] Mr. Hanna had employés listen to the effect of Mr. Reed on the crowds, he told my father. He never took Reed seriously as a possible President, his brothers assured Mr. Adler. I am told that a letter of Mr. Roosevelt to Nicholas Robertson, of San Francisco, makes a contrary assertion. But the letter dates from 1896, when Mr. Roosevelt was possibly influenced by his affection for Reed. It is well known that he wanted to see Mr. Reed nominated at Saint Louis in 1896.

A great malefactor rose in the East to collect upon himself the grievances of the West. President Grover Cleveland caused the repeal of the Silver Purchase Act in 1893, in the midst of the panic which sent young Bill McCready home from Saint Paul because his employer was ruined outright, and cost Henry Adler the favor of his bright lady, who, as Mark Hanna had warned him, wrung him as one wrings a moist rag and chucked him away when his income was suspended. In 1894 Mr. Cleveland sent federal troops into Illinois to aid in restraining the strikers at Chicago after Mr. George Pullman's stupidity brought about a general strike of railroad men, a thing costing more than has yet been computed. And here Mr. Hanna, furious in Cleveland, displayed himself in his odd duplex nature.

First he raged against Mr. Pullman for failing in common sense. The damned idiot ought to arbitrate, arbitrate and arbitrate! What, for God's sake, did the manufacturer think he was doing? He made a scene in the Union Club, surrounded by gentlemen who rather sympathized with Pullman. Mr. Myron Herrick tried to quiet him. Another friend claimed that Pullman had done fine things for his workmen. There was the town of Pullman, the model suburb, with its neat homes for workers and its pretty square and library. " Oh, hell! " said Marcus Hanna. " Model —! [8] Go and live in Pullman and find out how much Pullman gets sellin' city water and gas ten per cent higher to those poor fools! " He knew too much to take Mr. Pullman's claims as a philanthropist on the high plane. He knew too much about workingmen not to see that Pullman's stockholders, Eastern and midland, had forced the commonplace millionaire into a folly against the state. " A man who won't meet his men half-way is a God-damn fool! " His words sped out and came into Chicago; in 1896

[8] Primordial American noun, compound, meaning latrine.

there was a difficulty in collecting money for the Republican campaign fund from Mr. Pullman's office.

The odious and Eastern Cleveland went on affronting the West. He demanded of Congress that it help him get rid of the fluctuating currency which was making the Treasury a pool for capitalists who could collect gold on notes until the reserve of coin was low and then sell back to the government at their profitable convenience. He blundered and appealed to Wall Street for help in marketing bonds. Wall Street, in the person of Mr. John Pierpont Morgan, dealt out the bonds and collected handsomely for its services. Mr. Cleveland's second term of office was concluding in a series of crashes; it was Wagnerian music, politically expressed.

A certain madness, an apocalyptic tremor, passed about the world in this last phase of the nineteenth century. False scientists wrote novels on the end of the terrestrial globe, and flashy magazines printed them. An Englishman fancied the Martians invading London with poisonous smokes and flashing rays of heat that killed. Had the century failed, after all Macaulay had claimed for industrial machinery and progress, to make the world happier? Cheap men wondered what Christ would think of Chicago, as if the Nazarene would have concerned himself with Chicago any more than he valued things rendered to Cæsar which were Cæsar's anyhow. The disintegrating, halted Christian socialism of the century's middle period recurred in terms of emotion. Western speakers read *Progress and Poverty* again and there was talk in Kansas of the houses of Have and Want. Silly people in banks worried about revolutions. . . .

There was a nervous conversation at lunch in the Union Club at Cleveland. Someone got windy about a revolt. This Altgeld and that man Tillman from the South might

start something serious, with the Populists following them.
Mr. Samuel Mather laughed, saying that all the country
needed was some protection for its industries and solid
money. He left the room. Heads shook. Mr. Hanna took
his cigar out of his mouth and grunted, " Sam's right.
There won't be any revolution. You're just a lot of damn
fools."

That autumn all the youngsters who called him Uncle
Mark and hunted his advice on details of business had a
chill. Uncle Mark had quit! He had handed over his share
of Hanna and Company to his brother Leonard. He was
through. . . . He had taken a house in the South, at
Thomasville in Georgia. It was incredible. But it was true.
Mr. Hanna had retired from business. He really had not
time to manage Hanna and Company and squabble about
franchises of the street railways when he had to make William McKinley President of the United States.

III

THE Republican National Convention would convene on
June 16th, 1896, at Exposition Hall in Saint Louis, but Mr.
William Collins Beer arrived with the haste of all political
amateurs on the tenth of June. He arrived perspiring; heat
was already in possession of Saint Louis, and his room in
the Southern Hotel was a decorated oven. He was full of
ideas and advice which he yearned to bestow on the high
powers of the party at once. He wanted to have the United
States openly join the nations of Europe in declaring for
the gold standard in finance. The National Surety Company had transferred him to New York in 1893; he had met
Europeans and had dined with bankers and presidents of
life-insurance companies. His pockets were full of letters
introducing him to Eastern delegates, and he knew many
delegates from the states of Iowa, Minnesota, Nebraska,

and California. He wanted to meet the grandees. He was told that he must meet Mr. Hanna before he met anybody else.

He recoiled. Since April, Marcus Alonzo Hanna had been revealed in the newspapers owned by William Randolph Hearst as an amalgam of all sins. He was foulness compact. He was the Red Boss of Cleveland's politics. The town council trembled when he sent minions to address it. He had stolen a theater from poor John Ellsler, foreclosing a cruel mortgage and rejecting the man's pleas for time.[9] He ruled Cleveland from his office, terrorizing unions and ruining rival street railways. He sent poor sailors, forced on his ships by bestial labor masters, out to sea on the wintry Lakes, cold and starving, unpaid and mutinous. He had bought the poor old *Herald* and then had wrecked it, which meant that he had sold his newspaper after five years of steady loss, in 1885. He had corrupted William McKinley's government of Ohio. He was a hypocrite as well, affecting to be a strong churchman and drawing down the curtains of his house on the Lake when he had guests to Sunday dinner. Now the Red Boss lay in wait at St. Louis with a train of purchased Southern Republicans, ready to make McKinley the candidate of his party.

It was too wide an indictment for anybody to swallow whole, but Mr. Beer did not want to meet Marcus Alonzo Hanna. William McKinley was an old friend of his father. He would wait until he recognized some honest associate of the major. He hung about for two days, boiling his arguments for the gold standard in his head and drinking ice water. Then he gave in, and let Mr. Joseph Kimball lead him to Mr. Hanna's den on the floor below his own room in the Southern Hotel.

Mr. Hanna was a quiet object in a gray, plain suit, deep in a chair beside a bottle of mineral water, and placid as the

[9] See Appendix.

bottle, in a room packed with vociferous personalities. The only other placid thing in the room was a tall, comely gentleman, excellently clad, who leaned on a wall and fanned himself with a newspaper. Mr. Beer knew Myron Herrick by sight. They had met in the office of John McCall, president of the New York Life Insurance Company. But the other men were strangers, and, somehow, this heart of the great party wasn't imposing. Mr. Beer decided, suddenly, that the grandees were just noisy, worried men. They did not stop talking when he was presented to Mr. Hanna. Under cover of the noise Mr. Hanna's memory now ticked, adjusting itself to the problem standing before him, very hot.

"You from Ohio? . . . Son of Judge Beer?" The young man was startled. "H'm, your dad cost some friends of mine in the oil business a lot of money once." The young man was pleased. "Some Democrat judges," said Mr. Hanna, impersonally, " are a damn sight more honest than lots of Republican judges. . . . Let's see — " the memory caught at something — "Got an uncle down at Ashland, haven't you?" But, the young man thought, this is omniscience! "And now," said the Red Boss, "what's it you want to tell us about the platform?"

The amateur spoke. There had to be a statement in the Republican platform promising outright that the party stood for the gold standard. He had heard that Mr. Hanna was a bimetallist and he knew that McKinley had dallied with Free Silver in a cautious speech. He now attacked Mr. Hanna with statistics and financial reports. He soared into complexities of English banking and hopped the width of Europe to speak of Russia. He quoted from the resolutions of European conferences and congresses. He recited the wisdom of Mr. John McCall, although Mr. McCall was a Democrat. The grandees listened. Mr. Beer discovered in himself a talent for oratory and he talked and talked. Fero-

cious voices answered out of the jam. Two Westerners retorted with arguments from essays of theoretical professors. Mr. Beer's rapid tenor voice shut them up. He had
begun by talking to Mr. Herrick and Mr. Hanna. He was
now personally identified with the forces of sound finance;
he was the gold standard defending itself against Free Silver. He threw out an emotion while his collar wilted and
his clothes darkened with sweat. His throat was raw when
he stopped talking.

"Very interesting," said Mr. Hanna.

The others were more cordial. Mr. Herrick asked the
young man to dine. Mr. Beer walked, dripping, down the
corridor with Mr. Kimball, sure that he had saved
the United States from another panic. When Mr. Kimball
cackled and fell against a wall, he could not imagine what
was the matter with the gentle little man from Arizona.

"You're about the hundredth person who's made that
speech in there. Don't mind me!"

Mr. Beer went off to his bedroom and sternly took a
bath. His father had always warned him that Republicans
were coldly perfidious. He had been allowed to entertain
the Red Boss and the rest of them for half an hour. He
would leave Saint Louis directly. He would report to Mr.
McCall and the president of the National Surety Company
that Mark Hanna was a thug and a churl. He was moping
in fresh underclothes on his bed, waiting for a page to bring
him up more iced lemonade, when Mr. Hanna trundled in,
bearing a cigar and a long sheet of typed names.

"Know any of these men, son?"

The bruised amateur looked down the list. He saw that
this was the mass of the Silver faction in the party, delegates, bankers, editors of newspapers. Yes, he said, he had
met many of them on his trips for the National Surety. He
said so with a deal of injured dignity. Mark Hanna stared
at him.

503

" All these men are in town already. Go and talk to 'em.
Feed 'em. If you run out of money, come to me. If you
can't catch me, see Herrick. If he ain't around, get hold of
Andrew Squire."

Mr. Beer had plenty of money for dinners. But just
what did the man want? He asked, " Am I to say that
you — "

" You're not to say anything about me. You," said Mr.
Hanna, " go and talk gold to those men. Tell them everything you told us."

He was not even polite. He trundled out. But the dynamo in the gray suit had energized the bruised young
man on the bed. It is emblematic that Mark Hanna was one
of the first, if not absolutely the first, of industrialists to
attach a dynamo directly to a machine. He had the quality
possessed also by Theodore Roosevelt and Tom Johnson
in his times. He could energize. Mr. Beer pulled on his
clothes and went into operation, armed with many lozenges
for his delicate throat, certain that Mr. Hanna was for gold.
He commenced a round of the hotels and wallowed in the
society of men who wanted something done for Silver.

This Silver faction was partly made up of bimetallists,
men who believed, quite correctly, that there was nothing
wrong with a double standard of money. There was nothing wrong with bimetallism, except that international finance condemned it. The trouble of these gentlemen was
that finance was not international to them, but American.
They still did not comprehend what James Garfield had explained to Congress in 1868. Truly, they were victims of
their sentiment for the American life. Money-making was
the permitted field of the search for power in that America,
and they had grown up in that rhythm. Men worked; work
was life. And while that rhythm, now broken, lasted in its
strength, this American life satisfied; they were happy men,
memorable in their enthusiasms, more charming than their

504

sons who cannot believe in business as they believed.

But the bimetallists who thought that American interest was somehow damaged by submitting to the rules of world-finance were in a minority. The bulk of the Silver faction was made up, candidly, of the politicians to whom silver-mining was a home industry, a local issue. They wanted to see the Silver Purchase Act of 1890 restored and maintained; in other words they wanted the silver mines subsidized at the expense of the United States. They were bitten with fright and selfishness, of course, and among them moved quietly Mr. William Jennings Bryan suggesting that, if the Republican party rejected their patriotic enterprise on behalf of the plain people, they would find friends in the Democratic party.[10]

There were plenty of bitter Republicans entering Saint Louis from the East on every fast train, followers of Thomas Reed, and henchmen of Thomas Platt and Matthew Quay. They came to the convention knowing that this unknown monster of Cleveland had already secured William McKinley's nomination. His allies had caused the Republican conventions of nine states to pledge delegates to support Mr. McKinley, and the Southern Republicans of the " rotten boroughs," as Foraker called them, were loyal to the major. Mr. Hanna could thumb his nose at the Eastern bosses and the Eastern aspirants. His hero had refused to promise offices to Platt and Quay in exchange for their favors. All right, Mr. Hanna could do without the Eastern machines. His own machine supervened. The clever men of the party knew what had happened; Mr. Hanna, of Cleveland, Ohio, was the master of this occasion. But that was not enough. Mr. Hanna was doing what he should not; instead of being solemn and dignified, Mr. Hanna was amused. His mouth wiggled into grins as he stood in the

[10] Mr. Bryan was reporting the convention for a newspaper in Omaha. His own memoirs assert that he " conferred " with the Silver delegates.

lobby of the Southern Hotel with reporters purring and clawing his sleeves; he was openly entertained at his own show.

Meanwhile his human machine worked in the boiling of hot, discomfited men in those hot rooms and restaurants. Five unpaid amateurs were tackling the Silver faction. Mr. Beer spent all one night in useless argument with Richard Pettigrew of South Dakota, and crossed trails with another amateur in the rooms of Senator Teller of Colorado. Mr. Hanna himself was working out a subtle bit of fencing with a less public faction. Experts saw that a committee of the American Protective Association, the half-secret anti-Catholic society, was worming after Mark Hanna as he flitted from hotel to hotel. A messenger shot from Hanna's quarters to a quiet lawyer in Saint Paul on the fastest train and, suddenly, there was a vehement telegram from the great Monsignor Ireland demanding that the Republican party should not disgrace itself by any action against his sect. The telegram was published. There could be no further question of conciliating the A.P.A. Mr. Hanna was much surprised by Monsignor Ireland's telegram.[11] He was about to be described by a sensitive Eastern observer as " coarse, insolent and incapable of tact in the detail of politics. . . ." What is tact?

His machinery moved in triple time. He had three problems. He must conciliate the East, if he could. He must keep the Silver faction in the party, if he could. He must clearly have the convention declare for the gold standard in its published platform. A declaration for sound cur-

---

[11] Mr. Maury in *Wars of the Godly* correctly points out that Ireland's telegram kept the religious row alive and really strengthened the A.P.A. But the pressure on Mr. Hanna was serious. Many of the delegates from the central states were touched by Protestant bigotry. Senator Allison of Iowa had a violent scene with a man named Murchison who attacked him before my father and John Baldwin on behalf of the A.P.A. Saint Louis was full of religious busybodies, on both sides of the quarrel.

rency would be insufficient. So he blended two of his problems. Let the Easterners themselves force him to declare for gold, then, by all means. The grandees were heavily telling him that he must get a firm statement for the gold standard written into the platform, and they went on telling him so through Saturday and Sunday. Next autumn several dignitaries muddied the rill of history by declaring that they, severally, had caused the words " the existing gold standard must be maintained " to be written into the platform. Three Eastern politicians made this assertion and, in sketches of the episode, written by Easterners of recent times, their assertions still seem to be believed. But on Friday night Senator Redfield Proctor of Vermont told Charles Gleed, a Vermont man transplanted in Topeka, Kansas, that the wording of the sentence had been accepted by Mr. McKinley and Mr. Hanna before dinner. On Saturday morning William Merriam of Minnesota whispered to Mr. Beer that a gold standard plank was in the platform. At half past nine the young amateur telegraphed to the National Surety Company: " It is all right." However, the Easterners continued on Saturday and Sunday to force Mr. Hanna to declare for gold. Mr. Thomas Platt, Mr. Henry Cabot Lodge, Mr. Edward Lauterbach, and several others addressed this dunder-headed millionaire, with the authority of older politicians and cultivated financiers. His reluctance showed them what a fool he must be. They suffered a great deal.[12]

[12] " Why does Hanna not come out and tell these prominent burglars the truth? The gold standard sentence was in the platform by Friday night or else Proctor and Merriam are a couple of liars. He is pretty deep. . . ." Charles Gleed to William C. Beer, November 20th, 1896.

" I think Mr. Hanna was right to let it seem that the eastern end of the party forced his hand in declaring for the gold standard. Herrick and he had it all arranged when they came to Saint Louis. Lodge never got there until Sunday. He came on the same train I did. His claim is just one of his conceited pieces of bragging. I suppose he thinks he had something to do with it." Bruce Higginson to William C. Beer, August 1st, 1896.

HANNA

Late on Sunday night the dunder-headed millionaire made a play for Senator Cannon of Utah, the best speaker of the Silver faction. He did not know Senator Cannon, even by sight, and Cannon had pungently refused to meet the Red Boss. But William Beer had soothed and blandished a follower of Mr. Cannon, a jolly parasite named Ira Gillis, and he led this conquest to Mr. Hanna's rooms. Mr. Hanna received his callers informally, in a nightshirt, and demanded at once their opinion on his ankles. Some red blotches had appeared. Were they hives? He would not be assured that this was just prickly heat.

" A fortune teller told me this spring I was going to have a bad summer. I had hives all the summer of the Centennial. I can't stand 'em! "

He tramped the room, directing his attack on Mr. Gillis. Gillis could tell the Senator that Mr. McKinley would send a commission to Europe to find out whether an agreement in favor of international bimetallism could be reached. No reason why all that silver should be wasted. He and the major both hated to think of it. But you couldn't run the country on depreciated currency. He picked up a bit of cold toast from a tray. If all the nations of the world agreed this toast was money, it was money, and gold would be worthless as silver, and silver would be more worthless than it was now. Couldn't Cannon and Teller and Pettigrew see reason? . . . Mr. Beer saw this stout, worried man in the flapping nightshirt become dignified, leaning on a little table and holding a piece of greasy toast as he talked in harsh, short sentences. . . . Did the Silver Senators want to see another panic? Didn't they know that, back east and as far as Chicago, able workmen were starving and shopgirls going on the streets? He promised that the major would do what he could for Silver. And if Mr. Cannon had been reading the stuff in the newspapers about M. A. Hanna, let him wire any man in Cleveland, even

Tom Johnson, by God, and see if M. A. Hanna ever broke a contract! He had promised; he would have a commission sent.

"I've been in the coal and iron business pretty near thirty years. You go and roust out a man that's done business with me and see if I don't fill my contracts!"

Mr. Beer left him talking and did not see Mr. Hanna again until the convention assembled, but he saw Mr. Gillis and even tried his hand on the decorative Senator from Utah. He was sitting in the gallery close to Gillis when the gold plank was read out. Mr. Cannon's friend turned to grin at him. An hour later Teller and Cannon had made their speeches. The Silver delegates washed from the hall, and even Henry Cabot Lodge joined in the yells as the rebels stalked out.

Nominations were now in order. William Allison, of Iowa, was nominated by John Baldwin. Thomas Reed was proposed by Henry Lodge. Levi Morton, of New York, was inaudibly tendered by Chauncey Depew. Senator Joseph Benson Foraker of Ohio then put the name of William McKinley in nomination, never looking toward Mr. Hanna. The applause lasted twenty-five minutes. . . . The obedient Governor of Pennsylvania now nominated Matthew Quay, who had sense of humor and liked to display it indirectly. The roll of the states was called. Mr. McKinley had six hundred sixty-one and one-half votes. His nomination was made unanimous. Delegates bawled for Hanna, and people stood up in the galleries for a first glimpse of this new power. Young Bill McCready jumped, recognizing the plain citizen who had been so friendly at Saint Paul as the plump figure appeared on the platform. . . . Mark Hanna faced the crowd and barked out some limping sentences, his hands behind his back, his face watering his collar, and then he beamed at the collected party just as a child smiles when its birthday cake comes to the table,

People ebbed downward from the gallery. Mr. Beer saw a group around his wife's cousin, John Baldwin, who had nominated Senator Allison, and walked over to join it. He was standing with ladies in the medley when a tall, dramatic man shoved past him to shake hands with Mr. Baldwin, rolling out a flattery on " your beautiful oratorical effort . . ." in a wonderful, clear voice. Men from Omaha and Council Bluffs grinned at each other. Why couldn't Bill Bryan have said what he wanted to say without all that bosh about beautiful oratorical efforts? . . . But the ladies turned their little feathered hats as Mr. Bryan's curly dark head steered away into the press.

IV

" THE ODDEST thing about Hanna," Theodore Roosevelt said, on November 13th, 1916, " was that numbers of intelligent people thought him a fool. . . ." This impression, to be sure, had been riveted by the cartoons in the spring of 1896 producing Mr. Hanna as an obese moneybag or a stupid man lugging a hurdy-gurdy, with McKinley as a dejected monkey hitched to his master's wrist. None of that, though, excuses the subtle bankers and political lawyers in New York who, at a conference before the first of July, decided on McKinley's cabinet for him. Having decided on the cabinet, they went the further length of offering each other places in it, or " sounding out " various men to find that posts would be accepted. Colonel John McCook was airily appointed Attorney General of the United States in this manner, and Mr. Chauncey Depew, it was heard from the neighborhood of his offices, was to be Secretary of the Treasury. As for Mr. Hanna, he was said to be yachting off the coast of Maine, on the second of July, and they did not bother about him. Perhaps he would like to be an ambassador or something. Mr. Hanna was in

Cleveland, really, but, for all the New Yorkers cared, he might be at Monte Carlo. Out of sight was out of mind. Soon enough these smokes were blown askew. The voice of Mr. William Jennings Bryan sounded from Chicago, in the swells and pauses of a beautiful oratorical effort, and the East became poignantly aware of a great leader in the West, acclaimed as a new Lincoln, a son of the plain people, nominated by the ecstatic accord of the plain people.

At the time of Mr. Bryan's death, editors refused to print articles on his career in which commentators mentioned that his nomination by the Democrats at Chicago in 1896 wasn't a thunderbolt. But since 1925 Mr. Silas Kent and Mr. Charles Willis Thompson have asserted the truth: Mr. Bryan had a considerable following before he appeared in Chicago, and it had been guessed by several Republican observers that he might win the Democratic candidacy. Senator Allison of Iowa, among others, accounted Bryan a dangerous man in May of 1896. So did Harvey Scott of the *Oregonian*, out in Portland. So did Charles Gleed in Topeka, Kansas. So did Redfield Proctor in Vermont. Their letters on the topic exist. Nevertheless, the melodrama of his appearance and his famous speech are dear possessions of history, and your great-grandsons will probably read in schoolbooks that this handsome fanatic conquered the Democratic convention in 1896 by a single speech and so made himself a political hero. It will be true and untrue. He would not have been nominated except that he seized the nomination with cordial intent, and his speech was a deliberated, reliable method of seizure.

Properly analyzed, this address is an arpeggio of appeals to popular belief and prejudice, each paragraph calculated to rouse emotion. It contains a fuse for the conceit of the pioneer, a defiance of England, a gesture toward the cemetery, and a suggestion of Christian martyrdom. He

511

made the Republican party wicked by four strokes of the voice and lifted himself into the position he kept until death took the American people from him. He became a moral force, as uncritical persons understand morality, and his more critical opponents had to resort to calling him wicked in turn. That Mr. Bryan, enemy of capitalism, was the half-conscious agent of a faction of capitalists, the silver-miners, and that he proposed to crucify the plain people on a cross of depreciated silver are obvious facts. His sincerity is no longer important. " If you tell a crowd of Americans that you are a good man," said David Graham Phillips, " they will politely take you at your word. . . ." Mr. Bryan's virtue was announced. He was nominated for the presidency of the United States and at once began operations as an eager artist in success.

One of his most efficient enemies was a wrecked, fidgeting middle-aged lady in the small town of Canton, Ohio. She was effective in a quiet but condign manner. By direction of his friends Major McKinley stayed at home, speaking to deputations and pilgrimages from every quarter of the United States. These deputations couldn't get off the train at Canton without learning that McKinley was a devoted husband to an epileptic wife. Ladies often came with their own husbands to meet the Republican candidate and were impressed, although Mrs. McKinley was not displayed, and the curiosity of the deputations as to her health annoyed McKinley so acutely that several times he had her driven off to the farm of an old friend when his front lawn would be full of Republican pilgrims. But sympathy for the gentle little man poured out of Canton as the pilgrims retired. While women in crowds everywhere gulped as William Jennings Bryan spoke of God's will, and his curls glowed and his eyes flashed, other women talked of William McKinley's virtues. And everything was grist that came to mill in the summer of 1896.

THE HUMAN MACHINE

The general tone of talk at Republican headquarters in Chicago and New York was angry confidence. Of course McKinley would thrash Bryan, and thrash him completely. But there was an undertone. Mr. Hanna's machinery worked with a delightful smoothness. There seemed plenty of money for the pay of speakers, for brass bands, bunting, golden elephants of paper or metal, and posters. Only on July 20th the major was almost fantastically glad to hear that the population of Nantucket Island, off Massachusetts, was solidly Republican, and on July 29th Mr. Hanna acknowledged a load of Republican pledges and some news from Connecticut forwarded to him by way of Canton with a singular warmth. Everything seemed all right in New York. Clergy and bankers and owners of huge department stores denounced Free Silver cordially. Mr. Cornelius Bliss received journalists at the Republican bureau and talked with grave assurance. Good news was always coming in and going out. But on August 5th John Hay wrote to Henry White in London: " I find the feeling a little nervous; unnecessarily so, I think. I talked with Hanna and some of the Executive Committee, and while there is nothing like dread of defeat, there is a clear comprehension that Bryan will get the votes of a good many others of his kind, and that it will require more work than we thought necessary last spring to beat him. . . ."

Mr. Hanna came unostentatiously to New York on August 3rd and conferred with selections of the leaders. The feeling, as Hay wrote, was a little nervous. Americans were then more dignified, if they were men, than they are today and it was not considered form to display fright. It trickled out among the workers of the party that there was a good deal to be done. Mr. Hanna's idea of what was to be done scandalized Colonel John McCook so that he scribbled to William Beer: " I wish that Hanna would not talk so freely about money. But I know that we are going to

513

need more. It is disappointing that a Democrat like [John] McCall has more sense of the real situation than Mr. Depew. Depew's attitude is simply disgusting. It is turning out the stiffest campaign since the war. . . ."

It was, but the Lincolnian figure was not in the Republican party, and Mr. Hanna knew that a lot of money was needed against the shadow of the Liberator. Bryan's weakness, as Hanna knew, was what Harry Thurston Peck rhetoricized in 1905; Mr. Bryan had picked up the wrong weapon. He was making his campaign on Free Silver. " He's talking Silver all the time," said Mr. Hanna, " and that's where we've got him. . . ." He sat in a chair at the Union League Club with another bottle of mineral water at his elbow and faced the New Yorkers, his cane across his knees. The proper Republicans of the metropolis were upset and stood staring at the obtuse coal-merchant from Cleveland who thought they should raise three million more dollars for the campaign fund. Money! Wouldn't he see that revolt was threatening? It was very well to say that Mr. Bryan was not in favor of abolishing the Supreme Court or confiscating railroads and telegraphs. Those were notions of the Populists. But the Populists were backing this bastard Lincoln! Altgeld was a maniac, ready to plunder the cities in Bryan's name. A somber wave thundered from the West. And Mr. Hanna sat talking of speakers and brass bands and educational pamphlets on sound money when the world was turning upside down, as if mere words and music could stop this thing.

Something furious stirred the air around heads of children on sea beaches. Ladies were gasping, with hand on corsets, about rebellion and the horrible things John or Mason had told them about Mr. Bryan. Mr. Bryan was a black tower, like the Iron Man in *The Garden Behind the Moon,* smoking as he strode about in a clangor of bands, inciting revolution. You might be told that Mr. Bryan was a harmless person, normally resident in Lincoln, Nebraska, who thought the country would be better off if silver dollars were coined at a ratio of sixteen to one gold dollar. But even the voice of a father assuring you that he'd often talked to Mr. Bryan in Omaha and Lincoln without being damaged was not conclusive. Bridget could soothe. The matter was simple to her in the kitchen, because Monsignor Ireland himself had spoken against this crazy man from out west, and the saints were with Mr. McKinley, that was good to his wife in her trouble, and so don't you fret, and, for God's sake, be taking that dog out of this place, now! Still it was slightly awful to be a child in the summer of 1896.

The East took fright and high regions of the Republican party were troubled. Mr. Hanna did not seem to be spending enough money on New York. The metropolis heard that Mr. Hanna was trying to carry the midland states for McKinley. But the metropolitans saw no sense in that. John McCook was exasperated and delivered a whole lecture on the importance of the midlands to an audience in the Union League Club one afternoon, and Mr. Theodore Roosevelt followed up his stately exposition of the point with a few words. The metropolitans were not convinced. A young man of large means and advertised name drawled that he had arranged for a *maisonnette* in Versailles. If a man like this Bryan was going to run the country, he would certainly leave it. He then left the room. Mr. Roosevelt said in falsetto, " There might be compensations in seeing Mr. Bryan elected! " But it was a serious little meeting, for Mr. Bryan was soon to accept the Democratic nomination before a mob in Madison Square Garden. People were betting that the new Liberator would carry New York and Connecticut. And this fool of a Hanna was wasting money on the middle West!

Mr. Hanna returned to New York. He was there on Au-

515

gust 15th, again, in a gray suit, drinking mineral water. Also there was James J. Hill, the railroad king, who had words to say in certain offices. Mr. William Rockefeller did some rapid telephoning from his house in the Hudson valley. Mr. Cornelius Bliss went personally, in a closed carriage, from place to place around the lower end of the city. Late at night twenty or thirty checks were in Mr. Hanna's wallet, and a new phase commenced in the high regions of the party. The bluff of the Wall Street set had been called, in one day, and a number of men who'd been talking of the sums they had paid to the Republican campaign fund had now actually paid those sums. There was also a new tone in remarks made about the dunder-headed millionaire from Cleveland. " The feeling about Mr. H.," William Beer writes on August 20th, to Mr. Harvey Fleming in Kansas City, " has changed. He has made a lot of these people see that he knows what he is doing. But there is a bad scare here. . . ."

Pastors, politicians, and even some gentlewomen broke out and raved against Mr. Bryan. The scare was bad. Behind the plunging orator in his private car was this wave of queer names and uncomprehended identities, Altgeld, the anarchist, Debs, the socialist, Populists, and Silver Republicans. Bryan was cursed grotesquely, in speeches violent with fear. And under the fear was a little justification. An element of the Populists did a good deal of vicious talking on street corners and in railroad yards. Threats were chalked on coaches of the fast express trains. A spellbinder named Fletcher dropped in a fit as he howled against the Rockefellers in a crowd at Coney Island on the first of September. Cartoons showed Hanna and McKinley discussing policies across a whisky bottle. Slander, to be sure, was so current that it moved into McKinley's own party. Men who knew the candidate were cornered and asked, confidentially now, if McKinley wasn't pretty much of a sot. And wasn't there something funny about his wife? [13]

The failure of Mr. Bryan's speech of acceptance in New York, introduced at unutterable length by the Governor of Missouri, did not cheer the men at Republican headquarters. On September 8th John Hay wrote to Henry Adams: " He [Mr. Bryan] has succeeded in scaring the Goldbugs out of their five wits; if he had scared them a little they would have come down handsome to Hanna. But he has scared them so blue that they think they had better keep what they have got left in their pockets against the evil day." On the same day he wrote to Mrs. Charlton Paull: " And are you going to join the grand exodus from our wayward native land that is to occur when the Goldbugs are squashed under the heel of Silver's champion? Many of my friends are saving their money for the purchase of suitable residences in Paris. Shall we next meet on the Place de la République? " He might be gay on paper, but he was privately rasped. He broke out, in that week, dashing a newspaper from him, " They dare to call this mountebank a new Lincoln! " And this hurt, everywhere. It

---

[13] " I know that Mr. Hanna has refused to answer any of the libels as to himself. His position is sound. But I think this low campaign against Mr. and Mrs. McKinley ought to be dealt with. . . . The offices [of Wells, Fargo and Company] report that scandals are in circulation in Missouri and Kansas. Several men of some intelligence have asked me if it is true that Mrs. McKinley is an English spy. These reports prejudice a certain kind of second rate citizen intensely. . . ." Dudley Evans to William C. Beer, August 27th, 1896.

" Horrible stories are being told about McKinley's habits by Popocrats out here. He is called a common drunk and a deadbeat. A letter of Tom Johnson is circulated showing him up as a general reprobate who swindled the state of Ohio out of three millions on some deal for new poor houses. . . . You have no idea how the country brethren love free Silver. Tried to explain to one yesterday that 16 to 1 does not mean he will have 16 times the money he has now. He called me a liar. . . ." Nicholas Lemke, in Fresno, California, to William C. Beer, August 30th, 1896.

" We are all of the opinion that it would do harm to answer the slanders on Mrs. McKinley. My brother thinks it would make the matter worse. . . ." Howard Melville Hanna to Cornelius Bliss, September 1, 1896.

roused old generals of the Civil War; it disgusted a son of Robert Lee; it even made men shrug who had not loved Abraham Lincoln. Yet there it was, the image of the tall man from the West, the new folk-hero.

On the 9th of September William Beer was quietly summoned to the office of Cornelius Bliss in New York and there told that an idea, proposed to Mr. McKinley through Julius Whiting of Canton, had been approved at last by Mr. Hanna. Mr. Beer was to be allowed to conduct a special train containing some famous veterans of the Civil War through the West and middle West, making a demonstration for Major McKinley. Mr. Beer knew that his invention was already accepted by Hanna. Howard Hanna had sent him word from Cleveland that the generals were being collected. But he beamed on Mr. Bliss and said he was proud of the trust conferred on him by the party. He knew all the right things to say, by this time, for he had created an awkwardness at a luncheon by observing that some converted Democrats, speaking in the metropolis for Mr. McKinley on salary, were not worth what it had cost to convert them. This episode taught him that the inner mechanism of political conversion should not be mentioned abruptly. So he beamed at Mr. Bliss and reached for his hat. . . . The grandee twiddled a cigar on a brass tray, glancing at the shut door. As Mr. Beer had to report to Mr. Hanna in Chicago, would he — er — deliver a list of suggestions made by some — well — important people to Mr. Hanna. Bliss allowed his flat mortification to appear. But these people were handsome contributors to the funds, and. . . . Mr. Beer copied down a list of sixteen suggestions and told Mr. Bliss that he expected to be kicked out of Mark Hanna's office; the important people, vestrymen of correct churches and what not, were willing to turn the election into a religious feud. They had listened to anti-Catholic tattle. They proposed to antagonize every

Irishman in the United States by hinting that Monsignor Ireland's support of McKinley was insincere, and accusing prominent communicants of the Catholic Church of secretly aiding Altgeld's "German anarchists." Nevertheless, the list must go to Marcus Hanna, since these were important people, as importance was judged in New York. One of them gave exigent balls and another had been an ambassador, and another saw himself in Mr. McKinley's cabinet as Secretary of War.

Mr. Hanna was checking over a new pamphlet on sound money when the bearer of this idiotic document came before him on September 13th. After reading the suggestions he said nothing, but Mr. Beer now discovered that Mark Hanna's eyes seemed yellow when he was angry. He threw the paper on his desk and asked in a chugging, metallic voice, "Who gave you that God-damn stuff?" When he was answered, this unpoetic man leaned back in his chair and spoke in a figure. He was like a weight in the middle of a seesaw, he said, and both ends of the plank had damned fools on them. As for poor Bliss, he couldn't help himself. As for this lot of God-damn sheep in Wall Street, it would serve them right if Bryan kicked them to hell and gone. What were they made of? All you got out of most of them was a thousand dollars and a lot of condescension. If they had been allowed to nominate Tom Reed, Bryan would have walked over them. They could not even see the sense of his simple pamphlets against Free Silver. They couldn't see anything! Give him a farmer or a laboring man who wasn't a lunatic and he could make the man see the fallacy in Bryan's money scheme. "They'll read this stuff," he said, slapping the pamphlets. "It gets on to the table in the sitting-room and they read it!"

His breath gave out. He stopped. Then he was imperious. Mr. Beer was to tear up the list and not to talk about it. Mr. Hanna would send on some thoughts to New York.

519

His ugly mouth relaxed. He began to laugh. It was a funny world! Here he was, with his name mud in the Democratic papers, trying to keep the country out of a panic! He saw the humor of his own position: the Red Boss was the friend of the plain people in this pass, and their champion was their enemy. An irony made the pragmatist outweigh the idealist and moralist. By God, it was a funny world! . . . He chuckled, and roared for his secretary, dictating a curt order to all the railroads, commanding passage for General Alger and his party, and then rapidly told Mr. Beer how to get along with General Howard and General Sickles.[14]

The young amateur now entered on a crazy period of nights in a circle of cigars — he did not smoke — and heard the Civil War rehearsed in a purely professional way without compliments or sentiments. He dove from the train at all hours into towns still unknown to satire, hunting Bourbon whisky, bottled milk, liver-pills, and mineral waters for his convoy. He had to suppress the grandson of one hero who was learning to use a pea-shooter and tried its range on hats in Kentucky, where gray Confederate coats showed in the crowds alongside the halted train. He lay sleepless while a wooden leg which General Sickles sometimes wore got loose from its place in the darkness and rolled furiously down the line of berths as the train ascended slopes. He descended among the people with Republican pamphlets, or express agents sweated through the mob to meet him with fresh boxes of ammunition, buttons and leaflets and flags. He knew all the words of the

[14] This conversation is summarized from an extended report rendered by my father to the president of the National Surety Company. The report excludes any description of the questions submitted by the important personages to Mr. Hanna, which were naturally confidential as between Mr. Bliss and Mr. Beer. Mr. Hanna's order to the railroads is interesting, as it is dictated to the general managers of the lines, describing the railroads merely by initials, as " C.B. & Q." It was Mr. Beer's only authority for the transportation of the special train, but no manager questioned it, although the traffic of the roads must have been seriously distracted.

speeches that would be made and blessed General Howard for an impromptu, now and then. He fed bandsmen jujubes for their blasted throats and settled a quarrel between a cornet and a bugle over a wench in Nebraska. He struggled with the lunacies of reception committees and county chairmen. He played checkers with General Stewart, and ruined his palate for a day while testing a cocktail made by General Sickles. Outside the train a sentiment shouted, sometimes sobbed, as these old men spoke; inside it, Mr. Beer wondered why anybody ever went into politics. And were not unlimited monarchies the best governments, after all? And were not tribes in Africa happy without money, tariffs, and policies? He hated everybody on cold October mornings when General Sickles whistled an air from *Rigoletto* or General Howard spoke with feeling of the wronged Indians. But he was fighting Free Silver.

So the machine swept against the Democrats in an explosion of pamphlets, blue and gold emblems, placards, and voices. A dynamo whirred inside Mark Hanna's head. This man knew how to carry West Virginia? Send him speakers or money to hire them. Crowds in California liked a lot of music? Give it to 'em! . . . Two or three times in quiet rooms he let friends know his contempt for New York. It had taken Jim Hill and Bliss working like hell to make those sheep see what they must do for him. . . . But the top of the scare was passing. Money poured out of stately offices in New York and Boston. The oiled machine ran smoothly. On October 28th he thanked Henry Adler for a check, but returned it, writing: " It is all over. Reports are satisfactory just where we wanted them most." He had broken Mr. Bryan's sorceries in the middle states. There was jubilation already among his workers because now the farmers were scared of a panic, if Silver won. He threw away an affidavit brought to him by Bruce Higginson proving that Democrats had bought promises of votes in

Louisville. "What the hell of it? They're licked, anyhow!"

On Saturday before election day a parade of one hundred and fifty thousand men passed up Broadway in New York City. It included even the languid millionaire who'd been thinking of a *maisonnette* in Versailles. The city gasped at this monstrous production of so many well-dressed men, so many gilded elephants, so many buttons, so much colored bunting. It was mass production, politically applied, and it stunned watchers. . . . On the night of November 3rd the clubs in Chicago and New York were filled with men who never drank and were not drinking, but gabbled drunkenly among men who spilled champagne on the floors as they waltzed with each other, for it was over; McKinley was elected. Trains were creaking from the cities of Ohio toward Canton, loaded with Republicans who howled. . . . It was all over, but it did not seem true. A funny disbelief ran through the streets. Workmen who had been told that their jobs were lost if Bryan was elected were afraid to go home, as if he might win yet should they leave the telegraph boards or the saloons. And some emotions cracked in the darkness, since the new Lincoln had been madly followed, insanely trusted with a violence which would not be believed today. . . . A little girl watched the bonfires from her father's steps in southern Ohio, sleepily pleased that he had been returned to a petty office in the town, and a German stumbled up to her, mumbling, " Cross — golden cross — cross. . . ." It was the Populist who had been defeated today by her father. She was not afraid. He was a simple, big, dull creature. But when he carried her into a toolshed behind the house, she was scared and began to scream, wailing so that some of the man's friends heard her as they looked for him, worried by his daze at supper. When they broke in the door of the shed, he had driven one nail through her left hand

into the door itself: she was to be hung there, an expiation
for her father's sins. This golden cross burned his poor
mind. He was taken to an asylum. She grew up, and one
day watched Mr. Bryan's eyes as he stared at the long scar
trailing its purple down her hand on a balustrade in Florida. . . . There were suicides. Embittered men moved
from towns to escape chaffing. Reactions showed. Democrats bragged of pleasure in the Silver Knight's defeat.
Republicans denounced McKinley.

As for Mr. Hanna, he was now a huge grotesque, an
image of mud stained with dollars in the cartoons. He
swelled into national legend as a figure of gross wealth,
a fantasy of money's power and coldness. Some men had
grown fond of him, as men grow fond of a man who will
not be beaten, who shows himself resilient in the midst of
bad news, hard in a pool of cowardices. But he had been
little seen; he was a dot on McKinley's porch, a shape in
an office or in a smoky room of some hotel. The sensitive
John Hay stopped bantering and wrote his astonishment
to a friend in Paris: " He is a born general in politics, perfectly square, honest and courageous, with a *coup d'œil*
for the battlefield and a knowledge of the enemy's weak
points which is very remarkable . . ." and there were
other compliments. But members of a prim minority in
the Republican party were much offended. They had not
been consulted and, you see, they had not been flattered.
The proprieties had not been respected. Mark Hanna
simply unveiled the springs on which men are manipulated
into greatness.

" He has advertised McKinley," Theodore Roosevelt
told my father, " as if he were a patent medicine! "

This was Mr. Hanna's crime. He had openly made use
of the full powers of propaganda. He had dealt with politics as if the birth of a company was being arranged. He
had thrown a hundred thousand tons of advertising into

the nation, against Mr. Bryan's voice, bad logic, and good intentions. He had won, but he had upset these men whose fortunes he had certainly saved from a renewed panic and the domination of inexpert governors. He had made a President, and he had done it visibly. It is hard to forgive such realism. And now they wondered what he would do next.

CHAPTER IV

POWER, OF A KIND

COUNT CASSINI, ambassador of the Tsar, arrived in Washington ill-informed as to the political and animal life of the United States. When a little black and white beast minced from some bushes in a garden beyond Georgetown and ladies shrieked, the Russian advanced upon the peril affably and Senator Frye had to take his arm, explaining the inexplicable in frenzied words. Mr. Hanna picked up a pebble and aimed it at the skunk's shameless composure in the pathway.

" By God, he looks like an office-seeker! "

His pebble missed and the party retreated up the gardens. M. Cassini went on talking to a girl from Louisiana. He could not understand her prejudice against Mr. Hanna. Suppose, then, that the man had bribed town councilmen in Cleveland to renew franchises of his tramways? What else was expected of town councils? This was the habit of democracies; you put common people in your power and they, of course, hunted bribes and chances of blackmail. *Cela se voit!* . . . Miss Le Blanc retorted that Mr. Hanna was head of a capitalistic conspiracy seeking to control the United States. The foreigner shrugged. What of it? In a democracy the mob controlled or the rich controlled. There was no aristocracy to be responsible. There was no Church to advise. There was no *esprit de corps* of the educated. It came to a question between the mob and the

525

rich. Mr. Hanna appeared to him the best solution of the case, and how amiable a bourgeois, and what a good host, and what a quick wit! Miss Le Blanc gave it up, here, and allowed some other lady to attract the diplomat.

This was the spring of 1899 and Mark Hanna, for two years, had been a Senator. He had lately scandalized a dinner-party by observing that all questions of government in a democracy were questions of money, thus preceding Oswald Spengler in the opinion by two decades.[1] He would presently announce that communism seemed to him a method of increasing incompetence by making sure that nobody had any incentive to progress. Life, he thought, was a matter of competitions. All the men around Lyman Gage's dinner-table had got there by being better at their jobs than someone else. Miss Le Blanc sniffed, and the Senator's brown eyes settled on her.

" This sculptor in Paris you went to see, this man Roddinn, now. . . . Did you go to see him because he's the top of his profession or just because you wanted to have him say how good-lookin' you are? "

They sparred, the Southern girl declaring that Auguste Rodin had not come to fame through competition and the Northern plutocrat answering that the word " fame " itself implied a competition. But competition meant a hustle for prizes to her and she resented it, as she resented this society of hard diplomats and ladies always asking, " Who *was* she? " as if they were used to meeting people who, once, had been nobodies. And she recoiled from Marcus Hanna with a profound instinct of her vanishing kind; the daughter of a landholding society recognized an enemy of her traditions. Since the Black Death in the fourteenth century these

[1] " What is here described as Civilization, then, is the stage of a Culture at which tradition and personality have lost their immediate effectiveness, and every idea, to be actualized, has to be put in terms of money. . . . Democracy is the completed equating of money with political power. . . ." *The Decline of the West*, Volume II, page 485.

burghers, wielding massed money as a club, had come
pounding down doors and climbing walls into the sanctuaries of aristocracy. Etienne Marcel leading the guilds of
Paris to slaughter the well-born councillors of the scared
Dauphin was the prototype of this conquering class. There
were now no sanctuaries left; she had seen that in Europe.
Aristocratic society was at the mercy of the financier who
permitted its existence as a river permits a congeries of
water hyacinth to idle in à warm bayou; the landholders
were not important enough to be destroyed, at the end of
the nineteenth century. Land, once the title to all privileges
of earth, had fallen to be merely one form of speculation.
Mr. Hanna did not own fifty acres, although he was a stockholder in the use of thousands of square miles. But that
this powerful adventurer was just a stockholder made him
an ogre to the descendant of a lady whose head was struck
off in 1792 because she knew kings. All defensive fictions
of the declining landed power established Mark Hanna in
the wrong set. She looked at him with horror, and now
wonders why.

Mr. Hanna was an exception rather than a full member
of the plutocracy. He did not share the complete superstitions of his tribe. His provincial character exempted Hanna
from some ideas of the metropolitan capitalist in Europe.
He was, for instance, not an imperialist in the sense of
European and English plutocrats. And he still failed to
believe in revolutions. Instead of being high leader of the
capitalists managing the United States, so far as they did,
he was on poor terms with many of them and died suspected of gross treachery to capitalism by a lot of them.
He did not hold with several of their schemes for controlling peoples. His troubles commenced while he was advertising William McKinley from his rented house in
Georgia, in the spring of 1896.

As the decadent American sects took up fads, these were

utilized by prudent financiers and industrialists to mask their own wishes. Miss Frances Willard could proudly indicate on the roster of contributors to her Christian Temperance Union names of great factory-owners. In March of 1896 Mr. Hanna had to face a committee of Prohibitionists with letters of introduction signed by a Baptist millionaire. McKinley's backer might truthfully report that he himself had never tried wine until he was forty years old and that his candidate drank almost nothing, but his interview with the committee became a matter of tactful evasions. To get rid of them he asked if they had heard President Cleveland's answer to a like committee: " If you suppress the use of alcohol in America, you must seize Canada or build a string of forts all along the Canadian border." This gloomy challenge made the Prohibitionists argue among themselves until it was time to catch their train. Mr. Hanna shook hands with them, having promised nothing in the way of support for their cause.[2]

But another sectarian influence was not so easily steered out of Mr. Hanna's reception room at Thomasville. The question of Cuban independence brought itself to McKinley's manager half a dozen times before Grover Cleveland ironically presented a war with Spain to his inaugurated successor. Here again was a fad among the religious in small towns and a topic of orators in meetings of the American Protective Association. When some Catholic country had to be cursed, Spain often served as a butt of Protestant indignation. Mr. Hanna would make no formal promise of doing anything for the Cubans, but he was put strongly on warning that something might have to be done, and he

[2] Another version of Mr. Cleveland's remark is: " If the United States is to be cured of drinking beer, you will have to make a pie-crust of forts on the Canadian border and grab all the ships of Europe," this latter version being made in 1895 to Mrs. Stewart Warner. Mrs. Warner may well have reached Mr. Hanna with this witticism, as she visited Cleveland in 1895 and met Mrs. Hanna in society.

talked to McKinley frequently on the choice of consuls in the Caribbean countries. Three autographs dated in January of 1897 show him refusing consular posts near Cuba and one of these, addressed simply to " Dear Jones," contains a closing sentence almost rhetorical. " God forbid." he wrote, " that the United States be called on to intervene on behalf of these miserable people but if that need should arise it is to be hoped that our representatives in the region of Cuba will all be able men. . . ." Dear Jones, whoever he was, cannot have liked this eloquence, as it implied a doubt of his friend Mr. Huntley's ability. Mr. Huntley — whoever he was — would not do for a consulate in the tropics. But, as Theodore Roosevelt testifies in his memoirs, Mr. McKinley did find able men for the posts in Latin America. One of them was fairly ordered by Mark Hanna to leave a more profitable job for the consular service. He could not afford it? Very well, Mr. Hanna would take charge of his small capital and get it invested so that he need not worry, and he has not worried since 1897.

But able consuls in the tropics would not put off this question of Spain and her bullied colony. Mr. Hanna morosely grunted in Cleveland that the United States must not have any damn trouble with anybody. His language in February was heated by a social event, for it pleased a rich ninny in New York to give a ball so consummately advertised that it was talked of by positive princes abroad, while starving workmen fed at the bread-lines a few blocks from the hot hotel where ladies and stockbrokers sweated in their costumes, for one brilliant night. This did not gratify Mr. Hanna. His annoyance had, as so often, a doubled reason. He disliked the host of this entertainment, and the whole thing struck him as cruelly reckless. It would serve the New Yorker right if some terrorist heaved a bomb into the ballroom and blew dancers to spangles and red paste. " *Theory of a Leisure Class?* " he grunted, staring at a book in the library of Cushman Davis. "What's their theory? More damn fancy-dress balls?" The discipline of his mother's ancestors wrought in Mr. Hanna: men ought to work. Hearing that an agreeable young artist who sketched Mrs. Hanna that winter would paint perhaps only three portraits in six months, he rubbed an ear. What did the boy do with the rest of his time?

His own time was well taken up. Office-seekers had at him, now, in profusions of six or ten the day. The majestic tariff bill was being manufactured beforehand. The smart men rallied and came to call on Mr. Hanna with astonishing projects in mind, monstrous concessions of land to be dealt out by the government to the right people and quaintly arranged swindles of many kinds. Some of these propositions amused him so that he talked of them to his friends, and it can be certainly recorded that, about February of 1897, Mr. Hanna was offered shares in a company which proposed to secure from the government the whole western seacoast of Florida, with Mr. Hanna's assistance. Yet most of his time was taken by the office-seekers, and, before any announcement of Mr. McKinley's Cabinet had been made from Canton, cold information circulated in the East: Hanna was not doing the right thing by the metropolis.

The Eastern magnates were placidly neglected in the formation of the new President's immediate council. It is true that Cornelius Bliss, of New York, was made Secretary of the Interior after the appointment had been refused by John McCook, and that Theodore Roosevelt was to be Assistant Secretary of the Navy. But Mr. Bliss was not warmly friends with the Republican machine of New York, and Mr. Roosevelt was an amusing oddity who could be jocosely presented to strangers as " our police commissioner " or as Douglas Robinson's brother-in-law. He had no profession; his father, a secondary financier of the last generation, had left the vivid young man an income. He was erudite, as these Americans understood erudition, but that did him no good in the clubs, and he wrote books, which seemed strange. . . . These two appointments were all that New York got from Mr. Hanna's friend. The Secretary of State was old John Sherman, of Ohio, and his first assistant was William Day, also of Ohio. The Secretary of War was Russell Alger, of Michigan. The Attorney General was a Californian and, worse, a Roman Catholic. The Postmaster General came from Baltimore. The Secretary of Agriculture was a Scotch person out of Iowa, and — unbelievably! — the Secretary of the Treasury was a Democrat from Chicago, Lyman Gage. New York had certainly expected that Hanna would take the Treasury for his province. His own friends imagined that he might ask for the post. But he said to William Saunders, "Me in the Cabinet? All the newspapers would have cartoons of me selling the White House kitchen stove!"[3]

He had plenty of reasons for preferring to be a Senator. He must attend to the pruning of the tariff bill at close range. He knew that the power of declaring war lay with Congress. He liked the notion of being a Senator. So he became a Senator, filling John Sherman's place by appointment. The appointment lagged; Mr. Asa Bushnell, Governor of Ohio, hesitated for some awkward days and had to be civilly advised by Senator Joseph Foraker that Mr. Hanna must be appointed. It was done. He arrived at Washington and was sworn in at once. His tall hat shim-

[3] Mr. McKinley did offer the Postmaster General's place to Mr. Hanna in a preserved letter, and Hanna refused it. Several memoirs and notes on the period state that he wished to be Secretary of the Treasury, giving no authority for the statement. Mr. Croly makes no such point in the biography, and the testimony of Mr. Saunders, Mr. Leonard Hanna, and Mr. Joseph Kimball contradicts the legend.

mered with all those other hats of solemn gentlemen behind Mr. McKinley and Mr. Cleveland on the platform as the new President took oath of office.

The exaltation of John Sherman into the Cabinet was a privy scandal of Washington that spring. Distinction and experience had nothing to do with the case, in gossip. Mr. Sherman was hauled up to make place for Mr. Hanna in the Senate. But Mr. Sherman was offered the State Department before the tenth of January, and Mr. Hanna did not refuse a cabinet post until the middle of February. There was no question of a sudden lust for governmental powers on Hanna's part. A deeper motive was apparent to the retiring President. " I suspect," said Mr. Cleveland to Mr. Victor Ward, " that Hanna knows McKinley likes popularity too well." Mr. Hanna was placing himself where he could correct that tendency. Acts that might strain McKinley's will in case of a needed veto need never pass the Senate. His affection for the President was not blinding Mr. Hanna to some possibilities. He might be useful; he would be powerful.

Whatever he was to be, he was not noisy. Mr. Hanna appeared in the Senate and sat there, correctly sedate in his chair, much gazed upon by visitors in the gallery. He was obviously a plump man in his sixtieth year who seemed short unless he lifted his head to stare across the Senators at a speaker. The caricatured Hanna, described as a braggart in the journals, turned out to be a blunt, quietly amused personage at dinner-parties. He might get so enthusiastic as to say that Mr. McKinley's private secretary, George Cortelyou, was a fine boy or that he liked the Vice President's wife. Still, his monotonous voice did not rise in the Senate and a lady who met Mark Hanna at the end of March 1897 remembers mostly his silence.

Timidly invading Washington, Miss Edith Sims and her mother managed to find an Episcopal church on the morn-

ing after they arrived at the capital, and sat observing this
society. The widow and her daughter had been to Con-
stantinople, to Abu-Simbel down the Nile, and to Copen-
hagen. But they had never explored the United States. A
trip to Syracuse in 1870 convinced Mrs. Sims that she was
not quite safe far from New York. She came to Washington because her eldest daughter's husband had been transferred to duty at the War Department and she wanted to
be in the capital when Marion and the babies got there,
escaping from wild San Francisco.

Miss Sims presently was watching a lady seated three
pews away who looked back at her, or at her mother, with
a familiar sort of smile. She was not young, but she was
handsome, erect, and pleasant in a somber dress. She had
a little the look of those German great ladies one saw at
Baden-Baden, surrounded by mussy, shy daughters and
dogs. She smiled, though, in a special fashion and the girl
knew that her mother was watching the other lady's face.
Kate Richardson and Lottie Rhodes hunted each other
through the masks imposed by thirty-five years of living.
When the choir boys had taken themselves down the aisle,
Mrs. Sims and Mrs. Marcus Alonzo Hanna met with the
sentimental crash expected of such reunions in the latter
nineteenth century. Miss Edith was duly kissed and was
told — truthfully — that she looked like Mrs. Hanna's
youngest. She is still sometimes asked on trains if she is
not Mrs. Medill McCormick.

Senator Hanna was waiting for his wife at the hotel, with
another white waistcoat and top hat beside his Sunday
clothes. It was a thrill to meet Mr. John Hay, the new ambassador to England, and to be enveloped in his bantering
conversation. Mrs. Sims had met him, somewhere in Europe, and he pretended with great skill to remember all
about her.

Marcus Hanna pretended nothing. He was utterly silent,

with his cigar. But Mr. Hay babbled agreeably. He had
been dancing in and out of Washington for two weeks, talking to Mr. McKinley " around senators and through office-
seekers," and now he must go to luncheon with John Sherman. He said to Mrs. Hanna, " Smile at me, Mona Lisa, as
I go to this ordeal."

" John Hay, if you call me that again I'll be sorry Mark
didn't let them have Whitelaw Reid made ambassador to
England instead of you."

Senator Hanna grunted. Mr. Hay's eyebrows twitched.
Mrs. Hanna colored and then whispered that she didn't
think anybody heard her. The diplomat said it didn't matter, and went away. When she had her newly found old
playmate upstairs in her rooms, Mrs. Hanna chuckled. In
Washington, she said, you had to pretend not to know what
everybody knew, and, thank heaven, she was going home to
Cleveland tonight for some days. Then she began to talk
about the Senator.

" She was charming about him," says Miss Sims. " I
wrote down some of her stories a few days later in an irregular diary I kept in those days. But she was so upset
about his health. She asked us how we thought he looked.
I am afraid we were not of much comfort to her, as we had
never seen him before. She said candidly that she was
afraid he would overwork himself trying to manage the
Republican party in Cleveland and do his work in the Senate. My mother knew absolutely nothing about politics, and
neither did I. One of us innocently asked if Senator Foraker could not help Mr. Hanna in the Senate. Mrs. Hanna
had to explain that Mr. Foraker and Mr. Hanna were hardly
on speaking terms and that Ohio was divided between their
two factions. But she spoke very decently of Mr. Foraker.
She said that Mr. Hanna had been rather tactless toward
him at the Republican National Convention " — of 1888
— " where their quarrel began. Then she quite broke out

in regard to some of the politicians in Ohio. I find in my
diary: ' Mrs. Hanna said that she regarded many of Mr. H.'s
associates in politics as not worth his attention. They fawn
on him for campaign expenses and ask for favors while they
envy him. Interesting story: One of these politicians asked
Mr. H. to have a street in Cleveland paved past a certain
point. Mr. H. refused. The man then said, " I have helped
to have you granted franchises for your street-car lines and
now you will do nothing for me." Mr. H. answered that it
did not cost the city a penny to grant him a franchise, but
that it would cost a hundred thousand dollars to pave this
street, and that the man wanted it done to increase the value
of some real estate. Mrs. H. said that this man had now
turned into a bitter enemy of Mr. H. She does not believe
he will be really happy in Washington, away from his
friends in Cleveland.' She told several other instances of
these enmities that had come about through the Senator's
refusal of some political favor. I cannot pretend to recollect them. My mother asked her if Mr. Hanna had not great
power over Mr. McKinley. Mrs. Hanna said that he had
power, of a kind. I remember the qualifying phrase so distinctly. . . ."

Next day Miss Sims was taking snapshots of the White
House from its gateway when Senator Hanna bustled past
her. He said, " I'm Eliza crossing the ice, and there come
the bloodhounds." He fairly trotted up the drive. The girl
saw some gentlemen hastening toward her and was alarmed,
although they did nothing when they got to the gate. They
settled into a watchful group, strolling to and fro on the
sidewalk as they waited for Mr. Hanna's outcoming; she
had her first chance of observing the office-seeker's prowl,
that gait combining the hungry wolf's trot with the prouder
pace of a righteous woman about to vindicate her claim to a
new frock.

Mr. Hay, then, went to his duty in England and com-

535

menced the delicate performance of the task to which he had been appointed, while, in New York, men wondered why he had been appointed at all. Senator Hanna remained in Washington, beating off the bloodhounds and bluntly telling his private callers that the Dingley tariff was not an invitation to keep foreign goods out of the American market. "Mr. McKinley stands for protection, not exclusion," he told a furious maker of surgical instruments. The man yelled that he had contributed ten thousand dollars to McKinley's campaign fund, and this was how he was paid! Mr. Hanna's mouth became a line in his hot face. He shot a pointed finger at the loud person and shouted back, "Got your receipt? . . . You never turned in a cent!" His memory of fact was dangerous. A joke passed out around Washington. If you were claiming something from Hanna, you must have a receipt to show him.

The tariff was lifted. Mr. McKinley sent off his useless commission to Europe on behalf of bimetallism, as he had promised the Silver Republicans. There was a trivial improvement of business at large, but no boom. American confidence had been poisoned since 1890 and men of affairs did not brag of American opportunities as their fathers had bragged under Grant. Wall Street showed its discontent all summer long and, in the autumn, there were rumors of protests made by big men to the President, although what they protested to Mr. McKinley is now obscure.[4] Then, in October, Mr. Asa Barnes, lunching in the region of Wall Street with an importer of tobacco, heard the voice of Mr. Edward Lauterbach proclaiming from a table close to him that Mr. Hanna was to be dispensed with. It had been decided between a boss in New York and a boss in Pennsylvania that Mark Hanna was no good. He had not got some bills passed

---

[4] I judge from a note of Mr. Abner McKinley to my father that various steel interests had expected an enormous increase of the Navy to be made directly and that some representation of this kind was made to the President through Mr. Long, the Secretary of the Navy.

in which big men took an interest. He had loaded all these Westerners into the Cabinet. It was risky, said the agreeable Mr. Lauterbach, because Hanna was not so foolish as he looked and might not take his removal in peace. But he was to be spanked and returned to his coal bins in Cleveland.

To Asa Barnes this was awful. Mark Hanna had always been his fancy of a terrestrial god. Mark Hanna gave him dollars when he was a little boy in Cleveland for carrying notes to Miss Charlotte Augusta Rhodes. Mark Hanna noticed him slaving in a bank and planted him on better pay in the office of a coal mine. In 1894, when his small business in New York was nearly gone, a check had come from Hanna and Company, at the dramatic last moment, with a message telling him to hang on. Mark Hanna had limped out of a group of dignitaries in the autumn of 1896 to cross the lobby of the Holland House and shake hands with Mr. Barnes, as though the partner in a mere tobacco shop was someone very grand indeed. So the voice of Mr. Lauterbach sent Asa Barnes to the nearest telephone. Mr. Hanna was not in his office at Cleveland, but on a train somewhere. The tale was told to Mr. Leonard Hanna, who answered, " So we hear! " and then spoke busily about Wall Street's politicians. Mr. Barnes felt better. Christmas passed. Then, after New Year's Day, newspapers flashed headings. There was a revolt at Columbus, Ohio, against Marcus Hanna. State senators and assemblymen pledged to return Mr. Hanna to the Senate, by election, had fused with Democrats and Silver Republicans. The Governor and the mayor of Cleveland were mixed up in the fuss. All Ohio was boiling. Mr. Barnes packed his clothes and fled on the next train to Columbus.

When practical politicians turn fantastic, they outdo poets. Mr. Robert McKisson was a practiced and affable politician who wanted to be a mayor of Cleveland and applied to Mr. Hanna for backing. Mr. Hanna declined him.

537

He had no dislike for Mr. McKisson, but he preferred to back someone else. However, in 1895, Mr. McKisson got the Republicans of the big city to make him mayor, for the truth is that Mark Hanna's control of Cleveland was never so absolute as legend asserts, and Robert McKisson was then able to begin the contrivance of a personal machine for his own ends. This man is now such a shadow that the fact of his next performance seems sheer lunacy. He came to Columbus in the first week of January 1898, and there told a meeting of Democratic state legislators that he would have to be a Republican " before the people," but that, if they would send him to the Senate in Washington, he would act upon the principles of the Democratic party as set forth in the Chicago convention of 1896. This turned the stomachs of three Democrats and they refused to vote for the providential secret convert to Democracy. But Mr. McKisson was handsome and his voice soothed the rest of the caucus. On Monday, January 10th, it was known that he was the candidate for Senator against Marcus Hanna.

The details of this political cinema are fully given in Mr. Croly's biography of Mark Hanna except one feature of the muddle which was plain only to men who knew the Republican party in New York. Items of the party's metropolitan machine appeared in bars and hotels at Columbus, but their function was not discerned by Mr. Hanna's volunteers from the East. As Mr. Asa Barnes and Mr. Walter Held ranged the streets, they encountered these strangers, but never at Mr. Hanna's rooms in the hotel, where he smoked among his friends. For the five days ending with January 11th these spectators were visible. They were not helping Mr. Hanna's supporters to keep the wobbling assemblymen in line. They stood about. Mr. Held got in conversation with one of them and made nothing of his answers. He was just " watching the fight."

It was a fight. There are still five men living who tackled

the legislators for Mr. Hanna, and none of these used money. Mr. Lee Durstine operated on an assemblyman from Union County by means of the waverer's son; Mr. Barnes cornered Silver Republicans in bars and raved at them; Mr. Walter Held and his brother were effective as men are effective who stand six feet three and have thundering throats; another survives who had a pious uncle in the opposition and found the old man reasonable when it was explained to him that Mr. Hanna did not drink whisky. As for the rest of the doubtful voters, they may have been paid to be loyal to their pledges, or they may have been cowed by another force. The voice of the people is at least the voice of the people. All that week the people sifted into Columbus, and Hanna's friends amazedly heard farmers and Silver Republicans of the small towns demanding that Mark Hanna, the Cleveland plutocrat, be returned to his seat in the Senate.

Why? It had happened in September and October. Senator Hanna came before the plain people not as a smiling image in a white waistcoat behind other speakers on a draped platform, but as a speaker. He could not make an oration. He stood barking out short sentences at the crowds, challenging anybody to prove him an enemy of the labor unions or to deny that he paid the best wages in Ohio for a day's work. Farmers grinned when the Senator rubbed a fist on his red ear or said, " Wait a minute! " as he stooped to pull up a loose garter. He went on in this simple way: " Mr. Bryan said just one thing in his big speech at Chicago last year that strikes me as true. He said that farmers and workingmen are business men just as much as any banker or lawyer. Well, that's true. I like that. If you men will study business methods and learn how to look after your interests we won't have to hear any more wishy-washy stuff about how Wall Street's abusin' you. Now Johnny McLean went to the trouble to bring Mr. Bryan all this long way from

539

Nebraska — hope he got a pass on the railroad for him — to tell you that Mark Hanna is a labor crusher and God knows what all. My brothers and I employ six thousand men. Some of them are here in this crowd. Let any of them come forward and say that he hasn't had a square deal from M. A. Hanna and Company and I'll shut up! " It was not oratory, but the people stood silent under it and applauded it. They had heard Mr. Bryan's rhythmic nobility a few days before, in these same towns. But here was this plain man's frank attack on their pride. Were they not business men? " Bryan's mistake," says a witness, " was a constant appeal to self-pity. Mr. Hanna sounded grumpy and pretty bored with the whole thing. It may be strange that this was effective, but I certainly think it was. . . ." One must judge by the result. In the first week of January some of these plain people came to Columbus and cried in the streets that they wanted Mark Hanna sent back to Washington. Legislators heard, roared at them in the familiar speech of their town, that they had to vote for Hanna. This influence was unpaid, and it persisted through Monday, even after Democratic papers charged Mr. Hanna with attempting to bribe an assemblyman from Cincinnati through an agent.

Everything now had been done. A legislator had been kidnapped and drugged. There had been fights in bars and alleys. Armed guards were posted throughout the capital of Ohio. On Tuesday the legislators voted. A handkerchief waving from the steps of the State House announced to watchers in the street that Mr. Hanna was elected Senator, and the signal passed to his hotel. He said, " I'm too fat for a Juliet," staring down into the crowd. Then he sent word to Mr. McKisson that a baby in diapers would be able to beat him if he tried to be mayor of Cleveland again. Mr. John Farley, who defeated Mr. McKisson in the autumn of 1899, was no baby, of course, but the weakness with which the Republicans supported Mr. McKisson was notable, and Mr. Farley's friends had a lot of money to spend.

As to the spectators from New York, they had disappeared when Walter and Philip Held made a round of the hotels that evening, collecting some small bets. Four or five days later Mr. Edward Lauterbach idled up to Cornelius Bliss, lunching at the Lawyers' Club in New York with certain friends, and told the Secretary of the Interior that he knew a couple of men who were worried for fear Uncle Mark had been hearing nasty stories about them.

" They might send him a bunch of violets and a pretty note," Mr. Bliss suggested.

" I told them not to do it," Mr. Lauterbach said, " but they wouldn't listen to reason."

" You might tell Tom Platt to send a hymn book and some cigars along," Bliss laughed.

Everybody grinned around the table, all these powerful men were amused, watching the machinery twinkle. Power had become their amusement, though journals talked of their mania for money. Some of them had no money at all, but they had power. They would spend a month of intrigue on finding a place in a governmental bureau for a widow out in Oregon, and the point was not that they liked the widow. They had never seen the woman. But it was something to do, a minute display of force and craft.

They had talents for other games than this. One of them sang well and collected rare ballads in all tongues; one of them had five thousand books on history, bound in old Spanish leathers or Indian brocades and spun a theory of civilizations in a lisping drawl; one of them fascinated Bryce and afterwards Lord Haldane by the gay agility of his talk. But America did not summon them to show their power otherwise than among the machines erected as emblems of success. They worked. Leisure was for fools, women, and failures. And work, since they so believed, was their pleasure.

Their bodies thickened. They died at ages of fifty-two and fifty-three. They swooned on bright tables at meetings of directors and were lugged down to slick private cabs waiting on the slope beside Trinity Church. Courage might shred under the shock of a favorite daughter's death, and they were loaded on steamships for a weary trip abroad. They took no exercise and looked disapprovingly at John Jacob Astor sipping white wine at lunch while they tried to fire their energies with the alcohol of sweet food. They lurched off to Turkish baths where masseurs kneaded life into them before an evening conference in the yellow club-rooms beside Fifth Avenue. But this was their pleasure, although they did not live to explain it in memoirs. Few of them had time to make their wills, death was so importunate at the end, introduced by a secretary's scream or the rush of servants in some lobby to a tottering bulk in furs and a rolling hat. Wives shivered; doctors cursed them. They might drag out two months in Europe and be seen busy with American newspapers at Karlsbad or Vichy. But their game went on, a tangling movement of letters and messengers on the way to Washington or Cleveland or, later, to Oyster Bay. Most of them wanted nothing out of it save this thrill of making a point, an official had been created, or a bill, about which they did not care, had been killed in Congress. "See," one of them shouted to Stuyvesant Fish, "I got my man in!" He had put a collector of customs at a trivial port, to spite Thomas Platt, after spending ten thousand dollars on mighty dinners in Washington. This was pleasure, to be able to wave a telegram at Stuyvesant Fish in a club.

One of them saw Hanna buried and then gave up the sport. He roamed, and came yearly to a dive in Budapest where gypsy violins told him stories while he sat out nights

in the circle of his mistresses and their complacent husbands. One of them had a house in Spain and a room hung
with photographs of the men he had put in office. And one
of them, in much the finest, began to telephone one afternoon. His dry, Western voice sped through wires into offices, scaring old clerks as he summoned the dead to a meeting. A friend was told and brought a doctor in a closed car
to the door on Broadway, then intruded and found the tall
man raging. Some fool in the central at Cleveland was trying to tell him that Mark Hanna had died in 1904! But
this was 1896! The machinery of his mind had reversed,
as it broke, to the autumn of 1896. He could be persuaded
that Hanna was in town, in rooms at the Holland House;
the doctor and a hidden needle filled with sleep were waiting
in the car. After three days he joined the rest of them. . . .
But they had a good time. This was their pleasure. They
had power, of a kind.

II

A SUPERSTITION followed Mark Hanna from Cleveland into
Washington; he was " lucky." His disasters turned out
well. If a client of his ship-building company could not
pay for six vessels built at great cost, it would prove that
the client had an iron mine which Mr. Hanna could develop
for him and get back his money in no time. That the matter of finding capital for the development of the mine in a
panicky year was very difficult and that it took brains to do
anything with the mine at all were ignored in Uncle Mark's
legend. The " Hanna luck " saw him through anything, and
this luck was communicable. He lent or gave money to displaced workmen on the streets of his town in the winter of
1894. Some of them saved a silver dollar or a dime from
his gift for a luck piece. As he marched back into the Senate in 1898, elected to succeed himself, a Western Senator

leaned out of his seat to touch the jinni's shoulder for luck. Men smiled, but Mr. Hanna held a reception in the Marble Room at the end of the day's business. The affair at Columbus had echoed back favorably to these legislators. Senator Hanna was now Senator by election, after an awful fight for it, and they heard truly that he had shown good humor and pluck. " People are glad to have Warwick back," Thomas Reed wrote to a lady. " We need anybody divinely blessed with common sense at this time. . . ."

But Marcus Hanna needed something more than common sense, as the Congress assembled in 1898. He needed all those things possessed by Mr. William Jennings Bryan, arts of appeal and emotional display, the music of sentimental phrase, physical charm. He hadn't them. He was a business man in politics, able when it came to nursing the great tariff act along and a good persuader in conference. For once he wished to be an orator. He must try to head something back, cool a charge of the plain people, and every quality of his equipment was wrong. He had already been dramatized in the journals as Wall Street's man in Washington, and Wall Street was anxious to have no trouble with Spain, so the journalists declared. There was trouble with Spain already. Riots broke out in Havana; loyalists and a rabble of Spanish officials paraded the white streets yelling against McKinley, who dared to interfere in the island's government, and cheering General Weyler, who had established the reconcentrado camps, in which people died of starvation and stank of scurvy. Weyler had been recalled by the new premier, Sagasta, in the autumn of 1897 and hazy promises of autonomy were made to the Cubans, much too late. The insurgents would have full independence. Professor Sumner's outline of colonial history was filled: the island had been plundered and was now Spain's enemy.

Mr. Hanna read no foreign language and so was spared the exposition of European statesmanship which remains amply recorded in the journals and published correspondence of 1898. He was even able to maintain, up to the tenth of April, some belief in the good sense of Europe. His mind cut into the facts before the end of January. " I have just seen Mr. Hanna," Henry Adler wrote to his half sister, not knowing she had left Frankfort to join him, " and he seems to believe that a good deal of the sentiment against America is kicked up by financial elements in Germany and France. . . ." This was not what other Senators and members of the Cabinet believed. They believed and said that decadent, aristocratic Europe was trying to uphold monarchic Spain against American democracy. Under this babbling about chivalrous Castile they did not perceive plutocratic imperialists annoyed with America's invasion of a colonial question. The United States must not be allowed to trifle with empires; Spain's control of a colony must not be criticized. It was dangerous precedent. It was insolence. French royalists, Austrian landholders in debt to German banks, and the German highborn imperialists rallied to this whistle. The *Saturday Review* fell delirious in London and published marvels of that oddly vulgar invective which supplies the place of dialectic among English and American specialists in conservative refinement. But the continental show outglittered any British invention and is still quite interesting in its evasion of the patent facts: Cuba was in a condition of anarchy, its agriculture and industry both wrecked and its people two thirds adjudged rebels.

What European observers did not care to know was that American morality had become emotional again. The music of the Abolitionists pulsed up, after years, and the infecting notion of rescuing the oppressed flavored sermons. Religion, or rather the Protestant sects, had gathered the suffering Cubans into a topic of sentimental value. The plain people stirred, in the West, as the awfulness of Catholic Spain was revealed with pungency to ladies in black

silk who wanted to believe every word of it. Mr. Hanna
could beat down a Bryan, but he could not cope with women
who were asking the pastor to write to Mr. McKinley about
Cuba, and making children sign petitions to be sent to Congressmen. " You have no idea," Abner McKinley wrote on
January 26th, " of the pressure on William from religious
people. . . ." [5] Letters from English Methodists reached
the White House while an American squadron gathered at
the tip of Florida, in the last week of January. Before the
first of February, Mr. Hanna was denounced in a Baptist
church of San Francisco for holding Mr. McKinley back.
" By God," he said, " Christians are remarkable! "

Statesmen in Washington were also remarkable. A candid war party existed in the capital and gained allies in
the Cabinet. Simple jingos herded with humanitarians.
Cuba must be free. They learned how to pronounce the
phrase " *Cuba libre* " from officials of the Spanish ministry
and mispronounced it at dinners. Henriette Adler heard it
garbled in the heat of a reception on the night of February 9th as she backed from the active elbow of a burly
gentleman until she was against a wall and could not escape
his flailing sleeve. His teeth flashed and his eyeglasses
sparkled. He was alarming in the force of his objection to
Mr. McKinley's uncertainty. When his elbow ripped a
silken rose and some gauze clean from Miss Adler's shoulder, she said, " *Mon dieu!* " and this verbal velocity was
now aimed at her. He spoke in French with speed, abandoning all the nouns of his apology, but making himself clear.
Miss Adler liked him.

A lady called Nannie had a pin. Senator Orville Platt
and Senator Cushman Davis made themselves a screen for
the committee on reparations. Mr. Hanna came trundling
down the room to see what was being done to his guest, and
then the talk was a vortex. Miss Adler saw that these men

[5] Abner McKinley to Walter McCabe.

had a point to make with the Senator. The battleship *Maine*
lay in the harbor of Havana, sent there to notify Spain that
American citizens in Cuba were not to be molested. Senator Davis seemed to want Mr. Hanna to agree with him
on the value of this move. The burly charmer with the
teeth thought it a bully idea to send the *Maine* to Havana.
Mr. Hanna had no opinion, but stood with his chin sunk on
his white tie, staring at the talkers.

They seemed queer to Miss Adler, chattering as though
Europe did not exist for them. Surely they knew that
France and Germany would resent any assault on Spain's
imperial property? She said so, quoting what she had
heard in Paris two weeks ago. It did not seem to impress
the man with the teeth or the bald Senator from Minnesota.
Let France and Germany resent it, said Senator Davis. The
burly gentleman didn't think France serious in her talk.
But Spain must be kicked out of Cuba.

" I hope to see the Spanish flag and the English flag gone
from the map of North America before I'm sixty! "

Senator Hanna stared and drawled, " You're crazy,
Roosevelt! What's wrong with Canada? "

The Assistant Secretary of the Navy had not said that
anything was wrong with Canada except its English flag.
But he was in a state of mind about the foreign flags on
American soil just then and had written his prejudice that
day to his friend Moore. Mrs. Hanna explained Mr. Roosevelt to her husband's guest as they drove across Washington. He was really amusing and his wife was one of the
nicest women in Washington, but he did get violent about
things. Mr. Hanna grunted behind his cigar that, thank
God, they hadn't put Roosevelt in the State Department,
as Cushman Davis wanted done last year.

" We'd be fighting half the world," he brooded.

He sat with Miss Adler in the restaurant of the Arlington
over a pint of champagne and asked questions about the

feeling in Paris. Her half brother always spoke of Marcus Hanna as a comedian, but this grave, worried man of sixty said nothing funny. He had not liked the sending of the *Maine* to Havana. It was " waving a match in an oil-well for fun." And her reports of European opinion depressed him. We never got credit for our motives, he said. And what did she think of the French army? . . . They talked a long time.

" He was very frank, it seemed to me then. He said that Mr. McKinley had realized the possibility of this situation before he was elected and would do all he could to keep the peace. His own aversion to a war was very plain. He said the economic condition of the country was just beginning to improve and that a war was undesirable from every point of view. I have an impression that he hoped for an intervention of England, which was generally friendly, and some of the other Powers. Of course I had the European attitude in the question and thought that the reports of cruelty in Cuba were gross exaggerations. But Mr. Hanna assured me that reports of the American consuls and travellers bore out the worst statements. He was strongly in favor of getting the Cubans freed. But he said five or six times, ' I hate the thought of a war. You don't know what a big war is like. Suppose the French come in with Spain against us? ' . . ."

This notion of powerful allies joining Spain oppressed him. The *Maine* was destroyed on February 15th. On February 23rd Mr. Hanna's secretary telephoned to Mr. William Collins Beer, asking him to come at once to Mr. Hanna's office. The Senator abruptly ordered his caller to get back to New York and find out there what the biggest international bankers thought of the French sympathy for Spain. But Mr. Beer had come to Washington to pry, through the State Department, into the history of a bank in South America, for the New York Life Insurance Company. Very well,

Mr. Hanna would wire the damn thing's pedigree to John McCall before Mr. Beer could get to New York. He did so. Three days later, Mr. Beer reported that J. P. Morgan and Company did not take the French newspapers seriously, but that something might be feared from Germany in the way of interference. . . . In this transfer of opinions it seemed strange that Mark Hanna, Wall Street's tool, had to appeal to capitalists for opinion through the attorney of an insurance company. Why had not Mr. Hanna telephoned to Mr. Morgan?

" Too many damn ears on the wire! "

Men came into the smoky room. War had started for some of these legislators. There was a terrific oration on the strength of the Spanish fleet. Mr. Hanna listened, fiddling his cigar between his lips, until he had to grin.

" Bah! We can lick Spain in six months! "

But nobody believed that. The journals said differently. Mr. Hanna was left to his delusions and his cigar. The excited men walked down to the bar of the Raleigh, where it was argued that Mr. Hanna would force a war for the sake of his friends in the steel business. He gave out an interview, in two days, implying that he wanted no war just now. But next week Mr. Beer returned to Washington and found theorists in the Raleigh bar assuring each other that Mr. Hanna was trying to force a war for the sake of his friends in the railroad business. Then, in the first week of March, Mark Hanna became an unpatriotic demon trying to prevent a war in the name of Wall Street. He was nightly stealing into the White House and turning the President against the cause of freedom. He was willing to let Spain keep Cuba. He had not said any of this to anybody, but they were all sure of it in the Raleigh's bar.

Mr. Beer's head spun. He heard in Washington that Wall Street was solidly lined up against a war with Spain. He retired to New York and men grabbed his arm as he entered his club, asking what this insane Hanna meant by trying to head off the war? He noted that the solidarity of Wall Street was imperfect. John Jacob Astor wore a buttonhole of red, white, and blue flowers. John Gates, Thomas Fortune Ryan, William Rockefeller, and Stuyvesant Fish all were sounded, before March 24th, and were found to be feeling militant.[6] On March 28th it was announced by George Walbridge Perkins that John Pierpont Morgan was to put his yacht at the service of the government and that the financier saw nothing to be gained by more talk of arbitration. The news spread in the Lawyers' Club at noon, and men thought of their grown sons.

But McKinley waited. Mr. Hanna smoked cigars and growled in his office. Let the damn brokers go war crazy if they liked, this thing could be stopped. England was friendly. The Powers ought to interfere. Then the Pope made an error in dealing with the United States. He appealed to Spain and her antagonist in hope that Eastertime would not be defiled by an outbreak between two Christian nations. Archbishop Ireland went to Washington to plead for peace. Protestant pastors at once saw a profound danger to American independence which they must avert, and came to Washington by dozens. " Well," said Mr. Hanna, " that just about settles it! "

On April 7th the ambassadors of six nations, led by Sir Julian Pauncefote, presented a vacuous note to Mr. McKinley, stating that they hoped further negotiations would restore order in Cuba and maintain peace. The

---

[6] The great life-insurance companies made this inquiry. My father interviewed Colonel Astor and Mr. Ryan. It was his opinion that the steady opponents of the war among financiers were simply the life insurance men and small bankers. A carbon copy of a letter to his friend Dudley Evans of Wells, Fargo and Company, dated March 26th, 1898, says: " Nothing but war talk. Hill seems to be the only prominent railroad man who is fighting for peace. The Pennsylvania crowd say that nothing can be done to stop it since C. K. Davis and Alger are pushing the president. It can not be stopped from this end [New York] and I do not think Hanna can stop it in the Senate."

President longed for something else, a deliberate offer of
arbitration by a council of the Powers. He replied civilly,
twisting and reversing the phrases of the ambassadorial
twaddle, but presenting a counter comment on the note's
evasion. Their excellencies, he hinted, had not observed
that a humane cause was at stake in Cuba. This was rather
hard on the English diplomat, who had prevented a much
more insolent note, it is said, by informing the Conti-
nentals that England would not assent to an attempt at coer-
cion of the United States. The nations now symbolically
withdrew and Mr. McKinley waited for fresh news from
the civilized Old World in the morning. None came. Europe washed its hands of him and his affairs, he must have
thought. . . . About noon a letter arrived in Mr. Hanna's
office, where Joseph Kimball watched the Senator playing
solitaire on his desk. Hanna read the line from the White
House and made a noise inside his mouth, a swallowed
oath. He was beyond discretion. God damn the lot of
them! Why wouldn't they offer to arbitrate?

Here a high salesman in the White House would have
turned on Europe and called for arbitration, ignoring all
the rant of the French and German newspapers, asserting
the value of Cuba's case and forcing the tale of Spanish
stupidity on a table in full light. But McKinley had never
been abroad. He sensed that Europe was trying to bully
him, but he does not seem to have known that Europe could
be bullied back. And he was an American. The will of
majorities had a special meaning for him. War cries
banged in his ears. Roosevelt had said across a dinner-
table to Mark Hanna, " We are *going* to have this war! "
Cushman Davis, Alger, Frye, a mob of Congressmen and
officials, his own brother, and his friend Herman Kohlsaat
were telling him to go ahead. He delayed. He would not
send his message to the Capitol unless he heard that all
Americans were out of Cuba. Then, on April 11th, he sent

what it wanted to Congress, and so declined into an artist in popular government.

" If Congress had started this," Hanna said, " I'd break my neck to stop it." But his own President had let Congress have the lead. He sat glum in the Senate, approving when Teller of Colorado insisted that the Cubans must govern themselves when they were freed. He voted with the majority and walked through the Marble Room, staring at the floor, when the matter was concluded on April 19th. Reporters got some words out of him, but no sentiment worth print. A rumor lasted a few days. Hanna was said to have quarreled with Mr. McKinley. On May 2nd he was dining at the White House and the rumor wandered off in the herd of that month's lies.

He must have his say, though. " Now," he told some Senators and correspondents in the Marble Room, " look out for Mr. Bryan. Everything that goes wrong'll be in the Democratic platform in 1900. You can be damn sure of that! " They broke out in hoots of laughter. Bryan? What about the Silver Knight? Why, the man was a cipher! Uncle Mark was crazy. Only Senator Spooner shook his head. He thought that Bryan wasn't dead just yet.

" But," said Henry Cabot Lodge, " will not the Democrats hesitate before offering Mr. Bryan the nomination? "

" Hesitate? " Hanna growled. " Does a dog hesitate for a marriage license? "

He left the group. Senator Orville Platt asked the correspondents not to print Mr. Hanna's remark. He might not want it known that he thought such a thing. A solicitude for Mark Hanna grew among the Senators. He made no speeches, even in debates on the tariff, but they began to be fond of him. He was loyal to his President, and obliging about little jobs for a client of some friend, and his passion for arbitrating a row was useful in that nervous spring. And then he was an encyclopedia, ready in awkward moments of debate. Questions whispered along to his chair brought back a scribble of the number of negroes in Arkansas, the depth of Mobile Bay, or the size of a railroad station in Chicago. He was a good neighbor in the Senate and he gave a good dinner at his hotel. So they did not want to humiliate him by having it known that he was still afraid of Mr. Bryan.

Plutocratic imperialism now displayed itself in the Orient. In the first week of May it had to be admitted that something serious had happened between the Spanish and American fleets in the bay of Manila. On May 7th it was known that Commodore Dewey's ships had mashed up the defending flotilla and that Manila was due to be taken whenever American troops arrived. Within ten days Joseph Chamberlain and Lord Salisbury uttered speeches broadly friendly to the United States, and Americans in clever Paris heard that the Philippines were to be sold to England as soon as the subsidized Yankees had possessed the islands. The German official press twittered that Yankee insolence ought to be suppressed.[7] On June 3rd Vice Admiral Von Diederichs arrived at Manila and commenced his grotesque abrasions of neutral etiquette, facing the English commander, Chichester, past the American fleet. The situation was plain even to an eighteen-year-old seaman in the American pay. " These Dutch," he wrote to his mother in Fort Wayne, Indiana, " are trying to see if they can get up a fight with the English boats by busting all the rules. If we have a fight with them they can start a fight with England out of it and grab all this country out here." Seaman George P. Smith was in tune to the operations of imperialistic statecraft, which are those of eighteen-year-old boys.

---

[7] An editorial of the *Kölnische Volkszeitung* on May 7th is partly quoted in Peck's *Twenty Years of the Republic*. The files of this particular newspaper, from the moment of Dewey's victory to the signing of the peace with Spain, are luxuriously informative as to the quality of German propaganda, in 1898.

The game of grab, as glimpsed through portholes of his hot navigating home impressed him for what it was. On August 13th, if he was watching, he saw the British vessels steer forward between the rear of the American fleet and the moving German ships. Von Diederichs chose to follow the Yankee cruisers and transports steaming toward the city in assault, and Chichester chose to interfere. This ended the matter, in 1898, and historians may go on talking of the precise intentions demonstrated for a long time yet.

But the tension at Manila was quietly known in New York. The American plutocracy began to worry, not at all caring to have the United States drawn into a monstrous world war. In June, John Pierpont Morgan sent an agent to Washington to represent to Mr. Hanna that a victory in Cuba might make Germany recoil. Mr. Hanna rudely answered that he was not in the victory business. Still, a victory was supplied. On July 3rd Admiral Cervera led his squadron in flight from the bay of Santiago and it was destroyed by the blockading ships. Santiago fell. The war was all over. Spain had been licked in less than Mr. Hanna's six months.

He had not liked the war. " Oh, God," he said, reading the list of deaths at El Caney, " now we'll have this sort of thing again! " On the news of Santiago's fall the Senator swung out his cane among the ladies in a veranda and stood for minutes slowly stamping one heel on the floor. " Remember," he told a young girl, " that my folks were Quakers. War is just a damn nuisance. . . ." But in July he saw that the joke was on him, and he recognized the forces which had made his pacifism ludicrous. The United States had won something that could be assayed. European propaganda had vehemently advertised the wealth and the resources of the loathsome Yankee. Investors from France and Germany appeared in New York with notes introducing them to Mr. J. P. Morgan before the destruction of

Cervera's ships. All summer Herr Otto Heinrich was summoned from his desk in Dresden and brought to explain American securities to grave clients of his uncle's bank. He clicked his heels before a widowed countess and promised her that the city of Saint Louis was habitable and its bonds good. So the Hanna luck held. Mr. Hanna's President was now the ruler of a nation which, said a French statesman, " has entered the council of the Powers and is entitled, despite its youth, to the consideration of an equal. . . ." Its gunners could shoot and its bonds were good.

For all this, Mr. Hanna had not liked the war. Yet it did things for his President beyond the Mississippi; the West was pleased by this adventure; for twenty years every other lounger on a station's platform would tell tourists that he had been a Rough Rider in Roosevelt's regiment at San Juan Hill, and would accept a drink on the strength of that. The frontier was gone, and there was not much free land left to be parceled among sturdy men on the precedent of Mr. Lincoln's Homestead Act. Magnets which had drawn settlers to the West rusted out their attraction, but the strange thing called " earth hunger " still kept this Western population astir. A ghostly committee of Western legislators asked Mr. Hanna, in July, to find out whether Mr. McKinley would not keep the Philippine Islands.[8] The star of Empire was gone glimmering to its farthest and now beckoned from the Orient. Mr. McKinley had somehow led a war of expansion, without meaning to, and took the profits.

[8] Mr. Joseph Kimball was with Mr. Hanna when they called on him. Mr. Warren Watson informs me, in a letter dated July 1st, 1929, that: ". . . [in] the very first letters I received in Manila after the troops took possession of the town in 1898 was a funny request for information about ' farming land ' in the islands. The sender was a rolling stone whom I had occasionally helped with tiny loans when I was a clerk in Cheyenne, a typical ne'er-do-weel of the cow country. I do not care a straw what is now being said in histories of the period. The Westerners regarded the Philippines as a conquest and liked the idea of a colonial empire. . . ."

In the East, also, the war had done something unexpected. There was a new folk-hero born, and his rise amused Mr. Hanna, doubly. In the autumn of 1898 Senator Thomas Platt had to accept Colonel Theodore Roosevelt as the Republican machine's selection for Governor of New York State; an unlimited enthusiasm declared itself in the clubs while journalists caught up the commander of the Rough Riders into a glamour that ended by infuriating officers of regular troops which had also been employed in Cuba. Mr. Hanna was entertained so keenly that he laughed himself into an access of the cold indigestion that had troubled him ever since his typhoid fever of 1867. Why, the chilly metropolitans were like anybody else when it came to a military hero! They had made Roosevelt Governor of New York for charging a hill in Cuba. And how would Tom Platt get along with the crazy man? He wrote to Asa Barnes: " Mr. Roosevelt is really a very able man. He was a great help to Mr. Long last year in getting the navy ready for war. He took up a matter for me in a very effective way. . . .[9] I should expect to see him make a good record as governor unless he has bad times with Platt. He certainly did not ' shrink from office,' did he? "

Mr. Roosevelt unshrinkingly looked toward office and thus could not be sent to Paris with the commissioners as his friend Cushman Davis wanted when peace was discussed. Mr. Davis himself was selected and sailed with William Day, George Gray, and William Frye to join Whitelaw

[9] The case of the Gathmann torpedo, presumably. Mr. Hanna's passion for mechanics led him to interest himself in schemes offered to the Army and Navy in 1898. He rejected outright a grenade of the type afterwards used in the Great War, invented by a man named Vick Walter, of Chicago, saying that the cruelty of the device would damage American prestige! I have been shown a letter written by Secretary Long stating that Mr. Hanna had been of " inestimable help " in getting rid of " foolish inventions " tendered to the Navy Department. On the other hand, Mr. McKinley was rather given to clogging the department's work by sending along inventors and busybodies. Mr. Roosevelt complained of this in January of 1898 in a note to Jacob Riis.

Reid in France, remarking languidly that for once in his ill-spent life he would not be told by reporters how much he looked like the appalling Benjamin Butler. He was an obvious choice for this expedition, it seemed to Mr. McKinley, as he read French and Italian and, although Senator from Minnesota, suggested the heavy stateliness of an Eastern personage.

He was a personage, oddly forgotten by historians, a reformer, a jingo, an imperialist, and yet a critical patriot. It was Davis who launched an economist's demand for the control of big corporations in 1886, denouncing the theory of *laissez faire* as a profound economic fallacy spawned by Adam Smith. It was Davis who retorted in 1892 when a German imperialist invited the Reichstag to secure the decent dismemberment of the United States by planting colonies of civilized Europeans, commanded by their own ecclesiastics and speaking their own tongues, in yonder savage nation. The Senator from Minnesota thunderously told the Senate that this notion was less civilized than the political ideas of Confucius, and then was found by reporters in his office reading an unknown work named *The New Spirit*, by Havelock Ellis. He drawled that Dr. Ellis was a sort of improved Emerson and told the journalists where they could read the ideas of Confucius. The prose of *Moby Dick* moved him, but so did the rhythm of Tennyson's moral poems. He read constantly, slumped on a couch beside a box of violent cigars, and dallied with essays on Madame Roland and the law in the plays of Shakspere. He thought of a volume on musical instruments, described a history of prostitution in America that ought to be written by somebody else, and collected Napoleonana. But the war had done for him, he yawned. He would never amount to a damned thing, after the excitements and maladies of soldiering in the sixties. It took another war to rouse him. He set off for Paris ready to laugh aloud when the Spanish commission proposed that the United States accept the debts of Cuba along with Cuba.

John Hay's gay voice, meantime, had succeeded the politic silence of William Day at the State Department. The new Secretary talked so frankly that he seemed wholly indiscreet to callers. Yes, he had worked hard in England to secure the United States an open hearing in the newspapers. It had cost a pile of money. Such things did. But the sinking fund of the department had been at his disposal. He shrugged . . . " *Ça vous étonne, monsieur?* " . . . The superior Englishmen were on our side, but a friendly propaganda for use among the people had been necessary, and English dinners were expensive things. One talked best to journalists over champagne. . . . He was talking with Mr. Hanna, at lunch, when a wonderful interview of Cushman Davis reached him on December 12th, 1898. The Senator had been expansive to an English reporter, and had let his mind arrange a configuration of England, America, and Japan in the Orient, opposing the *Dreibund* of Germany, France, and Russia. To this marvel he added some thoughts on the utility of England as an ally, saying that the English had five hundred years of vigor left. " Heavenly union! " said Mr. Hay. " Davis has run amuck! " He hurried to the White House, paused in the telegraph room to tell Colonel Montgomery, " Do let me hear if Mr. Davis has another attack of statesmanship! " and then the door of Mr. McKinley's office shut on the Davis *Dreibund*.

The peace treaty was signed on December 10th, 1898 in Paris, and its terms promised Spain twenty million dollars for the Philippines. Now Mr. Hanna faced the revolt of the East. He knew that the West did not care, or favored keeping the islands. But only one Eastern Senator, Orville Platt, had been persistent in urging Mr. McKinley to hold the Philippines. Others had wavered and, outside the government, professors, editors, and a few bankers were protesting. They were not impressed by McKinley's prayers for guidance, and they did not know that Mrs. McKinley was charmed with the thought of Christianizing the Igorrotes.[10] Carl Schurz, William Sumner, Charles Francis Adams, William James, and Moorfield Storey were not infected by earth hunger. The Anti-Imperialist League was born at Boston in December of 1898. Senator Hoar and Thomas Reed headed the rebellion of Congress. Democratic legislators strayed, looking for a leader, when the treaty was sent to be ratified in January.

Leadership was bestowed. Mr. William Jennings Bryan appeared in the Marble Room and stood among the Democratic Senators, slowly gesticulating, beautiful, and still tanned a little by exposure in the camp of a volunteer regiment which he had peaceably commanded. His presence excited Mr. Hanna to telling Orville Platt that he'd like to see Mr. Bryan play Hamlet. Mr. Bryan's public performance had this purpose: the treaty must be ratified, to end the burden of war on the plain people. The people could then dispose of the Philippines by its sovereign will. He was well heard. On February 5th the treaty was ratified and an issue for the campaign of 1900 had been contrived. " This simple minded strategy seemed Machiavellian to him," says Charles Willis Thompson. " His idea was that if he could get the treaty ratified, the people would blame McKinley for it, because it was a McKinley treaty."

Mr. Hanna was not disturbed. On February 19th the New York Life Insurance Company learned, " He says that Bryan's trick can be discounted. McKinley consulted

---

[10] " Mrs. McK. talked ten to the minute about converting the Igorrotes. I hope you know how to spell the name of this tribe because your fond father does not. Anyhow she wants you and Alice to pray for the Igorrotes or Iggorotes. Tell your mother that Mrs. McK. asked for her. She was wearing a pink kind of dress with green spots. . . ." William C. Beer to his son, October 23rd, 1898.

hundreds of people of all kinds on his trip " (McKinley went to the Exposition at Omaha in October) " and finds western sentiment generally in favor of holding the islands. He implied that our good understanding with England would be damaged by letting Spain retain the Philippines, as they would be instantly sold to Germany. He said in a very forcible way, ' I wonder what these people in Boston would say if we listened to Hoar and turned the islands over to the natives. Why, Germany would take them in a month! Spain is selling all her other islands to Germany as it is. Hoar is crazy. He thinks Germany is just fooling.' He said a great deal more in the same strain. . . . I find a widespread feeling down here that Mr. Hanna is not much in favor of holding the Philippines but let himself be persuaded by Hay and [Orville] Platt. Hay is supposed to have practically pledged the country to keep the islands out of Germany's control.[11] Mr. Cortelyou had nothing to say on the matter. . . ." [12]

Now that Mr. Hanna had entered the sphere of conscienceless world-politics he dealt with it realistically. One's friends stood by one handsomely, in wars as in elections, and one paid them back. Let Hoar keep his illusions. But he was moved by the old Senator's tirades, because he liked the Yankee and enjoyed hearing him make an oration. He esteemed these men who could get up on their feet and become periodically eloquent. He always sat out a speech of Joseph Foraker, listening to his rival from Ohio with every attention. Mr. Foraker was abler and abler, now that the showiness of his time as Governor of Ohio had peeled

[11] Hay's letter to Mr. McKinley, dated August 2nd, 1898, states that " our English friends " would be disappointed if the United States relinquished the Philippines. Myron Herrick, in conversation with Mr. George Poldmann, in 1927, told him that Hay was obliged to argue Hanna into supporting the treaty. An autograph of Mr. Hay addressed to " Dear Hall," dated October 30th, contains the sentence, " I have had to talk Philippine business to Hanna for six hours."

[12] William C. Beer to George Walbridge Perkins, from Washington.

away from him. He talked simply, driving his sentences along in a pulsation of ready, sharp words, and men feared him. Even toughened journalists in the gallery would watch Foraker support a bill of the Administration on some trivial matter with an interest in his method. He was a lonely force in the Senate, an item of the machine, but a patent will, too little conciliating to be a leader and too cool to gather on himself the affection which came to Hanna or to Hoar and Orville Platt. And Mr. Hanna admired him, with detachment, since we have no other word for the mood in which the disbelieving mind observes the process of establishing belief.

Mr. Hanna believed in what Mark Hanna had done. His President was admired, and the business of the country swelled through 1899, fed by European investments, spilling manufactured products back into Europe. Industrialism's object was attained, and ever so comfortably. " The factories send up smoke; the workman's dinner-pail is full." Tariff had not brought revolution, and revolution did not come when the Congress fixed gold as the standard of value in the United States. The country bankers called on McKinley, and said, " God bless you! " in sincerity. Wages went up. Mortgages were paid off. A flutter of social display was constant. The intake of insurance companies was so rank that their presidents awarded to themselves salaries of invincible tragedians without a protest from charmed stockholders, and express companies showered free turkey and tinned oysters on clerks at Christmas. It was grand.

But the jinni in the midst of this golden vapor had moments of speculation. Mr. Hanna's general attitude toward workmen wasn't unctuous. He never flattered his engineers, his street-car hands, and his shipbuilders. He lent them money to set up a house or to send a promising boy to college, and he was not particular about being repaid.

561

His life was wound in a series of personal relations. This series included friendships with common mechanics and servants, for his cook adored him, and the waiters in his clubs sent roses to his funeral. People were people. He liked them, or he didn't. But what was all this bosh he began to hear at dinners where Eastern owners of coal mines and railroads prosed about " the lower classes? " " You mean working men? " he asked a Philadelphian banker. " Or do you mean criminals and that kind of people? Those are the lower classes."

This was not a pose. Mr. Hanna held and said repeatedly that a certain sort of workman would never get up in the world. God knew why, but they were born to be damn stupid folks. They stuck their fingers in machines, lost their pay envelopes and gabbled that the world owed every man a living when the foremen fired them. " I'll take back a drunk three times, but I won't have fools working for me. They get everybody in trouble." His mouth tightened when a young reformer, wiser since, protested an idea then afloat in social discussions, the castration of male morons. " It ain't pretty," said the pragmatist, " but what's the sense in increasing the supply of damn fools? We've got plenty." And what, he asked Jacob Riis, were you going to do with men who " won't save money, won't look after their kids, and won't stick to a job when they get one given to them? " So the mention of communism made him snort. What? Give all the damn fools in the world equal rights with good men? . . . By God, no!

But he detested this patter about the lower classes, so smoothly turned out by men who owned a coal mine or a railroad fed by coal mines. He viewed some of the great Pennsylvanian owners with a distinguished and rather visible contempt, not diminished by the fact that they rallied to his enemy Matthew Quay. " I hear," he said very suddenly to William Beer, " that there's going to be a revolu-

tion pretty quick, over in Pennsylvania. Heard of it? " Mr.
Beer had, because a friend who happened to be president
of the Pennsylvania Railroad Company was worried by
the talk in the coal country. " Hoh," said Hanna, " it'd
serve 'em all right! " This was in 1899. When the strike of
1902 did come, Mr. Hanna grunted his challenge to the
Pennsylvanians, " Serve 'em right if Roosevelt seizes the
mines. Go and tell Baer I said so! " [13] And so they had
been criticizing the Civic Federation and himself for trying
to avert the strike? " All right! You tell them that if I
hear any more of that kind of talk I will go to New York,
hire Carnegie Hall, and give them something to talk
about! "

If he could not stand the workman fool, he could not
stand the employing fool. In final fact he had an aversion
to fools. When Jacob Riis argued with him on the topic of
the Civic Federation, alleging that it was fatal for the delegates of the labor unions to come in contact with the rich,
who would be sure to overawe them, Mr. Hanna said, " But
the union men aren't fools, young man! " and scowled at
the journalist in plain offense. He was annoyed by the
superfluous fools who came calling at the White House to
take up the President's time. One day in May of 1899 he
stood watching a deputation of some kind filing out of the
place and said, " What would happen, do you think, if
some crank got in there with a revolver in his pants? "

III

In June he went abroad to see what Europe could do for
his rheumatism. Before leaving Cleveland he told the men

---

[13] Mr. Baer was the remarkable president of the Reading Iron and Coal
Company, who believed or said that God had put the operators in control of
the mines, and then told Mr. Roosevelt that coal-mining was not a religious
business. I happen to have heard Mr. Baer talk several times, and he remains
one of the most indurated specimens of the platitudinizing mediocrity I have
ever met.

of his street railways that they would be so good as not to join the strike planned by carmen of other lines in Cleveland. He then sailed and drearily took the cure at Aix-les-Bains, dodged up into Germany to consult American consuls about the law excluding American life-insurance companies from doing business in the Kaiser's territories, and then came home, uncured, and outraged by the absence of the American flag on the seas. " It's just a shame! " he cried, at luncheon in New York. " Where the hell are our ships? " Mrs. Hanna put her hands on her ears and hurried the Senator off to Cleveland, where Maggie, his legendary and noble cook, waited to soothe him with baked hash, stewed corn, and hot biscuit. His carmen, of course, had not joined the savage strike which scared the city while Mr. Hanna was away. He had gold coins added to the pay in a thousand envelopes on the next Saturday and bustled down to Washington to look at his President, wearying Charles Nolan on the train by a lecture about a subsidized shipping for the United States. He saw the American flag drifting on ships as they passed through a canal cut across Nicaragua or the isthmus of Panama. He talked half through the night, shoving his cane back and forth on the floor of his state room. . . . Europe? Oh, yes! Pretty interesting, but about these ships — [14]

In October the Democrats of Ohio hopefully selected John McLean, a rich and practical politician, as their candidate for Governor. Mr. Hanna used, against this serious antagonist, some of his technic for national elections. There were many hired speakers, much propaganda, and ample checks for workers. " Hanna is buying the cities

[14] He had proposed an act to subsidize a merchant marine in December of 1898. This became a mild mania with him for the rest of his life and he was admittedly tedious on the subject. A more interesting hobby was a notion of a governmental school for scientific research. He discussed this with Professor Langley and once with Henry Adams, at a dinner given by John Hay. Mr. Adams told Mrs. Charlton Paull that Hanna had quite an elaborate scheme for this school.

of Ohio," said Mr. Bryan. But it turned out that Mr. Hanna's candidate did best in the country or in little towns where Mr. Hanna made speeches, in the last weeks of October, while Mr. McLean's strength seemed to lie in the corrupt cities, not among the plain people.

In December some men in the lobby of the Raleigh at Washington were discussing McLean's defeat with Senator Richard Pettigrew of South Dakota. Mark Hanna was proving a good stump speaker. Mr. Warren Watson described the effect of Hanna's talks on the rural crowds in Ohio and praised the Senator's power of retorting offhand when he was heckled by Democrats in the audience. Mr. Pettigrew jeered; the Democrats were hired helpers from the Republican sty at Cleveland, he said, and Hanna drilled them beforehand in what they were to say. Would a thief like Hanna risk answering a sincere question, impromptu? Here a mild stranger outside the group said, " But, Senator, you wouldn't call Tom Johnson a thief for planting people in an audience? " Mr. Pettigrew denied that the Democratic reformer would do such a thing. The mild stranger meekly said, " But, Senator, he did it all the time in New York when he was campaigning for Henry George," (in 1897) " and I know he did, because he paid me ten dollars a meeting for asking him questions." Mr. Pettigrew got up and walked away.

Mr. Pettigrew had never forgiven Mark Hanna for ruining Silver in 1896. He was a quiet man, but he quarreled easily and carried a grudge to the public extreme of loud speech. " See," he said to Mr. Watson in a theater, one night, " there goes Hanna's wife. Every diamond on her is bought with blood! " Mr. Watson chuckled at this rhetoric, and Pettigrew would not speak to him for months. He was feared in the Senate, because he specialized in personal attacks. Having deserted the Republican party in 1896, he seemed to loathe everybody in it, except Hoar and Mr. Wilson, the Secretary of Agriculture. He pushed a scene with Henry Cabot Lodge in the Marble Room, in the autumn of 1898, by sneering at Theodore Roosevelt on some forgotten ground. Nobody was safe from him. " Here comes pale malice," Cushman Davis said, when Mr. Pettigrew strolled near him. " My God, Pettigrew," Senator Wolcott asked, " do you spit lemon juice? "

This character was perhaps a manufactured, defensive thing. Mr. Pettigrew could be kind, and his charities are remembered. He took care of poor relatives, bothered at home about sanitations and grain elevators in the small towns, and had friends who were appalled by his manner in the Senate. But his hatred of Marcus Hanna was acute, and it broke out once in December of 1899 before Oscar Underwood so flamboyantly that the gentleman from Alabama thought the Westerner mean and mad. They were standing on the steps of the Capitol, and close to them Mr. Hanna was comparing socks with Cushman Davis. A Yankee representative approached the jinni and put in a request of size, asking to have part of the Atlantic fleet sent to a port in Massachusetts for a celebration in the spring. Mr. Hanna thought and refused, rubbing an ear. The Congressman simmered and puffed steam. " You had a consul sent to Aix to doctor you! It doesn't matter what you get out of the government! " Mr. Hanna stiffened his neck and seemed tall. " It cost the government two dollars to send a cable. I paid his fare from Nuremberg to Aix an' back. Do you know what it'd cost in coal to send some battleships to this show? . . . No? Well, go and ask the Navy Department! " The Congressman was blown down the steps. But the gentleman from Alabama had to hear an oration by Richard Pettigrew on privilege and corruption. " He made it sound as though the whole consular service in Europe had been corrupted," Mr. Underwood said in 1919, " and if it had not been so foolish, it would have been pathetic to see an intelligent man so excited. But it was downright lunacy. He raved at me."

Mr. Pettigrew then moved to his doom. He sat in the Senate just ahead of Mr. Hanna, but never spoke to him. On June 5th, 1900, while Hanna was answering a charge of the Democrats for the Republican National Committee, Senator Pettigrew began fiddling a printed report, flipping its leaves so that men noticed it in his hands. It was the report of a minority in the Senate's committee on Privileges and Elections, asking an investigation of the tale that one of the assemblymen had been influenced to vote for Mr. Hanna in 1898 by unfair means. It was an inconclusive, wandering business, and the Senate had not bothered with the thing, as there was no real evidence of bribery set forth. But Mr. Pettigrew attacked Hanna with this clumsy bludgeon for ten minutes. The Senators grinned. Pettigrew was at it again. When the Senator from South Dakota ended his performance and sat down, they expected nothing.

But the Senate rippled as Hanna jumped up, yelling, " Mr. President! " and men hurried in to hear. He pinned together long sentences, comma by comma, and slung them at Pettigrew's shoulders in a continuous war song. He announced by the tone of his clattering words that he was sick of being lied about, caricatured, and called a knave, and a legend grew that he had cursed Pettigrew in the grandest manner, although he said little about the malignant orator. But he had found an eloquence. This was wrath. The indifferent god of the office-seekers had turned a new power loose. When he left the chamber, he pushed aside friends and went straight to the White House.[15]

[15] Colonel Montgomery told my father that Mr. Hanna's anger was cumulative in this case, as reports of Mr. Pettigrew's language about him had reached Mrs. Hanna, who was not well. Charles Willis Thompson in *Presidents I've Known and Two Near Presidents* points out that Mr. Hanna respected the dignity of the Senate. He disliked to hear personal attacks

He had not proposed to have this yarn spread in the campaign or to have it said that he was afraid to answer Pettigrew. In 1896 his friends persuaded him to keep still for McKinley's sake, when his son's lawyers had listed one hundred topics in an action for libel against Alfred Henry Lewis. But he was done with keeping still. He was going to " see about " this Pettigrew. When he had time, he would attend to the Senator from South Dakota. And there was Mr. Bryan. He would attend to Mr. Bryan. Immediately, he saw, there was a third case to be attended to.

Theodore Roosevelt, Governor of New York, went into the West and made speeches. The plain people called him Teddy — not that Mr. Roosevelt cared for the trick — and thrust up placards lettered " Roosevelt in 1904! " from crowds at stations. A constant need of self-assertion in Roosevelt's adolescence had given him a curious, unforgettable exaggeration of facial gesture and he had picked up from Senator Cushman Davis an excellent motion of the right hand in speaking. He drove forward whatever points he was making with a kind of stabbing thrust — the hand rose almost to the level of his shoulder and slanted down a trifle as the arm stretched. It was hypnotic and useful, for his voice was not pleasant when he spoke loudly, although its quality was charming in ordinary speech. Before New Year's Day of 1900, there could be no doubt that Mr. Roosevelt at last was a national personality, and in February Senator Thomas Platt had decided to transfer Roosevelt from the governorship to the vice presidency, for the convenience of Thomas Platt. This project seemed wisest to Mr. Platt, since it would cost an ugly, open battle

---

exchanged in the chamber. Mr. Pettigrew's speech reads unimpressively, as does Mr. Hanna's answer. The tones of the two men formed the melodrama of the episode. Mr. Pettigrew's feeling about the Silver issue was extravagant before 1896 and one of his relatives tells me that his hatred of Hanna was an obsession. He would believe anything said of Hanna, no matter how absurd.

in the Republican party to stop a second nomination of Roosevelt for Governor. He allowed it to be known that Mr. Roosevelt's friends were anxious to see him preside over the Senate.

Indubitably some of Mr. Roosevelt's friends wanted just that, and Mr. Roosevelt, in March of 1900, surprised John McCook by asking at a dinner whether it might not be better for him to accept the vice presidency rather than to disrupt the state's Republican party by a muddle over his reforming policies in New York's financial affairs. Colonel McCook advised him against the dull job in Washington, and then had a difficult hour with Mr. Platt when his advice was reported to the easy boss. But by May Mr. Roosevelt seemed to be set against the vice presidency and he appeared as the national Republican Convention collected itself in Philadelphia in June, with his mind made up: he would stay in his own state. Mr. Platt, however, had been busy. He had friends enough in the West to promote his wishes out there, and the natural feeling for the Rough Rider among the plain people was now solidified by some machine-made tacks and rivets. Western delegates got off the train at Philadelphia assured that dirty work was being done against Mr. Roosevelt, to cheat him of his dues. This feeling had caught even some of Roosevelt's intimate journalists, and they rushed about in the heat hunting Hanna to demand that he stop kicking their friend in the face, as one of them memorably put it. And in addition it proved that Mr. Matthew Quay had arranged a feeling for Roosevelt among the Pennsylvanian delegates.

" Our babe is in the manger," said Mr. Quay; " the kings have seen his star in the East and are come to worship him."

Mr. Roosevelt's sombrero passed among the Western delegates and the man under it assured his friends that he wanted to stay in New York for another term as Governor. Cynics chuckled a little about the soft and conspicuous hat.

It was an acceptance hat, said one of them to Arthur Dunn, and others wondered why Colonel Roosevelt wore this remembrance of the Cuban campaign. On Monday and Tuesday the hat was everywhere, and everywhere men pointed out to each other that Mr. Roosevelt's Eastern backers were very busy. On Wednesday morning Cushman Davis and Knute Nelson were hunting the Governor of New York, and Mr. Davis angrily bade Bruce Higginson tell Roosevelt that the Westerners would not stand for much more of this. The party wanted him to be vice president; the party might stop wanting anything of him, if he flouted its wishes. . . . Platt saw an advantage; messengers pounced on Mr. Roosevelt in the lobby of the Hotel Walton and drew him upstairs into Senator Platt's rooms. He rejoined Frederick Holls an hour later and said, nervously, that he must not disappoint his Western admirers.[16] That afternoon Charles Dawes telephoned to the President, reporting the tension in Philadelphia, and late that night Mr. Hanna invited the convention to nominate Mr. Roosevelt for the vice presidency unanimously. This was done.

" All right," said Mr. Hanna to a powerful man from New York; " all you gentlemen wanted Roosevelt out of New York. You've done it. Now, who's going to win your campaign for you? "

For three days there was an unreported, hot panic among the great powers. Hanna would not run the campaign, someone told someone. On June 21st Senator Thomas Platt was telephoning to most obscure men who were supposed to be on good terms with Hanna, asking the news. This one

[16] Mr. Kohlsaat's account of this episode differs trivially from a note of Frederick Holls to my father, written on Wednesday. In *From McKinley to Harding*, Mr. Kohlsaat quotes Nicholas Murray Butler as an authority and states that Mr. Roosevelt was obdurate until Platt sent for him. Mr. Holls wrote: " He was getting weak on Tuesday night. Platt sent [Lemuel] Quigg to find him. We happened to be standing in the Walton, with N. M. Butler. Roosevelt came to see me after an hour and seemed very nervous and strange. He said he had given in to prevent trouble with the western crowd."

remark of the fetish had caused such a rumpus among hardened, middle-aged capitalists and politicians. Everything would be lost without Uncle Mark. But on June 23rd there was sweetness blowing. Mr. Hanna had guffawed when he was directly asked if he wasn't going to play. The machine was being polished and oiled. Uncle Mark would do the right thing.

The incident did Mr. Hanna an indirect service. Journalistic certainties weakened a bit. It was plain, absolutely known, that Hanna had objected to Roosevelt's nomination, when the nomination was wanted by the chiefs of finance. Finance and the Westerners had forced Roosevelt on the Administration. Perhaps, then, the link between Hanna and Wall Street was not absolute? For the three years left to him, Mark Hanna was allowed to be fairly independent by some of the reporters. But when he died, the necessities of dramatizing him conveniently caused journalists to forget what they had learned at Philadelphia in 1900.

Mr. Bryan duly swarmed into sight, talking against imperialism, advocating more free silver, and, of course, anxious to preserve the nation from the Trusts. He was to be curiously supported, this time, by Richard Croker and Tammany Hall, while several inland bosses worked for him with a fair enthusiasm — nothing headlong or lavish, but a pleasing warmth. Mr. Hanna's machine then functioned, and the campaign went on smoothly and economically. Mr. Roosevelt was shot into the West and minor speakers were flicked into towns just after Mr. Bryan had made an oration or just before. Many babies were named for Mr. Roosevelt, but Mr. Bryan scored over him, in one instance. Mr. William Bryan Wells was born in the crowd listening to Mr. Bryan's remarks and, he is told, in a temperature of ninety-seven degrees. Roosevelt never had the effect on women which was at Mr. Bryan's constant disposal. In this campaign a Yankee virgin of seventy spent

571

incalculable money, buying and sending through the mails photographs of the Silver Knight to public schools and Sunday schools. On the other shore of the continent a widow of greater wealth paid the whole cost of the Democratic campaign in a city of twenty-eight thousand. Everywhere the female mind was at this orator's service; he was a religious symbol to uncounted lonely creatures.[17]

In September an unbelievable rumor crept; it was said that Senator Hanna was to go out on a tour of the Northwest, making speeches. This caused another unreported little panic at New York, where the wise men saw at once that Hanna would be murdered by some Populist if he set foot in Michigan or Wisconsin. New Yorkers could sit amused in cabs on Union Square listening to immigrant Socialists and even to Terrorists denouncing Wall Street, but, out there on the map, beyond Buffalo, there were terrible people ready to slay. Deputations addressed the President, saying that Mr. Hanna's life ought not to be risked. Mr. Henry Cabot Lodge put forth a special kind of pleading. He begged Senator Proctor of Vermont to use his large influence with Mr. McKinley to keep Mr. Hanna out of sight lest the good done by Theodore Roosevelt's speaking trip be lost to the party. The Senator from Vermont was tickled and didn't keep this plea to himself. It reached Mr. Hanna on October 3rd. He tossed Mr. Proctor's note to a caller and asked, " Isn't it nice to be told that you're not fit for publication? "

[17] It was my father's task in 1900 to find out for the Republican campaign committee just what the real capabilities of applicants for funds were. Hanna was determined to waste as little money as possible. In consequence Mr. Beer heard a good deal about the private mania for Mr. Bryan. He always asserted that people who had no connection with the Democratic campaign committees lavished enough money on Bryan to bring up the expenses of the orator's campaign in 1900 to the level of the Republican expense. In 1900 Mr. Hanna remarked to Mr. Walter Stoeffel that he knew of a widow in Cleveland who had spent a hundred thousand dollars on Bryan.

POWER, OF A KIND

The President sent the Postmaster General to discourage Mr. Hanna, with tactful oral messages. But the Senator sent back word that God hated cowards, and went off to attend to Richard Pettigrew and William Jennings Bryan in a private car, with assistants and a secretary, and nine reporters. He was announced by telegraph. If anybody was going to shoot him, he said, there was time to get the guns well loaded. "By heaven," said Tom Johnson, in Cleveland, "he has sand!" For all Americans are credulous about other Americans. As they had arranged a seraglio for Roscoe Conkling, delirium tremens for Grover Cleveland, originality and sincerity for William Bryan, and inhuman valor for Theodore Roosevelt, so they now built up an unqualified loathing of Marcus Hanna among the plain people. Dramatically, this should be.

The plain people was interested to look at Mr. Hanna. Wives fried breakfast at two in the morning and the buggies and spring wagons set off, filled with sneezing children, to the tracks eight miles away. Proletarians clotted at stations and piled on the roofs of freight houses, waiting for a mountainous brute in clothes splotched with dollar marks. Dollar Mark, the Red Boss of Cleveland, the fat brother of the Trusts in cartoons, was now to appear. An old man in a gray suit came limping out on the brazen balcony of the last car and told them that protected industry meant " more wages for the working man, more money in the banks, better prices for your crops." Smart lads swallowed twice and yelled questions at him, over the heads. What about the Trusts? "Well, what about 'em? All you boys have got foolish reading the papers. You'll see that big combinations of capital end up by forcing down prices. Why's one wagon company sell your dad his wagon ten dollars cheaper than the next one? That's what comes of these big combinations, in the long run. . . . Any old Grangers in the crowd, here? . . . Good morning. . . . I ask you this. Didn't

<label>573</label>

the Grangers combine to run prices up, so's your families could live comfortably, and didn't you fight the railroads like — like Sam Hill, to get rates regulated? Of course you did! It was sound business and good practice. Anybody abusin' you people now? All right, combine and smash 'em! . . . Combination is the life of business, and of politics, too! . . . Huh? Yes, I believe in capitalism. Set something up against it as a better system for promoting prosperity and I'll believe in that, when it works. . . . And now listen to Mr. Dolliver a minute. He makes a lot better speech than I do."

News returned to Washington. Nobody had shot the Senator, and crowds bigger than those greeting Mr. Roosevelt came to hear him. He meandered through Iowa, Michigan, Minnesota. Then he swept into Nebraska one morning. At Lincoln the crowd was immense. Mr. Hanna pounded his little fists on the railing and shouted at Mr. Bryan's neighbors that the Silver Knight's latest statement of Republican corruption was " false as hell." He had promised himself to denounce Bryan as a demagogue in his own town, and here he was doing it. Having done it, Hanna beamed at the crowd and blew his nose before resuming his graceless remarks. He was giving himself a good time.

Out in the press William McCready's old Populist father turned on his son and said, " But he don't look like he ought to, Billy! " The human image asserted itself against the cartoon, and in South Dakota it asserted itself at close range, since a law of the state forbade orators to speak from trains. Mr. Hanna trundled two hundred feet to a platform and spoke thence, while boys crept so near that they could smell his cigars. The demon pock-marked with dollars vanished in this sunlight; it was just a man standing there, without diamonds on his thumbs. . . . So Mr. Richard Pettigrew was defeated by a Republican candidate on election day, and the state of Nebraska was disloyal to Mr. Bryan.

Cushman Davis was dying all this while. When they told him that Mr. Hanna had started for a tour in South Dakota he said, " Captain Ahab is after his White Whale! " Mr. Hanna did not understand the allusion to *Moby Dick* and it had to be explained to him that a man named Herman Melville had written a tale of a crazy captain who chased a whale which once had hurt him. Oh? That reminded him. In 1896 some bookish person asked if he wasn't related to that Herman Melville, on account of his brother's name, and he had answered, " What the hell kind of job does Melville want? " Melville was dead, was he? That was why the bookish person laughed so. The Senator laughed, then talked on about Cushman Davis, and his eyes filled with tears. . . . Davis died. The newspapers forgot his speech against *laissez faire* in 1886 and twaddled about his books and a quarrel of his second wife with another legislator's lady in Washington. The man who had written twenty thousand letters to secure a law regulating capital's powers, who had done all he could to give the West its war in 1898 and then all he could to give imperialism its place among American policies, now vanished, and is nothing but a generous note in the memoirs of Theodore Roosevelt.

Senator Hanna rested, in his manner, at Cleveland and played bridge in the Union Club. He seemed, for the first time, an old man when Henry Adler made his last call at the house beside the Lake. Some rust now showed on the human machine. But the Senator was gay; his chase of Pettigrew had delighted him and he felt nothing but good humor toward Mr. Bryan. The orator always did the wrong thing. Free Silver was dead, and the people didn't care a damn whether the government kept the Philippines or set them free.

" And do you? "

" Not much," said Mark Hanna.

But why had he made such a kick against mentioning a

canal through Nicaragua in the Republican platform? Mr. Hanna would not answer until he was pressed. His mouth hardened. He hadn't wanted McKinley committed to a canal through Nicaragua or through the isthmus. But why not? Oh, he hated being bulldozed into a thing, whether he wanted it or not.

"Look," he said, "I've had enough things forced down my throat in this campaign!"

It was whispered about, in 1900, that a faint coldness grew between the Senator and his President. Mr. Hanna was no longer the minister without portfolio, distributor of federal jobs, but the leader of the Republican party in the Senate. This power, he told a friend, he would not exchange for the presidency. He was proud of it. He existed in the chamber and the Marble Room utterly apart from William McKinley. He had woven himself into the life of the Congress. And how? Well, he was a business man in politics. Let some Congressman run to him with the case of a shipmaster bullied down at Buenos Aires by the venal authorities of the port, and Mr. Hanna's telephone clicked. The Senator was speaking to the State Department, to Mr. Hay himself. Let some Democrat approach him in the Marble Room wailing that Hay and the President were dragging the United States into world-politics too far by demanding an open door for the trade of all nations in China, and people drew close to hear Hanna retort, for American trade. Nothing was too small to interest the Senator from Cleveland. He adjusted anything that was business. An engine driver had been crippled while helping to unload supplies at Tampa for the Army? All right! He would look after that, for Mr. Oscar Underwood, and he lectured the tall gentleman from Alabama on the dignity of engine drivers. "I've talked to hundreds of 'em. Never met one fool, either. . . ." A cargo of mahogany, the sorrows of an insurance company shut out of Germany, the complaint of a

lady whose son had been reprimanded at Annapolis for trying to invent a new torpedo, the inefficiency of a laundry
machine in a government hospital — bring him anything
that touched his instinct of a trader or that had to do with
a machine, and Mr. Hanna's voice would be loud for the
persons in trouble. A thousand such obligations bound Senators and Congressmen to Uncle Mark. He rose, in this simplicity, by his usefulness, and superstition clustered on him.
He was luck, he was force — and there was something else.
Dazedly and unwillingly, people came to see that the old
jinni loved his country, as he queerly loved his city and his
state. It was unaccountable, almost indecent, when he had
been dramatized as a mere plunderer. But there it was. " I
won't have an American abused," he growled, in the State
Department, " and I don't give a damn if he has a jail record
and ain't got a cent! You get those Swiss to let him loose! "

He towered. When there were rumors of descending tariffs and perhaps some regulation of business itself in the
summer of 1901, men at New York were afraid to ask the
jinni questions. They heard how he had yelled in a shop
at Washington when an American glove split on his hand
that the manufacturers were " squatting behind the tariff
like a lot of God-damn rabbits " and cheating the public
with bad goods. His paternalism might swell out and grow
critical, unless something was done about him. Suppose he
started his own war on protected industry? The alarmed
millionaires began to woo him with invitations and elaborated blandishments.

Then the murder of Mr. McKinley at Buffalo tossed all
calculations in a heap. Men who had wanted Roosevelt out
of New York because he intruded on matters of franchise
and seemed likely to regulate everything financial remembered Hanna's outcry to Arthur Dunn at Philadelphia,
" Don't you understand that there is just one life between
this crazy man and the presidency if you force me to take

577

Roosevelt? " Now they had something worse than a reforming governor on their charts of possible accident. All tendencies of political criticism in America latterly drifted toward a notion of central reform; the people were to look to Washington for redress of the balance between financial weight and popular weight. Finance had lifted Mr. Roosevelt's uncomfortable quality from the small area to the grand map. It was known that he thought a President entitled to powers of this critical kind. Now, what?

Of course he would discard Hanna, at once. Hanna had opposed his nomination at Philadelphia and Hanna would pay for that. The dramatization was swift. They didn't ponder enough on the new President's singular relation to the Congress. With Cushman Davis dead, Mr. Roosevelt had no spokesman in the Senate. There was Lodge, but the Yankee scholar was not a leader. Who was to be leader of the party at the Capitol? A story wandered loose in which Mr. Roosevelt and Mark Hanna were supposed to have come to terms on the train bringing McKinley's body from Buffalo, but that was sure to be a fake. No. Hanna was all over.

Late in November an agent went down to consult the Secretary of State for an insurance company on the case of a mess in China, with suspicion of European influence. Mr. Hay read the statements and then was evasive. Perhaps the President should see this. Could he arrange an appointment with Mr. Roosevelt?

" Certainly," said John Hay; " come along. The President and I are both lunching with Mr. Hanna."

CHAPTER V

JINNI

W HEN Lord Pauncefote died, in 1902, the President ordered the flag of the White House brought down to half-mast and thus presented Count Cassini with a topic. The Russian sat at luncheon and purred to his guests that Roosevelt had so honored the death of an English ambassador from a profound envy. Mr. Roosevelt would like nothing better than to be a great landholder, with horses and dogs. " *C'est son paradis laiteux. . . .*"

One of the guests laughed. Hadn't the President and the Attorney General just brought an action against the Northern Securities Company which must end in dissolving James Hill's huge combination of the northwestern railroads? Did that look as though he envied wealth? " You 'ave vulgar ideas," said the Count. Who had spoken of wealth? He was sipping brandy. After a little brandy the Russian ambassador did not care what he said about anybody. He smoothly chewed all Washington, the Cabinet, the insufferable Senators and their fat wives, those enraged cows the idiotic journalists, even dear friends of a handsome girl who was hostess at his embassy, and spat out the pulp. . . . Who had spoken about wealth? Bah! The President's milky heaven was to be such a creature as Cromwell, a false aristocrat who roused the filthy people to follow him. Had one not heard Mr. Roosevelt make a case for Cromwell? And then all that reverent babble about his mother's family in the South, with the lands and the hunting dogs! . . . He saw offended eyes, and turned the talk to himself, gayly deploring that he soon would be promoted. He would be minister of foreign affairs in Saint Petersburg, or maybe prime minister. " Then will come the dirty moujik with a bomb — and I shall go to heaven! " He faced the calamity, with a smile. They laughed. The Count was so amusing.

He came near to a sharp statement of Mr. Roosevelt's position in 1902. The plutocrats and their imitators had for some years busied themselves with a decoration of country-houses, gardens, horses, kennels, and bastard oak paneling. Ladies in 1902 were trying to use the word " bitch " technically without flushing; stockbrokers fitted on pink coats and fell off tall hunters in great quantity. Mr. Roosevelt seemed to be a shape in this movement. His horse on the driveway of the White House and his pleasant, simple estate on Long Island were possessions that tuned in this music of fresh wind. Abject journalists assured inland women that Mr. Roosevelt sprang from " two of the most aristocratic families in the United States . . ." and old ladies in New York or Georgia took that news as they might. An exacerbating dandy, who had lived within a quarter mile of Mr. Roosevelt all their two lives without meeting him, told James Huneker in the lounge of the Metropolitan Opera that the President was quite decently English. He shot and rode and all that, he'd taken a regiment to Cuba just as the best Englishmen took regiments to South Africa, and so he was quite all right.

This suggestion of the country squire rose wholesomely among moneyed men whose photographs betray hepatic insufficiency and social leaders in whose portraits faces seem masks of rosy dough stretched on wire. His other attributes soon made Mr. Roosevelt a sun god to many differing groups of Americans. He was antiplutocratic to weary theorists. His orthodoxy soothed clergymen worried by the swell of free thought. He was a model of sportsmanship useful to schoolmasters busily prodding introspective lads away from the amusements of intellect toward the baseball field. To the fathers of such lads he was the holy gospel of action, since nothing in the President's advice to the young could be construed as an encouragement of dreaming. He was food and light to sentimentalists; his qualities could be identified with almost any wish. The cult increased. He was advertised as a patent medicine, a panacea, until in his last phase youngsters went to call on Mr. Roosevelt well prepared to hate him.

They met a personage, charmingly alert, whose egotism floated in a tidal sweep of conversation which billowed twenty gayeties in an hour. If they were tactful they found that one must not argue when the Colonel happened to call Goya, Flaubert, or El Greco morbid rubbish, pronounced the renovated psychologies of Jung and Adler nonsense " and such dirty nonsense," or approved paste nymphs and useless flowers of his friend Saint Gaudens as " bully," in the nicest tone. They discovered, if they had a sense of like-ness, that they were hearing merits of Dickens, Thackeray, and Mr. Dooley extolled by their own father. He was gen-ially adverse to enigmatic discords of high art as was your uncle George. But they must not make a mistake in speak-ing of history. The man in riding boots could snap out the date of Louis the Fat, recollect after one blink the name of a peerage conferred on Nell Gwynn's brat or the number of men at arms seasick in the fleet of Medina Sidonia. He could extensively report the language of Oliver Cromwell to the silly Parliament. You found that history, to Mr. Roose-velt, consisted somewhat largely of facts in the lives of great popular leaders, and that most great leaders were popular leaders. Civilization was an eventual absolute and not a recurrent state in races. Morals were not customs of some period, but eternal verities, just as they were to your father.

. . . And you could not hate him, especially when he told you, one fist pelting into the other palm, that what the nation needed was action. Action!

Action was assertion. He was not impulsive, sane men saw, while fond journalists represented the President as a prancing kitten. But from resolve to effect, with Roosevelt, was a streak of exerted emphasis, and that this emphasis was right must not be questioned. " Why did you call Mr. Hill a fat spider, sir? " he was asked in 1902, when that epithet sent a friend of the railroad builder furious out of the White House. " But that's *my* way of putting it, Montgomery! " And this way of putting it was to annoy sensitive men who keenly wanted to admire Mr. Roosevelt, until January 6th, 1919, because it recalled too much of Roscoe Conkling and was too like those homely moments of Mr. Bryan's roadside invectivation when the orator forgot elegance and merely yelled names at his oppressors. Lenient psychiatrists tell us that this necessity of assertion was a survival, in the strong man, of the myopic, sickly child who had to feed his thin self-confidence by doing everything violently, so as to be sure of his heroic existence. Less friendly observers took it for a condescension to tricks of the ordinary political moralist who puts his enemy in the wrong by exploding him. Anyhow, it was a bully effect.

The trouble was that these effects began to influence Mr. Roosevelt's minor prophets when he was Governor of New York. " Forgive this short note," William James wrote, in 1900; " I have just escaped from an insufferable admirer of Mr. Roosevelt after a terrible trouncing. My offence was that I made a small objection to something in his last book. I am now in the condition of the feline caught too near the cream-jug. . . ." [1] As the cult expanded, an ugly swagger

[1] Unprinted, to a lady on her private affairs, October 11, 1900. I am permitted to quote a striking sentence at the close of the letter: " And so I have given you no real advice, as advice is never a realistic thing but a form of friendly hallucination which rises from the ego of the giver. . . ."

grew among the faithful. What T. R. did was right, what he said was bully, and what he was said to have said was sacred truth, even when he said in print that he had not said it, and so God damn you if you doubted anything. " Just two classes of Americans are not Roosevelt enthusiasts, fools and crooks! " The cheapness of that, its mendacity and its inferior bravado, sickened the scrupulous, as they were driven to note that Mr. Roosevelt, who had deprecated Hanna's advertisement of McKinley, did not seem to mind this sort of thing. No doubt it bored him, but he was engaged as virtue's impresario and perhaps he felt that his prima donna excused these flowers. The fine English art of bragging by indirections is not transplanted in America. Americans brag of themselves and their heroes with the simplicity of children and French patriotic statesmen. The damaging factor, in Mr. Roosevelt's case, was that a man of genuine sensibilities appeared to swallow this coarse diet and to thrive on it. " Remember Disraeli's advice about using a trowel," said the Attorney General, in 1903, taking a friend into the White House.

But, against all these semblances, Mr. Roosevelt was not immodest. He asked advice; he gallantly pointed out where he had accepted advice from his ministers; he would permit, up to a point, any amount of argument. Yet in these arguments his own sense of a conflict's violence led him to strain statements. Early in 1903 he strolled with several guests from his office into the dining-room of the White House and sank in his chair at the table, announcing, " I have just had the most *ter — rible* scene with Aldrich over the new act." Men who had been listening to a chat between the President and the Senator from Rhode Island over the draft of the Expedition Act stared at him. " But it was clearly evident," says one of them, " that Mr. Roosevelt really thought there had been a scene. Mr. Aldrich was in the best form possible. I cannot recall that he even put up a strong argument. Mr. Hanna winked at me across the table, without closing his eye. . . . Can it not be that Mr. Roosevelt imagined a kind of malevolence in his opponents and that it affected his thought during such scenes? . . ." [2]

Something affected the thought of Mr. Roosevelt's friends. McKinley hadn't been buried two months before a situation was arranged in melodrama between the White House and the Arlington Hotel. A hero confronted a purple demon; the President met the leader of his party almost daily and horrid battles took place. Details were known in the bars. Chairs had been upset; oaths hurtled. George Cortelyou was forced to drag the raving Hanna out of Mr. Roosevelt's office. " I have not heard such silly talk," said old Senator Vest, " since the boys had it that Mr. Cleveland was horsewhipping his wife every night." When Mr. Taft had become President a lady standing with Philander Knox at a reception asked if he, as Attorney General, had witnessed any of Hanna's rows with Mr. Roosevelt. " Yes," said Mr. Knox, " I did. Hanna got into an argument about the old Granger movement with Roosevelt. Roosevelt thought the Grangers were a lot of maniacs and Hanna thought they were useful citizens. They both got pretty hot. . . . And now," he concluded, glancing into the Blue Room, where Mr. Taft loomed amiably, " let us go in and eddy around the President. . . ."

But the boys had it that Roosevelt was fighting Hanna for permission to bring an action against James Hill's Northern Securities Company, the trust which would have placed all the railroads of the Northwest in the control of Hill and

---

[2] On the other hand, a real scene displayed Mr. Roosevelt at his best. Just after the settlement of the coal strike in 1902, Colonel Montgomery wrote to my father: " He came through it like a bird. We are all proud of him. He was justified in throwing chairs at them " — the operators — " but he even made excuses for Baer after it was over. They bullyragged him as badly as the war crowd bullied McKinley before the declaration in '98. I had to be in the room three times. It truly made me sick to listen to those men. . . ."

Morgan. Mr. Roosevelt had not to ask any permission for this action, and asked none. The Senator grunted, very coldly, in his parlor at the Arlington, " I warned Hill that McKinley might have to act against his damn company last year. Mr. Roosevelt's done it. I'm sorry for Hill, but just what do you gentlemen think I can do? "

Still, Mr. Hill's friends were aggrieved. The jinni ought to raise some smoke or waft away the papers of the action brought at Saint Paul. It began to be said in New York that he was selling out his friends to the President in exchange for federal jobs; he was trading loyalties for a postmaster-ship or a clerical place in the Treasury. He ought to do something, something final to stop all this. The exaggeration of what Mr. Roosevelt was doing leveled to the fantasy of what Mr. Hanna could do. For a superstition of the nineteenth century held all these talkers. They were like the credulous critics who established painters and novelists as unlimited, permanent qualities. Against the pullulating mediocrities created in literature and public life by the force of journalized sentiment, a man of any real power rose, in that century, to a tremendousness. Since Mr. Hanna made Presidents and governors, and led the Senate, he could do this other something. He somehow could abolish the presidential will.

Mr. Hanna laughed, turning the talk. A fortune teller had told him he would lose the rest of his hair and another tooth in 1903, he said. Or had his callers seen Maude Adams in her new piece? And what did they think of Clara Morris's yarn about McKinley in this magazine? And if they would excuse him, he had to drive over to see the President. But what was he going to do? . . . The Senator drew himself up and was tall in the smoke. " The Senate passed the Sherman Anti-Trust Law," he said; " how can I take it off the books? "

Meantime he had found a new plaything, although it

was not advertised. Having sported with money, with a city and a state, with extraordinary powers and dangers, he came to one of his last amusements. A few people noticed it, but not his own wife. A sentence would be shed with ash from his cigar, between two rambling jokes. Quentin Roosevelt had said a good thing for a baby, the other day, or Mrs. Roosevelt didn't like the baby to have too many toys, or the small boy was in a gloom because a pony had a sore foot. He walked up the driveway of the White House with men whispering at his other side and listened to the garrulous child that hung to his cane. " This is important, gentlemen. . . . I'll talk to you in a minute. Go on, bub."

Otherwise he did not cultivate elderly sentiment. He boasted that he would not build a dog kennel to his own memory. He yawned when a lady tendered him plans of a new orphan asylum, with a pavilion to be named for Marcus Alonzo Hanna. " Mr. Bryan would say I was corrupting the orphans, ma'am. . . . How would a check for five hundred do you? " This living body of Mark Hanna was all that he cared for as Mark Hanna. No monuments were to report his power. Wouldn't he look grand in a pair of wings sitting on the roof of an asylum named for him? Wow! And there was his check.

He had always given without any system, to a pair of begging nuns, or to a wretched old reporter, to a waiter at his hotel who had an ailing daughter, to anybody needing some money. In the autumn of 1902 while Hanna was helping Roosevelt to secure the committee of arbitration in the coal strike, he rolled up yellow bills, sitting in a cab on Pennsylvania Avenue, and tossed them into the hat of a man begging for the strikers. Let 'em have it. Some time or other there would be no more strikes. Business would be too finely adjusted to permit such waste. And coal would one day lose its value. There was enough water power in the one state of Pennsylvania to drive plants by electricity along the whole Atlantic seaboard. The government ought to take that up, some time. Enough would come back from even the lowest rates charged for this power to pay half the federal salaries — why the hell shouldn't the government run power plants? [3]

He was closely noticed, in these years. People who had not to talk to the Senator about a job or an act of Congress pondered him. One of them found that this pragmatist did not know of William James, save as one of those anti-imperialists up in Boston, but that he had studied out a difference in human natures for himself, much as James saw it. " See," he told a girl, " make your father find your brother something to do that's not real business. *The boy's all inside himself.* He can't run folks. He'll be a failure in business." Advice was wasted on a good, hard-headed man enamored of strenuous living for everybody in trousers. His eldest son must get out in the world and " do a man's work." There is a horripilant diary left to record the effect of a man's work on the young fellow at whom Mr. Hanna looked twice or so. The machinery of the strenuous life shook him for fifty months, and then all his notes on Kant and the diary's cover in the open drawer of his desk were stained by the discharged blood and the exploded brain.

But the extravert intelligence was happiest when he could deal with men who went in for achievements of fact. John Rockefeller, he said, was a kind of economic super-clerk, the personification of ledger-keeping. Coal Oil Johnny

---

[3] While revising this passage I have been privileged to listen to a redoubtable lawyer employed by a great coal-mining company as he expounded the horrors of " socialism " in an argument against the use of American water power as Hanna and a dozen others have prophesied it will be used. The gentleman talked through three cocktails about the nefariousness of governmental power plants. He is also in favor of Prohibition as a benefit to the laboring man, he has written strongly against the possible decrease of protective tariffs, and he hopes to be elected to Congress soon.

would never have been any good in Jim Hill's shoes, for instance. Charles Francis Adams was no business man at all, but a man who ought to have gone in for politics. John Hay, now, had found the real job of his life. The Lord had always meant Hay to be a Secretary of State. He was openly proud of having sent Hay to England in 1898. . . . As for the Lord, it seemed that this remote character had the function of an assembling engineer, who fitted the machine of destiny together and set it going. But what men did was of their own will or their peculiar folly. If they were idiots enough to excuse their failures by blaming God, it showed they were bigger fools than Mr. Bryan and Tom Johnson. Predestination? Swill! . . . Roosevelt was President by accident, wasn't he? " If you don't believe things happen accidentally, you're crazy as an Anarchist, by God! "

He admired Roosevelt's drive. The little cuss could work like a nigger, persuading and hinting until he got his way. He knew how to handle people. So did Mr. Hanna, and in 1902 the team of powerful men took all those malleable things at the Capitol and arranged them to their own wishes. They had come by power and used it. Both materialists, they made a double point in that high materialism which delights poets five hundred years after its force has thrown up that vastness of a wall against a flood, that roof, that pyramid. They chose to build.

II

OTTO PAUL HEINRICH left his young wife in a milliner's shop at Aix-les-Bains and ran out to stare at a profile, a cigar, and a white waistcoat in a victoria passing him. He had stopped being a journalist in 1896, when he permanently left America, but a craving roused again in August of 1899. He set off after the carriage and tracked it to a big hotel. Monsieur 'Anna would see no callers. Mr. Heinrich wrenched the neck of his conscience and threw the corpse away. He wrote on his card, " A friend of Hermann Kohlsaat " and sent it in to Senator Hanna. Doors flew open. Trying to remember the appearance of the editor whose name he had used, Mr. Heinrich came before Mark Hanna and demanded an interview.

Mr. Hanna would not be interviewed for any newspaper. Mr. Heinrich assured him that this was just a case of taking notes for a book on the United States. He had lived three years in America and meant to tell his experiences. Mr. Hanna hoped it would be a better book than Paul Bourget's *Outre-Mer*. He thought that about the wishy-washiest slop he had ever read. Mr. Heinrich agreed. He would have agreed to anything just then, with the Senator defenseless before him.

MR. HEINRICH: You do not care a great deal for books?

MR. HANNA: Not as a rule. I like some of Mr. Howells's, and I used to read Thackeray. But most of these popular books seem pretty thin to me. I don't like *Ben Hur* or Mrs. Grand's book [*The Heavenly Twins*], or things like that.

MR. HEINRICH: I suppose you prefer the newspapers?

MR. HANNA: I don't think much of most newspapers. They waste a lot of time. The editorials are too long. Editorials only ought to be printed about twice a week. I guess I am spiteful about newspapers because I made a fool of myself trying to run one.

[He then interviews his interviewer on German newspapers, down to the details of printing and the pay of typesetters. Mr. Heinrich struggles and changes the topic.]

MR. HEINRICH: I suppose you consider Mr. W. J. Bryan a very dangerous person.

MR. HANNA: Why should you think that? My friend Mr. Dawes has known Mr. Bryan for a long time. Dawes says that Mr. Bryan is a good fellow. I do not go around saying that people are bad because they oppose my friends in politics.

MR. HEINRICH: Still, you would have been afraid to see Bryan elected in 1896.

MR. HANNA: Of course. You know how bad the financial condition was in 1893, and from then on to the war. We are just getting back into shape now. Mr. Bryan's election would have brought on a panic.

MR. HEINRICH: I believe that is so. You believe that it is the business of your government to protect industries?

MR. HANNA: Yes. So does your Emperor.

[More conversation which was not written down. Mr. Hanna interviews Mr. Heinrich on the limitations of the Emperor's powers, or something of the kind.]

MR. HEINRICH: But I do not understand why Americans find the government ownership of railways so objectionable.

MR. HANNA: I will tell you. [His reserve, as usual, is breaking down under an agreeable presence.] I have been in the Senate for two years. You cannot understand how hard it is to get legislation pushed through Congress. Suppose that the government took over the railroads. We have just about one half of the mileage in the United States that is needed. If the government owned the lines it would be an awful job to get systems extended. Any fat-head [rendered as " sheep's head " in Mr. Heinrich's German] from Maine would be unwilling to see a new line put out in Minnesota. Senator Davis would have to fight for years to get such an act. Our nation is too big for one part to know what another part needs. Then, in case of strikes, what a terrible situation you would have! You know what Mr. Pullman's foolish friends made him do in 1894. Now, everybody blamed Mr. Pullman for refusing to arbitrate that strike. I blamed him myself. But it was one of his big stockholders who caused the trouble. Let us suppose the government owns the railroads. The unions ask for more pay. The case comes to Congress, and some silly Congressmen refuse to listen to reason. What have you got? Revolution!

MR. HEINRICH: But the people should not be allowed to strike.

[Mr. Hanna roars. He is then lectured on the rights of the State and the profound indecency of opposing the State, for quite a time.]

MR. HANNA: That may be true in Germany. But it would not do in the United States. Our working people are not so weak as that. I have been dealing with labor for thirty-five years. I should not be surprised to see the government take over the railroads in forty or fifty years. At this time it would be a bad thing. You forget how big our country is. The people in the East know nothing about it. That is why Mr. Reed would have made such a bad President. But he is a very clever [he probably said " smart "] man.

MR. HEINRICH: You mean that the provincial feeling of the various states makes legislation difficult? Enterprises are not nationally felt?

MR. HANNA: Yes. Now, as an instance, there are two good propositions in which Mr. McKinley takes a great interest. One is to do something for the irrigation of the dry states in the Southwest and the other is to have a serious discussion of a canal from the Caribbean to the Pacific. Senator Davis is opposed to a canal through Nicaragua. He may be right. He has studied the matter a great deal. But you cannot get a serious discussion of these matters from most of the members of Congress. [He then draws back into his reserve.] I am not criticizing Congress. The trouble is what I just said. It is the size of the country.

MR. HEINRICH [diplomatically]: I understand. Would

you be opposed to legislation determining the hours of daily labor?

MR. HANNA: Yes, if it was a case of national legislation. That is a matter to be fixed by the states. A great deal of the legislation proposed for the good of the working man is a case for the state and not for Congress. Conditions differ according to locality.

MR. HEINRICH: Did you ever read Henry George's book *Progress and Poverty?*

MR. HANNA: Yes, of course. Everybody was reading it when it came out. There is some good writing in that book. But I do not believe in Mr. George's principles. I do not think the single tax would do what he says it would. The final value of property is not in the land, but in the uses of the land. I have talked this over with many people. Mr. George's proposition is bad.

MR. HEINRICH: I agree. But you do not believe in most of the social reforms that are proposed?

MR. HANNA [very slowly]: No. They seem to end up in producing some kind of condition just as bad as anything we have on our hands now. Take the proposition of making all incomes equal, with the government owning all property. Now — [Mr. Heinrich interrupts to ask what party among the Socialists believes this.] But that has been talked of. You must have heard that. I heard John Ellsler talking about that many years ago.

MR. HEINRICH: Did Herr Ellsler write this in a book?

MR. HANNA [bored]: No, no. I mean the actor John Ellsler. [He is suddenly bitter.] He is one of the men I am supposed to have ruined. It was when he was producing a play of Mr. Howells's [October 25, 1878]. He was a very smart man, a great theorist.

MR. HEINRICH: A Socialist?

MR. HANNA: No! But he liked to talk theoretically. . . . But do you see where this proposition would end?

MR. HEINRICH: It appears to be like some of the English propositions. [They discuss the idea. Mr. Heinrich forgets to take notes for a while.]

MR. HANNA: That seems to me the defect. I know people who will do good work for nothing. But most people are not like that.

MR. HEINRICH: You think that special talent ought to be rewarded specially?

MR. HANNA: Of course I do! Suppose they had said to Henry George that he would not be paid more than a boy on a newspaper gets for writing his book! [He discovers that Mr Heinrich is translating his words into German.] I I wish I could speak some foreign languages —

But that was all. Mrs. Hanna came into the room, telling the Senator he was supposed to be taking a nap. Mr. Heinrich fled. His holiday was over. He and his pretty wife went back to their pretty apartment in Dresden, and Herr Heinrich attended to the English correspondence at the bank while Frau Heinrich worked on prophetic little shirts or practiced the piano. Only, a restless nibbling affected Herr Heinrich. He spun the commercial globe in his office, and the United States seemed a patch of raw, bright, alluring bulbs. He read over and over a copy of Rudyard Kipling's American notes picked up in a café. . . . In September his wife shed tears on the pier at Bremen. Otto had gone mad, her parents thought. He, so well placed at the office of his rich uncle, to return to that desolate and uncivilized Chicago! It was lunacy. The young man could not explain just why he wanted to go back. Something had taken him, while the Senator talked in the smoke of the cigar at Aix. In this way Mr. Hanna, without knowing anything about it, contributed a tall young machine gunner to the armies of his nation, in the year 1917.

This scant, unfinished interview raises two points. Mark

Hanna's interest in the irrigation of the Southwest does not appear in Mr. Croly's narration of his life. But he had shown an intelligent willingness to raise this topic during McKinley's presidency. In the spring of 1897 he brought his follower Joseph Kimball to the White House and made the President listen to the shy little man for an hour while the Westerner explained, stammering, the possible location of high dams and reservoirs. In the autumn of 1898 he had the visit repeated. Mr. Kimball stayed to luncheon, but the meal was interrupted by one of Mrs. McKinley's epileptic seizures. In 1899, before he had learned to use his voice in the Senate, he suggested an irrigation scheme to be introduced by Senator Spooner and turned Mr. Kimball loose on the clever man from Wisconsin. Other people were now attracted. Articles in magazines and newspapers were frequent.

" The thing is coming along," Mr. Hanna wrote to Mr. Kimball, in September of 1901. " I should not be surprised if it was seriously discussed in the short session. I would advise you to have a talk with Mr. Roosevelt when you come to Washington. He can do a good deal with some of the New York men if he wants." Mr. McKinley's death disheartened Mr. Kimball; he fancied that the power of Mark Hanna ended here, and was startled in the spring of 1902 when Mr. Elmer Dover wrote to him from Senator Hanna's office, saying that things were shaping for the passage of an act and that Mr. Roosevelt was working vehemently in its behalf.

The great proposal enchanted the new President, and all his dazing resources of conversation were behind the movement that took form in the Newlands Act. He summoned legislators; he dazzled callers; he wrote to powerful editors. But toward the end of May there was a hitch, a flare of provincialism. Some Senators and Representatives saw no sense in irrigating the deserts; the Southwest was too far

from their embarnacled, Yankee perception. Mr. Roosevelt
came, flushing and sweating, down the hallway, arguing
with a pair of these parochial statesmen and, twenty minutes later, tired callers in the outer office watched Mr.
Hanna pass through. Mr. Roosevelt had opened the brazen
bottle, evoking the jinni of the Arlington. His agitated falsetto broke out as the Senator approached.

" Uncle Mark, do you think you could explain to some
of these *complete* idiots that there is such a place as Arizona? "

Uncle Mark thought it possible, and did it in his own
manner. He roamed into the New Willard Hotel and summoned the bloodhounds of the lobby from their chairs with
a motion of his cane. He could command these men because they liked him, feared him, or might need something
from him. They had their orders promptly. They were to
go to work on Senator This and Mr. That. " Bring in some
scalps," said the Senator, " and make it fast." The bloodhounds wagged their frock coats and did what they were
told. On June 17th the Newlands Act, creating a huge reservoir of money from the sale of public lands, became a
law.

Mr. Hanna took no part in the debates, and journalists
wondered if he was not secretly in opposition to the measure, until Mr. Roosevelt set them right by a word to Arthur
Dunn. He had fulfilled his function in the unspoken treaty
between the White House and the Arlington Hotel, and the
credit could fall where it might. " People have not paid
much attention to this business," he said, " but I tell the lot
of you that it's a damned big thing."

So it was. It came on one man as a final release from a
course of action to which he had bound himself when he was
a boy. Mr. Joseph Kimball packed his modest trunk and
vanished forever from the city of Washington, where he had
spent months of each year since 1886, lurking in grand

offices with his black hat and his roll of plans spread on his
knees. Too shy, too gentle for the task he had set himself,
he had been obscure or ridiculous in this pale city. He was
pointlessly insulted by Thomas Reed and laughed at by
reporters who knew, from some profundity of their trade,
that it was impossible to irrigate the deserts of the West.
Until Mark Hanna took him up, he had been without a
powerful friend, a gray, slim figure in antechambers, a person known to secretaries and clerks as the fellow with the
irrigation scheme. But he had hung around, timidly badg-
ering Congressmen and Senators, and now other men triumphed for him. Mr. Hanna took him to the White House
to thank the President. Mr. Newlands sent him a cordial
line. He went back to his deserts and soon died. His name
means nothing, save to his children, written here, but it is
written to remind a few that a nation has — sometimes —
unselfish servants who are not paid. . . .

Mark Hanna's interest in a canal connecting the Atlantic
Ocean with its neighbor by way of Central America is a
more definite set of facts. He had periodically talked of
this since the Civil War. He bored his guest Henry Adler
by a long discussion of the matter in October of 1890, at the
Union Club in Cleveland. The affair presented itself to
him then merely as a technical topic. His mechanical intelligence was entertained by the possibility of cutting such
a canal. In the spring of 1896 he was talking of the canal
again, this time to Mr. Theodore Hamill, a youngster of
twenty who had lived in South America. In the autumn of
1897 Mr. Hamill appeared before him more seriously, full
of an agreeably piratical scheme of seizing the isthmus at
Panama for the United States, confiscating the property
of the French canal company, and building a canal. Mr.
Hanna must have enjoyed this project in patriotism, because he gave Mr. Hamill a note to Cushman Davis and sent
him across Washington to call on the Senator from Min-

nesota, who laughed outright, but kept the boy talking about the geological structure of the isthmus for some hours. Yet, however lightly Mr. Hanna took this chatter, he thought enough about Panama to address a letter in his own script to Senator Allison, asking what his real opinion of an interoceanic canal was. " I have recently," he wrote, " heard a lot about the Panama route which impresses me favorably. Mr. Henry Villard and some other solid business men in New York have been interested in the French concession. You know that Davis has no use for the Nicaragua route. He has been into the business very thoroughly and is dead against that project. I should like to hear from you on this point." [4]

Then, in 1900, he showed the frankest reluctance when Mr. McKinley was eager to include an interoceanic canal among the show pieces of the Republican platform. His objection was double. Mr. Bryan, he told one friend, was likely to grab at the plan as another gesture of imperialism. And he said to Myron Herrick, " It is bad business playing poker with other people's chips." The phrase echoed a long way, as did many of Mr. Hanna's rough figures. You must remember that his babyhood and young boyhood had been passed beside the ruinous canal at New Lisbon, the ditch into which so much money had been thrown. Age was not making Mr. Hanna cautious, but his President would be blamed if the canal through Nicaragua or the one through Panama, favored by Mr. Herrick, proved a failure.

He begged and ordered speakers to go easy on the topic. Neither the lordly contribution of the Panama company's American attorney to the campaign fund nor the pleasure of stealing a Democratic plank for his own party's platform made the canal dear to Mr. Hanna in 1900. He thought it bad politics, and said so, and his subsequent performance

[4] Mr. Oswald Villard tells me that his father had no interest in the French company, but that his name was used to promote sales of stock.

has thus been described by professorial historians as fla-
grant opportunism. But, in the technic of politics, he was
fully right in 1900. The canal was dangerous, although not
much attacked by the anti-imperialists, and the hazy condition of the whole scheme made it more ticklish still. It
haunted him, though — this gashing of mountains and
blending of seas. McKinley was not six weeks dead when
an engineer chatting with some friends about the route
through Nicaragua, in the Holland House, found a page
offering him a card; Senator Hanna wanted to know if he
might join a conversation that had drifted across the hallway to him where he sat with his cigar. It is not unlikely,
after all, that Daniel James Mason's denunciation of the
Nicaraguan scheme, fifteen minutes long, did as much as
anything to harden the Senator in favor of Panama. " You
are," he said, " a damned sight more enlightening about this
business than anybody I've listened to on it."

But he had heard a great deal about the business. In the
flux of easy satire since 1920 it has become strangely necessary to regard an American man of business as a jackass.
To assert the contrary for a number of dead men of business, some of whom had no favor among the sanctimonious,
is an exploit, here undertaken with a certain nervousness.
Quite independent of Myron Herrick, Nelson Cromwell,
and Colonel Bunau-Varilla, a quantity of political business
men in New York and Chicago moved in favor of the Panama Canal. They were not only independent of the French
Panama company, but they were independent of each other.
A few of them, such as John McCall, George Perkins, and
Thomas Fortune Ryan, directly approached Mr. Hanna.
Others approached Mr. Roosevelt. The feasibility of this
canal and its advantages over a canal through Nicaragua
were discussed at luncheon and dinner by men whose pockets would not swell by a dime's width if the canal was built.
It interested them; they liked to talk about it. John McCook

drew Edward Harriman into a chat, in 1901, and found that the dark collector of Western railroads was not at all averse to a Panama canal. Far from damaging his California properties, he said, a canal would help them. " People would get so sick of looking at water on the way out," he explained, " that they'd come home by rail." To this selected audience, then, it was exciting to hear privately, in March of 1902, that Mr. Hanna might oppose the measure languidly debated in Congress, empowering the President to arrange the construction of a canal by way of Nicaragua. But when Mr. Hanna appeared in the Senate on the fifth of June and spoke for Panama, his act bewildered half of the journalists and most of his friends.

He came into the Senate, followed by his secretary, whose hands were full of pamphlets, and commenced his conversational support of Senator Spooner's amendment to the Hepburn Bill before a scant gallery. Ten minutes passed; telephones had jingled and people hurried to the Capitol. Soon rules were broken. Ladies and diplomats, reporters, agents of the powers, all jammed the gallery's aisles. This plain old person in a dull gray suit was doing something and a drama heaped itself in the warm chamber while he drawled along, explaining this investment to the Senate without an eloquent phrase. He talked, glancing at two shreds of note paper scrawled with figures, as if some client had asked his advice about a sale of bonds. It seems the driest speech, and yet it thrilled. Up among the witnesses the Russian envoy began to murmur, " *Mais il est formidable!* " and this, they say, is true. Mark Hanna was formidable: he stood talking of costs and labor and convenience, the foreman of an age. Machinery spoke; the blue prints of engineers and the coal in bunkers found a voice here. A monstrous, docile power made itself heard. This was a job that the nation could take on, if it wanted to do it. This was work. He stood drawling, and another mood overcame people hearing him. He had spoken for an hour. It was seen that his ailing legs were stiffened under him as his face grew yellow, damp with effort. A woman gulped, so that Senators heard her, " Oh, do make him sit down! " and Senator Frye twitched in his chair. But he talked on. His report was not yielded; he would be heard out. His knees sagged at the last, and when he dropped into his chair a gasp of true relief whirled through the Senate before the applause began.

Gossip and rancor exploded in the hotels that night. This had to be explained away by Mark Hanna's enemies. They must find a dirty trick in it somewhere and, literally, by midnight men were assuring one another that Mr. Hanna was wrecking any hope of a canal by causing a deadlock between the Senate and the House. He was doing this, of course, on behalf of the railroads. If that story was not suitable, another served: he had been bribed by the attorney of the French Panama company to cause the United States to buy its worthless properties. In fact, everybody had been bribed. The Secretary of State, the Cabinet, Mr. Hanna, Mr. Spooner, the President's elder daughter, and Leonard Wood were sharing sums of thirty and forty million among them. " It is the most expensive lying since the Civil War," said Mr. Hay. " But where is the money supposed to be coming from? "

Meanwhile, at the Arlington, Mr. Hanna was tirelessly receiving callers. His control of his project was not complete. He could count certainly on the strong and utter opposition of Thomas Platt and Matthew Quay in his own party, and the perpetual protector of the Nicaraguan scheme was the agreeable Senator Morgan of Alabama, one of the most popular Democrats. As Hanna startled the public on June 5th, he now stunned experts by his private management of the affair. Congressmen and their friends were summoned to his rooms. The lobby took its orders. He promised nothing. No favors were to be doled out in exchange for obedience. " He has his campaign face on," said Senator Frye. On June 13th a Western journalist canvassed the House of Representatives and knew in advance that Nicaragua was done for. Mr. Hanna had won; it would be a Panama canal.

But he was paying for his conquest. Mrs. Hanna fretted and one of her friends found her quietly weeping on the afternoon of June 14th. He was killing himself, she said. He just would not realize that he was an old man now, and nobody could make him behave, not even Ruth. And the strain was extraordinary. He himself tried to slacken it, dashing along the Potomac in a fast launch one night, and stamping into John Hay's library one Sunday morning, saying that he was two thirds crazy, he was so tired. Mr. Hay was entertaining Daniel Hoyt Marvin with some literary gossip and Mr. Hanna listened to the talk a while. It recalled something he had meant to investigate.

" What about this poet Walt Whitman? "

" He's still dead," said Mr. Hay.

Mr. Hanna knew that. But someone had told him that a Postmaster General discharged Walt Whitman for writing a book. Mr. Hay handed him *Leaves of Grass* and the Senator examined it for half an hour silently, as if it were a report of bankruptcy proceedings. He put it aside with a snort.

" The Postmaster General must have been a fool."

He rode back with Mr. Marvin to the Arlington and took this stranger into his confidence on the subject of automobiles. His wife was the only person in the family who believed that automobiles would ever amount to a thing. His brothers and his son were skeptical. But he saw the automobile revolutionizing commerce. " It was just like reading," says Mr. Marvin, " one of those articles you see twenty times a year about what the automobile has done, but with every-

thing put in the future tense. His only error was that he
counted on a long war between the steam motor and the
gasoline motor. He said that someone would put a motor
on the market at prices suitable to small farmers and change
the whole nature of life in the country. I did not believe a
word of it, of course. This was my only encounter with
Mr. Hanna, and I thought he was going into softening of
the brain. . . ."

On June 19th he had his triumph. The Senate voted.
Mr. Hanna stood in the Marble Room with Senator Spooner
receiving compliments. Reporters and diplomats pressed
on him. He grinned with a particular sweetness when
Thomas Platt came up to make a chilly speech, for he knew
that Mr. Platt and Mr. Quay had been deviling the President
behind his back. They wearied Mr. Roosevelt until he arranged one of his amiable duplicities: Colonel Montgomery was summoned and stayed beside the desk while the
President importantly scribbled nonsense on a dozen telegraph blanks, the names of his children or sentences from
headlines of a newspaper. The bosses tired of his polite
inattention and left. Mr. Roosevelt lay back in his chair
and asked with violence, " Montgomery, does the spectacle
of human imbecility ever alarm you? "

This was known to Mr. Hanna, and his grin must have
burned Thomas Platt. But he triumphed affably. He said
to some Democratic Senator, " I'm sorry you wouldn't vote
with us. You'll find that we've sold the boys the best horse."
It was a business man's victory; he had sold the nation the
better of two propositions. It was victory on his own terms,
a solid argument of costs and convenience against oratory
and scandalous hints. " We've saved the Treasury about
seventy millions," he said, limping down the room on Mr.
Spooner's arm; " so let the dogs howl! "

The dogs howled and are howling yet, in cheap biography
and histories. This act so admired by men who hated Han-

na's power is slobbered with conjectures as to his motive. He did what he chose. But in America we have reversed Goethe's saying, " The doer is conscienceless; no one has a conscience except the spectator. . . ." Through all that June of 1902 spectators played the conscientious, linking the President and the Senator in a flurry of conscienceless accusations. Large things had been done, and they must be diminished by many little breaths; the quality, the fine heat of performance, must be cooled down. Gentlemen of the press and the bars knew all about it. The President had enormous holdings of dry land in the Southwest, or he had friends who had dry acres. Hence the Newlands Act. And Mr. Hanna was putting millions in his banks by this trick of Panama. So the dogs howled. But the hills were cleft and the oceans joined, where Hanna willed. Ships sail through this ditch of Panama, guarded by young Americans in badly fitting uniforms. High dams spill down their harvested flood for a harvest's good upon those plains where, when I was born, a horned skull might glimmer on unending dust, challenging man, and the train jarred past a ruinous house swept out by heat, past orchards murdered by the sun. These are facts, these achievements that once were dreams or trickeries of politicians. There could be no canal, it was innumerably proved in bars and drawing-rooms, and watering the desert was a child's notion. But the great ditch and the rills among trees all panoplied with fruit are facts. Let the dogs howl.

III

Hanna had fulfilled himself. It was felt. Anecdotes thickened on the Senator, envious or flattering. He was a national possession while reforming journalists raked him with the rest of the muck; he was a national disgrace while ambassadors and touring celebrities wanted interviews. He was more than ever the fetish of luck and force. His chuckling secretary showed privileged callers letters written in obscure houses and towns of the West, wheedling the Red Boss of 1896 to get a pension granted or to find an office. Mothers asked advice on proper books for growing boys, and to one such matron the old man wrote: "I have never been a great reader. When I do read it is generally something pretty practical. If your boy is a serious fellow, would suggest that you try to get him a very good book of Baron Humboldt. Either the book is named Cosmos or that is the first essay in it. You probably know this was a favorite essay with Mr. Lincoln. I admired it a great deal when I was a young fellow. I do not mean," he admitted, "that Mr. Lincoln and I grew up just the same way. . . ." But legend will have it that Mr. Hanna did not know the meaning of the word "cosmos," and legend prevails, in these cases. He will remain, then, a coarsely ignorant person, without intellect, yet somehow, a consummate manager of men, a comic *arriviste* at whose table members of the Cabinet, authors, scientists, actors, and painters cheerfully mingled. Oh, come!

Hanna talked plainly, but he talked honestly, and this honesty somehow accorded with a revolt of the sensitized against an insipid society. The old Senator spoke his mind. To people who did not confuse intellect with an appreciation of paper roses his mind was an interesting thing enough. He recognized the absurd in the creation of all these great fortunes; he did not gape at money, as money. One Western millionaire, he would say, had a bank slide on his head and sat up in the clay to see lumps of ore twinkling at him, and the anecdote is true. Another had a mother who gleaned a third of her boy's pay from his pockets by night, and returned him five thousand dollars of it when she heard of a good investment in stock of a steamship company, on the Lakes. He divided these goats from the sheep; the millionaires by chance did not rank with those banking or industrial plutocrats who knew what they were doing and deliberately did it. Also he disliked fussy shams. There was a giggle at Senator Spooner's house one night when Mr. Hanna glanced at an ideal restoration of the Roman Forum and said it looked a " second-rate World's Fair." Proper æsthetes shuddered when he called the rococo Library of Congress a German wedding cake, or they stared as politely as they could when he said his brother's new motor launch was a damned sight more beautiful than a lot of these foolish statues you had to look at. Everything hard, limbered, and strong pleased the Senator's mechanic eye; the prow of a motor boat, his slim daughter on a lean horse among the pines at Thomasville, the high line of a mast bearing a flag. Finally, he defended the interior economy of money-making itself, for one night in John Hay's library talk turned to intellectual achievements. Elihu Root and a lady survive from the group that laughed when the Senator claimed the invention of double entry book-keeping as a grand feat of intellect. Hanna growled, " Well, it is! " and went away with the Secretary of War. But Henry Adams roused in his corner and murmured to a woman, " Goethe thought it was, too . . ." and the murmur stays with her.

The Senator was not afraid of women. He dared even to scold one, if he liked her. The daughter of a friend came gleaming into Washington with ten trunks filled at Paris in the spring of 1903. Hanna took the girl, encased in a wonderful frock, to a dance given by naval officers. The Roosevelts appeared. Many partners said pretty things, and ladies purred over the French gown. Her exhilaration lasted until Mr. Hanna wanted to leave and led her down the room. She asked him confidently which was the best-dressed woman in the place. His head jerked sideways to a simple black robe in a knot of blue and gold uniforms. The girl saw nothing stunning about Mrs. Roosevelt's costume. It was just a nice frock.

" That's all that a lady has to have, sis."

A lady was a lady to the political pragmatist; the minister without portfolio was sedulous for the dignity of the lady in the White House. The harmless son of a military official was bouncing a tennis ball in the gutter of Dupont Circle one day of April in 1903 and the plaything hopped into a passing victoria. Quentin Roosevelt tossed the ball back, and its owner stood alarmed, wondering if this would cost his father a promotion, although Mrs. Roosevelt had smiled. Then a cane smote the end of his spine, and Mr. Hanna furiously grunted, " You! You ought to take your hat off when any woman speaks to you. When Mrs. Roosevelt speaks to you, keep it off a week! "

He was old. People saw it or would not see it, because his vivacity continued and his pace down to his chair in the Senate was stiffly competent. Seen from the gallery, Mr. Hanna was not unlike a finely adjusted toy in motion. His world amused him still, and he would dodge off on trips to look at things. Workmen in the plant of the Otis Elevator Company at Yonkers did not know the stout man in gray quietly poking among them, asking sensible questions about weights and slides, as if he was a graduated workman himself. But he was old. He talked, sometimes, a little wonderingly about other people's memories. His own was unimpaired. It puzzled him that Mel and Leonard should forget their father's swooning fit on election day of 1860. The whole family had been in the house, and how frightened they all were! But his brothers forgot that. . . . It distracted him, at breakfast in the Arlington, with men watching his lips. They had come down to head him against Mr. Roosevelt, but he would only talk to them of memory through the meal. . . . Take the nomination from Roosevelt in 1904? Rubbish! He was leaving for Saint Louis with the President in a day or two, to open this Fair. . . . He wanted to talk of his past.

Exasperation rose in New York. What did the old devil mean by speaking for the commercial treaties with Cuba, instead of against them, and why didn't he fight Roosevelt openly from the floor of the Senate on all these damned reforms? He had not stopped the act giving precedence to governmental actions in Federal courts, or the act punishing receivers of rebates, or the creation of the Department of Commerce and Labor.[5]

A simple explanation was, of course, that the leader of the Republican party thought Cuba entitled to reciprocal aid from the United States and believed some reform to be inevitable. But that was too simple. Perhaps — John Hay's ill health was known — Hanna wanted to be Secretary of State in a second Roosevelt administration. Edward Lauterbach had another theory: Hanna was turning State Socialist. That was what his Western irrigation scheme, his prophecy of power plants owned by the government, and his chat about the vanished Grangers with their ideas of co-operative grain elevators, co-operative banks, and sternly regulated freight rates, summed up to.

" To think," said a sporting banker, " that we sent this man to Washington to look out for us! "

" We did nothing of the kind," John Pierpont Morgan answered; " he sent himself. We did not know how to spell his name in '96." [6]

It had taken much persuasion to make financiers know that Hanna was not McKinley's ruler, but an adoring, diffi-

---

[5] In fact he pushed the creation of the new department. It had been discussed with McKinley in 1899 and 1900. It was favored in New York by John McCall, Darwin Kingsley, George Perkins, and several other less-known financiers. Howard Melville Hanna claimed in 1904 that his brother invented the department. Senator Hanna, in a letter to Mr. Jacob Bennett, dated October 1, 1900, says: " There should be a department capable of handling such situations as this [the threatened coal strike averted by J. P. Morgan and himself], and the matter is being put up to the President in a very strong way. . . ."

[6] *Ipsissima verba*, in latter March 1903.

dent friend. They were human financiers and doubted all sentiments except their own sentiments. Three of them had tried to have Whitelaw Reid made ambassador in 1897 to the court of Saint James, because they were fond of him. Mr. Morgan himself, striding on toes of clients in his waiting-room in a hurry to embrace a son just landed at New York, was a human and rather moving sight. But they could not credit that Mark Hanna had become fond of Theodore Roosevelt. . . . There must be something else he wanted. Meanwhile, why didn't he stop the President's uncomfortable activity?

" Can't you realize," a dry, Western voice asked, " that hundreds of men you all know and eat lunch with have been urging Roosevelt to enforce the Anti-Trust Law and the Interstate Commerce Law? "

They knew it, but did not want to know it. They were major capitalists. They sulked away from believing that hundreds of little rich men rejoiced quietly when the President moved to dissolve the Northern Securities Company. One of them certainly knew that the clumsy laws regulating commerce and the formation of trusts had been passed with the backing of minor capital at the end of the 'eighties. Little money had long fought big money, with the engines of democracy.

A phase of law ended in the United States. Capital was not at war with law, on the plan of Sumner and Spengler, but trying to maintain the elder code taken over from England in the eighteenth century, because old laws were too narrow to control capital, this floating, detached mass of power which illusively seemed free of the earth. Those old laws were written by learned clerks and abbots to whom money was just rent due proper landlords or tokens of gold exchanged by traders and merchants. This wealth in the hands of men without traditions and bound to no caste was not anticipated. The dead judges of the King's Bench could

not bind a casteless nation large as all Europe. Democracy
created American capitalists, as American capital once had
created democracy.

Money had stirred with every movement of the colonists
westward, always gaining strength. As the expansionist policy it had caused democracy to build its railroads, and as
democracy it had urged the Homestead and all like acts
granting free land in the West. As democratic morality it
destroyed the slaveholders of the South. As producing industry it had granted itself subsidies, acts for the purchase
of silver, tariffs and protections. As international finance
it had beaten down Free Silver in 1896. As " manifest destiny " it had, a little haltingly, approved imperialism. Its
private wars were clouded in moral issues and equivocations; its will speaks through shapes as various as William
Bryan, John Rockefeller, or the dreary Henry Ford. It
would make war soon on pleasure, learning, and criticism.
For what does demos care about aloof gayeties of the mind,
scholarship, frail dreams? Demos poor is wronged, and
demos rich is demos powerful to wrong demos. Money does
not rule democracy. Money is democracy.

Mr. Roosevelt, then, put the refreshed laws in force
against democracy, and democracy applauded. For eighteen months the financiers were highly disturbed, but, by the
autumn of 1904, they had sensed Roosevelt's limitation.
He wasn't imaginative, after all. They spent money on his
campaign for the next presidency in such bulk that his feeble opponent accused Roosevelt of blackmailing the great
corporations, which was untrue and superfluous. Still, in
the spring of 1903, rich men worried, and some of them
gave out solemn interviews. It was at once discovered that
a conspiracy against Mr. Roosevelt existed in Wall Street.
The word " conspiracy " was a bully effect.

For theatrical reasons Mr. Hanna had to be part of this
conspiracy. He was towering. He had smashed a heavy at-

tack of the Democratic party in Ohio, in the autumn of 1902. His popularity puffed. A lady strolling with Matthew Quay along Pennsylvania Avenue noted a huge truck filled with envelopes and wondered what the load was.

" It's just Hanna's mail going up to the Capitol," said Mr. Quay.

Mr. Quay knew precisely the situation between the White House and the Arlington Hotel. There need be no trouble if the President's satellites and Hanna's gang would let the two men alone. But the dear boys, he told Mrs. Warner, wanted to make a fight of it. He had warned the President that the regional bigwigs and little politicians who lunched with him one day would be hunting an invitation to breakfast next morning at the Senator's hotel. But there was going to be trouble, and soon.

" We have two Executive Mansions, and the President's friends don't like that."

Here, for six weeks, everything becomes misty, conjectural. It was heard in New York by the third week of April that a new leader of the Republican party had been found, in the person of Senator Joseph Benson Foraker. Prudent magnates sent messengers to conciliate and inquire what that meant. Mr. Hanna grinned. Mr. Foraker seemed " cold, and not in the least interested " to examining agents. Roosevelt was touring the country, explaining himself to the plain people. On May 3rd an obscure, clever man, secretary to a dull, rich Senator was beckoned by the Attorney General to enter his carriage on S Street. Mr. Knox observed gently that they were both indebted to Mark Hanna for great kindnesses. He wondered, staring away from his acquaintance, if Hanna knew that some " irresponsible people " were trying to bring about a breach between Mr. Roosevelt and himself. It would certainly be disastrous and it ought to be prevented. . . . Good morning.

Foraker's perplexity, on May 14th, shook some words out

of him. He was " expected " to get the Ohio State Republican convention to approve Mr. Roosevelt's presidency and to pledge itself to support his candidacy in 1904. He was " in a tight box." He pried off the lid, on May 23rd, by giving an interview in which he adroitly stated that Mr. Hanna's own retinue had raised the question of endorsing Mr. Roosevelt's candidacy in 1904 and, now that it was raised, the convention must endorse the President or refuse to endorse him.

Next morning the obscure secretary breakfasted with his Senator and the paragraph in the newspaper took the old Western adventurer's eye. Oh, so it had started! Well, Foraker would be appointed Chairman of the Republican Campaign Committee, if he could swing this trick for the Roosevelt faction. The President's friends were to repeat Hanna's performance of 1896. They would appear at the convention of 1904 with so many states pledged to the President that there could be no other candidate. Foraker would nominate Roosevelt and would mechanically be made Chairman. . . . This was being said everywhere. Washington was alert by noon. The President had struck at Mark Hanna. The jinni was to be cased in the brass bottle and chucked into the sea.

Hanna did not believe that. He assumed the trick to be Senator Foraker's invention and said so, in Cleveland. He had been joking with Roosevelt in March about the efforts of his own friends to get him to declare himself a candidate in 1904 and the President had asked to be a guest at the wedding of Ruth Hanna to Medill McCormick in June. Roosevelt would not do this to him. The men about him saw that his power of campaigns, its excitement and tension, was dear to Hanna. " By God, he can't mean to have Foraker run a campaign for him! . . . By God, I don't think he's in this! " He gave out an interview denying, for the fourth published time, that he wanted the presidency, and opposing

Foraker's suggestion. Now he telegraphed to Roosevelt, in Seattle.

" The issue that has been forced upon me in the matter of our state convention this year endorsing you for the Republican nomination next year has come in a way which makes it necessary for me to oppose such a resolution. When you know all the facts, I am sure that you will approve my course. . . ."

Mr. Roosevelt was not interested in the facts at all. Strategically remote from this incident in practical politics, he handled it with ideal cleverness. He proposed to be endorsed by the Ohio Republicans. He answered:

" Your telegram received. I have not asked any man for his support.[7] I have nothing whatever to do with raising this issue. Inasmuch as it has been raised, of course, those who favor my administration and my nomination will favor endorsing both, and those who do not will oppose."

The telegram was published instantly by the Associated Press. Experts differed as to its merits. Mr. Roosevelt's backers were thrusting him forward a year ahead of the convention which should endorse his candidacy. If Hanna now let him be endorsed it would impress the public as a deliberate plan to shut off any other choice in advance, and it would be taken as an act to strengthen Hanna's own candidacy for the senatorship in this year of 1903. Hanna refused fight. He telegraphed to the President, withdrawing his objection, on May 26th, and delicately added: " I have given the substance of this to the Associated Press."

[7] " ' I have not asked any man for his vote! ' Hurrah for George Washington! " Henry Watterson to Davison Weeks, May 26, 1903.

" I was terribly sorry to see Theodore descend to such an amazing quibble as his telegram to Hanna. You know I have no reason to love M. A. H. But he has been very dignified in his attitude since this happened. He knows perfectly that Theodore has been asking us all for our support next year. If Hanna had chosen to answer, his only course open would have been to say that he (Roosevelt) meant individual delegates in the Ohio Convention." John J. McCook to William C. Beer, undated.

His duller admirers saw that Mr. Roosevelt had planted one straight on the jaw of the Wall Street gang and had forced Hanna himself to approve his candidacy in 1904. That he had not published Hanna's telegram to him was another sound stroke in the game. They cared no more for the facts than the President cared at Seattle. His friends in Washington rejoiced. Senator Foraker, Henry Cabot Lodge wrote to the President, admired the telegram tremendously. Senator Foraker's way of showing this was odd.

" The whole business has been intensely disagreeable to me, for a number of reasons," he said in the first week of June.

His reasons he kept to himself. He stood on the stairs of his fine house in Washington and stared at a mosaic of Guido Reni's Aurora on the wall of the upper hallway, as he slapped the handrail. He rasped out that Mr. Roosevelt hadn't asked him to do anything. His callers watched him scowling until his small son decided to slide down the rail and gracelessly ended the serious conversation by bumping into the Senator. So ambassadors merely found that Mr. Foraker did not like the results of all this. As usual, they had seen Foraker in the yellow hallway of his house; one never got upstairs in this man's life. He received embassies on his doormat, and this embassy had been a failure. Foraker would not be reconciled with Marcus Hanna, and that was all. He led his child up the stairs. Agents of the most powerful banker and the biggest insurance company in America walked out of the house and reported that nothing could be done.

But much had been done. His brother Howard furiously circulated Mark Hanna's telegram to Mr. Roosevelt, advertising that Roosevelt had replied as to another kind of message. An impression grew among men who admired the President that he had been unscrupulous, and some said so, vigorously, in New York and Washington. They would not see Foraker or Lodge succeed Hanna as executive head of the party in the campaign of 1904. " And you can tell the President that," said Senator Orville Platt to Philander Knox, " as loudly as I am saying it to you in this room! "

On May 29th the President wrote an emollient letter to Mr. Hanna, a cadenza of soothing and smooth suggestions. " I thank you for your letter which gave me the first gleam of light on the situation. I do not think you appreciated the exact effect that your interview and announced position had on the country at large. It was everywhere accepted as the first open attack on me, and it gave heart, curiously enough, not only to my opponents but to all the men who lump you and me together as improperly friendly to organized labor and to the working men generally. . . . No one but a really big man — a man above all petty considerations — could have treated me as you have done during the year and a half since President McKinley's death. I have consulted you and relied on your judgment more than I have done with any other man. . . ."

This note bored the Senator's son. Two years later he wrote to Henry Adler: " Mr. Roosevelt soon sent father a conciliating letter, of which you will find a copy enclosed for your private file. But he does not explain why he did not give out the substance of Mr. Hanna's telegram correctly to the Associated Press when he published his own answer to it. The truth is that he had no explanation ready. He knew perfectly what Mr. Hanna's situation in regard to Mr. Foraker was. But he wanted to make a Rough Rider speech about his enemies in Wall Street to the crowd out in Spokane and he took this occasion to do it at Mr. Hanna's expense. Of course he had no time to learn the effect of Mr. Hanna's interview on the public. He answered father's telegram within a day of receiving it. He was consulting with two men who hated Mr. Hanna at the time, and admitted it in a letter he wrote to H. C. Lodge three or four days later. . . ." [8]

Mr. Lodge was rather indiscreet in the first week of June. Information passed from a brokerage in Boston to New York that the President's scholarly intimate claimed this whole arrangement of telegrams and challenges as his idea. The information was untrue, but Mr. Lodge did talk a good deal. An alarmed Attorney General began to send out rings of oil on the torn water. " Mr. Knox says the whole affair is a pure misunderstanding. He is doing his damnedest to patch it up. Lodge has been talking too much in Boston and some kind of letter he had from the President is being passed around. I am very sorry about the whole thing. . . ." [9]

Meanwhile in Cleveland it was raining daily. There were bets. The Hanna luck was to break: rain would fall on Ruth Hanna's wedding day, and the President would not appear. Magnates swarmed into the city under umbrellas on the ninth of June. Ladies prepared to wear a second-best gown. Then the sun rose decorously next morning and the rain ceased. The President's teeth shimmered on the veranda of the big mansion by the Lake and he said " Damn! " audibly,

[8] ". . . I thought the matter over a full 24 hours, consulting with Mellen, Byrnes and Moody. . . . I accordingly sent him my answer, and as you doubtless saw, made a similar statement for the public press, of course not alluding to the fact that Hanna had sent me the telegram — my statement simply going as one made necessary by Hanna's long interview in which he announced that he would oppose my endorsement by the Ohio Convention. . . . I made it " — the speech at Spokane — " particularly with reference to having a knockdown and dragout fight with Hanna and the whole Wall Street crowd. . . ." Theodore Roosevelt to Henry Cabot Lodge, May 27, 1903.

[9] Benjamin Montgomery to William Collins Beer, June 7, 1903.

A quotation from an official on duty in the White House should not be made without explanation. Colonel Montgomery wrote frequently to my father, but he scrupulously refrained from saying anything of business current unless the matter had become public property, such as the meal taken by Booker Washington with Mr. Roosevelt. He was warmly attached to Mr. Roosevelt, but viewed some of the President's maneuvers with regret.

catching his cuff in a twisted ornamentation of the newel post in the hall. Out under a tent on the lawn old Charles Foster lifted champagne to his lips, whispering, "To the next President — whichever one it is!" The conspiracy of business men to defeat Roosevelt in 1904 had learned of its own existence in March, but it was growing real. Senator Hanna bowed his most distinguished guest out of Cleveland, and the game continued.

"A case of Wall Street versus Theodore Roosevelt," said the Attorney General, in July, "has been made out. I think it can be settled out of court. But . . . it might be wished that the defendant would . . . exercise a little reticence."

The conspiracy took the form of daylit conversations openly carried on in clubs and restaurants by all kinds of men. But conspiracy was still the word at the White House. "I thought," mused a shrewd journalist from Kansas City, Harvey Fleming, "that conspiracies happened in dark rooms and nobody knew who was in them." Still, conspiracy was the appointed word. The President was having a knockdown and dragout fight with Hanna and the Wall Street conspirators.

"I'm the person who's going to be dragged out," said the Senator. "Don't these fools in New York know I'm sixty-six years old?"

These fools who wanted Hanna to take the nomination from Mr. Roosevelt in 1904 were mostly stockholders, not the major financiers. They were men more angered by some attitudes of the President than by anything he had done, against finance. "I have known Theodore for twenty-five years," one of them wrote to a son in Oxford, "without knowing that he hated corporations and wanted to see Wall Street smashed wide open.[10] But I should like to know what excuse he has for hating corporations. His father made

[10] This wish was reported into New York from Cheyenne, Wyoming, in June. It was widely quoted in private.

money out of them and he lives on it. . . . But what disgusts me, in this exhibition he has made of himself, is that he cries before he is hit. He has taken a leaf out of Bryan's book. It may please the Populists and the cowboys to see a President of the United States make a fool of himself talking cant. Could he name one real threat made against him by any responsible person? . . . Mr. Hayes was abominably libelled through his whole administration. But he behaved himself as a gentleman should. I cannot say as much for Theodore. Every decision and every piece of legislation is announced as if he had been obliged to enter the Senate and plead to have it passed. . . ."

Here the injustice is plain. Mr. Roosevelt's satellites were supplying their hero with airs of martyrdom. Horrible things were being done to the President by his enemies. Hill, Morgan, the Rockefellers, the steel-makers, and the grand butchers were " saying things." When the Republic of Panama appeared so suddenly in November, and Mr. Roosevelt caused it to be recognized, a plaintive journalist assured the world in the bar of the Raleigh that Hanna had forced this action on the President, a sentimental invention which annoyed Mr. Roosevelt into many words on November 22nd.[11] But what Mr. Roosevelt really said, about Wall Street and about his hypothetical enemies, was constantly whelmed and distorted in grotesque lies. " This wordy city," John Hay wrote to Mrs. Charlton Paull in the first of October, " poisons men, who might be friends, against each other. . . ."

The conspiracy of finance was formless enough until December, but the Senator had no peace from his proponents

---

[11] During the composition of this book I have been told at least ten times that Mr. Hanna forced the President to recognize the Republic of Panama. Mr. Roosevelt specifically denied, on November 22, 1903, that Hanna had even advised him to recognize the Republic. He said in 1911 to Mr. Charles Deshler at San Francisco, " Hanna did absolutely nothing to hinder me or to force our hand in that business." His denial in 1903 was made to a lady who sympathized with him on Mr. Hanna's reported brutality.

all through the autumn. They were at him in a hundred ways. Myron Herrick was asked to plead, and would not. John McCall, who was truly liked by the Senator, declined to bother him, saying that Hanna was too old to be made President. But loud conspirators would not be silent. They must have a yes.

"Conspiracy," Mr. Hanna said, in his rooms at the Arlington, "is the right word for it! They want to kill me!"

He growled that he was selling securities "to save Dan and the girls the bother." The whole business amused him. As soon as he told his bank to sell one famous stock, his very lawyers wanted to know if he was getting rid of this corporation's shares so as to be able to face the plain people with clean hands. That was pretty funny, wasn't it? . . . Well, he was off for Cleveland tonight. His campaign was booming. He was electing himself Senator and taking the governorship of Ohio for Myron Herrick. Tom Johnson was out on the stump already, shouting for municipal street railways and revised taxations. Johnson, he yawned, would stay mayor of Cleveland. That couldn't be helped. But the Democratic reformer's candidate for Governor would be wiped out. Herrick would sweep the state. . . . He limped downstairs and stood in the doors of the hotel. The funeral of a notable nothing was passing the Arlington.

"Drive him fast to his tomb," said my father.

"That from Shakspere, Beer?"

No, it was from *A Tale of Two Cities*. The old man nodded, repeating the words. Yes. He had not thought of the book in a thousand years. He stared after the funeral.

"Drive him fast to his tomb? That's where a lot of 'em want to see me!"

His maintained power had grown irksome to many people. Weak men and strong men both resent this amusement called success, and he had plangently succeeded for so long, and was succeeding still. His victory in November was sharp. Letters and telegrams from thousands demanded that he make himself President. Petitions came, signed by all these people in the South and West. It tickled him, and it seemed to puzzle him. He could understand those bully boys up in New York thinking they wanted him for President, but the Westerners? "I don't see that so well," he said, and lit his next cigar.

Be President? No! The answer went back to New York, perhaps twice a week in December. A committee up there was gathering pledges and money. Pity to waste their time so. No! . . . Meanwhile it all amused him, the messengers, the lickspittle orators, the embassies of Mr. Roosevelt's worried friends. He got tired, he told George Cortelyou, of going to the White House and being sworn in. His tonsils were calloused with telling damn fools he was too old, too fat to be President. Say, though, some of these gentlemen had corns on their tongues from lying to Roosevelt about him! . . . His eyes snapped. He marched into the Senate and grinned at the funny world. He was committing his last offense against the propriety of romantic politics: he disdained solemnity.

At the White House there was something going on for Hanna's diversion. Practical politicians called and lunched with Theodore Roosevelt. Rural editors were bobbing in and out. A boss from Cincinnati showed his gay eyes. Herman Kohlsaat grew exasperated, hearing the gossip in Chicago. Roosevelt must stop hunting delegates for 1904. He came to Washington and boldly lectured the President, declaring that Hanna was too old and too ill to be a candidate and that Mr. Roosevelt was making himself ridiculous by his nervousness. The President gave out word that he would not see men who had been brought to confer with him. Kohlsaat returned to Chicago. But, on December 20th, Senator Foraker exploded to a friend, "Root and Knox and Wayne McVeagh and I have all told him that Hanna does not mean

619

to fight him. But he is writing too damned many letters! "

For power begets superstitions. Something about this old man, with his stiffened legs and his sagging throat, worked on the President. He would not be satisfied. A terrible legend of force hung around Hanna. This same day the President thrashed up and down his office, talking trivial stuff to Mr. Beer. The question flashed after half an hour.

" Have you seen Senator Hanna since you came down? "

" Yes. On the street, for a minute."

" Did he say anything about the next convention? "

" No, sir."

" Oh. . . ."

But Mark Hanna's wife could not laugh. Her long training made her tactfully mute when questioners came at her. No, she would say, the Senator was not thinking of the presidency. He had said so. It was absurd for people to talk in this way, and so humiliating for the President! After Christmas she made one outcry, on the cold veranda beside the Lake. Wind hurled flakes upon her furs, and her friend shivered. But if she could only stay here! She would rather freeze in Cleveland than be at Washington. And those awful people were trying to kill him. And he would have to lead the campaign next summer! . . . But she came back to Washington and appeared at receptions, placidly correct, kindly, and so tired. She was not well and the Senator was ill. They went out together, to long dinners and the play. Talk swelled as the old man passed through murmurous alleys of hotels. . . . There he was. That was Mark Hanna!

Mr. Lytton Strachey, cleverest of biographers, patented a device at the end of his story about Queen Victoria, fancying thoughts that wheeled in the mind of the dying Empress, her life reversing until she came to the trees and grass of her babyhood at Kensington. Mr. Strachey did this much too well. Since his old Queen died so, a dozen famous men have died in print to the same music, or have passed a final,

measured paragraph reviewing their own times. Henry
James, Nathaniel Hawthorne, the great Swift, and François
Villon have been displayed on Mr. Strachey's patent, and
perhaps someone will set the needle on the plate of Marcus
Hanna's memories. But it is true, not fancied, that his youth
came back to him on the last night of January as he lurched
into his rooms at the Arlington.

There was a dinner of newspaper men. He must dress.
He left his train downstairs. It was not known yet that typhoid colored his face. The white-haired woman seated
with his wife stared at him entering and saw by the flush
and the blaze of his eyes that he was sick.

" Mrs. Balch is afraid you won't remember her, Mark."

He did not remember, yet. He stood looking at her, and
his eyes, as in 1865, seemed to go through her. She stammered that he had known her when she was a child and
walked toward this being in his yellow, splotched mask of
sickness, with his slim fingers thickened at the joints by
rheumatism. As she came, he altered. His memory caught
at her gait, or her voice, and he shouted, " Sawdust! "

He grew tall and glowed. He was her Mr. Mark again
who killed the rat on the wharf with his walking-stick and
gave her hearts of maple sugar from the tin box on his
desk. He babbled at her, question upon question. How was
— What was her brother's name? — Orion? And did she
live in California? Oh, and she should see the rat the Roosevelt kids had at the White House! It would scare her stiff.
. . . She was crying. He held her hands, and his fingers
burned her. A sense of death on his hands made Juliet Araminta choke. But she tried to talk.

" And you've got your canal now."

" Was I gassin' about canals back then? Honest? You
remember that? . . . How long ago it is! " he panted.

Men poured in, gentlemen dressed to dine. The child
who had loved him, and loved him now again, looked at

621

them with hate and heard suave voices urging Uncle Mark
to dress at once. He was swept away, and in half an hour
the Senator tottered into his chair at the gay dinner of the
journalists. She must leave for New York at midnight, hurrying to a nephew sick at West Point. But she had promised
to come back.

On the ninth of February she read that Senator Hanna's
illness had proved serious. The great Dr. Osler was in consultation, and the family had been summoned. Next morning she was back in Washington, one of the people drifting
incessantly to stare at the unresponding face of the Arlington.

Hotels jammed suddenly, and on Friday night the yellow
hall of Foraker's house was pungent with cigars. Furs were
sumptuous huddles on a bench and the Senator sometimes
stroked a black collar's softness with his light fingers as he
stood coldly listening to the cool flatteries of the powerful men, and coldly answering. The pastime must go on.
These lofty children played with power because they were
used to the game, and it was dear. Some of them came afterwards to think that Hanna had been more conscionable
than were they. He had played in a dream of advancing industry, of men and wealth in one blend, a smooth pulsation
of a grand machine. He had adored, and had been loyal,
when they played for the barren sake of egoism, to be known
as strong. So they spoke of him, afterwards, and perhaps
were not wrong.

Just then they must find a fresh alliance, and they had
come to make peace with Hanna's enemy, for the news was
bad at the Arlington. A courtly chatter ran in the group, an
insolent palaver about nothings. They had been brought
to call on Mr. Foraker, and that was all. And that was to be
all. They were told so, as they stood there.

A fair little boy strolled down the stairs and considered
these men with a child's impeccable contempt. It was time

for dinner, and the phonograph was broken, and an older boy set to amuse him on the landing was a weary bore. He was tired of this gathering. He yawned at them and leaned his blue clothes on the rail, waiting for them to have the sense to go.

"Well, Arthur, we're going to make your dad leader of the party."

"Mr. Roosevelt says there aren't going to be any more leaders when Mr. Hanna dies," said the child.

But outside in the city people stopped one another to ask what the news was at the Arlington. He had grown familiar to the simple, and it was known that he had open hands, that he was a kind father and the best of friends. A blankness hung in Washington as Sunday passed. He was fighting; there might be a chance. Pages from hotels and messengers on bicycles threshed before the Arlington that night, waiting. Reporters stamped cold feet and whispered that the big marine over there was an outpost of the White House, stolidly attending the death of Marcus Hanna. He stayed until midnight and then tramped out of their sight.

Monday was gray. The Senate idled. Lads ran in to mutter in some ear that it had not come yet. Senators walked out in the midst of speeches and found a telephone. Many dinners were canceled and a ball postponed before dusk, and at six o'clock watchers spread below the Arlington. The big young marine stood with his hands in his pockets close to Juliet Balch and may have seen that she was pale and weeping.

"Know him?"

"Yes. Are you a messenger from the White House?"

"No," he said. "Mamma wired me to be here. He was good to my folks out home."

Minutes marched. A new lad would come on his clicking bicycle, and a new cigar would glow among the reporters. Everything waited for the news. Carriages stopped and drivers bent down to ask if it was done. To his last he commanded a world's attention. People must wait and wait. It was half past six. It was twenty minutes to seven. A figure came through the brilliant doors and raised a hand. The young marine took off his cap and turned away. These living bodies separated and disappeared into the night.

APPENDIX

No terminal essay in condemnation or defense of Marcus Hanna was designed for this book. I must admit that the morals of leaders in a democracy do not interest me. If one man chooses to get in a dubious margin of votes for his candidate by handing a check of five thousand dollars to some discreet assistant and another rouses the same voters by yowling from the end of a train that his opponents are victims of a " seared moral sense " and yet a third assures dwellers in small towns that his heart is wrung when he hears the people of small towns criticized, I find no difference in morality among the methods displayed. Morality is an exaltation of personal taste, and taste is something usually sacrificed by leaders of mankind in the mass. The materials in condemnation of Mr. Hanna hugely exist in any large public library, written by men of unquestioned and also unexplored veracity. " Let the virtuous people stick to describing vice — which they can do well enough."

A current theory of history advises us that beyond democracy lies Cæsarism, the control of the ineffectual mass by the strong individual. My dissent from the theory has been twice implied in this sketch of Hanna's times. Democracy and Cæsarism seem to me coexistent. Democracy yearns for leadership and accepts many clever dictators before a Julius Cæsar declares the ideational ruin of the republic and sits on the wreckage to await his assassins. The characteristic of Hanna's bloodless adventure in government is this Cæsarism, and his charm lies in the candor of his approach to the mass. He appealed to materialists as a materialist; his pragmatism was not draped in virtuous pretenses. He grinned.

NOTES

Chapter 1

The episode of Hugh Jones is taken from a statement of his grandson, Mr. H. J. Tessman.

Leonard Hanna's cruise on the Lakes does not appear in Mr. Croly's study of Marcus Hanna, but is authenticated by a conversation of Mr. Hanna with Mr. Henry Adler in 1899.

There are several versions of Schuyler Colfax's conversation with Mr. Lincoln on the day of the assassination. Mr. Ernest Harvier, who had his information directly from Mr. Colfax, told me that Mr. Lincoln mentioned the immigrants particularly. Mr. Colfax saw the President before the Cabinet met in the morning, and again a little after seven at night.

Chapter 2

The intrigue which disposed of George Pendleton in 1868, at the Democratic convention in New York, is said to have been managed by Tammany Democrats under advice from Jay Gould and his associates. Mr. Peter Daly and Mr. George Grannis, who witnessed the convention, both told me that the swing to Seymour was contrived by the constant work of a man named Ledbetter, operating from the Saint Nicholas Hotel.

Hanna's performance at Warsaw was reported in New York by Mr. Conkling's friends as a deliberate trick of Garfield to cause Mr. Conkling to recognize him, Mr. Hanna acting as Garfield's agent, and in Charles Foster's version of the episode Mr. Hanna is said to have promised Garfield that he would ask General Grant to call at Mentor. I have adhered to Mr. Croly's narration of the matter.

Chapter 3

Mrs. McKinley's interest in the Orient peculiarly impressed my father and Mr. Charles Deshler, as well as Mrs. Saxton. Colonel Montgomery boldly declared that her incessant talk on the conver-

APPENDIX

sion of the islanders influenced the President to retain the Philippines. On the other hand a person as closely associated with the presidential family as William Day did not notice the obsession.

The accusation of having ruined John Ellsler always gored Mr. Hanna. Mr. Ellsler's daughter is not aware that her father ever borrowed money from Hanna. The Euclid Avenue Opera House was bought by Mr. Hanna at public auction, its sale being forced by Mr. Ellsler's creditors. Ellsler remained in charge of the theater to the end of the season, accepted a benefit at the last performance, and appeared as Mark Hanna's guest at a supper afterwards. Myron Herrick and James Dempsey, two men who knew Hanna intimately, both characterized this yarn as a complete invention.

The messenger who informed Monsignor Ireland's friends in Saint Paul that the American Protective Association was trying to procure promises from the Republican party is Mr. Walter Stoeffel. Monsignor Ireland was not aware that the information came from Hanna. Mr. Stoeffel was sent with a note signed by Myron Herrick to the house of an eminent Catholic lawyer in Saint Paul, received an answer, and returned to Saint Louis.

Chapters 4 and 5

From 1896 to 1904 my father was constantly employed by the New York Life Insurance Company and by George Perkins, of J. P. Morgan and Company, as a political observer. Copies of his long reports on events in which Mr. Hanna was concerned are filed among his papers. He was by no means intimate with Mr. Hanna and only grew to like him in the last years of their acquaintance. He often told me that Mr. Hanna's curious honesty about the shabbiness of some of his assistants was the first thing that gave him an affection for the Senator. Mr. Hanna would point out that a common politician was wholly scrupulous in his private life and wholly reliable when he was given money to spend. In the very intense campaign of 1899 in Ohio, for instance, Mr. Hanna gave several thousand dollars to a man of no character whatever to be spent on hire of carriages in rural districts on election day. The man afterwards presented all the livery bills, receipted, to the Senator, with five dollars in change. His accounts were precise to the penny. Mr. Hanna paid him two hundred dollars. The hanger-on immediately got drunk, and died of pneumonia in a public hospital.

627

HANNA

Mr. Beer was incessantly in Washington, after 1896, and it would have been possible to fill this book's latter chapters with wild gossip and perhaps some odd facts written to him by men of consequence or journalists. He aided in the lobbying for the Newlands Act, at Mr. Roosevelt's request, and was borrowed by Mr. Hanna for the battle over the Panama Canal. In the autumn of 1902 he was sent by Mr. J. P. Morgan to attempt the settlement of the coal strike through one of the more reasonable operators. He reported his failure to Mr. Roosevelt in person on the night of the old soldier's call described in the third chapter of this sketch. In the spring of 1903 he was used as an agent in the forlorn movement to reconcile Hanna and Foraker, and for the rest of the year seems to have spent most of his time informing various gentlemen in New York that Senator Hanna did not want to be President of the United States. It happens that he took me to Washington with him on the 9th of February 1904, and I am now the only person alive who heard Mr. Arthur Foraker's comment when George Perkins told him that his father was to be made leader of the Republican party.

In order to exhibit Marcus Hanna at close range I have added one of Mr. Beer's reports to this appendix. The campaign of 1899 in Ohio was bitter and costly. The Democrats and the independent Republicans spent enormous sums. A clerk in the office of Wells, Fargo and Company was offered one hundred dollars to vote the Democratic ticket. Unsigned private letters were circulated against McKinley and Hanna and sent particularly to clergymen. Mr. Hanna afterwards told my father that he regarded this as the most open use of money by the Democrats he had ever seen in Ohio, and that he suspected several eminent Republicans of assisting the opposition.

My indebtedness to Mrs. Henriette Adler Meyer for the use of her brother's papers, to Miss Alice Jayson for research, to Mr. David Saville Muzzey for some heartening advice, and to Mr. Charles Deshler and Mr. William McCready for most valuable information is here specially mentioned. Mrs. Henry Villard, Mrs. Juliet Balch, Colonel Benjamin Montgomery, and Mr. Oscar Underwood have now no use for my thanks.

APPENDIX

REPORT OF WILLIAM C. BEER TO JOHN McCALL

NEW YORK, November 11, 1899.

MY DEAR MR. McCALL: —

In obedience to your orders, I left New York on Tuesday evening, October 31st, for Ohio.

On Wednesday, in accordance with a suggestion from the White House, I stopped off at Pittsburg and called on President McCrea, of the Pennsylvania Lines West of Pittsburg. He, unfortunately, was out of town, but his representatives supplied me with transportation on all the Pennsylvania lines in Ohio, and also gave me a good idea of the situation, politically, from the railroad standpoint. Leaving Pittsburg Wednesday afternoon, I saw friends along the line and arranged for information and help in Columbiana, Mahoning and Stark, Trumbull, Wayne, Richland, Crawford, Ashland, Defiance, Williams and Lucas and several other counties. I stopped off at my father's home in Bucyrus, Crawford County, between trains, and ascertained from him the attitude of the Gold Democrats of the State, — he being in close touch with all of the leaders of that wing.

I went on the same day to Lima, Allen County, where I had arranged to meet Senator Hanna in the afternoon (Thursday). I found him at the supper table, at the Lima House, in company with Congressman Dalzell, of Pennsylvania, and several distinguished Ohioans. As soon as Mr. Hanna finished his meal, he sent his party out and came over to where I sat. I said, " President McKinley is anxious about Ohio." He answered, vigorously, " He has — good reason to be! " I then informed him that, by your orders and at the request of President McKinley, I had come to Ohio, being directed to report to him, Hanna, and do whatever I could in any direction, but principally among my friends in the various transportation companies. He em-

629

phatically assented to this suggestion, and having given me a general idea of the situation, he went off to the reception which had been arranged for him prior to the evening meeting, and told me to occupy his room in his absence, and start to work in any way I thought best. I thereupon wrote, by hand, twenty-two letters to railroad presidents, general managers, superintendents &c., and to Senator Platt and other prominent express officials. The letters were supposedly from Senator Hanna, and urged upon those gentlemen the extreme necessity of doing everything in their power to get every vote out among their employes and shop-men on election day.

On the Senator's return from his meeting, about 10:30, he read over the letters and signed all, except one to J. P. Morgan and a couple of railroad men whom he had seen personally, and with whom he had arranged that very matter, viz., the Lake Shore and the Nickel Plate Presidents. As soon as he signed the letters, I sealed them with sealing-wax and directed them, under private cover, to each man. After that was finished, the Senator leaned back and sketched to me, rapidly, the situation in the State. He said: " Please tell President McCall that I have had a very hard fight. I feel almost certain that we shall carry the State by a safe plurality. It has been hard work, and has nearly worn me out. We are having trouble in Cincinnati and some in Cleveland. Tell him that wherever I have been in the smaller towns and cities, I have called together the leaders, and have personally given out the necessary funds, one hundred dollars here, one hundred dollars there, and so on. I have seen to this matter myself in as judicious a manner as I could, and it has been placed as wisely as I could judge. You have noticed that I am to speak in Sandusky City to-morrow night. Well, I am going to leave here to-morrow morning at 8 o'clock and go to Toledo first. I have quietly summoned all our leaders there, — you know them, —

George Waldorf and the rest, — and am going to follow the same tactics which I used to beat Jones in the Convention, — to get the delegation, — you remember? They sent word to me a few days ago that if they had five thousand, they could buy up all of Jones' lieutenants, — his head men. Those fellows understand perfectly well that Jones can't be elected Governor, and that there will be no offices, and they are not in this for their health. They convinced me as to the scheme, and I sent them a thousand dollars yesterday, and will give them the rest to-morrow."

After some further chat on the subject of my duties, the attitude of various railroad men, &c., I asked the Senator point-blank what he thought the result would be. He looked at me for several seconds before replying, and looked rather queer, but, finally, said he thought the State would go about 25,000 or 30,000 for Nash. This did not agree with his first remark to me when I met him at the supper-table, and I knew he was giving me " taffy." I did not press him, however, and bidding him good-night, left his room with the letters, and, in company with the Senator's body-guard, Post Office Inspector Gaitree, went to the Lima Post Office and mailed the letters about midnight. I then took the C:, H. & D. train for Toledo about two hours afterwards, and arrived at Toledo at 7:30 Friday morning, procured a little information there, and left for Cleveland at 8:30 A.M.

You will remember I met you as I left my train, at 11:25 A.M. and immediately went uptown to the railroad and express headquarters' buildings. I had a letter from the Vice-President of Wells Fargo & Co., Col. Dudley Evans, to his Ohio Superintendent, Mr. T. M. DeWitt, and we spent part of the afternoon together, going around from place to place. We learned that the feeling in Cleveland among business men was very cheerful and sanguine for Republican success. They felt there was no particular doubt as to Ohio. Thought Cuyahoga County would give a safe Republican plurality, thought Jones would not have many votes in Cleveland, and the feeling was, in general, that the state was safe, and that Mr. McKisson and his friends would not poll a very heavy vote in Cleveland, as they would probably stay away from the polls.

Friday night, Superintendent DeWitt and I started for Cincinnati, as your orders were to take in the big cities first.

Mr. DeWitt told me that he felt confident most of his employes were safely for the Republican ticket, and went on to relate how they *could not* be otherwise, because Wells Fargo & Co. used them so well, and the men were fully conscious of the prosperity of the country and, consequently, of their Company; how the custom of the Company is to give each man a big turkey and a can of oysters and a bunch of celery on Christmas day, and this little custom made them all seem like one big family, &c., &c.

When we arrived in Cincinnati the next morning, we went immediately after breakfast to the General Agency of the Express Company, and taking the General Agent aside, inquired as to the attitude of the men. (There are over a hundred employes of Wells Fargo & Co. in Cincinnati.) Mr. Earle replied in rather an embarrassed manner, "Well, Mr. DeWitt, I think there are a very few for the Republican ticket, but most of them are for McLean, and a good many are for Jones." DeWitt was astounded, but after a hasty consultation, he arranged to have the men gotten together by Earle, so that he could address them in bunches and individually. While Earle was getting them together, Mr. DeWitt and I went over to call on our friend, the General Manager of the Cincinnati, Hamilton & Dayton System, Mr. C. G. Waldo. We found that Mr. Waldo had already heard from the letter which I wrote to President Woodford at Lima, (signed by Senator Hanna). He was very cheerful, however, and said that his men were all right, but that in deference to President Woodford's wishes, he had communicated with their route agents, superintendents, &c., but thought there was no cause for alarm. I convinced him to the contrary, and he set to work immediately. After he had finished dictating his telegrams, Superintendent DeWitt having left us, Mr. Waldo and I went over to call on President M. E. Ingalls, of the C., C., C. & St. L. R'y Co. (Big Four). Of course, you are well aware of President Ingalls' high standing in Sound Money circles. Like yourself, he has been a life-long Democrat. In Ohio, however, Mr. Ingalls has, among the best citizens, a reputation for " shiftiness."

As we had a most remarkable experience with him, I take the liberty of setting it out in full as nearly as I can recall his exact words. He said: " No, I am not taking any part in politics this year. I did in 1896, as everybody did. I have been rather sorry for it ever since. I spent over one hundred thousand of my own money, and devoted nearly all of my time to speaking and working for McKinley, and what was the good of it all? Why, afterwards when I recommended to them not to take sides with this old fellow Deboe over here in Kentucky, they wouldn't listen to me, and although I went to Washington and told the Pre — the Administration what I thought of it, my protest was unheeded, and they did as they pleased. No, I am not going to take any part, and they can get along the best they know how. Yes, there are a good many Republicans voting for McLean now, in fact nearly all my friends are for him, and I think he will carry the State. It is true there are a good many workingmen for Jones — why, my private secretary, Davie, who has been with me for many years, and has been a Republican always, is off this year. I said to him the other day, ' Davie, who are you going to vote for? ' He answered, ' Well, Mr. Ingalls, I am a Republican, but I can't vote for Nash, and I won't vote the Democratic ticket; I guess I will vote for old man Jones.' You see how it goes? Yes, a good many of our men are for Jones and McLean; I guess nearly all of them. My son, up in Cleveland, who is a good deal brighter fellow than his father, keeps me posted every day, and he says Hanna is going to lose the State sure this time, that everybody is for McLean up there. And, by-the-way, speaking of Hanna, now I like Hanna personally. He is a good fellow and all that, but I will say to you, — and this must not be told either to McKinley or Hanna, not at least until after election day, — the people are sick and tired of Hanna. They are sick and tired of Cox down here in Cincinnati, but the people of Ohio have revolted against Hanna, and I guess he is done for. They do not like his methods. McKinley is a nice, pleasant fellow, and I guess the people like him, but they want to show him this time, inasmuch as Hanna is running the campaign personally, that they won't have any more Hanna, and I guess they will do it. Yes, the State is going for McLean," and here he turned and shook his finger at me significantly, " and that means the jig is up with McKinley. He won't be nominated next year. You'll vote for Dewey next year, young man! "

Mr. Ingalls did not, of course, know that I came in any way from President McKinley. I had merely repeated verbatim your message to him as one Sound Democrat to another, and General Manager Waldo had been careful to introduce me as a New York Life man — a messenger from President McCall. At the conclusion of his address, Mr. Ingalls, after a moment's thought — apparently remembering whom I represented — said, " I am sorry I can't see my way clear to comply with President McCall's wishes. I haven't said to anybody how *I* will vote. Perhaps I shan't vote at all, but you can tell him I am not working this year."

Mr. Waldo, remembering President Ingalls' great influence in Cincinnati, left very much discouraged, but got his second wind, shortly afterwards, and started in with renewed vigor to get his men in line. He promised me to see, individually, every general manager in Cincinnati within twenty-four hours.

After leaving Mr. Waldo, I went to the Hotel and telephoned to an old-time friend, Mr. H. P. Boyden, formerly editorial writer for the " Cincinnati Commercial Gazette," now Comptroller of the City of Cincinnati, elected to that office by the Mugwump Republican-Democratic Fusion of two years ago. Mr. Boyden is perhaps the most intimate personal friend of President Ingalls. He had no idea of my errand in the city. To him I was merely a New York Life agent in the city on business. I invited him to dinner at the Grand Hotel, and after discussing other subjects of mutual interest, alluded to the political questions in Ohio, and asked him for some light on the subject, as I, being a New Yorker, was rather out of touch with the situation. Upon this theme Mr. Boyden spoke about an hour, and gave me the Mugwump Democratic side of the question in full. He said, in part, " It means that the people of Ohio are through with Mark Hanna. They have had all they want of Hannaism and Coxism. No, I have nothing against President McKinley. He is my personal friend. I like him. We all like him, but he has got to learn he must cut loose from Hanna, and, of course, we long-suffering Cincinnatians have decided that George Cox must understand that *he* has reached the end of *his* string. We have stood him as long as we are going to, and this alliance between the better class of the Republican party in Cincinnati and the Democratic party, has come to stay until Cox retires from politics. No, I do not feel that there will be disastrous consequences to the party in a national way. This is our own little fight in Ohio, and it had to come sooner or later. We may as well settle it right now, so as not to interfere with the success of the National ticket next year. Well, if it means disaster to McKinley, although I do not think so, let it mean so. It is a case of self-preservation. The party in Ohio must be purified. We have deliberately shut our eyes to the consequences. We shall carry Hamilton County against Hanna and Cox by 10,000 plurality, perhaps more, but certainly 10,000."

After leaving Boyden, I went to the headquarters of the U. S. Post Office Inspectors, to see how our case against the crank (Ireland) who is writing letters to Mr. Edward W. Scott, of the Provident Savings, was getting along. I found they had had some difficulty in finding the man, but finally learned that he is a " curbstone " broker. He has no fixed abiding place, so the Inspector says, and they have had hard work to run him down. It so happened that on the very day I was there, the Chief Inspector had located him, and had sent a man out to find him and give him a scare. He expected that within twenty-four hours at least, he would be able to prepare a final report on the case to be sent to the 4th Assistant Postmaster-General, who will, in turn, send it to us.

Afterwards I hunted up George Cox.

Cox said: " We shall carry Hamilton County certainly by 6,000, and if we can only get some money from Headquarters, we will carry it by more. The trouble has been here that we are fighting the Democrats, the Jones men and the Fusion Republicans in our own party, but we will win sure. We have been greatly hampered by lack of funds. There are 10,000 ex-city employes, all good, loyal Republicans, who have been walking the streets since the Fusion victory two years ago, and they are dead sore. You can't blame them. They have families dependent on them, and they haven't been able to find work. I guess a good many of them will work for McLean and Jones, if they can get something for doing so. Well, I cannot blame them, but if I had the money, I should at least induce them to stay away from the polls and not vote at all, if they did not vote with us. I have sent to Chairman Dick three times asking for money, but I haven't had a cent. They sent a man down here last week to help us collect money from our own citizens, and how much do you think he collected? Three hundred dollars. Our Committee was only able to collect seven hundred and fifty, and the Post Office employes here all hid themselves behind Civil Service, and how much do you suppose we got from that building? One hundred and fifty-two dollars and fifty cents. We have had some more in driblets, but nothing like what we ought to have, and I am fighting McLean's bar'l that way! If I had ten thousand, I would contract with Mr. Hanna to give him 10,000 majority from Hamilton County. If he will send me seventy-five hundred, I will give him 7,500 or 8,000 plurality. I will take whatever they send me, and be glad to get it. The more they send me, the better work I can do. Why, here we haven't got a daily morning paper in the city. McLean has bought the Republican paper, — The 'Commercial Gazette.' The only papers we have are evening papers. I sent to Dick and asked him to let me have twenty-seven hundred dollars to get out a morning paper for one day only, to-morrow, Sunday morning, the Sunday before election, and I would get out at least 5,000 copies and have them handed to the passers-by on the corners by boys. They would have been read by everybody, and would have done lots of good. But do you suppose he would give me a cent? No sir! How much do I think the State will go Republican? Well, it is a hard matter to say. Ninety per cent. of the railroad employes here are for Jones and McLean. The C., H. & D.? *Why,* I ought to know what they'll do. I am the largest individual stockholder in that railroad. I told you that ninety per cent. of those men are for Jones, and it is nearly the same with all the other railroads. What about the Big Four? Why, those men would follow Ingalls anywhere he would lead them. How is Ingalls this year? Why, for McLean sure. He is working day and night for John R. McLean. All his men are doing the same, too. As to the State? Well, of course I am paying more attention to Hamilton County than to the State, but I hear a good deal from up there. Of course, everybody comes to Cincinnati, and they tell me that we will pull through. How much do I think? Well," after a moment's hesitation, " I should say perhaps 10,000, or may be 12,-000, along there, perhaps 15,000."

As this was Saturday night preceding election day, I deemed it my duty to acquaint Senator Hanna with the state of affairs in Cincinnati at once. Cox intimated very plainly that he thought Dick was deceiving Hanna, and that the State was in such bad condition, that he wanted to keep the knowledge of it from Hanna, if possible. He said he thought Dick had not transmitted to Hanna one single message from him, Cox, and that as he, Cox, had not seen Hanna for several months, Hanna could not, of course, know how bad Cincinnati really was. Therefore, I left for Cleveland Saturday night within two hours after seeing Cox.

The next morning, Sunday, I drove out to the Lake Front, where the Senator lives, and was with him from 10:30 A.M. to nearly 1:30 P.M. I reported to him the situation in Cincinnati fully, and related the conversations I had had with Ingalls and Cox and Boyden as nearly verbatim as I could. He seemed greatly disturbed, and said that a week before that time, he had made out a check for five thousand, had mailed it to Chairman Dick with explicit instructions to send it to George Cox, and he supposed it had been done long ago. He said that he could not spare any more money. That he had used up all he had had from various sources, and now was drawing on his own funds. He said that his brothers had contributed six thousand, and that other public-spirited Republicans in Cleveland had done nearly as well. He denounced Cincinnati as a stingy city, and said what a shame it was, with the vast wealth of that place, they had the cheek to ask outside help, but that it had always been so. Said he would telephone to Cox immediately and to Chairman Dick. As to Ingalls, Hanna used some very forcible language in refuting that gentleman's statements. He said: " If Ingalls said he contributed one hundred thousand of his own money, or anybody else's, he is a liar. The fact of the matter is that in '96, Ingalls came to me with a cock-and-bull story about being able to carry Virginia, if we would help him. You remember what I did for him. How we poured the money into that State, and you know what good it did! Nothing!!! *He* contributed one hundred thousand? I'll bet he didn't contribute one hundred cents. Well, you can't expect anything more from Ingalls. His action is consistent with his character. Time and again he has come to me asking for favors, and I have done them always, and this is the reward. Why, not long ago, he came to me asking for a great, big favor from the Attorney General's Office — a very delicate matter, too — you know how peculiar our Attorney General is sometimes, and I went there in person and saw Griggs. I accomplished what Ingalls wanted, and now — !!! How much does George say he will give us from Cincinnati? Is that all? How much does George think we will carry the State by? 10,000?! "

The Senator went off into a brown study when I told him Cox's figures. He was silent for some time, but finally said, " I do not believe it. I think we will do better than that. We have a fine organization through the State in the rural districts, and will get out every vote. Wherever I have gone in places like Youngstown, and towns of that size, I have helped out the Committees with five hundred here and a thousand there, and I have neglected no place. Of course, all our money is gone now, and I won't ask Mr. McCall for any more. Of course, if you could get, say, twenty-five hundred more from some other sources in New York, it would be a great help, and I would send it right down to George Cox. He would use every cent of it right, and I believe it

would be a good thing to do. I can't let him have it myself.
I have told Dick that in cases where it is absolutely necessary, he should give the proper parties a reasonable amount,
and keep account of it and let me know. I will take care of it
here, and we will settle it up somehow when I come to New
York. I do not want to strain my friends in New York too
much, because I am going to ask them to help once more
next year. I can't ask John McCall for another cent. It
wouldn't be fair. He is too good a fellow. There is nobody
else like him in this country. There is only one John Mc-
Call. But if you could telephone there and have your folks
see somebody that would help us out to the extent of twenty-
five hundred it would do a great deal of good. The Catholic
vote is with us. All the head men in the Catholic clergy are
working with us, and John Farley, whom I helped in that
mayoralty fight, although he is a Democrat, has great influence with the Catholic clergy, and they are all with us,
and so is he. John is a good fellow. He is all right."

The Senator instructed me to try to communicate with
Vice-President Kingsley by telephone, and to let him know,
without fail, what answer I received, but to be very sure to
let Mr. Kingsley understand that if any money was forth-
coming, he did not wish it to be from the New York Life,
but only to be *collected* by Mr. Kingsley from such other
sources as he might see fit.

As you are probably aware, I followed the Senator's instructions, and received a reply next morning from Mr.
Kingsley to the effect that, being unable to communicate
with you, he did not see his way clear to comply with the
Senator's request. I met Mr. Hanna at the door of his office,
as he was going down to what he called the Ore Dump to
speak to a meeting of workingmen, mainly composed of iron
moulders, ore shovellers &c. He was in the centre of a
group of brawny foremen and bosses, with all of whom he
appeared on intimate terms. They were acting as a sort of

body-guard to him, as he anticipated a little trouble, perhaps, at the meeting. On receiving Mr. Kingsley's message, he replied quite cheerfully that it was all right, that he thought Cox could get along with the five thousand he sent him, and which had left Columbus by a special messenger Sunday night, in compliance with his telephonic instructions. He said: " Give my kindest regards to President McCall, and tell him I will see him when I come to New York."

I left Cleveland Monday afternoon, and went through Lorain and Huron and Seneca counties. I was glad to find that in the smaller places the voters were true blue, and the prosperity of the country was a greater argument for the Republican ticket, than anything which could be said against it by the traitors among the Republicans, or the followers of Jones or McLean. The farmers thought that the high prices of wool and wheat were better arguments than any cry of anti-Hannaism or anti-Imperialism. There were no voters for Jones in the smaller towns, except a very few of the riffraff, and perhaps one or two Anarchists that are to be found in every community.

During Sunday and Monday, the Republican farmers took a great brace. Election day was bright and clear, and almost to a man, the Republican and Sound Money Democratic farmers hitched up their buggies and started for town. The Republican organization, and for that matter the Democratic organization, had apparently ample means for livery hire, and the full vote was gotten out. Nobody was missed. The results were:

First — Republican gains through all the country districts. Thus proving that our strength lies outside of the big cities, and that the farmers of Ohio, if the present conditions continue, can be safely relied upon to carry that State for us next year, with an equally large plurality.

Second — That Ingalls and Boyden, and their friends, made good their threats against Hanna and Cox in Hamilton County, but they were able to do so only because of the large vote for Jones in Cincinnati. If Cox had been able to swing his customary vote with the laboring classes, he would have made good his promise. It is also my opinion that if he could have had five thousand dollars more than he had, he would have gotten a small plurality in spite of Jones and McLean.

THIRD — The disaster in Cuyahoga County is accounted for by the Republican leaders in the State, whom I saw after election, in just one word, " McKisson." This gentleman worked his game very cleverly and quietly, but it is evident now that his whole force voted for Jones by a pre-arranged plan. McLean ought to be more disappointed than Hanna about Cuyahoga County, for on Monday there were two headquarters opened in Cleveland for disbursing McLean's money. It was free as water. All in bright, new one dollar bills, fresh from the U. S. Treasury, and the word was given out that any respectable Democratic worker could have a reasonable amount of it. One of these headquarters was at the Weddell House, where I stopped, and all day long there was a ceaseless procession of " workers " up the stairs to that room and down again with smiling faces. The bar did a big business afterwards, and yet McLean came out third in the race.

FOURTHLY — It is evident to the Republican leaders that the campaign next summer must be in the country, in the district school-houses, or wherever a cluster of farmers can be gotten together to listen to bright, energetic, young Republican orators. There is in the big cities a deep-rooted conviction in the minds of most of the voters, that Hanna has certain methods which are wrong. No such feeling as this exists among the farmers, and to them George Cox is only a name. None of them have ever seen him, and they neither know or care anything about him.

I will say, in conclusion, that I reported daily, by letter, to President McKinley, addressing my letters to Col. B. F. Montgomery, at the White House. At the conclusion of my visit with M. E. Ingalls, I called up Col. Montgomery on the telephone (having been requested to do so, if anything startling should happen), and informed him fully as to that conversation.

After election day, I spent a day with my parents, part of another day in Canton with the President's friends, part of another day reporting to President McCrea, of the Pennsylvania Railroad, in Pittsburg, and then came directly to New York.

If I were to estimate the value of the results accomplished directly and indirectly by your assistance and agencies in the Ohio election, I should say, in all candor, that you supplied the margin of plurality.

Chairman Dick is not popular. Mr. Hanna is decidedly unpopular in the cities and county seats; but the effective aid given directly by you, and furnished by reason of your influence with corporations, is beyond estimate. Wells Fargo and Co.'s men all came over, and there are a thousand of them in the State. There are many more C., H. & D. employes. The express and railroad employes run into the thousands. The results of those letters were immediate. President T. C. Platt, of the United States Express, sent telegraphic orders to his superintendents, and it is quite easy to see where 25,000 votes were changed from Jones and McLean to Nash, within the week before election day.

I attach an informal note received to-day from General Manager Waldo, of the C., H. & D.

Very respectfully,

The Honorable
  John A. McCall,
    New York City.

PRINTER'S NOTE

This book was set on the Linotype in *Bodoni Book*, a printing-type so called after Giambattista Bodoni, a celebrated printer and type designer of Rome and Parma (1740–1813). *Bodoni Book* as produced by the Linotype company is not a copy of any one of Bodoni's fonts, but is a composite, modern version of the Bodoni manner. Bodoni's innovations in printing-type style were a greater degree of contrast in the " thick and thin " elements of the letters, and a sharper and more angular finish of details.

The book was composed, printed, and bound by The Plimpton Press, Norwood, Massachusetts. The paper was made by S. D. Warren Co., Boston. Typographic and binding design are by W. A. Dwiggins.